THE Almost COMPLETE HISTORY of THE WORLD

METRO BOOKS
New York

An Imprint of Sterling Publishing
387 Park Avenue South
New York, NY 10016

ISBN 978-1-4351-3793-6 (print format)

For information about custom editions, special sales, and premium and corporate purchases, please contact Sterling Special Sales at 800-805-5489 or specialsales@sterlingpublishing.com.

Manufactured in China

2 4 6 8 10 9 7 5 3 1

www.sterlingpublishing.com

THE Almost COMPLETE HISTORY of THE WORLD

75 INCREDIBLE EVENTS FROM ANCIENT TIMES TO TODAY

WRITTEN BY JOSEPH CUMMINS,
JAMES INGLIS & BARRY STONE

TABLE OF CONTENTS

The World at War 1901–1950

The Cold War and Beyond 1951–present

1301 BC — 500 AD

THE ANCIENT WORLD

The Almost Complete Annals

1274 BC

RAMESES II AND THE SECOND BATTLE OF KADESH

He is (my) brother, and I am his brother, and I am at peace with him (forever. And) we will create our brotherhood and our (peace), and they will be better than the former brotherhood and peace of (Egypt with) Hatti.

HITTITE VERSION OF EGYPTIAN–HITTITE PEACE TREATY

Rameses II, also known as Rameses the Great, was the third king of Egypt's Nineteenth Dynasty, and one of the greatest. His rule from 1279 to 1213 BC was the second longest in the history of the Egyptian Empire and included some of the most extensive and magnificent programs in its history.

Rameses' reign was also marked by conflicts with his neighbors—the Libyans to the west and the Indo-European Hittites to the north in an area occupied by present-day Turkey. His wars against the Hittites climaxed with the Second Battle of Kadesh in 1274 BC, the first battle in history with first-hand written evidence, and culminated in the world's first known peace treaty.

Rameses, meaning "fashioned by Ra" (the sun god, one of Egypt's most revered deities), was born into a non-royal family.

His grandfather Rameses I had attained power in 1293 BC, after a period of decline and loss of Egyptian influence under both Akhenaton and his son Tutankhamen. Akhenaton is best known for his highly individualistic religious beliefs, which focused on the worship of one god, Aton. His heir, Tutankhamen, died at eighteen; although his reign was brief, the splendors of his tomb were revealed to the world with its opening in 1922.

After some uncertainty and power manoeuvring, the Rameses dynasty took over and set about the task of restoring the empire's status. Since the death of Tutankhamen, various nearby states (from the region extending from present-day Sudan to Syria) had begun to seek opportunities to extend their own territories. The Hittites, skilled in the military arts, had been particularly troublesome during this period, fortifying their southern border with Egypt and making continual speculative sorties into Egyptian territory. The city of Kadesh, a long-time Egyptian possession that had recently defected to Hittite sovereignty, now lay just inside the Hittite border. It was a location of extreme strategic import, lying directly on the vital trade route that connected Europe to the Asian and African states.

This nineteenth century painting captures the wonder of Rameses II's imposing temple complex at Abu Simbel.

THE YOUNG RAMESES II

Two years after coming to power the elderly Rameses I installed his eldest son, Seti I, on the throne. Seti fought a series of partially successful wars against neighboring countries in western Asia, Libya, and Nubia (present-day southern Egypt and northern Sudan). He also managed to recapture Kadesh, which had repelled similar attempts by Tutankhamen and Horemheb (the last pharaoh of the Eighteenth Dynasty). Seti's son, the young Rameses II, was part of the victorious army, but the Egyptians did not sustain a permanent military occupation, and the Hittites reclaimed control within a few years. Hostilities ceased until after Seti's death in 1279 BC, perhaps because Seti had reached an agreement with Hittite ruler King Muwatalli on the position of the border between their empires.

Seti provided Rameses with an opulent lifestyle, including a personal harem. The young prince accompanied his father on military sorties, so that when he came to rule in his own right he was already an experienced warrior. He was given the rank of army captain at the age of ten (the rank was probably honorific, but the experience enabled the king-in-waiting to observe tactics and receive military training). Seti nominated Rameses as his successor at the unusually early age of fourteen, probably to ensure that he would succeed him as king—and around the age of thirty Rameses became pharaoh of Egypt.

In 1274 BC, five years into his reign, Rameses II set off into the Sinai desert across present-day Israel, Lebanon, and into Syria towards Kadesh. His army comprised some forty thousand troops and two thousand chariots. The Hittites, however, possessed some technological and strategic advantages. Many of their new chariots carried three men, rather than the traditional two. More importantly, the Hittites had set a cunning trap, luring Rameses forward into an ambush and separating him from the bulk of his army.

MARCH TO KADESH

The Egyptian army comprised four divisions, each named after an Egyptian god: Amon, Re, Ptah, and Seth. Rameses sent a division of about five thousand men to capture the nearby port of Sumur before returning to link up with the main army. Meanwhile the majority of his army turned inland and marched towards Kadesh. As he drew near Kadesh, Rameses captured

two Hittite spies who were masquerading as messengers, and extracted the "information" that Muwatalli's army was situated at Aleppo, hundreds of miles to the north. In fact, the Hittites were concealed in nearby mountains and valleys, waiting in ambush. Emboldened, Rameses and his troops forded the river Orontes about 7½ miles south of Kadesh, only to find that their retreat had been blocked and their fragmented army was now surrounded and vastly outnumbered by a superior Hittite army of about twenty-seven thousand troops and three thousand chariots.

The Hittites had used propaganda (and the crucial element of surprise) to seize the advantage. Rameses despatched messengers to hasten the return of the division sent to Sumur, but as the Hittites attacked, the Egyptian forces panicked and retreated in disarray. Amid the general mayhem, Rameses was unable to communicate with his troops, while Muwatalli's soldiers, too preoccupied with plundering the Egyptian camps to maintain surveillance, failed to detect that Rameses' reinforcements were rapidly approaching from the north and east.

Rameses was left with a small corps of personal troops who fought desperately until his Sumur troops arrived and his reunited company embarked upon a headlong counter-attack. Knives, maces, swords, spears, and longbows clashed as thousands of chariots engaged in battle. The Hittite three-man chariots, though more powerful and effective in open-plane combat, were now rendered vulnerable by their lack of manoeuvrability at close quarters, and suffered huge losses. Rameses retained control over the battlefield, but failed in his aim of taking Kadesh. Both sides had suffered failures of communication and good and bad exercise of central command. By this stage, both armies had suffered enormous casualties—the next morning the two sides agreed to an armistice and the Egyptians returned home.

Over the next fifteen years the Egyptians and Hittites fought a series of inconclusive skirmishes in the Kadesh region. The failure of the Kadesh campaign inspired some of the Egyptian-controlled states in the region to rebel against the central government. Rameses was forced to fortify the borders of the empire's Asiatic and African dominions at the same time as dealing with the Hittites. Eventually, like his father before him, he found that he could not retain control over territory so far from home in the face of continual insurrections.

A PEACE TREATY ... AND MONUMENTS IN STONE

Eventually concluding that the two kingdoms' mutual dreams of conquest were unattainable, Rameses and the new Hittite king Hattusili III, brother of Muwatalli, signed a peace treaty in 1259 BC, the first in recorded history. It contained eighteen articles, including requirements that are still found in treaties today—an amnesty for all refugees, exchanges of prisoners-of-war, and an agreement not to form alliances with each other's enemies. Two versions were recorded, one in Egyptian hieroglyphs, the other in Hittite cuneiform script. Most of the text is identical, with the exception that the Egyptian version claims that the Hittites relented and sued for peace, while the Hittite version claims the opposite.

Rameses was a master of self-aggrandizing propaganda. Scribes and poets accompanied him on his various military exploits—not to provide an objective, factual account, but to glorify his deeds and present them in the best possible light. Although the 1274 BC battle ended in a stalemate, Rameses' version of events claimed that he had won a resounding victory. He made the vainglorious boast that, even though his cowardly army had deserted him, he was nonetheless able to defeat the Hittites almost single-handedly (not crediting the reinforcements whose timely arrival had, in fact, saved the day).

Rameses arranged for numerous rock carvings and papyrus scrolls to record this and other sometimes-tenuous "victories." Such records are also found in the numerous temples that Rameses constructed—or co-opted from earlier times—to exalt his reign. Two major Egyptian narratives were made of the Battle of Kadesh. "The Poem" (a verse of which is reproduced below) is inscribed in the temples of Karnak, Luxor, Abydos, and the Ramesseum, while "The Report," a shorter version, is found in Luxor, Abydos, the Ramesseum, and Abu Simbel. A Hittite version was set down on tablets found in the Hittite capital Boghazkoy.

> Then the king he lashed each horse,
> And they quickened up their course,
> And he dashed into the middle of the hostile,
>   Hittite host,

> All alone, none other with him, for he counted
>   not the cost.
> Then he looked behind, and found
> That the foe were all around,
> Two thousand and five hundred of their chariots
>   of war;
> And the flower of the Hittites, and their helpers,
>   in a ring ...

A HITTITE BRIDE FOR RAMESES

With the peace formalities completed, the Egyptian and Hittite royal courts embarked upon a period of cordial relations. Rameses exchanged letters with Hattusili, discussing the possibility of a royal marriage to confirm the peace. In about 1245 BC a Hittite princess, given the Egyptian name of Maat-Hor-Neferure, arrived in Egypt to marry Rameses. This wedding was commemorated with inscriptions in numerous temples, including Karnak and Abu Simbel. It must have been a successful alliance, for Maat-Hor-Neferure was soon elevated to the status of Great Royal Wife, a title reserved for the highest ranked wife of the time (during his 66-year reign there were seven great royal wives).

Although incest was taboo in most ancient societies, including Greece and Rome, it was very common among Egyptian royalty. Rameses II is believed to have married several of his sisters and daughters. The major wives of kings were usually of royal blood, often their sisters or half-sisters. These marriages were profitable for several reasons. They blocked outsiders who might have designs on the throne, and produced royal children who would be eligible heirs.

They also ensured that a suitably trained princess would be available to become queen—the most important role available to an Egyptian woman. While the king could marry whomever he wished, a royal female was not permitted to marry below her status, so the field of potential husbands beyond her brothers (or father) was very limited. Egyptian princesses were also forbidden from marrying foreign monarchs, for fear their husbands or offspring might later lay claim to the throne of Egypt.

A TIME OF PROSPERITY

Despite the rich repository of records of Rameses' public life and achievements, little is known about his personal life. His first (and apparently favorite) queen was Nefertari, whom Rameses immortalized in the smaller Abu Simbel temple. She

RAMESES WAS A MASTER OF PROPAGANDA. SCRIBES AND POETS ACCOMPANIED HIM ON HIS VARIOUS MILITARY EXPLOITS TO GLORIFY HIS DEEDS.

bore him at least eight children in the more than twenty years of their marriage, and her ornate tomb in the Valley of the Queens at Thebes attests to her status. We know Rameses also married Isetnofret (among whose sons was Rameses' eventual successor, Merneptah) and Meritamun. The king maintained a large harem as well, comprising unattached female courtiers—including unmarried and widowed sisters, daughters and other relatives—foreign brides, upper class Egyptian women, and numerous consorts of unprivileged birth, including the servants of aristocratic ladies. Rameses is reputed to have fathered well over a hundred children.

Rameses took advantage of the relative peace of his rule by embarking upon a massive building program during which he oversaw the construction of a new capital, Per Rameses, in the Nile delta, and upgraded the ancient temple of Karnak, near Luxor. He also constructed the vast twin-temple complex of Abu Simbel, carved out of a mountainside in southern Egypt over a period of twenty years to celebrate his "victory" at Kadesh, and to commemorate himself and his beloved Nefertari. He built a temple complex, the Ramesseum, also near Luxor, which incorporated several 55-foot-high statues of himself, and included a writing school.

Rameses was idolized and imitated by later Egyptian kings, and his exploits lauded by leaders of foreign empires. But after his death the Egyptian empire gradually declined, succumbing in turn to the Persians, Alexander the Great and the Romans.

A note about dates: Dates in this era are disputed, and only approximate to within a few years, because witnesses and historians used various different systems to record events. To further confuse matters, at the accession of each new reign the Egyptian calendar reverted to Year 1.

431–404 BC
THE PELOPONNESIAN WAR

In the fifth century BC ancient Greece consisted of a group of warring city-states, the foremost being Athens, Sparta, Corinth, and Thebes. Peace was an occasional interlude between periods of war. The Peloponnesian War was a series of battles fought in three stages between Athens and Sparta (joined by their respective allies) from 431 to 404 BC. Athens was the dominant member of a group of city-states known as the Delian League, while Sparta led an alliance known as the Peloponnesian League, named after the peninsula on which Sparta was located. Athens, the most glorious city in the ancient world, was a flourishing democracy of perhaps one hundred thousand people, where decisions were made by its male citizens in public assembly. Sparta was an agrarian oligarchy governed by a small, aristocratic elite. Whereas Athens' strength lay in its navy, Sparta depended on a well-trained and disciplined army. Its military qualities had become legendary, attributable in no small way to the harsh and rigorous training young Spartan boys were subjected to when they left home at seven to live in barracks.

In 499 BC, though, the Greek city-states were united against a common enemy, the invading Persians. Eventually, they achieved victory over King Darius I at the Battle of Marathon in 490 BC. Darius' successor, Xerxes, invaded in 480 BC, but was driven out of the Aegean region by Athens and Sparta the following year. Following this victory, Athens became the pre-eminent state, forming an alliance with all the Mediterranean island states, many in Asia Minor, and most on the Greek mainland. Sparta, however, refused to join, preferring a policy of isolation and self-sufficient agriculture.

During this so-called "Golden Age," Athens became the world center of culture, a place where philosophy, literature, and drama flourished. Famous buildings, including the Parthenon, were built, and many eminent personalities emerged, among them the philosophers Socrates, and Plato, the historian and political analyst Thucydides, and the playwright Aristophanes. Athens continued to lead wars against the Persians, but some states became restive and, disapproving of Athens' increasingly imperialist outlook, tried to leave the alliance. They were unsuccessful.

When Athens destroyed the Corinthian fleet in 460 BC, Sparta seized the opportunity to join with Thebes and other states—and together they defeated Athens in 457 BC in the Battle of Tanagra. Sparta returned to isolation while Athens rose again to achieve a series of victories, both on land and at sea. But just a decade later, in 446 BC, Sparta again allied with other states to drive Athens from its mainland conquests. Facing revolts from its overseas empire, Athens was forced to sue for peace and agreed to sign the Thirty Years Peace Treaty with Sparta. Soon, however, the treaty was threatened by friction between the member states. In 435 BC Sparta's ally Corinth attacked the island state of Corfu, which in turn sought help from Athens. The threat of Athens' fleet was enough to deter Corinth, but other battles and sieges ensued over the next few years. Athens attacked another Spartan ally, Megara, 25 miles west of Athens, in 432 BC. This was the last straw for Sparta, which declared that Athens had breached the terms of the Thirty Years Peace and resumed all-out hostilities. This was the start of what is known as the Peloponnesian War.

THE BATTLE LINES ARE DRAWN

In the first phase of the war, Sparta invaded Attica, northeast of Athens in 431 BC, hoping to use the superior strength of

Pericles delivers the annual funeral oration for those killed in war against the backdrop of the newly built Parthenon.

its army to neutralize Athens' naval dominance. The Athenian leader, Pericles, determined to pursue a defensive strategy on land, while keeping his armies supplied with provisions and troops by sea. He cautioned the Athenian assembly not to become carried away with thoughts of expansion, but stated that the strength of Athens' navy gave reasonable expectation of a successful defence. Many, though, including Socrates, saw the looming war as an act of military madness, and probably doomed to failure.

Thucydides, who lived through the ensuing 27 years of warfare and documented it meticulously, says of this period:

> *The territory of Athens was being ravaged before the very eyes of the Athenians, a sight which the young men had never seen before and the old only in the Persian wars; and it was naturally thought a grievous insult, and the determination was universal, especially among the young men, to sally forth and stop it. Knots were formed in the streets and engaged in hot discussion; for if the proposed sally was warmly recommended, it was also in some cases opposed. Oracles of the most various import were recited by the collectors, and found eager listeners in one or other of the disputants.*

Their crushing defeat in the naval battle at Syracuse would prove the beginning of the end for the Athenians.

ASSAULT ON ATHENS

In 429 BC the Spartans quickly surrounded Athens, forcing its inhabitants to retreat behind the city walls. Plague soon broke out, causing a quarter of the population—including Pericles—to perish, and forcing the Spartans to retreat lest they also succumb. Thucydides also contracted the plague, but recovered. The following is an extract from his record of Pericles' famous oration on the occasion of the annual public funeral for the war-dead, in late 430 BC, in which he sets out the fundamentals of democracy:

> *Our constitution does not copy the laws of neighboring states; we are rather a pattern to others than imitators ourselves. Its administration favors the many instead of the few; this is why it is called a democracy. If we look to the laws, they afford equal justice to all in their private differences; if no social standing, advancement in public life falls to reputation for capacity, class considerations not being allowed to interfere with merit; nor again does poverty bar the way, if a man is able to serve the state, he is not hindered by the obscurity of his condition.*

The Spartans then besieged another Athenian ally, the city-state of Plataea to the northwest. By 427 BC they had starved Plataea into submission, massacring the entire population, and razing the city to the ground. Sparta also undertook annual attempts to invade Attica, but to no avail. Meanwhile Athens, undaunted by the loss of Pericles and the ravages of the plague, sent its navy on the offensive, wreaking havoc upon the Peloponnesian coast, destroying two naval fleets and blockading the Gulf of Corinth. Athens also quelled uprisings by Corcyra and the island of Lesbos.

OPPORTUNITY LOST

Pericles' successor, the hawkish Cleon, reversed Pericles' more moderate defensive strategy by launching unsuccessful attacks on Sparta's allies, Boeotia and Thebes. Athens next turned its attention to Aetolia to the north, securing a rare victory. In 425 BC the usual pattern of attack and counter-attack continued, as Sparta attacked Attica while the Athenian fleet cruised along the Peloponnese coast. The Athenian general Demosthenes established a fort on the southwest Peloponnesian coast at Pylos while the Athenian fleet drove the Spartan ships ashore on the nearby island of Sphacteria. Outmaneuvered, Sparta tried to sue for peace, offering its navy in return for Sphacteria, but Cleon demanded the return of all the lands Athens had relinquished at the end of the first Peloponnesian War in 446. Spartan king Agis demurred and the war continued, with Athens occupying Sphacteria and keeping the surviving Spartans as hostages.

The next two years saw a series of battles, with both sides experiencing victories and defeats. In 422 the Spartan general Brasidas defeated Athens at Amphipolis in Macedonia to the far northeast, though he and Cleon were both killed in the fighting.

A TRUCE AND A NEW GENERAL

In 421 BC the Peloponnesian War entered its second stage. The overly optimistic Fifty Years Peace treaty was signed, with both sides agreeing to hand back the territories they had gained, and the Athenians returning the Sphacteria hostages to Sparta. But in 418 BC Sparta's allies, Argos, Mantinea, and Elis, increasingly dissatisfied with the truce terms, formed a breakaway group which Sparta tried unsuccessfully to prevent. This alliance, with the assistance of Athens (under the command of the brilliant yet reckless general Alcibiades), turned on Sparta but was defeated at Mantinea in the largest battle of the war, with some ten thousand troops on each side.

DURING ITS GOLDEN AGE ATHENS BECAME THE WORLD CENTER OF CULTURE—A PLACE WHERE PHILOSOPHY, LITERATURE AND DRAMA FLOURISHED.

Sparta was again in control of the Peloponnesian League, and a period of relative peace followed. But in 415 Alcibiades (whose strategy invariably involved swift and aggressive action) persuaded the Athenian assembly that a threat by Spartan ally Syracuse, a city-state on the island of Sicily, to Athens' allies in Sicily offered an opportunity to conquer those areas of Sicily not already under Athenian control. Athens imported much of its grain from the island, and a total occupation would significantly increase its empire. This massive assault against Sicily launched the third and final phase of the Peloponnesian War.

BLOCKADE AND SIEGE

Athens besieged the Syracuse position, building walls to surround its landward border. This strategic advantage was lost when, in 413 BC, a combined Corinthian and Spartan fleet won a convincing naval victory, breaking the blockade and persuading the Athenians to withdraw. However, on the night of the planned retreat, an eclipse of the moon was interpreted as an evil portent, causing the Athenians to postpone the operation until the next full moon. This was a crucial strategic error—in the ensuing weeks the Syracuse fleet destroyed what was left of Athens' navy, killing its leaders and forcing a complete surrender.

The home situation was just as dismal for Athens. Sparta had once again declared war on Athens in 414, and succeeded in causing rebellion among some Athenian allies. Even the Persians came to Sparta's aid, providing funds as well as ships in return for recognition of their dominions in Asia Minor. Athens appeared to be doomed, and a coup in the city resulted in the suspension of democracy in favor of an opportunistic group known as the Four Hundred, who tried to sue for peace with Sparta. But, fortunately for Athens, it had preserved a fleet of a hundred ships and large reserves of currency specifically for use in a desperate situation such as the one it now faced. The fleet resumed operations in the Aegean Sea against the will of the Four Hundred, the troops disagreeing with the group's undemocratic structure. General Alcibiades had been branded a traitor, but nonetheless this charismatic soldier and politician retained a great deal of support. The Four Hundred were overthrown, democracy was restored and Alcibiades took charge of the Athenian fleet. From 411 to 408 BC Athens won a series of naval victories, causing Sparta to offer another truce. But the new Athenian leader, Cleophon, refused, and Sparta, under the command of Lysander, and boosted by the Persians' support (which had taken a long time to arrive), defeated Athens at Ephesus in 406 BC.

Alcibiades, whose leadership was always controversial, was sacked as the Spartans blockaded the Athenian fleet in the harbour of Mytilene on Lesbos. Athens managed to assemble another fleet, which won an overwhelming victory, causing Sparta to offer peace yet again. Cleophon again declined, letting slip another gilt-edged opportunity to save the Athenian empire.

By 405 BC the endgame was near. Lysander took his fleet to the Hellespont (now known as the Dardanelles), a narrow channel connecting the Aegean and Black seas, and a vital Athenian trade route. The Athenians attempted to engage him in battle, but Lysander refused, playing a waiting game until one night, in the harbour of Aegospotami, when the Athenians had been lulled into a false sense of security and sent most of their troops on shore leave, he attacked. He completely destroyed the Athenian fleet, ending Athens' lengthy era of naval supremacy. Lysander followed up this victory by besieging Athens and, in the spring of 404 BC, after a six-month blockade, starved it into unconditional surrender. Athens' defensive walls were completely destroyed and it lost all of its foreign territories. Sparta installed a puppet government known as the Thirty Tyrants, but this was overthrown by a popular uprising the following year and democracy was restored.

THE LEGACY OF ATHENS

Despite the war, Athenian artistic and intellectual life continued. Sophocles pondered the human condition and produced the dramatic masterpieces *Oedipus Rex*, *Oedipus Colonus*, and *Antigone* without ever mentioning the war. Aristophanes produced outrageous, hilarious, and often obscene satirical plays lampooning war and its advocates, and extolling peace. Thucydides kept analyzing, commenting, and recording contemporary history, giving us a vivid, comprehensive, and meditative record of the war. Socrates, despite speaking against many of the manifestations of the war (and predicting Athens' defeat), nonetheless served heroically in several campaigns, and never stopped trying to convince people that the good of the soul is the supreme good, and that rigorous, sceptical debate and dialectic are the keys to intellectual advancement. His execution after the war in 399 BC for supposedly corrupting the morals of youth can be seen as symbolic of Athens' fall from grace.

Athens never regained its political power, and poverty became widespread in Greece as the draining economic effects of the long war became manifest. Although Greek cultural and artistic pre-eminence continued, its city-states proved unable to unite against common foes, and its declining political influence led to eventual occupation by Macedonia, and later Rome. ❧

274 BC
THE REIGN OF EMPEROR ASHOKA

The Emperor King Ashoka (304–232 BC), also known as *Devanampiya Piyadasi* ("Beloved-of-the-Gods") and Ashoka the Great, was the third monarch of the great Mauryan dynasty that had come to rule most of the Indian subcontinent. He ruthlessly conquered a vast domain that included present-day Afghanistan, Pakistan, Nepal, Iran (Persia), and most of India. British author and historian H. G. Wells wrote of him: "In the history of the world there have been thousands of kings and emperors who called themselves 'their highnesses,' 'their majesties' and 'their exalted majesties' and so on. They shone for a brief moment, and as quickly disappeared. But Ashoka shines and shines brightly like a bright star, even unto this day."

In 262 BC, eight years after his accession, Ashoka sought to further expand his empire, and his armies attacked and conquered the Kalinga region, roughly corresponding to the modern east-Indian state of Orissa. But in the wake of the bloody battle, contemplating the horrors he had unleashed, he experienced a spiritual epiphany that led to a complete turnabout in his outlook. Ashoka spent the rest of his life applying pacifist and humanist principles of justice and virtue to his administration, and helped the fledgling religion of Buddhism to expand throughout India and nearby states. (Buddha died in about 480 BC.)

Ashoka's grandfather, Chandragupta, had established a large empire in northern India, which was further expanded by Ashoka's father, Bindusara. Little is known of Ashoka's early life, but upon Bindusara's death he embarked on a two-year war of succession that led to his ascent to the throne.

On his accession, partly achieved by ruthless elimination of all potential opposition (including his stepbrothers), Ashoka found himself leader of a great empire which already stretched from northern India to the southern border of modern Karnataka state, eastward to Calcutta and Bangladesh, and as far west as southeast Afghanistan.

However, he had even greater imperialist designs. He embarked upon a series of battles that extended his domain, and then set his sights on Kalinga, which had declared itself independent during the reign of Chandragupta and resisted several unsuccessful invasion attempts by Bindusara. Ashoka determined to regain control over the region, which was abundant in precious ores and rich farmlands, and was strategically situated on the busy Bay of Bengal trading route leading to the Krishna River valley, which held vast reserves of gold and precious stones. Ashoka's war against the king of Kalinga—the bloodiest in India's history—was successful, but at the cost of over one hundred thousand lives. Legend has it that, after the war, he ventured into the shattered streets of Kalinga and, seeing only smouldering buildings and countless corpses, cried "What have I done?" In the aftermath, Ashoka's contemplations caused him to renounce his expansionist policy and determine to rule by compassion and education, rather than by conquering territories and repressing the masses.

CONVERSION TO BUDDHISM

Another factor may have led Ashoka to Buddhism. According to legend, Mauryan princess Maharani Devi, the wife of Ashoka's brother, whom he had killed during the war of succession following the death of their father, fled with a maid in order to protect her unborn child. When eventually the exhausted princess collapsed under a tree, the maid ran to a nearby Buddhist monastery to seek help from a doctor or priest. Meanwhile Maharani Devi gave birth to male and female twins, Mahindra and Sanghamitra, who were brought up and educated at the monastery.

When Mahindra was about thirteen years old he met Ashoka, who expressed surprise that such a young boy was dressed as a sage. When he revealed that he was in fact Ashoka's nephew, Ashoka was overcome by remorse and compassion, and allowed the twins and their mother to move into his palace. Mahindra, by now more a monk than a prince, advised Ashoka to embrace the Buddhist dharma and renounce war. *Dharma*—Law, or Truth—does not have a direct English equivalent, but may be roughly translated as referring to the inherent order and harmony in nature, and a life lived in accordance with that order. Mahindra and Sanghamitra were opposed to war so they asked Ashoka for permission to join the sangha (Buddhist monastic community), which he reluctantly approved. They went on to establish Buddhism in Sri Lanka. Henceforth Ashoka, who had been known as Chandashoka, "Ashoka the Cruel," became known as Dharmashoka, "Ashoka the Good."

Ashoka, who had been born a Hindu, began to study Buddhism under the guidance of the great Brahmin Buddhist sages Radhaswami and Manjushri. For the rest of his reign he pursued *ahimsa* (the policy of non-violence that in the twentieth century found expression in Mahatma Gandhi's quest for India to gain independence from Britain). He freed his prisoners-of-war and returned control of their territory to their rightful rulers. He abolished the unnecessary hunting, slaughter, branding and mutilation of animals. Limited hunting was allowed for nutrition where necessary, but Ashoka promoted vegetarianism, and eventually adopted the practice wholeheartedly. All wildlife was protected under law—Ashoka was perhaps the first ruler in history to introduce animal conservation measures. He embarked upon a large

The Lion Capital of Ashoka has become an enduring symbol for India as its national emblem.

public works program, building universities, irrigation, and navigation canals, and free rest houses and hospitals for travellers and pilgrims. He abolished slavery and treated everyone as equal, regardless of religion, politics or caste. Prisoners were released for one day per year. He abandoned the long-standing Mauryan policy of invading weaker kingdoms, instead favoring trade and negotiation.

THE EDICTS

Ashoka now began to formulate his Edicts, which are the earliest decipherable Indian written works. They are written on rocks, mountains, and stone pillars, the last bearing testimony to the technological and artistic dexterity of ancient Indian civilization. The pillars, between 40 and 50 feet high, and weighing up to 50 tons, were excavated from quarries to the south of Varanasi. Some were transported 100s of miles. Each pillar was originally capped by a headstone representing an animal such as a lion, bull or horse. Few headstones have survived, but the extant examples are recognized as artistic masterpieces. Both the headstones and the pillars have retained an extraordinary mirror-like sheen that has survived centuries of exposure to the elements.

Ashoka's Edicts fall into several categories. Some refer to the activities of the Buddhist *sangha*, and are addressed to local

Detail of a relief sculpture at the Great Stupa built by Emperor Ashoka at Sanchi.

government officers or monks. The so-called Minor Edicts describe Ashoka's general commitment to Buddhism and to other philosophical issues, while the Major Rock Edicts and the Pillar Edicts are more wide-ranging and comprehensive. In general they emphasize the importance of open-mindedness in regard to differing belief systems, and define social ethics as a respect for parents and teachers. They also highlight the necessity for harmonious relationships between family members, teachers and students, and employers and employees.

The following extract from Minor Edict 2 describes the kinds of harmonious relationships that should exist among all living creatures:

Father and mother should be respected and so should elders, kindness to living beings should be made strong and the truth should be spoken. In these ways, the Dharma should be promoted. Likewise, a teacher should be honored by his pupil and proper manners should be shown towards relations. This is an ancient rule that conduces to long life. Thus should one act …

23

Kalinga Rock Edict 1 provides guidance on how to live one's life with wisdom, compassion and discipline:

All men are my children. What I desire for my own children, and I desire their welfare and happiness both in this world and the next, that I desire for all men. You do not understand to what extent I desire this, and if some of you do understand, you do not understand the full extent of my desire. You must attend to this matter. While being completely law-abiding, some people are imprisoned, treated harshly and even killed without cause so that many people suffer. Therefore your aim should be to act with impartiality. It is because of these things—envy, anger, cruelty, hate, indifference, laziness or tiredness—that such a thing does not happen. Therefore your aim should be: "May these things not be in me." And the root of this is non-anger and patience. Those who are bored with the administration of justice will not be promoted; those who are not will move upwards and be promoted. Whoever among you understands this should say to his colleagues: "See that you do your duty properly. Such are Piyadasi's instructions."

Some Edicts were positioned in significant locations, such as Buddha's birthplace, while others were located in large population centers where they would be widely read. They appear to be written in Ashoka's own words rather than in the formal style of a royal proclamation, and their informal and personal tone provides a glimpse into the personality of this multi-faceted man. The style is at times repetitive and Ashoka often refers to his good works, although not necessarily in an egotistical way. The Edicts suggest a keen sensitivity and a concern that those who read of him in the decades and centuries to come would think of him as a sincere person and a good governor.

One of the Edicts in Afghanistan is written in both Greek and Aramaic, indicating that the Greek empire had expanded to this region, and that the Greek population within his realm converted to Buddhism. Most edicts are written in Brahmi, the root script from which all Indian and many Southeast Asian languages evolved. In eastern India the edicts are written in Magadhi, which was probably the official language of Ashoka's court. In western India an early form of Sanskrit is used.

ASHOKA'S LEGACY

Ashoka was responsible for the first attempt to formulate government along Buddhist principles; he played a seminal part in helping Buddhism spread throughout India and abroad, and built the first major Buddhist monuments. It is apparent that he considered his reforms part of his duties as a Buddhist. Nevertheless, he was not intolerant of other religions; rather, he encouraged everyone to practise their own religion with the same sincerity that he demonstrated in his own practice.

Ashoka ruled over his empire for only forty years, and within fifty years of his death the Mauryan Empire had ceased to exist. Nevertheless, legacies of his rule can be seen all over India today. The Ashoka Chakra, the 24-spoked Wheel of Dharma, can be seen in the center of India's national flag, and the famous Lion Capital of Ashoka, the four sculpted lions standing proudly back to back that once adorned the top of the Ashoka Pillar at Sarnath, has since become the national emblem of India and can be seen today in the Sarnath Museum.

The Sarnath pillar also contains an Edict that sums up the theme of "unity in diversity" that so perfectly captures the Indian attitude to its religiously disparate society: "No one shall cause division in the order of monks." ❀

259–210 BC

QIN SHIHUANGDI AND THE CREATION OF A UNIFIED CHINA

China's first emperor was born Zhao Zheng around 259 BC, the son of Zichu, a prince of the royal family of the Qin state. His mother was a former concubine of a rich merchant named Lu Buwei. He ascended the throne in 245 BC at the age of thirteen and ruled with the help of his mother and Lu Buwei until 238 BC, when he rose to full power after a successful coup. He then executed his mother's lover, Lao Ai, who had joined the opposition, and exiled Lu Buwei.

In the third century BC China consisted of a group of seven independent states that had been constantly warring for more than 250 years. Zheng was born in Zhao state but his family, suffering persecution, fled to neighboring Qin state. He began his conquest of the states in 228 BC by successfully invading Zhao with an army of five hundred thousand troops. (In comparison, at about the same time, Rome was fighting Carthage with a mere six thousand troops, while, in the early nineteenth century, Napoleon's army at its height numbered about one hundred thousand.) He identified those Zhao responsible for his family's exile and tortured them before publicly killing them, often by dragging them behind a horse.

Zheng achieved loyalty with a mixture of reward and punishment; successful troops were awarded land, money, promotions, and publicity. This had the effect of improving bravery, morale, and recruitment rates. But failure was punishable by death. Success was measured by the numbers of enemy killed—calculated by the number of victims' heads which the returning armies carried as proof. The armies were divided into groups of ten; if just one member was killed, the other nine were required to obtain the head of an enemy, otherwise they would all be killed.

In 225 BC Zheng attacked Chu state deploying only two hundred thousand men, but suffered an almost complete rout, losing all but about ten thousand troops. Realizing his error, he called upon one of his great generals, Wang Jian, who advised him to re-attack the following year with some six hundred thousand troops. This time the Chu, complacent and flushed with victory, were easily defeated, causing Yan state to pre-emptively surrender—or so it seemed. In fact, the capitulation was a ruse, and Yan emissaries tried unsuccessfully to assassinate Zheng. Enraged, Zheng invaded Yan and crushed it in a mere four weeks.

HEAVY CASUALTIES AND TRIUMPH FOR ZHENG

By using espionage, bribery, and ruthlessly effective military tactics, Zheng eliminated, one by one, the remaining six rival states. His defeat of Qi in 221 BC saw China united for the first time in its history, albeit at the cost of well over a million lives. Following these triumphs Zheng renamed himself Qin Shihuangdi (*shi*, the first; *huang*, august or great; *di*, son of

秦始皇

姓嬴名政始目始皇乙卯即王位庚辰併天下稱皇帝
在位三十七年居王位二十五年即帝位十二年壽五十

廿

heaven)—in other words, the first God-sent ruler of a unified China. *Qin* (pronounced "chin") gave his name to the new integrated power.

But treason and treachery followed as rulers of the defeated states plotted their retribution. Recognizing the threat they posed, Emperor Qin forced them to relocate to his own court, along with one hundred and twenty thousand aristocratic families, so he could keep an eye on them. He also imposed standardized systems of currency, law, measurement, and language—which still exist to this day.

Qin now embarked upon a huge capital works program. He organized the construction of a canal system that linked the Lijang and Xian Jiang rivers and used the canals to transport food and arms to his troops. He also decided to build a great wall—to join sections of wall built by previous provincial administrations—to keep out marauding Mongol "barbarians" to the north. When completed, the wall measured over 3000 miles and stretched from Mount Jeyshi in present-day North Korea to Linshao in western China. It was built with local materials: stone in some places, compacted earth and wood in others. It measured 20 feet high and up to 16 feet wide, with beacon platforms 26 feet high placed along its length within sight of each other to enable communication by smoke signal in daytime and by fire at night. It was the world's first communication highway, and it enabled messages to be sent from one end of the wall to the other in just a few hours. To construct the wall Qin conscripted up to seven hundred thousand soldiers, peasants, and criminals, each with a support staff of up to five who were responsible for providing food, building materials, horses, camels, carts, and other essentials. Well over one million workers died during construction of the Great Wall of China, which progressed at an average rate of almost 1 mile per day for ten years. The bodies of many of the dead were used as filler within the walls.

BURNING THE BOOKS

To emphasize his status as the "first" emperor, Qin ordered the burning of most traditional books of wisdom (with the exception of those on the topics of agriculture, medicine, and divination). Qin became obsessed with the quest for eternal life, apparently believing that he would be able to retain power even after his death. He traversed his kingdom seeking the

> QIN BECAME OBSESSED WITH THE QUEST FOR ETERNAL LIFE, APPARENTLY BELIEVING THAT HE WOULD BE ABLE TO RETAIN POWER EVEN AFTER HIS DEATH.

elixir of life, ingesting mercury-laced potions prepared by his numerous doctors in the belief that this poison, in combination with other substances, held the secret.

By 213 BC Qin suspected everyone of plotting against him, including his most loyal eunuchs, ministers, courtiers, and priests (many of whom he ordered killed), and he surrounded himself with sycophants who fed his megalomania. When Confucian scholars warned him of genuine plots to overthrow or assassinate him, he ordered the live burial of 460 of them and banished the remainder to wall-building duties—a death sentence in itself. (When he was compared to Qin, Chairman Mao Zedong, leader of the People's Republic of China from 1943 to 1976, replied: "He only buried 460 scholars alive; we have buried forty-six thousand scholars … You intellectuals revile us for being Qin Shihuangdis. You are wrong. We have surpassed Qin Shihuangdi a hundredfold.")

A RULE MARKED BY SUSPICION AND PARANOIA

Qin also killed most of the country's pre-eminent intellectuals and military officers. The populace grew ever more restive as Qin ignored the prevailing Confucian precept that good governors attract good portents and popular support. He became convinced that even the spirit world was against him; he was in control of his empire, but not of himself. He suffered hallucinations and came to believe that he would live forever (even though his body might die) and that, in any case, he could become lord of the underworld if he took sufficient resources with him. He ordered more and more additions to his mausoleum, including terra-cotta warriors, who were intended to ensure that his power would last for ten thousand generations.

Qin had begun construction of his mausoleum in 220 BC, the year after he came to power, and just ten years before his death. It took an estimated seven hundred thousand conscripts to build what is the largest pyramid on earth in terms of surface area. Its circumference is three-quarters of a mile, its height 250 feet. In comparison, the Great Pyramid at Giza in Egypt rises to almost 500 feet. The mausoleum is aligned to the north star, reflecting Qin's belief that his heaven-sent authority was the center of the universe. It is surrounded by two perimeter walls that mark the limits of the inner and outer city.

FIGURES IN TERRA-COTTA

In between the walls of the pyramid, to the west of the sarcophagus, is a series of pits. One contains bronze horses

China's first emperor, Qin Shihuangdi, whose reign was both bloody and visionary.

(and the remains of real horses), chariots, the remains of various rare birds and animals, and pieces of gold, bronze and jade. Archaeologists have dubbed this area "the zoo." Nearby are eleven shallow graves containing the skeletons of prisoners bound hand and foot, and to the southeast ninety-one small pits house the "royal stables," complete with bronze chariots, terra-cotta horses, the remains of real horses, and terra-cotta figures of grooms. The chariots feature paper-thin bronze umbrellas less than $1/12$ inch thick to protect the drivers from the elements. Scientists today have no idea how the ancient metalworkers were able to manufacture such delicate and precise creations. No tools or technology capable of engineering such a feat have ever been discovered, although the technological methods they used to make many of the chariots' moving parts are still in use today. Another pit holds sixty-eight soldiers who are taller than the massed warriors: 6 feet 2 inches compared with 5 feet 8 inches. Archaeologists presume that this is the command center for the highest-ranking warriors. Yet another pit contains some very unusual clay figures—acrobats, jugglers, and other entertainers who are spinning, jumping or dancing.

To the northwest lies a palace, a miniature model of the empire that Qin created, complete with mountains and valleys, and lakes and rivers of mercury. The mausoleum is yet to be unearthed, but architects' plans describe how its ceiling is studded with pearls and other precious gems to emulate the pattern of stars in the sky. Whale oil lamps caused the "stars" to shimmer and reflect in the mercury lake below. Concubines who had not borne children to Qin were interred next to him, to accompany him into the afterlife and perhaps provide him with heirs.

The smelting methods used to manufacture the arrows, arrowheads and trigger mechanisms were remarkably advanced. A similar crossbow design did not appear in Europe until some 1000 years later. The arrow shafts were made of iron doped with carbon in a blast furnace, indicating history's first use of steel. This technique next appeared in Scandinavia about 800 BC, a thousand years later, and in the rest of Europe about 300 years after that. The bronze tips of the arrows were coated in corrosion-proof chromium, a technique that did not appear in the West until the nineteenth century. These items, despite being buried for more than two thousand years, are still in perfect, untarnished condition. The precision and consistent proportions of the triangular arrow bolts indicate extremely advanced metallurgical techniques. The perfect consistency of the weapons' components meant that parts were interchangeable—a valuable strategic asset that allowed rapid running repairs in the heat of battle. Qin had created the world's first military–industrial complex.

QIN'S MAUSOLEUM IS PROTECTED BY A SERIES OF BOOBY TRAPS COMPRISING PHALANXES OF CROSSBOWS WITH BRONZE-TIPPED ARROWHEADS.

PREPARATION FOR THE AFTERLIFE

An army of terra-cotta warriors, each weighing about half a tonne, is contained in four pits to the east of the central tomb complex. They were transported, presumably by horse and cart, from the firing kilns several miles away. The torsos were constructed using coils of clay mixed with white quartz dust that were pressed together then forced into a mould. (Exactly the same technique is used to make terra-cotta today.) The limbs were constructed the same way and then attached to the body. The hands and feet, moulded separately, were inserted into holes in the limbs and secured with slip (wet clay). The bodies were then clad in handmade clay pieces fashioned to resemble the various soldiers' uniforms. Before the head was added, the bodies were slowly dried in a warm kiln then baked at 1000°C (1800°F) for five days. The heads were then fired before being loosely placed on the bodies; they are removable. The heads are as individual as the bodies are similar. Each was moulded and sculpted separately by artisans who created individual facial features and expressions, hairstyles and headgear. Some look serious and sombre; others appear amused, bewildered, startled, or sad. The 'hair' on some of the soldiers was colored with charcoal. After firing, some (perhaps all) of the soldiers were brightly painted.

The troops were then placed in formation, and the pit covered with pine logs. A layer of plaster powder was sprinkled on top, then a layer of woven hessian-type material. The plaster hardened as it gradually absorbed moisture. Finally, a layer of earth about 5 feet thick was placed over the matting, concealing the fruits of the world's first mass-production assembly line.

The actual mausoleum is protected by a series of booby traps comprising phalanxes of crossbows with bronze-tipped arrowheads, which are set up to be activated by tripwires and also by the opening of the entrance door. (This is one reason why the area remains for the present undisturbed; another is that we do not yet have the technology to prevent the paint from dissolving almost as soon as it comes into contact with air.) After Qin's burial, at his instruction, one of his trusted lieutenants sealed the door to the tomb from the outside, entombing all the workers who had built the mausoleum in order to keep its location secret.

THE END OF QIN

Qin died suddenly in 210 BC, probably as a result of mercury poisoning, and was succeeded by his eighteenth son Huhai, who was not nearly as competent as his father. He was unable

to prevent civil revolts and invasion by the other resurgent states, starting with the Zhao.

Three years later the Qin Empire collapsed, heralding the start of the Han Dynasty, which lasted four hundred years. The Han reintroduced the teachings of Confucianism from the earlier Zhou Dynasty, but preserved most of Qin's economic and political reforms. Thus Qin's work has carried on through the centuries and become an enduring feature of Chinese society. His widespread reforms had created the world's greatest nation-state. Giant projects like the Great Wall and the canal systems provided unprecedented security to the populace, particularly the peasant classes. But in the process, the dynasty had become terminally fatigued.

Qin's historical legacy is mixed. He achieved greater power than Napoleon Bonaparte and controlled more territory

One of the terra-cotta regiments buried with Qin Shihuangdi which would help continue his domination in the afterlife.

than Alexander the Great. He commanded the biggest army in history. Some regard him as an imperialist megalomaniac who enslaved his people, brutally eliminated his opponents and imposed his views on the entire population. Others point to the efficiencies and economies of scale resulting from his standardization of language, writing, weights, measurement, and currency, and the newfound security experienced by most of the citizenry. The Chinese government has said that Qin's necropolis may remain forever unearthed. He has attained a kind of immortality after all. ❧

218 BC
HANNIBAL CROSSES THE ALPS

In the third century BC, the ancient North African kingdom of Carthage fought the up-and-coming power Rome for control of the Mediterranean basin. This lengthy and bloody conflict took three wars—known as the Punic Wars—and one hundred years to resolve. In the end, Rome was the victor, Carthage, famously, the loser, the once-grand old city burned literally to ashes, its people sold into slavery, its very earth sown with salt, so that nothing could ever grow there again. After this victory, Rome was well on its way to establishing its thousand-year empire, while Carthage became merely an echoing and distant memory. Except, that is, for one man: Hannibal Barca, whose extraordinary feat of crossing the Alps with a large army—and a herd of battle elephants—has captured human imaginations for 2500 years.

It's doubtful whether we would know anything about Hannibal were it not for a dogged Greek-born historian named Polybius, who, writing 50 years after the event in his *History of the Roman Republic*, even tried to trace Hannibal's route and talk to descendants of those who had fought with the legendary Carthaginian. What a word picture Polybius paints. He reports that, as Hannibal stood in the foothills of the Alps, with mountains of indescribable height looming behind him—mountains no army had ever crossed—he addressed his

---

Hannibal's elephants were battle-hardened war machines, but did not fare well in the subzero temperatures during the journey across the high Alps.

nervous troops in this way: "What do you think the Alps are? They are nothing more than high mountains ... No height is insurmountable to men of determination."

Hannibal had come up with an extraordinary military and logistical plan: a way to attack Italy, not by sea, which the Romans with their powerful navy could readily guard against, but from the north, after travelling through mountains many thought impassable. But it was not just his logistical adeptness that motivated his army to travel 1000 miles through hostile territory, from Spain, across the Pyrenees and through southern France to Italy. It was also the fact that he was one of the most determined and inspiring leaders in history, driven by what may have been a passionate hatred of Rome, but was certainly a passionate need to win at any cost.

"I WILL USE FIRE AND STEEL"

The Punic Wars—the name comes from the Latin word *Punicus*, meaning "Phoenician," for Carthage began as a Phoenician colony in the seventh century BC—were about territory and wealth. In the third century BC, Carthage, located in modern-day Tunisia, controlled much of the islands of Corsica, Sardinia, and Sicily, south-eastern Spain, and a good deal of the North African coast to present-day Israel. Rome, on the other hand, was just emerging as the conqueror of many of the city-states of the Italian Peninsula, and wanting to extend its dominion into the Mediterranean. The First Punic War began in 264 BC as a battle for control of Sicily and lasted twenty-three years. Carthage lost and was pushed out of Sicily and forced to pay a huge indemnity to the Romans. It

turned its attention to building up an empire in Spain, but the Romans weren't about to let that happen either.

In 221 BC, Hannibal Barca, the twenty-five-year-old son of a legendary Carthaginian commander, took control of Carthaginian forces in Spain after his father was killed fighting the local tribes. He immediately began an aggressive campaign against some of the wild Celtiberian tribes to the north; when he besieged the city of Saguntum (now Sagunto in Spain), which the Romans thought was rightfully theirs, they demanded that he be brought to Italy in chains. But Hannibal scoffed at the emissaries who demanded that he give himself up and break off the siege, and in 218 BC the city fell to the Carthaginians in an orgy of slaughter. Diplomatic relations between Carthage and Rome were then broken off and the Second Punic War commenced.

It was said that when he was still a child Hannibal had sworn an oath that "as soon as age will permit ... I will use fire and steel to resolve the destiny of Rome." The Romans who met him reported back that he was indeed possessed of a fiery hatred of Rome. Whatever it took now, Hannibal was not about to allow Carthage to lose another war to Rome, for he knew that it would mean the utter destruction of his homeland. Soon, he began to put his plan for an overland attack on Italy into motion.

A sixteenth-century depiction of the battle of Zama in 202 BC, where the Romans finally defeated their great Carthaginian rival.

A POLYGLOT FORCE

Estimates vary regarding the size of Hannibal's army: ancient sources put it as high as one hundred thousand, but it was probably between forty and fifty thousand, including ten thousand cavalry. It was a polyglot force—Celtiberian tribesmen, Berbers, and Numidian cavalry from North Africa, Gauls from southern France, Greek infantry. All were mercenaries, commanded by Carthaginian officers—yet Hannibal, through extraordinary charisma, as well as common sense when it came to dealing with soldiers, managed to keep them in line.

Famously, Hannibal also brought forty war elephants with him on his journey across the Alps. Elephants had been used in combat for thousands of years by the time Hannibal employed them and were a potent force, the tanks or armored cars of their time. They were especially useful against isolated communities that had never seen them before, as Hannibal must have suspected would be the case with the tribes he would run up against on his journey. Hannibal's elephants

THE PANIC SET IN AS VISIBILITY GOT WORSE. THE ROARS OF THE ELEPHANTS THAT THUDDED DOWN THE SIDES OF THE GREAT PEAKS TO THEIR DEATHS WERE ESPECIALLY TERRIFYING.

were African forest elephants. Now extinct, they were about half as high as the Asian elephant, although they were relatively speedy and more manoeuvrable.

As he led his army out of New Carthage (the modern-day town of Cartagena) in the spring of 218 BC, heading up the east coast of the Iberian Peninsula to Gaul, Hannibal knew that he needed to make his journey in time to cross the Alps before winter set in, or he and his men would almost certainly perish there. After crossing into Gaul and fighting off a warlike tribe near the Rhône River, Hannibal's cavalry scouts had the misfortune to encounter troops under the Roman commander Publius Cornelius Scipio, who happened to put into the nearby port of Massilia (now Marseille) on his way to attack Spain. This chance meeting changed Hannibal's entire approach to crossing the Alps, for he could not now cross via any of the more accessible passes in the Maritime Alps near the Mediterranean because he felt sure the Roman fleet was dogging him. So he made a detour north, up the Rhône River, and then turned right and headed down a river valley through mountains that rose about 5000 feet high. It was now nearly the end of August, and he had little time left to make it over the Alps before the winter set in at high altitudes.

At this point, the strategy must have begun to seem reckless, even to the leader himself. Yet one of the reasons why Hannibal is considered such a brilliant leader by historians is that he never once considered turning back, not even now when he knew the Romans were aware of his presence and he had lost the element of surprise.

INTO THE ALPS

After Hannibal made his stirring speech, his forty thousand or so men, along with elephants, horses and retainers, moved into the Alps. As the soldiers climbed, they wound their way through ever-narrower defiles and canyons. Above them on cliff ledges were wild tribesmen, the Allobroges, whose shadowy presence was frightening and who soon launched an ambush that caught the Carthaginians in a gorge, but which Hannibal was able to bloodily repel.

A bust of Hannibal, now in the Museo Nazionale in Naples, Italy. Hannibal Barca was Rome's sworn and deadly enemy.

HANNIBAL CROSSES THE ALPS

After a week or so, Hannibal approached the tallest mountains in the French Alps, the last barrier between the fertile valleys of Italy. These mountains were 13,000 feet tall, a truly awe-inspiring sight, some with snow on their peaks even in September. If the Allobroges had been bad, the tribesmen who inhabited this region were worse. In writing of Hannibal's journey, the Roman historian Livy called them "shaggy, unkempt men perched upon the crags above, more horrible to look at than words can tell." It seems, from the accounts of Livy and others, that this unnamed group was populous—and obviously not afraid to take on a large force of men in ambush.

Surprisingly, these tribesmen sent a delegation to Hannibal, claiming that they were impressed by the way he had defeated the Allobroges and offering to lead him to an easy pass to Italy. Hannibal acquiesced to this, warily, even asking for hostages to guarantee the Carthaginians' safe passage. However, there is evidence he may have been lost, and felt that following these men was his only choice.

The tribesmen led the Carthaginians through the mountains for about two days, then steered them into an extremely narrow ravine with a high wall on one side and a fast-flowing stream on the other. As the Carthaginian column entered this ravine, the tribesmen moved to block the front and back entrances, while others crept up high on the cliffs. At a signal, they pushed piles of rocks and logs down upon the soldiers and shot arrows to stampede the animals.

It was a horrible slaughter, with men crushed by rocks, or caught between the hooves of elephants and horses. It is possible that the army might not have survived except for the forethought of Hannibal. To protect against just such an attack, he had placed his heavy infantry at the front and back of the column. These soldiers were able to repel the tribesmen attacking at those points and eventually help the middle of the column fight its way though the pass. They were aided in this by the elephants, which badly frightened the barbarians, sending them reeling out of the way when they charged. After a long day's struggle, the Carthaginians escaped.

A HIGH AND DESOLATE PASS

But the hardest part of the journey was yet to come. The Carthaginians now had to cross one of the highest passes in the Alps. In attempting this, men by the hundreds, weak and exhausted, began to slip and fall, and their cries echoed across the mountains, horrible music to the ears of those left climbing. According to at least one chronicler, a snowstorm now hit the column, causing more men to stumble over the precipices. The only thing each man could see through the blinding blizzard was the man directly in front of him.

Panic set in as even that small amount of visibility began to dim. The roars of the elephants that thudded down the sides of the great peaks to their deaths were especially terrifying. The falling elephants were joined by many of the pack animals, who broke through the first soft layer of snow with their hooves, became stuck in the ice beneath, and were finally pushed off the sides by soldiers impatient to get through. The soldiers themselves were burdened by supplies in heavy packs, and one tilt off balance could send them, too, hurtling into the dark ravines.

Hannibal, who usually travelled at the rear of the line, strode past his terrified soldiers, exhorting them to move, reminding them, even with the wind howling in their ears, that the beautiful valleys of Italy awaited them. "The mighty barriers we have scaled are the walls, not only of Italy, but of Rome itself," he told his troops. "It is only one battle when we get down on the plains, or at most two, and the great city will be ours."

After three days, they reached the top of the pass and could look down upon the Po Valley of Italy. But the descent—down slippery, rocky slopes, where the back of the column trod on icy slush churned up by the front—cost even more lives than the climb. Finally, however, the army reached the lower slopes and entered a temperate zone—which must have seemed like Eden to them. Trees and grass grew in abundance, and there was fresh game and fruit. Filthy, emaciated, and traumatized, they must have looked worse than any of the "barbarian" peoples who had tried to impede their progress. But they had made it.

> HANNIBAL LOST AS MANY AS TWENTY THOUSAND MEN IN HIS JOURNEY ACROSS THE ALPS.

TAKING THE BATTLE TO ROME

The cost of the journey had been high indeed. Estimates vary, but it appears that in the Alps Hannibal lost perhaps twenty thousand men. Only three elephants—perhaps just one—survived. Despite this, Hannibal had achieved his objective and was now in a position to attack the Romans. After resting his remaining twenty-six thousand troops for nearly two weeks, Hannibal brought them to their feet and marched them south through Italy.

Hannibal was to spend the next fourteen years campaigning there, where he won numerous victories. This included his bloody and historic success at Cannae in 216 BC, where his force massacred fifty thousand Roman soldiers in one day. But he was never able to get the city-states of the Italian Peninsula to side with him, and Rome, after an initial shock, was able to rally, finally defeating Hannibal in 202 BC at the battle of Zama, in North Africa.

Soon thereafter, the Carthaginian commander went into exile. Rather than be captured by the Romans, he committed suicide on an obscure island. Despite this, no one could say that Hannibal had ever really been defeated.

44 BC
THE ASSASSINATION OF JULIUS CAESAR

At dinner, the man suddenly asked his companions what manner of death they might hope for, and answered his own question by saying he wanted a quick, unexpected end. After he went to bed, the windows and shutters of his house were blown open, as if by a fierce wind, except that the night was calm. In his sleep, the man dreamed he was flying above the clouds, skimming, lighter than air, and he awoke just as he was reaching out to touch the hand of Jupiter.

That morning was the Ides, or middle, of March. As Julius Caesar rubbed the sleep out of his eyes, his wife, Calpurnia, told him that she had dreamed of his lifeless body lying bloody in her lap. She begged him not to go to meet with the Roman Senate, as he had planned to do. Her exhortations gave him pause; Calpurnia was not prone to hysteria. Moreover, Caesar recalled a soothsayer, Spurinna, recently telling him that danger would befall him no later than the Ides of March.

When Caesar's close aide Mark Antony arrived at his house, Caesar instructed him to postpone the visit. But then another friend arrived and convinced Caesar it would not be seemly for the *Pater Patriae*, or "Father of the Fatherland," to cancel a meeting with the Senate. The friend's name was Decimus Brutus, cousin of another Brutus who awaited Caesar on the Senate floor, and he had murder in his heart.

Caesar listened to this man and left his home for the last time.

A CAUTIONARY TALE?

It is no wonder that omens (real or imagined) surrounded the death of Gaius Julius Caesar. The most pivotal figure in the thousand-year history of Ancient Rome was born in 100 BC in the month of Quintilis, a month that was later named after him: July. (No one really knows, however, if he was born by Caesarean section.) Caesar was altogether extraordinary. He was a brilliant military leader—brave, imaginative, beloved of his men—who advanced the fortunes of Rome immeasurably by conquering Gaul. He was also a fine writer, whose tales of his conquests, while sometimes self-serving, are always gripping. And he was a superb administrator who, despite being a patrician himself, sought ways to spread the wealth of Rome around.

Of course, the man had his faults. The story of the assassination of Caesar can be seen as a cautionary lesson in what happens if you fail to heed warnings, if you take personal hubris to excess. Shakespeare understood that Julius Caesar is a perfect figure for drama. His play about the Roman leader, which is one of the greatest tragedies in literature, focuses on a question all human beings ask themselves: can we ever change our destiny?

The story of Caesar's assassination also continues to fascinate us because of its political ramifications and ethical implications. The achievements of Caesar, and his popularity at the time of his death, make his killing, on the face of it, puzzling. Yet the assassins claimed to be acting for the good of Rome and most historians have argued that this was the case (though some, more recently, have claimed the opposite). This in turn raises the broader question, still much debated and just as pertinent in our own time, of whether it is acceptable to murder an individual or individuals for the benefit of the majority—whether it is justifiable, in other words, to kill in the name of democracy.

CONQUEROR OF ADVERSITY

As his litter was borne along the bustling streets of Rome, a man raced up to Caesar holding a note and thrust it into his hands, begging him to read it. Caesar took the note and pocketed it, waving the man off. He was possibly a servant in the house of one of Caesar's enemies, or a repentant conspirator—historical sources vary. In the note, the plot against Caesar was revealed, but Caesar seems to have dismissed the man as some favor-seeker and tucked the note away without reading it. Whether he felt any disquiet at this point, following the earlier warnings and dreams, we do not know. But we know that Caesar was a man who had faced adversity before, and had always triumphed. Perhaps it was this confidence that pushed him on, to his death.

Caesar was a member of one of Rome's original aristocratic families, the Julii. The Julii were not of the ruling oligarchy, the *nobilitas*, but they were well connected—fortunately for Caesar. When he was only sixteen, he ran afoul of the tyrant Sulla during a civil war that pitted supporters of aristocratic rule against those who favored a more democratic approach—an early instance of Caesar's populist leanings. Sulla ordered Caesar's arrest, but Caesar escaped to the Sabine region of Central Italy. Caesar's relatives prevailed on Sulla to spare him, but Caesar sensed that it would be prudent if he spent some time away from Italy, and so he joined the army, beginning a distinguished military career that would catapult him to power.

Caesar spent two years campaigning in Asia Minor. When Sulla died in 78 BC, he returned to Italy and built up a reputation as a politician. In 63 BC, he went to Iberia (present-day Spain) as governor and was instrumental in putting down rebellions there. By 59 BC, he had returned to Rome and attained the prestigious position of co-consul with Marcus Bibulus. However, true power resided with what modern historians call the First Triumvirate, formed by Caesar and his allies Licinius Crassus and Gnaeus Pompeius Magnus (Pompey).

The members of the Senate and the most powerful aristocratic families were at this time broadly divided into two opposing camps: the *optimates* (literally, "the best men"), who distrusted the populace and wanted to hold power close to the ruling oligarchies; and the *populares*, the reformers, who sought (or pretended to seek) to improve the lot of the common people. Caesar was a *popularis*, and, as part of the First Triumvirate, he tried to pass a law that redistributed land

to the poor, thus endearing himself to the underprivileged of Rome, the *proletarii*, or plebs. Whether Caesar was trying to create a power base for himself as a future dictator, as his enemies (and many historians) claimed, or whether he was a genuine populist reformer, is still a matter of controversy.

Caesar may have had a popular following, but at this point he didn't have an army. However, his heroic campaigns in Gaul, from 58 to 50 BC, not only won him and Rome great riches, but also earned him the loyalty of his legions. This aroused the fear and envy of the Senate, where Pompey had recently joined the *optimates* faction. It demanded that Caesar return to Rome and disband his army. Instead, Caesar marched across the Rubicon River in northern Italy with his legion—a violation of Roman law—and began a civil war that resulted in the ouster and death of Pompey and many of his supporters.

By 46 BC, Caesar had returned to Rome in triumph, and in the next few years he was showered with honors by the Senate, including the title of Dictator for Life. There was some suggestion that these flowery honorifics were, in reality, sarcastic bestowals by a group of senators who, increasingly, resented Caesar's power and popularity, and what must have seemed to them an almost socialistic redistribution of wealth. For, during this time, Caesar gave allotments of land to thousands of his army veterans and also to eighty thousand of the plebs of Rome—and made a point of giving even more farmland to twenty thousand Roman families with three or more children (in fact, as the historian Plutarch said, he provided "almost the whole of [the province of] Campania" to the poor). He also set up public works projects, such as draining marshes and repairing towns and cities, as a way of providing work to the unemployed. On occasion, he even doled out cash to soldiers and citizens straight from the treasury.

For a long time, historians have seen the plot that arose against Caesar as an attempt by patriotic (even democratic) Romans to stop a despot, but there is now a very strong point of view that those who decided Caesar must be stopped were the opposite of democrats—were in fact rich nobility out to stop what they feared would be a wholesale power shift from the haves to the have-nots.

> WHETHER CAESAR WAS TRYING TO CREATE A POWER BASE FOR HIMSELF AS A FUTURE DICTATOR, AS HIS ENEMIES (AND MANY HISTORIANS) CLAIMED, OR WHETHER HE WAS A GENUINE POPULIST REFORMER, IS STILL A MATTER OF CONTROVERSY.

A bust of Julius Caesar. An outstanding general, politician and writer, Caesar has fascinated generations of historians.

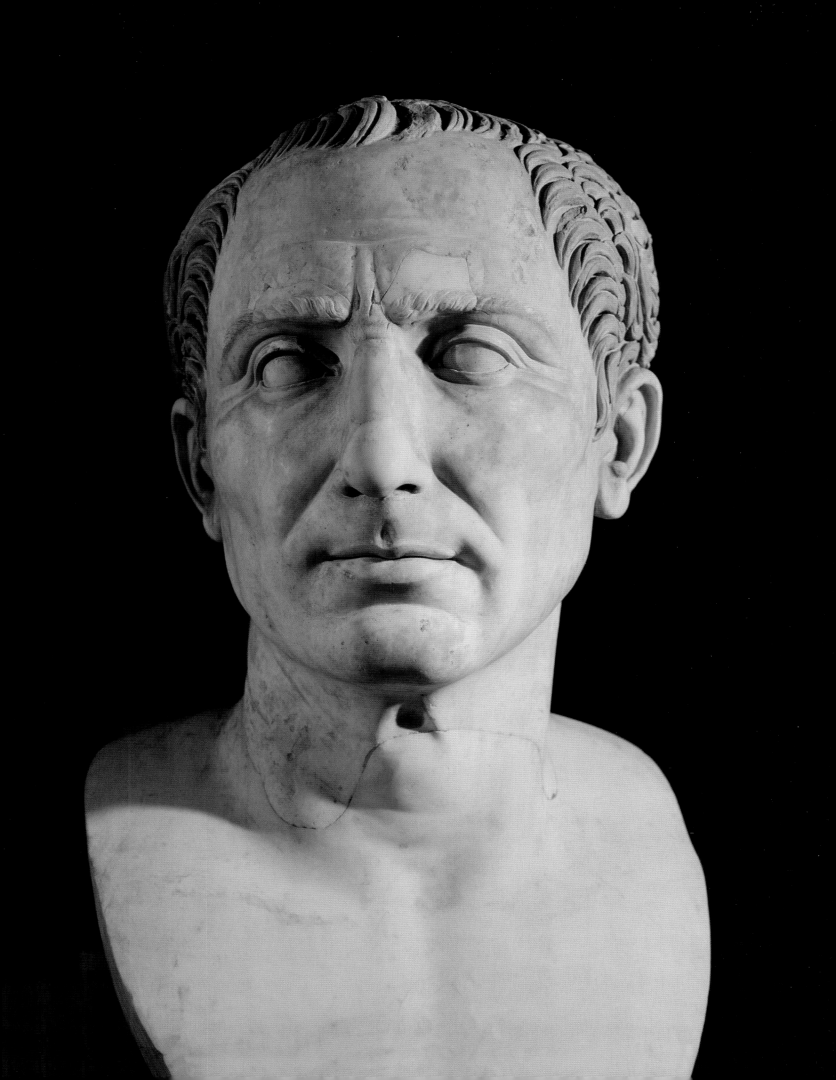

THE LIBERATORS

As Caesar travelled to the Senate on March 15, 44 BC, the note that might have saved him tucked deep in his robes, the men who would kill him awaited nervously. Most of what we know about the plot to kill Caesar as well as his actual death comes from Caesar's biographer Suetonius and the Roman historian Plutarch. (Shakespeare's play, *Julius Caesar*, although obviously fictionalized, is a fairly faithful rendering of Plutarch's version of the story.) The plot had begun with Gaius Cassius Longinus, who harboured an enormous grudge against Caesar, whom he called a tyrant, but whom he may also have feared was going to weaken the powerful aristocracy, of which Cassius was a prominent member.

Cassius' most important ally was his brother-in-law, a young nobleman named Marcus Brutus, who happened to be the son of Caesar's longtime lover, Servilia, and who may have held grudges against Caesar that were other than political ones. The conspiracy then grew to include sixty mainly aristocratic Romans, not all of whose names have come down to us. One was Decimus Brutus, a distant cousin of Marcus, who was in fact a close friend of Caesar's; others included Tillius Cimber and Publius Casca. These men called themselves "the Liberators," and, over a period of months leading up to March of 44 BC, met secretly, a few at

The Death of Caesar, by Vincenzo Camuccini (1773–1844). The assassination has provided a rich subject for painters through the ages.

a time, in each other's houses. While they railed against Caesar's supposed tyranny, they, as members of the Roman Senate, had a great deal to lose by Caesar's land distributions and his reforms. They all had their sweetheart deals with contractors and public officials, for one thing. For another, they feared that the great, unwashed rabble now following Caesar so slavishly might ultimately gain power and turn on them.

Something, obviously, needed to be done. Knowing that Caesar was leaving the country with his army on March 18 to attempt to suppress rebellions in parts of Asia Minor, the conspirators decided to take drastic action on March 18—the Ides of March—when Caesar would address the Senate.

"THE IDES OF MARCH HAVE COME!"

Accompanied by Decimus Brutus, Caesar arrived in front of the Senate House mid-morning. Climbing the steps, he confronted Spurinna, the soothsayer, who had warned him of danger.

"The Ides of March have come," he told Spurinna jokingly.

"Yes, they are come but they are not yet passed," Spurinna is supposed to have replied.

If he pondered that answer, Caesar gave no sign of it. He went up the steps of the Senate and onto the floor—without bodyguards, as usual, since he considered having them as a sign of fear. The Senate stood in respect. Caesar sat down in his chair but was almost immediately surrounded by the conspirators, who began to ask him questions, to distract him. Tillius Cimber handed him a petition to read. As Caesar waved it away irritably, Cimber suddenly yanked Caesar's robe off his shoulders, a signal that the attack should begin (and a potent symbol, for his purple robe was the symbol of Caesar's dictatorship).

The first blow was struck from behind by Publius Casca, but his nervousness caused him only to graze Caesar's shoulder. Caesar retaliated by jabbing Casca's arm with the stylus he used for writing, crying out, "You villain, Casca! What are you up to?"

He then tried to burst through the circle of assassins surrounding him, but was stabbed in the face by Cassius. Then Decimus Brutus, who had lured him out that day, plunged a knife into his side. Whirling desperately, but trapped on all sides, Caesar fought as hard as he could, uttering guttural cries, striking out with his stylus. The assassins slashed and stabbed in a frenzy, so much so that they wounded several of their own members.

Marcus Brutus was one of the last to plunge his knife into Caesar. Shakespeare has the dying dictator cry, "Et tu, Brutus?" but this is an invention. Suetonius claims that Caesar's last words, directed at Brutus, were, in Greek: "And you too, my child!" Plutarch merely says that Caesar wrapped his toga around his head and died at the foot of a statue of Pompey, with twenty-three stab wounds in his body.

UNINTENDED CONSEQUENCES

When they were done, the conspirators turned to the rest of the Senate, displaying their bloody knives and claiming that they had slain a dictator as a legitimate act of tyrannicide (tyrannicide being legal under Roman law). But the senators were terrified and fled the Senate House. Anger and fear then swept through the city, paralyzing Rome. By the next day, when Mark Antony gave his funeral oration for Caesar, the common people of the city had turned against the senators, even those who had not helped kill their idol.

With Mark Antony in control of the legions—and Caesar's anointed heir Octavian soon to be a formidable presence—Brutus and his co-conspirators were forced to flee the country. Thirteen years of civil war followed. In the end, the Roman Republic was no more. Imperial Rome, with Octavian as emperor, had begun, and would last for five hundred years of absolute rule.

The assassins, whether they were acting out of self-interest, or in a true belief that Rome faced a tyrant, had ironically changed the course of Roman history and halted the Republic in its tracks. Had Caesar not been killed, who knows what would have happened? The most likely outcome is that Caesar would have become a sort of benevolent dictator, using the devoted masses as a power base to keep the aristocrats in line, but at the same time greatly improving the lot of the *proletarii*.

For six days after Caesar's violent death, a comet appeared in the skies above Rome. Some people believed it was Caesar's spirit, flying through the sky, as in his dream. And in coins minted after the assassination, the comet is always shown. That's a sign of the power of Caesar's name, then and thereafter, whether he was a tyrant or *popularis*, or a little of both. ✦

30 BC
THE DEATH OF CLEOPATRA

In 30 BC the last pharaoh of the ancient Egyptian Empire committed suicide—bitten by an asp that she had smuggled into her Roman-guarded prison. Cleopatra had a charismatic personality, was a born leader and an ambitious monarch, and one of the most dynamic rulers in the ancient world. Her reign was one of skilful opportunism, initially co-ruling with her father, then with her brothers, and later in alliance with the Roman juggernauts Julius Caesar and Mark Antony. When she and Antony pitted Egypt against the mighty Roman Empire, she set a course for one of the most dramatic downfalls in history.

Cleopatra VII (69–30 BC) was the last of seven Ptolemaic Egyptian queens of the same name. She ruled from 51 to 30 BC and, with the assistance of Roman leaders Julius Caesar and, later, Mark Antony, extended the reach of the Egyptian Empire. But her downfall led to end of the Ptolemaic line, and marked the start of Roman rule over Egypt. The Ptolemaic line had been ruling Egypt since the brilliant military ruler Alexander the Great, king of Macedon, conquered the region almost three hundred years earlier, uniting Europe and Asia for the first time. Ptolemy, one of Alexander's generals, took control of Egypt after Alexander died.

Cleopatra was bright, politically astute, and well educated; she was said to be the first Ptolemy to actually learn the Egyptian language (the Ptolemies' native language was Greek) and she was fluent in at least seven others. Cleopatra was also reputed to be a brilliant singer and orator, and very witty. Several contemporary accounts claim that she was not physically attractive in the conventional sense, but more than made up for it with her many other skills. There is no shortage of evidence that she was a superb and successful seductress.

AN APPROACH TO CAESAR

Cleopatra first ruled in association with her father, Ptolemy XII, who came to power in 80 BC. When he died in 51 BC, the eighteen-year-old Cleopatra shared the throne with her twelve-year-old brother Ptolemy XIII. The first three years of their reign were blighted by many problems, including economic difficulties, famine, drought (which prevented the River Nile from flooding and caused crops to fail) and political struggles—including civil war caused by Cleopatra's obvious intention to rule in her own right. When Ptolemy's supporters succeeded in ousting her from power in 48 BC, Cleopatra tried to muster support for a rebellion but eventually was forced to flee for her life to Rome, which at the time held a tenuous control over Egypt. She set her sights on Roman ruler Julius Caesar, determined to gain his favors by any means necessary to secure his alliance in her quest to wrest power back from her brother—even if it meant delivering to Rome full control over Egypt.

Greek historian Plutarch, writing over one hundred and fifty years later, describes how Cleopatra charmed Caesar with her beauty:

She took a small boat, and only one of her confidants, Apollodorus, the Sicilian, along with her, and in the dusk of the evening landed near the palace. She was at a loss how to get in undiscovered, till she thought of putting herself into the coverlet of a bed and lying at length, whilst Apollodorus tied up the bedding and carried it on his back through the gates to Caesar's apartment. Caesar was first captivated by this proof of Cleopatra's bold wit, and was afterwards so overcome by the

Ever the artful politician, Cleopatra summons Mark Antony to her barge.

charm of her society that he made a reconciliation between her and her brother, on the condition that she should rule as his colleague in the kingdom.

AN ALLIANCE IS FORMED

Cleopatra's connection with Rome had first been forged through Roman leader Pompey, who had been appointed as her guardian when her father died. After Pompey was defeated by Caesar at Pharsalia (in northern Greece) in 48 BC, he fled to Egypt, where he was murdered at the behest of Ptolemy XIII—probably in an attempt to please Caesar and gain the support of Rome, to which Egypt was heavily indebted. This was a disastrous blunder, for when Caesar arrived in Egypt two days later and Ptolemy presented him with Pompey's pickled head, Caesar was enraged. Although they were political enemies, Pompey had been a high-ranking Roman consul, and the husband of Caesar's only daughter Julia, who had died while giving birth to their son.

As a result of the alliance between Cleopatra and Caesar, who was thirty-one years her senior, Cleopatra gained supreme power. Six months later Ptolemy XIII drowned in the Nile while trying to escape the combined forces of Cleopatra and Caesar. His youngest sister, Arsinoe IV, who had been proclaimed queen by the people of Alexandria, was captured and taken to Rome. Caesar was afraid that his affair with Cleopatra, by now an open secret, would further inflame Egyptian (and Roman) hostility. Knowing that it was an Egyptian tradition for royal siblings to marry each other, and that in former times pharaohs had commonly married their own daughters and sisters (an arrangement which Romans considered grotesque and degenerate), the lovers arranged for twenty-two-year-old Cleopatra to enter into a sham marriage of convenience with another, younger brother, Ptolemy XIV.

CLEOPATRA HAUGHTILY REFUSED TO MEET MARK ANTONY AT HIS COURT; INSTEAD SHE SUMMONED HIM TO HER MAGNIFICENT BARGE WHERE HE FOUND HER DRESSED AS VENUS.

DEATH OF CAESAR

In 47 BC Cleopatra bore a son to Caesar, whom she named Ptolemy Caesarion. But, against Cleopatra's wishes, Caesar refused to appoint Caesarion as his heir, naming instead his grand-nephew Octavian—a decision which would, in time, rebound disastrously. Cleopatra and Caesarion went to live with Caesar in Rome in 46 BC, their open association causing a great scandal. There were whispers that Caesar intended to install himself as king of Rome with Cleopatra as his queen. After Caesar was murdered by his opponents in the Senate

in 44 BC, Cleopatra and Caesarion fled back to Egypt. Soon afterwards her brother Ptolemy XIV died in mysterious circumstances—possibly poisoned—and Cleopatra set about regaining power, installing her toddler son as co-ruler.

By now the brilliant but debauched Roman general Mark Antony, having defeated Caesar's assassins Brutus and Cassius, ruled the eastern section of the empire of the Roman Republic. Concerned that Cleopatra might be making strategic alliances with his enemies, Mark Antony summoned her to Rome. She made a spectacular entrance—before working her magic on the married Antony just as she had on Caesar. She haughtily refused to meet him at his court; instead, she summoned him to her magnificent barge where he found her dressed as Venus (the goddess of love and beauty), reclining sumptuously on silken pillows and being fanned with gold-plated peacock feathers by young boys dressed as Cupid, her handmaidens dressed as mermaids with silver threads plaited through their hair. Plutarch chronicled the next stage of Cleopatra's seduction of Antony:

The following day, Antony invited her to supper, and was very desirous to outdo her as well in magnificence as contrivance; but he found he was altogether beaten in both, and was so well convinced of it that he was himself the first to jest and mock at his poverty of wit and his rustic awkwardness. She, perceiving that his raillery was broad and gross, and savored more of the soldier than the courtier, rejoined in the same taste, and fell into it at once, without any sort of reluctance or reserve. For her actual beauty, it is said, was not in itself so remarkable that none could be compared with her, or that no one could see her without being struck by it, but the contact of her presence, if you lived with her, was irresistible; the attraction of her person, joining with the charm of her conversation, and the character that attended all she said or did, was something bewitching.

A NEW CONSORT

Cleopatra and the besotted Antony soon returned to Egypt, spending the winter at Alexandria. In December 40 BC she bore him twins: Alexander Helios (Sun-god) and Cleopatra Selene (Moon-goddess). Cleopatra catered to Antony's every whim; at one feast she ordered her servants to cook twelve pigs at different times, so that one of them would be ready whenever he wanted it.

Shortly afterward Antony returned to Rome, correctly assuming that his political opponents would be taking advantage of his absence, and resumed married life with his wife Octavia Minor. But in 37 BC he returned to Egypt to rejoin Cleopatra and meet their children for the first time. They had another child, Ptolemy Philadelphus. Meanwhile, alarm was growing among Romans that Antony had abandoned his empire for a life of hedonism with an Egyptian. To make matters worse, Antony's co-ruler Octavian, was slandering Antony and boosting his own power base. Fearing Egypt's wealth and power, the Senate was intent upon gaining complete domination of the province (at this stage Rome was levying taxes on Egypt but did not hold full political control). Antony, however, still enamoured of his Egyptian lover, bestowed on Cleopatra huge areas of Cyprus, Lebanon and Syria, and appointed their children as monarchs of these and other countries. This was too much for Octavian and the Senate (and for Octavia Minor, who was furious that Antony had deserted her).

THE END OF A DYNASTY

Rome declared war on Egypt, eventually defeating Cleopatra and Antony's forces at the Battle of Actium in 31 BC. Believing that Cleopatra was dead, Antony committed suicide. Cleopatra fled to the luxurious mausoleum in Alexandria that she had constructed for herself and her treasures, where she remained under house arrest by Octavian's soldiers. Rather than face her inevitable fate, and perhaps preferring death to defeat, Cleopatra arranged for a venomous asp (a traditional symbol of Egyptian royalty) to be smuggled into her room in a basket of figs. One morning Octavian's soldiers found her dead; on her arm were two pinprick marks from the fangs of the asp. Caesarion was pronounced pharaoh by the Egyptians, but Octavian had him imprisoned, then strangled. (It is reputed that his name too closely resembled "Caesar" and that Octavian, also known as Augustus Caesar, was advised that "it was a bad thing to have too many Caesars.")

Octavian declared himself Pharaoh of Egypt on August 30, ending the Ptolemaic reign and the last of the Egyptian dynasties forever. ✹

79 AD
THE DESTRUCTION OF POMPEII

Just before noon, towards the end of a hot summer's day on the west coast of central Italy, the long-dormant volcano Mount Vesuvius burst into life with a deafening bang followed by the release of a tall, white cloud of smoke. The sky turned dark and the sun disappeared as dirt, mud and red-hot boulders were hurled into the air. Blown by the prevailing northwest wind, the debris began to rain down on the nearby Roman city of Pompeii, which had a population of around twenty thousand people. Burning pumice stones followed by ash then rained down, and the air became poisoned with the acrid, deadly fumes of sulphur dioxide and hydrochloric acid. Those who survived the initial downpours and did not flee immediately were asphyxiated as they sought to escape—before being buried under a shroud of ash. After the poisonous gases came a rain of mud and damp ashes, which solidified as it cooled and preserved everything on which it fell.

We do not know how many people died, but the toll certainly measured in the thousands. Pompeii gradually faded from memory until 1748, when archaeologists began digging through layers of debris, unearthing human forms captured at the moment of death. After the ashes had solidified around the bodies, all but the skeletons had decomposed. Archaeologists poured plaster of Paris into the moulds to produce perfect copies of amazingly intricate detail. Individual hairs, facial lines,

Nineteenth-century artist James Hamilton's dramatic interpretation of the destruction of Pompeii.

fish scales, grains in loaves of bread, and other such details of animal and vegetable matter were seen. The health, and even the profession of the victims, could be ascertained by study of the skeleton—young men with osteoarthritis caused by hard work were probably slaves, while skeletal indentations made by sharp objects indicate the body of a soldier, undoubtedly on leave.

The Pompeiians were obviously taken completely unaware by the disaster, even though the warning signs were well documented. We know from the reconstruction works in progress that Pompeii and the surrounding areas had experienced a devastating earthquake sixteen years earlier, in 63 AD, after a long period of seismic inactivity, and there had been lesser quakes in the intervening period. For example, in one house archaeologists discovered a baking oven that had incurred major cracking, been repaired and plastered over, and then damaged again. But there had not been a major eruption since about 1800 BC, which lulled the locals into a false sense of security. We now know that long periods of quietude followed by earthquakes are strong portents of an imminent, catastrophic volcanic eruption, as was the case with Krakatoa in 1883; but the Romans, though aware that Vesuvius was "alive," knew nothing of this. Local citizens often took recreational strolls inside its crater. The Romans had so little experience of volcanic eruptions they did not even have a word for "volcano" in their lexicon, much less "eruption."

THE FATEFUL DAY

On the morning of the explosion, bread was baking in ovens as donkeys, attached by harnesses to grain mills of interlocking stone wheels, plodded their circular route around the bakery yard. The central fish market was a hive of activity as the morning's catch was cleaned, scaled and sold. Shops and market stalls were in full swing and the numerous wine bars, or *thermopolia*, were serving luncheon snacks of fruit, fish, salads, nuts, and hard-boiled eggs. Wine jars in the cellars bore the world's first-known advertising pun, Vesuvinum—a combination of "Vesuvius" and the Latin for wine, *vinum*. Oil lanterns hung from the ceilings and bronze containers for drinks were set into the bar, coins lying alongside them in readiness for the drinkers' next order—a custom still evident today. Families were preparing lunch and the public heated baths, their fires lit earlier that morning, were starting to fill with customers wishing to perform ablutions or escape the heat of the day. At the Temple of Isis, priests were preparing to eat their lunch of eggs, fish, nuts, and lentils. Street vendors were selling various products, including flatbread, pies, poultry, and fish.

Workers were cleaning at the city's cultural venues such as the Odeon and the Great Theatre. The Odeon was a small, covered concert and poetry theatre that featured intricate carved figures "holding up" the stone walls at the end of each row of the stone terraced seats; the Great Theatre was a large open-air amphitheater that hosted plays, pantomimes and gladiatorial bouts. Cloth covers had been erected to provide shade for the spectators.

Although the Romans were often flippant in their artistic depiction of gods, religion was nonetheless deeply entrenched in their everyday life. The state-approved religion honored Olympic gods and emperors, and many household shrines displayed religious art. Many Romans belonged to various mystery cults, worshipping exotic foreign gods or goddesses, such as the Egyptian fertility goddess Isis.

THE CATASTROPHIC ERUPTION OF VESUVIUS LASTED TWO DAYS, EXTINGUISHING LIFE, DESTROYING BUILDINGS, HOMES AND MONUMENTS, AND LEAVING SURVIVORS VULNERABLE TO LOOTING AND STARVATION.

POMPEII'S ART WORKS—HIGH AND LOW
Many of Pompeii's buildings featured superb wall frescoes and intricate mosaics on the floors and walls. Depictions of snakes representing domestic protector-gods were a common feature of the fresco art. One magnificent mosaic on the floor of the luxurious private house known as the House of the Faun consisted of about one and a half million stones measuring on average less than a quarter of an inch. The mosaic depicted the Battle of Issus (333 BC) in which Alexander the Great defeated the Persian king Darius III. Pompeii's library held thousands of books made of rolls of papyrus, a paper made from processed marsh reeds.

The Romans had a far more permissive attitude to sexual matters than we do, and the numerous brothels contained frescoes advertising and illustrating the cost and particular services available within for both men and women. Pompeii was a booming sea port, and crews of military and merchant ships availed themselves of its erotic services when they took recreational shore leave. The wage of even the lowest-paid prostitute was more than triple that of an unskilled labourer. Erotic art and frescoes were very widespread throughout the city, but much of what may appear pornographic to modern eyes was in fact fertility imagery, representing respectful supplication to various deities such as Priapus, always depicted with a very over-sized erect penis. Many household items, such as salt-shakers and lamps, also had sexual motifs.

Graffiti was widespread in Pompeii, covering many external and internal walls of both public and private buildings. In the red light district, comments such as "I came here, screwed many women, then went home" and "Atimetus got me pregnant" were scrawled on the walls. Some graffiti (and more permanent art works) cast aspersions on the poor quality of nearby business competitors' merchandize. Other popular graffiti subjects were businesses advertising daily specials, political slogans, election campaign material, and magic spells and invocations (the new heretical cult of Christianity had, as yet, few adherents). One city wall displayed the droll message "I wonder, oh wall, that you have not fallen in ruins from supporting the stupidities of so many scribblers."

LIVES OF LUXURY AND PLENTY
An iron chest discovered in the house of Lucius Caecilius Jucundus, a banker, contained 132 wooden writing tablets covered in a thin layer of beeswax. Into the wax were carved such records as receipts and account details, signed by the banker and many of Pompeii's well-to-do citizens. One of Pompeii's most opulent buildings was a villa owned by the aristocratic Vetti brothers who made their fortune selling wine and other beverages. Situated in the center of town, it featured a large, central, beautifully landscaped garden surrounded by a peristyle, or group of columns. Trees and herbs were arranged around stone tables, statues and mosaic pathways. In the house of another nobleman, Lucius Secundus, one

wall featured a huge fresco showing lions hunting various kinds of prey, reflecting the popularity of African landscapes throughout the Roman Empire, which by this time stretched as far as northern Africa.

The house of Marcus Loreius Tiburtinus had a huge rear garden with water channels, magnificent landscaped beds of edible and ornamental plants, wooden lattice fences and an open-air dining room, or *triclinium*, with ornate fresco-covered walls. Some houses contained industrial workshops—fullers cleaned and dyed cloth, while mechanics' shops maintained and repaired chariots and carts. Warehouses held clay pots containing wine, grains, olive oil, vegetables and honey. Beekeeping was practised in and around Pompeii, and honey pots were labelled with the type of honey and its origin, for instance Corsican, thyme, or crystalline. Many Pompeiians adorned themselves with magnificent gold jewelry. The rich noblewoman Poppaea Sabina owned a magnificent, spiral upper-arm band in the shape of a snake, with intricately carved scales, eyes and other details.

At the nearby coastal town of Herculaneum (which would soon be buried by the lava flow rather than the pumice and ash that choked Pompeii), a festival to honor the memory of Octavian, Rome's first emperor, was under way as local fishermen sold the morning's catch.

Volcanic clouds billow ominously above the idyllic town of Pompeii and its unsuspecting inhabitants.

FOOD, FESTIVALS AND GATHERINGS

Most food consumed at Pompeii came from the surrounding region. The Bay of Naples provided fish, crustaceans and other seafood, which were also farmed in ponds. Game such as pigs and deer were hunted in the nearby mountains, while the countryside contained fruit and vegetable market gardens, and cattle and poultry breeding farms. Vineyards flourished on many nearby farms and covered the hillsides on the outskirts of the city, while the foothills of Vesuvius, with its rich volcanic soil, produced wines of excellent quality. Grapes were pressed on farms and in the city itself.

Under Roman law, cemeteries had to be positioned outside the city walls. Pompeii's cemeteries were situated outside the Gate of Herculaneum and the Gate of Nuceria, and featured many impressive stone mausoleums holding the remains of the rich. Those who lived well died well, while the ashes of less wealthy citizens and slaves were buried in clay urns.

The Pompeii Forum was a large and important public meeting place, typical of those found in Rome and other cities throughout the empire. It was used for public meetings, court hearings, political rallies and markets. Pompeii's citizens enjoyed sports, both as participants and spectators. Inside the public gymnasium, or palaestra, men wrestled, boxed, jogged or lifted weights. Outside they participated in sports such as javelin and discus. Lessons were available, and competitions held. There were several public baths, including a complex comprising a 100-foot swimming pool with adjoining saunas, a ball court and a designated women-only area. The baths were a popular gathering place where people met friends, drank wine or sought sexual partners. The amphitheater featured spectator sports including animal hunts, gladiator fights and chariot races. On the day of the explosion, sixty-three people died in the adjoining barracks, including two prisoners in their cells.

AN EYEWITNESS ACCOUNT

We have an excellent eyewitness account of the explosion, recorded twenty-five years later by the philosopher, administrator and poet Pliny the Younger, for the great Roman historian Tacitus. Pliny's uncle, Pliny the Elder, a naval commander who wrote the thirty-seven-volume *Natural History*—the longest scientific treatise in Latin that has survived from antiquity—was killed in the explosion, as he and his fleet attempted to assist fleeing citizens. Pliny was just seventeen years old at the time, and was stationed at Misenum, some 18 miles distant, so he had a grandstand view of the catastrophe. He was forced to flee for his life the next day as the deadly eruptions continued. The following extracts from his letters are from a translation made by William Melmoth in 1746.

Pliny describes the initial ash cloud and the upheavals that transformed the landscape:

And now cinders, which grew thicker and hotter the nearer he approached, fell into the ships, then pumice-stones too, with stones blackened, scorched, and cracked by fire, then the sea ebbed suddenly from under them, while the shore was blocked up by landslips from the mountains ...

He then describes the perilous situation confronting his uncle as he attempted to assist those escaping the conflagration:

The house now tottered under repeated and violent concussions, and seemed to rock to and fro as if torn from its foundations ... It was now day everywhere else, but there a deeper darkness prevailed than in the most obscure night; relieved, however, by many torches and diverse illuminations. They thought proper to go down upon the shore to observe from close at hand if they could possibly put out to sea, but they found the waves still run extremely high and contrary. There my uncle, having thrown himself down upon a disused sail, repeatedly called for, and drank, a draught of cold water; soon after, flames, and a strong smell of sulphur, which was the forerunner of them, dispersed the rest of the company in flight; him they only aroused. He raised himself up with the assistance of two of his slaves, but instantly fell; some unusually gross vapor, as I conjecture, having obstructed his breathing and blocked his windpipe, which was not only naturally weak and constricted, but chronically inflamed. When day dawned again (the third from that he last beheld) his body was found entire and uninjured, and still fully clothed as in life; its posture was that of a sleeping, rather than a dead man ...

AFTERMATH

The catastrophic eruption of Vesuvius lasted two days, extinguishing life, destroying buildings, homes and monuments, and leaving survivors vulnerable to looting and starvation. The traumatized survivors chose not to rebuild Pompeii and it faded from memory until the mid eighteenth century, when archaeologists began their systematic excavation of the city and its splendors became known to the world once more. ✸

476 AD
THE FALL OF
THE ROMAN EMPIRE

Had there been no Rome and Roman Empire there would be no us. Founded around 510 BC, the Roman Empire had by the third century AD extended across millions of square miles, to the Rhine and Danube rivers in the north, North Africa in the south, Spain in the west and Constantinople, and beyond in the east. Throughout this territory, the Romans paved roads (some still in use today) through trackless wilderness, constructed towns and built aqueducts to water them. Roman government held sway and the Latin language grew in influence.

The city of Rome itself, with its public baths, sewer systems, glorious buildings and flourishing arts and poetry, was not only the center of Western civilization, but in a sense helped create it. Our Western systems of law, our cultures and our languages—it is estimated that fifty percent of the words in English, for example, are of Latin origin—derive from ancient Rome. Even our sense of empire. These days, it's considered a bad thing to have an empire, but Rome's thousand-year hold over the world probably did more good than harm.

Not surprisingly, the rulers of this magnificent empire attained godlike status. Some, such as Julius Caesar and Octavian, even claimed they *were* gods. Even the less effective, more disreputable emperors like Nero had an air of grandeur about them.

So, given all these great accomplishments, how did Rome end up in 476 AD being ruled by Romulus Augustus, a twelve-year-old boy? His first name, fatefully enough, was the name of the legendary founder of Rome, but people mocked him and called him *Momyllus*, which means "little disgrace"—that's

when they weren't sarcastically calling him *Augustulus*, which means "little emperor."

BARBARIAN INVASIONS

The eighteenth-century historian Edward Gibbon wrote a famous masterwork, *The History of the Decline and Fall of the Roman Empire*. Gibbon attributed Rome's "fall" partly to the "barbarian" (from the Latin word for "bearded") tribes who had long been bubbling and boiling around the edges of the northern Roman Empire, but also to the Romans themselves, whom, he claimed, became lazy and self-satisfied, depending on hired mercenaries (in some cases the same barbarians who would turn on them) to do their fighting. Many contemporary scholars, however, have rejected Gibbon's arguments about barbarian hordes as overly simplistic and paternalistic. Was Gibbon not merely viewing the barbarians from a contemptuous Roman point of view? Barbarians were, after all, mainly Germanic tribes on an empire-building mission of their own. In the view of some of these modern essayists, the Roman Empire never "declined"; it was merely transformed, becoming an amalgam of Germanic and Roman influences.

This provides us with a kinder, gentler—not to mention more politically correct—end to the Romans. But it ignores the very real trauma felt by this thousand-year-old civilization at the time. It also overlooks the impact of the subsequent decline of Western (read: Roman) learning, when much classical knowledge—including records of what was happening in the fifth century as Rome neared its end—was not "transformed,"

but irrevocably destroyed. As a result, Europe entered what has come to be known as the Dark Ages.

NEPOS USURPED

Romulus Augustus reigned from October of 475 to September of 476. Not much is known about him, except that he was thought good-looking. He was a kid caught in a big trap, really, one from which he was going to be lucky to escape alive, given the chaotic conditions prevalent in Rome at the time. Romulus had been named emperor by his father, a general named Flavius Orestes, who was part German and part Roman and yet had been named Master of Soldiers—commander in chief of the Roman army—by the then-emperor, Julius Nepos.

This was a sign of the deep barbarian infiltration of Rome, and a mistake on Nepos' part. For Orestes subsequently led a combined group of barbarian auxiliary forces against the emperor, sending him into exile (there are some who say that Nepos was really the last Roman emperor) and putting his own son, Romulus, on the throne. He probably did this so that he could rule from behind the scenes. But if he was expecting a bright new era in Roman history (or even just greater spoils), he was to be sorely mistaken.

A SLOW DECLINE

Rome had, in fact, been sliding from power since the middle of the fourth century, when the Huns, a nomadic people from Central Asia, had appeared on the Eurasian steppes and pushed other tribes westwards in front of them. One of these tribes was the Visigoths, who settled on the banks of the Danube in about 376 AD, living there on the sufferance of Emperor Valens, head of the Eastern Roman Empire (the Roman Empire had been divided into two halves, Eastern and Western, by the Emperor Diocletian, in 285 AD, to make it easier to govern).

Valens' corrupt officials treated the Visigoths in a high-handed way, as if they were inferiors, stealing money from them and not listening to their complaints. As a result, they revolted, and defeated and killed Valens in the historic battle of Adrianople in 378, then swept with a vengeance through the Eastern Empire. The next emperor, Theodosius I, finally made peace with the Visigoths in 382, but only after ceding them the territory they had seized—Thrace (now northern Greece and the Balkans). Rome looked eastwards nervously.

Less than twenty years later, a charismatic young general named Alaric arose from one of the royal families of the Visigoths. Alaric was trained by the Emperor Theodosius and served as one of his top commanders, but after Theodosius died

The Colosseum and the Arch of Constantine, by Giovanni Paolo Pannini (1691–1765), ponders the glory that was Rome.

he turned on the Romans. He first invaded Italy in 400 AD, but was defeated by the Roman general Stilicho in the Piedmont region, possibly because the Romans had captured his wife and family, and were holding them hostage. Around 408, Alaric tried again, this time in the middle of a civil war—a propitious time for an invasion, as it turned out. Alaric even briefly aligned himself with forces under his old foe General Stilicho, but, after Stilicho was murdered by the Romans, Alaric turned with purposeful vengeance and marched on Rome.

In August 410, panic gripped the citizens of Rome as Alaric settled in for a siege. The Emperor Honorius fled to Ravenna just as Rome began to starve. Thousands of slaves left their masters and slipped out through the city's gates, seeking better employment with the Visigoths. Honorius refused to bargain with Alaric; meanwhile, the people of Rome, suffering from a plague, began to die by the scores. According to some sources, cannibalism was practised. Finally, someone—legend has it that it was a rich Roman noblewoman who could no longer stand the plight of her city—opened the Salaria Gate, and, for the first time in seven hundred years, Rome was in the hands of a foreign invader.

As far as sackings went, Alaric's was relatively mild. Many Roman citizens were enslaved, but because of this there was a glut of slaves on the market and they could be bought back

Present-day Rome's Largo Argentina was the site of the ancient Roman senate.

from the barbarians very cheaply. What the Visigoths were mainly interested in was food, and after obtaining what little they could from the starving Romans, they set off south to sack more fertile parts of the country. But Alaric died of an illness shortly thereafter, and the threat was temporarily dispelled.

THE EMPIRE DISINTEGRATES

The respite for Rome was relatively brief, however, for soon it had to deal with Attila and his Huns, who had moved out of Asia pillaging and conquering. While they did not build great cities like the Romans, the Huns—particularly the charismatic Attila, who saw himself as a world leader—were intent on assimilating conquered peoples. After first invading the Balkans and Gaul (where they were defeated at the battle of Châlons), they headed for Italy. In 452, Attila cut a great swathe of destruction through the northern part of the country before heading for Rome. It is said that Pope Leo I then met with Attila and persuaded him not to attack the city, although it is more likely that Attila turned back because famine and disease were by then tearing his army apart. In any event, the Imperial City was spared.

Attila died the next year, and the power of the Huns waned, but in 453 the Vandals dealt Rome a devastating blow. The Vandals were a tribe from eastern Germany whose very name is now synonymous with wanton destruction. After taking a roundabout route to Rome—through Spain, hopping across the Mediterranean, devastating North Africa, and then sailing to Italy—they spent two full weeks sacking Rome and did not refrain from murder and plunder, before returning to North Africa.

Over the next twenty years, the Imperial City and the Roman Empire disintegrated. With the Italian Peninsula devastated by barbarian onslaughts and civil war, the struggling Roman government was unable to levy enough taxes to keep a standing army in the field. Increasingly, it depended on barbarian mercenaries. The Roman government was weak and obviously up for grabs. It was at this point, 475 AD, that Flavius Orestes was appointed—ironically, to protect the Roman emperor. As soon as he could, he betrayed him.

ROMULUS IN EXILE

After Flavius Orestes appointed Romulus emperor, he, too, fell prey to the tumultuous politics of the time. He had double-crossed the barbarians who had fought for him, refusing to give them land to settle on, and they joined forces and rose against him, led by the Visigoth Odoacer (a name that has numerous spellings). Orestes was captured and quickly beheaded on August 28, 476. Then Odoacer marched on Ravenna, where Romulus Augustus held court, and immediately deposed him, in the autumn of 476, as easily as a big kid pushes a little one out of a sandpit.

Odoacer then sent an arrogant note to Emperor Zeno of Constantinople—then head of the Eastern Empire—to the effect that there would be no need to appoint a new Western emperor: he, Odoacer, would now rule. It is a sign of how insignificant a threat Romulus was that Odoacer did not bother to have him killed—he simply pensioned him off to Campania in southern Italy.

The fall of the Roman Empire was so quiet, one commentator has written, as to be "noiseless." But this was because by the time Odoacer pushed Romulus out, the power of Rome was already gone forever, lost in war and strife. The Eastern Empire, protected by better luck, a great wall built around Constantinople, and water (the Bosphorus separates Constantinople from Europe, and the barbarians were notoriously poor seamen) survived until the Ottomans conquered it in the fifteenth century. But the Western Empire was gone. For a time, Roman bureaucracy kept the streets paved, the water flowing through the aqueducts and the books safe in their grand libraries, but these things were not of value to the new owners of the empire, and gradually fell into disuse and disrepair.

Some aristocratic Roman families cooperated with the Germanic tribes and thrived, but many of the inhabitants of Rome and other major Italian cities were enslaved. Others were left alone to work for their new masters, but because the barbarians had redistributed the land among themselves, these former Roman citizens were left in a condition approaching serfdom. Times changed. Coins were not minted. The famous Roman pottery, which had spread across the empire, stopped being made. Local economies declined severely, as did the population of Europe. The great civilization of classical antiquity now entered a steady decline. The Dark Ages, which would last until about 1000 AD, had begun. ❧

501–1500

THE MIDDLE AGES

The Almost Complete Chronicles

610
THE CALLING OF MUHAMMAD

The prophet Muhammad (meaning "praised" or "glorified" in Arabic) was born in 570 in the desert town of Mecca, in present-day Saudi Arabia. According to tradition, he received a series of visions from the angel Gabriel, which he recorded and passed on to a small group of disciples. His revelations are found in the Qur'an, the sacred scripture that Muslims consider to be the final revelation of God. Together with the record of his acts and the 114 *suras* (verses) he composed, it forms a guidebook of divine and moral direction for humankind.

At the time of Muhammad's birth the Arab world was made up of various warring states. Muhammad's parents died when he was very young; he was brought up by his grandfather, then by his uncle Abu Talib, whom he accompanied on business trips to Syria, where it is said he came into contact with the teachings of Nestorian Christian monks. The monks were part of the eastern tradition of Christianity advanced by Nestorius, Patriarch of Constantinople, in the fifth century. In 583 one of these monks, Bahira, predicted the twelve-year-old Muhammad's future as a prophet to Abu Talib after experiencing divine manifestations in his presence.

As a young man Muhammad entered the service of the rich widow Khadijah, a merchant who organized trade caravans. When she was forty years old and he twenty-five, she proposed and they were wed. Their happy marriage of twenty years

A **sixteenth-century Persian painting** showing Muhammad's ascent into heaven.

produced three sons (who died during childbirth) and four daughters—including Fatima, who married Muhammad's adopted son Ali. This union produced Muhammad's only future bloodline.

MUHAMMAD'S RETREAT

Muhammad, despite being a respected and successful member of the community, found it difficult to accept the prevailing polytheism and superstition practised by some Arabs, and became attracted to the ideas spread by Jews and Christians. He would often retreat to a mountain cave outside Mecca to practise asceticism and meditation. One night in 610, at forty years of age, he dreamt he was gripped around the throat by a strange being who ordered him to read a cloth scroll covered in symbols. Upon awakening he felt that a book had been written in his heart, and saw in the distance an angel, later identified as Gabriel. Convinced he was going mad, he returned home and related his experience to Khadijah, who reassured him—and became his first disciple. More visions followed, which Muhammad related to a small but growing group of converts including Ali, his son-in-law Uthman, and his future fathers-in-law, Abu Bakr and Umar (they later became the first four Muslim caliphs or leaders). After three years of regular visions, Gabriel ordered him to begin a public preaching career.

Muhammad delivered sermons on the evils of materialism, the wrath of God and the imminent Day of Judgment. His statements were largely scorned, not least because they endangered Mecca's religious—and hence economic—status quo. His followers (known as Muslims, "those who give their souls to God") were persecuted although Muhammad himself, despite suffering constant insults and threats, was protected by his membership of the powerful merchant clan Banu Hashim.

MUHAMMMAD'S SUPPORT GROWS

As Muhammad's followers grew in number, they became a menace to Mecca's rulers, who depended for their livelihood upon the Ka'bah, a shrine made of granite that housed numerous statues representing over three hundred tribal gods. Muhammad now threatened to overthrow the shrine and rededicate it as an Islamic house of worship. His condemnation of traditional religion was a particular threat to his own tribe, the Quraysh, who profited by their guardianship of the Ka'bah, and thus had much to lose. They offered him entry into the inner circle of merchants, the kingship and a lucrative, prestigious marriage, but he refused.

In 619, the "year of sorrows," both his wife Khadijah and his uncle (and leader of the Banu Hashim clan) Abu Talib died. The new clan leader was Abu Lahab, who was a sworn enemy of Muhammad and withdrew the clan's protection. Muhammad was now in great danger, since the removal of protection meant that, should he be murdered, retribution for his killing would not be required under law. However, he was able to find another guardian, Mut'im ibn Adi, and the protection of his clan Banu Nawfal.

Muhammad now experienced his most famous and intense vision, as Gabriel teleported him on the back of the winged horse Boraq from Mecca to Jerusalem (this event is referred to as the *isra*, meaning night journey), where he prayed in the ruins of a temple. He ascended to Heaven (the *mi'raj* or ascension), where he saw the throne of God and the prophets Moses and Jesus, and was told that he held similar exalted status. God then imparted to him the five daily prayers that are, to this day, the practical basis of Muslim religious observance.

FLIGHT TO MEDINA

In 622 Muhammad and his followers fled Mecca, an event described as the *hijra* or emigration, to Yathrib (soon renamed Medina, "city of the prophet"), about 185 miles to the north, whose citizens had asked Muhammad to help mediate in their internal disputes. While his fame as a negotiator, judge, and sage continued to grow, along with his group of followers, the Meccans still considered him a threat. Between 624 and 627,

MUHAMMAD HAD AN ARMY OF MORE THAN TEN THOUSAND FOLLOWERS—THEY CAPTURED MECCA AND DESTROYED ALL THE IDOLS AND PAGAN IMAGES.

in a series of battles between the people of Medina and the Meccans, Muhammad displayed great political and military ability as he won significant victories over the Meccans. This helped to confirm the authenticity of his calling. In the first of these encounters at Badr, south of Medina, in March 624, just 313 Muslims defeated an army of one thousand Meccans. After the Muslims' victory in Medina in 627 over a combined Meccan–Jewish army at the Battle of the Ditch, a truce was called. Muhammad then sought the endorsement of Medina's thriving Jewish community, pointing out that he shared their monotheistic viewpoint and accepted the legitimate authority of all the biblical prophets, including Jesus. But the Jews, disagreeing with his interpretation of the scriptures, refused to be a party to the treaty—so the Muslims beheaded the men and enslaved the women and children.

In 629 Muhammad made the first *hajj* (or pilgrimage) to Mecca, a tradition still carried out annually by hundreds of thousands of pilgrims. He then created the *suras*, a series of precepts that are usually placed at the beginning of the Qur'an. The following year the Meccans broke the truce, but by now Muhammad had an army of more than ten thousand followers. They conquered and captured Mecca, destroyed all the idols and pagan images in the Ka'bah and elsewhere, and either killed or expelled the Jews who were agitating against them. Muhammad held that the Jews had persecuted the exalted prophet Jesus and his mother, but had in fact failed to kill him—a ghost had been crucified in his place.

A NEW FAITH TAKES HOLD

Muhammad had clearly defined the decrees of the new faith and now enjoyed increasing power. His religion had gradually become more Arabic in tone, and from this time became centered on Abraham, father of the Jews, and his son Ismael, precursor of the Arabs and believed to be the founder of the Ka'bah. From now on, Muslims would face Mecca when they prayed; previously they had directed themselves toward Jerusalem.

By 631 Muhammad's influence and support extended over most of the Arab world, thus ending what he called "the age of ignorance." In March 632, at the age of about sixty-two, he preached his final sermon to some two hundred thousand people at Mount Arafat, which was about 12 miles east of Mecca. On June 8, at Medina, he died suddenly in the home of Aishah, the favorite of his nine wives and the daughter of Abu Bakr, one of his original followers. His body lies in a tomb at Al-Masjid n-Nabawiy ("The Mosque of the Prophet") at Medina, which

was built next to his home and is venerated throughout Islam. Muslims believe that a prayer in this mosque is worth at least a thousand prayers in any other mosque, apart from the Ka'bah.

Muhammad left as his successors his daughter Fatima—who had two sons—and his several wives, who included the daughters of his advisers, the caliphs Umar and Abu Bakr. Two separate factions emerged from this group, the Shiites and the Sunnis, setting in train a power dispute that is still evident today (notably in the sectarian bloodshed that blights modern Iraq). The minority Shiites held that future caliphs should be selected from the descendants of Fatima whereas the Sunnis recognized the lineage of the four caliphs.

ISLAM AFTER MUHAMMAD

Islam, which means "surrender (to the will of God)" had already enjoyed a remarkably rapid expansion, which after Muhammad's death continued apace. Within a century Islam had spread its influence over large swathes of the Western world. After Muhammad's death, Sunni caliph Abu Bakr took only two or three years to consolidate Islam in Arabia by completing the task of uniting the numerous disparate tribes. After he died in 634 Muhammad's other father-in-law, Umar (an astute military commander), became caliph and conquered Jerusalem, Syria, Lebanon, Armenia, Egypt, much of North Africa, and most of Iraq and Persia (Iran). He was assassinated in 644, whereupon Muhammad's son-in-law Uthman took over, conquering Cyprus, the Caucasus, more holdings in North Africa, and the rest of Persia.

Over the next fifty years Islam spread to the remainder of the Middle East and to modern-day Pakistan, Uzbekistan, Kazakhstan, and Tajikistan. Almost thirty years after the death of Mohammad, Ali (Mohammad's cousin as well as Fatima's husband) succeeded Uthman after Uthman was killed in a

Muhammad proved to be a great military as well as religious leader, and led his followers to conquer Mecca.

civil war, but was himself assassinated in 661. His successor Muawiyah I, the governor of Syria, founded the Sunni Umayyad dynasty which ruled until 750, conquering Gibraltar, Catholic Spain and Portugal on the Iberian peninsula (with the help of the recently converted North African Moors), as far north as the Pyrenees mountains, the border between Spain and France.

This expansion of Islamic control continued more or less unchallenged until the French defeated the Muslim armies at the Battle of Tours in 732. Meanwhile the Shiites were fighting to secure various regions of Syria and Iraq against Sunni control. Shiite caliph Husain, a son of Fatima and Ali, was killed in Iraq at the Battle of Karbala in 680; his martyrdom is still mourned by modern Shiites.

MUHAMMAD'S TEACHINGS

The reasons for the extraordinarily rapid expansion of Islam are similar to the reasons that Muhammad's teachings were so vehemently opposed by the entrenched powers during his lifetime. He preached against the corrupt ruling hierarchies (which were based on class differences) in favor of the rights of the masses. He also spoke against many widespread Arab customs, including female infanticide, the vastly inferior status of women, and slavery. He abolished numerous tribal customs—which had led to endless conflicts—in favor of a single unifying Islamic law. He preached the virtues of modesty, fairness, respect, honesty, generosity of spirit, universal (rather than authoritarian) justice, and government based on merit rather than power, wealth or status. ❦

747–814
THE CROWNING OF CHARLEMAGNE

On Christmas Day in 800, while Charlemagne, king of the Franks, knelt in prayer in Saint Peter's in Rome, Pope Leo III placed a crown on his bowed head. With this act Charlemagne was appointed the first modern Emperor of Romans.

Charlemagne, also known as Charles the Great (742–814), was a descendant of the Germanic tribes called the Franks who raided much of Europe from the third century onwards; they soon carved out a strong presence, gradually acquiring influence in Spain, Belgium, France, the Rhine regions and parts of Italy. One notable leader, Clovis, in 496, interspersed a career of conquest with his conversion to Catholicism. Almost three hundred years later, Charlemagne transformed Western Europe into a Christian empire that stretched from the west coast of France to Germany, the Low Countries (present-day Belgium, the Netherlands, and Luxembourg), northern Spain, and Italy.

Charlemagne's birthplace is uncertain, but was probably in or near the town of Aachen (known by the French as Aix-La-Chapelle) near the border of Belgium, Germany, and the Netherlands. His father Pépin III, unkindly known as Pépin the Short, and his grandfather Charles Martel were both rulers of the Frankish world. Martel had started the process of transforming Europe, operating from the standpoint that Christianity was not only the one true religion, but also the most effective force for political unification and peace. He was largely responsible for stopping the spread of Islam into Europe. Pépin continued the process, as did the young Charles, who therefore inherited an established tradition by which a king's

significance was gauged by his success at war. This required him to formulate a method of government that would be able to maintain power over an increasingly fragmented population.

Charlemagne and his forebears believed that the Catholic Church should be reformed and reorganized under the aegis of the pope. They assisted the popes of the day in their struggles against the temporal rulers of Rome, the Byzantines, receiving in return papal recognition of their right to rule, and support for their European military campaigns. This in turn assisted their rise to power as founders of what became known as the Carolingian (named for Charlemagne) dynasty. When Pépin died in 768, Charles and his brother Carloman each inherited half of the Frankish empire, following the tradition of the existing Merovingian dynasty. Three years later, when Carloman died, Charles took over the entire kingdom, inheriting great riches and a formidable army.

CHRISTIANITY IS ENFORCED

Eighth century Western Europe was a largely heathen world, with many warring tribes and kingdoms. Charlemagne embarked upon a series of military operations, starting with the Saxons in northwest Germany. The Saxon wars lasted thirty-three years as Charlemagne rampaged across their lands, burning towns and massacring the inhabitants in persistent attempts to force Christianity on them. These campaigns

The oldest cathedral in northern Europe, at Aachen (Aix-la-Chapelle) in Germany, was built by Charlemagne in 792.

marked one of the few occasions on which Charlemagne was not completely victorious; he actually defeated the Saxons several times, but did not maintain a strong enough occupying force to prevent them reverting to their previous beliefs and way of life.

Although Charlemagne generally respected the traditions and customs of the territories he conquered, providing his new subjects embraced Christianity, at times his resolute drive for domination spilled over into cold-bloodedness. His religious self-assurance led to his belief that ends, no matter how ruthless, generally justified the means. His nephews mysteriously disappeared while under his custody, and he deposed his cousin in order to conquer Bavaria. When his illegitimate son Pépin the Hunchback led a rebellion against him in 792, Charlemagne quashed the insurgency with great brutality. During one of the periodic Saxon rebellions, when they renounced Christianity and his authority (yet again), Charlemagne regarded it as heresy as well as treason, killing four thousand Saxons in one day in an attempt to discourage such uprisings in future. After Pope Gregory III approved and blessed his conquest of Byzantine Italy, he reneged on his promise to increase papal landholdings, deciding to keep Lombardy for himself.

SUPPORT FOR THE POPE

Charlemagne turned his attentions to Italy, where the papacy's sphere of influence had shrunk to only a small portion of land around Rome and was under continuous threat from the Lombards, a Germanic people who were at war with both Rome and Byzantium. In 773 Pope Hadrian I appealed to Charlemagne, who quickly defeated the Lombards. Charlemagne's second eldest legitimate son Carloman was granted the title King of the Lombards and took the name Pépin, while the pope regained power over northern Italy.

From Italy Charlemagne moved on to Spain, where he experienced partial success in annexing the northern area near the Pyrenees mountains, but failed in attempts to head south and conquer the Iberian peninsula. Southern Spain, controlled by the North African Moors, resisted several invasion attempts, and succeeded in maintaining its Islamic faith and control for several centuries to come. But Charlemagne was able to create a buffer between Africa and Europe; in 781 he created the kingdom of Aquitaine, which was ruled by his son Louis. The western Frankish empire was now largely peaceful, so Charlemagne stormed north in a successful attempt to subdue the fiercely independent Bavarians of western Germany. This brought him up against the Avars, central Asian nomads who

had occupied the lands around the river Danube and had their eye on further westward expansion. Charlemagne succeeded in looting and conquering their lands, and forcing them to convert to Christianity.

In 799 Pope Leo III, following a Roman insurrection against him, sought Charlemagne's protection. Although Leo was generally popular, members of the Roman nobility had attacked him during a procession, threatening to blind him and rip out his tongue. According to contemporary reports, the two leaders had arranged to have Pépin installed as king of Italy and Aquitaine. But on Christmas Day 800 at St. Peter's Basilica in Rome, when the moment came, Leo placed the crown on Charlemagne's head instead, pronouncing him in traditional Roman terms *Imperator Romanorum* ("Emperor of the Romans"). This placed Charlemagne in an invidious position as it guaranteed the fervent opposition of the Romans—they looked very poorly on an attempt by an outsider to inherit the authority of the Caesars.

The Byzantine rulers of Italy already had a Christian leader in Constantinople and did not recognize papal authority, so Leo's actions were technically illegal and without authority. After his agreement to guard the pope, Charlemagne was not amused at this very public anointing and exposition of his role. But his irritation may have been feigned; although he had gone to Rome to restore the political equilibrium of Christianity, and despite the fact that Leo's actions had actually destabilized it, Charlemagne made the most of the situation, intending to restore unity by proposing marriage to the Byzantine Empress Irene. But the scheme was abandoned when Irene was deposed soon afterwards. Nonetheless, Charlemagne's armies continued to sweep through Europe, conquering many other tribes, including the Bretons on the western Frankish coast in modern Brittany, the Huns in western Asia, and the Danes.

ADVANCES IN EDUCATION, ART AND ARCHITECTURE

The church and Charlemagne enjoyed a symbiotic relationship; they gave stability to each other's jurisdiction and quest for power. As each new area of Europe was conquered, Charlemagne murdered any leader who did not convert to Christianity and installed a new one, usually a high-ranking church official. Charlemagne employed church leaders as educators who used the Bible to teach morality in the numerous educational institutions he established. This was an important factor in aiding Charlemagne's genuine aim to improve the education of

> CHARLEMAGNE'S RELIGIOUS SELF-ASSURANCE LED TO HIS BELIEF THAT ENDS, NO MATTER HOW RUTHLESS, GENERALLY JUSTIFIED THE MEANS.

the people at a time when, other than members of the clergy, very few people were educated.

Another beneficial consequence of this policy was that Charlemagne was provided with ever-increasing numbers of educated people who proved very useful in assisting his administration. Although himself virtually illiterate (despite being fluent in Latin and able to speak some Greek), he standardized western European language by reviving Greek and making the study of Latin compulsory in all his institutions. He founded the Palace School in his hometown, Aix-La-Chapelle. Many of the scholars brought to teach there were foreigners, including Italians, Spaniards, and Irish who together developed a new style of script known as Carolingian minuscule, characterized by simple, rounded letters, which made it easier to learn, read, and write.

Charlemagne attended the school, studying Latin, Greek, grammar, rhetoric, dialectics, and astronomy. He tried to learn to write, but was not very successful, being a very late starter—although he was very articulate and eloquent in speech. His sons and daughters attended academic classes, as well as studying the traditional Frankish pursuits of riding and hunting for boys, and cloth-making for girls. The education systems were very similar to those followed by classical Greek and Roman scholars. A teacher would read a text then explain

On Christmas Day 800, Pope Leo III crowned Charlemagne Emperor of the Romans in Saint Peter's Basilica.

it. The class then discussed the material, applying analytical, logical, and disciplined reasoning.

Charlemagne introduced standard trading laws across his kingdom and stabilized coinage, regulating the amounts of silver and gold contained in each denomination. Since the fifth century, coins had been minted by many different manufacturers—with the result that their actual value varied greatly. Money was now publicly guaranteed and controlled by one source, rather than many.

Charlemagne also had a significant influence on architecture and art, restoring ancient Roman traditions. He commissioned impressive chapels for monasteries, providing large spaces where the masses could worship. The early constructions were mostly made of wood because it was a familiar material to the nomadic people of the time. But the need for defence and durability caused a return to stone construction, resulting in the resurrection of the Roman style of churches, monuments, gardens, and arches. Aesthetic adornments, such as mosaics, gilding, marble statuary, ivory carvings, and paintings were other architectural features of the period. Precious gems, gold, silver, frescoes, terra-cotta,

THE CROWNING OF CHARLEMAGNE

and plaster were also incorporated into the designs of churches, monuments and other buildings.

HONORING PAST ACHIEVEMENTS

Charlemagne attempted to honor traditional Frankish customs while responding resourcefully to new social forces. Intellectual and artistic stirrings were occurring throughout all of Latin Christendom. There was a growing desire to re-establish contact with the Classical past, which was seen as a fundamental requirement for the revitalization of Christian society. Charlemagne possessed the personal qualities to successfully confront such a challenge. He was the supreme warrior chief, with an imposing physical presence and charisma, and possessed a remarkable constitution. Renowned for his personal courage and iron will, he loved action and physical pursuits of all kinds—fighting, travelling, hunting and swimming—but he was also a popular court companion, generous with gifts and skilful at establishing and maintaining friendships. He married five times, owned several concubines, and sired at least eighteen children, whose interests he oversaw conscientiously. These traits commanded respect, loyalty, and affection. He was a natural leader, capable of making and acting on informed decisions and proficient at persuading others to assist him.

NEW THREATS FROM THE SEA

Although Charlemagne's armies were virtually invincible on land, the same could not be said for his navy. Vikings were attacking from the north while Spanish Muslims harried him from the south. Finding it difficult to repel advances on so many fronts simultaneously, in 811 Charlemagne began a concerted but unsuccessful military and diplomatic campaign to persuade Byzantine Emperor Michael I in Constantinople to recognize his Roman holdings. He planned to divide his empire among his three legitimate sons in the traditional way, but two of them, Charles (the eldest) and Pépin, died before him. In 813 he arranged for his son Louis, king of Aquitaine, to succeed him. He tried to confirm his religious primacy by holding the ceremony in Germany (as far as possible from Italy, the center of Christian rule), and did not ask the pope to perform and legitimize the accession, as would have been expected.

When Charlemagne died in 814 Louis inherited a festering and complex (indeed byzantine) series of rivalries that, without Charlemagne's strong guidance and charisma, he was unable to negotiate. Nor was he able to effectively retain control over the many disparate tribes that had united under his father. It turned out that the empire's strength had rested not on its institutions and systems, but in its leader. Upon Louis' death in 840, his three sons inherited various separate parts of the kingdom, but the lack of effective leadership they (and, in turn, their sons) displayed, led to the fragmentation of the previously united kingdom and its overthrow by the Frankish nobility in 880.

CHARLEMAGNE'S LEGACY AND A NEW EMPIRE

Nonetheless, Charlemagne's legacy lasted for centuries. The ambition to increase his empire was driven (and tempered) by his unswerving devotion and his desire to spread the Christian religion and use it as a source of peace and unity. His legislative system, constitution and governmental practices were used as the model by the French Capetian dynasty that ruled from 987 to 1328. His Carolingian empire eventually provided the model for the Holy Roman Empire, which was highly influential around the world until its dissolution in 1806. He revolutionized European cultural and spiritual life, and the relationship between politics and religion. He left behind thriving libraries, cathedrals, and monasteries, and introduced schools and universities, which researched and taught many disciplines, including architecture, visual arts, and history. He set up systems whereby eminent scholars educated the clergy, who in turn set up schools. He was extraordinarily persistent, compassionate in his actions (with a few exceptions that he deemed necessary in order to eliminate entrenched harmful practices), and perhaps wiser than any other ruler of his era.

In January 813, aged seventy-two, Charlemagne contracted pleurisy and died a week later in the forty-seventh year of his reign. He was buried in Aachen Cathedral. His body was exhumed in 1215 on the orders of Frederick II and placed inside a gold and silver casket. ❧

1043–1099
EL CID AND THE CONQUEST OF VALENCIA

Rodrigo Díaz de Vivar, the popular hero of the chivalric age of Spain, was one of the most complex military leaders of the Middle Ages. At various times he led armies on behalf of both the Christians and the Muslim Moors, who were fighting for control of Spain and the Iberian peninsula. Both groups—as well as warring with each other—were deeply divided within themselves. This led to a constantly shifting series of alliances between kingdoms, which often made it difficult to tell who was fighting whom.

Rodrigo's sobriquet "El Cid," which he acquired during his lifetime, is a combination of the Spanish *el* (the) and the Arabic *cid* (lord), which seems appropriate since, alternately, he served both Christian Spain and the Moors. Sometimes the epithet *campeador*, a Latin word that roughly translates as "master of military arts," is added to his name, further reflecting the multicultural nature of his exploits. His reputation has contradictory aspects—he was known for his diplomatic skills, his courage, and his innate fairness, but also for being a duplicitous, opportunistic, cunning, and ruthless man.

BEGINNING OF A LEGEND

El Cid was born about 1043 in the village of Bivar in northern Spain. His parents were minor nobility—his father Diego Laínez Díaz was an administrator in the Royal Court and a soldier. The young Rodrigo trained in knightly and military arts at the court of Prince Sancho, the eldest son of the reigning King Ferdinand I of Castile and Léon, and distinguished himself as a formidable soldier, winning the respect of his peers and mentors. When Ferdinand died in 1065 he was given command of Sancho's army.

Before he died, King Ferdinand allocated different areas of his kingdom to each of his three sons. His second (and favorite) son Alfonso was given the kingdom of Léon (a substantial area in the north) and the recently conquered Moorish kingdom of Toledo. García, his youngest son, was granted Portugal, Seville, and the western province of Galicia. Sancho, despite being his first-born, was granted the smaller areas of Castile and Saragossa. (His two daughters, Urraca and Elvira, were granted power over all the monasteries, on condition that they did not marry or bear any offspring.) Sancho was displeased with this arrangement, and told Ferdinand that he refused its terms on the grounds that it was unfair to him, the eldest son. But the old king refused to waver. Furthermore, he told the sons that they would be disinherited unless they deferred to Rodrigo, effectively placing him *in loco parentis*, even though he was about their age.

Sancho appointed Rodrigo as commander of his army and determinedly went about increasing his territory. In 1067 Rodrigo led Sancho's Castilian armies in a successful campaign against the Moorish city of Saragossa in northeastern Spain, extracting a promise of loyalty and immediate payment of the first annual tribute (tax) installment. A contemporary Jewish chronicler attributed the success of the operation exclusively to Rodrigo, dubbing him *Cidi*, or "my Lord."

WAR BETWEEN THE BROTHERS ESCALATES

After Ferdinand's widow died in 1067 Sancho abandoned his adherence to his father's allocation of territory and, by

1068, Castile was at war with Léon, which was ruled by his brother Alfonso. El Cid (as he was increasingly known) defeated Alfonso's army at the brief war of Llantada Plain on July 19, 1068 but Alfonso, reneging on an agreement that the loser would surrender and throw in his lot with the victor, fled south. He mustered his forces and successfully attacked the Moorish state of Badajoz, extracting a promise of future tributes even greater than those the state was already paying to the third brother, García. Inevitably, the war between the three brothers escalated; Sancho pretended to side with García against Alfonso, all the while awaiting his opportunity to annex García's domains of Portugal and Galicia.

It is not known whether El Cid tried to mediate in these internecine battles, as he had promised Ferdinand, but in 1071 Sancho and Alfonso defeated and captured García, and split up his lands between them. Songs of the period say that it was El Cid himself who captured García and delivered him to his brothers; perhaps he saw this as a way of ending the civil war that was destabilising Christian Spain. In any case, he stayed faithful to the eldest brother, Sancho, who escalated his war against Alfonso now that García was, to all intents and purposes, out of the picture.

Several border skirmishes led to the battle of Golpejera in which El Cid played a crucial role in Sancho's victory. During the battle Sancho was heard to comment that *he* was worth a thousand men—and Rodrigo another hundred. El Cid's humble reply was that he was only equal to a single man, and the rest was up to God. Alfonso was taken prisoner, perhaps by El Cid, and exiled to Toledo. Sancho declared himself King of Léon, which made him ruler of the largest kingdom in Spain. But Urraca, who, some historians believe, held an incestuous infatuation for her brother Alfonso, organized a rebellion against the new king. While Sancho was waiting to visit Urraca's castle at Zamora an assassin murdered him. El Cid gave chase but the perpetrator escaped into Zamora where he was given refuge. Alfonso crowned himself King of Léon, Castile and Galicia, and sought El Cid's support. El Cid agreed, but not before forcing Alfonso to declare before his subjects that he had nothing to do with his brother's murder.

Despite this public humiliation, Alfonso honored El Cid by arranging for him to marry his niece, Ximena Díaz. This had the effect of demonstrating the high esteem in which El Cid was held by the king, and was also designed to help heal the schism between Castile and Léon, though it did little to dispel the ongoing suspicion and mistrust between two strong individuals. Ximena bore El Cid two daughters, Cristina and Maria, and a son, Diego Rodríguez.

EL CID HAD NO PROBLEM RAISING AN ARMY—MANY WERE KEEN TO SERVE UNDER SUCH A SUCCESSFUL AND RENOWNED WARRIOR.

INTRIGUES AT COURT

Despite his marriage, El Cid's status at Alfonso's court was shaky. His enemies whispered to Alfonso that he was an unrepentant secret supporter of the Castilians who resented being ruled by the king of Léon, and they reminded him of the humiliation El Cid had subjected him to after Sancho's death. El Cid, for his part, disapproved of the influence of the nobility over Alfonso, and probably resented losing the position of Ensign (or Commander) of the Royal Armies that he held under Sancho. His inclination to humiliate powerful leaders probably contributed to his impending exile.

Alfonso exiled El Cid in 1081 after he invaded Alfonso's Moorish kingdom of Toledo. After several unsuccessful attempts to heal the rift, El Cid aligned himself with Moktadir, the Muslim king of Saragossa—whom he had helped defeat in 1067. The king jumped at the chance to employ the services of such a successful Christian warrior and El Cid served him, and his successor Motamid II, for the next ten years. This experience no doubt gave him an insight into the byzantine and ever-changing intricacies of Christian–Muslim and Spanish–Arabic politics, which would hold him in good stead in his future exploits.

In 1082 El Cid routed Moktadir's enemy, the Moorish king of Lérida, and his Christian allies, including the King of Barcelona. Two years later, despite being vastly outnumbered, he conquered an army that was led by the Christian king Sancho Ramírez of Aragón. His appreciative Muslim masters rewarded him greatly for these victories.

EL CID SETS HIS SIGHTS ON VALENCIA

But in 1086 Alfonso swallowed his pride and requested El Cid's assistance—his forces had been almost completely annihilated by the invading Berber Muslim Almoravids from Morocco. El Cid spent a short time at Alfonso's court in 1087 until, under the influence of El Cid's opponents, old animosities surfaced and Alfonso imprisoned his wife and children, and banished El Cid to Saragossa. El Cid took no part in the war that was raging as the Almoravids threatened the very existence of Christian Spain. After a period as a mercenary, offering his skills to whoever would hire him, he decided to attempt an invasion of the prosperous Moorish kingdom of Valencia, ruled at the time by a Muslim–Christian coalition.

The Castilian military leader Rodrigo Díaz, or El Cid, is one of the most celebrated knights in history.

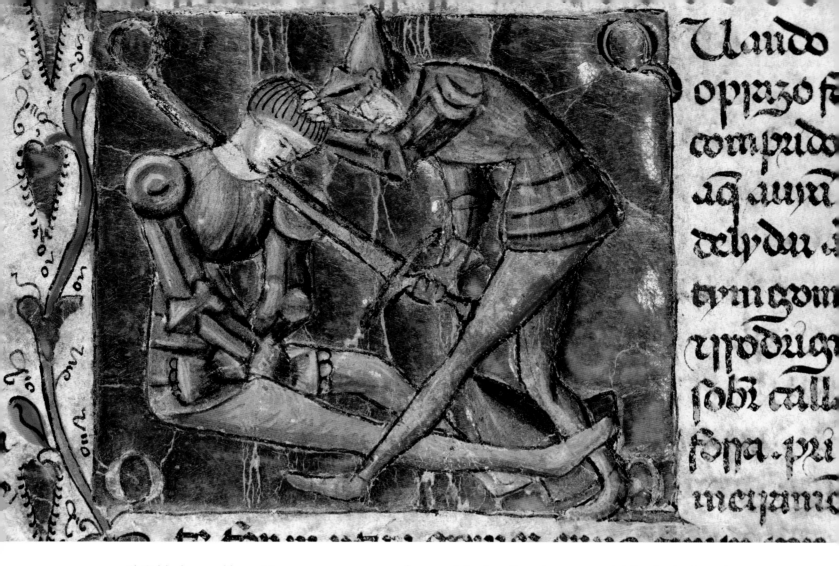

A fourteenth-century manuscript illumination from the *Chronicles of Spain* showing El Cid in battle.

El Cid had no problem raising an army—many were keen to serve under such a successful and renowned warrior. They invaded the kingdoms of Deria and Lérida, capturing two castles and appropriating a cave full of treasure belonging to the lord of Lérida. With his forces boosted by the enemies of the vanquished Lérida, and new recruits attracted by the handsome wages he was now able to offer, El Cid set off for Valencia. Al-Kadir, the faint-hearted and indecisive ruler of Valencia, agreed to restore the tribute he had been paying to El Cid before his second banishment. But trouble loomed in the form of Berenguer, the powerful Count of Barcelona, who had been captured by El Cid in an earlier battle. Berenguer had formed a partnership with the Moorish lord of Lérida, and had tried to enlist the support of Alfonso. Much to the surprise of almost everyone, Alfonso refused. Nonetheless, El Cid's forces were so outnumbered as to make the prospect of victory, even for such an excellent leader as El Cid, very remote. El Cid's troops left Valencia and set up camp in a nearby valley, fortifying its three entrances with wooden bulwarks. Berenguer and El Cid exchanged a series of letters, accusing each other of treason and cowardice.

Meanwhile El Cid had allowed several of his men to desert, carrying the misinformation that he was preparing to make his escape through one of the passes leading into the valley. This had the desired result. Berenguer split his forces into three, one guarding each of the entrances to the valley. A chaotic night battle followed, during which El Cid was wounded. The men blundered back and forth in the darkness but, despite El Cid's incapacitation, his troops were able to hold sway. They captured Berenguer and five thousand troops with the loss of very few of their own. This latest stunning victory led to the leaders of east and southeast Moorish Spain voluntarily offering to install El Cid as their warlord, with the payment of huge tributes in return for his future protection. Eventually Berenguer was ransomed and in 1096 his son Ramón was married to El Cid's daughter Maria as insurance against future discord.

A COMPLEX NETWORK OF ALLIANCES

El Cid's influence in Valencia grew, but his huge domain, with its many complex and uneasy alliances, was proving increasingly difficult to control. The Almoravid Berbers had renewed their attacks from the south and there was an ever-present danger that El Cid's Moorish vassals would request aid, or simply change their allegiance. He played a delicate balancing act, striving not to offend or overpower either Moors or Christians, and balancing mercy and justice to such a successful degree that even Alfonso, impressed by his triumphs, ceased his attacks on the Moors and sought treaties. The Berbers continued their attacks in ever-increasing numbers and, even though Alfonso and El Cid were to some extent united again, captured large tracts of land in Alfonso's Moorish fiefdom of Granada and Andalusia to the south.

The threat of a total Muslim conquest of Spain loomed large, and only El Cid stood in its way. From his base in Valencia he began to negotiate with Christian princes, encouraging them to enter into treaties with Muslim lords to unite against the common foe. Alfonso, although still mistrustful of El Cid, eventually succumbed to the reality of his popularity and power, and reinstated him to his court. But it was El Cid who was seen as the true leader, and Alfonso's influence gradually waned.

In 1092 El Cid journeyed north to Saragossa to plan the renewal of his assaults on the Almoravids, but in his absence their leader, Yusuf, stormed northward, capturing several Christian strongholds along the way, including Granada. When news reached El Cid he returned and began to raise an army to reconquer the city he had so recently ruled. After a complicated series of battles and sieges lasting almost two years, Valencia succumbed to El Cid on June 15, 1094. Although he nominally ruled in the name of Alfonso, he was now effectively the king of Valencia. He sent for his wife and children to join him and they took up residence in the palace. Christian knights and Muslim warriors from all over Spain flocked to his banner and soon he commanded a force of some eight thousand Christians, and twenty-five thousand Muslims.

But there still remained the matter of Yusuf. In late 1094 the Almoravid leader amassed a force of some 180,000 under the stewardship of his nephew Mohammed and ordered them to crush El Cid forever. But at the Battle of Cuarte near Valencia in December, the Christian forces led by El Cid defeated the Almoravids using unconventional tactics. They cut a path through the massed opposition troops with a force of heavily armored, mounted knights, then swiftly turned around, trampling the chaotically disorganized Berbers underfoot. In 1096 Valencia's nine mosques were converted into Christian churches under the bishopric of French priest Jerome, and an uneasy peace ensued for nearly three years until, in 1097, Yusuf's army returned to southern Spain. El Cid remained in Valencia waiting for an attack that never came. His son Diego, however, was slain by Yusuf's troops and El Cid was inconsolable for months afterwards. In 1098 he attacked and besieged the Moorish forces at the castle of Murvideo, south of Valencia, and by the middle of the year the starving Moors had collapsed and El Cid was again triumphant. He had avenged the death of his son and showed yet again that Valencia was invincible so long as he was alive to rule over it.

El Cid died unexpectedly at Valencia on July 10, 1099. His wife Ximena succeeded him but was able to rule for barely three years, even with the aid of Alfonso, who at last realized that he was largely helpless without the assistance of his famous knight. Valencia was soon besieged by the Almoravids, and Alfonso decided that it was impossible to defend unless he maintained a huge army there. He evacuated then burned the city. On May 5, 1102 the Almoravids finally succeeded in occupying Valencia, which remained in Muslim hands until 1238. El Cid's body was taken to Castile, where it was buried in the San Pedro de Cardeña, a monastery near Burgos.

Most of the lands won by El Cid also returned to Muslim rule and, without El Cid, Alfonso was unable to make any further inroads against the Moors. El Cid's remarkable legacy was recorded in numerous songs and poems and, although there were many more wars between Muslim and Christian to come, Spain gradually evolved into a cultural melting pot of East and West, a process started by El Cid. ❧

1066
THE BATTLE OF HASTINGS

In the early light of the October morning, the Saxon shield wall on the crest of the hill must have seemed impenetrable to the Normans gazing up the slope. The English *thegns*, or landed aristocrats, loyal to their Anglo-Saxon King Harold were covered with chain mail, wore strong helmets and carried swords and long, double-edged Danish axes. They had planted their heavy semicircular shields on the ground, interlocking them so that there was not an inch of space between them. Behind this barrier were the so-called levies, the English peasants who, under the feudal system, were obliged to fight for their king. And, at the center of the line, astride his horse and protected by his bodyguards, was King Harold Godwinson. It was his intention to hold firm and triumph, or die.

Arrayed against the Saxons, at the foot of the hill, were the forces of the invader, William the Bastard of Normandy, soon to be known by the far more flattering sobriquet of William the Conqueror. William's forces were equal in number to the Saxons, but far more mobile and professional, including as they did cavalry and archers, and experienced Italian mercenaries. There were arrayed in three divisions or "battles": Bretons on the left, Normans in the center, and French on the right. It was William's intention to shatter the English shield wall, kill Harold, and take his crown.

....

A vivid illustration of the battle of Hastings from a fifteenth-century French manuscript, the *Chronicle of Normandy*.

The battle began with a song. According to a legend, William's minstrel and knight, Ivo Taillefer, begged his king to allow him the honor of charging the English first. William granted his request, and Taillefer sped his horse towards the Saxons, where he tauntingly tossed his sword in the air while singing what was probably an early version of the epic *The Song of Roland*. When an enraged Saxon soldier charged out to challenge him, Taillefer decapitated him and took his head as a trophy—and as proof that God was on his side.

The Saxons believed differently, of course. As the Normans rushed up the hill, they shouldered close behind their shield wall and cried, *Ut! Ut!* Meaning "Out! Out!"

THE MEN FROM THE NORTH

At this moment, around 9 a.m. on the morning of October 14, 1066, the future of England hung in the balance. The Anglo-Saxons had controlled the country since the fifth century, after migrating there from Scandinavia or Germany, but they were now faced with a mass invasion of their lands by the Normans from northern France—who intended to stay.

The Normans had recently emerged as a formidable regional power. They were descended from Vikings who had occupied the Seine River valley in the ninth century—their correct name, *Normanni*, means "the men from the north." In the tenth and early eleventh centuries, they had conquered much of northwestern France while developing a reputation as skilled and ferocious warriors, united by strong kinship ties. The feudal system, which obliged tenant farmers and knights to fight for the landholders, provided

manpower and supplies for the Norman campaigns, but led to an unceasing quest for more land. By the mid-eleventh century, England, just a short distance across the English Channel, had become a tempting target. All the more so because the Duke of Normandy, William the Bastard (so named because of his illegitimate status), saw himself as the country's rightful ruler.

A PROMISE AND AN OATH

Strong links between England and Normandy had developed following the coronation of King Harold's predecessor, King Edward the Confessor, in 1042. Prior to assuming the throne, Edward had spent twenty-five years in exile in Normandy, where his mother had taken him to escape a Danish invasion and subsequent period of Danish control. On his return to England following the reinstatement of Anglo-Saxon rule, he had taken with him a group of Norman advisers. This upset the Anglo-Saxon aristocracy, who rallied round Godwin of Wessex, a powerful English lord. Aided by William, Edward expelled Godwin from the country in 1051. But after Godwin's death, his son, Harold Godwinson, managed to return to England. There he regained much of the power lost by his father, so much so that King Edward—not the most strong-willed of rulers—made him a chief adviser.

In 1064, Harold was shipwrecked off the French coast and captured by the Duke of Normandy. William claimed that Edward had promised England to him in 1051 in return for his aid in expelling Godwin, and he had long since set his eyes on its throne and rich lands. He forced Harold to swear an oath on a saint's relic to support his "claim" to the throne once Edward, childless and purportedly celibate, died.

On his return to England, however, Harold simply explained that the oath had been forced from him under duress, and Edward himself denied making any promises to William. So, following Edward's death on January 5, 1066, there being no other heir, and with the full support of the kingdom's most powerful nobles, Harold was crowned king at Westminster Abbey.

This infuriated William. And William was not a person to trifle with. Just a boy when he succeeded his father as Duke of the Normans—"I was brought up in arms from childhood," he told people—he had had to be courageous and wise beyond his years just to survive. Sincerely believing that God was on his side, he resolved to amass a great seaborne army, take England by force, and depose Harold.

HAROLD BESIEGED

William's invasion fleet was an incredible one for the time—six hundred ships, which were to hold seven thousand men in all, including knights, archers, and infantry. For months, the coast of Normandy rang with these shipbuilding efforts. Meanwhile, to help justify his attack, William sought the support of Pope Alexander II, drawing attention to the fact that the prelate who had crowned Harold, Archbishop Stigand of Canterbury, had not been formally recognized by the Pope. Alexander, who was keen to establish alliances with powerful figures outside the Holy Roman Empire, agreed, and he sent a papal banner in support. This, in turn, helped William rally troops from all over northern France and beyond. The fleet was finished in early September, and when favorable winds arose on the 27th, William and his men set sail for England.

King Harold already had his hands full, because he was fighting off not one invasion force, but two. For there was another claimant to the throne, King Harald III Sigurdsson of Norway, who was descended from King Canute, once the ruler of both Scandinavia and England. Joining forces with Harold's estranged brother, Tostig, Harald III invaded England in September, landing in the northeast and defeating the armies of two northern earls before making camp at Stamford Bridge, near York. Harold reacted swiftly, marched north with his army and, on September 25, defeated and killed both Harald and Tostig at the battle of Stamford Bridge. This was a major victory for England, and also marked the last time a Scandinavian army would attempt to invade the country.

William landed on the southeast coast of England three days later. Needing as quick a victory as possible, since he was operating on foreign territory, far from his base of supply, he and his forces began pillaging the land, hoping to draw Harold into battle. It worked: Harold raced down from York, stopped in London to gather more forces and then headed with all speed to the little village of Hastings, in East Sussex. There he arrayed his forces across the Hastings–London road, on Senlac Hill, about 8 miles north of the town, a site now known as Battle Hill.

Harold's force of about seven thousand men was set up across the crest of the hill, with its flanks anchored on either side by woods and the massive forest of Anderida at his back—on the face of it an impregnable position. But Harold's forces were not as strong as they seemed, as they had been weakened both by losses at the battle of Stamford Bridge and by the reluctance of local peasants to fight another pitched battle.

"I'M ALIVE!"

After Ivo Taillefer made his fabled charge (one account has him riding into the Saxon lines and killing another two Saxons before being killed himself), William gave a command and a shower of arrows fell upon the English. The Saxon soldiers ducked beneath their shields as the arrows fell, and were little harmed—the Normans were shooting uphill and the distance was hard to gauge. In any case, since Norman archery tactics depended on shooting back arrows already fired by opponents, and since the Saxons were without archers, the Normans were soon forced to stop firing in order to conserve their ammunition.

William then had his infantry charge straight up the hill at the densely packed English army, but these foot soldiers were unable to break through the shield wall and fell back, with many dead and wounded. Their retreat almost became a rout. At one point, the English right wing began to pursue the Bretons falling back on the Norman left, and although their commanders checked this advance, it was noted with interest by the Normans.

A rumor then rippled through the panicky Norman ranks that William was dead and he was forced to doff his helmet and ride in front of his lines, yelling, "I'm alive! I'm alive!" But he was faced with a problem: time was on Harold's side, not his. The longer the battle continued, the more likely it would be that reinforcements would come to Harold's aide. As the day wore on, repeated attacks on the shield wall produced nothing but a growing pile of dead Normans.

The Bretons had continued to observe that when their men retreated, the English right wing was likely to pursue, at least partway down the hill. So, at William's behest, the Bretons staged a feigned retreat and when the Saxons pursued, the Norman cavalry charged and slaughtered them. This happened at least twice during the course of the long battle, seriously weakening the English line.

AN ARROW IN THE EYE?

By late afternoon, the battle had come down to a bitter, brutal clash of two armies. The shield wall had fallen back on itself and tightened up as losses increased. But still the English and King Harold held on, even though the gaps in their lines were now filled with peasant levies whose fighting value was questionable. For his part, William knew that if night fell and he had still not found a way through the shield wall, he would be forced to retreat from the battlefield, leaving his forces in a vulnerable position.

> AS THE NORMANS ADVANCED, HAROLD LOOKED UP INTO THE SKY AND WAS PIERCED BY AN ARROW THAT HIT HIM DIRECTLY IN THE EYE.

Before preparing for one last assault, he ordered his archers to shoot another volley, this one high over the Saxon lines, where it fell, wreaking havoc among the closely packed forces. As the Normans advanced, King Harold, who was rallying his troops, looked up into the sky and was pierced by an arrow that hit him directly in the eye. Some stories have it that he pulled it out and continued fighting, half-blind, blood spurting down his face, flanked by his bodyguards, until he was cut down by a Norman knight. But there are numerous versions of Harold's end, some of which have his body hacked to pieces. The Bayeux Tapestry shows a figure being struck through the eye with an arrow, but some historians think this is not Harold, or that the arrow was a later addition to the tapestry—in medieval times, a missile in the eye was considered a just punishment for traitors and liars.

However it happened, Harold died on the field and the Saxons, having no king left to fight for, fled down the back of the hill and into the forest pursued by the Normans. William was triumphant: England was his. That night, William the Conqueror camped on the battlefield, at the spot where he later ordered the building of Battle Abbey, his thanks to God for his victory.

Courage is an essential attribute for a king and William certainly had that—three horses were killed under him that day. But so is luck. And William's luck may well have included an arrow that found its way to the eye of the king of England.

A FUSION OF CULTURES

Since there was no one left in England who was strong enough to oppose William, he had himself crowned king on Christmas Day, 1066, although he soon faced several rebellions and did not secure England until the 1170s. With the Norman Conquest complete, England changed forever. Land was given to the Norman lords who had participated in the conquest, a traumatic process for the Saxon owners. (There was so much squabbling among the Normans over who owned what that the Domesday Book was created to solve the disputes, in turn becoming an invaluable record of the period.) However, the Normans left intact the Anglo-Saxon legal system—sheriffs, courts, taxes, names of counties.

In the longer term, the Norman invasion changed the English language—infusing it with French and Latin—and ensured that Catholicism would be the state religion (until the sixteenth century). It also tied England more strongly to the continent.

The Saxons had trouble adapting to the rule of the man they considered a tyrant. But was William such a tyrant? Probably not. Although he met the fierce resistance of the north of England after Hastings with blood and fire, he also knew when to be merciful, and he understood how to administer and apply laws.

William the Conqueror died in 1087, still holding the lands he had conquered. No one really knows what would have happened had William failed to conquer England, but the melding together of these two strong peoples created one of the most extraordinary cultures in the Western world. ❧

1095-1291
THE CRUSADES

On a cold November day in 1095, Pope Urban II gave a powerful speech in France that had a momentous impact on the subsequent history not only of Europe, but also of the Middle East. Facing a crowd of clergy and other important church officials at the Council of Clermont in Auvergne, Urban described what he saw as a disturbing development: the encroachment of Muslim Turks on Byzantium, the former Eastern Roman empire, whose Emperor Alexius had sent the Pope an urgent plea for help. But it was not just, or even chiefly, the Muslim Turks threatening Asia Minor that concerned Urban, but the forces of Islam that held the holy city of Jerusalem and "the Holy Sepulchre of the Lord, possessed by unclean nations." The Pope went on:

> Your brethren who live in the east are in urgent need of your help, and you must hasten to give them the aid which has often been promised them … The Arabs have occupied more and more of the lands of those Christians … They have killed and captured many, and have destroyed the churches and devastated the empire. If you permit them to continue thus for awhile with impunity, the faithful of God will be much more widely attacked by them. On this account I, or rather the Lord, beseech you as Christ's heralds to publish this everywhere and to persuade all people of whatever rank, foot-soldiers and knights, poor and rich, to carry aid promptly to those Christians and to destroy that vile race from the lands of our friends.

Urban whipped the crowd into a frenzy, promising them that "all who die by the way, whether by land or by sea, or in battle against the pagans, shall have immediate remission of sins." His listeners shouted over and over again, *Deus lo volt!*— "God wills it!" And so the Holy Wars began.

A MIXED LEGACY

The popular view of the Crusades in the West was shaped first by the romantic literature that sprang up while the Crusades were occurring, and later by Hollywood. Early on, Crusaders were portrayed as soldiers of God on a divine mission to reclaim the Holy Land. However, some representations of the Crusaders in today's literature and in films present the European knights as bloodthirsty thugs out only for gold and land, God or Allah be damned. Despite these stereotypes, however, the extraordinary importance of the Crusades in history remains. Scholar Thomas F. Madden has written that "whether we admire the Crusaders or not, it is a fact that the world we know today would not exist without their efforts."

In the century before the Crusades, Christian Western Europe was recovering from the ravages of the Dark Ages and fighting off attacks from various invaders—Vikings from the north, Magyars from Central Asia, and various Muslim peoples from North Africa, some of whom were fighting their way up the Iberian Peninsula. However, as the century came to a close, the fortunes of Western Europe changed. More efficient farming techniques, most notably the introduction of a more efficient plough, improved living conditions and in turn gave rise to rapid population growth. The consequent revitalization of the economy bolstered Europe's armed forces. At the same time, reformist popes were seeking a way to turn Europe's nobles away from the internecine warfare of feudalism—and confront Islam in the Holy Land.

A nineteenth-century portrait of King Richard I, also known as Richard the Lionheart, the most famous, if not the most successful, Crusader.

THE CRUSADES

AN ELECTRIFYING EFFECT

Pope Urban repeated his speech several times throughout 1095 and 1096, and sent forth his clergy to spread the word all over Europe: all who wanted to fight the Muslims and return Jerusalem to the True Cross were to swear a pilgrim's oath and make their way to Constantinople by August 15, 1096, on the Feast of the Assumption, and from there set out for the Holy Land. In return, they would be granted indulgences for the remission of their sins. It's not known what Urban expected when he made this plea—some historians think his main aim was to unite warring European nobles—but there is evidence that he thought a few thousand knights at most would answer the call.

Instead, over one hundred thousand people joined the initial wave of the First Crusade, known as the "Peasants' Crusade." Despite the Church's efforts to harness and control this gathering—Urban futilely decreed that no women, monks or children should take part—huge numbers of peasants and land-poor knights streamed east towards Constantinople, electrified by a new piety, filled with millennial dreams and seeing their pilgrim's oath as a sure road out of their impoverished lives. A charismatic and zealous monk known as Peter the Hermit was one of their leaders. Peter, preaching throughout northern France, told mass gatherings of peasants to meet in Cologne,

This fifteenth-century illustration shows the soldiers of King Baldwin I, the first Christian king of Jerusalem, battling with the Turks.

Germany, in April, well ahead of Urban's proposed rendezvous. Leaving from there in two different groups, this ragtag Crusade headed for Byzantium.

RIVAL RELIGIONS

As it is today, Jerusalem was a city holy to both Christians and Muslims. The Christians revered it as the place where Jesus was crucified and the site of the Church of the Holy Sepulchre. For the Muslims, it was the city where the prophet Muhammad was taken on a mystical night journey before being raised up to Heaven to meet the prophets Abraham, Moses, and Jesus. The Muslims knew it as *al-Quds* ("the Holy Place"). When they captured it from the Byzantines in 638, they built one of the world's most beautiful places of worship: the Dome of the Rock.

The idea that European Christians ("Franks," as the Muslims knew them) simply set out at the end of the eleventh century to retake Jerusalem for no reason other than fervent anti-Islamic sentiment doesn't portray the entire picture. For, at the time, Islam did pose a very real threat to Christianity.

The older of the two religions, Christianity had arisen in the first century AD and spread to all parts of the Roman Empire (which then included Jerusalem and Palestine, out of which the Romans had pushed the Jews). At this time in the history of the Catholic Church, the religion was spread peacefully, by missionary work. By the seventh century, when Islam began to flourish on the Arabian Peninsula, the religion of Jesus Christ was the predominant belief in Europe and the Mediterranean basin.

But not for long. Emerging in the early seventh century, Islam taught that while Christians and Jews might live peacefully and practise their religion under Islamic rule, Christian states must be replaced by Islamic ones. Muslim forces took over Palestine, Syria, and Egypt, crossed to Spain, and defeated Christian forces on the Iberian Peninsula. By the mid-eighth century, they had launched raids into France.

Conflict between the two groups continued for the next two hundred years. The Arabs were conquered in the eleventh century by the Turks, but the Turks then converted to Islam and carried on the battle with the West. The Byzantine Empire—the surviving eastern half of the Roman Empire based in Constantinople—was threatened when the Turks conquered Asia Minor. Looking across the Bosporus Strait in 1095, the Byzantine Emperor Alexius I Comnenus decided to make a plea to Western Europe for help in fighting the Turks. It was this plea that prompted Urban's speech.

PEASANT AND LAND-POOR KNIGHTS STREAMED EASTWARDS, ELECTRIFIED BY A NEW PIETY.

DESTRUCTION OF THE PEASANT'S ARMY

The undisciplined army of pilgrims launched by Urban's plea made its way across the Rhineland in the spring of 1096. One group, whipped to a frenzy by an anti-Semite German count named Emicho, participated in horrific slaughters of Jews—whom they considered to be enemies of Christ—in the German towns of Metz, Worms, and Mainz. Arriving near Constantinople in the summer of 1096, the tattered army of the Peasants' Crusade engaged a force of veteran Turks, and was quickly demolished.

However, this army of peasants was followed by a much more formidable group of soldiers led by great European nobles including Count Robert II of Flanders, Count Stephen of Blois, and Godfrey of Bouillon, the Duke of Lorraine. In large part motivated by piety, these men put aside their differences, raised a powerful cohort of knights and made the long, extremely arduous journey to the Holy Land. There,

they allied themselves with the Fatimid rulers of Egypt (not the first time Christians and Muslims would make temporary marriages of convenience during the Crusades) to defeat a large Seljuk Turk force outside Antioch. Then they turned on their allies and wrested Jerusalem from the Fatimid Muslims in 1099. When the Crusaders entered the city, they massacred Muslims and Jews alike.

THE SECOND CRUSADE

The First Crusade had been successful beyond anyone's dreams, liberating the Holy Land in near record time, opening Jerusalem to Christian pilgrims, and founding a new Christian realm in Palestine. Divided into four states (the counties of Edessa and Tripoli, the Principality of Antioch, and the Kingdom of Jerusalem), it consisted of a narrow finger of land between the Mediterranean Sea and the Jordan River. It was a sliver of Christianity surrounded by enemies, notably the Seljuk Turks in Syria in the north and Fatimid Egypt in the south.

In the middle of the twelfth century, Arab leaders arose who sought to unify the Islamic world. One of them was Imad Ad-din Zangi, a Seljuk Turk who seized Edessa, the northernmost of the Crusader States, on Christmas Day, 1144, and murdered all its European Christian inhabitants. This prompted the ill-fated Second Crusade, preached by the fiery monk Bernard of Clairvaux and led by French and German armies under King Louis VII and the Holy Roman Emperor Conrad III. This was nearly a complete disaster—one of the lowest points was a foolish attack on Damascus, a Muslim-controlled city that had up to that point been a supporter of Christian Jerusalem—and the Christian forces retreated in disarray.

Heartened by this victory, Islamic forces under such leaders as Nur al-Din, the son of Zangi, attacked Crusader outposts. Thus the pattern for years of warfare was set, with Crusader castles being besieged by "Saracens," as the Franks called the Muslims (a word deriving from a Greek term that means "easterners"), and other Crusaders riding to the rescue.

Slowly, the Saracens whittled away the Christian holdings in the Holy Land. In 1174, Nur al-Din died and was replaced by the legendary Salah al-Din Yusuf Ibn Ayyub, known to history as Saladin, the most ferocious Islamic leader of his age or of almost any other. Saladin had fought as one of Nur al-Din's lieutenants, although he had spent a good deal of time trying to wrest power from his leader and his family. On succeeding Nur al-Din, Saladin portrayed himself as the unifier of Muslims and set out to drive the Christians from the Holy Land.

In this he was almost entirely successful, defeating two armies sent from Jerusalem at the battle of Hattin, near the Sea of Galilee, and finally entering Jerusalem in triumph in 1187. After this, only a few Christian cities held out, notably the port city of Tyre. Saladin had, for the time being, stamped out the foreign presence in his land.

THE THIRD CRUSADE

The Third Crusade is probably the best known in the popular imagination of both West and East, pitting against each other as it did two famous warrior-kings, Saladin and King Richard I, the Lionheart, of England (although the two never met in personal combat, as medieval legend liked to have it). With the Crusader States in Palestine teetering on the edge of extinction, Richard joined forces with Emperor Frederick Barbarossa of Germany and King Philip II of France to raise a sizeable army. Here, the stereotype of a hungry nobleman heading to the Holy Land to seize land and enrich himself can be put to rest, since much recent research of medieval records shows that crusading was an extraordinarily expensive business for any prince, and was mainly undertaken at this point in time out of piety and hope for remission of sins—a not inconsiderable reward.

From the beginning, though, the Third Crusade was marred by ill fortune. Frederick fell off his horse and drowned while crossing the Saleph River in Anatolia, in 1190. Richard and Philip, once the closest of friends, began arguing as they sailed to the Holy Land. Once there, they managed to retake the city of Acre from Saladin, but Philip, ill and unhappy, then left the Crusade.

It fell to Richard to advance the cause, and he proved himself the leader history and folklore has painted him: bold, intelligent and extremely brave. He swept along the coast of Palestine, leading his men to victory after victory. But when-ever he struck inland to attack Jerusalem, he was unable to secure his supply lines against his marauding enemy. Ultimately, he was forced to make a truce with Saladin, whereby the latter allowed unarmed Christian pilgrims free access to the Holy City, but only on condition that Richard and his forces left the Holy Land.

THE LATER CRUSADES

There were four more Crusades in the thirteenth century, but none was ultimately successful. By 1291, the date conventionally given as the end of the Crusades, Islamic forces had succeeded in ousting all Christian forces from the former Crusader States. The Middle East was now completely controlled by Islamic rulers and would remain that way until the nineteenth century. However, the battle between Christianity and Islam went on elsewhere for hundreds of years, resulting in the fall of Constantinople to the Turks in the fifteenth century and the near-fall of Vienna in 1529 to the armies of Suleiman the Magnificent.

Paradoxically, despite the almost total victory of Islam over the Christian armies in the Holy Land, it was Europe that benefited the most from the Crusades. Exposure to Islamic science, mathematics, art, and military science invigorated European culture. The increased traffic between Europe and the Holy Land stimulated trade, and Europe came to best the Islamic world economically. In contrast, a resentful Islamic world retreated into isolation, the once sophisticated courts of the Muslim realms becoming cultural and economic backwaters.

Today, eight hundred years after they officially ended, the Crusades are still a matter of speculation and controversy. Just after the terrorist attacks of September 11, 2001, when President George W. Bush referred in a speech to "this crusade, this war on terrorism," there were many in the Islamic world who felt this raised the spectre of Christian knights invading Muslim lands in an attempt to destroy a religion and a way of life. And so perhaps the most lasting effect of the Crusades was to have sown the seeds of suspicion between Islam and Christianity. ✺

1162-1227
THE RISE OF THE MONGOL EMPIRE

The Mongol Empire under Genghis Khan and his children was the largest contiguous empire in history—in terms of land conquered the empire was four times larger than the empire of Alexander the Great—and extended from Korea in the east to Poland in the west, and from the Russian Arctic in the north to Vietnam in the south. Genghis Khan came to power by uniting many of the nomadic tribes of northeast Asia. His disciplined army grew to include Tartars and Turkish warriors, and a multitude of religions as he conquered civilizations across Asia and Eurasia, making him one of the greatest tacticians of all time.

Few details are known of Genghis Khan's early life. Born in Mongolia in about 1162, the son of Yesukai, the khan (leader) of the local Yakka clan, he was named Temujin. When he was thirteen years old his father was poisoned by the rival Taidjut clan, whose khan, Targutai, claimed all the Yakka territory. Temujin inherited his father's leadership, in the Mongol tradition, but most of his clan members refused to be ruled by a mere boy and defected to other clans. Temujin's enemies attacked his weakened clan and the young khan was forced to become a fugitive, continually fleeing from one refuge to another on the fringes of the Gobi Desert with his few remaining loyal clan members. Temujin managed to win a series of tribal battles and regain some territory for his clan. He formed an alliance with Toghrul Khan of the Kerait tribe,

an erstwhile ally of his father, and together they fought more successful campaigns. During times of peace, Temujin worked on organizing his tribe into a ruthlessly effective fighting force in preparation for battles to come.

By 1206 he had succeeded in uniting or overcoming six major tribes and numerous smaller ones, and at a council of Mongol chiefs was recognized as khan of the united tribes. It was at this point that he took the new title of Genghis Khan.

A DIVINE POWER

Genghis had an unshakable belief in his own divinity, and assumed that all states were already subject to his rule, even before being conquered. As long as foreign rulers accepted this simple and, to him, self-evident reality, everyone was happy. As his empire grew, his power and fame led many (such as the northern Chinese) to believe that he must indeed possess a divine power. He rewarded loyalty and bravery among his subjects, and furthered his aims by various means, including blackmail; for instance, his bodyguards were often the sons of his senior officers, effectively making them hostages. He was good at delegating, leaving large tracts of territory under the aegis of trusted officers as he expanded the empire elsewhere. He was physically fit well into his sixties, remaining simple in tastes and habits, retaining the elements of his inherited nomadic life and avoiding the trappings of luxury. He was famous for his self-discipline, never indulging in anger or losing his temper. He was as accepting of the peoples he conquered as he was of his own; he rewarded merit and talent without prejudice, bestowing power and privilege where he saw it being most effective for his ends. Possibly

With an unwavering belief in his own divinity, Genghis Khan meted out punishment to those who threatened his rule.

bag was used to carry reserve supplies of water, and to keep weapons and clothing dry during river crossings.

Most food was obtained from the land, but the soldiers also carried emergency supplies of dried milk curd, which was dissolved in water as required until it had the consistency of syrup. Troops also drank mare's milk, and occasionally carved a slice of flesh from the rump of a living horse (a practice that apparently was not fatal). In times of extreme need the soldier would cut his horse's jugular vein, suck out some blood, then reclose the wound with stitching.

MILITARY TACTICS: INGENIOUS AND RUTHLESS

Mongol boys were taught riding and archery from a young age and could hit targets at a distance of more than 650 feet, even while on horseback. Every soldier had at least one reserve horse, enabling the armies to travel large distances quickly. A favorite tactic was to retreat as soon as the enemy attacked or stood its ground, luring it into an awkward strategic position from which it could be surrounded and massacred. The mass slaughter of defeated victims was a necessary strategy because the Mongols were usually numerically inferior to their opponents and Genghis simply could not supply enough personnel to maintain an occupying force while his armies continued their expansive campaigns; he could not risk insurgencies by defeated enemies.

Genghis learned siege techniques from the Chinese, whose mercenary soldiers he welcomed and employed for the information they could provide. He once offered to end a siege at the city of Hsian if its leader gave him thousands of cats and pigeons. The commander complied, hoping and expecting that Genghis would then go away. Instead, Genghis attached a small flaming torch to each animal, then released them. The cats rushed back to their homes, squeezing through gaps in the wooden walls, while the pigeons returned to their nests. The city burned to the ground.

Various ploys were used to create the illusion that the army was much bigger than it appeared. In one such ploy, the troops would advance along a very broad shallow front. Realistic fake armies of man-sized puppets on horseback were constructed. Then, at night, each soldier would light several torches, placing them some distance from each other to give the impression that each torch represented one soldier. Spies, often disguised as merchants or traders, would spread false rumors ahead of advancing armies, implying they were much larger than in actuality; they also provided Genghis with accurate information about the strength and position of the enemy.

GENGHIS KHAN WAS GOOD AT DELEGATING, LEAVING LARGE TRACTS OF TERRITORY UNDER THE AEGIS OF TRUSTED OFFICERS AS HE EXPANDED THE EMPIRE.

SCIENTISTS MEASURE AN EMPEROR'S LEGACY

In March 2003 the American Journal of Genetics published a remarkable report by twenty-three geneticists who had been studying DNA from about two thousand Eurasian men. They found that, despite the enormous area under study, which stretched from the Caspian Sea to the Pacific coast of east China, more than a hundred of the men, or about eight percent, contained the same DNA. This meant that people from the sixteen disparate groups studied had a single common male ancestor. Extrapolating this to the rest of the population in the region gives a total of some 16 million descendants.

They were studying the Y chromosome, and although everyone has their own unique DNA pattern, enough characteristics survive through the generations to allow researchers to group us in family trees. The DNA information also allows a reasonably accurate estimate of when the common ancestor existed. The team allowed thirty years between generations, dating the common ancestor about one thousand years ago. But if we allow a more realistic twenty-five years between generations, the date becomes 850 years ago—exactly the period of Genghis Khan's rule.

When the researchers superimposed a map of the area they were studying over a thirteenth-century map of Genghis' empire, the fit was perfect. This proved that the common ancestor was either Genghis or one of his immediate ancestors—in any case we know that Genghis was responsible for dispersing the DNA signature across central Asia and north China between 1209 and his death in 1227. Part of the spoils of war were the most beautiful of the vanquished women, and Genghis, though not a libertine as such, was anything but celibate. Furthermore, he was able to display authority and generosity at the same time by allocating women as rewards to his most loyal and senior offspring and officers. He had access to hundreds of women during his forty-year period of empire-building.

THE ACHIEVEMENTS OF GENGHIS KHAN

In 1995 the Washington Post dubbed Genghis Khan "the most important man of the last 1000 years," on the grounds that for the first time "a single species fully exerted its will upon the earth." Most people in 1200 were unaware of any other continents or even other societies or countries. Though Asians traded with the eastern reaches of the fading Byzantine Empire, they knew almost nothing of the European lands to the west. With the exception of a few Viking explorers, Europeans were unaware of America's existence. Genghis Khan's legacy was to unite East and West into one realm, absorbing (and transforming) what we now know as China, Russia, Tibet, Afghanistan, the eastern part of Iran, Syria, Turkey, Ukraine, Hungary, and Poland. He facilitated the spread of Islam and Christianity from the Middle East to the Pacific Ocean. He established new trading routes, and reopened old ones, such as the Silk Road, whose use had been severely limited by the rise of Islam in the seventh century. Genghis had no argument with any religion or its adherents; his sole ambition was earthly power and as long as a group accepted his rule and heavenly authority—and there were of course very strong practical reasons for doing so—he was mostly tolerant of beliefs and the devotional practices of others.

When Genghis Khan died in 1227, his empire stretched from the Pacific Ocean to Poland. His sons and grandsons continued to expand it, and by the time Marco Polo arrived in 1274, Genghis Khan's grandson Kublai Khan had extended it to include all of China as well as Turkestan, the rest of Persia (modern-day Iran) and the area covered by the former Soviet Union. Caravans and couriers traversed his entire empire in peace, allowing the free flow of ideas and merchandize between East and West. Numerous Chinese inventions found their way to Europe during Khan rule, including gunpowder, movable print type, noodles, tea, and paper made from wood pulp.

Just how Genghis Khan died has long been a matter of dispute. Some stories have him falling from his horse while being chased through Egypt, whereas others say he was killed in battle with the Tanguts of western China. There is no reliable record of where Genghis Khan's body was buried. China and Mongolia, each determined to be the true heir of his tradition, have conflicting stories about his death. The Chinese emphasize the glorious trappings at his funeral, while Mongolians hold that in accordance with tradition his corpse was transported across the Gobi Desert to a secret, unmarked resting place in Mongolia. ❧

1215
MAGNA CARTA

In January of 1215, a group of noblemen, mainly barons from England's northern counties, gathered together for a secret meeting at Dunmow Castle in Essex, the home of Lord Robert Fitzwalter. As well as Fitzwalter, who had organized the meeting, those in attendance included several influential figures, such as Eustace de Vesci, Lord of Alnwick Castle, and Geoffrey de Mandeville, the Earl of Essex, and at least one important cleric, Giles, Bishop of Hereford. At that moment, England was extraordinarily tense, on the verge of the chaos that precedes a civil war. Armed bands of the barons' men roamed the byways, trying to keep order.

The barons were in a state of great anger about this lawlessness, and they laid the blame for the situation squarely at the door of the ruler of the realm, King John. At their meeting, they resolved that they must confront him and demand changes that would improve their lot and the lot of their subjects. In particular, they wanted an end to the heavy taxes John was placing on his people in order to pay for his failed war against France. Before the barons disbanded, they stood together solemnly and took an oath that they "would stand fast together for the liberty of the church and the realm."

A few days later, the barons arrived at Windsor Castle, where knots of worried royal advisers were meeting hourly with the king. Reluctantly, John agreed to hear them out. It was not a happy meeting. To prove the seriousness of their intent, the barons had come armed, and their contempt for the king was palpable. Once in his presence, they set out their demands for reforms to the laws regarding the distribution of land to, and the taxes levied on, the nobility. If they did not receive these and other concessions, they warned the king, they would go to war against him.

These were no empty threats, and John knew it. Ultimately, they would constrain the king to concede—to a degree unprecedented in England or in any other Western realm of the Middle Ages—certain basic civil rights, not only to his barons, but to all of his subjects. And this concession would be enshrined in one of the most extraordinary and important documents of all time: Magna Carta. In turn, Magna Carta (properly speaking, "the" is not attached to these two Latin words meaning "Great Charter") would become a symbol of civil rights, and subsequently be the basis for common law in England and, later, for the U.S. Constitution and Bill of Rights.

A DISASTROUS RULE

Was there ever a king in English history so hated and scorned as King John? It's hard to think of one who really comes up (or down) to his standards of cowardice, betrayal, greed and incompetence, so much so that even in this age of revisionist history, John resists rehabilitation. It can be said, however, that John came by treachery naturally. He was, after all, a member of the Plantagenet noble family, rulers of England since 1133, and a notoriously treacherous bunch. His three older brothers had all rebelled against his father.

John was born on Christmas Eve, 1166, the youngest of eight children of Eleanor of Aquitaine and King Henry II of England. Despite the fact that John was Henry's favorite child, the king had kept no royal land to give his youngest son, who thus became known to many as John Lackland. Aggrieved, John joined with his brother Richard to rebel against his father in 1189; this armed revolt ended with Richard, the elder and more powerful brother, being named Henry's successor. When Henry died, Richard—soon to be

King John signing Magna Carta at Runnymede on June 15, 1215. Within months, John sought to annul the charter.

known to history as Richard the Lionheart—became king. Knowing John to be untrustworthy, he confirmed him as Lord of Ireland and married him off to a rich woman, on the condition that he stay out of England while Richard was away on the Crusades. True to form, John agreed—and then immediately broke his promise.

Worse yet, when Richard was captured and imprisoned on his way home from the Third Crusade, John refused to help ransom him and, indeed, allied himself with Richard's enemy, King Philip II of France, to seize Richard's lands in Normandy. Richard made his way back in 1194, and forced John to relinquish these lands. But when Richard died in 1199, without a legitimate son, John had himself crowned King of England. He managed to gain King Philip's support for this by ceding him large tracts of French land in Normandy. However, he then upset Philip and all of the French aristocracy by annulling his existing marriage and wedding the barely pubescent Isabella of Angoulême—right under the nose of her fiancé, and one of Philip's vassals, Hugh IX of Lusignan. In response, Philip began a campaign to oust John from his remaining French possessions.

WEARING THE COST OF INEPTITUDE

Not only did John then fight an inept military campaign against Philip and steadily lose English holdings in France, but he also demanded financial support for his ill-advised ventures from his own nobles, in the form of "scutage"—a fee paid in lieu of military service. Despite the fact that this form of payment had either fallen into disuse or was used to levy only very mild fees, John had increased the rates of scutage eleven times during his fifteen years in office.

And this wasn't the only financial burden the barons had to carry as a result of John's fecklessness. Earlier, he had alienated Pope Innocent III by insisting on filling, and thereby profiting from, ecclesiastical offices. (Essentially, John would insist on a fee from any prelate who sought a higher office, usually in the form of Church lands or money raised from Church land.) In response, the pope held not only John, but the entire country, excommunicate, meaning that no one could get married or buried or be baptized in a church. To have this ban lifted, John was forced to pay the pope the large sum of one thousand marks per year. Much of the money he recouped from his barons.

John was bleeding the kingdom, and particularly his barons, dry. He was also losing the trust of his people, who had seen him break his word over and over. Popular myths sprang up that spoke of people banding together against the king to achieve freedom—one was the legend of Robin Hood. So while it was the barons who led the revolt against John, largely for their own reasons, popular consensus supported them.

THE MARCH ON LONDON

When the barons met King John in January of 1215, they demanded reforms that had been enshrined in King Henry I's Coronation Charter (or Charter of Liberties) of 1100. In particular, they alluded to a promise made by Henry, to "all his barons and faithful men," to abolish "evil customs" that had oppressed them—in particular, abuses by the king when it came to the unequal handing out of royal land and extracting money from his barons through taxes. Henry had put these tenets into writing due to a possible threat to his throne, but had subsequently ignored them almost completely.

John paid little attention, either, and after the January meeting, both sides prepared for war, filling war chests with money and arming their followers. John gathered those barons still loyal to him and swore them to a new oath of fidelity, not just to their king but also "against the charter." He sent emissaries to Pope Innocent in Rome, seeking to sway the Catholic leader to his side. In early March, in a brilliant public relations stroke, he began wearing the white cross of the Crusader, and made all his men wear it, writing to the pope that his baronial enemies were "worse than Saracens"—the name used by Crusaders for Muslims.

Naturally, this did not please the barons. In May, led by Fitzwalter, they marched on London. Fitzwalter and Eustace de Vesci had very personal reasons for wanting to temper John's power. Fitzwalter claimed that the king had attempted to rape his daughter; de Vesci declared that John had seduced his wife. Whether this was true or not, no one knows. But such tales brought sympathy to the barons' cause. When they marched on London, the citizens opened the gates of the city. The barons occupied this seat of the Crown without a fight on May 17. Now there was no way John could avoid negotiating with the rebels. Moving beyond their initial demands, the barons drew up a series of articles, which they sent to the king. Emissaries went back and forth. By June, the barons had what they wanted: a document that would curb the king's power to do damage to their lives and estates.

THE CHARTER APPROVED

To make the document official, King John and his barons met "in the meadow which is called Runnymede between Windsor and Staines on the fifteenth day of June." 1215—a

> POPULAR MYTHS SPRANG UP THAT SPOKE OF PEOPLE BANDING TOGETHER TO ACHIEVE FREEDOM—ONE WAS THE LEGEND OF ROBIN HOOD.

field alongside the Thames River, about 12½ miles southwest of London. John attached his seal to the so-called Articles of the Barons, and ordered that the document be copied and distributed. In return, on June 19, the barons swore their fealty to John.

Magna Carta questioned the authority of a king to rule solely as he pleased—in 1215, an extraordinary question indeed. As a corollary to this, it also guaranteed the cornerstone of modern civil rights, the right of *habeas corpus*—meaning "you shall have the body"—which signified that the Crown could no longer keep a free man imprisoned forever without trial. Other articles dealt with maintaining the barons' property rights, limiting scutage, and limiting certain of the king's feudal privileges. But the articles became extraordinarily important for one simple change, made at the last minute. In stipulating to whom the provisions of the charter applied, the barons altered the term "any baron" to "any freeman." As a result of this seemingly minor change, the rights of all English people were, for the first time, written in law—and the foundation stone of modern ideas of freedom was laid.

THE AGREEMENT ANNULLED

Yet a great historical irony of Magna Carta is that, while it accomplished many things, it did not accomplish what it set

In his play *The Life and Death of King John,* Shakespeare had John poisoned in a monastery. In reality, he died of dysentery.

out to do in the short term: avert a civil war in England. At the time, no one really believed that the agreement—dubbed the "Great Charter" to differentiate it from the Coronation Charter of 1100—would hold. Part of the problem were articles 52 and 61, which indicated that if there were any disagreement about a plan made by the king, it "would be settled by the judgment" of a committee of twenty-five barons—all of whom were John's enemies, naturally. King John had signed Magna Carta because he had been forced to, but no king could be expected to have his power abrogated in such a way. This was the ostensible reason why John, almost as soon as he returned from Runnymede, rejected the charter and in September convinced Pope Innocent, whose temporal influence extended across much of Europe, to annul "the shameful and demeaning agreement forced upon the king by violence and fear."

The barons, naturally, were infuriated by this—once again, the treacherous King John had broken his side of a bargain. A bloody civil war then raged throughout England, with the rebels obtaining the support of the French against John (in return for promising Prince Louis, later King Louis VIII, the

English throne). John campaigned destructively, torturing captured prisoners and extorting money from civilians to finance his army. At least two-thirds of the baronage of the country fought against him, including many men who had formerly been close to him. But then, in October of 1216, John died of dysentery and the war came to an end. John's nine-year-old son became King Henry III, the rebels were restored to their lands, without paying a penalty for treason, and Prince Louis ultimately withdrew his claim to the throne.

AN ENDURING SYMBOL

Yet Magna Carta survived. To gain support among the nobility for the new monarch, Henry III's regents revised the document to exclude provisions calling for "rule by barons" and reissued it in 1217, and again in 1225. The 1225 version is the best known today. However, Magna Carta remained relatively inconsequential in English law until the seventeenth century, when Sir Edward Coke, who had been Queen Elizabeth's attorney general, as well as a leader in Parliament in opposition to King Charles I, resurrected Magna Carta in order to show that even the Stuart kings must be held accountable under law.

The charter was then exported with British colonists to North America—and there, in the mid-eighteenth century, adapted by American radicals, who were enraged at the levying of taxes against them when they were not afforded a seat in the British parliament. The rebels held that Magna Carta forbade "taxation without representation." This was not literally true, but the Americans continued to believe regardless that Magna Carta protected their liberties—the seal adopted by the colony of Massachusetts on the eve of the Revolution showed a militiaman with a sword in one hand and Magna Carta in the other. From these ideals, in just over ten years, the U.S. Constitution would be born and, in turn, greatly influence other constitutions around the world. ❧

C. 1295
THE TRAVELS OF MARCO POLO

Marco Polo is undoubtedly the most famous Western medieval traveller along the Silk Road—exceeding all other travellers in his determination, his writing and his influence. His journey through Asia lasted twenty-four years, taking him further than any other traveller from Europe, beyond Mongolia to China. He became a confidant of Kublai Khan, travelled the whole of China and returned to Venice to tell the tale with the publication of *The Travels of Marco Polo*.

Marco Polo was born in Venice in 1254. Little is known about his early life, but his family had been successfully trading with the Middle East for a long time, amassing substantial wealth. When Marco was six years old his father Niccolo and uncle Maffeo went to Constantinople on business. When unrest broke out there in about 1261, the Polos decided to sell their property holdings and convert their capital into precious stones. They set off for modern-day Bulgaria where they commenced trading with Berkhe Khan, ruler of the western regions of the Mongol Empire. They managed to double their wealth, but when war blocked the path of their return to Venice they decided to head east to China carrying messages and gifts for Kublai Khan from Berkhe and other leaders. At the time Kublai, grandson of the great conqueror Genghis Khan, ruled over an empire that encompassed Mongolia, modern-day Korea, China, North Vietnam, Tibet, northern India, the Balkans, the Caucasus, Persia (Iran), Turkey, Poland, southern Russia, and everywhere in between.

The travellers arrived at Kublai Khan's magnificent summer palace at Shangdu on the vast Mongolian Plain in 1265.

(Shangdu was the model for Xanadu, celebrated in Samuel Taylor Coleridge's poem "Kubla Khan," published in 1816.) They were very well received, and when they departed for the return journey they were given Kublai's ambassadorial protection. The Mongols had recently come into contact with Islam and Christianity, and were interested in learning more about these religions, so Kublai gave them a letter addressed to the pope in which he requested one hundred educated priests and some oil from the Holy Sepulchre lamp in Jerusalem.

In 1269, when the brothers arrived back in Venice, they found that Marco's mother had recently died. When, in 1271, they decided to return to China, the young Marco accompanied them. Pope Gregory X gave them his credentials, along with gifts including precious gems, and the requested holy oil. He also assigned two friars to accompany them, authorizing them to ordain priests, consecrate bishops and grant absolution, but they fled soon after the expedition began.

MARCO'S EPIC JOURNEY BEGINS

The travellers began their journey in a fast galley supplied by the Christian king of Armenia. They arrived on the Levantine coast of the Mediterranean, then set out across Syria toward Iran. As they neared the Caspian Sea, Marco reported a strange and wonderful black oil seeping from the ground, which the locals burned for light and heat. At Kerman in Persia, at the crossroads of the great east–west trading routes, they saw vast warehouses containing spices from India, incense from Oman and India, metalwork from Damascus, and porcelain and silk from China. Soon they passed across one of the most inhospitable places on earth, the Dasht-e Kavir, the great salt desert in central Iran. Marco reported that swallowing even a small mouthful of the salt would make a person violently ill for days.

Leaving the edge of the known European world, they headed through the mountains of Afghanistan, exposed to the burning heat of the sun during the day and freezing cold at night, and under constant threat of bandit attack. Amazed at the height of the mountains, they were even more amazed when, after several weeks' travel, they started to ascend even higher. The locals claimed that it was the highest place in the world, and they were not far wrong; this mountain range was the Hindu Kush and just to the south was K2, the second-highest peak in the world. To the north lay the Pamirs, lofty mountains completely unknown to Europeans until Marco reported them (they would not be explored for another six hundred years). As they descended to the foothills of the Tibetan plateau they joined the Silk Road, passing through a number of cities more than a thousand years old. Eventually they reached the Gobi Desert in Mongolia, a trackless wasteland that took them thirty days to cross. After a journey of almost four years they were now in China. The twenty-year-old Marco Polo would remain there for about fifteen years.

MARCO IS PRESENTED TO KUBLAI KHAN

In Shangdu, Niccolo and Maffeo renewed their acquaintance with Kublai Khan, whom they had first met at Shangdu in 1266. The return of the Venetians was celebrated with much "mirth and merry-making." They presented the papal gifts—along with the young Marco, to whom Kublai took an instant shine—and were "well served and attended to in all their needs." Marco turned out to be the best gift of all; he would soon make known to the world the power and the glory of the great Khan. Although he did not speak Chinese, Marco, apparently an excellent linguist, could speak several other languages, including Turkish, Farsi (Persian), and perhaps Mongolian. He soon learned the languages of other places where Kublai sent him on various diplomatic and exploratory missions. Marco "learnt in a short time and adopted the manners of the Tartars, and acquired a proficiency in four different languages, which he became qualified to read and write."

Kublai loved hearing stories of the various far-flung reaches of his empire, so he sent the trusted Marco on numerous information-gathering assignments. He went to Yunnan in southwest China, where he reported on "snakes and great serpents of such vast size as to strike fear into those who see them, and so hideous that the very account of them must excite

---

The epic journey of Marco Polo opened up the world for the map makers of medieval Europe.

the wonder of those to hear it ... some of them are ten paces in length ... the bigger ones are about ten palms in girth. They have two forelegs near the head, but for feet nothing but a claw like the claw of a hawk or that of a lion. The head is very big, and the eyes are bigger than a great loaf of bread. The mouth is large enough to swallow a man whole, and is garnished with great pointed teeth."

Marco was also amazed to discover that in many places corpses were burned rather than buried, as cremation, once popular in Venice and Europe in general, had died out about eight hundred years earlier.

He was also amazed to observe coal—"stones that burn like logs"—as it was not used in Venice with its temperate Mediterranean climate. (He had obviously never been to England where coal was just as commonplace as in China.) He also exposed the myth that salamander lizards were fireproof and lived in fire, a misunderstanding caused by the fact that they often scurried out from under the bark of logs when they were placed on a fire. He gleefully reported that a "salamander is not a beast as commonly believed" but a type of rock. Asbestos was unknown in the west, and he reported that a gift of fireproof cloth had been sent as a present to the pope. Strangely, Marco made no mention of tea, which was very commonly used in China and did not appear in the west for another two hundred and fifty years. Perhaps he did not like it. Not so strangely, he made no mention of gunpowder or its obvious value for warfare. Since he was in prison in Genoa, which was at war with Venice over control of the lucrative Mediterranean trade routes at the time he wrote his book, he doubtless did not wish to reveal the existence of such a valuable weapon to the enemy.

Marco's travels took him to Myanmar (Burma) and other places in the distant south, far from Mongolia. He may have been entrusted with administrative duties, for example the collection of taxes and revenues from trade in goods such as salt and iron. It is not known what Marco's father and uncle were doing during this time; however, Marco was certainly making himself at home. But, ultimately his desire to return to Venice grew. Unfortunately, Kublai Khan was so enamored of him that, for a long time, he refused to allow the Polos to leave and, without his consent and support, the long and hazardous journey would not have been possible.

Eventually, however, in 1291, an opportunity arose when the ruler of Persia, a grand-nephew of Kublai, lost his wife and wished to marry a woman from the same tribe. He asked Kublai for help and an appropriate girl was chosen. Pointing out their excellent knowledge of the lands between China and Persia, the Polos succeeded in being chosen for the task of escorting and protecting the bride-to-be on her journey, after which they would be permitted to travel on to Venice.

RETURN TO VENICE

From the southern Chinese port of Zaitun (Quanzhou), they travelled in a fleet of fourteen large junks via Vietnam, the Straits of Malacca, and Sumatra, where bad weather forced them to remain for five months. With no option but to camp among cannibals on the Sumatran coast, they protected themselves by constructing a fortress surrounded by pointed sticks and guard towers. They eventually continued their voyage across the Bay of Bengal and through the strait between India and Sri Lanka, where they made landfall. Marco was fascinated by the variety of high-quality gems—rubies, sapphires, amethysts, topazes, garnets and pearls. At the city of Chennai in India he was amazed at how long pearl divers could hold their breath as they collected oysters from a depth of more than 65 feet, as they still do today.

The party continued its voyage via the coast, ending their journey at the port of Hormuz in Persia. From there they travelled overland to Trebizond on the Black Sea, where they delivered the bride before continuing overland to Venice. When they arrived in 1295 they caused a sensation when they cut open the seams of their bizarre oriental clothes to reveal that the linings were stuffed with gems.

MARCO POLO'S DESCRIPTIONS OF CHINA AND ITS RICHES INSPIRED CHRISTOPHER COLUMBUS.

Soon afterwards, in 1297, Polo was imprisoned in Genoa after being captured during a sea battle in the Mediterranean. He dictated his story to Rustichello, one of his fellow prisoners-of-war and a popular writer of romances. Marco was released after the war ended in the summer of 1299, returning home to Venice to live with his father and uncle, who had bought a mansion with their profits. In 1300 he married the noblewoman Donata Badoer, who bore him three children. He died in his home on January 1324 at the age of 69, and as he lay dying he is reported to have said: "I didn't tell half of what I saw, because no one would have believed me." Marco Polo was buried in Venice in the Convent of San Lorenzo.

His descriptions of China and its riches inspired Christopher Columbus to try to reach it by sea, travelling westward in 1492. He owned a heavily annotated copy of Polo's book. Marco Polo's epic journey also greatly assisted the development of European cartography and helped make possible the accuracy of the famous Fra Mauro map (created around 1450), one of medieval Europe's most detailed maps of the known world and seen by many as an improvement upon the map that Polo had brought home from Cathay (China). ✸

Marco Polo departs from Venice on his twenty-four-year round trip to the court of Kublai Khan.

THE TRAVELS OF MARCO POLO

1297

WILLIAM WALLACE AND THE FIGHT FOR SCOTTISH INDEPENDENCE

Sir William Wallace, also known as Brave Heart, was one of Scotland's greatest heroes. A fearless knight and landowner, he led the Scottish resistance through a long, and ultimately successful, fight to free Scotland from English rule. For such a revered hero, his origins are shrouded in mystery and controversy. Probably born in the town of Ellerslie in Ayrshire, he was the landless younger son of a minor nobleman who, without patronage, privilege or inherited power, rose to become the political and military leader of his country. At the time, Scotland's fortunes were at their lowest ebb; the Scots were suffering under England's rule and their independence had been virtually obliterated.

Wallace was born into an era of relative stability and peace. Scotland was ruled by King Alexander III, who had successfully repelled English claims to sovereignty. But when, in 1286, Alexander fell off his horse and died without heirs (apart from Margaret, his four-year-old granddaughter), a series of contenders to the throne came forward. From this time onwards, Scotland's natural leaders—earls, barons, landowners, and priests—began continually betraying their countrymen to the English, in return for the retention of their own assets and status. The English king Edward I took advantage of the power vacuum by arranging for Margaret to marry his son Edward, agreeing that Scotland would remain an independent state. The Scottish lords set up a provisional government to rule un-

til Margaret came of age, but Margaret died in 1290 at the age of seven. The claimants to the throne invited Edward to arbitrate, and he installed John Balliol as ruler on November 17, 1292 on the condition that Scotland recognize Edward as Lord Paramount of Scotland. The Scottish reluctantly agreed, presumably because they reasoned that, under the circumstances, they would be easy pickings for the English if they refused, and because a civil war between the various claimants (who included Robert the Bruce, who much later became king of an independent Scotland) loomed as a real possibility.

TENSION MOUNTS

The English king proceeded to make life difficult for the new King John, undermining his reign and embarking on a series of "divide and conquer" deals with Scottish nobles to establish English authority over various areas of their domain. By March 1296 John had had enough and renounced his homage to Edward, who responded by sacking the border town of Berwick-on-Tweed and massacring most of its residents, even those who surrendered or fled. In April he defeated the Scots at the Battle of Dunbar in the town of Lothian; in July he forced John to

An etching of the Scottish patriot and national hero, Sir William Wallace.

abdicate. Many Scottish nobles were imprisoned, and the remaining 1800 or so were forced to pay taxes to the English. As a final insult, Edward purloined the Scottish coronation stone, known as the Stone of Destiny, from its location at Scone Palace, and took it to London. Scotland's subjugation was almost complete; the time was ripe for a savior to arise to unite the oppressed, alienated populace against the common enemy. The stage was set for William Wallace.

THE ART OF WARFARE

In the late thirteenth century, war was not a matter of technology or science, but mostly of raw strength in hand-to-hand combat, individual courage, and adroitness in the use of the weapons of the day—the dirk (a long, straight dagger), the broadsword, battle axe, and spear. The longbow had only just been invented and, as one of the first weapons capable of killing at a distance, it was frowned upon under the international rules of war. Soon enough it would transform warfare, as did the introduction of guns and gunpowder a century later. But the wars between England and Scotland were fought at close hand by relatively small numbers of men in bloody combat. The successful war hero would have to possess military expertise, extreme moral and physical courage, and a spiritual commitment to duty.

William Wallace rallies his men and leads the charge against the English at the Battle of Stirling Bridge.

Wallace displayed all these traits, along with a fierce desire to defend and protect the interests of his beloved Scotland when many others were all too willing to compromise their country and countrymen for their own self-interest.

The town of Stirling was of great strategic importance, buttressed on the south by one of the most unassailable castles in the British Isles, and situated on a high peak overlooking the plain of the vast river Forth. It was the gateway to the highlands, and formed a natural barrier that effectively prevented the wild Highlanders from swarming over the Lowlands at will. The crucial point of the gateway was the narrow wooden bridge that spanned the Forth just above the town. This bridge was critical in any conflict against invaders from the south; all the lands north of the bridge still remained in Scottish hands, apart from Dundee which was holding out against an English siege. English commander John de Warenne, Earl of Surrey, decided to send reinforcements to Dundee to finish off the resistance, but to do so he would need to cross the heavily defended Stirling Bridge. He led a large army through the center of the country, planning to seize the bridge before pouring north into the Highlands. The stakes were high—if the English won, Wallace would be reduced to a mere political leader. If Wallace won, he would be in a strong position to expel the English and take over as leader of all Scotland, which had never before stood up to the might of an English army. It is highly significant that the common people, the lesser gentry and the peasantry were prepared to rally under the Wallace banner. It is also a tribute to the leadership abilities of the youthful Wallace that he was able to persuade them to risk everything against the experienced warrior Warenne, and the most battle-hardened army in Europe.

THE STAGE IS SET AT STIRLING BRIDGE

The English contingent comprised around one thousand cavalry and fifty thousand troops drawn from England, Wales and Ireland. Eight thousand reinforcements were also heading north. This intimidating force included veterans of campaigns in the Holy Land, France, Wales and earlier Scottish battles. It was heavily armed and had never known defeat. The Scots, on the other hand, had performed poorly at Dunbar, where they demonstrated lack of discipline and poor tactics, as the English were well aware. Furthermore, the Scottish gentry were generally lying low, ignoring the young nonentity. Cowed by the recent successes of the English, they were no doubt fearful of the consequences if, as they expected, the English were victorious. Nor would they be likely to serve under an untitled leader, even if he won. In addition, many of the Scottish leaders were in Flanders, assisting Edward in a simultaneous campaign against France. Yet, despite these seeming obstacles, Wallace was able to tap into the indomitable spirit of his countrymen, who had been enduring the contempt and brutality of the English for seven years and hence had little to lose if they risked their lives to rid themselves of English tyranny.

At Stirling Bridge the Forth was about 100 feet across, slow-moving but very deep; there was no other way to cross the river. At the north end of the bridge a causeway traversed a wide, low-lying area of swampy marsh. The bridge was barely wide enough for two horsemen to ride shoulder to shoulder; the causeway not much wider. The marsh was too soft to allow horses to operate at all. The English gave the Scots the chance to submit, which was common medieval practice. On September 10, 1297 Warenne sent his herald to Wallace to demand his surrender, which was not forthcoming. That evening Warenne ordered his troops to be ready to cross

IN THE THIRTEENTH CENTURY, WAR WAS NOT A MATTER OF TECHNOLOGY OR SCIENCE, BUT MOSTLY OF RAW STRENGTH IN HAND-TO-HAND COMBAT.

the bridge at dawn the next day. Accordingly, at daybreak, about five thousand foot soldiers, including a Welsh archery contingent, crossed the bridge; but the exhausted Earl was still asleep, and no further commands were issued. Confused and lacking support, they re-crossed the bridge. It was a moment of high farce, and a harbinger of the tactical failures to follow. Once Warenne finally arose, he held a parade to confer knighthood on a number of his troops, many of whom would be dead by day's end. Still the Earl dithered, and failed to issue orders to advance. Across the river in the distance he could see the summer sun glinting on Scottish spears, and it must have occurred to him that the Scottish position looked invincible. They were positioned in the foothills of Abbey Craig, a sheer cliff which of itself would have halted his advance soon after he had breached the northern bridgehead. He would have noticed that the surrounding bog would not only have hindered his armored troops: it would have been impossible for his mounted cavalry to traverse. The Scots had the opportunity to retreat into the foothills if necessary, but once Warenne had crossed the bridge, retreat would have been impossible in the face of his own advancing forces.

TENSION MOUNTS AS TACTICS ARE ARGUED

But Warenne's army was fired up for battle, and as time passed the soldiers' frustration grew. The Earl sent two Dominican friars over the bridge and causeway to offer terms for surrender, but Wallace sent them back with the message that he was inviting Warenne to attack as soon as possible, and that they were more than prepared for the fray. Unnerved, Warenne called a conference of war to discuss the matter. One participant was Scottish nobleman Sir Richard Lundie, who had betrayed the Scots earlier that year at the battle of Irvine by surrendering without a fight (along with all the other Scottish gentry). Lundie was very familiar with Stirling and its surrounds, and cautioned that to advance would be suicidal. He pointed out that progress across the narrow bridge would be very slow, and that once they reached the northern bank of the Forth they would be surrounded, with no chance of retreat. He requested command of a group of five hundred knights and foot soldiers who would ford the river at a nearby shallow point he knew of, and mount a rear-guard attack. In that case, it would be the Scots who were constricted by the inability to escape, and Warenne's troops would be able to cross the bridge safely.

The war council descended into confused disarray as the two cases were loudly argued—until the English Treasurer,

Hugh de Cressingham, had his say. He was a physically repulsive man, grossly obese and pompous, and hated by the English almost as much as by the Scots. Having exchanged priestly garments for chain mail, he became a grotesque figure who surely attracted the contempt of the professional soldiers in his charge. He shouted down the tumult and, ever mindful of his duty to the royal coffers, reminded Warenne how much the war had cost already, and suggested that they advance without further ado. The Earl was irritated by this interruption, and by the substance of the argument, considering it a minor irrelevance when so much was at stake. But in the end, tired of the inconclusive arguing, he issued the command to cross the bridge. At the front was Sir Marmaduke de Thweng, who rode ahead of the troops with a small contingent of knights. Their task was to secure the northern end of the causeway in order to protect the advancing troops behind. Cressingham followed just behind, along with various other nobles and flag-bearers. The Scots resisted the temptation to rush headlong into battle as they had done at the Battle of Dunbar, rather maintaining their positions in the foothills. They held their nerve as more and more English troops reached the northern bank and spread out over the marshes.

This was Wallace's great advantage—he could choose against what odds he would fight. At about eleven o'clock he made the prearranged signal of a single horn blast and the Scots poured forth en masse with spine-chilling war cries, wielding their comparatively few swords and spears as they swarmed down the mountain and into the midst of the English troops. The men on the right flank cut a swathe through the less manoeuvrable English cavalry and succeeded in taking the northern bridgehead, thus cutting off all chance of retreat. Panic reigned as the fleeing English came up against their fellows still trying to advance across the bridge; many fell or jumped into the river where they drowned, weighed down by their armor. The main mass of the Scottish forces ran headlong into the midst of the English forces, spears levelled. Their lack of armor or heavy weapons proved an advantage as the unwieldy Englishmen struggled in the marshy ground. The English infantry, disoriented and unfamiliar with the territory, were reduced to a confused rabble as the Scots stabbed and hacked their way through the lines. Thweng was one of the few to stay in control; he charged and managed to scatter the Scots who were guarding the causeway, but the English advance had halted and all around him wholesale slaughter was occurring. With screams of "On them! On them!" the Scots killed virtually all the English troops who had crossed the bridge, including about three hundred Welsh archers and five thousand infantrymen. A bare few managed to strip off their armor and swim back across the river, including Thweng. Scottish losses were very few.

WALLACE'S CHANGING FORTUNES

Warenne ordered a hasty retreat, leading the remnants of his army hastily southwards. The Scots followed and harried them for a long way, stealing their pack animals and killing stragglers. Then, in October, Wallace invaded northern England, ravaging the counties of Northumberland and Cumberland (for reasons that are not clear, as it seems there was little strategic benefit in doing so). When he returned to Scotland in December he was knighted and proclaimed Guardian of the Kingdom, ruling in the name of John Balliol. But many nobles resented him, and King Edward, after returning from his Flemish campaign, invaded Scotland on July 3, 1278. On 22 July, with a much bigger army than Warenne had deployed, his troops routed Wallace's forces at Stirling in the Battle of Falkirk, ruining Wallace's military reputation.

Nothing is known of Wallace's activities for the next four years. Although the Scottish nobles surrendered to Edward in 1304, the English continued to pursue Wallace unremittingly. On August 5, 1305, he was arrested near Glasgow and taken to London, where he was illegally condemned as a traitor to the king even though, as he correctly pointed out, he had never sworn allegiance to Edward. Following a travesty of a "trial," he was publicly hanged, cut loose before his strangulation was complete, disembowelled while still alive, decapitated then quartered by four horses, one tied to each of his limbs. His preserved head was placed on a pike on top of London Bridge.

The violent and pitiless nature of his death, and the ongoing agitation of the Scots for freedom from English rule, ensured a legendary status for this warrior hero, whose exploits have been celebrated across the centuries in poetry and song. ❧

1347–1349
THE BLACK DEATH

All over Europe, doctors refused to heal the sick, priests ran from the dying whose souls they were supposed to save and parents fled their children. People ate, drank and made love manically. In Italy, groups of desperate people lay with their faces over foul and bubbling sewers, hoping that the stench they inhaled would somehow ward off the dread disease.

Everywhere, the dead were buried six deep—stacked, in the words of one Italian chronicler, "like lasagna." But soon such descriptions stopped and even writing stopped. Those who survived became simply too weary, too numb, too familiar with horrible death to comment further.

In five years, beginning in 1347, one-third of Europe—twenty-five million people—died of bubonic plague. Even this figure does not reflect the true horror of the situation, for many villages and towns lost eighty percent of their populations. A world that had burst forth from the Dark Ages and was moving forwards into a new era suddenly found itself pockmarked with deserted farms, abandoned villages, collapsed churches and zombie-like survivors. Two centuries later, the name Black Death ("black" referring not to the color, but to something awful or evil) was coined for this pestilence; but, at the time, people in Europe called it *la moria grandissima*, or *la très grande mortalité*, or the *huge mortalyte*. Meaning, the Big Death.

A DEVILISH DISEASE
Bubonic plague changed the course of world history and haunts humankind to this day. All subsequent epidemics—smallpox, cholera, influenza, AIDS—are a reminder of the terror of the Black Death, the spectre of a world strewn with dead bodies, defenceless against an invisible killer. Even today, when medical treatment is light years ahead of what was available in the fourteenth century, with every new epidemic—be it AIDS or bird flu—we subconsciously fear the return of the Big Death.

For those experiencing this extraordinary plague in the mid-fourteenth century, the effect was horrific. No wonder they flagellated themselves through the streets, praying to God or trying to appease the Devil. Though it wasn't known at the time, the devil in this case was a hardy rat flea known to scientists as *Xenopsylla cheopis*, a ravenous little creature that lived (sometimes by the hundreds) on black rats and other rodents. *X. cheopis* carried a virulent plague bacillus known as *Yersinia pestis*. When *X. cheopis* chomped down on human flesh (which it was increasingly likely to do when rats began to die off, either from the plague or from hunger), *Y. pestis* entered the human body and the effects were deadly.

The illness caused by *Y. pestis* took two forms. Bubonic plague was caused by direct contact with the fleas and resulted in egg-shaped lumps, or buboes, at the site of the flea bite, usually in the armpit or groin area, followed by black-purple bruising and a horribly foul stench arising from the victim. It had a mortality rate of sixty percent and killed within five to seven days. But the main form of the medieval plague seems to have been the pneumonic variety, which infects the lungs and is then spread from person to person through the air, without the aid of *X. cheopis*. The Italian cleric Matteo Villani, writing in 1348, quite accurately depicted the course of pneumonic plague: "[The victims] began to spit blood and then they died—some immediately, some in two or three days … And it happened that whoever cared for the sick caught the disease from them or, infected by the corrupt air, became rapidly ill and died in the same way."

A CREEPING PESTILENCE
In the Dark Ages, Europe's climate had been markedly cold, but in about 1000 ad it warmed up. Combined with improvements

in agricultural technology (a new type of plough, for one), this led to marked increases in food production. By the beginning of the 1300s, populations had grown rapidly and urban centers were thriving and densely inhabited. At the same time, advances in shipbuilding and navigation sent traders far across the known world. Soon after the start of the fourteenth century, Europe was hit by what has become known as the "Little Ice Age." Devastating storms and frigid weather destroyed crops. About 1315, a famine struck Northern Europe, which significantly weakened the survivors' immune systems.

Meanwhile, deep in Asia, bubonic plague was beginning its march. China was then involved in a lengthy and bloody war against the Mongols, during which great swathes of the countryside were laid to waste. Rats, no longer able to feed themselves in the forests, headed for populated areas. As the creatures starved and died, *X. cheopis* sought new hosts. The humans they encountered, their immune systems weakened by starvation, other diseases and stress, were perfect targets. By the 1330s, the plague had laid China to waste. Records are nowhere near as complete as those left in Europe, but historians estimate that China lost 35 million people out of a total population of about 125 million. Some scholars go further and say that one out of every two people in China died.

Near the end of the 1330s, *X. cheopis* began to travel. It went with traders as they followed well-worn routes across the wide plains of Mongolia and Central Asia. By 1345, the plague had hit the lower Volga River and by 1346 the Caucasus and Crimea. By the spring of 1347, it had travelled to the outskirts of the town of Caffa on the north shore of the Black Sea, a bustling trading center, leased by Genoese merchants from the local Mongols, where goods, people and ideas from East and West met. When some Genoese traders ran afoul of the local Mongol ruler, he besieged them in their town, but soon *X. cheopis* hit his troops and began cutting down his soldiers by the thousands. So as to make his Genoese enemies share his pain, the Mongol leader ordered the stinking, plague-ridden bodies of his dead catapulted into Caffa, and the Christians inside began to die.

The decimated Mongol army finally gave up the siege and left. The panicked Genoese then tumbled out of the town—those who were still living—boarded ships and headed for Italy. They stopped at Constantinople and other ports, spreading the plague into each town, and then finally arrived in Italy in the autumn of 1347. It isn't quite certain how even a few seamen survived such a long trip, alive and surrounded by plague—possibly they had stronger genes than others—but as the ships from Caffa pulled into the port town of Messina, in Sicily, those onshore were horrified. Vague rumors had reached them of this horrible pestilence in the East, but now, here it was, right before their eyes. An Italian friar later wrote that the sailors in these dozen or so ships carried "such a disease in their bodies that if anyone so much as spoke with one of them he was infected … and could not avoid death."

DEADLY TENTACLES REACH OUT

On maps historians have created, the Big Death looks like a multi-tentacled monster holding the world in a dreadful embrace. One tentacle reached south and west from Constantinople to cause horrible suffering in Damascus, Jerusalem, and Cairo, while another groped northwards from Messina, reaching central and northern Italy in early 1348. Not surprisingly, the plague tended to follow medieval trade routes.

The Italian writer Giovanni Boccaccio (1313–75) lived through the plague in the city of Florence. He brilliantly captured the experience in his famous *Decameron*, the story of ten well-born young people trapped by the pestilence in a villa. In the introduction to this work, Boccaccio describes the terror in the city, where people were afraid "to speak or go near the sick" or even to touch their clothing. People espoused different philosophies. Some lived moderately "forming small communities … shutting themselves up in their houses where there was no sickness … avoiding all excess, allowing no news or discussion of death." But some did exactly the opposite, thinking "the sure cure for plague was to drink and be merry." Neither approach did much good, though: the Black Death killed three-quarters of the population of Florence.

NEAR THE END OF THE 1330S X. CHEOPIS BEGAN TO TRAVEL—FOLLOWING MEDIEVAL TRADE ROUTES.

DECIMATED POPULATIONS

From Italy, the tentacles split off: one going north into Germany, another west to France and Spain. From France, the pestilence leaped across to southern England, landing there in the summer of 1348. It probably entered the country through the port of Bristol, which lost half its population, and then spread outwards, flourishing in the foul conditions of most medieval towns of the era, where sanitation was highly primitive. The disease arrived in London in November. Those who became infected lived scarcely two or three days, and soon London had lost one-third to one-half of its population. While the plague was a democratic killer, generally the poor died faster than the rich. This was no doubt because immune systems were compromised by poor nutrition; chroniclers at the time noticed this, as well: "The one who was poorly nourished with unsubstantial food fell victim to the merest breath of the disease."

Even harder hit were the villages of rural England, where a community of, say, two hundred people might be wiped out.

The lifeblood of this society—its farms, livestock and rural workers—was destroyed. Records describe one sad and horrible symbol of this: a mad peasant who, for years after the plague hit the county of Durham, in northern England, wandered the roads, calling out for his wife and children, who had died.

Historians estimate that the population of England and Wales in the early fourteenth century, before the plague struck, was six million people. It's possible that the plague killed fifty percent of this population; numbers did not rise to the same level again until the mid-seventeenth century.

A WORLD TRANSFORMED

The plague quieted down over the winter of 1348, giving false hope that it had passed, but sprang up again in 1349, burning through England to Scotland, leaping to touch eastern Ireland, then crossing the North Sea to Scandinavia, before devastating Moscow in 1352 and heading south. Finally, it died out near Kiev—exhausting itself on the endless and relatively empty Russian steppes.

The world was devastated, but the plague had brought a strange blessing. Europe had been overpopulated as the 1300s began, with people beginning to fight over resources. Now, there was a ghastly amount of room. The few remaining farm workers were much in demand and could therefore insist on better wages and conditions. As a result, the standard of living of ordinary country dwellers improved.

The Big Death instilled in people paradoxical desires. One was to live life to the fullest—men and women began to marry and start families earlier. It also created an obsession with death and dying. One reflection of this was the new popularity of morality plays. For performances of one, *The Dance of Death*, people would gather, often in a graveyard or church, and take macabre pleasure in a spectacle that included a dancing skeleton choosing audience members and leading them to a grave. This would be followed by a sermon, the gist of which was usually close to the following inscription from a tomb of the period: "Dust you are, unto dust you return, rotten corpse, morsel and meal to worms."

The plague was to return again in 1362 and in numerous smaller yet still devastating reoccurrences for centuries thereafter, right up until the 1600s. Another wave of plague swept through Asia late in the nineteenth century, and it was then that the role of *Y. pestis* and *X. cheopis* was discovered. Although this last plague pandemic was contained, *X. cheopis* still exists in wild rodents, and hundreds of plague cases are reported each year. These can be treated with antibiotics and further global outbreaks have been kept at bay, but the dread fear of the Big Death still remains. ❧

1415

THE BATTLE OF AGINCOURT

We few, we happy few, we band of brothers;
For he to-day that sheds his blood with me
Shall be my brother; be he ne'er so vile,
This day shall gentle his condition:
And gentlemen in England now a-bed
Shall think themselves accursed they were not here ...

WILLIAM SHAKESPEARE, HENRY V

King Henry V's unexpected, underdog victory at the battle of Agincourt made him a hero to the English people—and to anyone who has read William Shakespeare's play *Henry V* and thrilled to his "band of brothers" speech. While his triumph did not win England the Hundred Years' War, it saved his kingship, and furthermore became the battle by which England symbolically defined itself for the next five hundred years. This in turn helped English leaders inspire their people in times of crisis ranging from the Spanish Armada invasion of 1588 to the Battle of Britain in 1940.

Of course, the speech is pure fiction and the real-life Henry V was neither the raucous "Prince Hal" nor the good King Harry of Shakespeare's portrayal. He was instead a fairly brutal bloke who fought his way onto a throne he might otherwise have been excluded from, and thereafter invaded a country he had no right to invade. In other words, Henry was not unlike most other rulers of his time.

On the muddy field at Agincourt on October 25, 1415, however, Henry V was extremely brave and extremely lucky—not a bad combination.

LANDING AT HARFLEUR

One morning in August 1415, in the French port of Harfleur in the English Channel, French soldiers manning the town garrison turned their eyes seawards and suddenly saw, to their astonishment, a vast fleet of ships approaching. Quickly noting that the fleet was flying the English red cross of St. George, the French defenders sounded alarm bells, which in turn echoed out over the choppy waters of the Channel to the invading force.

Leading the three hundred English ships was the twenty-eight-year-old King Henry V, who had come to reclaim land he thought belonged to the English throne. His struggle was the continuation of what would become known as the Hundred Years' War, a series of conflicts between England and France that continued for 116 years. It had begun in 1337, when the English King Edward III grew tired of French attacks on English territory on the French mainland. One way to stop this, he figured, was to give himself the title of "King of France," on the somewhat far-fetched grounds that he was the only surviving male heir of his maternal grandfather, the deceased French King Philip IV. This would legitimize a war against France. Naturally, this was something that the *real*

king of France, King Philip VI—Philip IV's nephew—was not happy about.

The conflict waged back and forth for seventy-five years or so, but by the time of Henry V's reign the French were in a weakened state—and Henry had decided to take advantage of this.

His twelve thousand troops and huge siege engines took the port of Harfleur in five weeks, but at great cost. The French garrison put up a strong defence, but finally capitulated, after which Henry expelled all the French inhabitants, planning on filling the town with English immigrants and turning it into an English port of entry in France.

During the siege, however, dysentery had ravaged Henry and his men, costing the lives of perhaps two thousand soldiers. Henry had been planning a major campaign in France after taking Harfleur, but now, with his army weakened, he decided to head north to winter at the English-held port of Calais. Leaving a small force behind to fortify Harfleur, he set off with nine hundred men-at-arms—mounted knights—and five thousand archers, shadowed by a French army that was at least four times larger.

This situation might have fazed a less determined king, but not Henry V, who had clawed his way to the English throne. Shakespeare's description of him as a madcap partier who made a pious reconciliation with his father, King Henry IV—the prodigal son, returning—has only a kernel of truth. Henry, born probably in 1387, had become a hardened warrior by the age of sixteen, when he commanded his father's forces at the battle of Shrewsbury. He may have led a somewhat raucous life, but when the ageing and ill Henry IV would not anoint him heir to the throne—not because of hard partying, but because they had serious political differences—there was no pious reconciliation. Instead, Henry forced his way into his father's bedchambers, followed by armed men, and, using threats, induced Henry IV to make him his heir.

And so it was that in 1413, after his father's death, Henry V became King of England.

THE WAITING GAME
The French forces, perhaps twenty-five thousand strong, were led by the Constable of France, Charles d'Albret. D'Albret was

> HENRY'S TWELVE THOUSAND TROOPS AND HUGE SIEGE ENGINES TOOK THE PORT OF HARFLEUR IN FIVE WEEKS, BUT AT GREAT COST.

no military genius, but he was smart enough to understand that time was on his side. He didn't want to risk incurring a loss similar to the one suffered at the battle of Crécy, in 1346, another vital engagement of the Hundred Years' War, where Edward III's knights and archers had beaten off repeated French frontal attacks. So he rode hard on the English, keeping them away from favorable river crossings, harassing their flanks and making sure their sickly and starving troops did not receive supplies.

Henry doggedly marched his men on towards Calais, finally crossing the Somme at a ford near St. Quentin, but found his way blocked by the French near the village of Agincourt. It was now October 24 and the French and English were, at last, facing each other. Henry had, however, manoeuvred his army so that he had one crucial advantage: his men were at the head of a long, narrow strip of land flanked on either side by thick woods. He might have been outnumbered, but he was not going to be outflanked.

FOR ENGLAND AND ST. GEORGE
The night before the battle, it rained, hard. The French, certain of the annihilation of their foe—for how could twenty-five thousand not crush six thousand—drank and partied and shouted taunts, with French knights throwing dice for the opportunity to be the first to kill or capture the English king.

On the English side, Henry ordered strict quiet. He also commanded his troops to make their confessions to the priests travelling with the army, take a last communion and prepare themselves for their possible deaths. Whether a pose or genuine, Henry presented himself as a religious man. He wore his hair in the short, pious style of monks, anointed himself with religious oils, spent hours in prayer and had taken as his role model St. George, the warrior-saint. In fact, the English troops all wore the red cross of St. George, which had been used as a symbol of English patriotism at least since the First Crusade in 1099—indeed, its use here helped establish it as the potent icon of English nationalism it remains today.

Did Henry make a "band of brothers" speech that night, as the rain poured down and the gibes of the French echoed around the English camp? Almost certainly not. But as light dawned the next day, he did something even more significant. He put on a royal coat over his armor that bore not only the three leopards that were another symbol of England but also the three gold fleur-de-lys of France, as well. This act of almost unimaginable arrogance in the face of an overwhelming foe,

---

This fifteenth-century depiction of the battle of Agincourt shows captured French knights being led away by an English soldier.

on enemy ground, inspired the English troops greatly. As did something a medieval soldier would take note of: as Henry rode out in front of his line of troops that morning, he wore no spurs, a sure sign that when the battle was joined he intended to fight on foot.

HENRY'S LETHAL WEAPON

In fact, all of Henry's men would fight on foot that day. At the center of his line were his dismounted men-at-arms, who wore full armor and carried swords, as one might expect, but whose main weapons were axes and maces, which were needed to batter through an opponent's armor. On either side of the men-at-arms was Henry's most lethal weapon: his five thousand archers.

These were English longbowmen, the finest archers in the world. They were well paid, professional and highly skilled, and the French feared them greatly. The longbowmen could shoot their deadly broadhead arrows as far as 1000 feet. At 180 feet, they could drive an arrow through any armor. They had decimated the French on any number of occasions and they knew that they could expect no mercy from their enemy, who had hung three hundred English longbowmen after a French victory earlier in the Hundred Years' War.

To protect against their being ridden down by French knights, Henry had ordered the longbowmen to fashion wooden stakes, which would be placed in the ground in front of their ranks – a stroke of innovation that would help win the battle for him.

STARTING WITH A STANDOFF

Facing Henry's army were three lines of French knights, dismounted men-at-arms in the front, then cavalry, then Genoese crossbowmen. After some fruitless negotiations—Henry refused to make a deal or concede defeat—the two forces stared at each other across the narrow, ploughed field for hours, a typical medieval stand-off. Finally, around noon, Henry realized that he had to make a move. Pointing his men onwards, he led them at a slow march towards the French forces.

When Henry's army arrived within 985 feet of the enemy, the English archers drove their stakes into the ground and let loose a volley. Thousands of arrows clouded the sky at once, arching up and up, then falling straight downwards, planting themselves in the backs of horses, glancing off French armor with a clang or, where a knight was unlucky enough to look up at the wrong moment, striking through a visor slit.

Enraged, the French cavalry charged along the flanks, determined to destroy the English archers. But the ploughed ground of the field, perhaps 2500 feet wide, was soft and wet from the rain, bogging down the horses and causing some to slip and fall. Also, the woods on either side kept the

horsemen hemmed in, unable to flank the English lines. As the French neared the enemy lines, the English longbowmen unleashed a deadly volley of arrows that cut through the cavalrymen's armor. Then the survivors were brought to a sudden halt by the wooden stakes. The longbowmen rushed out to surround them and, using sidearms such as long knives, axes and heavy, long-handled mallets, literally hammered the French into the ground.

Now the main French force engaged the English line of men-at-arms, and a ferocious battle ensued. Medieval close combat relied on brute strength: the aim was to knock your opponent down and beat him to death with mallets or battle axes, or find an opening in his armor, through joints in the plate or the visor, and stab him until he stopped moving. At Agincourt, on the ploughed fields slippery with mud and blood, some knights fell beneath piles of other knights and suffocated. The Duke of York, the most prominent Englishman to die that day, lost his life this way.

HENRY MAKES HIS MARK

At this point, the real Henry V began to resemble the legendary Henry of Shakespeare, for his gallant presence was felt everywhere on the field. The English soldiers saw him race to and from crisis points on the battlefield. Most of the time, he was accompanied by his bodyguards, but no bodyguard kept Henry from direct action. At one point, he raced to the aid of his brother Humphrey, the Duke of Gloucester, standing over the man's wounded body and, joined by his royal party, fighting off the Count d'Alençon and as many as eighteen French knights who had sworn an oath to kill him. A French knight charged in, eager to claim the English king as his prize, and a blow from the man's battle-axe knocked part of Henry's crown from his head and dented his helmet (today, you can see it on display at Westminster Abbey). But Henry and the English stood fast.

Gradually, the French retreated and Henry and his surviving force were left on the bloody field, surrounded by piles of dead and groaning men. Henry ordered his soldiers to begin taking the fifteen hundred or so French prisoners to the rear, but then heard the news that a French raiding force was behind his lines and sacking his unprotected baggage train. Fearful that the remaining French—who were formed into a battle line that alone outnumbered the English forces—would now assault him from the front, Henry made a brutal decision: he ordered the French prisoners slaughtered. No English man-at-war would perform this deed, as it was against the rules of chivalry (it may also have angered them because dead knights would bring no ransoms). So two hundred longbowmen went at the prisoners with knives and mallets. When news of this reached the French, they retreated, leaving the way open to Calais. The battle was now over.

SHAKESPEARE'S PORTRAYAL OF HENRY V ENSURED THAT HE BECAME A LEGENDARY FIGURE IN ENGLISH HISTORY.

A POTENT MYTH

Agincourt was a stunning English victory, as well as a terrible French defeat—French casualties included half of the nation's fighting nobility, including three dukes, ninety counts and about fifteen hundred knights. The English lost perhaps four hundred men.

Directly after the battle, Henry marched to the English port at Calais, but, with his sick and tired army, was in no position to follow up on his victory and march on Paris. But two years later, in 1417, Henry invaded France again and won a series of victories against a French foe weakened by internal dissension. Thereafter, he was able, with the Treaty of Troyes in 1420, to have himself recognized heir to the throne of France and regent—the king, Charles VI, having ceded his rule as a result of his debilitating mental illness. To cement the deal, Henry married the king's daughter, Catherine of Valois, on 2 June 1420. But just as he was about to achieve his goal of becoming dual king of both countries, he died of dysentery, aged thirty-four, seven weeks before Charles' own death, in 1422.

Henry V then passed into history, his story being repeated in various medieval chronicles. When it reached William Shakespeare, he seized upon it to provide his seminal portrayal of the warrior king who overcame the odds to become a symbol of England's fighting spirit. Even if Shakespeare's portrayal departs from reality, it is easy to see why Agincourt, and King Henry V, represent victory and brotherhood right down to the present day. ⚜

A portrait of King Henry V of England. Henry's tonsure and pious pose belie a brutal and determined character.

1431
THE EXECUTION OF JOAN OF ARC

Pushing and shoving to obtain the best vantage points, ten thousand spectators gathered in the main square of Rouen, in northwestern France, on the morning of May 30, 1431. For weeks, they had watched the trial of the Maid, as she was known, and heard ever more outlandish stories of her past. At the center of the square were four large platforms. On one sat the Maid's judges, on another her guards, on the third the Maid herself alongside her preacher, and on the last a wooden stake, which was planted in a mounded plaster base to raise it high, so that it was visible to everyone in the crowd.

Before the Maid was brought to the stake, ceremonies were performed. There were sermons, speeches, and prayers. It all took so long that some of the eighty English soldiers guarding the Maid began to taunt her and the cleric who was praying with her: "What, priest, will you make us dine here?" Finally, however, the Maid was chained to the post, with her arms high above her, and the crowd gasped as the wood was set ablaze.

THE VARIOUS LEGACIES OF JOAN

Saint, heretic, schizophrenic, feminist icon, illiterate shepherd girl, savior of France—you can take your pick when it comes to Joan of Arc. She has been the subject of countless studies, the protagonist of novels, plays and operas, the basis of medical and

---

Joan of Arc at the Coronation of Charles VII (1854), melds the warriorlike and saintly sides of Joan.

psychological speculation, and the object of ongoing religious veneration. The Catholic Church canonized the Maid, as she was known, in 1920, and held her up as an icon of both womanly purity and strength. She has long been venerated by liberals and socialists in France for her humble origins and empathy for the poor, but also by conservative-patriots as an example of early French nationalism. As a further example of the contradictory ways in which Joan has been used as a symbol, during the Second World War both the Vichy Regime (which cooperated with the Nazis) and the French Resistance used her image as an icon.

And all this for an illiterate country girl who was perhaps nineteen when she died. Yet the kernel of who Joan of Arc really was will always elude us—just as it did her inquisitors—since her shape shifts as ours does.

CAPTURE OF THE "SORCERER"

When Joan of Arc fell into the hands of the English occupiers of the French city of Rouen in 1430, it was as if she had been taken by the devil, for these men meant to do her a great deal of harm. "Fell into the hands" makes it sound like Joan's capture was merely a fortune of war and it was not. In fact, having been captured fighting a valiant rear-guard action against Burgundian French forces (who sympathized with the English) at Compiègne, she was sold to the English by her French captors for a goodly sum.

The English wanted to put to death this "sorcerer," as they called her, for she had been a great hindrance to their efforts to conquer France—in particular, she had been instrumental in making sure the French dauphin, or heir to the throne, Charles VII, became king of the country, rather than Henry VI, the young son of Henry V. But the English did not want to execute the Maid themselves, lest the French people who sympathized with Joan disapprove. Therefore, they brought together a panel of judges, chief among them Pierre Cauchon, Bishop of Beauvais, and had them try her on religious grounds, for heresy. After all, here was a woman who said God spoke to her on a daily basis.

VOICES IN BELLS

Joan of Arc (Jeanne d'Arc) was born, probably in January of 1412, to Jacques d'Arc and Isabelle Romée, at Domrémy, on the Meuse River. The family owned a small amount of land, and Joan, along with a sister and brother, grew up helping to farm and to tend flocks, although Joan proved to be hopeless when it came to chores. This was partly because of her piety, which made itself evident when she was very young. Whenever a bell sounded for mass, she would drop whatever she was doing and head for the village church.

By the time Joan was thirteen or so, however, these innocent village bells signified something else: when the child heard them, she also heard voices from God. The voices (later accompanied by physical manifestations) were mainly those of three saints: St. Michael, St. Catherine and St. Margaret. Eventually, these voices informed her that she needed to save France—a country that, at the time, was quite in need of a miracle or two.

Joan of Arc grew up during the endgame of the Hundred Years' War, a perilous time to be living in France. England had just won a major victory at Agincourt, controlled the cities of Paris and Reims, and, as Joan was hearing voices from God, was besieging Orléans, the last loyal French city north of the Loire. English raids into the countryside—known as *chevauchées*—devastated the lives of poor farmers. To make matters worse, the French King, Charles VI, was quite insane—Joan may have heard voices, but Charles VI thought he was made of glass—and a vicious internal struggle for power was taking place, with one faction, the Burgundians, siding with the English against the real heir to the French throne, the Dauphin Charles.

Into this desperate and chaotic situation stepped Joan, at the age of perhaps sixteen. Her saints had told her to drive the English out of France and bring the dauphin to Reims (the traditional site for French coronations) to be crowned. It is perhaps a sign of how desperate the French were that the

dauphin actually met with Joan when she secretly left her home village and asked to see him at the French court at Chinon. Or it was a sign of how impressive Joan was, for this young woman, who by now was dressing in men's clothes (including armor, shield and sword) in order to fit in with the rest of the army, was supreme in her confidence that the English siege of Orléans could be raised with her help.

Indeed, Joan not only lifted the siege at Orléans (despite being wounded by a crossbow bolt in the neck), but also helped capture several other towns in the English occupied zone, and finally escorted the dauphin to be crowned King Charles VII at Reims. She even led a failed attack against Paris (where she was wounded once again) before being captured. Joan's actions during this period had frustrated the English, who had been on the verge of success in France, but were now forced on the defensive—and by a woman, no less.

How did this peasant girl acquire enough military leadership and tactical acumen to win victories and bedevil the English? The short answer is, no one knows. Traditional historians, perhaps less inclined to give a woman credit for military skill, assumed she was merely a banner-waver during these campaigns—close in on the action, to be sure, but not a planner. But more recently, some historians have concluded that she may in fact have been a skilled strategist, not merely an icon. Quite possibly, she simply displayed enough leadership qualities that the troops were willing to follow her and do her bidding.

THE JUDGES AT THE TRIAL WERE CONFRONTED WITH JOAN'S STUBBORN INDIVIDUALITY— HER SINGLE MOST EXTRAORDINARY TRAIT.

IMPRISONMENT AND TRIAL

At Joan's trial, which began on January 13, 1431, this extraordinary military career was put on display by examiners, who were prosecuting her as much for the fact that she wore men's armor and clothing, wielded a sword in combat, sat perfectly atop a horse in a man's war saddle and led men into combat, as for any perceived religious apostasy. When the examiners asked her if she had ever been in a place where English were killed (a coy way of getting her to admit killing an Englishman), she replied bluntly: "In God's name, yes! How gently you talk! Why don't they leave France and go back to their own country?"

During the trial, Joan was kept in a large tower of Rouen Castle, called the Tour du Trésor, later named the Tour de la Pucelle (the Tower of the Maid) after her. She had made several escape attempts before she arrived in Rouen, and so inside her tower room she was placed in leg irons that were chained to a huge piece of wood. An iron cage was also made for her, in the shape of her body, but whether it was used is uncertain. She was

guarded twenty-four hours a day by a squad of English soldiers.

The trial itself consisted of repeated interrogations, many taking place in the royal chapel of the castle. Aside from Cauchon and the other judges, there were numerous assessors (learned men charged with giving an opinion of the accused, although they had no say as to her verdict) and other onlookers.

From the beginning, the judges were confronted with Joan's stubborn individuality, her single most extraordinary trait, evident in a situation in which she was under extreme pressure. When asked to swear an oath to tell the truth, she replied: "I do not know what you will ask me about. Perhaps you will ask me things which I shall not tell you." (She finally agreed to take a very limited oath.)

After questioning her on her childhood and military matters, the examiners returned over and over again to the subject of Joan's voices. She could not (or would not) quite say what the saints she claimed to have seen looked like (although she described Michael as being quite handsome), and became irritated when pushed on the subject: "I have told you all I know about that and rather than tell you all I know I would prefer you cut off my head!" The judges continually set traps for her, at one point asking her if the voices told her to wear male clothing: "All that I have done is by the commandment of the Lord," she replied. "And if He had commanded me to

This fifteenth-century tapestry shows Joan arriving at Chinon for her audience with the dauphin on March 6, 1429.

take another dress, I should have taken it."

And when she was asked if she believed that she was in a state of grace—essentially a trick question, for no true believer would really claim to know to whom God had given salvation—Joan gave an answer worthy of Solomon: "If I am not, may God put me in it; and if I am, may God keep me in it."

RECANTATION AND EXECUTION

Joan was proving no pushover; so much so that the embarrassed Bishop Cauchon decided to stop holding semi-public sessions of the trial. Still, the strain on Joan was enormous. Not yet twenty, without legal defenders or representation of any kind, she had only herself and her voices to rely on. And, while the voices came to her in prison—indeed, during the trial itself—she sometimes said that they were inaudible or confusing.

Battered on all sides, faced with a horrible death by burning, she agreed to publicly renounce her voices and make penance for the error of her ways. She did so on May 24, in the town's cemetery, with an executioner's wagon nearby, ready to take her to be burned if she faltered. She was then sentenced to life imprisonment. She made her recantation wearing women's clothing, possibly to show that she was cooperating with the authorities.

However, Joan could not keep this charade up. By the following Sunday, once again wearing men's clothing, which she apparently still had in her possession, she announced that she was hearing her voices again. There is some historical evidence that Joan was sexually assaulted in prison after her recantation, while wearing women's clothes. This is not conclusive, but if it is correct, it might explain why Joan put on men's clothing again; it is also possible that it was the trauma of the assault that resulted in the return of her hallucinations.

Whatever the case, on May 29, the court sentenced her to be burned at the stake, the next day. Despite the fact that Joan must have seen this coming, she was distraught on the morning of her death. "Am I to be treated so horribly and cruelly that my body, which has never been corrupted, must today be consumed and reduced to ash. Ah! Ah! I would seven times rather be beheaded than to be thus burned," she cried out, and could not be comforted.

Just before 9 a.m. on May 30, Joan was placed in a cart and brought to the marketplace, surrounded by English guards. She was now, at this final moment, dressed in women's clothes—wearing a black shift with a black kerchief over her head, and she wept profusely. After a priest gave a sermon, a mitre was forced on her head and she was proclaimed a heretic and an idolater.

Now the religious men present, including Bishop Cauchon, left her to the secular authorities, although one priest accompanied her to the scaffold. As Joan was chained to the stake, it appeared that she had begun hearing her voices again; those nearby heard her call out to St. Michael. She also exclaimed "Rouen, Rouen, shall I die here?" as if she could not believe her fate. She begged for a cross and one was shown to her.

Then the fire was lit. The huge noisy crowd fell into perfect silence as the Maid's shrieks and pleas rose up to the heavens. As the flames enveloped her, she began to cry out for holy water. Her suffering lasted a long time—the executioner later explained that the stake was placed so high up he could not reach the young woman to mercifully strangle her, as was customary in such cases. He was so moved by her plight that he wept. Yet by order of the authorities, he was ordered to rake the fire back after Joan died, so that the crowd could truly see that she was dead.

Then she was burned to ashes, and the ashes thrown into the Seine. All except her heart, which—according to a legend that sprang up—could not be burned at all. ❧

1440

THE INVENTION OF THE PRINTING PRESS

It is easy to appreciate how the compass revolutionized navigation and gunpowder transformed warfare, but the changes wrought by the printing press extend into almost every field of human activity, even into consciousness itself. Communications theorists often refer to the last five hundred years as the Gutenberg Age. The explosion in knowledge and social change that flowed on from the availability of inexpensive, mass-produced books was unprecedented in human history. Not until recent decades, with the rise of television and then the internet, has human civilization been so greatly affected by a new communication medium.

The term "Dark Ages" was coined by Petrarch, Europe's most renowned fourteenth-century scholar. He saw himself as living in an age where learning was such a rare and precious thing that the few books in existence shone like lights "surrounded by gloom and darkness." Like many scholars, he spent much of his life wandering across Europe searching for small, scattered text collections and tattered manuscripts, in order to reproduce them.

ARMIES OF SCRIBES

Copying by hand meant that armies of scribes—almost invariably monks—had to spend their time preserving knowledge, instead of extending it through writing new books. Equipped with only quills and ink pots, their years were consumed by the tedious, seemingly never-ending task of copying, and they frequently changed the text as

carelessness or opinion interfered with their work. It was even harder to accurately reproduce more challenging technical information, such as maps, tables, diagrams and sketches of natural phenomena. Knowledge was constantly being lost as manuscripts went missing or were destroyed by accidents of history. The Renaissance (or "rebirth") is the name later given to one of several revivals of learning that occurred after the Dark Ages. This great revival, an effective transition from the medieval to the modern world, was given impetus by Gutenberg's printing press.

Following the ravages of the bubonic plague (the Black Death), which killed about a third of the population of Europe, the late fourteenth century was a time of growing prosperity. Many new churches and noble estates were built, and copies of the Bible were hard to find. Scribes could not meet the demand, and many people were experimenting with ways to produce books more quickly. The first to make the breakthrough and print an entire book was a secretive, determined man named Johannes Gutenberg. Ironically, if it weren't for his court records, we would know almost nothing about him at all, because he kept his work secret for decades, fearing that it would be stolen and copied.

GUTENBERG'S "SECRET" BREAKTHROUGH

Little is known about Gutenberg's life. In about 1398 he was born to a family of coin makers and goldsmiths in Mainz, Germany, and the precision metalwork skills he learned at home were at the heart of his innovation. Printing itself had been invented by the Chinese centuries earlier—text was carved into wooden

blocks that were covered in ink and then pressed onto paper. Carving out enough pages for a whole book was not much faster than hand copying, however, and few woodworkers had the level of skill needed to make letters the same size and keep them perfectly aligned. Moreover, wood is too soft to maintain its shape if pressed repeatedly. Gutenberg's breakthrough was movable metal type. Drawing on his experience as a goldsmith Gutenberg created individual letters made of metal that were arranged on a frame, coated with a black, oil-based non-running ink that he invented, then placed into a modified wine press. Gutenberg's letters were made from a combination of tin, lead and a crystalline solid called antimony. His lettered plates were durable and could be used for hundreds of printings, resulting in the production of books on a scale that had never before been achieved. His new method was several hundred times faster than hand copying, and few major improvements were made on it until the nineteenth century, when the introduction of steam power enabled automation of the printing process.

Gutenberg also split his letters, which were designed in the round, cursive handwriting style of the time, into upper and lower case and included punctuation such as commas and semi-colons. All his letters were precisely the same height and individually hand cast, and his screw-type press was designed to transfer the text evenly onto paper (and occasionally the more expensive vellum). Gutenberg took almost a year to create a total of some 270 characters for the first printed Bible.

THE EXPLOSION IN KNOWLEDGE AND SOCIAL CHANGE THAT FLOWED ON FROM THE AVAILABILITY OF MASS-PRODUCED BOOKS WAS UNPRECEDENTED IN HUMAN HISTORY.

GUTENBERG LOSES A LIFETIME'S WORK

With the aid of about twenty men in his workshop, Gutenberg completed the printed Bible in 1455. He made 180 copies in the first year—the same time it took a monastery to produce a single copy. By this time, however, Johann Fust, the financier who had bankrolled Gutenberg's years of experimentation, lost patience with waiting for a return on his investment. Fust successfully sued Gutenberg, seized everything in the workshop, and went on to make a fortune printing Bibles and prayer guides. It had taken Gutenberg his entire life to accumulate the tools in his workshop and construct his famous press, and now it had been taken away from him. Gutenberg's fame did not spread far in his lifetime, but he did receive a pension for his achievements from the

Johannes Gutenberg inspects a page proof from his miraculous printing press.

town authorities, along with 440 gallons of wine. A friend later gave him a press, and he spent his last days as a humble bookseller, and died in 1468.

His invention, however, was an idea whose time had definitely come. By 1500 practically every European city had a printer's workshop, and over twenty million books had been printed. Like the Gutenberg Bible, three-quarters of those books were in Latin, the language of religion and academia, but, by the end of the century, publishers were already reaching out to the masses of Europe by publishing books in languages that people actually spoke. While most early printed books were reproductions of old texts—Bibles, works by Greek and Roman authors, and so on—vernacular books emerged to cater to popular tastes, and the idea of reading for pleasure took hold. Illustrated travel guides, popular histories, collections of ballads and short stories, books on astrology, etiquette, mythical animals, costumes, playing chess, and so on, were soon inundating the market.

THE SPREAD OF BOOKS AND THE RISE OF LITERACY

As books became readily available, more people had the chance to become literate, and were willing to pay for them. These factors fed into each other, constantly expanding the market for books, the number of readers, and the range of titles—and this process has never really stopped. At the dawn of the Gutenberg Age, literacy was rarely found beyond the university towns and monasteries. But soon literacy spread to the nobility and wealthier merchants, then to skilled tradesmen and small shopkeepers and other members of what we could call the middle class. In many households it was the women who first learned to read, and it became a common pastime for women to read aloud to their families during the long winter nights. Until universal primary school education was introduced in the nineteenth century, many of Europe's poor could not afford schooling and thus remained illiterate, but even the poor were served by chapbooks—small pamphlets with illustrations, song lyrics and news items.

Besides reading for pleasure, there was a great desire for practical knowledge. The first centuries of printing saw an incredible number of publications aimed at those who wanted to learn how to play an instrument, give a sermon, run a farm, balance accounts, brew beer, identify plants, and so on. Students who had previously been forced to learn their crafts orally were now in the novel position of being able to outshine their teachers, assuming they could get their hands on particular books.

What little knowledge of the workings of nature was often located in ancient texts or practical crafts, and printers collected and published such information in a genre known as *libri secretorum*, or "books of secrets." These were eclectic collections of everything from medical prescriptions and technical formulas, to recipes, parlor tricks and jokes. Advances in chemistry, for instance, owe a great deal to the publication of guides to dying fabrics—but this information was mixed with advice on how to breed multicolored horses, create men out of clay, or get chickens to lay eggs the size of human heads. The later development of the scientific method by Francis Bacon, with its emphasis on observation and experiment, was spurred by the need to separate the useful "secrets" from the claptrap. This ensured an ever-faster accumulation of discoveries that could be applied to the creation of new technology—another process that shows no sign of stopping.

IMPACT ON THE CHURCH

Yet it would be a mistake to think that the shift from a medieval to a modern world was at all smooth or straightforward. Vernacular Bibles allowed many more people to read the Bible for themselves, and controversies erupted over the accuracy of Bible translations, the role of priests as interpreters of divine truth, and pretty much every other aspect of Catholic teaching and practice.

A key issue was the role of indulgences, documents promising forgiveness for sins that could be bought from licensed church authorities, usually professional pardoners. Indulgences had long existed, but it was not until the advent of printing that they could be easily mass-produced, and Gutenberg himself was printing them long before he finished his Bible. Pious Christians were scandalized to see pardoners hawking their wares for profit, promising, for example, that for a few coins, dead relatives could be released from hell even if they had committed murder. In 1517 Martin Luther, a German professor of theology, became so outraged by this and other clerical abuses that he nailed an indignant protest—the 95 Theses—to a church door. Within a few days, several printers were selling copies of this document, and within fifteen days of its appearance it had reached every part of Germany.

Pope Leo X ordered Luther to renounce his views, but his defiance remained and grew more radical, leading to his denunciation as a heretic. Many had defied the popes in the past, but they had always lost because heretical ideas had travelled too slowly to escape church repression. Within a couple of years, however, Luther was a bestselling author, and he had literally armies of supporters. Similar movements emerged in other countries, especially England and Switzerland, and a split developed between the Catholic kingdoms of the south and the followers of new, Protestant creeds in the lands to the north.

THE PRINTED WORD FUELS NATIONALISM

Another source of tension was nationalism itself, which was also fired by printed material in a number of ways. Maps in Gutenberg's time were rare, very basic, and filled with errors, and the ones that were any good were among the most prized state secrets. Ships' crews frequently had to rely on accounts from other mariners. But mapmaking flourished as printing presses spread, and ships' captains were invited to send corrections to Europe's cartographers. A century after Gutenberg, Mercator created a very modern world map, one that took into account the curvature of the earth and thus allowed accurate navigation at sea. And then, with political atlases widely available, people began to see themselves as members of states, where previously they had tended to identify themselves with their local region and their place in the social ladder.

This shift in consciousness accompanied the emergence of vernacular literature, which destroyed the Latin monopoly on educated thought. Now the Bible, current affairs, philosophy, and a thousand other topics could be read in people's own national language, which was frequently the dialect of national capitals. This development was encouraged by national governments, hoping to extend their power, and added another dimension to the religious strife. In 1549, for instance, the English prayer book, *The Book of Common Prayer*, was created and imposed across the kingdom, replacing Latin as the language of worship. It was wildly unpopular in some areas of the countryside, and helped fuel a rebellion in Cornwall, where a minority language held sway. The English-language Bible was also a prime factor in accelerating the religious Reformation promoted by King Henry VIII. The masses could now read the word of God for themselves, rather than depend on the translations provided by clergymen who could speak Latin. In another seismic shift, the Pope's authority gradually lessened as people came to realize that the Bible attributed holy authority to God alone, not his human servants. ❧

1453

THE FALL OF BYZANTIUM AND THE RISE OF THE OTTOMAN EMPIRE

On May 29, 1453, twenty-year-old Sultan Mehmed II triumphantly rode his white horse down the avenue that ran through the center of Constantinople and watched as the Islamic soldiers of his victorious Turkish Ottoman army sacked the city that had been the capital of the Roman Empire throughout the Middle Ages. According to Nicolo Barbaro, a witness from the city-state of Venice, blood flowed through the streets like water following a downpour and corpses floated out to sea like melons along a river. Tursun Beg, an Ottoman administrator, wrote that the soldiers "took silver and gold vessels, precious stones, and all sorts of valuable goods and fabrics from the imperial palace and houses of the rich. In this fashion many people were delivered from poverty and made rich."

Mehmed rode on to the Cathedral of Holy Wisdom, or Hagia Sophia, the leading church of eastern Christendom and the seat of the Ecumenical Patriarch. It had been built nine hundred years earlier by Byzantine emperor Justinian, and boasted the largest dome in Europe. Mehmed dismounted and, as a gesture of humility before God, poured a handful of dirt over his turban. The Greeks had long considered the shrine a symbol of heaven on earth, and the temporal throne of the Christian God, but now the cathedral was being re-consecrated as the Aya Sofya mosque. Hundreds of Greeks who had taken refuge inside were rounded up and slaughtered. But when the Sultan saw one of his soldiers hacking at the marble floor he stopped him, saying "Be satisfied with the booty and the captives; the buildings of the city belong to me." Watched over by golden mosaics of Jesus Christ, the Virgin Mary, Greek Orthodox saints and Byzantine emperors, he offered a prayer of thanks to Allah, begging for his eternal blessing and protection.

A MAGNIFICENT WALLED CITY

Constantinople (now Istanbul) had been the center of the Christian world in the east, largely because of its strategic location on a triangular peninsula on the geographic boundary of Europe and Asia. On its north was a scimitar-shaped harbor 3¾ miles long and ⅔ mile wide, known as the Golden Horn because the setting sun bathed its waters in a golden light.

Constantinople was founded by the Greeks in about the seventh century BC. In 324 BC the Roman emperor Constantine the Great declared it to be "New Rome" and for the next thousand years it served as the eastern capital of the Roman Empire. It was the largest and most advanced city in Europe. In 1203 the French knight-crusader Geoffrey de Villehardouin wrote that his fellow crusaders were filled with wonder "when they saw these high walls and these rich towers by which it was completely enclosed and those rich palaces and those lofty churches of which there were so many that no one could believe it unless he had seen it with his own eyes." The walls, built in the fifth century ad, were indeed magnificent, stretching from the Golden Horn to the Sea of Marmara and completely enclosing the city, which was fortified by moats, parapets and one hundred and ninety-two towers. They were essential to the security of Constantinople.

But in 1204 the city was finally sacked, not by enemies but by so-called friends—fellow Christians of the fourth crusade, backed by Constantinople's commercial enemy, the seafaring state of Venice. The Byzantine Empire regained power in 1261 but in the following period the city endured continual attacks from Muslim enemies and civil wars between rival emperors. Constantinople's Greek population dwindled from four hundred thousand to about fifty thousand. They still proudly referred to themselves as Romans, in commemoration of the Roman Empire's first Christian emperor Constantine (272–337), after whom the city was named. But by 1453, Constantine XI's kingdom had dwindled to the city, a few islands, and part of the Peloponnese in southern Greece. The powerful seafaring states of Venice and Genoa had taken over all the commerce in the region and Constantinople was surrounded by foes on all sides. It was ripe for the picking.

THE OTTOMAN THREAT

Mehmed's father Murad II was a man of peace and scholarship. A friend of Constantinople, he led a contemplative life, but Mehmed was ambitious, conceited and trusted no one. Constantine was well aware of the imminent threat he posed so in January 1453 he enlisted the help of Genoese nobleman Giovanni Giustiniani—an expert in defending walled cities—and his seven hundred well-armed troops. He persuaded the ever-bickering Genoese and Venetians within the city to unite under his command against the common enemy. But the Turks had a formidable new weapon on their side—an awesome bronze cannon designed by Hungarian engineer Urban, who had initially offered his assistance to Constantine in return for the funds needed to build the behemoth. But Constantine could not even afford his asking salary, let alone the construction funds, so Urban approached Mehmed, who granted him four times his asking wage and all the other necessary finance. The cannon's barrel was over 26 feet in length, with a bore of 23 inches. Stuffed with more than 110 pounds of gunpowder, it could propel a 550-pound stone cannonball over a distance greater than two-thirds of a mile.

On April 2, 1453, Mehmed and his troops set up camp outside the city and began their barrage. Constantine had installed a huge chain boom across the harbor entrance, guarded by his strongest galleys. Over the next few days, the Turks tried but failed to breach the harbor boom, but did succeed in demolishing a small section of the wall. Urban's cannon was yet to arrive so Mehmed decided to postpone his attack for a few days. He was well aware that the siege would be a daunting task, despite his far larger army of eighty thousand men. The weakest section of the city wall was the Golden Horn, where the shore was dotted with warehouses and wharves. Mehmed decided he could breach it once he gained control of the harbor, so he put his fleet of several hundred vessels under the command of Suleiman Baltoghlu, the governor of nearby Gallipoli. But until Baltoghlu secured the harbor, Mehmed would have to concentrate his attack on the heavily fortified landward walls. Inside the surrounding moat, a series of walls ranged from the relatively low Mesoteichion wall to walls as high as 60 feet, with towers interspersed along their length.

Mehmed concentrated his attack on the Mesoteichion wall, the weakest part of the walls.

THE BATTLE ESCALATES

On the second night of the attack Constantine oversaw repairs to the section of the wall that the Turks had destroyed that day. All able-bodied citizens—women, men and children—participated in filling the breach with wood and stones, and by morning the repairs were passable, if not perfect. While Mehmed waited for Urban's cannon, he ordered his soldiers to fill in the moat—no small task as it ranged in depth from about 25 to 165 feet, and could be flooded from tanks within the city. For several days the Turks worked with bundles of sticks, barrels and tree trunks, rushing the moat under a barrage of stones, arrows, and walnut-sized bullets, then scurrying back to their trenches. The defenders retaliated using mechanical engines and catapults to release boulders and darts—as well as Greek fire, an incendiary substance that burned on water as well as land.

By April 12 Mehmed's reinforcements, including Urban's cannon and fifty smaller cannon, had arrived. The monster weapon had been manufactured at Adrianople, the Turkish capital, then hauled over 800 miles on a wooden raft, by thirty carts drawn by sixty bulls, and assisted by four hundred men. The gun took so long to reload that it could be fired only

THE STREETS BECAME RAGING TORRENTS AND SEVERAL CHILDREN WERE SWEPT TO THEIR DEATH. THAT NIGHT AN OMINOUS, UNNATURAL GLOW ILLUMINED THE HAGIA SOPHIA.

Sultan Mehmed II, victor at Constantinople in 1453 and the greatest ruler of the Ottoman Empire

seven times a day. The defenders tried to reduce its impact by hanging sheets of leather and bales of wool over the walls, but this proved ineffectual. The cannon was unpredictable—after each deafening blast and discharge of pungent smoke it would recoil violently, often toppling off its wooden platform. To prevent it splitting or melting, oil was immediately poured down the barrel. Unfortunately for Urban, its inventor, it backfired early in the siege, killing him.

Meanwhile Baltoghlu, having received reinforcements, launched another attack against the harbor boom. His fleet now consisted of six two-masted triremes (with three tiers of oarsmen), ten biremes, almost a hundred other galleys and longboats, and numerous smaller craft. Constantinople's sailing fleet consisted of twenty-six large battleships, of which ten were anchored outside the chain boom to guard the 1300-feet wide harbor entrance. Despite being vastly outnumbered, Constanine's forces were able to force Baltoghlu to retreat by using the height advantage of their battleships to send down a hail of javelins, arrows and large rocks projected by catapults.

Mehmed decided to concentrate on a land attack. On the night of April 18, having succeeded in filling in the moat, he launched an attack on an ageing section of the wall. Waves of Turks swarmed towards the city under a hail of weaponry

The siege of Constantinople, which lasted for just over a month, ended the thousand-year-old Byzantine Empire.

but were eventually repelled. Once again Mehmed had been thwarted—he had lost over two hundred men, the heavily armored defenders had lost none.

AN ECLIPSE RECALLS A FEARFUL PROPHECY
The battle raged for another five weeks—after which several harbingers of imminent doom appeared. On May 24, there was a lunar eclipse, recalling a prophecy that Constantinople would fall under a waning moon. The next day, in a plea to the Lord, it was decided to remove the city's holiest statue from the church of Hagia Sophia and parade it through the streets on the shoulders of the faithful. Every citizen—including every soldier (except for a skeleton crew who remained on the walls)—joined the sombre parade. Suddenly, to everyone's horror, the icon tumbled off its stand. It took several minutes to restore its position, at which time a massive thunderstorm struck. The streets became raging torrents and several children were swept to their death as the populace fled for shelter. The next day the city was enveloped in a dense fog, which was

extremely unusual at that time of year. That night an ominous, unnatural glow illumined the Church of the Hagia Sophia. It was noticed by the Turks in their camps and alarmed the troops—until the muezzins, whose responsibilities included leading the daily prayers to Allah, convinced them that it was an omen that the true light of God would soon shine from the church. Constantinople's counsellors begged Constantine to order the evacuation of the city, but he refused. The dispirited Turks also seemed no closer to achieving their aim, and had heard rumors that Christian reinforcements were on their way from Venice.

On May 5, Mehmed offered to spare the city if its inhabitants surrendered, but Constantine refused. For one thing, he could not afford the enormous annual tribute Mehmed demanded. He sent back a compromise offer—he would hand over all his personal riches, but not the city. But Mehmed replied that the citizens must surrender and convert to Islam, or be killed. Thus the negotiations broke down. The next night, by torchlight, the Turks amassed materials to fill the moat, in preparation for a final, massive attack. On May 27, all the cannon were focused on the Mesoteichion, by now unstable from the constant bombardments. Urban's cannon blasted holes in the wall three times, and each time the wall was repaired. Mehmed promised all his troops that they would be given the run of the city for three days, free to plunder and rape to their hearts' content. Morale soared.

That night ten thousand torches blazed as the Turkish troops set about filling the moat and gathering weapons. The exhausted defenders made no attempt to stop them; many knelt and prayed. At midnight all work abruptly stopped; Mehmed had ordered that there would be a day of rest and religious observance before the final offensive. Shortly after 1 a.m. on May 29, a fanfare of drums and trumpets announced that the onslaught was about to begin. The Turks began bombarding the Mesoteichion wall, but were repelled by Giustiniani and his men.

Simultaneous attacks commenced on the sea wall, which faced the Golden Horn, but once again the defenders were able to repel the invaders. Mehmed's battle plan was to allow the Christians no relief, to wear down the resistance of the tired, hungry defenders by sheer force of numbers. Wave after wave of his troops advanced, with the dead immediately replaced by others. It was a high-priced strategy in terms of casualties, but Mehmed was taking advantage of his great numerical superiority. He positioned armed troops behind the front lines whose job was to kill anyone who hesitated or retreated. Ottoman troops surged over the moat and through the breaches created by the cannon. They grappled with the defenders on the outer wall and swarmed up ladders placed against parts of the wall that were still intact. Just before dawn Giustiniani, who had been leading his troops from the Mesoteichion for more than six hors, was wounded. Constantine pleaded with him to stay at his post, but to no avail; his injuries had incapacitated him. He and his bodyguards fled to the harbor and boarded a Genoese ship. Once his soldiers realized that their leader was gone they lost heart and the defence faltered. The demoralized Genoese and many others fled. A group of soldiers led by a giant Turk named Hasan managed to climb to the top of the outer wall. Hasan was killed, but the followers succeeded in swarming over the wall, then through the damaged inner wall and into the city.

Meanwhile about fifty Turks had broken in through a small gate further up the hill. It had not been properly bolted and yielded to their pressure. They were the first invaders to enter the city; fortunately for them, they had not been noticed in the fierce battles for the walls, otherwise they would have been easily overpowered and killed. But it was too late—they had mounted the turret over the gate and raised the Ottoman flag above it. Their emboldened comrades yelled the news that the city was taken and the defenders retreated as more and more of the invaders flooded through the walls, smashing them as the Christians withdrew. Constantine tried to lead by example, leaping into the fray and fighting bravely as a common soldier, but to no avail. He was killed after throwing away his royal regalia and charging defiantly into a mass of advancing Turks.

END OF AN EMPIRE

The locals began rushing to their houses in a vain attempt to save their families. The Venetians and Genoese who had escaped the slaughter fled for the safety of their ships. The commanders of the fleets hacked away the boom protecting the harbor and, their vessels packed with refugees who had managed to swim to the ships, sailed away, along with a bare few of the emperor's ships. They were the lucky few who avoided the terrible fate that awaited the Christian survivors now at the mercy of the rampaging Turks. The Byzantine Empire, which had survived for over a thousand years, was no more.

1478–1530
THE SPANISH INQUISITION

On February 6, 1481, seven people were marched out from the Cathedral of Seville, led by chanting, black-robed Dominican friars. The seven were dressed in yellow robes, held votive candles—and wore nooses around their necks. And, as they were marched towards an open field outside the city, they were followed by a howling mob.

These seven people (six men and one woman) were *conversos*, Jews who had been converted to Christianity. They were being rounded up because they had, or were suspected of having, "relapsed," or secretly begun to practise their Jewish faith again. The *conversos* were the prime target of the Spanish sovereigns, King Ferdinand and Queen Isabella, who wanted nothing more for their country than that all worship the same God. Out of this desire was born the Spanish Inquisition, which was to have an infamous effect, not just on the *conversos*, but on Spain and the Catholic Church, as well.

The Spanish Inquisition (from the Latin word *inquisition*, meaning "examination") lasted officially for almost four hundred years (it was not abolished until 1834), but was most active from 1480 to 1530. Not only did it result in the persecution and death of thousands of Jews, but it also led to the exile of almost half the Jewish population of Spain. Recent historians have posited that the role of the Catholic Church was a less active one than previously believed and have placed a good deal of the responsibility on Ferdinand and Isabella, and it is certainly true that the pope who first authorized the Inquisition was aghast at the horrors he had helped set in motion. But the official Church did little to stop the persecution and the fact remains that the prime instruments of the Inquisition—the face it showed to the public through its inquisitors and through those who publicly harangued the people about to be executed—were Catholic clergy.

"THEY AMOUNT TO THE SAME"

Ferdinand and Isabella of Spain were the most glamorous monarchs of their time, and the most focused. The theme of their entire reign can be summed up in one phrase: unity for Spain. They married in 1469, royal cousins from the powerful provinces of Castile and Aragon, and following their coronation in 1475, oversaw the epic last stage of the eight-hundred-year-long *Reconquista*—the ouster of the Moors from Spain, which was completed with the conquest of Granada in 1492.

Tanto monta, monta tanto, Isabel como Fernando was their motto: "They amount to the same, Isabella and Ferdinand." And being devoutly religious Catholic monarchs, Isabella and Ferdinand both wanted all of Spain to worship Christ. In earlier times in the history of the Iberian Peninsula, three religions—Judaism, Islam and Christianity—had lived together in a peace which, if by no means perfect, had been a workable one. But increasingly, in the late fourteenth century, Jews had been subjected to vicious pogroms in which thousands were massacred. Surviving Jews found themselves ghettoised and in many instances forced to wear red badges denoting their religion.

While many Jews fled the country, many more converted to Christianity. Known as *conversos* or "New Christians," they became a burgeoning new class in Spanish society, often holding high positions, not just in government, but in the Church itself. However, the anti-Semites in Spain, particularly among the clergy, never accepted or trusted the *conversos*. One such man, Friar Alonso de Hojeda, prior of the Dominicans in Seville, had the ear of Queen Isabella and, in 1475, came to her with an alarming report.

Francisco Goya's *Inquisition Scene* (c. 1816) captures the macabre and at times absurd nature of the religious persecutions.

Hojeda said that he had evidence that, in the province of Seville, more and more *conversos* were reverting to their original faith. Some had had their children circumcised, others secretly celebrated the Jewish Sabbath, still others sat *shivah* for their dead and practised kosher customs.

Was any of this true? Quite possibly, given that a large group of *conversos* had converted merely as a practical matter, to save their families from exile or worse. But much of it was no doubt paranoia, fuelled by anti-Semitism or even a greedy desire for Jewish property. In the next few years, however, reports from Dominicans in other provinces came into the royal court, giving detailed examples of the perfidy of these "crypto-Jews" and urging Isabella and Ferdinand to take strong action.

The monarchs were sufficiently concerned that they visited some of the provinces in question to see and hear for themselves. Isabella (whose chief confessor, Friar Hernando de Talavera, was himself a *conversos*) was not at first convinced, but Ferdinand was, and ultimately brought Isabella into the fold. The two monarchs turned to Pope Sixtus IV, who, on November 1, 1478, issued a papal bull authorizing an inquisition. Not the first inquisition, of course—there had been others in history, going back to the twelfth century, when the Albigensian heresy was rooted out in France—but the one that was to become the most famous. It would take two years to get underway, but when it did, its purgative flames blazed high.

THE PUBLIC BURNING

The place that the *conversos* were being marched towards on February 6, 1481 was merely an open field, which the Inquisitors referred to as "the stage." But it very quickly became known as the *Quemadero*, or burning place. In the middle of the field were wooden stakes (later, these would be changed to stone ones so that they did not have to be continually replaced). The swelling crowd had come to watch these *conversos* burn.

Before that happened, there was to be some preaching. And the preacher was none other than Friar Alonso de Hojeda. Hojeda's sermon to the seven condemned *conversos* at Seville was a grandiloquent one, filled with exhortations to those who were true in their faiths to seek out idolaters and persecute them. The good friar quoted from the apocryphal preachings of St. Peter, which painted a picture of heretics "hanging by their tongues … and under them a fire flaming and tormenting." When Hojeda was finished, a civil authority read out the details of each charge—one of the prisoners had eaten unleavened bread and kosher meat, another had attended a secret Jewish service, and so on.

Hojeda and his fellow Dominicans next offered the *conversos* kneeling before them a chance to repent their sins. This would not save their lives, but it would allow them the grace of being strangled before the fire reached them. Very soon, these first seven victims of the Inquisition at Seville repented and received this small mercy.

Satisfied, the Dominicans ordered that the *conversos* be chained to the wooden stakes. Loyal Catholics then stepped forwards eagerly to pile wood high around the victims—the Dominicans had promised that performing this service would lead to indulgences for the remission of sins. Then, masked executioners whose normal task was to dispatch criminals came forwards, and with quick efficiency garroted each prisoner with a length of leather rope. Finally, the flames were lit and the public burnings began.

THE GRAND INQUISITOR

A week later, Seville's second auto-da-fé began, but Friar Alonso de Hojeda was not present. On the day after his passionate sermon, he had become ill with what turned out to be bubonic plague, and he died before the next auto-da-fé could take place. Those who were inclined a certain way saw this as the hand of God upon him, but he was soon forgotten. For another Inquisitor was to gain prominence in Spain who would become the driving force behind the Spanish Inquisition. He was the Dominican Tomás de Torquemada.

Born in 1420, Torquemada was the nephew of an influential cardinal and theologian. He was a strange-looking man: tall, thick-browed, with a squashed and flattened nose, he resembled the sparring partner of some pugilist—not a star boxer himself, but a man who possessed dogged qualities of perseverance.

Since 1452 the prior of the monastery in Santa Cruz in Segovia, Torquemada was a confessor of both Isabella and Ferdinand, who admired him for his holiness. He never wore shoes, slept on bare wooden cots, wore hairshirts and refused to touch meat. His modesty caused him to turn down an archbishopric offered him. But when the job of Grand Inquisitor was offered to him in 1483, he did not turn it down. This is interesting in light of the fact that most historians believe that Torquemada's maternal grandmother was a *conversos*.

Torquemada has come down in history as a bloodthirsty fanatic, but this is an inaccurate portrayal. Instead, he was the Adolf Eichmann—the Nazi functionary who oiled the bureaucratic wheels behind the Final Solution—of the

POPE SIXTUS IV, WHO HAD APPROVED THE INQUISITION, WAS HORRIFIED BY THE SEVERE TORTURES BEING METED OUT TO GET SUSPECTED HERETICS TO CONFESS.

Inquisition: the organizer, the man who set up procedures, the bureaucrat who made sure the paperwork was in order before the heretics were strapped to the rack. Under Torquemada, the Inquisition spread across Spain, from one Holy Office in Seville to nearly two dozen around the country.

SO MANY TO BE JUDGED

The first year of the Inquisition, after February 1481, was so harsh that even Pope Sixtus IV became alarmed. The pope was genuinely horrified by the "severe tortures" being meted out to get the suspected heretics to confess. In a papal brief issued just before Torquemada was appointed in October of 1483, Sixtus explicitly rebuked not only the Inquisitors, but also Ferdinand and Isabella, who were, in practice, in charge of the whole affair. And, in a bull issued in April of that year, the pope went further, demanding that justice be given to *conversos* like any other suspected criminals—for instance, the right of counsel, the right to confront those who had accused them and the right of appeal. But this bull was for all intents and purposes ignored after Sixtus died in 1484. This is because his successor, Innocent VIII, was susceptible to pressure from Spanish diplomats, who put forward the case that the Inquisition was a matter for Spanish authorities to handle alone.

An auto-da-fé procession taking place in Spain in the late 1400s, as depicted in a nineteenth-century engraving.

Ferdinand had informed Torquemada early in 1483 that he and Isabella now wished to expel all Jews (*conversos* or not) from the Kingdom of Spain, and so Torquemada had been preparing for this massive task. At the end of 1484, he gathered all his appointed Inquisitors about him in Seville and issued a set of instructions on the procedures that needed to be followed during the arrest, interrogation and imprisonment or execution of heretics. Once again eerily foreshadowing the "banality of evil" of the ordinary means by which the Nazis went about their Holocaust, these instructions were all about efficiency and rapid processing. Everything went far more easily and cost less if the suspected heretic confessed quickly (expenses—paid for by Isabella and Ferdinand—were a big concern as the Inquisition wore on), so steeper penalties were put in place if he or she did not recant within thirty days. No one was allowed to confront their accuser. If the Inquisitors—a panel of Dominican clergy, usually—found that the *conversos* had made only a "partial" confession, torture could be used. The Inquisitors even developed their own chilling terminology: those who agreed to adhere to the One True Faith after torture

THE SPANISH INQUISITION

or imprisonment were said to have "reconciled," while those who died in the flames were said to have been "relaxed."

Three tortures in particular were favored. In one, the accused was strapped upside-down on a ladder with a cloth over his or her face; then water was forced down the prisoner's throat until he or she passed out. In another, the prisoner had a rope tied to the wrists and weights attached to the feet, then was pulled up before being dropped suddenly. Last but not least was the rack, on which the prisoner's wrists and ankles were stretched and twisted.

Torquemada's instructions also set out procedures for the requisition of the property of the accused, which went either to finance the Inquisition, or directly to the crown, which received a third of all confiscated goods and properties, and usually granted some portion of that to wealthy nobles. This has led one historian to call the Inquisition "a vast land grab from wealthy and prominent landholders."

THE BLACK LEGEND

The Spanish Inquisition did not officially end until the last Holy Office disappeared in 1834. Torquemada died in 1498, after helping institute what would become Ferdinand and Isabella's Alhambra Decree of March 1492, which ordered the expulsion of all Jews and Muslims from Spain within three months. Weakened by years of relentless Inquisition, perhaps forty thousand, or half the Jewish population of Spain, emigrated to Portugal, North Africa or the Ottoman Empire, particularly Constantinople or Greece. In these places, they continued to speak a Judaeo-Spanish language and practise ancient customs which are continued by Sephardic communities in these areas to this day. Others chose to be baptized during this three-month period, in order to keep their homes and possessions, and in turn became fresh targets for the Inquisition.

In all, between 1480 and 1530, perhaps two thousand heretics, mainly *conversos*, were relaxed at autos-da-fé. In recent years, many Catholic scholars have mounted a revisionist campaign that claims that the Inquisition was not nearly as bad as many people believe, was in fact a "black legend" invented by Protestant writers after the Reformation. These revisionists point out that not as many people died as was once claimed, that torture was relatively infrequent, and that Ferdinand and Isabella, not the Church, bear the chief responsibility. There is some truth to these claims, in the same way that there is truth to the claims that Torquemada was the manager of the Inquisition rather than a torturer. But the Catholic Church's (at the very least) tacit acceptance of Ferdinand and Isabella's persecution and ousting of the Jews fostered what historian Joseph Perez has called "the development of the insidious prejudice of blood purity," a prejudice that subsequently spread outwards from Spain.

Whether or not the influence of the Church was less than people initially believed, the Inquisition increased the tensions between the Church and the Jewish religion, tensions that were further exacerbated by Pope Pius XII's failure to help Jews during the Holocaust. The Spanish Inquisition remains a dark stain, not just on the glittering reputations of Isabella and Ferdinand, but also on what had shown itself to be a cruel and intolerant church. ❧

1492

COLUMBUS ARRIVES IN THE AMERICAS

[We] set sail on Friday, August 3, half an hour before sunrise, steering for the Canary Islands of your highnesses, thence to proceed until I arrive in the Indies and fulfil the embassy of your highnesses to the Princes there ... My plans involve such close attention to navigation and hard work that, considering all, I shall have to forget about sleep.

This passage in Christopher Columbus' journal is obviously written for the ears of his mentors, King Ferdinand and Queen Isabella of Spain, containing as it does a level of sycophancy that might impress a modern junior executive. Still, it rings with history. Columbus was setting off on a voyage that was the most important ever undertaken. Never before or since in the history of the world has such a vast discovery of unknown territory been made. Those on the continent of Europe whose eyes had been turned inwards, or to the East, suddenly found a fertile new ground for nation-building. Within a few short years, Spain, France, England, Portugal, and the Netherlands were involved in a fierce race to grab as much land in the Americas as possible, and the balance of power was permanently altered in Europe.

For those who lived in the Americas, however, Columbus' landing would have to be called a singular disaster. Decimated as much by European disease as European steel (many native cultures were killed by smallpox before any of their individual members even saw a European), their way of life would be completely destroyed.

FINDING A WAY EAST

It wasn't as if the two worlds had never touched before, of course. The Chinese of ancient times may have travelled to Central America. The Vikings had crossed the Atlantic (at the time generally referred to as the "Ocean Sea") numerous times, sailing to Labrador and Newfoundland, and possibly points further south, in the years between 1000 and 1300 AD. But, with the exception of one, short-lived settlement in Newfoundland, these journeys were trips to pick up timber or find good fishing, and contact with this unknown world was not exploited.

Columbus' infinitely more sophisticated voyage came about because of a desire by European countries, in particular Portugal and Spain, to find a sea route to Asia—to the "Indies," as India and China were known. Pioneering a route to the lucrative trade goods of the East that avoided the long overland journey through Central Asia could bring fabulous wealth. Fabled mariners, the Portuguese had led attempts to reach the Indies by heading east via Africa and the Cape of Good Hope. But with most people of learning having accepted that the world was round, attention began to focus on the idea of reaching the East by sailing west. Attempts had been made as early as the late thirteenth century—but it was a voyage fraught with extreme peril.

ROYAL APPROVAL

About forty years old at the time of his legendary voyage, Columbus was born in Genoa, Italy, a city with a long-established seafaring and mercantile tradition. He probably went to sea by the age of ten and in later years plied the Mediterranean for various Italian city-states before going to work for the Portuguese and their king, John II. Columbus proposed to King John that he should sail across the Western Sea to the Indies, but John rejected the proposal, being certain that the way to the East lay east via Africa. So Columbus took his idea to Ferdinand and Isabella, heads of a newly unified Spain following the expulsion of the Moors, and they agreed to back him.

Columbus was an odd figure, a mixture of arrogant loner and supplicant, an idealist convinced of his ideas, and an opportunist out to become "Admiral of the Ocean Sea," as he asked his sponsors to name him. Yet he was an undeniably brave and brilliant seaman. He knew from his extensive seafaring experience that two different wind systems operated in the Atlantic, forming a circulation. The northeast trade winds (*las brisas*) would push him across the ocean from the latitude of the Canary Islands, and the southwesterly trades, which blew further north, would push him in the opposite direction. The question was, would they be strong enough to get him back home?

SECRETLY MAKING HEADWAY

Setting sail on August 3 from Palos in Spain, Columbus had with him three ships: the *Niña*, the *Pinta*, and the *Santa María*; his crew consisted of ninety men. The ships were caravels, two- or three-masted sailing vessels, although the *Santa María* may have been a *não*, a larger and heavier vessel, since, although it was Columbus' flagship, it always lagged behind the other two. At the beginning of the ocean crossing, heading west from the Canary Islands, Columbus recorded nothing but good sailing weather—strong westerly winds, blue skies, flying fish leaping through the air. "The savor of the mornings was a great delight," wrote Bartolomé de las Casas, Columbus' biographer, who abstracted the explorer's journal (the original no longer exists).

Columbus' crews were provisioned for a year, but he expected the voyage to take only a few weeks, since the geographies he had consulted had said that the Ocean Sea between Europe

No verified likenesses of Columbus exist, so even Sebastiano del Piombo's now-famous portrait was probably based on guesswork.

and the Indies must be very narrow at the twenty-eighth latitude, which was the latitude Columbus was following from the Canary Islands. In the first ten days of his voyage, the trade winds sped him along for 1160 nautical miles. On his best day he made 174 nautical miles.

This speed was a mixed blessing, however, for Columbus expected the outlying islands of the Indies to appear any day, and they did not. Concerned that his crew might begin to become fearful, he lied to them about the distance they had covered each day, always telling his men they had travelled a lesser distance.

BEWILDERED AND BECALMED

In the third week of September, Columbus' ships encountered an alarming phenomenon: the Sargasso Sea. Looking like a great meadow of yellow and green grass, the Sargasso is made up of sargassum, a thick weed. It is harmless to ships, but since no European had ever sailed through it before, the men did not know that. They were also much disturbed because they thought such weeds must presage land, yet there was no land to be seen.

Around this same time, the trade winds seemed to falter, and the ships were forced to sail much more slowly, tacking to find a breeze. They travelled only about 250 miles in five days, and the sea was so smooth the men were able to shout between vessels to each other, and dive off to go swimming.

On September 25, a lookout on the *Pinta* shouted "Tierra! Tierra!" and everyone believed they saw a high mountain in the distance. Columbus even sank to his knees to thank God. But it turned out to be a mirage.

DESPAIR—THEN JOY

While Columbus recorded in his journal that "the sea was like a river" and the air "sweet and soft," the men were growing suspicious. To these sailors, Columbus was a foreigner, a Genoese, and not a very likeable one at that. As the ships moved further and further into the unknown, with no sight of land, they began to grumble openly. He tried to placate them (even as he continued to lie about the distances they were covering), but by October 10 (when the ships were about 200 miles from the present-day Bahamas) had agreed that he would turn back within a few days if land were not spotted. He wrote in his journal: "Here the men could no longer stand it; they complained of the long voyage."

> THE TEMPLATE WAS SET: INDIANS WERE CAPTURED AND ENSLAVED, AND WOULD ACCOMPANY EUROPEANS ON A SINGLE-MINDED HUNT FOR GOLD.

COLUMBUS ARRIVES IN THE AMERICAS

Because of his desperation to find land, he ordered that the ships sail at night, a dangerous prospect in unknown waters if land is thought to be near. All hands therefore kept a sharp lookout. Around 10 p.m. on October 11, Columbus thought he saw a light flickering in the distance, but wasn't sure. (No one has ever decided what this light could have been, since Columbus was still too far from shore to have seen a fire.) But around 2 a.m. on October 12, Rodrigo de Triana, lookout on the *Pinta*, saw a white-sand cliff or beach gleaming in the distance and cried out "Tierra! Tierra!"

This time it was no false alarm. Columbus soon pulled alongside in the slower *Santa María* and marked the distance to this welcome apparition as about 6 miles. The ships tacked back and forth, waiting for dawn.

The voyage from the Canary Islands had taken five weeks. Steering through uncharted waters, using celestial navigation, and dead reckoning, Columbus had managed to find the optimal course to the Americas—a course that Spanish ships would follow for centuries to come.

A MOMENTOUS MEETING

Columbus had brought his men to an outlying island of the Bahamas, probably Watlings Island, though this is still debated.

In this artist's impression, a priest blesses Columbus and his fleet as they depart from Palos, Spain, on August 3, 1492.

The island, which Columbus was to name San Salvador, was a low, curving landmass about 13 miles long by 6 miles wide, protected by a coral reef. Once daylight arrived, Columbus and his men sailed their ships to an opening in the reef and entered a shallow bay. Floating in azure waters, off a beach of glistening sand, they suddenly saw a group of naked people run down to the shore and stare in astonishment at the Spanish ships.

Columbus, on the *Santa María*, ordered a longboat dropped to the sea, and he and a group of armed men rowed to shore. The captains of the other ships followed suit. Columbus carried the royal banner, while others in the party carried flags bearing green crosses and the letters F and Y (the initials of the Spanish king and queen). Once on shore, they fell on their knees and praised God for their salvation.

Ignoring the naked people approaching, Columbus took possession of the island in the name of Spain. Then he turned his attention to the islanders, who turned out to be friendly and gentle, and were probably Taino or Arawak Indians. Although the Indians had never seen men like these or ships of such size, they showed no fear. According to Columbus, some of these people thought the Spanish were gods and threw themselves on the ground with their arms outstretched. Columbus spent a great deal of time describing them in his journal (much more so than the island itself, which probably disappointed him—it was not as lush as he had thought the Indies would be). The Taino wore their hair cut into a fringe over their eyebrows and long down their backs, painted their bodies and their faces white, black or red and had skin coloring that was neither black nor white. They reminded Columbus of the Gouache Indians of the Canarys—an ominous reference, for the Gouache were being hunted to extermination by the Spaniards.

Columbus passed out beads and "red caps" to these people, and accepted parrots, balls of cotton thread and javelins in return. The Indians appeared to be poor, but one thing caught Columbus' interest: many of them had gold hanging from holes pierced in their ears or noses. Asking about this using signs, he thought they told him that the gold came from an island to the south, where there was a great king. So, after spending three days on San Salvador, Columbus decided to leave and seek this island. He took seven Indian men with him as guides, giving them no choice in the matter. Thus the template was set for the conquest of the Americas: enslaved Indians accompanying Europeans on a single-minded hunt for gold.

SHORT-LIVED GLORY, LASTING FAME

Columbus continued exploring the islands for three months, hoping to find gold and the fabled land of the Indies or of Cipangu (Japan), which he also thought might be in these latitudes. At first it was a fruitless search. One of his captains, Martín Pinzón aboard the *Pinta*, abandoned Columbus and went off to search for gold on his own. The *Santa María* ran aground on Hispaniola (now in Haiti and the Dominican Republic) and had to be abandoned. But Columbus was able to find gold on that island and even left a small European settlement behind. In January of 1493, he sailed north, found the southwesterly trade winds, and headed back to Spain, rejoined by Pinzón in the *Pinta*, who had also found gold.

When he arrived back in Spain, Columbus was given honors beyond his wildest imaginings. He was awarded the rank of "Admiral of the Ocean Sea" and made viceroy and governor of all the lands he had discovered. He was to make three more voyages to the Caribbean, though he never gave up insisting the Americas were the Indies, despite growing evidence to the contrary. Unable to renounce an idea that was obviously wrong, and angered by the Spanish government's refusal to give him ten percent of all gold found in the New World as he had requested, Columbus died embittered and estranged at the age of fifty-five, in 1506. Meanwhile, and especially after Hernán Cortes landed in Mexico in 1519, Spain reaped the benefits of Columbus' momentous discovery. Wealth poured into its treasury, enriching and empowering the nation far beyond its previous status, just as it was about to take its position as a pre-eminent power in Europe.

Columbus had not found the Indies, nor had he really found a "new" world. Instead, as the historian John H. Parry has put it, he "established contact between two worlds, both already old." But from that moment of contact, the modern world—one of extraordinary interchanges between far-flung cultures, both for good and ill—has sprung. ✀

1501–1900

THE EARLY MODERN ERA

❧ The Almost Complete Charters ❧

ERDINANDVS *Magallanus à Rege Portugalliæ offensus, Carolum V. Imperatorem adit, atq; illi demonstrat Moluccas Insulas Castellanorum iuris esse: sperare se, nauigatione ad Occidentem facta, fretum inuenturum in Occidentali India, per quod in mare Australe penetraret, & inde ad Moluccas insulas peruenire posset: Ea autem via minoribus sumtibus, & minore difficultate, aromata, aliasq; Orientis merces inuehi posse. Carolus ex eorum sententia qui rerum Indicarum Concilio præerant, illi naues instruit quibus eum præficit. Is Hispali soluens, post longam nauigationem tandem fretum inuenit centum decem leucas in longitudinem patens, binas in latitudinem, interdum plures, cui, ab Inuentoris nomine, Magallanici cognomen inditum.*

1519 MAGELLAN CIRCUMNAVIGATES THE WORLD

Perhaps the greatest journey in the age of discovery was Ferdinand Magellan's circumnavigation of the world. On September 20, 1519, after convincing the Spanish king to fund the expedition, the Portuguese explorer Magellan set sail from Spain with five ships to find a westward route to the Spice Islands. By November he had reached South America, and the following year he rounded the Strait of Magellan and entered the Pacific Ocean, arriving in the Philippines in March 1521. Although Magellan did not make it home—dying in battle in the Philippines—he did circumnavigate the globe by passing the easternmost point he had visited on an earlier voyage. On September 6, the last remaining ship, in his fleet, the Victoria, loaded with spices, arrived in Seville under the leadership of Sebastián del Cano and history was made.

Ferdinand Magellan was born about 1480, the son of Rui de Magalhães and Alda de Mesquita, members of the Portuguese nobility. He spent his childhood in the northern Portuguese state of Minho, and at the age of eleven was enrolled in the Royal School for Pages where he studied etiquette, music, fencing, dancing, astronomy, cartography, and navigation.

Theodor de Bry's sixteenth-century allegorical rendering of Magellan's incredible voyage.

These subjects reflected Portugal's status as a great seafaring nation—since the 1430s the Portuguese had been colonizing the west coast of Africa, setting up trading centers and proving that humans could actually live in the tropics (previously regarded by Europeans as uninhabitable).

By the time Magellan entered page school, his countryman Bartholomew Diaz had travelled south, rounded the Cape of Good Hope at the southern tip of Africa and, sailing in a north-easterly direction, discovered an ocean route to India and the Far East. This was significant because the overland trade routes across Europe and into western Asia were controlled by middlemen in the Middle East, making goods far more expensive. By the time such goods as silk, porcelain, and spices reached Europe their price was a hundred times greater than the cost at the source.

EARLY CAREER

During Magellan's first year at school the Genoese navigator Christopher Columbus, sailing under the flag of Portugal's bitter naval and trade rival Spain, reached the islands of the New World in the Caribbean. A few years later Portuguese explorer Vasco da Gama sailed around Africa to India and then to the Molucca Islands (known as the Spice Islands), at the southern tip of Malaya. When da Gama returned home, he brought such riches of spices, silk, emeralds, and pearls that overnight Portugal was transformed from one of the poorest to one of the richest countries in Europe. Magellan started dreaming of leading his own expedition ship to the east, but obstacles were put in his way. For some reason the supervisor of the page school, Duke Manuel, brother-in-law of Portuguese King John II, took an enduring dislike to Magellan. A page needed royal patronage in order to gain employment at sea, and his hopes faded further when the king was assassinated in 1495 and Manuel ascended to the throne. For the next nine years Manuel thwarted all Magellan's attempts to go to sea on one of the many ships that sailed from the port of Lisbon to the Spice Islands.

MAGELLAN'S FIRST EXPEDITION TO THE EAST

In 1504 Magellan saw his opportunity. Manuel ordered Admiral Francisco Almeida to India with the largest fleet ever to leave Portugal—twenty-two small, highly manoeuvrable caravels and some two thousand men. Magellan took leave from his inconsequential job at court, concealing his reason for doing so, and signed up as a common sailor on one of the caravels. Almeida's mission was to destroy the Arab trading centers on the east coast of Africa and the west coast of India, in order to gain control of lucrative commerce routes. The armada spent eighteen months in the Indian Ocean, attacking numerous African ports, setting up sieges and blockades, and driving the occupants—those who survived their massacres—into the inland jungles. Magellan proved to be an excellent sailor and soldier, and was promoted to captain of a barge equipped with six cannon. He and his small crew sank over two hundred Arab craft and Magellan was rewarded with another promotion, to captain of a segment of the fleet. In early 1509 the armada was involved in one of history's bloodiest sea battles off the Malabar Coast of south India, eventually taking over all the trading ports in the region. Magellan was seriously wounded and spent five months in hospital.

The fleet then sailed to Malacca on the southwest of the Malay Peninsula, where Magellan was again wounded in a skirmish with the local sultan, from whom he acquired a thirteen-year-old slave named Black Henry, who would remain with him from that point on. Magellan captured a Malaccan caravel and embarked on a journey to the Philippines. He displayed his honesty by reporting back that he had found some islands, but did not claim them because they belonged to Spain. (This was based on the Treaty of Tordesillas, brokered by the pope and signed by the kings of Spain and Portugal, under

WHEN VASCO DA GAMA RETURNED HOME, HE BROUGHT SUCH RICHES THAT PORTUGAL WAS TRANSFORMED FROM ONE OF THE POOREST TO ONE OF THE RICHEST COUNTRIES IN EUROPE.

which the non-Christian world was divided by an imaginary line from pole to pole. Lands to the west of it belonged to Spain; to the east, Portugal.) Magellan's naval superiors, infuriated, sent him home to be punished by King Manuel, who was only too happy to comply. Magellan was demoted, put on half pay and sent as a soldier to North Africa, where the Portuguese were at war with the Moors. He was wounded in action by a spear to the right knee, leaving him lame for life. He was also accused of treason for supposedly trading with the Moors, and then sent home. The charges were eventually dropped but Magellan's star had waned to the extent that he saw no future for himself in Portugal. He requested command of a caravel and, when Manuel refused, asked permission to seek another master. Manuel replied, "Serve whom you will, Clubfoot, it is a matter of indifference to me."

MAGELLAN SEEKS PATRONAGE TO FULFILL HIS DREAM

Magellan hatched his plan to reach the East by travelling west from Europe, believing that he could find *El Paso*, a passage through the Americas to the Far East. He had no chance of receiving Portuguese royal patronage for such an expedition, but fortunately made the acquaintance of two wealthy and powerful Spanish brothers, Duarte and Diogo Barbosa. They arranged his marriage to Diogo's wealthy daughter Beatriz, then introduced him to King Charles I of Spain, better known as Charles V, emperor of the Holy Roman Empire. The king, delighted to be told that Magellan had not attacked his holdings in the Philippines, gave him five tall, square-rigged sailing ships, fully equipped with captains, crew and supplies. Magellan chose the 110-tonne caravel *Trinidad* as his flagship, and one of his countrymen, John Serrano, and three Spaniards to captain the carracks *San Antonio*, *Victoria*, *Concepcion*, and *Santiago*. At the last minute he also received a passenger, Venetian nobleman Antonio Pigafetta, who was actually a spy sent by the rulers of Venice to report on any new trade routes to the East discovered by the expedition. Pigafetta did us a favor by keeping a detailed diary, the only surviving account of the journey.

The fleet, with about two hundred and seventy men, set off on September 20, 1519, sailing south down the coast of West Africa, then crossing the Atlantic to South America. In January Magellan thought he had discovered *El Paso*, but it turned out to be the estuary of the Rio de la Plata, the dividing line between present-day Uruguay and Argentina. Disappointed but not

discouraged, they headed south and soon found themselves in the icy, stormy waters near the Antarctic. On March 31 they anchored in a bay that Magellan named St. Julian, not far from the Falkland Islands, to sit out the southern winter—but unrest was growing among the crew. Food was running low, largely because about one-third of the provisions had been stolen by secret agents of King Manuel before they set sail. In addition, the Spanish crewmembers, who resented being under the command of a Portuguese captain, began to hatch plans for a mutiny. They had already tried to take control of the expedition in the Atlantic by murdering Magellan, who got wind of the plot and saved his life by agreeing to follow their sailing orders for a while. But he was still in a highly fraught position. Pigafetta's diary describes what then took place:

On the night of April 1–2, (Spanish captain) Cartagena boarded the San Antonio and forced her ship's company to acknowledge them as their leader. By dawn the Spaniards had seized three ships, leaving Magellan in charge of just the Trinidad and the Santiago. But Magellan was equal to the task of restoring his power. He sent some of his men to the Victoria to announce that they wished to join the turncoats, but once aboard they pulled out concealed weapons and recaptured the ship. Magellan then covered the harbor entrance with the three

Magellan was killed on the Philippine island of Mactan, after getting involved in a local dispute.

ships he now controlled, leading the outnumbered rebels to surrender. Cartagena was court-martialed then left to die on an uninhabited island; another Spanish captain, Mendoza, died in the fighting while the third, Quesada, was executed. The latter two were strung up and left hanging on the Trinidad as a warning to the rest of the crew that Magellan was in control.

Magellan had thwarted the mutiny, but still faced the bitterly cold winter ahead. The crew constructed wooden huts while the mutineers were forced to clean the ships' hulls, in chains and often up to their waist in freezing water. They would not be unchained until the start of summer when the journey resumed.

THE DISCOVERY OF EL PASO— AND A VAST OCEAN

When the ice floes eventually started melting, the fleet set southward once again. The wonderful day came on October 21, 1520 when they finally discovered *El Paso*, the winding, mountain-edged waterway across the southernmost tip of South America that we now know as the Strait of Magellan. By the time they reached the western end of the passage on November 27, the fleet had been reduced to three ships. The *Santiago* had been wrecked on a sandbar, while the *San Antonio* had mutinied, deserted, and headed back across the Atlantic for Spain. Now that they had traversed *El Paso*, Magellan was certain that they would soon reach the Spice Islands—but the world turned out to be much larger and the journey ahead much longer than anyone had imagined. Finding himself at the edge of a large, peaceful sea, Magellan wrote: "we are about to stand into an ocean where no ship has ever sailed before. May the ocean be always as calm and benevolent as it is today. In this hope I name it *El Mar Pacifico* [Pacific Ocean]."

On January 25 they found a small island where they were able to stock up on water and food. They set sail after a week but soon the food ran out again, and Magellan knew that they would all die unless they could find land within two days. On March 6 they had the good fortune to come across the island of Guam. They were attacked by natives in a flotilla of canoes, waving spears and clubs and bearing oval shields. Magellan fired the cannon on them, causing them to retreat into the jungle, and the crews feasted for a few hours on the food they found in the natives' huts before resuming their voyage with stolen food. Nine days later they discovered a series of wooded islands where they rested for a few days and replenished their supplies. On March 28 they were approached by eight natives in a large canoe. Magellan's young slave Black Henry hailed them in Malay, the language of his native Malacca. They replied in the same language and Magellan realized that they had finally reached the Philippines—the very islands that he had approached from the opposite direction in 1511. The first circumnavigation of the world was complete.

A FATAL ENCOUNTER IN THE PACIFIC

Magellan befriended Columbu, the rajah of the island where his ships were anchored. He and many of his people soon converted to Christianity, but the rajah told Magellan of some islands nearby where the locals refused to convert. Magellan, like all Spanish explorers, was commissioned to bring souls to God, and decided that they must be punished. A group of his men were sent to attack the island of Mactan. They destroyed the villages and killed the warriors, but the Mactan's leader stood firm. On April 26, 1521, Magellan led a force of some sixty men onto Mactan, where they were met by an opposing force of about three thousand. Too late Magellan realized that he had been led into a trap, and he ordered a retreat. Most of his men escaped back to their boats, but Magellan and about twelve of his men were left stranded. The Spaniards who had escaped refused to come to the aid of their Portuguese captain, and he was stabbed to death. In the words of Pigafetta:

The natives continued to pursue us, and picking up the same spear four or six times, hurled it at us again and again. Recognizing the captain, so many turned upon him that they knocked his helmet off his head twice, but he always stood firmly like a good knight, together with some others. Thus did we fight for more than one hour, refusing to retire any farther. An Indian hurled a bamboo spear into the captain's face, but the latter immediately killed him with his lance, which he left in the Indian's body. Then, trying to lay hand on sword, he could draw it out but halfway, because he had been wounded in the arm with a bamboo spear. When the natives saw that, they all hurled themselves upon him. One of them wounded him on the left leg with a large cutlass, which resembles a scimitar, only being larger. That caused the captain to fall face downward, when immediately they rushed upon him with iron and bamboo spears and cutlasses, until they killed our mirror, our light, our comfort, and our true guide.

THE *VICTORIA* LIMPS HOME

Magellan's remaining men accepted an invitation to a feast by the rajah of Cebu, who got them thoroughly drunk and killed most of them. Juan Carvalho took command and ordered the burning of the *Concepcion*, along with all Magellan's records, in the hope that evidence of their treachery would be destroyed. The *Trinidad* and *Victoria* set sail, running amok around the southwest Pacific for four months, plundering and attacking ships and harbors. On November 8, they reached the Spice Islands and were welcomed by the king of Tidor, who invited them to stay and trade. In February 1522 they set off for the long return voyage, stocking up (according to Pigafetta's record) with "many bahars of cloves, plumage of the terrestrial bird of paradise, roots of ginger dried in jars … very many quintals of pepper … sandalwood, white gold … robes of silk …" The *Trinidad* headed east for the Spanish port of Panama, but was captured by a Portuguese fleet in the Pacific, and all on board were hanged as pirates. The *Victoria* headed west for Spain on February 13 and, after a gruelling voyage during which many of the men died of starvation and scurvy, finally arrived at San Lucar harbor in Spain on September 6, 1522.

Of the two hundred and seventy men who had set out, only eighteen returned alive. The *Victoria* had survived an epic journey of around 34,000 nautical miles around the world, discovering half a world never before traversed by Europeans. ❧

1519–1521
THE SPANISH DEFEAT OF THE AZTECS

After Christopher Columbus discovered the New World in 1492, stories of wealthy empires and fabulous riches encouraged many Europeans to travel across the Atlantic Ocean in search of their fortune. Spaniard Hernán Cortés was one of these thousands of adventurers, and perhaps the luckiest. By an amazing stroke of coincidence, he was mistaken for a god by the Aztec occupants of Central America, leading to his conquest of Tenochtitlán, the Aztec capital, in 1521 and the eventual Spanish occupation of much of South America and the Caribbean. The treasures plundered by Cortés and succeeding Spanish conquistadors (conquerors) and brought back to Europe were so great that the fragile economy of sixteenth-century Europe almost collapsed, while the lives of the people of the New World were changed forever, and great civilizations, such as the Aztecs, were destroyed.

Hernán Cortés was born in 1485 in the Spanish town of Medellin, to a family of "little wealth but much honor," according to his secretary. At the age of fourteen he commenced studying law and classics at Salamanca, in western Spain. He left before graduating and joined the Spanish navy as a clerk. In 1504 he travelled to the island of Hispaniola, a recently conquered Spanish colony in the Caribbean, where he worked as a farmer and trained as a soldier before joining the army of Diego Velázquez, participating in the conquest of Cuba in 1511; he was subsequently appointed mayor of the Cuban city of Santiago. By 1518 Velázquez was governor of Cuba and Cortés one of his most trusted allies. He originally commissioned Cortés to explore the Mexican coast, but changed his mind, perhaps

fearing that the ambitious Cortés would assume governorship of the mainland. But Cortés, mutinously, decided to go anyway, setting off with his mutinous fleet of some eleven ships, six hundred men, sixteen horses (unknown in the Americas at the time), numerous steel swords and shields, and about twenty guns, including a bronze cannon. The fleet made landfall on the Yucatan Peninsula, far from the center of the Aztec empire, and proceeded to sack the Mayan town of Tabasco. Cortés had heard many tales of fabulous riches further to the west and determined to claim and plunder the territory in the name of Spain and Christianity.

AN ASTONISHING CIVILIZATION

The fierce Aztecs ruled an empire encompassing most of Central America where they had created an astonishing civilization. On an island in the middle of Lake Texcoco, in modern-day Mexico City, stood a beautiful and opulent city with a population of some 250,000, making it one of the largest in the world. Tenochtitlán was just one of several such Aztec cities. Its two-storey royal palace contained hundreds of rooms, a three-thousand-seat hall, and walls covered with paintings, stone and wood carvings and solid-gold panels. It was surrounded by gardens with ponds and fountains, and a large zoo where its ruler Montezuma kept exotic birds and animals.

The Aztecs practised human sacrifice as part of their religion, often using captured soldiers from nearby states. Their need for a constant, daily supply of human hearts to offer to the sun-god Huitzilopochtli made them very unpopular with their neighbors—a situation which Cortés

would use to good advantage. Montezuma, who lived in an opulent palace in the center of Tenochtitlán, enjoyed god-like status and ruled a vast army.

The Aztecs believed that Quetzalcoatl ("Feathered Serpent"), a god who opposed human sacrifice, would one day return to punish them in what they called a "1-Reed year" on their calendar. These occurred every fifty-two years, and it so happened that 1519 was a 1-Reed year, and that Cortés made his appearance at the coastal town of Vera Cruz on April 22, the very day predicted by the prophecy. It was believed that Quetzalcoatl would be recognized for his white face and wearing dark clothes with a feather in his cap—just like a conquistador in uniform.

There had been other recent portents of evil for the Aztec world. A blazing comet crossed the skies; temples were hit by lightning, causing many to burst into flames; Tenochtitlán was hit by several unprecedented floods; and some said they had seen the water in Lake Texcoco boil.

When Montezuma's envoys met Cortés, they were overcome with both reverence and terror. It would not do to harm one of their most revered deities, but, on the other hand, if the newcomers with their terrible weapons were hostile, the Aztec empire was in grave danger. They presented Cortés with gifts including twenty women and a huge, solid-gold disc of the sun, the size of a cartwheel. One of the women was Doña Marina, who would learn Spanish and go on to accompany Cortés as adviser and translator in his future exploits. She also became his mistress and bore him a son.

Montezuma hoped that the strange intruders would be impressed, take their gifts and leave the Aztecs alone, but the ploy merely reinforced Cortés' determination to complete his terrible ambitions. He destroyed all but one of his boats, offering his troops a last chance to return to Spain, but none took up the offer. In any case, retreat or escape was now impossible for the Spanish contingent—it would be death or glory. Cortés wrote to Spanish King Charles V: "I intend to advance and see him [Montezuma] wherever he might be found and bring him either dead or in chains if he will not submit to your Majesty's crown." He correctly predicted that victory, and booty, would prevent him being punished for his mutiny against Velázquez.

THE AZTECS BELIEVED THAT THE GOD QUETZALCOATL WOULD ONE DAY RETURN TO PUNISH THEM, AND WOULD BE RECOGNIZED FOR HIS WHITE FACE AND DARK CLOTHES.

The Aztec capital of Tenochtitlán, where Montezuma welcomed Cortés, was larger than any European city in the 1500s.

AN INVASION, A MASSACRE AND A FAREWELL TO MONTEZUMA

Cortés' army began the trek to Tenochtitlán, receiving support from tribes who had suffered at the hands of the Aztecs. En route, they invaded the powerful state of Tlaxcala and gave the Indians their first sight of the awesome power of European weaponry. Though outnumbered by at least fifty to one, the Spaniards quickly won an overwhelming victory. The vanquished Tlaxcalans agreed to join his cause against the hated Aztecs. Cortés marched onwards to the city of Cholula, where Montezuma's agents tried to poison him. Cortés responded by massacring the city's entire population as a brutal demonstration of power before continuing onwards to Tenochtitlán. Montezuma's spies had told him of the Tlaxcalan alliance; so, rather than fight such a formidable force, he invited the Spaniards to cross the narrow protective causeways that led to Tenochtitlán. Upon meeting Montezuma, Cortés feigned friendship, but soon made him a hostage in a bid to protect his position, surrounded as he was by a quarter of a million furious Aztecs.

At the beginning of 1520 Cortés received word that a Spanish force was on its way from Cuba with a royal contract to imprison him and confiscate his bounty. He and most of his troops headed off to the coast, leaving Tenochtitlán in the hands of just eighty of his men. Cortés managed to defeat his would-be gaolers, and persuaded most of them to switch allegiance and join his cause in the battle for Tenochtitlán. But when Cortés returned, he discovered that there had been an uprising, and that his countrymen and his hostage Montezuma were under siege. The greatly outnumbered Cortés convinced Montezuma to address the furious mob from a tower in an effort to placate them, but they stoned him to death. On June 30, 1520, Cortés tried to escape with his men under the cover of darkness. He got away, but about two-thirds of his men were killed, and many others wounded. Some drowned as they swam across Lake Texcoco, weighed down by the gold that they had pillaged from Montezuma's palace. The dead Spaniards were offered as sacrifice, and their skulls and those of their horses were displayed on the enormous skull-rack in Tenochtitlán's main square. The remaining troops were pursued by hordes of Aztecs but, on reaching the other end of the causeway, the Spanish turned around, attacked and somehow emerged victorious. This awful night became known as *La Noche Triste*.

The Spaniards had another, invisible ally: they had inadvertently infected the city's population with smallpox,

THE SPANISH DEFEAT OF THE AZTECS

CONQVISTA DE MEXICO POR CORTES. 7.

which rapidly decimated the population and severely weakened the Aztec military force. Montezuma's successor, his brother Cuitlahuac, died of the disease after reigning for just 80 days.

Slaughter on the causeway—the Aztecs were no match for the sophistication of the Spanish weaponry.

RETURN TO TENOCHTITLÁN

Cortés, after reaching the safety of the coast, rounded up a seventy-five-thousand-strong army of Cuban mercenaries, Tlaxcalan volunteers and more new arrivals from Spain. On April 28, 1521 he returned to Tenochtitlán with 86 horsemen, 118 crossbowmen and musketeers, 700 swordsmen, his new native army, and 18 cannons. They were confronted by troops who no longer believed in the divinity of the interlopers. The Aztecs' primitive weapons included wooden swords edged with razor-sharp obsidian, wooden clubs known as *macanas*, lances, and axes. Some used bows, but their arrows were unable to penetrate the Spanish steel coats of armor.

Cortés and his brigands swarmed to the edge of the causeways and began their attack and siege on Tenochtitlán. The troops were split into three sections. Cortés' deputy, Pedro de Alvarado, took 30 horses, 18 bowmen, 150 Spanish infantrymen, and 25,000 Tlaxcalans along the northwest causeway. Cristóbal de Sandoval led 30 horses, 18 bowmen, 150 infantry and, 25,000 Tlaxcalans down the southwest causeway. Gonzalo de Sandoval advanced along the southeast causeway with 24 cavalry, 4 musketeers, 13 bowmen, 150 infantry, and 30,000 foot soldiers, while Cortés commanded 13 recently constructed brigantines which contained the remaining Spanish musketeers and archers. He left one causeway free hoping that the Aztecs would escape, rather than fight to the death, but few took this option. The Spanish first destroyed the city's fresh water supply; the Aztecs responded by showering them with the arms, legs, and heads of the Spaniards they had captured and sacrificed. The defenders hoped to demoralize the Christian Spaniards, knowing how appalled they were by the practice of human sacrifice, and screamed "Bad men, your blood appease our gods and will be drunk by our snakes." This psychological ploy would be used, unsuccessfully, for the duration of the siege. When the brigantines entered the lake from the river, the Aztecs attacked them with more than five hundred canoes but were repelled by Spanish gunfire. The Aztecs managed to slow the progress of the ships, and of the advancing causeway troops they were supporting, by driving wooden stakes into the bottom of the shallow lake. Many tried to swim out to the ships and surprise them, but this was rarely successful. Meanwhile, famine increased as the besieged city was unable to import foodstuffs from the surrounding countryside.

DEFENCE OF THE CAUSEWAYS

By June 9 the Spaniards had made some progress along the causeways; Alvarado in particular had advanced 1300 feet. Their progress was slowed by the Aztecs' destruction of the wooden bridges on the walkways, which they were forced to painstakingly repair time and again as the defenders destroyed by night what they had constructed by day. As the troops reached the edge of the city, they destroyed every house and used the material to repair the gaps in the bridges. The ships prowled the lake, smashing every canoe they could find, and stringing up the captured Aztec warriors from their masts. The Aztecs were not used to this style of battle—their custom was to capture prisoners from enemy states in a form of limited, ritualistic warfare with neighboring, loosely allied states, then offer them up as sacrifices—but they soon learned. They gleefully sacrificed all their prisoners, accompanied by the ominous pounding of a gigantic drum which the invaders learned to hate, knowing that their comrades' living hearts were being ripped out by priests encrusted in Spanish blood. Conquistador and diarist Bernard Díaz del Castillo wrote this gruesome eyewitness account:

> We saw them put plumes on many of them, and then they made them dance with a sort of fan in front of Huitzilopochtli. Then, after they had danced, the priests laid them on their backs on some narrow stones of sacrifice and, cutting open their chests, drew out their palpitating hearts which they offered to the idols before them. Then they kicked the bodies down the steps, and the Indian butchers who were waiting below cut off their arms and legs and flayed their faces, which they afterwards prepared like glove leather, with their beards on, and kept for their drunken festivals. Then they ate their flesh with a sauce of peppers and tomatoes.

SIEGE OF THE CITY

At one point Cortés was almost captured after he advanced too far past the nearest opening in the causeway. He was ambushed by Aztecs, who killed many of his men and drove him to the edge of a 65-foot gap. But his life was saved by a comrade who severed the arm of an Aztec chief who was hauling Cortés towards a canoe. The Aztecs bombarded Cortés with Spanish heads as they cursed him and taunted him with the claim that they had killed Doña Marina. But Cortés and the invaders, having crossed the causeways and invaded the city, were gradually destroying Tenochtitlán, forcing its ever-decreasing defence forces into a small area near the city center. Many of the starving Aztecs were little more than skin and bone, but they fought to the death nonetheless. Many were also dying of disease, particularly smallpox to which they had no resistance—unlike the Spaniards.

Cortés' three columns burned everything in their path as they advanced toward the marketplace in the city center. When they smashed the gigantic holy pyramid of Huitzilopochtli, they found at its apex a mountain of clotted human blood, whipped corpses and heads, and some the identifiable remains of their recently slain comrades. The carnage became enormous as the Aztec defiance wilted. On some days the Spaniards captured and massacred over ten thousand prisoners; at this point even the resolute, hard-hearted Cortés lost his stomach for the slaughter, and began trying to persuade King Cuauhtémoc (who had ascended the throne after the death of Cuitlahuac from smallpox) to surrender. But the Aztec king threatened to kill any of his countrymen who retreated, or dared to advocate peace. Not until the city was almost completely controlled by the Spanish was the king captured as he tried to escape in a canoe. The Spaniards tortured him until he revealed the location of the gold and other riches that they had gathered before they fled on *La Noche Triste*. Cortés led the final attack on August 13, 1521, and the Spanish victory was complete.

AFTER THE CARNAGE

Within forty years of Cortés' conquest of Tenochtitlán, Spain had plundered over 100 tons of gold—more than double the amount previously held in the whole of Europe. They also pillaged some 7000 tons of silver, and other riches in the form of precious stones, artefacts, woods, spices, food (including chocolate) and animal skins. Within eighty years, three-quarters of the Aztec population had died of smallpox and other imported diseases. It would be another three hundred years before Mexico regained its independence from Spain.

Meanwhile, Cortés was appointed governor of "New Spain," as the region was now called. Christian churches replaced Aztec temples and, in 1540, a new Spanish viceroy was appointed and Cortés returned to Spain. He died, poor and in debt, at Castilleja de la Cuesta, near the town of Seville, on December 2, 1547.

147

1533

HENRY VIII MARRIES ANNE BOLEYN

In 1527 a young woman at the English court, Anne Boleyn, caught the eye of the sovereign, King Henry VIII. When she refused to become his mistress Henry determined to seek an annulment of his marriage to Catherine of Aragon. The pope in Rome, however, refused this request—leading to a stalemate as both Henry and Anne refused to compromise their positions, setting in motion the end of Catholicism in England.

Henry Tudor was the second son of Henry VII, and, after the death of his elder brother, Arthur, in 1502, knew that he would one day be king. In his youth he was a keen student of a wide variety of learning, particularly the explosion of new, empirical knowledge that was beginning to appear across Europe. In addition to intellectual pursuits, he also became skilled in the various physical accomplishments expected of a nobleman, and by the time he ascended the throne in 1509 he was an accomplished athlete, jouster, hunter and dancer. He was very popular with the masses and widely admired for his excellent physique and appearance: he was an unusually tall 6 feet in height, powerfully built and very handsome.

A TUMULTUOUS TIME

On June 11, 1509, soon after his accession, Henry married his brother Arthur's widow, Catherine of Aragon. While the marriage seemed a successful one, she proved unable to provide a male heir, suffering several stillbirths and infant deaths, and produced only one living girl, Mary, born in 1516. While there was no legal hindrance to a female monarch, the fragile and treacherous nature of royal politics in Europe meant that a king was far preferable in terms of providing future stability. Contemporary wisdom held that a woman was too weak to rule alone, and would need to marry into another royal family, thus risking instability or war as the new king exercised his right to rule.

Henry eventually tired of Catherine, and her failure to produce a male heir, and embarked upon a series of unconcealed affairs with ladies of his court—which Catherine, by and large, endured with a stoic and gracious understanding. In about 1526 his attention was taken by Anne Boleyn, one of his wife's maids of honor. Henry had had an affair with Anne's elder sister, Mary, in 1520. Anne, daughter of aristocrat and successful diplomat Sir Thomas Boleyn, had spent much of her youth in France, eventually serving as a maid of honor for several years at the French royal court of Francis I, as her sister had done. She returned to England in 1522, taking up residence at Henry's court. The manners and style she had acquired in France did not go unnoticed, and she quickly gained a reputation as a most accomplished and intelligent courtier. She had received an excellent, wide-ranging education in the Netherlands and France, was fluent in French and Latin, and soon attracted numerous young suitors. She became secretly engaged to Henry Percy, son of the Earl of Northumberland and a famous debaucher, but when Henry discovered this he ordered the Archbishop of

A defiant Henry VIII presents his second wife, Anne Boleyn, to the court in 1533.

York, Cardinal Wolsey, to prevent the marriage. Henry had effectively delegated to Wolsey the power to rule England, freeing the king to concentrate on more hedonistic pursuits.

THE PURSUIT OF ANNE BOLEYN

Henry became completely besotted with Anne, but she refused his advances. Previous mistresses had rapidly succumbed to Henry's charms, but Anne was made of sterner stuff. Henry's usual practice was to discard and marry off his mistresses when he tired of them and Anne was determined to avoid that fate. Although Henry pursued her fervently, she kept him at arm's length, telling him she would not be seduced as an unmarried woman. She knew of Henry's disaffection with Catherine, and no doubt saw an opportunity to take advantage of his passion and to become queen. Anne's brother and her sister Mary were renowned for their promiscuity, and her mother's reputation was also suspect. King Francis had mentioned to the Duke of Norfolk "how little virtuously Anne had always lived." Her refusal to submit to Henry's advances, therefore, was almost certainly the result of calculating ambition rather than an inherent sense of morality.

Meanwhile, Henry had other concerns about his marriage. The Bible's Book of Leviticus warns that a man who marries his brother's wife (as Henry had) will be punished with childlessness and Henry, despite having received permission from Pope Julius II for the marriage, began to suspect that Catherine's failure to produce a son might be God's work. In addition, the leader of the French embassy, Gabriel de Grammont, Bishop of Tharbes, had told Henry that, even though the pope had permitted his marriage to Catherine, he was not sure that it was legitimate under canon law. From now on Henry wanted to do everything according to the precepts of church law.

A REQUEST FOR AN ANNULMENT

On June 22, 1527 Henry told Catherine that he had sent an envoy to Rome to ask Pope Clement VII for an annulment. This was the beginning of what became known as "the Great Matter"; it would dominate the court—and English domestic and foreign policy—for the next decade. Catherine and Henry continued to keep up appearances, dining together in public and maintaining courteous relations. Cardinal Wolsey's spies (at Henry's behest, and bribed by money, gifts, and sex) were keeping Catherine under surveillance and scrutinizing all her letters before they were sent. But as the pope had been recently imprisoned by Catherine's nephew and ruler of the Holy Roman Empire, King Charles V, Henry and Wolsey soon realized that he would probably be unwilling—or unable—to agree to an annulment. Henry thus put Wolsey in charge of facilitating the divorce. Wolsey, who was jealous of Anne's increasing influence, nonetheless had no choice but to comply. Anne would soon gain her revenge against Wolsey for disallowing her earlier marriage to the Earl of Northumberland.

Anne continued to play hard to get. When Henry became too ardent, she would retreat to her family home until Henry begged her to return to him. The Vatican archives contain seventeen letters from Henry to Anne dating from 1527 to 1529. In one he says: "Hence shall my heart be dedicate to you alone, greatly desirous that so my body could be as well ... Written by the hand of the servant who in heart, body and will is, Your loyal and most ensured servant, H." In another letter he ends with: "wishing myself, specially an evening, in my sweetheart's arms, whose pretty dukkys [breasts] I trust shortly to kiss." (We know that Anne somehow resisted these passionate beseechings, because other letters, according to a 1530 report by the Spanish ambassador, provide proof. And in 1531 Henry, who did not hide his affairs from Catherine, swore to her that he had not committed adultery with Anne.)

In 1528 the pope, wishing to play for time, sent his envoy Cardinal Lorenzo Campeggio to England to hear Henry's arguments for annulment, and to try to broker a reconciliation between Henry and Catherine. By now the Great Matter had led to the formation of three factions in a fierce power struggle among the nobility, and in the court and the houses of Parliament. One bloc comprised followers of Cardinal Wolsey and supported Henry, another secretly supported Catherine but wanted to get rid of Wolsey, while a third faction, which would soon become the most powerful, supported Anne and also wanted an end to Wolsey's influence. The last group attracted many who had long sought a way to end Wolsey's monopoly of power; they saw Anne as the key.

STORMY NEGOTIATIONS

Campeggio quickly realized that the king and queen were irreconcilable, so he suggested that Catherine enter a convent, which would clear the way for Henry to remarry. Catherine refused outright, and Campeggio reported to Clement that Henry "sees nothing, he thinks of nothing but Anne; he cannot do without her for an hour. He is constantly kissing her and treating her as if she were his wife."

> THE ENGLISH PUBLIC LOVED CATHERINE AS MUCH AS THEY HATED ANNE. AFTER CATHERINE'S EXILE, THE CITIZENS OF LONDON RIOTED TO SHOW THEIR DISAPPROVAL.

On May 31, 1529 the English church leaders, led by co-judges Wolsey and Campeggio, convened to consider Henry's case for annulment. Catherine refused to recognize the court and made a dramatic exit. The case went ahead anyway, but after weeks of inconclusive discussion Campeggio announced on July 23 that the case must now adjourn to Rome. Henry stormed off in fury, and blamed Wolsey for his failure to stage-manage the proceedings more effectively. Wolsey was demoted, stripped of his government office and property, and exiled to Yorkshire. Henceforth his influence would decline until his death on November 29, 1530 as he was travelling from Yorkshire to London to face charges of treason—which would undoubtedly have led to a death sentence.

STALEMATE—AND AN EXECUTION

The next few years were marked by stalemate, as Henry and the pope both dithered. Henry could not see a way to annulment, while Clement's hands were tied by his reluctance to offend Henry or Charles V. Henry exiled Catherine to remote Kimbolton Castle in Cambridgeshire. (For the rest of her life, Catherine of Aragon referred to herself as Henry's only true common law wife. She died from cancer, alone and still in exile, in January 1536.)

Anne's execution at 8 a.m. on May 19, 1536 was the first public execution of an English queen.

Meanwhile Lord Chancellor Thomas More told Henry that he would not support the divorce, but did support Henry in his persecution of Lutheran heretics. In 1530 he refused to sign a letter asking the pope for an annulment. In 1531 he requested Henry to permit his resignation after being forced to sign an oath declaring the monarch "the Supreme Head of the English Church," but Henry declined. However, in 1532 More was allowed to relinquish office after claiming illness. After refusing to attend Anne's coronation in 1533, he was found guilty of high treason and beheaded.

The English public loved Catherine as much as they hated Anne. After Catherine's exile and, as Henry and Anne's relationship became increasingly public, citizens in London rioted to show their disapproval of the union. Anne became known as "the great whore" and Henry's urgency to sort out the annulment situation increased. He realized how much he had depended on Wolsey to run the ship of state as he found himself barely capable of organizing the daily affairs of the court, let alone the religious, political and romantic storms that raged all around. Anne's position was unchanged; until she had a ring on her finger and a crown on her head, her bed was off limits to the king.

Henry was becoming increasingly paranoid and megalomaniac, when an ally appeared in the form of Thomas Cromwell—an urbane, well-travelled banker, parliamentarian and former servant of Wolsey. Henry appointed him to the Privy Council and he quickly became as indispensable to Henry as Wolsey had been. In Italy Cromwell had become familiar with the writings of Machiavelli, whose pragmatic, often brutal ideas about politics and the supremacy of the state he began putting into practice. One of his closest friends was a minor cleric, Thomas Cranmer, whom Henry appointed Archbishop of Canterbury. Cranmer advised Henry that God is the only authority, and that no human, not even the pope, could replace His word. This, of course, was music to Henry's ears. In August 1532 he appointed Anne to the high nobility, meaning that any child she bore would qualify for accession to the throne. In January 1533 he married her, very recently pregnant, in a secret ceremony which Cranmer and Cromwell pronounced legal under both clerical and common law. Anne Boleyn had achieved her ambition. The pope responded by excommunicating Henry from the Catholic Church, but by now papal authority in England was so diminished that nobody in power took any notice.

ANNE BECOMES QUEEN

Henry now resumed his sexual affairs but Anne, unlike Catherine, did not turn a blind eye. Henry brusquely reminded her that she owed her position to him, and should "shut her eyes and endure as her betters had done," or he would send her back whence she came. Still unpopular among the general citizenry, Anne's only hope was to deliver a male heir but, unfortunately for her, she gave birth to Elizabeth on September 7, 1533. Anne became increasingly miserable and demanding, as the carousing Henry became ever more autocratic and preoccupied with his religious and political machinations.

By October 1535 Henry was involved with Jane Seymour, one of Anne's ladies-in-waiting. Unlike Anne she was demure, tactful and submissive—traits Henry had come to admire in a woman. He now wanted to be rid of Anne as much as he had wanted to have her in the first place. Following a miscarriage in early 1536, he alleged that she had seduced him into marriage by using witchcraft. Jane started using Anne's delaying tactics, refusing Henry's lavish gift in March of a purse of gold sovereigns, on the grounds that she was unmarried. Their affair continued, but in secret. By now

Catherine was dead, opening the way for Charles V of Spain to form a strategic alliance with England. He still refused to recognize Anne as the legitimate queen, but let it be known that he would approve a new wife. Henry decided to eliminate Anne, and ordered Cromwell to produce evidence of crimes that would enable him to sentence her to death. Cromwell duly produced "evidence" that Anne had committed adultery on twenty-two occasions, including with her own brother George, Lord Rochford. Most historians agree that all the charges were fabricated.

A SERIES OF EXECUTIONS

On May 2, Anne was arrested and transported to the Tower of London to await trial. Over the next few days, five of her co-accused, including her brother, were also arrested and incarcerated. All, including Anne, were found guilty and condemned to death. On May 17, the men were executed, even as Cranmer annulled Henry's marriage to Anne and declared their daughter Elizabeth a bastard. Anne was executed two days later, not by the usual rusty axe, but by an expert French swordsman whom Henry, in a gesture of "compassion," had retained for a fee of £24. On the scaffold she made a speech in praise of Henry, probably in an attempt to protect Elizabeth. She was buried in the Tower's chapel of St. Peter. The next day, May 20, 1536, Henry and Jane Seymour were formally betrothed. Jane gave birth to a son, Edward, on October 12, 1537, and died twelve days later from an infected placenta.

AFTERMATH

Henry went on to plunder many of England's churches, and confiscate their assets and land. The reformation of the church under Thomas Cromwell continued as Henry gradually attained more power than any other English monarch before or since. But by the time of his death on January 28, 1547, Henry had become paranoid, obese, and generally unsightly—the result of a life of dissipation, over-indulgence, and debauchery. The many portraits of him over the years attest to this gradual deterioration.

His reputation also suffered because of the many people he had put to death—it is estimated that he had executed more than 70,000 people, including two of his wives—and the fact that he had virtually bankrupted the country by waging continual wars. He is the perfect embodiment of nineteenth-century English historian Lord Acton's dictum: "Power tends to corrupt; absolute power corrupts absolutely." ❧

1572

THE ST. BARTHOLOMEW'S DAY MASSACRE

The French Wars of Religion were an ongoing conflict between French Catholics and the Huguenots that erupted in 1562 with a massacre of Huguenots by French troops in the town of Vassy outside Paris. The Huguenots (the origins of the name remain uncertain) were French Calvinist Protestants. Their beliefs were based on the notion that salvation could be achieved through individual faith alone, without a Church hierarchy as intermediary. The religious conflict would continue, albeit with numerous periods of ebb and flow, until 1598. Catholic France was first confronted with Protestant ideology in the 1520s, but Protestantism had failed to attract the level of support in France that it had in England and throughout Scandinavia. Furthermore, it was strenuously opposed by the French monarchy and much of the country's Catholic nobility.

There were seventeen million Roman Catholics in France in the 1560s and just over a million Huguenots; yet, despite this seeming disparity, life in sixteenth-century France was increasingly characterized by rising Catholic–Protestant tensions. In 1561, the sermon of a Protestant minister preaching in the city's 5th arrondissement was interrupted when a group of Catholics rang the bells of a nearby church to drown him out. In the melee that followed, more than a hundred people, mostly Huguenots, were killed. The following year a force of sixteen thousand men, led by Catholic nobleman Anne de Montmorency, defeated an eighteen-thousand-strong Huguenot army at the Battle of Dreux. Tensions subsided, however, with the signing of the Edict of Saint-Germaine in 1570, engineered by Catherine de Medici to promote tolerance between the country's Protestant and Catholic factions.

A ROYAL MARRIAGE
BRINGS RISING TENSIONS

Although it was a walled city, religiously conservative, and an intellectual and religious bulwark against Huguenot encroachment, Paris was not immune to Protestant influences. In August of 1572 hundreds of Huguenots had flooded into the city to celebrate the marriage of Marguerite of Valois, the Catholic sister of the King of France, Charles IX, to the Huguenot Henry III of Navarre, which was to take place with the usual pomp and ceremony on August 18. In sixteenth-century Europe marriage was often seen as a means to overcoming religious differences and to create convenient alliances, but this was not destined to be one such an occasion. The proposed marriage of Marguerite and Henry brought consternation to the city's Catholics. Henry, though baptized a Roman Catholic, had been raised a Protestant by his mother Queen Jeanne III, the inspiration of the French Huguenot movement. Jeanne III had declared Calvinism (a form of Protestantism inspired by religious reformer John Calvin) to be the official religion of Navarre, a small kingdom on the Atlantic coast straddling the Pyrenees between France and Spain. Henry had only recently ascended to the throne upon his mother's death in June, and French Catholics were nothing short of horrified at the prospect of Henry, through marriage, placing himself in line to become a future king of France.

Catherine de Medici, the mother of King Charles IX, had pushed hard for the marriage between her daughter and Henry. Never claiming to understand Huguenot theology or motivations, she appeared to be driven only by a desperate desire to further the interests of her own line, the House of Valois, with little regard to the wider consequences of the marriage. Though she failed to gain papal approval for the union, Catherine nevertheless convinced Cardinal de Bourbon to marry the couple, and the day of the wedding came and went without incident—even though the ceremony at Notre-Dame cathedral was boycotted by the Paris *Parlement*. Three days later, on August 21, long-simmering hatreds were brought to the boil with a failed assassination attempt on the Huguenot leader Admiral Gaspard de Coligny, political head of the Calvinist Party. Coligny had remained in the French capital to discuss Huguenot grievances over the Edict of Saint-Germaine and was returning to his rooms at the Hôtel de Béthisy when he was shot in the arm by an unknown assailant.

The admiral was carried to his lodgings, where a bullet was taken from his elbow and a pair of scissors was crudely used to amputate an injured finger. Coligny, who was among the most respected of the Huguenot leaders and enjoyed a close relationship with King Charles, was visited by the king who gave the admiral his word—very likely born out of fear of imminent, city-wide Huguenot reprisals—that whoever was responsible for the shooting would be quickly and unsympathetically brought to justice. The king and Coligny were undoubtedly close friends. But there were some in the French government, and in particular the aristocracy, who thought them too close, and they worried about the implications for Catholic France should Coligny convince Charles to convert to Protestantism. The capital had long been rife with rumors that the Prince of Condé, Louis de Bourbon of the Protestant House of Bourbon, planned to kidnap Charles and convert the impressionable, twenty-two-year old king to Protestantism once away from the influence of his advisers. With so many Huguenots still in Paris in the wake of the royal wedding, circumstances had delivered those in the government of Charles IX an unprecedented opportunity to eliminate the entire Huguenot leadership with one swift, decisive blow.

LEADERSHIP ELIMINATED

On the morning of Sunday August 24, St. Bartholomew's Day, Coligny and dozens of others in the Huguenot hierarchy were murdered in a series of coordinated assassinations that could only have been organized at the very highest levels of the French government, although whether or not Charles himself had personal knowledge of the plot remains open to question. The signal to commence the killings came with the ringing of the church bell at Saint Germaine l'Auxerrois not far from the Louvre. Coligny ordered his valet to assemble the guards the king had made available for his protection, but was horrified to learn it was these very guards who now were intent upon ending his life. When confronted by his assassin, the fifty-six-year-old Coligny is said to have pleaded, "Young man, reverence my grey hairs." But to no avail. He was stabbed in the chest with a dagger, his body thrown from an upper storey window. Moments after his lifeless corpse struck the pavement below, his head and hands were severed from his body and the head taken to Catherine de Medici. Hours later, the decapitated torso of Gaspard de Coligny was seen on the end of a rope being dragged by groups of ragged-looking children around the streets of Paris. It was finally brought to the gallows at Montfaucon and strung up ingloriously by the heels. Catherine later had his head embalmed and sent to Pope Gregory XIII, though there is no historical document that suggests he ever took receipt of it. Nevertheless, Gregory was so delighted by the news of Coligny's demise that he ordered hymns of praise to be sung throughout Rome.

Meanwhile Coligny's fellow Huguenots were being killed wherever they were found. François III de La Rochefoucauld, a confidant of Coligny and member of a famous French noble family that could trace its aristocratic roots back to 1019, had dined with King Charles himself just the previous evening—and yet he was stabbed in the heart after six masked men burst into his room. Charles de Teligny, a member of the staunchly Huguenot Rouerque family and son-in-law of Admiral de Coligny, was killed by a musket shot in the corridors of the Louvre after he refused to recant his Huguenot beliefs. The Marquis de Renel was chased to the bank of the River Seine before being shot by his own cousin, Louis de Bussy d'Amboise, as he attempted to cast off in a boat. His body was then thrown into the river.

A LOCAL BUTCHER NEAR THE PONT NEUF BOASTED TO THE KING THAT HE HAD GLORIOUSLY DISPATCHED ONE HUNDRED AND FIFTY HUGUENOTS IN A SINGLE EVENING.

SLAUGHTER OF THE HUGUENOTS

Contemporary and historical accounts are in agreement that these targeted slayings were a premeditated act calculated

The rampage began with Huguenot leaders hunted down and murdered, even in their own homes.

merely to eliminate the Huguenot leadership; they were never meant to escalate into a citywide conflict. Catholics and Huguenots had already fought three civil wars, and nobody wanted a fourth. What was to follow, however, was an unprecedented wave of bloodshed. Historians suggest that when the head of Coligny was put on a spike and shown to the Paris mob, it released a rage that had been simmering for decades. In the mistaken belief they were acting on behalf of their king, the mob took over from the royal troops and began seeking out and killing the city's Huguenots.

Peter Ramus, the French humanist and reformer who had converted to Protestantism in 1561, spent the first two days of the massacre hiding at the back of a bookshop on the Rue St. Jacques before making his way under cover of darkness to his home, where he was found and stabbed to death on August 26. The wife of King Charles' very own *plumassier*, who was in charge of the king's ornamental plumage and feathers, was taken from her home on the Notre Dame bridge, a well-known Protestant enclave, stabbed, and thrown still alive into the river. Paris had become a city in which reputations and innocence counted for nothing. The young and the old, women and children, were dragged from their homes and killed in the streets. Horse-drawn carts soon filled with the bodies of the slain and were hauled to the River Seine, into which they were

In one of the most horrifying holocausts in history, as many as fifty thousand Protestants were killed in the massacre.

thrown without ceremony. One particularly gruesome story tells of a little girl whose parents were both killed before her. She was then dipped in their blood and cautioned that the fate that befell her parents would also be hers if she ever dared to become a Huguenot. Paris had gone mad.

Such vast numbers of bodies were thrown into the river and left there for so long that the city's residents refused to eat fish taken from the river for months to come. The injured, bound hand and foot, were thrown still breathing from the city's bridges. Doors were battered down and citizens were dragged into the streets regardless of what their religious convictions might be. Huguenot houses were burned to the ground, reflecting the Catholic belief that fire purifies heresy. Even the entrances to the king's palace became smeared with blood. Huguenots fled their homes in the thousands and were even chased from the gates of the city into the surrounding countryside.

Estimates of the total number of deaths varied widely. Official records of the numbers killed were never kept, and there was the problem of the many wild and exaggerated claims of slaughter, each one more gruesome than the last. A local butcher near the Pont Neuf boasted to the king that he had gloriously dispatched one hundred and fifty Huguenots in a single evening. One man, a gold and silver artisan called Crozier, boasted that he'd killed four thousand Huguenots by dressing himself as a hermit and luring them into his hermit's enclave where he then proceeded to murder them one by one. What is not in dispute is that city officials offered its grave diggers a premium to bury the growing piles of corpses that littered the city's streets.

THE VIOLENCE SPREADS

In the wake of the massacre King Charles wrote to the governors of France's provinces and regional cities stressing that what occurred was not the result of religious intolerance but a response to a direct and personal threat posed by Admiral de Coligny and his followers upon the royal family. He directed that any armed retaliation by Huguenots in the provinces should be handled with care and diligence and not be used as a further pretext for murder. Over the course of the following six weeks, however, the exact opposite was to happen. The violence in Paris was repeated throughout the towns and villages of France. In Rouen in Normandy, those Huguenots able to escape the killing fled the city, taking its Protestant population from more than sixteen thousand to just over three thousand. Similar accounts were received from Tours, Angiers, Toulouse, and all the way to Lyon in the south. In Lyon almost the entire Huguenot population of five thousand were killed, maimed, or forced to flee for their lives. Among the dead was the French composer Claude Goudimel. The River Rhône flowing south from Lyons, like the Seine, was so polluted by corpses that downstream in the Mediterranean city of Arles the people refused to drink its water.

There were massacres in Orleans, Bordeaux, Angers, and also in Nîmes. At Nîmes, five years earlier, Huguenots had proved they were capable of those same murderous excesses when they massacred one hundred Catholics in 1567. In the town of Meaux, northeast of Paris, about two hundred Huguenots were herded into the town's prison, then brought out one by one into its central courtyard where they were either stabbed or beaten to death. The Duke of Anjou (one of a group of powerful nobles opposing the Huguenots) wrote a letter to Count de Montsoreau, the governor of Saumur in the Loire Valley, which said, in part: "You must go at once to Saumur with all your supporters and kill any Huguenots you find there." Across France anywhere between five thousand and fifty thousand people were murdered, depending upon whether one chooses to believe the accounts of Roman Catholic apologists

or Huguenot survivors. The general consensus of modern scholars puts the figure at around twenty thousand.

The atrocities of the Saint Bartholomew's Day massacre, however, do not tell the whole story. Amidst the bloodshed there were also many isolated acts of defiance, heroism and tolerance. The governor of Auvergne, for instance, thought a letter given to him, supposedly signed by the king, ordering him to kill the Huguenot population there, to be a forgery and refused to hand them over. The governor of Bayonne, Viscount Orte, responded to an order to round up the Huguenots there by writing a letter to King Charles claiming not to be able to find a single executioner among Bayonne's citizenry willing to carry out the deed.

AFTERMATH OF THE MASSACRE

The consequences of the Saint Bartholomew's Day massacre were far reaching. Huguenots, who had always believed in the good faith of the monarchy, did so no longer. Their trust had been irrevocably betrayed and their leaders began referring to Catherine de Medici as "that Jezebel." They abandoned their founder John Calvin's injunction to remain loyal subjects to their king and took up the revolutionary's mantra of justifiable rebellion should a king or queen sufficiently disregard what is in the best interests of their subjects. Huguenot leaders who previously enjoyed little or no influence in decision-making because of their radical, militant positions were once again being listened to. The massacre may have brought joy to the papacy in Rome, but the general response amongst France's Protestant allies and Catholics abroad was that of horror and disgust.

Throughout September 1572, with their leadership now decimated and their way of life in disarray, Huguenots withdrew to their provincial fortress towns such as Nîmes and La Rochelle, accompanied by thousands of moderate Catholics. In the country's southwest hundreds of sympathetic Catholics were seen alongside Huguenots fleeing Toulouse for the nearby Protestant stronghold of Montauban, and before the end of the year the Catholics and Huguenots of France would be embroiled in yet another bloody civil war, ignited when the nominal capital of the Huguenots, La Rochelle, denied the king their taxes as a protest against the massacre.

War was declared on the port city in November 1572 and it was laid siege to in February 1573. By May, however, with the city continually being resupplied from the sea and after heavy losses on both sides, the siege was abandoned. Over the next seven years there would be three more bloody conflicts—the Fifth War (1576), the Sixth War (1577), and finally the Seventh War (1580), culminating in the ascent to the throne of the Protestant king, Henri de Navarre. ❧

1588

THE DEFEAT OF THE SPANISH ARMADA

The weather had been unseasonably cold all that spring and summer of 1588, with heavy storms and rain squalls rolling across England and turning the Channel into a cauldron of choppy waves and gale-force storms. The morning of July 29 dawned to unpromising grey skies. Mists hugged the ocean surface and fast-moving showers raced across the waves. Still, the watchers stationed at Lizard Point in Cornwall, at the southwestern tip of England, squinted dutifully off into the distance.

Later that morning, one of the guards, peering through his telescope, spotted the dark shapes of dozens of ships far out over the water. This was what they had been waiting for. Within minutes, torches were touched to piles of resin-soaked brush that stood at the ready. First one beacon burst into flame, then another and another, until a glowing necklace of fire lit up the southern English coastline, all the way from Cornwall to Plymouth, in whose harbor lay the English fleet. The fires were an alarm call, warning of the approach of the Spanish Armada, the great invasion fleet that had been expected for some time and which, the English knew, posed the most serious threat their nation had faced for centuries.

For their part, the Spanish in *la felicísima armada*—"the fortunate fleet"—could see the glow of the fires and guess what they portended. The Spanish high command sent out

---

Philip II of Spain. Philip saw himself as a protector of Catholicism and resolved to restore the religion to England.

an English-speaking captain in a small tender, who returned that night with four terrified English fishermen in tow. They revealed that the English fleet led by the Lord Admiral, Charles Howard, Second Baron Howard of Effingham, and his famous second-in-command, Sir Francis Drake, was coming to make a fight of it.

The ensuing naval battle would become a part of English folklore—it has long been recounted how Drake calmly continued his game of bowls after hearing the news of the Armada's approach, and how the whole of England reacted to the dark news with pluck and courage. But the battle also had a very real effect on subsequent events. Although more Spanish ships were eventually lost to gales and storms than to English cannon fire, England's victory began its rise to the status of a first-class naval power; it also marked a major shift in naval strategy, away from close-in fighting to the use of accurate, long-range cannon fire.

DEEP DIVISIONS

Long-standing differences and a succession of disputes led to this extraordinary battle between England and Spain. In a sense, the countries and their differences were embodied by their two rulers—Elizabeth I of England and King Philip II of Spain. Elizabeth, daughter of King Henry VIII, was a Protestant, while Philip was a staunch Catholic who had once had close ties to England. He had been married to Mary Tudor, Elizabeth's Catholic predecessor, and had even intervened with Mary to save Elizabeth's life after a Protestant plot to put her on the throne instead of Mary was uncovered.

But after Mary's death in 1558 and Elizabeth's accession to the throne, the two monarchs and their countries had become enemies. This was partly the result of religious differences and partly because England had begun to flex its muscles, particularly at sea, which put it at odds with Spain, then the most powerful seagoing nation in Europe. English seafarers like Sir Francis Drake attacked Spanish shipping, seemingly with impunity; Elizabeth publicly turned a blind eye to such affronts to the Spanish pride and purse, but privately profited by them.

NO ORDINARY FLEET

The huge Spanish fleet that entered the Channel on July 29 was 125 ships and thirty thousand men strong. About twenty-five of the ships were mighty fighting galleons, the rest armed merchantmen, transport ships and pinnacles for swift scouting and message-bearing between the larger ships. The Armada was commanded by the Duke of Medina-Sidonia aboard his flagship, the *San Martín de Portugal*. Philip had appointed Medina-Sidonia to the job after the previous commander, the

Marquess de Santa Cruz, had died unexpectedly. Medina-Sidonia had a high social standing in Spain and was a brilliant administrator, but he was not an experienced sea admiral, although he had very able advisers.

As the Spanish ships passed by, the English fleet left Plymouth and deliberately fell in at the rear of the Armada so that it had the wind behind it and therefore an advantage if the Spanish turned to fight. Lord Admiral Howard was aboard his flagship, the *Ark Royal*, Drake was on his ship, the *Revenge*. The much lighter and more nimble English fleet contained thirty-four royal warships and almost two hundred other vessels.

However, most of these were small, privately owned and lightly armed pinnacles. In fact, although the English fleet was sizeable, it was in a desperate position. For the Armada was no ordinary fleet of warships, but rather the most potent invasion force that had ever been pointed at England. Of its thirty thousand men, only seven thousand were sailors, the rest soldiers. The ships contained powerful land artillery, siege equipment, six months' worth of food and wine, and tons of ammunition. At this point, however, the immediate

objective of the Armada was not to fight the English fleet, but to head north and rendezvous with a second Spanish force in the Netherlands.

This painting of the clash of the Spanish and English fleets captures the tumult of the battle, albeit in a fanciful composition.

"GOD'S OBVIOUS DESIGN"

The Netherlands, or Low Countries, as it was also known, was the flashpoint in the feud between Philip and Elizabeth, a place where their contrasting cultures and religions clashed. It had been under Spanish rule for some time, and the Dutch Protestants there had been persecuted for their religion and forced into the role of second-class citizens. Under William of Orange, the northern provinces revolted. When the southern provinces declared their loyalty to Philip by signing the Union of Arras on January 6, 1579, seven of the northern provinces declared their independence a few weeks later with the Union of Utrecht, regarded as the founding document of the modern Netherlands.

In response, Philip had William of Orange assassinated in 1584, and, thereafter, Spanish control of the region began to increase once more. But in the following year, Elizabeth, alarmed at the Spanish presence so close to her northern shores, openly sent an army to the Netherlands after years of covert aid to the Dutch rebels. This helped the Dutch force a stalemate between rebel forces and those of the Duke of Parma—and enraged Philip.

Then, in 1587, Elizabeth's execution of her cousin, the Catholic Mary, Queen of Scots, who was plotting against her, greatly heightened religious and political tension. In her will, Mary left her accession rights to the English throne to Philip, formerly her brother-in-law. Philip and his advisers subsequently convinced themselves that the security of Spain relied upon the destruction of Elizabeth's regime and the restoration of a Catholic monarch to the throne of England. Even the pope agreed. It was, as one Spanish noble put it, "God's obvious design" that Spain rule England.

PACKING FOR AN INVASION

The invasion strategy had been cobbled together from two separate plans. The aggressive and strategically astute Duke of Parma had suggested placing thirty thousand men in seagoing barges in the Netherlands and making a surprise assault across the Channel. The Marquess de Santa Cruz, who commanded Philip's Atlantic fleet, wanted instead to take a huge invasion force of some fifty-five thousand men from Spain and land in England or possibly southern Ireland.

It was Philip who decided to merge the two plans. The Armada was to sail up the Channel with part of the invasion force. When it reached Flanders, it would protect Parma's men as they crossed to Kent, then unload its own forces. In total, some fifty thousand well-provisioned Spanish troops would then find themselves ashore in England, a force that Elizabeth would be hard pushed to resist. Many in Philip's court envisioned a slaughter of the English. Some of the Spanish commanders even brought their finest china with them, thinking they would need it once they settled comfortably into English castles.

The only problem was, the massive build-up of the Armada had become the worst-kept secret in Europe. The English had already delayed the action once in the previous year when Sir Francis Drake had wreaked havoc among the Spanish ships at Cadiz, and Drake had sortied out twice in the summer of 1588 to attack the Spanish fleet on its own coast, only to be forced back by storms.

So when the sails appeared off Plymouth, the English, refitting in port, knew what was afoot. They also knew that if they did not stop the Armada before it reached the Netherlands, an invasion of England would almost certainly occur.

NEW RULES OF BATTLE

When the Spanish fleet saw the English coming out for them, they formed with startling precision into a crescent, something that had obviously been practised, with the heaviest warships on the two horns of the crescent, and the slower ships within. The English attacked at about nine in the morning of July 31, just off Plymouth. Divided into two groups, one headed by Lord Howard, the other commanded by Drake, they struck at the flanks of the Spanish in single file, discharging their cannon at long distance.

This cannonade may be thought of as the opening blow of modern naval warfare. Traditionally, ships tried to get close

to each other, attach themselves to the enemy with grappling hooks, and fight what were essentially mini-infantry battles at sea. But the English, under the influence of a radical naval thinker named John Hawkins (who was in Drake's group at the battle), had recently overhauled their strategy, tailoring their ships to move fast, and so avoid being boarded, and to cannonade with accuracy. An English innovation helped greatly here—the replacement of fixed gun mountings by moveable carriages, which allowed cannon to be reloaded more rapidly.

On July 31, however, the cannonading had little effect initially. The English were skittish, perhaps overawed by what must have looked like an extraordinary metropolis of ships, a veritable city on the sea. One powerful Spanish galleon came out almost tauntingly and challenged three English ships—Drake's *Revenge*, Martin Frobisher's *Triumph*, and John Hawkins' *Victory*—to close and do battle. The English declined the invitation, preferring to lob shots from a distance.

As the engagement continued, the Spanish remained in control, outmaneuvering Howard and Drake. On August 6, after a week of running battle, Medina-Sidonia anchored his fleet off the port of Calais, waiting now for word from the Duke of Parma that he was ready to invade. The English, who were nearly out of ammunition, waited offshore, plotting their next move. In the meantime, Queen Elizabeth, needing to stir her people, famously appeared in front of her troops at Tilbury, telling them: "I know I have the body but of a weak and feeble woman, but I have the heart and stomach of a King, and a King of England, too! And I think it foul scorn that Spain or Parma or any prince of Europe should dare invade the borders of my realm!"

> VICTORY OVER THE SPANISH ARMADA PROVIDED THE ENGLISH WITH AN ENDURING PATRIOTIC MYTH—MUCH LIKE WASHINGTON'S VICTORY AT TRENTON OR THE FRENCH STORMING OF THE BASTILLE.

FLUSHING OUT THE ENEMY

Unfortunately, despite the months of planning, the Duke of Parma had been slow in putting together his own invasion force, and his twenty thousand men were now being blockaded in their ports by Dutch rebels. To make matters darker for the Spanish, the water along the Flanders coast was so shallow that the deeper-draught Armada vessels could not strike close enough to shore to breach the blockade—something that the Spanish planners should have foreseen.

Around midnight on August 7–8, as Medina-Sidonia pondered his next move, the English sent eight fire ships into the anchored Spanish fleet. These vessels were not just drifting old pinnacles filled with pitch and tar, but warships running at full sail, holds full of gunpowder, ready to be set alight by their suicidally courageous crews, who leaped off at the last possible moment. Two of the English fire ships penetrated the Spanish defences, wreaking havoc. The Spanish ships were forced to cut their anchor cables to escape and move to the open ocean— exactly where the English wanted them.

THE BATTLE OF GRAVELINES

On August 9, the English closed in for a pitched, decisive battle off Gravelines, a town in the far southwest of the Spanish Netherlands. The engagement lasted eight hours, with English and Spanish ships engaged in ferocious cannon duels, tacking back and forth in the shallow waters. Finally, the effect of the cannonading took its toll on the confused and scattered Spanish fleet. Four vessels were lost to English gunfire and the entire fleet was very nearly stranded on the sandbanks off Flanders.

When the wind turned to the west, pushing the ships off the sandbars, Medina-Sidonia was faced with a choice: cross to invade England on his own, return south through the channel, or head north and west, around the British Isles. With the prevailing winds against him, he chose this last course. Unfortunately for the Spanish, he did not know two things: one, Howard's English fleet was out of ammunition and could not have withstood a Spanish attack; and two, horrible gales would face the Spanish on the west coasts of Ireland and Scotland.

During the long return voyage, thousands of Spanish sailors drowned in storms, and hundreds were killed by scavengers along the British coastlines. By the time it returned to Spain, the Armada had lost about half its invasion fleet, as well as fourteen thousand soldiers and seamen. During the battle, the English had lost only seven ships.

A PATRIOTIC MYTH

In the short run, the victory saved England from a Spanish invasion and a Roman Catholic monarch on its throne. It also helped preserve an independent Netherlands. Of the two royal adversaries, Elizabeth was to live longer, until 1604, while Philip, blinded by cataracts and with a crippled arm (probably from a stroke), died in 1598.

Eventually, the defeat of the Spanish Armada was seen as marking the beginning of English supremacy over the seas, which reached its full fruition after Admiral Lord Nelson's victory at Trafalgar in 1805, as well as the demise of Spain as a great naval power. But more recently, historians have concluded that Spain's demise did not really begin until the end of the Thirty Years' War in the middle of the next century, and that England achieved its pre-eminence on the high seas only after a long period when the Dutch—whom they had saved—ruled the oceans.

Regardless of this, victory over the Spanish Armada provided the English with an enduring patriotic myth—much like Washington's victory at Trenton or the French storming of the Bastille—that would be summoned back into the public consciousness again and again when the country faced dark days in the future. ❧

1614—1615
TOKUGAWA AND THE SIEGE OF OSAKA CASTLE

In Japan, the period from the mid fifteenth century through to the beginning of the seventeenth century is known as the Age of Warring States. It was an era of sporadic civil wars fought between feudal lords called *daimyo* that ended with the siege of Osaka Castle in 1615. The daimyo fought one another in open defiance of the nominal rule of the emperor and the country's shoguns or military dictators, whose influence had been in decline for more than a century.

Born in 1536, Toyotomi Hideyoshi joined the Oda clan as a servant and sandal bearer, and rose to become a trusted general to Oda Nobunaga, one of the country's pre-eminent warlords. In a country long beset by feudalism Nobunaga was slowly establishing himself as one of Japan's most influential leaders, aided by Hideyoshi, who proved himself an adept negotiator and military strategist, convincing many samurai ("those who serve") to defect to Nobunaga and thus avoiding many a bloody conflict. Hideyoshi also presided over many pivotal battles and conquered the western Chugoku region for Nobunaga in 1576. By the time of Nobunaga's death in 1582 he had conquered more than a third of the country. Hideyoshi then became Nobunaga's successor, though because of his peasant origins could never hope to become a shogun. Nevertheless he did achieve the title of retired regent, or *taiko*, and in 1583 he began the construction of a castle at Osaka.

CONSTRUCTION OF THE CASTLE BEGINS

The Osaka castle would be based on the design of Nobunaga's great castle at Azuchi. It would mimic its extensive use of granite blocks in its 20-foot defensive walls and would have a massive central tower to afford its cannons maximum range; a series of irregularly shaped battlements would provide its defenders with a multitude of retaliatory options when under siege. There would, however, be one significant difference. Osaka castle would be on a far grander scale than Azuchi, and would be the most impressive castle ever constructed in Japan.

The castle, when completed, must have seemed impregnable. A complex arrangement of wet and dry moats surrounded inner walls that rose behind each other in tiers topping out at a staggering height of 395 feet. Its central tower (*tenshu*) rose up five storeys and was part of an integrated series of multi-layered defences that included towers and ramparts, all set within an outer perimeter wall with a circumference of almost 9 miles. Immediately to its west was the Sea of Japan; to its north, the convergence of the Yamato, Temma and Yoda rivers created a muddy expanse of rice paddies and shoals that made any approach all but impossible. To the east, the Huano River provided a further natural barrier.

THE GROWING POWER OF IEYASU TOKUGAWA

When Hideyoshi died in 1598 he left behind his only son, the five-year-old Hideyori. Hideyoshi had established a Council of Five Elders to rule in his son's place until he came of age, and of those five one was Tokugawa Ieyasu. Tokugawa, born in 1543,

Portrait of Shogun Tokugawa Ieyasu in court dress.

was an old ally of Nobunaga. He emerged as the dominant member of the council and cleared his way to become Japan's undisputed shogun after the Battle of Sekigahara in October 1600, which led to him consolidating his power throughout western and central Honshu. In 1603 Tokugawa revived the title of shogun and established the Tokugawa shogunate. He also arranged for his daughter to marry Hideyoshi's heir Hideyori, then just ten years old, in the hope of averting an eventual conflict. However, a confrontation between the ageing Tokugawa and the young Hideyori, whom Tokugawa had allowed to remain in his father's castle in Osaka, became increasingly likely. In 1611, after a meeting in Kyoto in which Tokugawa could see for himself the threat posed by his young rival (and the Toyotomi clan that he headed), he began to devise a plan that would remove Hideyori from his castle stronghold.

By mid 1614 it was clear to everyone that war was inevitable—with the exception of the somewhat naïve Hideyori, who even refused a delivery of English gunpowder because he couldn't foresee a use for it. When Tokugawa heard that Hideyori had turned the carts of gunpowder away from the gates of Osaka Castle he astutely purchased the gunpowder himself, as well as five British guns, which included four 4000-pound giants that could shoot 18 pounds of shot and were considered superior in range and firepower to their smaller Asian alternatives. By July

During the siege of Osaka, Tokugawa wiped out the Toyotomi family, effectively eliminating any rivals to his reign.

Hideyori had learned that Tokugawa was planning an assault on the castle and sent out a call for *ronin*, wandering samurai and swordsmen not aligned to any master or feudal lords, to join him in the defence of the Toyotomi clan. In no time at all the young Hideyori had almost ninety thousand men at his disposal, veteran fighters mostly, who had previously refused to align themselves with anyone but who now had thrown their lot in with the House of Toyotomi. Some of Hideyori's new recruits were Christian samurai who had suffered sporadic periods of persecution under Tokugawa's rule and considered him to be a "devil of war." There were also thousands of men who had been ruthlessly displaced by Togukawa's men after the Battle of Sekigahara fourteen years earlier. This decisive battle had been vast in its scale, and there were many who were eager for an opportunity to exact some revenge.

All that Hideyori was lacking was a commander able to lead his men in battle. Although he had been trained in many of the disciplines of the samurai, the one thing he lacked was experience on the battlefield. Though unable to find anyone with the sort of battlefield experience he was looking for, Hideyori was fortunate in acquiring Sanada Yukimura, a defensive specialist who helped turn the already heavily defended castle into an impenetrable edifice. One of Yukimura's first ingenious acts was to trade thousands of his men's samurai swords for spades—and to put the samurai to work beyond the castle walls digging a ditch linking the Nekoma Stream with the Ikutama Canal just beyond its western wall. This created a moat more than 235 feet wide and 37 feet in depth. He also built an outer wall or barbican. Despite Yukimura's emphasis on defence, however, he also had something of a reputation as an audacious offensive tactician; he tried in vain to persuade Hideyori to launch a raid on Kyoto and to convince the emperor to declare Tokugawa a traitor. But Hideyori rejected the plan, preferring instead to ensconce himself behind the walls of his castle and wait for Tokugawa to come to him.

THE WINTER SIEGE

In November, with almost one hundred and ninety-five thousand troops at his disposal, Tokugawa began what was to become known as the Winter Siege, focusing on eliminating a number of outposts east of Osaka Castle that guarded the castle's approaches and looked over its various supply routes. The first to fall, on November 19, was Kizu Fort, a small cluster of fortifications at the mouth of the Kizu River garrisoned by eight hundred men; six days later the village of Imafuku with its six hundred defenders was taken. Tokugawa's forces were well armed and many carried arquebuses, low-velocity Portuguese-designed muzzle-loading muskets that fired shot that could pierce armor if fired at very close range. More of Hideyori's outposts succumbed to Tokugawa's samurai, and by the beginning of December the armies of the Tokugawa shogunate had marched within sight of Osaka Castle.

Despite repeated shows of strength and a string of small victories, Tokugawa decided he would attempt to infiltrate into Osaka Castle and take it by stealth rather than rush headlong into an armed conflict. He had successfully managed to bribe a low-ranking commander, Nanjo Tadashige, who promised he would open the castle gates and permit the shogun's troops entry. The bribe, by all accounts a moderate sum at best, came close to paying off, but Tadashige's treasonous act was uncovered at the eleventh hour and he was executed.

On December 20, Tokugawa, still keen to avoid a long siege and costly battle, initiated a series of overtures to Hideyori by dispatching a merchant from Kyoto to the castle gates with the offer of a negotiated settlement. No reply was received. More offers were sent, but each one was met with silence.

TOKUGAWA ADVANCES ON THE CASTLE

Now impatient to test the defensive capabilities of the castle, Tokugawa decided he would make an attack on its southern flank, which just happened to be the one commanded by Yukimura, who was defending the southern perimeter with more than seven thousand men. Tokugawa launched the assault in two waves, the first with twelve thousand troops under the command of Maeda Toshitsune, an able but unremarkable general, and the second consisting of ten thousand Red Devils from the Ii clan, commanded by Ii Naotaka and Tokugawa's grandson, Matsudaira Tadanao.

On January 3, Toshitsune's samurai began to advance. The red flags attached to the tops of poles fastened to their backs waved in the breeze as a single, undulating river of red. They approached the walls of the castle in tight formation but were driven back under a withering onslaught of arrows and musket fire as they were scaling the castle walls. Naotaka's Red Devils, with their trademark red breastplates, fared a little better, managing to penetrate the castle's Hachomeguchi gate and the outer defences constructed by Yukimura known as Sanada's Barbican, further along the southern flank. Their progress, however, was halted by more than eight thousand heavily armed Toyotomi troops under the command of Kimura Shigenari who fell upon the Red Devils' tightly packed formations. Hundreds were felled by Shigenari's muskets, and lead shot from the defenders of the pierced barbican wall, and the Red Devils were forced into a headlong retreat that turned into a rout. The attack had been a disaster, but Tokugawa was not easily dissuaded. On the following day, another attack was mounted, this time on the Tanimachiguchi gate, by a four thousand strong force led by Todo Takatora, a loyal and fearless samurai whose family had been in allegiance with the Tokugawa clan since the mid 1590s. Takatora's troops managed to briefly gain a foothold on the castle ramparts, before they too were driven back in yet another fierce counterattack. Tokugawa was now convinced that the castle would not fall to assaults by ground troops.

At the same time as the failed attacks were taking place, Tokugawa had ordered the construction of a network of ramparts and battlements that had all but encircled the castle, into which he now began to place his three hundred cannon.

> BY 1611 TOKUGAWA COULD SEE FOR HIMSELF THE THREAT POSED BY HIS YOUNG RIVAL AND BEGAN TO DEVISE A PLAN THAT WOULD REMOVE HIDEYORI FROM HIS CASTLE STRONGHOLD.

167

The time had come to demonstrate the massive superiority he enjoyed in artillery over his besieged opponent. The majority of his cannon were of English and Dutch origin and included 3½-inch sakers and 5½-inch culverins. These cannon were both capable of long-range bombardment and far superior to Hideyori's smaller, breech-loading swivel guns, which were barely able to fire beyond their own outer defensive walls.

On January 8 the bombardment began, but it soon became apparent that even Tokugawa's culverins were no match for the thick walls of Osaka Castle. Although the bombardment was unsuccessful, it did have the effect of significantly unnerving Hideyori's mother, who now urged her son to seek a diplomatic end to the siege.

Diplomacy was also on the mind of Tokugawa. Although he had his enemy surrounded and his own troops dug in, he was looking forward to a long and tedious and morale-sapping siege in what had so far been a bitterly cold winter. Tokugawa offered Hideyori any fiefdom in Japan as well as a guaranteed revenue should he voluntarily leave Osaka Castle. He also insisted that Hideyori allow him to fill in the castle's moat and demolish the barbican. Finally, on January 22, Tokugawa received a letter signed by Hideyori saying he was prepared to put aside any thoughts of rebellion against the Tokugawa shogunate, and Tokugawa agreed to withdraw his troops. The Winter Siege, or *Fuyu no Jin*, had come to an end.

THE STAGE IS SET FOR THE SUMMER SIEGE

Hideyori, however, had been emboldened by his successful resistance and chose to remain defiant. In Tokugawa's absence Hideyori made repeated attempts to interfere with the filling in of the castle moat, and spent the spring of 1615 gathering even more troops to his side. By the end of April he began striking out again at Tokugawa's outposts, setting the stage for the *Natsu no Jin*, the Summer Siege, which would prove to be the final act in the siege of Osaka Castle and bring about the end of Hideyori's stubborn defiance.

The Summer Siege began as a series of running battles as Hideyori went on the offensive—but things did not go well for him. On May 24, on the approaches to the Tokugawa stronghold of Wakayama Castle, a force of five thousand men loyal to Tokugawa defeated Hideyori's three thousand men. On June 2, not far from the imperial tombs at Domyo-ji, a further force of three thousand—this time commanded by Sanada Yukimura—confronted the ten-thousand-strong army of one of Tokugawa's most accomplished strategists, Date Masamune, and suffered heavy casualties. Yukimura retreated hastily to the supposed safety of Osaka Castle, but when he arrived was confronted with the sobering sight of 150,000 Tokugawan samurai in the fields to the south of the castle preparing for one mighty, final assault on Hideyori's stronghold. The coming battle, the Battle of Tennoji, would be the last large-scale samurai confrontation in Japanese history.

Yukimura steeled the remnants of his army for one last fight but was himself suffering from exhaustion and unable to go on. When confronted by a Tokugawa samurai, Yukimura admitted who he was and slowly removed his helmet. Moments later, in full view of his troops, he was beheaded.

A BRUTAL CONCLUSION

Tokugawa then ordered the commander of the Red Devils, Ii Naotaka, to fire on the castle's wooden keep with his artillery. Soon flames were engulfing the castle's inner courtyards. Hideyori, in one last desperate attempt at freedom, rode out to confront the enemy but was literally chased back into the castle, allowing the enemy at his heels to enter the grounds. The following day the once impregnable Osaka Castle was in flames. Almost all of its defenders were slaughtered, including Hideyori's mother, his young son (who was, ironically, Tokugawa's grandson), and Hideyoshi's wife, Yodogimi. Hideyori committed *seppuku*, a traditional samurai suicide involving disembowelment.

With the final destruction of the powerful Toyotomi line, the Tokugawa clan was able to establish an uninterrupted line of shogunate rule, ushering in a period of relative peace and prosperity in Japan that would last for more than two and a half centuries. Tokugawa Ieyasu proved to be a master politician as well as a fine military strategist who won far more battles than he lost and possessed a sweeping vision for a unified Japan. Not long after the siege of Osaka Castle, Tokugawa retired to Sunpu Castle, where he died on June 1, 1616. In 1617 his remains were taken to Nikko Tosho-gu shrine in Tochigi Prefecture, where they remain to this day. 🔹

1666
THE GREAT FIRE OF LONDON

ondon in the mid-seventeenth century, with a population of about half a million, was a great and thriving metropolis, one of the most important urban centers in the world, and yet it covered an area so small it represents only a tiny semicircle on a map of the present-day city. Old London—essentially medieval London—was surrounded by walls 33 feet high, a vestige of the days when outlying highwaymen often raided the city. Within the walls, rich and poor lived closely together in startling contrasts. The poor inhabited tumble-down garrets made of wood, while across the street might be the home of a wealthy and mighty banker. (Another quarter of a million people lived in wooden shanties in the out-parishes or suburbs that had sprung up outside the city walls.) Most people ate bread or grains or whatever they could steal, yet the wealthy feasted daily on rich fare almost beyond our imagining—everything from pheasant's tongue to salads of selected flowers to huge sides of beef and pork.

Yet the great leveller was the London streets. They were so narrow that houses on either side seemed to lean over, lending a strange darkness to the byways below. This was not a planned city, with squares and parks and grids, but a haphazard one, with side streets ending in blind alleys without names. Open sewers ran down the middle of the roads. There were no footpaths. Not only did pedestrians have to beware of fast-moving horses and carriages, but they had to keep a sharp eye out lest a window open above and a chamber pot of "night soil" be emptied on their heads. The streets were in general so foul that many people wore small metal platforms that fitted to the bottoms of their shoes, which they would then remove before entering their homes.

In 1664, a writer named John Evelyn published a pamphlet called *Fumifugium*, dedicated to King Charles II, in which he warned of the dangers of so many open fires and furnaces in such a "wooden … and inartificial congestion of Houses." A few days later, on September 2, 1666, when a great fire rose up from a baker's oven and smote London a blow of "infinite mischief," Evelyn was there to watch his warnings gain the status of prophecy.

WARNINGS IN THE SKY?

Actually, there were other signs and portents in the year before the fire, celestial events, which, it was decided, portended momentous things. In December of 1664, and yet again in March of 1665, comets were seen in the night sky over London and there was much debate over what they meant. Samuel Pepys, the famous diarist and then Secretary of the Admiralty, went out one night to view one of these heavenly visitors, noted how close it seemed to London's rooftops, and reported that people felt "it imported something very peculiar to the city alone."

To Puritans and other supporters of Oliver Cromwell, until recently head of state, the comets were a sign that God himself was unhappy with the return of the Stuart monarchy in the form of King Charles II. But to many astrologers, the comets predicted a return of the plague, the deadly disease that had sporadically appeared in London since the Black Death of the fourteenth century, most recently in 1625. Each reoccurrence, the astrologers said, had been presaged by a comet.

Of course, this was sheer poppycock, but the plague did return, and with a vengeance. Beginning in about April of 1665, London was stricken by a horrible outbreak of bubonic plague. The Great Visitation, as it became known, killed perhaps seventy-five thousand to one hundred thousand people, causing horrible scenes of suffering. The rich and prominent, including Parliament and the king, fled the city. The poor died in droves, to be dragged out and dumped on carts and buried in mass graves. People driven insane by the final stages of the disease accosted others on the street, trying to infect them.

The plague raged until the winter of 1665–66, then seemed to subside. By the summer of 1666, plague deaths were still averaging about thirty or so a month, but they seemed to be mainly confined to outlying suburbs. Merchants returned, warehouses filled up again with goods, commerce restarted. By September of 1666, London was breathing a wary sigh of relief.

And then the king's baker forgot to douse his fire.

THE BAKER'S HOUSE

Thomas Farynor, baker to King Charles II, usually doused the fire in his oven before going to bed at night, but on Saturday September 1, he appears to have forgotten to perform this basic task. At about two o'clock on Sunday morning, he was awakened by a fire that was already engulfing the first floor of his house. Reacting quickly, he was able to get himself, his daughter Hannah, and a manservant onto the roof, but a maid, afraid of heights, refused to accompany them, and thus became the first victim of the fire.

Farynor lived on Pudding Lane, about 100 feet or so from Thames Street, a busy thoroughfare lined with warehouses, which ran along the river wharves. Pudding Lane was typical of hundreds of London side streets, so narrow a hand barrow could barely fit through it, according to one contemporary observer. The houses were all of timber that had been weatherproofed with pitch. It had been a hot, dry summer and it did not take long for the blaze to spread. Farynor and his companions were able to escape, scrambling over rooftops, but the blaze ate the houses behind them as a fresh wind blew up. The next street west, Fish Street Hill, ignited as piles of straw in the yard of an inn exploded into fire.

IT HAD BEEN A HOT, DRY SUMMER IN LONDON AND IT DID NOT TAKE LONG FOR THE BLAZE TO SPREAD.

Charles II by the studio of Pieter Nason (1612–90). At the height of the fire, Charles took to the streets to rally firefighters.

BLUDDER'S BLUNDER

At about four o'clock in the morning, after bucket brigades had failed to douse the blaze, local constables woke the Lord Mayor of London, Sir Thomas Bludworth (known to those who didn't like him much as "Bludder"), and warned him that a fire was spreading. Apparently, Bludworth had been out carousing the night before and didn't much like being dragged down to the scene of what was, to his eye, merely another London blaze. He took a quick look around Pudding Lane, and then made the remark for which his name was to live on in notoriety. "Pish," the hungover Mayor said. "A woman might pisse it out!"

And then he went back to bed. But by 7 a.m. on Sunday, when Samuel Pepys climbed the Tower of London to get a better view, an east wind that he described as a "gale" had stirred the fires into one "lamentable" conflagration. Tongues of flame had sped down Pudding Lane and Fish Street Hill and devoured warehouses full of oil, brandy, pitch and tar, and mounds of coal and piles of lumber. Explosions rang out as the flames then engulfed the ancient church of St. Magnus Martyr.

FIREFIGHTING, LONDON-STYLE

There were fire engines in mid-seventeenth-century London, but they were rudimentary ones—essentially large pumps mounted on carriages, which could shoot out relatively strong streams of water. Moreover, there was no London fire brigade; instead, the vehicles were privately owned or sponsored by local parishes. In all the chaos, contacting the owners and obtaining permission to use the pumps proved almost impossible. And any pump companies that did get into action found themselves hampered by large crowds wandering the narrow streets, which were also clogged with furniture people had dragged from their burning homes in the hope of salvaging something from the blaze.

The normal strategy for fighting fires in London was to create fire breaks—empty areas over which a fire cannot travel, for lack of fuel. This was done by pulling down buildings with fire-hooks—huge iron hooks attached to long poles or ropes, which were routinely kept in public buildings. Fire workers would frantically sink the hooks into the top beams of houses and pull them down, collapsing the house. The next step was to clear the debris, creating a barren stretch.

Unfortunately, by the time Bludworth finally ordered this to be done, he had the demolition started too close to the fire, so that the flames either ate up the buildings as they were being torn down, or blazed through debris that had not yet been cleared. Consequently, as Samuel Pepys observed, "an infinite great fire" was soon headed right at London Bridge.

THE GREAT FIRE OF LONDON

OLD LONDON BRIDGE

The London Bridge that spanned the Thames at the time of the Great Fire was an extraordinary structure, lined with houses and shops separated by a passageway only a few feet wide. The fire attacked the bridge greedily, leaping from rooftop to rooftop, as people fled the span in panic. Onlookers thought the entire bridge would collapse. Indeed, the fire seemed intent on heading for the south shore of the Thames, but was slowed by an empty area. A few sparks reached the south side of the river, causing several houses to go up in flame, but the blaze was ultimately checked there.

Seeing the fire speed across the bridge was enough for Pepys, who, taking advantage of his status as a senior naval official, urgently requested an audience with the king to advise him of the dire seriousness of the situation. Flames were now roaring to the north and west through London, leaping high into the air, sucking oxygen out of the atmosphere—Pepys even noticed pigeons simply dying where they stood, like canaries in a coal mine. King Charles told Pepys to command the Lord Mayor to spare no effort in demolishing huge swathes of the city to halt the fire, but when Pepys returned and found Bludworth, the mayor was practically hysterical and of little use to anyone.

By Sunday evening, boats carrying families and their belongings swarmed across the river to the south bank, where

The Great Fire of London, by the Dutch artist Lieve Verschuier (1630-86), shows the city blazing out of control while residents flee.

onlookers lined the shore, watching the extraordinary blaze. It was, as one observer remarked, like seeing "a foretaste of the Last Judgment."

DEVOURING A CITY

Monday dawned a hot, dry, sunny day, and as a powerful east wind drove the fire on through London, houses, churches and buildings went up in explosions of flame. A fire storm had been created, with oxygen from the high winds feeding the flames. The dark cloud rising above London could be seen in Oxford, 60 miles away. Citizens no longer made any attempt to fight the fire, but now fought fiercely to get away. The rich were willing to pay the poor almost any sum to help cart their belongings from the city, which engendered the line in John Dryden's later poem "Annus Mirabilis," about the events of 1666: "The rich grow suppliant, and the poor grow proud."

It was essentially every man for himself. With no one in charge of the firefighting—Bludworth seems to have fled—

the king stepped in and put his brother, the Duke of York, in charge. He created fire posts around the city, and the men at these posts tried to create fire breaks by pulling down houses. But the blaze moved too fast, and eventually gunpowder was used to blast out fire breaks.

It was a time like no other. An East India Company warehouse full of spices blew up into smoke and the smell of incense drifted across the city. The king himself rode with his guards through the blazing ruins, carrying with him a bag of silver coin to pass out to heroes.

CONSPIRACY THEORIES

As the fire continued to consume London on the Tuesday, rumors of arson spread through the town. The smell of incense proved to some that the blaze was the work of the Catholic Church. Others blamed the Dutch, with whom the British had fought a war for naval supremacy, or England's perennial enemies, the French. "Many Citizens, having lost their houses and almost all that they had, are fired with rage and fury," wrote one chronicler. "Arm, Arm, Arm doth resound the Fields and Suburbs with a dreadful voice." Mobs roamed the streets, attacking anyone who appeared to be Dutch or French. King Charles sent armed troops out to save the foreigners from such attacks. Later, the government was forced to go through a lengthy investigation of the causes of the fire, just to prove there was no conspiracy.

Finally, by Wednesday, the wind had died down and, with it, the fires. Two hundred thousand homeless Londoners looked in astonishment at their great city, now turned to ash and charred wood. About 13,000 houses, 87 parish churches, St. Paul's Cathedral, the Royal Exchange, the Custom House, all the city prisons, and the General Post Office had been destroyed.

John Evelyn walked the ruined streets of the city he had tried to save from fire and noticed that those around him, wandering in shock, looked like "men in some dismal desert." The official death toll, amazingly, stood at four, but no one really believed this—you could smell the death in the smouldering ruins—and today it is thought that thousands must have died.

A NEW LONDON

If the Great Fire had a silver lining, it was that, from then on, far more attention would be paid to fire safety. In 1667, a Rebuilding Act was passed, and Londoners set about with a will to make their new city a shining one. Ten thousand houses were built in less than eight years—and by ordinance, they were made of brick. The old pestilential open drains disappeared. Streets were widened and provided with footpaths for the first time. Insurance companies, which had lost heavily in the fire, now realized that it would be to their benefit to hire and train competent firefighters. When the new London arose, it was not only a far more beautiful city—the great architect Christopher Wren designed forty-nine new churches, as well as a new St. Paul's Cathedral—but also a far safer one.

There were some who felt that getting rid of the old wooden houses also helped get rid of the plague, which disappeared at about this time. More likely, rats died fast enough, trapped in the fire, to reduce the incidence of the disease. Despite these benefits, however, the Great Fire of London remained a feared and almost apocalyptic event, one that fulfilled earlier warnings: "All astrologers did use to say Rome would have an end and Antichrist come, [in] 1666," said mystic Anthony à Wood, "but the prophecie fell upon London."

1692
THE SALEM WITCH TRIALS

*If it was the last moment I was to live,
God knows I am innocent of any thing of this nature.*

ELIZABETH HOWE, EXECUTED JULY 19, 1692

The Salem witch trials hold great historical significance for America. They mark a defining moment in the shift from Puritanism, with its values of kinship, minimalism and devoutness, to the new, evolving world of individualism, sophistication, competition and freedom of personal belief. They also clearly illustrate the methods by which human groups initiate, rationalize and escalate persecution. Because so few people were involved, the trials illustrate with particular clarity the processes that humans have always tended to use against those they wish to marginalize, demonize or annihilate.

Witch hunts were the result of superstition and a general climate of persecution. In seventeenth-century Salem, as elsewhere, fear of the devil—and of divine punishment for heresy—led to an environment where many feared the influence of witches on god-fearing members of Christian society. Witches were believed to reject Jesus Christ, worship Satan, and make contracts with him in return for riches or supernatural powers. They were also believed to fly at night to secret trysts, or "sabbats," where they indulged in orgies, defiled crucifixes and used demons to help them undertake various evil acts. They supposedly changed form into other humans or into animals, and abducted children in order to eat them. No doubt some people did worship the devil or try to use witchcraft to cause harm, but despite the lack of any empirical evidence, sorcery and other specifically defined "supernatural acts" were forbidden under law in Europe and America.

EARLY SIGNS OF DISCORD AMONG THE FAITHFUL

Many of Salem's citizens were descended from the Pilgrim Fathers, plain-living English Puritans who had sailed to nearby New Plymouth in the *Mayflower* in 1620 to escape persecution at the hands of the recently formed Church of England. By 1690 a commercial elite was developing as debate raged over how independent the small Salem Village (now Danvers) community should be from New Plymouth. Two of Salem Village's most prominent families, the Porters and the Putnams, were involved in a power struggle over control of the village and its church.

Harvard University dropout and failed businessman Samuel Parris, following the invitation of Putnam clan leader Thomas to take up the position of minister at the Salem Village church, arrived in Salem with his family in 1689. He accepted, but only after negotiating an unprecedentedly generous contract which,

George Jacobs pleads for mercy after he is accused by his grand-daughter Margaret (center), acting to save her own life.

among other things, required the parishioners to supply him with free firewood. Putnam also agreed that Parris could own the pastor's house, which traditionally remained the property of the town. The appointment outraged the Porters and many other community members.

THE FIRST "SYMPTOMS" OF WITCHCRAFT ARE MANIFEST

In January 1692 Parris' daughter Betty and niece Abigail started having strange seizures—throwing things about, gibbering incoherently, contorting their bodies and crawling under furniture. The following month Parris' Caribbean slaves, John Indian and his wife Tituba, used their knowledge of voodoo to bake a "witch-cake" with the girls' urine, which they fed to the family dog. This was designed to break whatever spell was affecting the girls, as dogs were commonly believed to be "familiars" (servants) of Satan. Soon other children, including Mary Lewis, Ann Putnam, and Elizabeth Hubbard, began to exhibit similar symptoms of madness. When pressed, they accused Tituba and two others, Sarah Osborne (who had married her black slave and rarely attended church) and Sarah Good (who was poor and often begged food from her neighbors), of bewitching them. The three women (all fitting the stereotype of a witch) were charged with witchcraft, interrogated for several days by magistrates, then jailed on March 5.

The two girls then accused a respectable churchgoer, Martha Carey, of bewitching them. On March 21 she was examined and imprisoned. On the same day Ann Putnam's mother, also named Ann, began having similar seizures, and blamed seventy-one-year-old Rebecca Nurse. Three days later Rebecca was imprisoned, along with Sarah Good's four-year-old daughter Dorcas. By the end of April, as the accusations, examinations and imprisonments continued apace, twenty-three more alleged witches had been imprisoned. They included John Proctor and his wife Elizabeth, Bridget Bishop, Mary and Phillip English, and Giles Corey. Several of them had been accused by Thomas Putnam. On May 4, George Burroughs, who had served as Salem Village preacher between 1680 and 1683, was arrested in nearby Maine following allegations of witchcraft, and imprisoned in Salem.

THE ACCUSED ARE TRIED

On May 14, Sir William Phipps arrived from England to take up his appointment as governor of Massachusetts, accompanied by Increase Mather, who became a minister in Boston. By the end of May about forty more people had been imprisoned in Salem. On June 2, Governor Phipps appointed a court, led by Deputy Governor William Stoughton, to try the alleged witches. If found guilty, the only way an accused could avoid the death penalty was if they were pregnant, or had pleaded guilty in the first place. Bridget Bishop was found guilty of witchcraft and, on June 10, became the first fatality when she was hanged on Salem's Gallows Hill. Nathaniel Saltonstall, a member of the judges' panel, resigned the same day. Increase Mather and his son Cotton produced a report titled *Return of the Ministers Consulted*, which advocated both "caution" and "speed and vigor" in the witchcraft trials. On June 29, Sarah Good, Rebecca Nurse, Sarah Wildes, Susannah Martin, and Elizabeth Howe were tried and found guilty; they were hanged on July 19.

John Proctor, a farmer who had been outspoken against the witchcraft proceedings from the outset, was also the first male accused of witchcraft. On August 5, he and his wife Elizabeth, along with George Burroughs, John Willard, George Jacobs, and Martha Carrier, were brought to trial and found guilty. All but Elizabeth (spared because she was pregnant) were hanged on August 19.

Between September 9 and 17, fifteen more Salem residents were tried and condemned to death. Five were spared, either because they confessed or were pregnant, but on September 22, Martha Corey, Mary Easty, Margaret Scott, Alice and Mary Parker, Ann Pudeator, Samuel Wardwell, and Wilmott Reid were hanged. These would be the last hangings. On September 19, Giles Corey, who had refused to enter a plea or attend the court, was pressed to death—the statutory penalty for refusing to stand trial, which until then had never been used in Massachusetts. Corey, a supporter of the Porter faction and critic of the entire proceedings, had been accused by Ann Putnam and imprisoned in April. He was stripped naked and a board was placed upon his chest. As more and more boulders were added to the board in an attempt to elicit a confession, he asked only that more weight be added in order to hasten his death.

HYSTERIA SPREADS

By now members of nearby communities in Andover, Ipswich, and other rural areas of Massachusetts were being accused, arrested and examined as the witchcraft hysteria spread. In October the afflicted girls were summoned to

> WITCHES WERE BELIEVED TO REJECT JESUS CHRIST, WORSHIP SATAN AND MAKE CONTRACTS WITH HIM IN RETURN FOR RICHES OR SUPERNATURAL POWERS.

Andover, then Gloucester, where they made more than fifty accusations. But they went too far, stimulating a backlash when they named several highly respectable and prominent churchgoers (as many of the Salem accused had indeed been), including Lady Phipps, the governor's wife. Many of those who disagreed with the whole proceedings had remained silent, noting the deadly fate of John Proctor and others who had spoken out. The young accusers had been particularly harsh in their accusations against anyone who cast aspersions on their allegations.

On October 2, Increase Mather preached a sermon called "Cases of Conscience Concerning Evil Spirits Personating Men," which shed grave doubt on the accuracy of "spectral visions" such as were claimed by the Salem girls. He said: "It were better that ten suspected witches should escape, than one innocent person should be condemned." Five days later, merchant and astronomer Thomas Brattle wrote a long letter to an unknown recipient, which argued fervently against the trials and convictions. We may assume that he intended it to be circulated in the hope of influencing Governor Phipps over the future of the trials. He wrote, "I cannot but condemn this method of the justices, of making this touch of the hand a rule to discover witchcraft; because I am fully persuaded that it is sorcery, and a superstitious method, and that which we have no rule for, either from reason or religion."

VOICES OF REASON

At last voices of reason were starting to be heard above the hysterical tumult. Finally, on October 12, Governor Phipps forbade any further imprisonments at Salem, and on October 29 officially dissolved the court. In November the afflicted girls were again summoned to Gloucester, but this time their fits and accusations were ignored. After this they did not make, nor were asked for, another accusation. In May 1693 Phipps ordered the release of all the convicted witches remaining in jail, thus ending the entire sordid episode. Nineteen people had been hanged and one pressed to death, while five had died in jail.

AFTERMATH

Though the trials and their attendant horrors had come to an end, the repercussions were felt for years to come. The burden on the accused and their families was severe. In addition to the great emotional distress they had suffered, there were economic consequences. Those who remained in jail were obliged by law to pay for their food and "lodging." Until these debts were discharged, they could not secure their release. Also, many had their properties confiscated by the authorities. Fields and their crops were left untended or laid to waste while buildings fell into disrepair.

In the years that immediately followed, Salem failed to prosper, and many saw this as punishment for the great wrongdoing perpetrated by the accusers. Relationships between the Reverend Samuel Parris and his community had been irrevocably undermined, and three years after the trials ended the disgraced minister agreed to remove himself from his post.

On August 25, 1706, Ann Putnam recanted her accusations, in the form of a confession read out to the Salem congregation by the Reverend Thomas Green, who had replaced Parrish. She did not take responsibility for her actions, but at least blamed her delusions on Satan, rather than on humans. Her confession said, in part:

> I desire to be humbled before God for that sad and humbling providence that befell my father's family in the year about '92 … it was a great delusion of Satan that deceived me in that sad time, whereby I justly fear that I have been instrumental, with others, though ignorantly and unwittingly, to bring upon myself and thus land the guilt of innocent blood … ❧

1759
THE BATTLE OF QUEBEC

On the night of September 12, 1759, a flotilla carrying the cream of the British army in Canada floated up the St. Lawrence River, right under the noses of the watchful French guarding the citadel city of Quebec. A quarter-moon had arisen around ten o'clock, which provided enough light for the fleet to steer by, but not so much that it might be clearly seen. Moving under the towering cliffs of Quebec, the British continued west to a cove called the Anse au Foulon, landing in the dark perhaps two hours before dawn. They looked up from the beach to see a sheer rock face some 165 feet high, with a narrow path winding across its face. The path had been pointed out to the British a few weeks earlier, probably by a French deserter.

With haste, yet trying to be as quiet as possible, the detachment of perhaps two hundred Light Infantry crept up the path; when a French sentry challenged them, a French-speaking Highlander told him with some indignation that they were reinforcements sent from up the river. This fooled the French soldier long enough for the British to reach the top of the cliff and overwhelm the French garrison on guard duty.

One of the officers who accompanied the first companies to the top of the cliff was their brilliant, cold commander in chief, General James Wolfe. He had donned a new uniform for what he was certain would be the defining moment of his military career. Plagued by illness and possessed of a dark soul and temperament, he had convinced himself that he would die in the coming battle, and had hinted as much when he gave his personal effects and a picture of his fiancée to a Royal Navy

Benjamin West's *The Death of General Wolfe* (c. 1771), a romanticized version of the British leader's demise, helped immortalize the event.

officer for safekeeping. Yet now, as thousands more British troops climbed the cliff, following those who had so easily taken the guard-post, he may have thought for a moment that he might yet escape the fate he had foreseen for himself.

A PIVOTAL MOMENT

The battle for possession of Quebec—which controlled the St. Lawrence River, the water highway by which the interior of the North American continent and its rich fur trade could be accessed—came three years into the Seven Years' War, as France and Great Britain, age-old rivals, engaged in a global struggle for supremacy. Beginning in 1753, the war was fought on two fronts. In Western Europe, Great Britain and Prussia were pitted against France, Austria, Russia, and Sweden. Britain and France continued the battle on the second front, in North America. Known as the French and Indian War due to the French use of Indian allies, it was fought mainly in what would become New York, New England, and Canada.

The French had had the best of it up until Wolfe's arrival at the Anse au Foulon. They and their Huron and Abenaki allies had destroyed a force under General Braddock at Fort Duquesne, on the Pennsylvania frontier in 1755. The next year they had made inroads into what would become northern New York State, capturing Forts Ontario, George and Otswego. And in August of 1757 they had captured Fort William Henry on Lake George.

The commander of the victorious French forces at Fort William Henry was a man named Louis-Joseph, the Marquis de Montcalm. He guaranteed the safety of the British troops and civilians inside the fort after they surrendered. But as soon as the British were allowed to begin their journey to British lines, the Abenakis set upon them, killing 180 in cold blood and taking perhaps 500 as slaves. When he heard about this, Montcalm raced out on horseback to restore order. Montcalm's brave and judicious actions were the only bright spot in an ugly episode that became a rallying cry for British and Americans.

ON THE PLAINS OF ABRAHAM

After the advance company of the British had scaled the cliffs and neutralized the small French outpost, the rest of the British force—about five thousand men—made its way up and marched to the Plains of Abraham, southwest of the city. The Plains of Abraham were named, not after the biblical figure, but after a farmer named Abraham Martin, who had been given this long piece of land west of Quebec in the 1650s. On September 13, as the sun rose over these plains, the French beheld an astonishing sight: thousands of red-coated troops who had formed up in a line two deep that extended all the way across the thousand-yard-wide plains. These men were 550 yards from Quebec's western wall. On their right were cornfields and then the cliff-edge over the St. Lawrence. On their left was a forest.

The French leader, the Marquis de Montcalm—the same Montcalm who had tried to stop the massacre at Fort William Henry—was stunned when he rode his horse out in front of the French lines. He kept staring at the seven battalions of British troops as though, one observer noted, "his fate was upon him." Despite the fact that Canadian irregulars and French Indians sped to the cornfield and the forests to begin picking off British troops, Montcalm seemed frozen.

Far across the plain, his counterpart, General Wolfe, with little regard for his own safety and perhaps deliberately tempting fate, strode up and down behind his men, whom he had ordered to lie down. Montcalm and Wolfe could almost certainly not see each other, but their lives and deaths would be forever intertwined on that day.

In some ways, they presented a study in opposites. Montcalm was a decent man; not a brilliant commander, but a strong and intelligent one. Born in 1712 (which made him fifteen years older than Wolfe), he was the product of wealthy royal French parents and a classical education. His father died when he was a young man, leaving him a fortune, which, unfortunately, was riddled with debts. Friends arranged a marriage for the young marquis to a rich heiress named Angelique Louise Talon du Boulay; surprisingly, the union of convenience turned into a happy marriage, producing ten children to whom both parents were devoted. Montcalm, however, was away much of the time, fighting wars. He was

> THE MARQUIS DE MONTCALM WAS A DECENT MAN; NOT A BRILLIANT COMMANDER, BUT A STRONG AND INTELLIGENT ONE.

wounded on several occasions and showed such conspicuous gallantry that he was promoted to major general. In 1756, he arrived in North America and led French troops to a series of stunning successes before being placed in charge of the all-important fortress of Quebec.

Major General James Wolfe was a more complex, more troubled man, and had had a far more mercurial rise than Montcalm. Thirty-two years old, he was the son of an undistinguished army general. His looks were the first thing most people commented on: he was tall and gangly, with a pinched face, pale skin, and a mop of red hair, which he refused to cover with a wig. He had made his reputation with the British army in Scotland in 1746, fighting the Jacobite rebellion, and a cruel reputation it was—Wolfe thought nothing of burning villages or executing civilians. Cold and egotistical, unable to connect with men or women, and prone to maladies that left him ill much of the time, Wolfe was bad-tempered, but a powerful fighter, which he had proved during the successful siege of the French fortress of Louisbourg, Nova Scotia, in 1758, a victory that opened up the approaches to the St. Lawrence for the British Royal Navy.

Despite protests from rivals, some of whom thought Wolfe mad, King George II put him in charge of the invasion force that was to attack Quebec. "Mad, is he?" the king famously said. "Then I hope he will bite some others of my generals."

DILEMMAS ON BOTH SIDES

Wolfe had been besieging Quebec for three long months—"burning and laying waste the countryside," as his orders to his scouts read, blockading the St. Lawrence and hoping to starve the French garrison out. But his forces had not been quite strong enough to do this, and so he had settled on a last gambit before winter set in: all-out attack on Quebec.

Mad or not, Wolfe had taken an extraordinary chance. As the French cannon lobbed shots at his lines, he knew that somewhere west of him was a French force of some three thousand troops commanded by Louis-Antoine de Bougainville, a man who would later become one of the most brilliant explorers in French history, and who now, Wolfe assumed, was on his way to reinforce the French garrison. If so, British forces would be caught between the cliffs, the French in Quebec, the snipers in the woods and Bougainville approaching from the rear. To avoid this trap, he was going to have to order his 4500 troops to attack soon, charging directly at Quebec's defences.

French commander the Marquis de Montcalm famously tried to halt an Indian massacre of British prisoners at Fort William Henry.

Montcalm, too, was having his anxieties. His forces equalled Wolfe's, but he had far fewer regular army troops, being dependent on unreliable militia as well as scouts and Indians. It seemed that his best move would be to retire behind Quebec's walls to await the coming of Bougainville and his relief forces, but there were two problems with this strategy. Quebec's defences at this point in the city walls were weak, since it had been assumed no one would be able to scale the cliffs. Secondly, where was Bougainville? No one knew. Montcalm paced up and down impatiently. "Is it possible Bougainville doesn't hear all that noise?" he asked an aide.

A PERFECT VOLLEY

Bougainville later claimed he received too little notice to muster his forces for an attack on Wolfe. Whatever the case, by 10 a.m., he had still not shown up. Montcalm thus made a decision which, while understandable, was almost certainly the wrong one. Instead of retreating within the walls of the city, he chose to attack Wolfe's forces.

When Montcalm gave the order to attack, the French forces, cheering and whooping, charged at the British lines. But here the lack of discipline among the militia showed, for they were either ahead of or behind the regular forces, and they did not

fire in volleys at the British lines a few hundred yards away, instead kneeling and snapping off single shots whenever they could. The regular British troops simply waited for the French to get within 100 feet and then fired what one British officer later called: "the most perfect volley ever fired on a battlefield."

The effect on the French was devastating. The British then moved forwards and fired yet another volley and this became the pattern of the battle. Steadily, the French withered under such a terrible onslaught of lead at such close range, and those who survived turned tail and ran. The British gave fixed bayonets and charged, chasing the French back towards the city.

But Quebec was temporarily saved by the fifteen hundred or so French irregulars and Indians in the woods off the British left flank, who poured fierce fire into the British and forced them to stop and re-form several times. This allowed the French army in the field to escape, for the time being, to a fort upriver. Quebec remained strongly garrisoned, however, and for the moment, the British, still concerned about the threat from Bougainville, did not attack.

THE BATTLE OF QUEBEC

TWO LEADERS IMMORTALIZED

Probably just as the British charge was beginning, James Wolfe, who had continued to recklessly expose himself, was shot in the chest and bled to death. However, he lived long enough to hear an aide cry, "They run!" Wolfe asked who ran, and the aide said: "The enemy sir. Egad! They give way everywhere!" Wolfe, ever the commander, gave orders to cut off the enemy's retreat, then said, "Now, God be praised, I can die in peace." A few moments later, he was gone. His was and remains one of the most famous last moments in British military history, immortalized in art and literature, most notably in Benjamin West's famous painting, *The Death of General Wolfe*.

Remarkably, at about the time Wolfe was hit, Montcalm also suffered a mortal wound, either from sniper bullets or grapeshot, and had to be helped back into the city. He died the next day and was buried in the yard of an Ursuline convent. He, too, passed into legend, staring fixedly at the sky in numerous French paintings, the most famous being Jean-Antoine Watteau's *The Death of Montcalm*, which has the General dying on the battlefield, flanked by Indians, instead of at the convent. Ironically, although the battle was one of the most pivotal in North American history, its prominence in the public imagination derives mainly from these stirring but inaccurate portrayals.

The British did not enter the city that day, but the French finally surrendered. The British lost six hundred and fifty men, the French a few less, but the British triumph was great. Although the French would try in vain to retake Quebec in 1760, after Wolfe's posthumous triumph the French empire in North America was as good as lost. Wolfe's great gamble at the Anse au Foulon had paid off. The British now had complete control of Canada and would soon gain control of New England and New York. The battle of Quebec had determined that North America would be a British, not a French, continent. ❧

1776

WASHINGTON CROSSES THE DELAWARE

George Washington's crossing of the Delaware River to attack British forces at Trenton, in what is now the state of New Jersey, on Christmas Day of 1776, is a legendary event in U.S. history. And Emanuel Leutze's 1850 painting *Washington Crossing the Delaware*, which now resides at the Metropolitan Museum of Art in New York, is one of the most famous pieces of art in America. However, for some Americans, Leutze's painting is infamous for the number of factual errors it contains. Leutze has the crossing happening as the horizon glows with light, when in fact it took place in the middle of a dark and sleety night. Washington is standing at the prow of a rowing boat; he probably was standing, but in a high-sided, flat-bottomed ore-transport barge. The American flag depicted is wrong —the "Stars and Stripes" did not exist at the time of Washington's crossing. Poor Leutze was even mistaken about the ice, some historians quibble—the sharp floes he depicts are more akin to those found on the German-born Leutze's native Rhine than to the flat sheet ice of the Delaware.

With all these errors—and many more—why in the world is the painting so famous? Because, details aside, Leutze captures the *spirit* of the whole affair, the determination, desperation and dignity of these men as they rowed into the fight of their lives. For had George Washington failed in his crossing of the Delaware, it is entirely possible that America's fight for independence could have failed, as well.

ON THE RETREAT

The War of American Independence, in which Great Britain's thirteen American colonies sought to push off the rule of the motherland and govern themselves, had begun in the spring of 1775 with armed skirmishing between American irregular troops and the British army near Boston. Full-scale war soon followed, with New York State becoming a key battleground. In a campaign beginning in August 1776, George Washington and his rebel force, the Continental Army, were pushed out of Long Island and New York, and harried southwards, first into New Jersey and then into Pennsylvania, towards their base at Philadelphia, by aggressive British forces under General Sir William Howe. By December, half of Washington's army had been killed, wounded, captured or deserted, leaving him with perhaps five to six thousand men, many of them injured. On December 13, the British even captured one of America's top commanders, General Charles Lee—whom they believed in every way to be George Washington's superior in military thinking and tactics.

As soon as the Delaware River—the broad river that formed the borderline between New Jersey and Pennsylvania—froze, Howe planned to brush aside the ragamuffin army in front of him and easily sweep down the river to take the rebel capital, from which the Continental Congress had already fled. After this, the war would be over.

Washington had yet another problem: most of the men in his volunteer army had enlisted for only a year, meaning that they could legally leave on December 31, just a week away. If he was going to strike at the British, he had to do it at once. Not only Washington but all of his men understood this, which

is why the password for the Christmas mission Leutze later depicted would be "Victory or Death."

A BLOODY TRAIL

Just before the crossing, George Washington readied to mount his horse and inspect the two thousand four hundred shivering men forming on the Pennsylvania side of the Delaware River, near McKonkey's Ferry, approximately 8 miles upriver from Trenton. At that moment, a Continental officer from Philadelphia rode into camp with a letter for Washington. How on earth had the man found them, Washington asked? Easy, he replied; he had followed the bloody footprints left in the snow by Washington's soldiers.

Bloody footprints pretty much seemed to sum up the situation George Washington and the Continental Army were now in. Before heading with his men to the transports that would take them across the Delaware, Washington sent a notification to the head surgeon of the Continental Army, telling him to expect heavy casualties. At six o'clock, it was already dark and sleeting heavily, and the men standing on the banks of the river, which was fast moving and swollen, were freezing. Still, there were a few lighter moments. One soldier noticed how red Washington's nose looked in the cold and later wrote: "[His nose] was scarlet in the wind … He was not what ladies would call a pretty man." Washington himself, watching his nearly 310 pound artillery commander, Colonel Henry Knox, enter one of the boats and try to sit down, joked: "Shift your tail, Knox, and trim the boat."

The width of the Delaware at this point was only 985 feet, but the fast-moving water, filled with ice (and, in Leutze's defence, some of it may have been craggy, since it may have washed into the Delaware from streams along its banks), crashed into the boats, and freezing rain and snow blew hard into the men's faces. The plan was for the entire force of two thousand four hundred (plus horses and eighteen cannon) to cross by midnight. But, despite the best efforts of the Massachusetts soldiers (fishermen in civilian life) to whom Washington had assigned this task, each separate crossing took much longer than expected, and the operation was not completed until three o'clock in the morning of December 26.

Washington stood on the banks of the Jersey shore, supervising the landing, his cloak wrapped around him. He seemed to onlookers to be extraordinarily determined. He may have been thinking about certain lines from the patriot writer Tom Paine's *The American Crisis*, the first issue of which had just been published. "These are the times that try men's souls.

Washington Crossing the Delaware (1851) by Emanuel Leutze: the details are wrong but the spirit is captured brilliantly.

The summer soldier and the sunshine patriot will, in this crisis, shrink from the service of their country, but he that stands it now, deserves the love and thanks of man and woman." Just over two days before, on December, Washington had formed the very troops now crossing the Delaware into ranks, and had these soon-to-be famous sentences read to them.

There were no summer patriots with Washington on that freezing night. And, despite the desperation of his crossing, it had sound military strategy behind it.

VITAL INTELLIGENCE

The British, having chased Washington into Pennsylvania, had formed a line of outposts nearly 80 miles long, extending all

Jean-Antoine Houdon's bust of Washington (1786-93) was based on casts and sketches made during a visit to Washington's home in 1785.

the way from Burlington, New Jersey, to the Hackensack River in New York. The deeper the British forward lines were placed in New Jersey, the further away they were from their supply base in New York.

When Washington had first crossed into Pennsylvania that fall, he had used his network of spies and scouts to carefully survey the British positions. They had noted that the British had placed 1500 German mercenaries in Trenton under the command of Colonel Johann Rall (sometimes spelled Rahl), and that these Hessians, as they were known, were so confident that they had not bothered to dig or erect barricades. Washington's spies had also told him that Rall, although a soldier who had served with some distinction in previous battles, was given to drinking and lax discipline when away from the direct gaze of his supervisors. Washington also noted that Trenton was at least a half-day's march from the nearest British outpost, leaving it relatively isolated. So, as well as his own force, he planned to have two smaller forces cross the river downstream, one to engage the British at Bordentown as a diversion and stop them coming to Rall's aid, the other to block the retreat of the Hessian forces from Trenton.

MOVING ON TRENTON

In normal conditions, a 8-mile march would have been nothing to a hardened Continental soldier, but on this freezing cold night, the trek to Trenton was extremely difficult. Moving through a forest of black oak and hickory, the soldiers followed a path that was rutted and crisscrossed with tree roots, as an ice storm raged. Bringing up the rear of the line were cannon, which had small torches stuck in their touch-holes for guidance; one Connecticut private later remembered how these lights "sparkled and blazed in the storm of the night." At one point, messengers brought news from one of Washington's officers that the rain and sleet had ruined their powder. Washington merely said: "You have nothing for it but to push on and use the bayonet."

By coincidence, this march on Trenton was populated with men who would later become important figures in American history. Along with Washington were a future president, James Monroe; a future Chief Justice of the United States, John Marshall; Aaron Burr, a future vice president; and the man Burr would later famously kill in a duel, Alexander Hamilton, a future Secretary of the Treasury.

At about eight in the morning, having divided his troops into two columns and sent one to attack from the north, Washington finally arrived at Trenton. He was at least two hours off schedule, having planned to attack before dawn, but the storm had worsened and the only guards standing duty were pickets posted in small houses perhaps half a mile from town. Washington's men drove the pickets in with a clatter of musketry, and the battle for Trenton began.

The sound of shots and yells awoke Colonel Rall from what most sources state was an alcohol-induced stupor. The good colonel had spent much of Christmas night drinking, and so had missed a chance to discover Washington's plans. For a Tory farmer—loyal to the Crown—had come to Rall's quarters that night to tell him about the attack, but Rall had refused to see him. Frustrated, the man had written what he knew on a piece of paper and passed it to Rall via a guard, but (much like Caesar ignoring a similar note handed to him on the Ides of March) Rall had stuck it in his pocket and forgotten about it.

Now it was too late. Some of the Hessian troops began firing from the windows of their quarters, as others raced half-dressed into the streets, only to be cut down by disciplined Continental fire. Hundreds more Hessians were rallied by their officers and began forming near a church, but Henry Knox lined six of his artillery pieces up on King and Queen Streets, and fired at them with devastating effect. American infantry seized most enemy cannon before they could be fired, or shot their crews as they lined up and tried to fire them (Lieutenant Alexander Hamilton led a brave charge which destroyed one Hessian battery).

Washington's other column moved in from the north, boxing the Hessians in. Rall tried to lead a charge of his panicked men, yelling, "All who are my grenadiers, forward!" He started to ride his horse at Continental lines, but his men would not move from cover, and Rall was shot twice and knocked onto the snowy streets of Trenton. Mortally wounded, he was carried into a church and placed on a pew.

TRENTON WAS A PIVOTAL VICTORY, ACHIEVED AT THE DARKEST HOUR OF THE WAR OF INDEPENDENCE.

DUMBFOUNDED BY VICTORY

Everywhere, groups of Hessians, surrounded by Continental troops with bayonets drawn, were surrendering. Washington at first seemed almost dumbfounded by his victory. He ordered a battery of guns to fire upon a Hessian position, and the gunner said to him, "Sir, they have struck." "Struck?" Washington replied, as if he could not assign a meaning to the word. "Yes. Their colors are down." At last, Washington understood. He turned to one of his young officers, Major Wilkinson, and shook his hand: "This is a glorious day for our country."

Four hundred Hessians had escaped before the Continental noose tightened, but more than nine hundred were captured, while about fifty had been killed or wounded. Washington's losses were amazingly light: three dead (one of whom had frozen to death along the line of march) and six wounded. Along with the prisoners, Washington had captured six artillery pieces and a thousand badly needed muskets, and seven wagonloads of powder and ammunition. And this had been achieved without the support of Washington's two other contingents, which had been unable to cross the Delaware and create diversions downstream.

Colonel Rall, dying in a nearby house, was visited by Washington, who spoke with him through an interpreter. Rall had by this time seen the note that he had failed to read, and thus knew that he had given away his command, and his life, because he had been so careless.

"THAT UNHAPPY AFFAIR"

Crossing the Delaware and defeating the Hessian forces at Trenton gave Washington and his Continental Army an all-important victory at a time when the American forces were at a low ebb. Following it up with victories at Trenton when British forces counterattacked on January 1, and at nearby Princeton on January 2 and 3, Washington was able to save Philadelphia. "The enemy was within 15 miles of Philadelphia," Henry Knox wrote his wife, "they are now 60 miles." Eventually, following a bloody conflict that continued until 1783, Americans would oust the British from America and win the right to govern themselves.

Though the triumph at Trenton was followed by other, greater, battles, it was a pivotal victory, achieved at the darkest hour of the War of Independence. Washington himself, with modesty, called the strike at Trenton "a lucky blow." But the disgruntled British Secretary of State, Lord George Germain, later summed up the British view of the battle: "All our hopes were dashed by that unhappy affair at Trenton." ❧

1788
THE FIRST FLEET

On August 18, 1786 English home secretary Thomas, Lord Sydney of Whitehall, wrote to the Lords Commissioners of the Treasury outlining his plan to overcome the growing problem of chronic overcrowding in English gaols. Felons had previously been sent to North America, but that option had been closed after the American victory over the British in the War of Independence in 1776. The gaols were full to overflowing, as were the numerous rotting prison hulks moored in various harbors and rivers. England was undergoing an industrial revolution which saw a transition from an agrarian-based economy to an industry-based one centerd in cities, towns, factories and workshops. By the late eighteenth century this revolution was well under way, with the result that millions of workers had lost their jobs, to be replaced by machines. While the rich were getting richer, the unemployed working class was growing in leaps and bounds.

London's population had doubled between 1750 and 1770 as people flocked from the countryside to seek nonexistent work. Many resorted to what we would call petty crime, most often theft of food and other essentials. The government's response was to introduce the death penalty for numerous crimes, including smuggling, forgery, burglary, larceny by servants, petty theft and horse-stealing. But judges were reluctant to send offenders to the gallows, and they commuted many sentences to transportation to America, even after that was no longer possible.

In 1770, acclaimed English explorer Captain James Cook led an expedition to the south seas during which he discovered new lands and claimed territories for Britain. He had made landfall at Botany Bay, on the east coast of the continent that would be named Australia. His official botanist, Joseph Banks, had returned with hundreds of new plant species. As the government considered its options for transportation, the *Journal of the House of Commons* recorded Banks' opinion:

> … the place …, best adapted for such a purpose, was Botany Bay, on the coast of New Holland, in the Indian Ocean, which was about seven months voyage from England, that he apprehended there would be little possibility of opposition from the natives, as during his stay there in the year 1770, he saw very few and did not think there were above fifty in the neighborhood, and had reason to believe the country was very thinly populated, those he saw were naked, treacherous, and armed with lances, but extremely cowardly…

THE TRANSPORTATION SOLUTION

Lord Sydney was secretary of state for the Home Office in the government of William Pitt the Younger and was responsible for solving the convict problem. He became an advocate for transportation to Botany Bay, and Parliament adopted his recommendations, less than a year before the departure of the largest migration fleet in history.

The great southern land was already well known in Europe before Captain Cook's exploration—more than fifty Dutch, Portuguese and Spanish ships had landed on various parts of the continent over the previous three hundred or so years, but none had set up colonies. Britain hoped by settling the land to solve their convict problem and claim the land outright.

The fleet comprised the naval escorts HMS *Sirius* and HMS *Supply*, the convict transports *Alexander*, *Charlotte*, *Lady Penrhyn*, *Friendship*, *Scarborough* and *Prince of Wales*,

Of the 1400 or so who landed, nearly 800 were convicts, the remainder marines and officials.

and the food transports *Golden Grove*, *Borrowdale* and *Fishburn*. The largest, the *Alexander*, was just 115 feet long and less than 33 feet wide. The fleet was placed under the command of Captain Arthur Phillip, a relatively undistinguished naval officer who nonetheless turned out to be a good choice; he would also become the first governor of the colony of New South Wales. On board were more than one thousand four hundred passengers, including nearly eight hundred convicts, several hundred soldiers, marines and officers, some family members and the ships' crews. Of the convict contingent, nearly two hundred were women, important to the colony according to Lord Sydney because "without a sufficient proportion of that sex it is well known that it would be impossible to preserve the settlement from gross irregularities and disorders." The fleet also took tools that would be needed to create the new settlement, including 300 chisels, 175 saws and hammers, 140 knives and drills, and an assortment of wheelbarrows, grindstones, fish hooks, and ploughshares.

Almost sixty percent of the convicts had been sentenced for stealing food or other goods of relatively minor value. Thirteen percent had been convicted of breaking and entering or burglary, and fifteen percent were guilty of highway robbery, with violence or grand larceny. The remainder had

The First Fleet explored coastal inlets in Sydney Harbour before settling in Camp Cove.

been sentenced for swindling, receiving stolen goods, forgery or some other crime. A West Indian, Thomas Chaddick, was sentenced to seven years' transportation for stealing twelve cucumber plants. Thirteen-year-old Elizabeth Hayward was transported for stealing a silk bonnet and a linen gown worth seven shillings.

THE FIRST FLEET SETS SAIL

In late 1786 the convicts began to be loaded onto the ships. They were shackled below decks, and many died of disease or malnutrition even before the fleet departed. Finally, on the morning of May 13, 1787, the First Fleet left Portsmouth Harbour, bound for New Holland. Less than a week into the voyage, the crew of the *Friendship* went on strike, demanding an increase in daily meat rations from one and a half to two pounds. But it was not physical hunger that the sailors wanted to satisfy—even though a wall had been built to separate the crew and convicts, the sailors had already knocked a hole in it; their intention was to use the meat as a bribe for sexual favors from the female prisoners. Phillip refused to increase the rations, but promised a pay rise.

By the time the fleet reached Tenerife in the Canary Islands to re-stock with fresh food and water, eight convicts had died of pneumonia and dysentery, but thereafter the general health of the prisoners improved. From Tenerife the fleet sailed to the Cape Verde Islands off the west coast of Africa, where they planned to replenish their supplies, but Phillip decided against landing due to light winds and strong currents. They headed across the Atlantic to Rio de Janeiro, enduring plagues of rats and insects in the stifling tropical conditions. Phillip compassionately ordered the opening of the hatches above the convict quarters after many of the prisoners began suffering from dehydration, fainting fits and convulsions.

The conditions below decks were generally atrocious. Most of the time the prisoners were locked up in total darkness as the risk of fire prevented the use of candles or torches. Lice, fleas, cockroaches and other vermin flourished on all the ships, and the rotten water in the bilges filled the airless quarters with an overpowering stench. The open-air exercise areas were only a few feet long because convicts were prevented from reaching the quarterdeck by a high wooden wall topped with metal spikes. John White, chief surgeon of the First Fleet, reported that "when the hatches were taken off the stench was so powerful that it was scarcely possible to stand over them."

The fleet reached the Portuguese-run port of Rio de Janeiro on the east coast of South America on August 6. Phillip was very well received, having previously served in the Portuguese navy in its war with the Spanish. The ships were repaired, particularly the flagship *Sirius*, which was leaking badly. The convicts were held below deck, but the crews enjoyed shore leave during the month-long stay. They stocked up on rice, coffee, cocoa, fresh meat, various fruits and vegetables, and 65,000 litres (over 14,000 gallons) of rum.

On September 4, the ships set sail on the prevailing westerly breeze for the Cape of Good Hope at the southern tip of Africa. The weather mercifully cooled, but at times the seas were so rough that Lieutenant Ralph Clark wrote that "those marines sleeping with the convict women were washed out of their beds." They arrived at the Cape on October 13, staying for four weeks and stocking up with provisions that included over five hundred animals—cattle, pigs, horses, poultry, goats and sheep—for use not only as food on the voyage, but also to stock farms at the new colony.

On November 13, aided by brisk westerlies, they set off across the Indian Ocean on the final, longest leg of the voyage. There was a general outbreak of dysentery, which caused the death of a marine private named Daniel Creswell. At the end of November, Phillip split the fleet into two, the fastest ships going ahead to scout for suitable locations for the new settlement. The *Supply*, along with the three fastest transport ships, set off with some convicts who had carpentry or gardening skills to help prepare for the arrival of the others. On January 3, 1788 the leading group saw land which they knew to be Van Diemen's Land (now Tasmania), discovered and mapped by Dutch explorer Abel Tasman in 1642. It took them another two weeks, struggling against northerly winds, to sail the 620 miles to Botany Bay, where their gruelling voyage finally ended on January 18.

WHEN THE ABORIGINAL PEOPLE SAW THE SHIPS ARRIVING IN BOTANY BAY, THEY GATHERED IN LARGER NUMBERS AROUND THE SHORE, BRANDISHING SPEARS AND SHOUTING FOR THE FLEET TO GO AWAY.

LANDFALL AT BOTANY BAY

The new arrivals' first encounter with the natives was friendly. They were naked and armed with spears, but pointed the unarmed newcomers to a freshwater stream. These good relations would not last for long. The second division arrived just the next day, having encountered much more favorable conditions en route. The voyage had actually been very successful—no ships were lost, and fewer passengers died than on most of the fleets that would bring about 160,000 more prisoners to Australia over the next fifty years (the exact number is unknown, due to lack of accurate records). Just sixty-nine people had died—many before the fleet had left Portsmouth—of the more than fourteen hundred who had set out. They included forty convicts, five children of convicts, one marine, a marine's wife, and a marine's child.

When the Aboriginal people saw the extra ships arriving in Botany Bay, they gathered in larger numbers around the shore, brandishing spears and shouting "*Warra, warra*" ("Go away"). These are the first recorded words spoken by black to white in Australia. Several spears were thrown; one of the marines answered with a blank pistol shot. But soon peace was made, as the Aborigines admonished the spear-throwers and accepted conciliatory gifts of beads from Phillip.

Phillip quickly decided that Botany Bay, with its poor shelter and sandy, barren soil, was unsuitable for settlement. On January 21 he and a group of his men sailed north and entered Port Jackson, which Cook had mentioned in passing, but did not enter. Phillip called it "the finest harbor in the world"; Chief Surgeon White was even more enthusiastic, dubbing it the finest "in the universe."

They explored several coves, eventually finding a hospitable location with deep water close to the shore, and fed by a small river. Phillip named it Sydney Cove. Arthur Bowes Smith, captain of the *Lady Penrhyn*, wrote:

The finest terra's, lawns and grottos, with distinct plantations of the tallest and most stately trees I ever saw in any nobleman's ground in England, cannot excel in beauty those which I saw. Nature now presented to our view … the stupendous rocks from the summit of the hills and down to the very water's edge hang'g over in a most awful way from above, and form'g the most commodious quays by the water, beggard all description.

EARLY HARDSHIPS

They returned to Botany Bay and, on January 25, after being delayed for several days by a fierce storm, the fleet set sail for Port Jackson and began to set up the new outpost—the most distant colony ever established by a founding state. The next day Phillip raised the British flag and the new settlers began unloading the ships, starting with the livestock that had not starved or been eaten on the way. The female convicts were left on board as land was cleared and a tent town erected. On Sunday, February 3, the chaplain, Reverend Richard Johnson, conducted the first church service under a large tree overlooking the bay. Ten days later the female convicts were brought ashore during a wild storm, giving rise to scenes of unrestrained licentiousness as the seamen shared their grog rations. The officers were powerless to keep apart the men and women; as Surgeon John Smith wrote: "it is beyond my abilities to give a just description of the scene of debauchery and riot that ensued during the night" and Captain Watkin Tench recorded: "When landed their separation became impracticable, and would have been, perhaps, wrong … What was to be attempted? To prevent their intercourse was impossible."

The first few weeks were marked by numerous summer storms. On February 1, marine Ralph Clark wrote: "I never slept worse my dear wife than I did last night—what with the hard ground, spiders, ants and every vermin you can think of was crawling over me." The fierce summer winds killed many of the newly planted crops as the temperature reached 109°F (43°C). The local gum trees turned out to be difficult to use for building, their timber so hard that English tools were barely strong enough to make an impression.

The newcomers could have gleaned much useful survival information from the Aborigines, but their attitude of racial superiority prevented them from seeking advice, even though the British government had sought good relations with the locals: "to conciliate their affections, enjoining all our subjects to live in amity and kindness with them." By and large the two groups kept out of each other's way at first, although later in the year there were several incidents where Aborigines or settlers died, usually following theft of each other's property. Hostilities gradually increased, leading to the uneasy relationships that would endure for the next two centuries. Imported cholera and influenza, previously unknown, also took a terrible toll on the locals, who had no resistance to these diseases. Although this was accidental, and the settlers had no wish to add tribal warfare to the colony's numerous problems, within a year the surrounds of Sydney cove were littered with decomposing native corpses.

Morale in the fledgling settlement was appalling, fuelled by hunger, malnutrition, disease, and by cruelty inflicted by officers on marines, and marines on convicts. Realizing that the colony faced starvation unless more stores arrived soon from England, Phillip allocated the same rations to convicts and employees alike, regardless of status—this caused further resentment. Things would not start to improve until the arrival of the Second Fleet in June 1790.

Yet despite these brutal and unpromising beginnings, the colony very slowly began to prosper. Army officers were given land, many assisted by convicts who, on emancipation, acquired their own smallholdings. The young country attracted new settlers wishing to take advantage of the opportunities offered by cheap land and labor, and a range of other commercial enterprises.

Convicts continued to be transported to Australia but, by the mid nineteenth century, attitudes towards transportation had begun to change. There were many more free immigrants living in Australia, along with a number of former convicts, and they were concerned about the negative influence of a large criminal population in the increasingly prosperous colony. In Britain, social reformers voiced their concern at arbitrary and inconsistent sentencing and the inhumane treatment of prisoners aboard the convict ships. The number of transportation ships dwindled until, in 1868, eighty years after the arrival of the First Fleet in Botany Bay, the last convict ship left Britain for Australia. ❧

1789

THE STORMING OF THE BASTILLE

The storming of the bastille on July 14, 1789 is renowned and celebrated as the heroic uprising that kick-started the French Revolution by conquering an infamous symbol of oppression and liberating many of the French Crown's most hard-done-by and mistreated victims. But as with many legends of the French Revolution and other uprisings in history, the reality was somewhat different, and nothing highlights this better than the scenes that immediately followed the liberation.

When the mob broke through the gates of the infamous fourteenth-century jail and the garrison had capitulated and was dragged off to its fate, the prison was discovered to be almost empty. Unknown to the attackers, the government had scheduled the building for demolition and only six prisoners were left in all of its many cells and chambers. (There would have been seven, but the Marquis de Sade, its most famous inhabitant, had been transferred elsewhere a week before.) Four of the prisoners were forgers. Two were insane. Of these, one, the Comte de Solages, had been committed by his family for libertinism and incest. The other was a deranged Irishman known to history only as Major Whyte.

Of the six inmates, only this lunatic fitted the picture most people had of prisoners in the Bastille: men or women who had been wronged by the Crown and sentenced to a living death in the great prison's dungeon. Unlike the other inmates, who had been in the prison but a short time, Whyte had languished for decades and was gaunt, white-haired and had a beard down to his waist. So he was paraded in a cart through the streets while crowds gathered and cheered at this perfect symbol of the oppression of the King of France. And because it was Major Whyte's particular delusion that he was Julius Caesar, this suited him perfectly: thinking the crowds were applauding the dictator of Rome, he smiled broadly and waved his hands in grateful thanks wherever he was taken.

INEVITABLE BUT UNFORESEEN

The French Revolution was, as Alexis de Tocqueville later wrote, both "inevitable yet … completely unforeseen." Arising in a France wracked by extreme poverty, the Revolution was to change the face, not only of France, but of Europe. When the revolutionaries subsequently came to power, established a constitutional democracy, and executed France's formerly untouchable monarchs, it sent shockwaves through nearby nations, which feared such progressive ideas might be exported. And not just ideas. As the French Revolution went careening out of control and thousands of nobles and alleged counter-revolutionaries were executed, it seemed to observers that such change must inevitably be accompanied by violent bloodshed.

Later, Revolutionary France would fight wars with England, the Netherlands, Austria and Italy and, ironically, its success in these wars would see its great general, Napoleon Bonaparte, ultimately become a dictator, thus subverting the ideas of the Republic. But the French Revolution, like most revolutions, began out of a genuine desire to reduce hunger and injustice.

"RAVENOUS SCARECROWS"

In the early spring of 1789, France, a country of about twenty-six million people, suffered from a level of poverty that horrified even hardened foreign observers. One English writer, travelling through the countryside, described seeing everywhere starving peasants who looked like "ravenous scarecrows." There were numerous reasons for this level of poverty, but heavy taxes were chief among them. These taxes were almost universally borne by the peasantry and poor urban workers, rather than by nobles (who could take advantage of any number of loophole exclusions) or the rich and powerful Catholic Church, which owned ten percent of the land, yet paid no taxes at all. The taxes were particularly onerous in the city of Paris, where every foodstuff, dried good, barrel of wine or mooing, baaing, clucking head of livestock coming into the city for sale was stopped at a "customs barrier" and its owner forced to pay an excise tax.

With a staggering national debt of around forty-six million *livres* and a struggling and uncertain tax base, France was in terrible shape. King Louis XVI had inherited this situation when he ascended the throne in 1774, but had been unable to do much about it. Although not the beast he was later made out to be, he was an uncertain king who was not by inclination sympathetic to the needs of the common people.

Prior to 1789, France already had a constituent assembly—made up of the First Estate (the clergy), the Second Estate (the aristocracy) and the Third Estate (the middle class and the peasants)—but it hadn't met since 1614. Under pressure, Louis XVI called together this Estates-General to deal with the crisis of the worsening economy and starving peasantry. The Third Estate clamored for reform, but was stifled by the clergy and the nobility. On June 17, 1789, led by a group of radical Parisians, it broke off and formed the National Assembly, whose purpose was to create a French constitution. An increasingly powerless Louis was forced to accept this development.

Soon, liberty was in the air in Paris. Fiery debates took place on street corners and ordinary people—merchants, students, farmers from the countryside—began to sense that they now might have a say in their own futures.

CITIZENS TAKE UP ARMS

The incident that sparked the storming of the Bastille was the dismissal of Jacques Necker, Louis XVI's finance minister. The king's conservative advisers had urged him to fire Necker, who had shown sympathy for the plight of the French people and

had approved of the formation of the National Assembly, and Louis did so on July 11. By July 13, crowds carrying wax busts of Necker (who had fled to Belgium) were demonstrating in the streets of central Paris.

Rumors spread that Louis XVI was about to unleash his Swiss and German mercenaries on the crowd, since his own French-born army could not be trusted to fire on their compatriots. Inflamed by this and intoxicated with the sudden feel of freedom in the air, the demonstrators—the citizens' army, as they called themselves—became desperate for arms to defend themselves. Shortly after dawn on Tuesday July 14, they gathered in front of the Hôtel des Invalides, a military complex and hospital, demanding weapons. With the guards standing by, they then broke into the basement and took over 28,000 muskets and ten cannon.

The only problem was they had very little powder and ball with which to fire their weapons. Fearing that the ammunition might be used by the rebels, the commander of the Invalides had sent it to be stored protectively in the stark fortress of the Bastille—all 19,850 pounds of it.

To the mob, the Bastille was not only a source of powder and ammunition, but also a symbol of the longstanding aristocratic political and social system, the so-called *ancien regime*. An enormous building with eight rounded towers and walls 80 feet high, the Bastille (from a French word meaning "castle" or "fortress") had been built in the fourteenth century as a military stronghold and used as a state prison thereafter. It had more recently gained a sinister reputation as a place that housed those who had committed political crimes, real or imagined, against the Crown. Along with de Sade, famous prisoners had included the writer and philosopher Voltaire; the journalist Simon Linguet, whose writings had been published in 1782 and helped inflame the mobs gathering on July 14; and a prisoner who wore a velvet mask and whose identity was never discovered, though he was subsequently immortalized in literature and film as the "Man in the Iron Mask."

THE NERVOUS GOVERNOR

The governor of the Bastille was Bernard Jordan, the Marquis de Launay, who had actually been born in the prison—his father

LIBERTY WAS IN THE AIR IN PARIS. FIERY DEBATES TOOK PLACE ON STREET CORNERS AND ORDINARY PEOPLE BEGAN TO SENSE THAT THEY NOW MIGHT HAVE A SAY IN THEIR OWN FUTURES.

A reasonably accurate depiction of the taking of the Bastille. Note the prison's enormous rounded towers, which stood 80 feet high.

A 1786 portrait of King Louis XVI. After trying unsuccessfully to flee the country in 1791, Louis was guillotined in January 1793.

was the previous governor. His forces in the prison amounted to eighty-two pensioned-off soldiers, or *invalids*, who could not be counted on to fight a pitched battle in the best of circumstances, let alone against many of those who were their friends and neighbors. But Launay also had a command of thirty-two professional Swiss soldiers, who would become the core of any defence he could offer, as well as thirty or so cannon, many aimed right out the upper embrasures at the crowd now approaching.

The Bastille was entered through a small gate that opened into an outer courtyard, the Cour de Passage, which was lined with shops. Here, in more peaceful times, prisoners were allowed to mingle with their relatives and walk or smoke. The thick gate to the inner courtyard of the prison lay across a drawbridge over a dry moat. Once through that, any attackers would have to brave still another moat and drawbridge before arriving in the Bastille proper.

In an attempt to avert confrontation, certain Electors—members of the new National Assembly—raced ahead of the mob to speak with Launay, at about ten o'clock in the morning. Pointing out that the cannon poking out of the upper embrasures could be seen as an act of aggression, they asked him to withdraw the guns, which he did. While these negotiations were going on, however, a crowd of about a thousand arrived outside the walls of the Bastille, crying "We want [the] Bastille! Out with the troops!"

Impatient with the pace of the negotiations going on inside the prison, a few of the demonstrators leaped onto the roofs of the shops lining the Cour de Passage, climbed up onto the undefended lower ramparts and jumped to the ground inside the inner courtyard. There, they grabbed sledgehammers and smashed the chains holding the drawbridge up. It came crashing down across the moat—killing one rioter who could not get out of the way in time—and the mob surged into the inner courtyard.

At this point, about 2 p.m., someone opened fire. It has never been discovered who fired the first shot—some in the mob, unaware of how the drawbridge had been let down, were certain that the Swiss soldiers had lured them into the courtyard to be slaughtered, while the Swiss troops later swore the first fire had come from the rebels, who had aimed at the guards on top of the towers. In any event, bullets and cannon shot began to fly, as the demonstrators scattered to the side of the courtyard.

Some of the Electors tried to effect a cease fire over the sound of battle, but could not make themselves heard. Makeshift pallets carrying the wounded began to emerge onto the streets from the smoky courtyards. Inside, Launay was frantic. Despite there being numerous French troops stationed nearby, none had come to his aid—both because many within the ranks of the infantry sympathized with the rebels and because of the curious vacuum of power that had opened up in central Paris, which had been virtually abandoned to the mob.

THE FORTRESS FALLS

Finally, reinforcements came—but not to Launay. At about 3:30 p.m., the mob was joined by about a few hundred *gardes français*, soldiers of the rebellion's "new militia," formed from any man or woman who could acquire a gun, as well as deserters from Louis XVI's forces. They brought with them not only more muskets, but also two cannon, including, ironically enough, a silver gun given to the king by the Raj of Siam, which Louis had largely used as a sort of toy. It had been looted from the royal warehouse and now stood ready to bring down the Bastille.

Led by two veteran officers, the militia members set up the guns in the inner courtyard, aiming them directly at the wooden bottom of the raised drawbridge (the walls of the prison were too thick for cannon shot to penetrate). On the other side of the gate, Launay lined up his own cannon. Perhaps 100 feet apart, the forces of old and new faced each other.

Shortly thereafter, convinced of the hopelessness of his situation, Launay decided to concede defeat. At first, the crowds would not accept his surrender (which would have guaranteed safe passage for the prison defenders) and kept on firing. Desperate, Launay wrote a note, which he had passed out to the crowd: "We have 9000 kilograms [19,850 pounds] of powder. We shall blow up the garrison and the whole neighborhood unless you accept our capitulation." But when the officer in charge of the rebel guns made as if to fire

them into the gates, Launay gave up without condition. The drawbridge was opened and the mob poured into the Bastille.

A SYMBOL OF FREEDOM

The rebels disarmed the Swiss soldiers and led them through the streets, stoning them and screaming at them. The soldiers survived, however, unlike some of the *invalides*, who were mistaken for prison wardens and hung or beaten to death. Launay, too, suffered a horrible fate when the mob stabbed and shot him to death and then carved off his head to put on a pike.

Eighty-three members of the mob died, but the victory of the crowd was great. On the evening after the fall of the prison, huge crowds thronged Paris, shouting, celebrating and firing their guns in the air. Thereafter, those who had taken part in the assault were given the title *Vainqueur de la Bastille* and marched on every anniversary of the event for as long as they lived.

The king announced that he would recall Jacques Necker. Louis even wore a tricolor cockade, the symbol of the Revolution, as he approved a new government. However, many nobles were appalled at the violence (which would later claim the king's life, as well as that of his wife, Marie Antoinette), and began fleeing the country.

During the next decade, France would be radically transformed. More widespread mob violence would turn the Revolution very ugly, very soon. The Reign of Terror that began in 1792, in which thousands of those suspected of "counter-revolutionary" sympathies were killed—a terror that foreshadowed similar blood-lettings after the successful rebellions in Russia and China in the twentieth century—was to forever besmirch the ideals of the Revolution. Not only that; the Terror pushed away countries (especially America, which had just undergone its own successful revolution) that might otherwise have been sympathetic.

But on July 14, 1789, it was truly the common people who took the first step towards a republic. And ever since, Bastille Day has been celebrated annually in France as the day when the French people, at least symbolically speaking, won their freedom. ✤

1815

THE BATTLE OF WATERLOO

It's just possible that the Battle of Waterloo is the most famous battle in the history of the world. Sure, it has a few strong competitors—Cannae, Gettysburg, the Somme, D-Day. But Waterloo is one of the very few battles in world history that decided the outcome of a war on a single day. Had Coalition forces not stopped Napoleon at Waterloo, the map of Europe would have been drastically redrawn, with, just possibly, Napoleon presiding over a French empire on the Continent. The mighty clash at Waterloo also encouraged war planners for years to come to plot massive set-piece battles that might end conflicts at a single, bold stroke. This shining chimera was to cause much carnage when World War I began.

To this day, the very name of the battle is synonymous with crushing defeat and personal downfall—with overreaching ambition being thwarted. But things could have gone quite differently on that June day of 1815 in Belgium, as even the victorious British commander would acknowledge. If it had, we might be sitting in a very different world today.

A QUIET MORNING

On the morning of June 18, a few miles outside the Belgian village of Waterloo, one hundred and forty thousand men faced each other over a piece of land 2 miles wide and about ⅔ mile across. On the north side, drawn up along and behind a ridge, was the Army of the Seventh Coalition, which contained forces from Great Britain, the Netherlands, Belgium and Germany, totalling about sixty-seven thousand men. Their commander was the Duke of Wellington, the most successful British general of his generation. An allied Prussian army under Field Marshal Gebhard von Blücher was not far away. To the south across the field were seventy-three thousand French troops commanded by Napoleon Bonaparte.

It had rained heavily and both armies had spent the night miserable and cold in the open fields around Waterloo. The open land separating the two armies had become a morass of mud. After dawn, the skies cleared and the sun came out. The British readied themselves, certain that the notably aggressive Napoleon would attack their positions, and then … nothing happened.

As the hours wore on without action, soldiers relaxed, wrote letters, tried to catnap. Among the French forces, word went around that Napoleon was waiting for the fields to dry, in case the mud slowed any attack, particularly one made by artillery or cavalry. This was a perfectly reasonable assumption, except that it wasn't really like Napoleon. Those who knew him had never seen him slowed by inconveniences like muddy fields. And the longer the delay, the greater chance that von Blücher's Prussian forces would be able to reinforce Wellington's troops—the very thing Napoleon wanted to avoid. Many in the French ranks began to ask, what was the matter with the emperor?

Napoleon Crossing the Alps (1801), one of five versions of the same portrait painted by the French artist Jacques-Louis David.

AFTER ESCAPING FROM ELBA IN FEBRUARY 1815, NAPOLEON LANDED IN FRANCE, WHERE HE WAS MET BY A REGIMENT OF SOLDIERS SENT BY LOUIS XVIII TO CAPTURE OR KILL HIM.

THE THREAT TO EUROPE

This confrontation in Belgium represented the culmination of almost two decades of conflict in Europe. War had broken out between France and most of Europe after the French Revolution in 1789. These hostilities had briefly ended in 1802, but under Napoleon, who had seized power in 1799 and had himself proclaimed emperor in 1804, the fighting continued, with most of Europe attempting to check Bonaparte's attempts to seize more and more territory. Wellington was later to say "France has not enemies. We are the enemies of one man only," and there is some truth to this. The wars had been fought against Napoleon, not against France.

Wellington was notably successful in his early encounters with the legendary general. Taking control of British, Portuguese and Spanish forces in the Peninsular War, he ousted Napoleon from Spain and Portugal. Then, in 1814, after Napoleon's disastrous attack on Russia left the French army at fewer than one hundred thousand men, Coalition armies occupied Paris, and Napoleon was forced to abdicate and surrender unconditionally, on April 11. The Treaty of Fontainebleau exiled him to the tiny Mediterranean isle of Elba. In the wake of Napoleon's resignation, royalists grabbed power in France and Louis XVIII, brother of Louis XVI, was restored to power, supported by Coalition powers that wanted a stable monarchy in France. Europe breathed a sigh of relief, and most of the armies disbanded.

But not for long. After escaping from Elba on February 26, 1815, Napoleon landed in France, where he was met by a regiment of soldiers sent by Louis XVIII to capture or kill him. These men had previously been Napoleon's Fifth Regiment and were led by his former subordinate, Marshal Ney. In true Napoleonic fashion, the general leaped off his horse, approached the regiment and cried out: "Soldiers of the Fifth, you recognize me, if any man will shoot his emperor, he may do so now!" The soldiers spontaneously rallied to Napoleon and marched on Paris with him. Louis XVIII fled, and Napoleon, using the same charisma that had brought the Fifth Regiment to his side, raised an army consisting of many of his old imperial soldiers.

It was a time of profound fear and distress among the Coalition powers in Europe, probably not rivalled until the ascendancy of Hitler in the late 1930s. Here was a man many considered a dangerous megalomaniac, returned from what was supposed to be permanent exile, who had, with astonishing swiftness, raised an army of 140,000 men. He needed to be stopped, and immediately, or the very future of Europe was at risk.

As it happened, representatives of Britain, Austria, Prussia and Russia were meeting in Vienna when the news came that Napoleon had escaped. The swift response of these countries was to assemble another coalition—the seventh to fight Napoleon—and declare war on France on March 25. The intention of the Seventh Coalition was to surround France on all sides, march on Paris, and destroy Napoleon once and for all. But the only force ready to fight was Wellington's Anglo-allied army in Belgium, although the Prussian force commanded by von Blücher would soon be on its way to join the British commander.

Napoleon, meanwhile, decided to strike at Belgium and capture the port of Brussels. He deployed his army along the French border and sent Marshal Ney to attack the Prussians. After fierce fighting, the French forced von Blücher's army to retreat—but did not destroy them— and Napoleon brought his army, on the evening of June 17, to the village of Waterloo.

PAINFULLY AFFLICTED

Forty-five years old as the engagement began (just a few months younger than the Duke of Wellington), Napoleon was in a state of odd indecision on the morning of the battle. He arose quite early, having spent the night in a farmhouse, and conferred with his generals over maps. "We have ninety chances in our favor," he said, "and not ten against us. I tell you Wellington is a bad general, the English are bad troops and the whole affair is nothing more than a picnic."

But his behavior belied such confident words. After reviewing his troops, he did not give any order to attack and simply brushed off every commander who suggested he do so, giving as his only excuse the fact that the ground was still too muddy to manoeuvre. Finally, he asked his aides to take him to a small inn at the rear of the lines, where he dismounted his horse and sat on a chair, at one point putting his elbows on his knees and placing his face in his hands. One of his staff officers later wrote that he seemed to be in a stupor.

It began to dawn on those around him that Napoleon was ill, although no one dared ask if he was and he never said so. But years after his death, his brother, Prince Jérôme, and his personal physician, Baron Larrey, revealed that the emperor

suffered fiercely from an affliction he found embarrassing to admit to—hemorrhoids, which if aggravated by long periods of sitting on a hard surface, such as a saddle, can became painfully prolapsed. He may have also suffered from cystitis, a bladder infection that makes urinating painful and causes high fevers, and is aggravated by cold, wet conditions. It had struck him before, most notably at the battle of Borodino.

Historians have also speculated that Napoleon, whose formerly taught physique had suddenly become pudgy, suffered from a pituitary disorder, which can cause weight gain, as well as indecisiveness and blurry thinking. Whatever was happening, it wasn't until around 11:30 a.m. that Napoleon roused himself from his lethargy and ordered that the attack begin with a cannonade.

THE THUNDER OF ARTILLERY

Some Coalition troops later claimed they were relieved that hostilities had finally begun. This was their moment to oust Napoleon, who, to some of the younger troops, had been a bête noire from infancy, a figment of evil used by nursemaids to frighten them. The relief of the troops to finally get the action underway turned to horror, however, as 9- and 13-pound French cannonballs flew through their ranks, wreaking havoc. One raw British recruit watched his sergeant major literally cut in half by a ball.

But here is where the Duke of Wellington's foresight came into play. He had personally suggested the ridge amid the farmers' fields near Waterloo as a place to make a stand against the French, and one of the reasons was the protection offered by its reverse slope. Now, he ordered that all of his men lie down behind it. To the watching French, it looked like the Coalition line, mainly British at its center, had simply disappeared. Although the artillery assault was the worst many a veteran soldier could remember, the ridge was their savior. Most of the cannonballs flew over the men, who tucked themselves as close as possible to the back of the ridge line, and landed well to the rear. The balls that did most damage were those that hit the top of the ridge and bounded across the supine soldiers.

When the barrage ended, after perhaps half an hour, the Coalition infantry raised their heads.

THE DUKE OF WELLINGTON LATER SAID OF THE BATTLE, IT WAS THE NEAREST-RUN THING YOU EVER SAW IN YOUR LIFE.

Denis Dighton's *The Battle of Waterloo*
18th June 1815 depicts the Duke of Wellington amid the chaos of the battle.

HALTING THE CHARGE

Even to men half-deaf from gunfire, the sound of the charge was recognizable. First, the *rat-tat-rat-tat* of drums, then bugles, ragged shouting, and finally, stronger and more unified, the cry "Vive l'Empereur!" When the Coalition forces rushed to reoccupy their lines at the center of the ridge, they saw, coming directly at their left center, three columns of French infantry, each twenty-four ranks deep and one hundred and fifty soldiers wide. These were flanked by cavalry on either side. This was the classic and deadly formation of the French Grand Army, the one that had won battles all across Europe: for Napoleon used these shock columns to punch rapidly through enemy lines, destroying all cohesion in a moment.

The French soldiers marched, as one British officer said admiringly, "as if on parade," directly at the Belgian division commanded by Sir Thomas Picton. Unnerved, the Belgians turned and ran, leaving a great hole in the center of the Coalition lines. But all was not as it seemed in the French ranks. Because of the deafening noise, men could not hear their leaders, and when the other British ranks opened fire, the columns started veering to the right and into a row of double hedges. Here, Picton had stationed the only men he had left, a troop of Scottish infantry, and he ordered them to attack just as a French bullet struck him and killed him instantly.

The Scots opened up from in front of the hedges, three thousand rifles pouring a volley into the French columns at close range. The French outnumbered the Scots many times over, but because of their column formation could not bring as many rifles to bear in reply. Next, the two forces hit each other, hard, and the combat turned into hundreds of deadly hand-to-hand melees in the swirling smoke, fought with rifle butt, sabre, pike and fists. Then, as the French wavered, there came an amazing sight: leaping the hedges, as if in a steeplechase, the British cavalry arrived, led by the Scots Greys, in a charge that utterly destroyed the French advance.

ON THE RUN

Heavy fighting now swirled around three isolated farmhouses and their outbuildings—Hougoumont, La Haye Sainte and Papelotte—which were ready-made defensive positions. At about three in the afternoon, Napoleon sent Marshal Ney to capture La Haye Sainte and after a bloody fight, the French infantry managed to tear it from British hands. French artillery was then emplaced there, aiming directly at the Coalition-held ridge. But when Ney asked for backup, Napoleon said he had none to spare. For arriving on the French right were the Prussian forces under von Blücher.

These were the reinforcements Wellington had needed and prayed for. Napoleon was appalled, for a force under one of his commanders, the Marquis de Grouchy, was supposed to have blocked these troops; but Grouchy had failed, allowing himself to be held up by other Prussians in a pitched battle at nearby Wavre while von Blücher made his way to Wellington.

Napoleon sent one last roaring attack of his elite forces, the Imperial Guard, against the Coalition-held ridge. But while some managed to break through, the rest were overwhelmed and began to flee. Seeing this elite corps on the run, the French lines broke, pursued by the Coalition cavalry. Napoleon's army was now in flight and Napoleon himself, bitter, broken and ill, retreated with it to Paris.

FINAL EXILE

On the battlefield that night lay forty thousand men, dead and horribly wounded. The subsequent looting has passed into legend. Ghoulish Belgian peasants stripped thousands of dead men bare, while Coalition soldiers wandered through the night, sometimes even robbing and killing their own. Officers, with their purses and gilded swords, were especially good sources of booty. The French wounded could expect no aid, and died, screaming for water.

The very next day, Belgian civilian sightseers came out to wander the battlefield, holding handkerchiefs over their noses against the unpleasant smell. They knew that Napoleon had finally been defeated here, this time for good, and that therefore history had been made.

Napoleon managed to escape from the battlefield, pursued by Coalition forces. With defeat inevitable, he abdicated, then made an attempt to flee to America, but was captured by the British and forced to surrender aboard a British warship on July 15. The ailing general was exiled once again, this time far away, to the tiny South Atlantic island of St. Helena, where he was to die in 1821, possibly poisoned, possibly, finally, a victim of the many ailments that had begun to plague him at Waterloo.

Europe had been saved, but the political effects of the battle of Waterloo would be long lasting. Horrified by the way in which Napoleon's re-emergence from Elba had once more stoked the fires of rebellion, Europe's leading powers became fiercely conservative. Signs of social change and moves towards democracy were quickly stamped out. Traditional monarchies were restored and bolstered across the continent, nationalist and republican movements quashed.

Supporters of the old order well knew how close they had come to catastrophe. As the Duke of Wellington said of the battle of Waterloo itself, it was "the nearest-run thing you ever saw in your life." ❧

1836

THE BATTLE
OF THE ALAMO

Late in the evening of March 5, 1836, so the story goes, Lieutenant-Colonel William B. Travis, the commander of a small garrison of over one hundred and eighty volunteers manning the Alamo mission in Texas, called them together, took out his sword, and drew a line in the sand. He then asked anyone who wished to stay and face the army of the Mexican General Antonio López de Santa Anna—which by then had all but surrounded their isolated outpost—to cross the line and stand with him. But he warned that whoever did so faced the likelihood of being killed or captured. All but one, a former lieutenant in Napoleon's Grande Armée named Moses Rose, stepped over the line and into history. Later that same evening Rose made his own way into history, crossing silently through the Mexican lines to freedom and everlasting notoriety as the so-called Coward of the Alamo.

No documentary evidence survives to support the "line in the sand" story. It may well be apocryphal. Rose, who settled in Louisiana and eventually faded from history, later swore that Travis did indeed draw the line, and Susannah Dickinson, the wife of the Alamo's artillery officer Almaron Dickinson and one of twenty women and children to survive the battle, also claimed to have seen Travis draw his sword and use it to make a sweeping gesture in the sand. That such an incidental moment should achieve the mythic proportions it has in the history of America—and of Texas in particular—might at first glance seem surprising, but nothing about the Alamo story is inconsequential. In the reverential retelling of the events leading up to March 6, 1836, every decision, every

command, every gesture and every shot is an intrinsic piece of the legend and a treasured reminder of what it means to live free.

THE ALAMO'S SPANISH ORIGINS

In the early 1700s the Spanish government controlled a large area that swept north from Mexico and included present-day Texas. It began to establish a series of Catholic missions across eastern Texas that were intended to serve as a buffer against the growing French settlements in Louisiana. The isolation of the missions, however, required the establishment of a way station to assist in the adequate provisioning of these new outposts, and in 1718 an expedition led by Martin de Alarcon, the governor of Spanish Texas, arrived at the banks of the San Antonio River. Construction soon began on a new mission, San Antonio de Valero. When floods from a gulf hurricane demolished the mud and straw structure in 1724, it was relocated to the other side of the river, which was less prone to flooding. Over the following decades this building grew into a collection of more than thirty adobe structures that included storerooms, homes for its missionaries and its growing population of Indian converts, and a chapel.

The mission complex was continually being reinforced and strengthened to withstand raids by the local Apache and Comanche Indians, but, with the population overwhelmingly converted to Roman Catholicism, the mission, which had been secularized in 1793, was abandoned.

Early in the new century the old mission was given a new name, the Alamo, most likely after a nearby grove of

cottonwood trees known as *alamo* in Spanish. Responsibility for the mission was transferred from Spain to Mexico after the Mexican Revolution in 1821.

TEXAS COLONISTS TAKE OVER THE ALAMO

In a series of battles and sieges during 1835, Texan revolutionaries inflicted a series of defeats upon the Mexican military culminating in the Siege of Bexár, staged in San Antonio de Bexár (present-day San Antonio), Texas. The Mexican forces, under General Martín Perfecto de Cos, brother-in-law of Santa Anna, surrendered on December 10 and, four days later, Cos marched his remaining eight hundred troops from San Antonio back to Mexico. This defeat represented the end of any Mexican armed presence in Texas and led many Texans to believe that the days of armed conflict with Mexico were over.

James Clinton Neill, a Texas revolutionary and politician, took command of the old mission on December 21, 1835. He was appalled at what he found and immediately set about strengthening its defences. Neill had inherited a strategic outpost that was woefully undermanned and lacking in even the most basic of supplies. He wrote to Sam Houston, then a major general in the Texas army and soon to be the first president of the Republic of Texas, pleading for extra provisions as well as an increase in the numbers garrisoning the outpost, which he claimed wouldn't last four days if placed under siege. "Unless we are reinforced and victualled," he wrote, "we must become an easy prey to the enemy, in case of an attack."

But no help was forthcoming. Instead, on January 19, Jim Bowie, the legendary Texan pioneer and soldier, arrived with fifty men and a note from Houston to salvage the mission's artillery and blow the Alamo to pieces—a difficult order to obey when a shortage of horses meant hauling artillery away on gun carriages was next to impossible. Both Bowie and Neill, convinced of the mission's strategic importance, thought the order ridiculous and replied they would rather perish defending it than surrender it to the enemy. On January 26, the mission's garrison passed a resolution in which they vowed to defend rather than destroy the mission.

NOTHING ABOUT THE ALAMO STORY IS INCONSEQUENTIAL— EVERY DECISION, EVERY COMMAND, EVERY GESTURE AND EVERY SHOT IS AN INTRINSIC PIECE OF THE LEGEND.

Davy Crockett, folk hero, frontiersman and defender of the Alamo, shown in heroic pose.

DAVY CROCKETT RIDES INTO TOWN

In early January Davy Crockett had arrived in Texas from his home in Tennessee and signed an oath to defend the Provisional Government of Texas (declared in November the previous year) for a period of six months. He and a small group of Tennesseans rode into the town of San Antonio on February 6, and were met there by Jim Bowie. Bowie convinced them to ride with him to the Alamo as volunteers. On February 14, James Neill went on furlough to visit his sick family in Bastrop and to seek out supplies and reinforcements. He left the Alamo under the command of the garrison's highest ranking officer, William B. Travis, a cavalryman who had arrived at the mission the previous week with thirty volunteers. Twelve days later fourteen hundred troops under the command of the self-styled "Napoleon of the West," General Antonio López de Santa Anna, arrived to reassert Mexican control over its rebellious northern state.

Santa Anna was one of the great and enduring figures in Mexican history. Born in Vera Cruz on February 21, 1794, he joined the colonial Spanish Army in 1810 and rose to the rank of captain. In 1822, together with Guadalupe Victoria, he signed the Plan de Casa Mata, which led to the abolition of the monarchy and the establishment of the Republic of Mexico. In 1828 he took part in the coup that overthrew the government of President Manuel Gómez Pedraza and in 1833 was elected president of Mexico. Far more than just another general, Antonio López de Santa Anna was the embodiment of the Mexican nation.

Extending over 3 acres, the collection of buildings that constituted the mission complex (it included palisades, barracks and a chapel) had been fortified over the years to withstand attacks by Indian raiders—but its walls and defences were ill-equipped for the artillery that Santa Anna was bringing. Its perimeter of almost 1300 feet would also be impossible to adequately defend with the number of men at Travis' disposal. Furthermore, there were no firing ports (or openings) built into its walls through which a rifleman could project the barrel of his gun and shoot while still being protected. This meant a walkway had to be constructed that allowed its defenders to shoot over the walls; however, this left their upper bodies horribly exposed to enemy fire.

SANTA ANNA'S UNEXPECTED ADVANCE

Santa Anna, however, was so enraged by what he saw as nothing more than armed acts of rebellion against the Mexican government that he wrote a tersely worded letter to

the U.S. president, Andrew Jackson, stating that he regarded any "foreigners" who might be captured in future battle to be "pirates" and they would be treated accordingly. He would be taking no prisoners. The letter reached Washington in January but seems not to have been widely circulated. It is all but certain that the volunteers within the walls of the Alamo had little idea that, once they stepped over Travis' line in the sand, their chances of survival were nil. By mid-February Travis had heard talk that Santa Anna was marching in the direction of San Antonio but wasn't expecting him to advance north until early spring and discounted rumors of his approach as unfounded. It proved to be a grave miscalculation. On February 16, Santa Anna crossed the Rio Grande and, on the evening of February 21, with his troops camped along the banks of the Medina River just 25 miles away, all but ten of the Alamo's garrison were enjoying a raucous night with the residents of San Antonio celebrating the birthday of George Washington.

On the evening of February 22, Santa Anna arrived at Leon Creek, a mere 8 miles from the Alamo and word of his advance spread to the residents of San Antonio. When scouts sent out by Travis returned claiming to have seen advance elements of Santa Anna's Delores Cavalry, his volunteers did all they could in what little time they had to fortify their position. Cattle were brought into the compound; food was scrounged

Defenders of the Alamo are overrun in a withering assault by Santa Anna's troops, leaving only seven Texan survivors.

from surrounding houses; and San Antonio's blacksmith shop was raided for anything that might prove valuable in a long siege. Some men, such as Alamaron Dickinson and Jim Bowie, brought family members in to the perceived safety of the mission, and Travis hurriedly dispatched couriers to the garrison at Gonzales 70 miles away to plead for reinforcements.

COLONEL FANNIN'S DOOMED MISSION

When news of the Alamo's plight reached members of the Provisional Government, recruitment drives were begun and reinforcements assembled, but none would arrive in time to help. Colonel James Fannin Jr left Goliad (to the southeast of San Antonio) on February 28 with more than three hundred men and four cannon, but the rescue attempt would prove a disaster. A shortage of horses meant Fannin was forced to rely on oxen to pull the artillery. Wagons broke down while still within sight of Goliad and the expedition took six hours just to cross the San Antonio River. Oxen wandered off into the night and many of the men under his command had even forgotten to bring any provisions for the journey. Fannin's mission ground to a halt. The defenders of the Alamo were on their own.

The siege began on February 24. Santa Anna positioned his artillery of 8-, 6- and 4- pound cannon within 330 yards of the Alamo's southern and eastern walls, too far to do any real damage to its defensive walls but intimidating nonetheless. The following day, under cover of artillery shells, Mexican troops moved to within 100 yards of the Alamo's perimeter and took shelter in a series of small mud huts, but were driven out the following morning. On February 26, the Alamo's artillerymen exchanged fire with some Mexican guns until forced to cease firing in order to conserve their low reserves of powder.

The next day, having heard of James Fannin's failed rescue mission, a group of approximately fifty men left Gonzales and reached the Alamo in the early hours of March 1. Not realizing in the darkness that the men were Texans, the Alamo sentries fired at them. One man was wounded, but their pleas quickly convinced those inside that they were Texans, not Mexicans, the gates were opened and the men were allowed in. According to the majority of historical accounts, the Alamo was now garrisoned by over one hundred and eighty men.

THE TROOPS DIG IN

In the midst of the siege on March 2, unbeknownst to those inside the Alamo and even to Santa Anna himself, Texas was declared an independent republic by the convention of 1836 delegates meeting at Washington-on-the-Brazos, a small town on the Brazos River in eastern Texas. The men of the Alamo, although they could not have possibly known it, were now fighting not only for their lives, but also for the world's newest nation, the Republic of Texas.

Any hopes those inside the Alamo might have had of holding on until reinforcements could arrive were dashed when, on March 3, a thousand Mexican troops arrived and paraded through San Antonio's plaza. This brought the total strength of Santa Anna's army to two thousand four hundred. The Mexicans were in high spirits, celebrating the defeat of a small force of Texans at the Battle of San Patricio, though in truth it was more of a skirmish than a battle, with just twenty Texans killed out of a complement of sixty. Nevertheless, the Mexican marching band played long into the night, and all those inside the Alamo could do was sit and listen.

THE FINAL ASSAULT

Sporadic artillery bombardments continued throughout March 4, and on March 5, Santa Anna announced to his staff that the final assault would begin the following day. When his aides asked why he did not prefer to wait until the arrival of his 12-pound cannon he replied: "What are the lives of soldiers than so many chickens?" So it was, with the mission all but surrounded and with food and water quickly running out, Santa Anna, rather than waiting out the enemy, chose instead to sacrifice his men in a dramatic, bloody and glorious finale.

At 5 a.m. on Sunday March 6, approximately eighteen hundred Mexican troops advanced in formation on the Alamo and were hit with a withering onslaught of cannon and musket fire. Their ranks staggered, but they regrouped and drove relentlessly forward. Travis was among the first to be killed, felled by musket fire while defending the north wall. Abandoning the mission walls the defenders withdrew to the inner courtyard and barracks, but the cause was hopeless. Jim Bowie, bedridden with a mystery illness, was bayoneted to death. The chapel was the last building to fall. Only seven men survived the battle, including by most accounts Davy Crockett, but all seven were subsequently executed on the personal orders of Santa Anna.

The siege of the Alamo had lasted thirteen days and was as much a tragedy as it was a heroic sacrifice. If the Texas Provisional Government hadn't been in such disarray, reinforcements could have been despatched sooner and the slaughter avoided. But it was not in vain. The battle ignited a righteous anger that spread across the fledgling nation, helped inspire a Texan victory at the decisive Battle of San Jacinto (Santa Anna and his troops were thoroughly routed), and etched into American history that famous call to arms: "Remember the Alamo!" ❧

1845–49
THE IRISH POTATO FAMINE

During the cool, wet summer of 1846, those Irish peasants who had managed to stave off starvation since the fall of 1845, mainly by selling their livestock and eating corn imported from America, waited anxiously for their potato crops to come in on fields and garden patches all over the country. Surely the potato would not fail again, would not turn black and stinking on its vine due to some unknown disease, as it had done the previous year.

At first, the crop seemed healthy and the people rejoiced that the blight would not continue. But by September, potatoes began to die in the west of Ireland; then, the malevolent disease moved across the country, at the rate of 50 miles a week, until no potato remained untouched. One parish priest wrote: "In many places the wretched people were seated on the fences of their decaying gardens, wringing their hands and weeping bitterly." Government officials estimated that there were only enough potatoes left in Ireland to feed people for one month. Black '47, as the Irish would later refer to the year of 1847, was about to begin.

A DRAMATIC IMPACT

It is impossible to overestimate the importance of the so-called Great Famine or Great Hunger in Irish history, but the following statistics convey the magnitude of its impact. In 1845, the population of Ireland was about eight million. Six years later, it was five and a half million. About one million died of starvation and disease. The other million and a half emigrated—mainly to Britain, Australia and America.

The effect of this population loss was extreme. It left Ireland an impoverished country for generations to come—indeed, it would take until the beginning of the twenty-first century for a resurgent Ireland to build its population levels back to those of 1845. It also began the rise to prominence of Irish communities in countries around the world, most notably the United States and Australia. In addition, it precipitated the growth of Irish nationalist movements like the Fenian Brotherhood and the Land League of the late nineteenth century. The latter, notably, would preach that the only way to avoid another dire famine was to wrest Irish land from corrupt English lords.

KING POTATO

As the Irish consumed their last supplies of potatoes and the winter of 1846–47 began, they started to eat nettles, turnips, rotten cabbages, seaweed, even grass. Those who lived along the west coast could stare out at a sea teeming with fish, but they had no way to harvest them—their tiny round boats, or coracles, were too flimsy for the deep water the fish inhabited.

Few countries were as vulnerable to famine as Ireland. It had been dependent on the single crop of the potato since the 1590s, when this marvellous, life-giving tuber was imported from South America, where it had first been cultivated in the highlands of Peru. In the cool, wet climate of Ireland, it thrived. Indeed, potatoes grew so easily there, and with so little labor, that they were planted in what were called "lazy beds." One acre (0.4 hectares) of the very scarce farmland in Ireland could bring up to 11 tons of potatoes a year, enough to feed a large Irish family easily.

It has been estimated that by the mid-nineteenth century three million Irish survived on potatoes alone, with perhaps a little cabbage and buttermilk added. One adult Irish person would generally eat up to 13 pounds of potatoes a day. Potatoes were rich in protein, carbohydrates and Vitamin C—if poverty forces you to eat just one food, the potato is not the worst choice you can make.

Unfortunately, not only did the Irish cultivate only one food source, but they grew only one variety of potato, called Lumpers. It produced a high yield but was vulnerable to being completely destroyed by blights; and since it was not

Sir Charles Edward Trevelyan, who pronounced himself unmoved by the sufferings of the starving Irish.

genetically diverse, a single blight could wipe it out. The cause of the blight that began at harvest time in September of 1845 was a killer fungus called *Phytophthora infestans*, which had been brought from America on ships to England, and then blown on an ill wind across the Irish Sea. This fungus not only killed the potatoes, it turned them black and rotten, leaving them putrefying in their beds. What's more, it returned with a vengeance the following year.

The winter of 1846–47 was the worst anyone could remember: freezing cold, with one blizzard and sleet storm after another, very unlike the usual mild Irish winter. People began pouring into government poorhouses, but these places were hellholes, rife with disease and desperation. In one poorhouse in Skibbereen, in Cork, fifty percent of the children admitted in late 1846 died. The chief magistrate of Cork, a man named Nicholas Cummins, wrote in horror of a visit to one poorhouse: "Six famished and ghastly skeletons to all appearances dead were huddled in a corner on some filthy straw. Their sole covering what seemed a ragged horse cloth. Their wretched legs hanging about naked above the knees. I approached with horror and found by a low moaning that they were still alive. They were in fever. Four children, a woman and what had once been a man … in a few minutes I was surrounded by at least two hundred such phantoms … Their demoniacal yells are still ringing in my ear and the horrible images are fixed upon my brain." Stories like this had been coming out of Ireland for a year—and now people were dying, truly, by the thousands. Why wasn't anyone doing anything about it?

"THE ENGLISH GAVE US THE FAMINE"

The Irish had been fighting the English occupiers of their country on and off for two centuries before the famine. As recently as 1798, an army of Irish peasants under an Anglo-Irish lawyer named Wolfe Tone had risen up against the English. Forty thousand of them were killed before Britain put down the rebellion. Even after the 1801 Act of Union integrated Ireland into Great Britain, the Irish were still considered poor cousins. Catholic Ireland remained under the control of an Anglo-Protestant landlord class which owned vast tracts of land. These were divided into tiny parcels by middlemen and sublet to tenant farmers. It has been estimated that over 90 percent of land in Ireland in 1845 was split up into plots of 12 hectares or less, and that perhaps four hundred thousand Irish peasants lived on plots of two hectares or smaller.

There is a saying among the Irish that "God gave us the potato blight, but the English gave us the famine." The prevailing stereotype of the Irish amongst the British landlords (most of whom seldom visited their holdings) was that they

THE IRISH POTATO FAMINE

were superstitious, cunning, lazy and dishonest. When the famine first hit, the British Prime Minister Sir Robert Peel attempted to help those in need by repealing the duties on imported corn, paying for Indian corn (maize) to be imported to feed the hungry, and setting up other relief efforts. But even this mild and inadequate response met with opposition in Britain, and Peel was voted out of office in the summer of 1846.

A CRUEL AND BIGOTED RESPONSE

Without Peel's leavening hand, control of the Irish was left entirely up to the Assistant Secretary of the British Treasury, Charles Edward Trevelyan, who visited Ireland only once during the famine. He claimed that, unlike the majority of those who witnessed the suffering at firsthand, he was unmoved by the experience—and that this made him better able to make decisions. One of his first was to halt shipments of government food, for fear that the Irish would become "habitually dependent." The only option left to the bulk of famine victims was public works relief. In the winter of 1846–47, seven hundred thousand Irish—men, women and children—found work breaking stones with hammers, transporting the pieces in baskets and laying roads. But the pay was so poor that not enough food could be bought to assuage hunger pangs, and so, in turn, the people grew too weak for such hard labor.

The cruel and bigoted response of Trevelyan and others like him infinitely worsened the suffering. As 1847 wore on, there were scenes, especially in the west, that were comparable to those of the plague years of the fourteenth century. Villages were depopulated, with survivors too weak to bury the dead, who lay on the roadways. There were reports of cannibalism. There were outbreaks of typhus, dysentery and something called famine dropsy (hunger oedema), which causes the limbs and the body to swell and ends with the victim dropping dead suddenly. And the situation didn't just affect the peasantry: over two hundred Irish doctors died in 1847 alone.

As all this occurred, the Irish watched while shiploads of Irish grain and livestock were sent to ports all over Europe. For while one crop had failed, others had thrived, and the British needed to turn a profit, "thus inflicting upon the Irish people," as one Irish politician wrote at the time, "the abject misery of having their own provisions carried away to feed others, while they themselves are left contemptuously to starve."

There were food riots in ports in Cork, where mobs tried to storm warehouses and take grain. In County Waterford, British troops guarding a food shipment were stoned; in return, they fired indiscriminately into a crowd, killing two people and wounding numerous others. Six landlords were shot and killed, murdered along dark roads. The British responded by sending more and more troops to Ireland.

KEEPING THE PEOPLE ALIVE

In June of 1847, the British government, influenced by outrage at home and abroad, decided to "keep the people alive," as Trevelyan put it. While still not providing any direct aid, it passed the Temporary Relief of Destitute Persons (Ireland) Act, also known as the Soup Kitchen Act, whereby soup kitchens were set up to feed the starving for free, but only through the auspices of international groups like the Quakers or the private British Relief Organisation.

The demand for soup far exceeded the ability of these groups to provide it, but by the summer of 1847, as another potato crop was anxiously awaited, three million people were kept alive in this way, on a pound of "stirabout" and a 3½ ounce slice of bread per day. In September, the potato crop appeared—and this time was without blight. But so few farmers had been able to afford seed to plant the previous years (or had been to busy doing public works projects) that the crop was comparatively tiny. Consequently, landlords decided that they needed to turn to other sources of income—wheat or livestock. But to create the larger fields needed, they had to destroy the dozens of tiny farms and potato plots on their lands—farms to which the starving Irish were desperately clinging.

The solution for the landlords was to evict their Irish tenants on grounds of nonpayment of rent and send them out to wander the roads or knock on the doors of the poorhouses. Some paid to send their peasants on ships to North America. These "coffin ships," as they were known, were overcrowded and pestilential. In the summer of 1847, forty ships containing fourteen thousand Irish waited under quarantine on the St. Lawrence River to enter Canada at Quebec; hundreds died of typhus, their bodies thrown overboard to float past the horrified eyes of the Canadians.

FLIGHT AND REBELLION

Ultimately, during Black '47, about one hundred thousand Irish went to Canada. Half of them walked across the border to the United States (which had more stringent immigration regulations and would not allow disease-carrying ships to enter). There, they paved the way for a great wave of Irish emigration to America, consisting of hundreds of thousands of men and women anxious to leave anything to do with Great Britain behind and find work in a new and bustling country. By the 1870s, Irish immigrants would control the inner political workings of some of America's largest cities, including New York, Boston and Chicago.

Black '47 was the worst year of the Famine, but when it was over the Irish continued to suffer. In 1849, after another failed potato crop, things became so bad that young Irishmen got themselves arrested in the hope of being transported to Australia, where at least they would be fed. Still more waves of Irish left the country for America.

Others, tired of the oppressive rule of the British and their inhumane response to the famine, proposed drastic action. In the middle of the Great Hunger, in 1848, a group of rebellious young Irish nationalists formed the Irish Confederation and plotted throughout the summer of 1848 to rise against the British. But, heavily infiltrated by the British secret police, unable to secure arms and also underestimating an exhausted populace's willingness to revolt, the rebels were quickly overcome after a few minor skirmishes. Their leaders were arrested and sentenced to transportation to Australia. However, their writings would influence a future generation of rebels, both in Ireland and America, who would fight to cast off British rule.

The 1850s brought normal harvests of potatoes, and, with the diversification of crops, the expansion of railways for transporting food and the politicization of the working class, the spectre of famine was gradually diminished. Politizisation led to agitation for land reform, notably by the Land League movement in the late 1870s, and gave the Irish a greater awareness of the importance of controlling their own destinies. In this sense, a line can be traced from the Great Hunger to the events that brought about independence in 1921 and the creation of the Republic of Ireland in 1949. ❋

1854

THE CHARGE OF THE LIGHT BRIGADE

Theirs not to reason why,
Theirs but to do or die:
Into the valley of Death
Rode the six hundred.
ALFRED, LORD TENNYSON, "THE CHARGE OF THE LIGHT BRIGADE"

There are monuments aplenty to meaningful deaths in war, but Tennyson's poem "The Charge of the Light Brigade" provides history with a dramatic recounting of the opposite: the sacrifice of hundreds of good men by criminally stupid officers in a futile, meaningless attack. Most people today would know nothing about the Charge of the Light Brigade were it not for Tennyson's poem. It brilliantly captures the bravery of the "six hundred" to be precise, six hundred and seventy three cavalrymen of the British Light Brigade as they galloped down a valley near Balaklava, on the Crimean Peninsula, under murderous fire from their Russian adversaries. Even so, although the poem also says "not tho' the soldiers knew, someone had blundered," it doesn't come close to capturing the true nature of this debacle.

Beginning in 1853, the Crimean War pitted the Imperial Russia of Tsar Nicholas I against Great Britain, France and the Ottoman Empire, which aimed to block Russia's attempts to expand its sphere of influence into the Middle East. Most of the fighting centered on the Crimean Peninsula, which thrusts southwards from the Ukraine, then part of the Russian Empire, into the Black Sea. In 1854, Great Britain, France

and Turkey invaded Crimea with an allied expeditionary force intent on besieging the Russian port of Sevastopol. On October 25, the Russians attempted to break the siege by attacking the nearby port of Balaklava, from which the allied forces got their supplies.

THE THIN RED LINE

These attacks were repulsed by extraordinarily brave actions on the part of the British army and cavalry. The Ninety-third Highlanders stood their ground against the Russian onslaught, earning the famous nickname "the thin red line" from William Howard Russell, often called the first war correspondent, who was on the scene reporting for the *Times*. (Actually, Russell, watching from nearby heights, depicted the Ninety-third as "a thin red streak tipped with a line of steel," the red referring to their uniforms, the steel to their bayonets, but the phrase was at once condensed into "thin red line" and is still used to describe valiant stands.) In addition, in an extraordinary uphill charge, the so-called Heavy Brigade of about five hundred dragoons, or mounted infantry, attacked a charging Russian cavalry formation of three thousand horses, engaging them in ferocious hand-to-hand combat.

"UNUSUALLY STUPID"

At that moment, about ⅓ mile away from this desperate see-saw battle, stood an extraordinary figure, James Thomas Brudenell, the Seventh Earl of Cardigan, commander of the Light Brigade, so-called because its members were true cavalry, less heavily armed than the Heavy Brigade. He turned to a fellow officer and said, "Those damn Heavies will have the laugh on us this day." But it never occurred to him to leap on his horse and lead his men to join the battle. As he explained later, he had not received orders to do so.

This was typical of Cardigan. Fifty-seven-years-old in 1854, an immensely wealthy aristocrat, he has been described by the British historian Cecil Woodham-Smith as "tall, handsome, opulently dressed, carrying himself with a mixture of arrogance and self-importance said to make one lose one's temper just to look at him." Cardigan, who wore, at casual moments, the sweater that he popularized was also, as Woodham-Smith puts it, "unusually stupid … The melancholy truth was that his gorgeous head had nothing in it."

Cardigan had had a checkered career in the British Army (which had not fought a war since the battle of Waterloo). He had been publicly reviled for such excesses as fighting duels and having a man under his command flogged on Easter Sunday. But, despite this, he had steadily advanced himself, by dint of the perfectly legal practice of buying commissions, and was by this time a major general. After each day's campaigning, he retired to his private yacht in the Black Sea, there to drink champagne and have his uniforms freshly pressed.

WHOSE SIDE ARE THEY ON?

While Cardigan leaned on his horse and made comments about the fight between the Heavies and the Russians, as if he were at a sporting event, sixty-six-year-old Fitzroy Somerset, Lord Raglan, watched from the Sapoune Heights, an imposing escarpment high above the raging battle. A career officer, Raglan was the commander of the British forces in the Crimea and he had seen action forty years before at the battle of Waterloo, where he had lost his right arm serving under his hero, the Duke of Wellington. Unfortunately, Raglan had little command experience and also possessed the embarrassing habit of referring to France (Britain's ally in the Crimea, but a foe in earlier wars including the Napoleonic Wars) as "the enemy," for which he had to be corrected time and again by his staff.

From his bird's-eye viewpoint, Raglan could see the Heavy Brigade breaking the will of the Russian cavalry and forcing them into a retreat. The Russians subsequently streamed back along the Causeway Heights, a low line of ridges stretching above the beaches of the Black Sea. On their advance, the Russians had captured British redoubts complete with artillery that had been emplaced there; now, Raglan and his staff could see them attempting to remove these guns as they fell back. Anxious to stop the Russians from retreating with British artillery, Raglan issued orders to Lord Lucan, commander of the British cavalry division, to attack.

PLODDING AND UNIMAGINATIVE

Fifty-four-year-old George Bingham, the Third Earl of Lucan, was the third sorry figure in the trio of British aristocratic officer dunces at Balaklava. Lucan had been retired from the army for nearly twenty years before being called to duty in the Crimea; he had paid £25,000 to purchase a colonelcy, much of which had been extracted penny by penny from the peasants who farmed his vast Irish estates. Plodding and unimaginative, he was the polar opposite of Lord Cardigan, who was his direct subordinate. The two men happened to be brothers-in-law. They also hated each other passionately and had done so for thirty years.

Lucan's cavalry division was positioned at the mouth of what was known as the North Valley, which was about ⅔ mile wide. On his right were the Causeway Heights, from where the Russians were removing the British guns. On his left were the Fedioukine Hills, where there were more Russian guns emplaced. About a mile away, at the far end of the valley, were heavy Russian guns and Russian troops. Lucan now received a series of confusing orders from Raglan ordering an attack by his light cavalry against the Russian guns, but could not understand them and asked for clarification. Why would Raglan order an attack by cavalry along a mile of open ground exposed to Russian fire on three sides?

TRAGIC CONFUSION

The answer was, he had not. Raglan wanted Lucan to attack to his right, against the gun emplacements on Causeway Heights. But because Lucan did not have Raglan's bird's-eye view of the land, he could not understand what his commander was talking about.

> AFTER EACH DAY'S CAMPAIGNING, CARDIGAN RETIRED TO HIS PRIVATE YACHT TO DRINK CHAMPAGNE AND HAVE HIS UNIFORMS PRESSED.

The imposing but witless Seventh Earl of Cardigan, James Thomas Brudenell, led the disastrous Charge of the Light Brigade.

This romanticized illustration of the charge shows the moment when the survivors reached the Russian gun emplacements.

After repeated delays and requests for clarification from Lucan, an impatient Raglan finally sent an officer by horse to speak directly to Lucan. This man was a key figure in the whole affair, the thirty-six-year-old Captain Louis Nolan, an aide de camp with a wide knowledge of cavalry tactics. He had been enraged by Cardigan's failure to pursue the retreating Russians and he blamed this failure squarely on Lucan, Cardigan's commander. Arriving with frothing horse at Lucan's position, he verbally and with some impatience delivered Raglan's order for Lucan to attack the Russian guns.

Angered by this junior officer's air of insolence, Lucan replied: "Attack sir? Attack what? What guns, sir?" And Nolan, instead of pointing at the Causeway Heights, flung his arm in the direction of the Russian emplacements at the end of the North Valley: "There, my lord, is your enemy, there are your guns!"

Nolan's words and tone were so insubordinate that members of Lucan's staff felt that he should be placed under arrest. To this day, no one knows quite what Nolan was referring to when he pointed. He certainly knew that Raglan did not intend for Lucan to charge his men right down the valley, but those present, along with Lucan, took his gesture to mean just that. It is possible that his arm-waving was simply gesticulating, meaning nothing at all. But the men on the ground could not see the Russians with their captured guns on the heights, so it

is easy to understand why they might have assumed that he was directing them to the far end of North Valley.

In any event, Lucan accepted that he was being forced to make a suicidal charge, and spurred his horse over to see his hated brother-in-law, Lord Cardigan.

INTO THE VALLEY OF DEATH

Had Cardigan and Lucan been on better terms, it is possible that they together might have made some sense of these puzzling orders. Instead, they spoke stiffly, in military formalities. Lucan told Cardigan of Raglan's orders and instructed him to lead the charge with the Light Brigade while Lucan followed with the Heavies. Taken aback, Cardigan remonstrated: "Certainly sir, but allow me to point out that the Russians have a battery in the valley at our front and batteries and riflemen on both sides."

Lucan replied: "I know it, but Lord Raglan will have it. We have no choice but to obey." At this, Cardigan saluted, wheeled his horse around and ordered his brigade to make ready to attack. An aide heard him mutter: 'Well, here goes the last of the Brudenells."

Cardigan next divided his brigade of six hundred and seventy three men into two lines, but then Lucan, countermanding Cardigan's orders, stepped in to divide it into three. When the lines were ready, Cardigan marched about five horse-lengths out in front of his men and raised his sword. He said, quite calmly: 'The brigade will advance. Walk, march, trot'. A trumpet blew, and they were off.

NO LOOKING BACK

While Cardigan's intelligence and leadership skills can be fairly impugned, his bravery cannot. Erect in his saddle, wearing a resplendent (and freshly pressed) uniform of red, blue and gold, riding a beautiful chestnut mare, he led his men down the valley, never once looking back.

Shells began bursting among the lines, shattering men and horses. Whenever a man fell, the ranks parted around him and then closed again. The Russians, who were able to bring about fifty guns to bear on the charging British horses, were astonished when the attacking cavalry did not wheel into the hills, but instead kept going straight down the valley.

During this early stage of the charge, an inexplicable thing happened. Captain Nolan, Raglan's aide de camp, rode his horse out in front of Lord Cardigan (an unforgivable breach of etiquette) and, crossing the British line of advance, turned in his saddle, waved his sword, and began shouting something. Was he trying to lead the charge, as the enraged Cardigan thought? Or was he finally urging the British to veer off to the right to attack the Causeway Heights?

No one will ever know, for in the very first volley of shells, Nolan became the first casualty of the charge, as a hot metal fragment tore into his heart. In a scene of sheer horror, his sword fell to the earth, but, with the right hand frozen in an upright position, his body was carried by his horse back through the ranks of the brigade while issuing a bone-chilling and seemingly endless shriek. This caused the ever-empathetic Cardigan to declare: "Imagine that fellow screaming like a woman when he was hit".

GONE IN A CLOUD OF SMOKE

Despite this distraction, Cardigan led his men on. Shells and bullets whizzed by but he was not touched, despite the fact that he was weirdly alone, out in front of everyone. His men were now being hit by the guns at the end of the valley, as well as from the sides. As more and more men fell, those who came behind were forced to trample their bodies to keep going. After eight minutes that must have seemed like an eternity for the attackers, and with the first line about 90 yards from the guns at the end of the valley, Cardigan raised his sword to lead the final attack. Then, all at once, the guns blazed in unison, and the first line of the Light Brigade seemed to simply disappear.

Cardigan later claimed that he felt the flames of the cannon singe his legs. In any event, he picked a gap between two guns, kept on going through a cloud of smoke and found himself on the other side of the Russian guns, face to face with a troop of Cossack cavalry. As extraordinary coincidence would have it, one of the Russian officers, Prince Radzivil, recognized Cardigan from the social circles of London, and ordered his men to capture the earl, not harm him. Cardigan evaded them and galloped back the way he had come. On the way, he passed some of his soldiers clashing with Russian troops. Their position was precarious and they were soon forced to retreat, however, back through the curtain of fire and steel that constituted the 'Valley of Death'. Cardigan never seems to have felt any duty to his men to rally them or help lead them back. In fact, he arrived at British lines well before most of the stragglers. Only one hundred and ninety five men survived, leading to rumors that he had not even made the famous charge at all.

THE CHARGE IMMORTALIZED

After Russell's report in the *Times* and others that followed, the Charge of the Light Brigade became a major point of controversy and public debate. Blame was variously assigned: to Lord Raglan for giving confusing orders, to Lord Lucan for not clarifying them, to Lord Cardigan for not communicating with his commanding officer.

But ultimate blame lay with an official system that allowed unqualified aristocrats to purchase officer ranks and be placed in charge of the lives of thousands. In fact, this system was abolished after the Crimean War, as a direct result of the debacle of the Light Brigade. And while the stupidity of senior officers was highlighted, the bravery of the men of the Light Brigade did not go unnoticed, and the British public began to demand better treatment for the ranks, in terms of food, medicine and nursing care. So, in the end, some good did come out of one of the most famous military disasters in history. ❧

1863

THE GETTYSBURG ADDRESS

The speech was just 272 words long—ten sentences—and it took Abraham Lincoln at most three minutes to deliver it. Yet it became and remains a rallying call for Americans, and one of the most eloquent, powerful and influential expressions of the value of freedom and democracy ever made.

The date was November 19, 1863, the place a once-sleepy hamlet called Gettysburg in the rolling farmland of southern Pennsylvania, in the north-eastern United States. About twenty-three thousand people were in attendance, but only fifteen thousand of these were alive. The rest were some of the dead of the ferocious battle of Gettysburg fought the previous July, who were in the process of being transferred from their hasty battlefield graves to more suitable accommodation in the new cemetery the President of the United States had come to help dedicate.

As Lincoln sat on the dais at the new cemetery, waiting literally for hours to speak, he had, on two sheets of paper tucked in his inside jacket pocket, what amounted to a prophecy. The Gettysburg Address spoke to a country that Lincoln envisioned rising like a phoenix from fire, blood and ashes. It would be a country that was no longer merely a union of disparate states, but a nation. There was no surety in the summer of 1863 that this nation would come into being—quite the opposite possibility, that the Union would shatter into pieces, was the one many people contemplated. Such an outcome could have had a dramatic effect on world history and the global balance of power, even to this day.

"A NEW NATION"

Fought in high, hot summer, the battle of Gettysburg pitted the invading Southern forces of General Robert E. Lee (approximately seventy thousand in all) against the defending Union Army of about ninety thousand, led by the newly appointed General George Gordon Meade, the latest in a string of commanders that Abraham Lincoln had turned to in increasing desperation. The war had begun in 1860, but the conflict had been coming for decades.

Upon freeing themselves from British rule in 1776, America's first thirteen states had asserted in the Declaration of Independence that all men—including the slaves used in America since the seventeenth century—were born equal and should be free. In the industrialized North, this goal was embraced. But in the agrarian South, where cotton was the main crop and enslaved Africans did much of the work, the institution of slavery was retained and defended.

Northern antagonism to slavery steadily increased, and things came to a head as America expanded westwards in the 1850s. Were the new territories, as they became states, to be "free" or slave states? When no agreement on this issue could be reached, the Southern states seceded from the American Union and formed the Confederate States of America. Soon after, war began.

President Abraham Lincoln, whose address at Gettysburg has proved one of the most influential speeches in history.

"A GREAT CIVIL WAR"

At the battle of Chancellorsville in Virginia, early in May of 1863, a badly outnumbered Lee had defeated the Union forces. Thereafter, the Confederate general invaded Pennsylvania, planning on capturing the state capital of Harrisburg or even the major urban center of Philadelphia. With Philadelphia, which was only about 150 miles from the Union capital of Washington D.C., in hand, Lee could cut off Union supply lines and even surround Washington, ending the war at a stroke. But the Union, with its back against the wall, blocked Lee at Gettysburg, fighting well and desperately over three days and finally inflicting casualties on the South of twenty-three thousand killed, wounded or captured. Although Meade's forces lost even more, Lee could ill afford these casualties in the manpower-poor South, and he was forced to retreat on July 4. Although the over-cautious Meade missed an extraordinary opportunity to follow and finish off his opponent, the North had won a great victory.

"A GREAT BATTLE-FIELD OF THAT WAR"

When Meade finally moved south after Lee, he told Lincoln: "I cannot delay to pick up the debris of the battlefield." And

Confederate dead, swollen by the heat, lie unburied on the battlefield at Gettysburg, as Union troops and sightseers stand by.

quite a debris it was. Eight thousand human bodies and the corpses of three thousand horses still lay unburied, rendering the ridges and farmlands of Gettysburg a wretched, stinking mess. Burial parties were hastily recruited from civilians and Confederate prisoners, but with few resources available and time pressing, the most they could do for the human dead was to lightly cover them with earth. (The horses were burned in great piles south of the town.) Soon, relatives of Union soldiers who had fallen began to scavenge through the shallow graves, looking to identify their loved ones or at least find mementos. In the process, bodies became unburied, and arms and legs and even heads protruded from the ground, becoming food for pigs, crows and masses of buzzing flies.

Obviously something had to be done about this, for even then everyone knew that Gettysburg was a major turning point—a "Waterloo," as the *New York Times* called it. You could not have the semi-buried corpses of Union heroes littering the landscape.

So an interstate commission was set up (for the cost of burying these dead would fall on all the northern states whose soldiers had died there), seven hectares of land were bought for a cemetery, and William Saunders, cemetery landscape architect, was chosen to design the plots. The time-consuming process of digging up the dead (some already twice buried), identifying what states they were from, and placing them in the thousands of coffins provided by the Federal Government, now began. (The Confederate dead stayed in their field burial plots, until their bodies were repatriated to the South some ten years later.)

"WE HAVE COME TO DEDICATE"

So it was that when the principal speaker came to the podium on November 19, he looked out over a brilliantly landscaped cemetery. Saunders had shaped the Soldier's National Cemetery at Gettysburg (now called the Gettysburg National Cemetery) so that the dead were arranged in a series of semicircles around a central monument to their valor. The reburial process was still in progress and would not be completed until the following spring.

The principal speaker was not, however, Abraham Lincoln, but the orator, former senator, cabinet member and Harvard president Edward Everett. Indeed, not only was he the principal speaker, but he was allowed to deliver thirteen thousand words over two hours. His prominence at the event fuelled one of the many myths about Gettysburg: that Abraham Lincoln was deliberately snubbed by its organizers, many of whom were from an opposing political party, the Democrats. In fact, at this time presidents had little involvement in state affairs and the organizers weren't even sure that Lincoln would turn up for a ceremony managed by a state government.

In any case, Everett was a famous orator who specialized in battlefield topics and had previously dedicated monuments at such War of Independence sites as Lexington, Concord, and Bunker Hill. At Gettysburg, he provided what the historian Garry Wills has called a kind of "docudrama" for his listeners—a sort of re-enactment of what happened on the battlefield, the fruit of his careful study of the events of early July. His speech was well received. When he finally sat down, Abraham Lincoln stood up.

"ALTOGETHER FITTING AND PROPER"

Lincoln may have been casually invited to make a "few appropriate remarks," as the dedication organizers had put it to him, but he was not about to let this opportunity pass

> FOUR SCORE AND SEVEN YEARS AGO OUR FATHERS BROUGHT FORTH ON THIS CONTINENT A NEW NATION, CONCEIVED IN LIBERTY, AND DEDICATED TO THE PROPOSITION THAT ALL MEN ARE CREATED EQUAL ...

by. Here, at last, was a major victory for his administration that he was keen to exploit for propaganda purposes. People, in America and in Europe, needed to be reminded that the Union would be victorious. But moving beyond the immediate political implications, Lincoln carefully wrote his short speech to expound upon a glorious vision of an America with a bright future ahead of it beyond these dark days.

The care that went into the writing of the Gettysburg Address puts to rest another myth that has since arisen—that Lincoln scrawled it on the back on an envelope on his train ride from Washington to Pennsylvania. On any number of levels, this is highly unlikely. Lincoln was a careful organizer who understood the power of words better than almost any U.S. president before or since. It seems highly improbable that he would have left such an important task to the last moment, let alone until a train ride that would have involved meeting and greeting any number of politicians and well-wishers travelling to Gettysburg.

The best evidence has Lincoln working on his speech for several days at the White House before he set off. In crafting it, he drew upon broad but not formal learning. Unlike Edward Everett, Lincoln had not had a university education. Far from it. He had had perhaps one year of grammar school, put together a few months at a time while he worked on various farms in Kentucky, Indiana, and Illinois, and he was essentially self-taught. But what an education he had given himself: large doses of the Bible, Shakespeare, history, literature and the law.

Arriving the night before the speech was due to be given, Lincoln stayed at the house of David Wills, prime mover behind the cemetery and its dedication, and there he may have added a few finishing touches.

"FOUR SCORE AND SEVEN YEARS AGO"

Another myth that surrounds the Gettysburg Address is that Lincoln spoke hurriedly and essentially mumbled his address, so that few present could hear it. In fact, Lincoln (a former amateur actor who loved to recite Shakespeare) was known for his ability to project. True, he did not have Everett's stentorian tones—Lincoln had a high-pitched, twangy, backwoods Kentucky drawl, but it apparently carried quite clearly to all areas of the great crowd.

Everett's speech, though finely written and topical, was of the moment, whereas Lincoln's address was for the future. He began by harking back to a time eighty-seven years earlier—

deliberately using biblical language ("four score and seven years ago") to provide a timelessness and importance to his counting of the years—when America was born with the idea, put forth in the Declaration of Independence, that "all men are created equal." Now, Lincoln went on, this basic premise, important not just for Americans, but for "any nation" that desired freedom, was being put to the test. Through the extraordinary sacrifices of those who had died at Gettysburg, American ideals had been, for now, defended, but this cemetery dedication, this "consecration" (with its sense of the sacred, of hallowed ground), would be of little use, unless the living carried on with the sacrifices necessary for a "new birth of freedom": a unified nation that was truly "of the people, by the people, for the people."

Summarizing his nation's history, from first birth through a painful struggle to an envisioned rebirth, Lincoln made every one of his few words count.

"THE GREAT TASK"

Yet another myth that has arisen around the events at Gettysburg was that Lincoln left the dais disappointed with both his speech and its reception. This was promulgated in part by his friend and bodyguard Ward Lamon, who claimed Lincoln had muttered to him afterwards that the speech was a "flat failure" and "fell upon the audience like a wet blanket." In fact, most historians consider the memories of the dramatic and self-aggrandizing Lamon suspect. Contemporary newspaper reports show that Lincoln was interrupted five times for applause in only three minutes. These accounts were mainly quite laudatory—the *Chicago Tribune* said, "The dedicatory remarks by President Lincoln will live among the annals of man." Indeed, Edward Everett wrote Lincoln the very next day to say: "I should be glad, if I could flatter myself, that I came as near to the central idea of the occasion, in two hours, as you did in two minutes."

Everett had it exactly right. Lincoln's prophetic speech not only focused the minds of Americans on the purpose behind this horrible war, but was a text future Americans could return to again and again, to find meaning in the struggles they found themselves engaged in. Moreover, the Gettysburg Address would soon be adopted internationally as a symbol of freedom and equality. As early as 1865, in an address before an international conference of workers, Karl Marx praised the Gettysburg Address and Abraham Lincoln as being instrumental in defeating "the slave driver" of the South. When Winston Churchill addressed a special meeting of the U.S. Congress on December 26, 1941—just after America had declared war on Japan and Germany—he said: "I have been in full harmony all my life with the tides which have flowed on both sides of the Atlantic against privilege and monopoly and I have steered confidently towards the Gettysburg ideal of government, of the people, by the people, for the people." And even today, the Gettysburg Address, which has been translated into more than thirty languages, continues to inspire people around the world.

THE TWO HUNDRED AND SEVENTY-TWO WORDS THAT MADE HISTORY

No one really knows exactly which text Lincoln used at Gettysburg, because at least five known copies of the address exist, in Lincoln's hand, each with minor differences. However, the version below is the one most widely accepted and used, since it was the last copy written out by Lincoln personally, to be lithographed for sale and distribution in February 1864, to benefit a charity.

Four score and seven years ago our fathers brought forth on this continent a new nation, conceived in Liberty, and dedicated to the proposition that all men are created equal.

Now we are engaged in a great civil war, testing whether that nation, or any nation, so conceived and so dedicated, can long endure. We are met on a great battle-field of that war. We have come to dedicate a portion of that field, as a final resting place for those who here gave their lives that the nation might live. It is altogether fitting and proper that we should do this.

But, in a larger sense, we can not dedicate—we can not consecrate—we can not hallow—this ground. The brave men, living and dead, who struggled here, have consecrated it, far above our poor power to add or detract. The world will little note, nor long remember what we say here, but it can never forget what they did here. It is for us the living, rather, to be dedicated here to the unfinished work which they who fought here have thus far so nobly advanced. It is rather for us to be here dedicated to the great task remaining before us—that from these honored dead we take increased devotion to that cause for which they gave the last full measure of devotion—that we here highly resolve that these dead shall not have died in vain—that this nation, under God, shall have a new birth of freedom—and that government of the people, by the people, for the people, shall not perish from the earth. ❧

1876
CUSTER'S LAST STAND

Oh, what a slaughter how Manny [sic] homes are Made desolate by the Sad disaster eavery [sic] one of them were Scalped and otherwise Mutilated but the General he lay with a smile on his face ...
—Private Thomas Coleman, B Company, Seventh Cavalry, U.S. Army

It took place on a hot, dusty Sunday morning near an obscure river in a remote part of the American West 130 years ago—and yet we still can't forget Custer's last stand. Why? The name may have something to do with it. 'Last stand' has an epic ring to it, although many think it implies that Custer was the last man standing on the battlefield, which was certainly not so. Perhaps it's because everyone on one side of the battle—General George Armstrong Custer and two hundred and ten members of his Seventh Cavalry—was massacred. Battles where nobody among the defeated survives to tell the tale have a way of capturing the human imagination; only half the story is brought home, the rest resides with ghosts. Had Custer been defeated, but with much of his command left alive, would we remember the Battle of the Little Bighorn in the same way?

Almost certainly, the battle's fame has something to do with the fact that it marked the beginning of the end for the thousands of Sioux warriors who surrounded Custer that day—in fact, for all the Indian peoples of America. Following the defeat, public outcry turned George Armstrong Custer into a martyr whose spilt blood had to be revenged. An expanded American army fiercely hounded the great Sioux leader Sitting Bull and his people afterwards; while Sitting Bull escaped to Canada with a small band, most of the Sioux were forced to surrender and ended up on reservations. And within fifteen years of Custer's death, the battles had faded into legend.

MOVING WEST

In the late 1860s, America's westward expansion, slowed considerably by the Civil War (1861–65), had begun again in earnest. The new drive west was fuelled by gold strikes in Colorado and Montana, but also by white settlers hungry for the rich farmland of the Great Plains, which spread from the Mississippi River all the way to the foot of the Rocky Mountains.

The tribes that ranged the northern Great Plains were called the Lakota, although the whites and the tribe's other foes referred to them as the Sioux, from an Ojibwa word meaning "serpent" or "enemy." The Sioux were a close-knit, wandering tribe, which followed the herds of buffalo and worshipped *Wakan Tanka*, the Great Spirit. By the 1860s, however, the Sioux found a formidable foe swarming into their lands—white men, whom they called *wasichus*, meaning, literally, 'you can't get rid of him'. The *wasichus*, the Indians felt, simply didn't listen very well. So they tried to underscore the point that white people were not welcome on the land they were trying to preserve— by slaughtering miners and other incomers, sometimes by broiling them over open fires.

In 1868, the U.S. government and the Sioux signed the Second Treaty of Fort Laramie. In return for a cessation of attacks against whites, the government would cede the Sioux much of western South Dakota and eastern Wyoming, and keep settlers and miners away from the Sioux's sacred *Paha Sapa*, or Black Hills. By 1876, however, after the discovery of gold in the Black Hills, fifteen thousand white miners swarmed through Sioux territory. Using Sioux attacks on settlers as a pretext, the administration, under President Grant, sent troops

223

to the region with orders to push the Indian tribes further west. This put the Sioux on a collision course with one of the most controversial military figures in American history: George Armstrong Custer.

DARING AND DASHING

In June of 1876, Lieutenant Colonel George Custer's regiment of the Seventh Cavalry set off as one arm of a three-pronged expedition to find the Sioux, who were rumored to be encamped along the Little Bighorn River in what is today the state of Montana. Brigadier George Crook's command would move up from the south, Colonel John Gibbon's regiment would approach from the west, and Brigadier General Alfred H. Terry's group, which included the thirty-one officers and five hundred and sixty-six men of Custer's Seventh Cavalry, would approach from the east. But Crook was delayed by a battle with the Sioux, and it was only Terry and Gibbon who rendezvoused late in June. They decided to send Custer down the Rosebud River with his regiment, while they travelled along the Bighorn and Little Bighorn Rivers, hoping to trap the Sioux between them.

Before the Seventh Cavalry galloped off, swallowtail flags snapping in the breeze, Gibbon called out jokingly to Custer, "Custer don't be greedy! Wait for us!" Custer wheeled his horse and waved, replying in the same vein, "No, I will not!"

This kind of comment was characteristic of George Armstrong Custer, who was born in 1839, in a small Ohio town, one of five children of a blacksmith father. Custer graduated from West Point in 1861, last in his class. But the Civil War was starting and every man was needed, so he was hurried into combat as a raw young cavalry officer. Despite his poor performance at the academy, Custer was a revelation on the battlefield. He quickly earned a reputation as a fierce fighter in the Union Army; from the First Battle of Bull Run and the Battle of Gettysburg to the denouement of the war at Appomattox, Custer played a critical role in defeating the enemy. During the war, he was promoted from first lieutenant to brigadier general (the youngest in the Union Army)—an unheard-of rise in rank.

Not only was Custer brave, but he also had dashing style. His long, curling blonde hair and fair, youthful complexion caused some troops to snicker, "Who is this child? Where is his nurse?" But Custer ignored them and even added to the controversy by designing his own uniform made of black velvet with a brilliant crimson scarf tied round his throat.

Custer's contempt for danger also made him controversial. His cavalry units suffered extraordinarily high casualty rates,

even by the bloody standards of the Civil War, because he was known to charge into situations where another commander might proceed more cautiously. Despite this, he was offered another commission after the war ended, as Lieutenant Colonel of the newly created Michigan Seventh Cavalry.

ON THE TRAIL OF THE SIOUX

After parting from the army regiments at Yellowstone River, Custer moved his Seventh Cavalry up Rosebud Creek in the direction of the Bighorn Mountains, scouting out Indian trails as they went. All trails seemed to point in the same direction—to the valley of the Little Bighorn River, which the Indians called the Greasy Grass. Custer assumed there was a village there, but he had no idea of its size.

On the morning of June 25—a bright, hot, clear Sunday—he took his command over the Wolf Mountains and down into the valley of the Little Bighorn, about 15 miles from the Indian base. Since he still wasn't completely sure of the location of the village, Custer chose to divide his command into three sections, headed by himself and two other officers, Major Marcus Reno, a nervous, excitable soldier, and Captain Frederick Benteen, an indisputably brave fighter who, however, hated Custer with a passion because of what he considered to be Custer's vanity and posturing.

Custer put three companies (about one hundred and forty men) under Reno and three under Benteen. Five companies, about two hundred and ten men, he kept with himself. The plan was for Custer to approach the village from the north, and Reno from the south. Benteen, trailing, with pack mules laden with ammunition, would be available to either column, as needed.

What Custer did not know was that the Sioux chiefs had decided to band together for protection against the *wasichu* soldiers and had been gathering in the area for months. Now, spread out across a plain on the west bank of the Little Bighorn was a large mass of Indians, an estimated two thousand of whom were warriors. And they knew Custer was coming.

FIRST SKIRMISHES

Reno's men, advancing in three long columns, crossed the Little Bighorn River and then spread out into a line abreast

> CUSTER'S CONTEMPT FOR DANGER MADE HIM CONTROVERSIAL. HIS CAVALRY UNITS SUFFERED EXTRAORDINARILY HIGH CASUALTY RATES.

General George Armstrong Custer, in a pose that captures some of the self-confidence and haughtiness for which he became renowned.

and moved to a gallop. When they neared the village, they were horrified by what they saw: instead of just one village, it was a huge conglomeration of Indian tents extending for about 3 miles along the banks of the river—six villages in all, set up in large, interlocking circles.

At once, a swarm of Indian warriors rose up to meet the advance. Reno, whose conduct on this day would later be the subject of much speculation and of an official inquiry, led a panicked retreat back across the river and up the banks of a steep bluff. His men finally reached the top and formed a defensive line, where they were joined by Captain Benteen's contingent. Together, their two commands made a stand on the bluff.

Meanwhile, Custer led his five companies to a place that was parallel to the village and across the river from it, in a shallow depression that bisected the small ridges that rose from the water's edge. Indians in the village could not see his horses at first, just a rising cloud of dust moving across the river. Turning left and heading towards the water, Custer's men saw Reno's first skirmish with the Indians and heard the sounds of shots popping. The raw recruits began shouting and cheering. Most of them were poorly trained German or Irish immigrants, fighting not for love of country but for thirteen dollars a month, a bed and three square meals a day.

TOTAL ANNIHILATION

There is still some question about Custer's exact movements, but it appears that, after sending a messenger to tell Benteen to reinforce him, he wheeled his command away from the river and ended up crossing it further north, leading his force onto a ridge above the village, about 3¾ miles from where Reno and Benteen were locked in battle. More and more Indians now flocked in Custer's direction, like "bees swarming out of a hive," as one Sioux later described it. They fired arcing showers of arrows or made quick, rushing attacks on the cavalry, most of whom had dismounted and shot their own horses to use for cover. A cloud of grey dust and black gunpowder began to obscure the battlefield as the charging Indians gradually divided Custer's forces. Figures dashed in and out of the cloud as if through artificial night, and gun barrels blazed yellow in the dimness.

The squads and platoons of the Seventh Cavalry disintegrated quickly under the onslaught, with perhaps six or seven "last stands" occurring at various ridge tops. Individuals were then cut down by Indian warriors, who appeared like wraiths out of the smoke and dust. Indian veterans of the battle later told how many of the soldiers did not appear to know how to fight. In their panic, some of these raw recruits even began shooting themselves.

The total annihilation of Custer's force probably took no longer than two hours. One last Indian charge, led by the famous war chief Crazy Horse, swept over the battlefield, and the last survivors went down, shot or speared or clubbed. After that, there was silence and drifting smoke.

At the bluff, Reno's and Benteen's men continued to fight for their lives. They managed to hold off the Sioux attack for the rest of that day and into Monday afternoon, June 26, when the Sioux, fearing the approach of more soldiers, packed up their tents and moved off to the south in a massive cloud of dust.

"THERE HE IS, GOD DAMN HIM"

On the morning of Tuesday 27 June, a forward unit of Brigadier General Terry's cavalry, comprised of one lieutenant and his Crow Indian scouts, rode cautiously through the valley of the Little Bighorn River and saw on a distant hillside numerous objects. At first they thought they were buffalo carcasses and skins drying in the sun. But soon they realized with horror that the objects were the stripped bodies of Custer's entire command, along with their horses.

At the site, in the hot June sun, the stench was terrible. Sioux squaws, who had swarmed over the battlefield soon after hostilities had ceased, had horribly mutilated the bodies of the slain. Five companies lay dead, a total of two hundred and ten men in all (plus another fifty-three members of Reno's command had died during his desperate fight). Custer's body was discovered near the crest of a hill, surrounded by the slaughtered members of his staff. The corpse was reclined, semi-upright against the bodies of two slain soldiers. He had been shot in the left side near the heart and in the left temple.

Captain Frederick Benteen rode down from what would become known as Reno's Hill to examine the body of his old commander, and decided that the killing shot near the heart had been fired from a rifle at fairly long range. The shot in the temple had been a Sioux coup de grace later. Although the public was told afterwards that the Indians had not mutilated Custer's body as a sign of respect for his heroic stature, in fact, after death, his left thigh had been gashed, a finger cut off and an arrow had been driven through his penis. In 1927, a Cheyenne woman named Kate Bighead, who had been present on the field after the battle, told a researcher that the Indian squaws had also punctured Custer's ears with a sewing awl, in order to make him hear better the next time.

But, of course, there would be no next time. An onlooker recalled Captain Benteen rising from Custer's recumbent form and exclaiming, "There he is, God Damn him, he will never fight anymore." ❧

1879
THE ZULU WARS

When the great Zulu ruler King Shaka kaSenzan-gakhona was assassinated by members of his own family in a coup in 1828 he is said to have used his dying breaths to warn them that they would never rule the land as he had done. White men, he said prophetically, would one day come "like locusts" and devour the kingdom that he had created.

Although the Dutch had settled the southern regions of the African continent as early as 1652 and the British gained their foothold around Cape Town in 1806, the landlocked kingdom of the Zulu had remained unaffected by European colonialism. A former Royal Navy lieutenant, Francis Farewell, established the first commercial ties with King Shaka in 1824. Natal was annexed to the Crown in 1843 and for the next thirty years the relationship between the colonial British and the kingdom of Shaka kaSenzangakhona was amiable and profitable.

When diamonds were discovered in Kimberley in 1868, however, British government strategists began to reassess the traditional view of southern Africa as being little more than a colonial backwater and began to examine ways in which their control of the region could be strengthened.

BRITAIN MOUNTS AN OFFENSIVE
In late 1878 a series of unresolved border disputes between the Zulus and white farmers in the Transvaal provided the British government with the trigger to wipe the Zulu nation from the map of Africa. An ultimatum was handed to Zululand's monarch Cetshwayo kaMpande in December 1878, demanding that the Zulu army and its hierarchy be disbanded, and that certain Zulu warriors responsible for various border incidents involving the apprehension and detention of British citizens be handed over for trial. Cetshwayo did not acknowledge the

ultimatum, and provided the British with the excuse they were looking for to invade.

On January 11, 1879 the 24th Regiment of Foot under the command of Lieutenant-General Frederick Augustus Thesiger, Second Baron of Chelmsford, invaded Zululand. He divided his force into three columns: the Central Column crossed the Buffalo River at the Rorke's Drift; Northern Column forded the Ncome River 40 miles north, and the Coastal Column of 2700 men crossed the Tugela River. The objective of these three columns was the Zulus' royal capital, Ulundi, 35 miles to the northeast. Ten days later, on January 20, after their crossing at Rorke's Drift, the Central Column passed by a hill to the east called Isandlwana, where Chelmsford decided to make temporary camp. Little did he know that the first major battle of the Anglo-Zulu War was just two days away, and that it would end in the worst ever defeat for the British Army in a fight against a technologically inferior enemy.

THE BATTLE OF ISANDLWANA
After ten days of marching, the Central Column had covered just 10 miles and made camp beneath the isolated sphinx-shaped hill of Isandlwana, believing that the Zulu army was still days away. Britain, however, was about to be dealt its largest ever military defeat at the hands of a native militia, as twelve thousand Zulu warriors closed in, having covered 50 miles in a mere five days, from Ulundi.

On January 22 British scouts discovered twelve thousand Zulus, under the command of Prince Ntshingwayo, one of the most able military strategists in the Zulu kingdom, sitting quietly in a valley adjacent to Chelmsford's troops. The Zulus' original plan was to attack forward elements of Chelmsford's force the following day; now that their position was revealed, Ntshingwayo was forced to issue orders to assume the Zulus'

traditional "buffalo horn" formation. He also chose to bypass Chelmsford's 2500-man-strong Central Column, which had marched out at dawn in search of his army, and instead to attack the approximately 1200 men left to guard the Isandlwana camp under the command of Colonel Henry Pulleine.

Pulleine was a bureaucrat with little field experience and, instead of organising a defensive perimeter with Isandlwana at their backs, he ordered his troops to assume a standard firing line. It was a decision that would cost his men their lives. The Zulu attack was methodical, swift and brutal and, despite the Zulu "chest" taking heavy casualties, the "horns" were able to envelop the British line and break through on both its right and left flanks, at which point the British line collapsed. As discipline broke down small groups of British troops formed into a disparate collection of "last stands," firing until their ammunition was exhausted and they were simply overwhelmed. Forced back to a tributary of the Tugela River, the last vestiges of Pulleine's battalions were cornered and slaughtered as they tried to make their way across. British losses included 802 non-commissioned officers, fifty-two officers and 470 native Africans. Only fifty-five British soldiers managed to escape. Zulu losses were approximately 2000 killed.

As if the losses at Isandlwana were not enough, when Lord Chelmsford's column returned to the encampment they were able to see beyond the Tugela River to where, in the distance, smoke was rising from the old mission station at Rorke's Drift.

DEFENCE AT RORKE'S DRIFT

In the afternoon of January 22, after Pulleine's troops had been encircled at Isandlwana, four thousand five hundred Zulus under the command of Cetshwayo kaMpande's younger brother, Prince Dabu-lamanzi, chose to descend upon the one hundred and thirty-nine soldiers left to man an old mission station at Rorke's Drift. Commanding officer Lieutenant John Chard of the Royal Engineers had transformed the church into a storeroom and the house of its resident minister, Otto Witt, into a hospital.

In the morning gunshots could be heard coming from the direction of Isandlwana, 13 miles away, and the garrison started fortifying the mission by using mealie bags and biscuit boxes to create defensive walls linking the church and the hospital. Five hundred Zulus descended on the mission from the south while the main body attacked the British defences with gunfire from the west and northwest. The hospital became the focus of the battle after Zulu warriors set it alight. The British withdrew from the building, fighting almost hand-to-hand with the advancing warriors as they

went. Three patients had to be left behind and were stabbed to death.

Fighting continued until well past midnight, but the Zulus couldn't break the British line despite the British being pushed back into a small fortified area around the old church. Through the night the Zulus would withdraw, engage in a war dance and beat their spears and shields on the ground—and attack again. The following morning, upon seeing the approaching relief column of Lord Chelmsford, Dabulamanzi ordered a withdrawal, and the Zulus turned and left the battle. British casualties were fifteen killed and thirteen wounded, and the battle at Rorke's Drift went into the history books as a classic example of defensive warfare.

Twenty-three Victoria Crosses, the highest military award for bravery in the British Army (instituted in 1856 by Queen Victoria), were awarded during the Zulu Wars. Of those twenty-three, eleven were awarded at the Battle of Rorke's Drift, the most ever received by a British regiment in a single engagement; another five were awarded to those involved in the defence of the hospital, including Alfred Henry Hook, who was wounded in the scalp by a Zulu spear and retired from the army in June 1880.

Accounts at the time put Zulu losses at three hundred and seventy, but the real figure will never be known. Wounded

In nearly twelve hours of fighting 120 British troops shot down 500 Zulus at Rorke's Drift.

Zulus were later bayoneted or shot where they lay by the relief force, whose men had witnessed the disembowelment of British troops at Isandlwana. In an interview with the newspaper Western Mail in 1914 Samuel Pitts, a private who fought at Rorke's Drift, claimed the actual number of Zulu dead was in the vicinity of eight hundred and seventy five.

Eshowe, Intombe and Kambula Also on January 22, a Zulu force numbering six thousand attempted to block the advance of the Coastal Column, under the command of Colonel Charles Pearson. Pearson was on the way to the KawMondi Mission Station at Eshowe, from where he planned to advance on the capital, Ulundi. Pearson made it into the mission only to be besieged for ten weeks by twelve thousand Zulus under the command of Prince Dahilamanzi in what became known as the Seige of Eshowe, until relieved by Lord Chelmsford on April 3. In that time thirteen hundred Zulus and forty-four British were killed.

To the north of Zululand was a region of disputed territories, with the town of Luneberg at its center, a white settlement that was under constant threat of a Zulu attack.

The decision was made to reinforce the town, and eighteen wagons of supplies and ammunition were despatched, along with the one hundred and six troops of the 80th Regiment under Captain David Moriarty, who would be stationed there until war's end. The wagons, however, began to founder in a series of heavy rainstorms that had swollen the Intombe River and separated the convoy. On March 12, the Zulus ambushed the wagons and killed seventy British troops.

The Battle of Kambula on March 29 is considered the turning point in the conflict, when an attack on the British camp there resulted in the deaths of over a thousand Zulus, with British casualties of thirty-eight killed and forty-three wounded. The Zulus, despite being armed with captured British rifles, were unable to break through the *laager*, a hexagonal-shaped fort of interlocked wagons. The adjacent *kraal* (an Afrikaans word for cattle enclosure) could not, however, keep the Zulus out and was the scene of heavy hand-to-hand fighting before the British troops could withdraw to the relative safety of the *laager*. Despite several Zulu charges on the tightly drawn wagons the British lines held, aided by the canister shells of its artillery projected in a devastating arc that decimated the Zulus' tight formations. When the Zulus were at last forced to retreat they were chased down by cavalry units for more than 7 miles, constantly being shot at and even speared with their own discarded iron spears.

There were other battles of course, but after Kambula the result was never in doubt. The Zulus were a motivated, mobile fighting force and their leaders proved themselves adept strategic thinkers, but even the finest strategy is rarely a substitute for superior weaponry. Spears and cowhide shields were no match against Gatling guns, 7-pound artillery shells and long-range rifles. But it wouldn't be until the Battle of Ulundi on July 4 that the military power of the Zulus would be smashed once and for all.

BRITISH TROOPS APPROACH THE ZULU CAPITAL

On July 4, 1879 the Frontier Light Horse, a British cavalry regiment consisting of one hundred and fifty six officers and men under the command of Captain Robert Barton of the Coldstream Guards, was steadily advancing across a wide plain toward Zululand's capital of Ulundi. The Frontier Light Horse included forty scouts, seventy Transvaal Rangers, about a hundred Cape Colony volunteers, a contingent of Border Horsemen and more than two hundred and fifty native troops from the Transvaal. At the same time, four thousand

two hundred troops under the command of Lord Chelmsford looked on from the surrounding ridges. Chelmsford had been sending out scouts since first light in the hope of locating the army that he knew would be defending the Zulu capital, but by 8 a.m. no sightings of the enemy had been reported. It was now up to the Frontier Light Horse to approach the city and flush the warriors out, and up to Chelmsford to end the six-month-long Zulu Wars.

The Frontier Light Horse crossed the Mbilane stream with nothing, it seemed, between them and the city. But from the surrounding grasslands fifteen thousand troops of the Zulus' inGobamkhosi regiment suddenly arose to the cavalry's north, south and east and began to thump the ground with their feet and shields. If the Zulus had been armed with modern weaponry the Frontier Light Horse would have been slaughtered, but the regiment was able to retreat to the lines of the British infantry before the Zulus could close the noose. As the in Gobamkhosi advanced, Chelmsford's infantry formed a defensive square four rows deep, with the first two rows in kneeling positions, supported by rapid-fire Gatling guns and artillery fire directed almost point-blank into the ranks of the advancing Zulus. Discipline saw the British prevail. The sequence of firing—first the front row, then the second, third, fourth, returning to the first again—proved impenetrable, and no Zulu could get closer than 30 yards. A reserve of Zulus charged the square's southeast corner but fell to the British 9-pound artillery shells and the withering fire from the infantry. It was hardly a fair fight.

SPEARS AND COWHIDE SHIELDS WERE NO MATCH AGAINST GATLING GUNS, ARTILLERY SHELLS AND LONG-RANGE RIFLES.

THE CHARGE OF CHELMSFORD'S VETERAN CAVALRY

When the Zulu ranks finally broke and began to retreat, Chelmsford ordered his cavalry, the 1st King's Dragoon Guards, the veteran 17th Lancers (many of whom had participated in the Charge of the Light Brigade during the Crimean War), the colonial cavalry and a contingent of native cavalry that had been raised in Natal Province, to set off in pursuit. The bloody chase did not end until every Zulu warrior was killed. Not even the wounded were spared the wrath of the British, keen to take their vengeance for the slaughter of their troops at the Battle of Isandlwana. British losses amounted to ten killed and about eighty wounded. Zulu losses were in the thousands. Lord Chelmsford ordered Ulundi to be razed to the ground, and the Zulu capital burned for days. The Anglo-Zulu Wars that began in January of 1879, and lasted for six bloody months, were over.

For the most part the Zulu Wars had been a series of murderous, suicidal charges, with spears and cowhide shields proving no match for rifles and British discipline. In hindsight, of course, had the Zulu leadership been able to depart from their "buffalo horns" tactics and learn to use the thousands of rifles they acquired from their victories on the battlefield, they would certainly have been able to put up more resistance. But to the Zulu a rifle was little more than a kind of super throwing stick, to be fired occasionally but ultimately to be discarded in favor of spears and shields. It was this inability to alter their traditional approach to warfare that helped bring the Anglo-Zulu Wars to a relatively swift conclusion.

In the wake of the Battle of Ulundi the Zulu armies were disbanded and their chiefs submitted en masse to British rule. The British withdrew from Zululand shortly after the conclusion of the battle and the once-proud Zulu nation was divided into thirteen separate "kingdoms" each ruled by pro-British sympathizers. The Zulu king, Cetshwayo, fled but was eventually captured on August 8, and spent the next four years living as an exile on Robben Island. He died in February 1884. On 20 May 1884 the Boers supported the installation of Cetshwayo's son, Dinizulu, as ruler over one of the thirteen kingdoms, but he was never formally recognized by the British.

Tensions between the Boers and the British resulted in the First Anglo-Boer War (1880–81), where the Boer fought to regain the independence in the Transvaal which they'd lost in 1877, and the Second Anglo-Boer War (1899–1902), which saw the Boer republics eventually become British colonies. ❧

1883
THE ERUPTION
OF KRAKATOA

Beginning in the early morning of August 27, 1883, in Indonesia's Sunda Strait between Sumatra and Java, a series of eruptions, the like of which had never been seen or heard in recorded history, tore through the atmosphere. The explosions of rock and magma that rose from the depths of Krakatoa Island were heard 3000 miles to the west on the Indian Ocean island of Rodrigues and 2200 miles to the south in the Western Australian city of Perth, where citizens mistakenly identified the sound as cannon fire. It was, in effect, a very large cannon. The Krakatoa eruption was the equivalent of 10,000 Hiroshima-style atomic bombs, and the 3.8 cubic miles that the island lost that day, quite apart from what collapsed into the caldera, was spread over a staggering 1½ million square miles.

The cataclysmic events and horrifying statistics that followed the Krakatoa eruption are almost too numerous to name. Estimates of the actual death toll from the explosion and subsequent tsunamis are as high as one hundred and twenty thousand, but it is generally accepted that at least thirty-six thousand people perished in an estimated three hundred villages along the coastlines of the Indonesian islands of Java and Sumatra—in the tsunamis that the eruption generated and the pyroclastic flows that raced across the Sunda Strait and onto the Indonesian coast. Floating pumice in the Sunda Strait was so thick it hampered the progress of ships, and as much as a year later skeletons floating on "pumice rafts" were being swept ashore on the coastline of East Africa. Five cubic miles of rock and pumice were thrown into the air when two-thirds of Krakatoa disappeared, and the island was reduced in

height from 1475 feet above sea level to 820 feet below. Three thousand people, the entire population of the island of Sebesi, Krakatoa's nearest inhabited neighbor almost 8 miles to the north, were killed instantly.

UNIMAGINED DESTRUCTION ON A VAST SCALE

Ash from the eruption fell on the surrounding islands and killed every living thing, every blade of grass and every insect. The ash cloud rose to a height of 50 miles and then began to spread around the globe, darkening the skies and resulting in spectacular red sunsets that prompted the great English poet of the Victorian era, Alfred, Lord Tennyson, to compose the poem "St. Telemachus," which read in part:

> Had the fierce ashes of some fiery peak
> Been hurled so high they ranged about the globe?
> For day by day, thro' many a blood-red eve,
> The wrathful sunset glared.

Tidal surges, possibly caused by the shockwaves that travelled seven times around the earth, were recorded in Alaska and the English Channel, and ships anchored in the coastal waters off South Africa swayed at their moorings. Krakatoa was a global event such as the modern world had never seen, and its effects on climate and vegetation would last for years.

The eruption of Krakatoa was thousands of years in the making. Krakatoa Island, Verlaten Island, Lang Island, and a small volcanic outcrop called Polish Hat were all that remained

after the eruption of Ancient Krakatoa approximately 60,000 years ago. In 1883 Krakatoa Island was home to three volcanoes: Danan, Rakata, and the most active, Perboewetan. Since the collapse of Ancient Krakatoa, the chambers beneath these three volcanoes had slowly been filling and heating up, resulting in the build-up of enormous amounts of pressure. Three months before the eruption smoke began rising from Perboewetan for the first time in more than two hundred years, reaching a height of over 6 miles. Steam began venting from the volcano's slopes and shockwaves from the explosions rattled windows in the capital of Batavia. Towards the end of May all measurable volcanic activity had subsided. On 27 May, eighty-six volcano watchers arrived at Krakatoa Island on the *Loudon*, climbed to the eastern rim of Perboewetan's crater and peered into its black heart—a remarkably foolish act by any standard. On June 16 a series of small eruptions began anew. More steam vents had formed between Perboewetan and Danan to the south, and the eruptions became so intense that high tides were reported in several Javanese and Sumatran ports. By June 19 much of Perboewetan's upper cone had been blasted away.

VIOLENT EXPLOSIONS

In early August a Dutch engineer, Captain H. Ferzenaar, visited Krakatoa and noted that two new steam vents had opened up on the north face of Danan and that part of its crater had collapsed. He also recorded that an additional vent had opened on Perboewetan and went on to write in his diary that, in his opinion, it was now too dangerous to send anyone onto the island; and, indeed, Ferzenaar was the last human being to leave a footprint on Krakatoa. The Sunda Strait had busy shipping lanes, which ensured that Captain Ferzenaar's sighting would not be the last. On August 12, a Dutch ship, the *Prins Hendrik*, reported columns of steam and ash rising 2 miles into the atmosphere.

By August 26, the eruptions were virtually continuous. Ships within a 12-mile radius of the island began to report heavy falls of volcanic ash as well as large pieces of solidified volcanic rock crashing onto their decks. The volcanic rock, or pumice, was the result of rapid cooling and depressurization. In Batavia that afternoon, ash was reportedly falling in the streets, while pressure gauges in the city recorded increasingly violent explosions throughout the day and into the evening. The explosions were so loud they woke people from their sleep in Australia's Northern

THE CATACLYSMIC EVENTS AND HORRIFYING STATISTICS THAT FOLLOWED THE KRAKATOA ERUPTION ARE ALMOST TOO NUMEROUS TO NAME.

Territory. During this first phase of the eruption, which lasted until the early hours of August 27, it is estimated that between 2–3 cubic miles of pumice, rock and magma were ejected into the atmosphere. As spectacular as this undoubtedly was, it was nothing in comparison to what was soon to come.

At 5:30 a.m. on August 27 the first of a series of four massive explosions began to tear Krakatoa Island apart. The explosions were of such intensity that they shattered the eardrums of sailors on ships in the Sunda Strait. Then, at 10:02 a.m., Perboewetan and Danan collapsed and the island began to disintegrate. Rock fragments (tephra) mixed with superheated ash raced down the flanks of the volcanoes towards the sea and were propelled as far as 25 miles across the Sunda Strait—with such ferocity that they did not stop until they hit the Indonesian coast. This pyroclastic flow reached temperatures in excess of 1300°F—temperatures so extreme that it boiled the seawater over which it was moving, allowing the gases to ride a self-made cushion of air that increased the speed and the distance it was able to travel. The pyroclastic flow didn't stop until, like the tsunamis, it hit the coastline which was only 25–30 miles away. It is estimated that around four thousand five hundred people who were fortunate enough to survive Krakatoa's tsunamis were soon afterward burned alive by its gases.

The force of the pyroclastic flow's impact becomes obvious when one reads the testimony of the Beyerinck family. Willem and Johanna Beyerinck and their three children lived in the Sumatran coastal town of Ketimbang but also had a small hut on the slopes of Radja Bassa 1300 feet above the village. Willem was the area's comptroller, a civil servant responsible for the dispensing of law and order, and tax collection on behalf of the Dutch colonial government.

A FAMILY'S ACCOUNT

A detailed diary kept by Johanna Beyerinck provides a valuable insight into the events of August 26 and 27, 1883 and the ordeals she suffered in the week that followed until her family's rescue on 1 September.

By August 26, the rumblings of Krakatoa had filled Johanna with a sense of dread. Unable to ignore her feelings, she convinced her husband Willem to make his apologies at the opening of a small market in the nearby village of Tjanti, and they returned home to their government house in Ketimbang. That afternoon, with Krakatoa obscured by thick black smoke that was hiding an ominous, blood-red sun, Johanna again pleaded with Willem, this time to make for a small hut the

A **view of Krakatoa** during the 1883 eruption—one of the most catastrophic explosions in recorded history.

THE ILLUSTRATED LONDON NEWS

No. 2316.—VOL. LXXXIII.   SATURDAY, SEPTEMBER 8, 1883.   WITH TWO SUPPLEMENTS   SIXPENCE. By Post, 6½o.

ISLAND OF KRAKATOA, IN THE STRAITS OF SUNDA, THE CENTRE OF THE LATE VOLCANIC ERUPTION, SAID TO HAVE DISAPPEARED.

family had above the town outside the small village of Amboel Balik. Though initially concerned at creating a panic should the populace see him fleeing into the hills, increasingly erratic wave surges convinced Willem to head for higher ground.

That evening at 8 p.m., as the family were busily packing their suitcases, a small tsunami struck their house, demolishing the staircase and hastening their departure. Three thousand villagers joined them. It took three and a half hours to reach the hut, trudging through ankle-deep mud, and when they got there Johanna put her exhausted children to bed as the terrified villagers huddled outside. By this time the roof was covered in a thick layer of ash and pumice, which continued to fall throughout the night and, unbeknownst to those inside, began to kill those outside the hut in their hundreds.

During the night, a thousand people perished in the ash and pumice that fell on and around the Beyerincks' hut, preserving the victims just as they had been when they drew their last breaths. Bodies, Pompeii-like in their last desperate, grotesque and pathetic poses, were everywhere. A week after the skies cleared, the body of a man was found, his arms stretched out in front of him as he tried in vain to crawl through the choking fumes that took his life. The deaths of the Ketimbang villagers on Radja Bassa were the only recorded deaths attributable to the eruption itself, not to its many after-effects.

The eruption made headlines around the world.

The next morning, August 27, the day of the final eruption, Johanna Beyerinck emerged from her hut to see fire raining down from the sky. Some of the surviving villagers raced to Ketimbang, only to return a few hours later with the news that the entire village had been washed away. Then, at precisely 10:02 a.m., the eruption and the shockwave that travelled around the world launched a pyroclastic flow that surged towards the Sumatran coast. Miraculously, it had drained itself of its deadly intensity just as it reached the front door of the Beyerincks' hut.

Johanna, protected by the walls of the hut, described how her sarong was almost burned from her body, and how the hot ash was so thick she could barely see her hand in front of her face. Willem closed the door to the hut and plunged the family into darkness. The ash took its toll on the couple's three-and-a-half-year-old son who died the next day. Overcome with grief and unable to stand the confines of the increasingly suffocating room any longer, Johanna stumbled out into what was once a green, verdant forest and was now a grey, still world devoid of life. It was only then that she noticed large swathes of skin hanging from her body.

I noticed for the first time that my skin was hanging off everywhere, thick and moist from the ash stuck to it. Thinking it must be dirty, I wanted to pull bits of skin off, but that was still more painful. My tired brain could not make out what it was. I did not know I had been burned. Worn out, I leaned against a tree.

— From the diary of Johanna Beyerinck, 1883

TSUNAMIS OF ROCK AND MOLTEN ASH

The four explosions on August 27 that ripped Krakatoa Island apart each created its own tsunami, generated by several cubic miles of rock and magma entering the ocean and displacing equal volumes of water that then raced towards the low-lying villages of Java and Sumatra with devastating speed. They were reportedly over 100 feet high. Nine out of every ten people killed that day lost their lives to the monstrous tsunamis, which were of such ferocity that the steamship *Berouw* was picked up and deposited almost a mile inland, with its entire crew of twenty-eight subsequently lost.

Blankets of pumice choked the waterways of the Sunda Strait for weeks afterwards. Hundreds of bodies were washed up on Javanese and Sumatran beaches and thousands of head of cattle were swept into the sea. Sailors described how buckets lowered over the sides of their ships would come back up laden not with water but with a thick sludge of pumice and ash; they told of floating pumice, thick enough to carry tree trunks, that was still being found on the world's oceans more than two years after the eruption. The sulphur dioxide propelled into the atmosphere mixed with water vapor to produce vast amounts of sulfuric acid—on such a scale that for the twelve months after the eruption it is estimated the amount of sunlight reaching the earth was reduced by as much as 13 percent, and the earth's temperature dropped by almost half a degree Celsius.

Willem and Johanna Beyerinck, their two remaining children, and some two thousand native Indonesians stayed for three nights on Radja Bassa before deciding to make their way down from their mountain sanctuary and back towards the coast. They passed paddy fields and collapsed villages and along the way met a group of survivors who had taken refuge in a nearby river.

Progress down the mountain was slow but, on August 30, the Sunda Strait came into view and the sun was at last visible through the clouds of ash. Johanna stood and faced the sun, and gave thanks to God for delivering her family. On 1 September the ship *Kederie*, which had been trying for days to find a path through the choking sludge of volcanic pumice to the coast, finally managed to get a boat to shore where the village of Kali Antoe used to be and where the Beyerinck family and the survivors of Ketimbang had emerged, blistered and bloodied, from the jungle.

WHY KRAKATOA?

The islands of the Sunda Strait and the islands of Java and Sumatra sit over two convergent tectonic plates, the Indo-Australian Plate and the Asian Plate, with the crust of the Indo-Australian Plate pushing beneath the Asian Plate to its north along the Sumatra–Java trench. As the rocks of the uplifted Asian Plate slip across the Indo-Australian Plate, its rocks are heated by friction and begin to melt, occasionally rising to the surface in the form of molten magma and ending their journey in the form of a volcanic eruption. Volcanoes of this type often occur along oceanic trenches and are known as "andesites," after the volcanic Andes Mountains in South America which were formed in the same manner.

Along the line of the Sumatra–Java trench a string of islands has been born, including Krakatoa and Anak Krakatoa, the "child of Krakatoa," which first broke the surface in 1927 and is today in an almost constant state of eruption and growing at the rate of 22 feet a year. ❧

1901–1950

THE WORLD AT WAR

❦ The Almost Complete Bulletins ❧

1912
THE SINKING
OF THE TITANIC

On May 31, 1911, the hull of the world's largest luxury liner, the *Titanic*, was launched in the River Lagan in Belfast, Ireland. Her manufacturers, Harland & Wolff, boasted that she was "virtually unsinkable". It was not their custom to have ship-naming ceremonies, so rather than the traditional smashing of a bottle of champagne across the bow of the ship, three rockets were fired into the sky. The large crowds along the river bank cheered as the ship's 26,000-tone hull began to slide down its greased slipway into Belfast Harbour.

The next day the *Belfast Morning News* published the following editorial comment:

> ... *It is difficult to understand why the owners and builders named the ship* Titanic. *The Titans were a mythological race who came to believe they'd conquered nature, who thought they'd achieved power and learning greater than Zeus himself, to their ultimate ruin. He [Zeus] smote the strong and daring Titans with thunderbolts; and their final abiding place was in some limbo beneath the lowest depths of the Tartarus, a sunless abyss below Hades.*

STATISTICS OF TITANIC PROPORTIONS

The gigantic ship had become the talk of the town as her 882-foot long hull took shape on the riverbank, held together by more than three million steel rivets. Over the ensuing months the empty hull was transformed into an ornate floating palace. Twenty-nine boilers and one hundred and fifty-nine furnaces were installed to provide the steam power for the ship's engines. Carpenters, metalworkers, engineers, and decorators spared no expense as they installed first-, second- and third-class cabins, restaurants and ballrooms, a gymnasium, library, hospital, and the world's first on-board swimming pool. State-of-the-art electronic navigational and communications equipment was installed in the wireless room; the ship's 10,000 light bulbs were linked by 200 miles of wiring. The manufacturers were confident of the *Titanic*'s seaworthiness because inside the hull were sixteen watertight compartments separated by bulkheads, and she was designed to stay afloat even if up to four of the compartments became flooded. But there was a fatal design flaw—there was a gap above the bulkheads, which did not reach all the way to the top of the hull. This meant that if one compartment became flooded, it would overflow into the adjacent compartment, then the next, and so on until all were flooded—which is exactly what happened. It beggars belief that such an apparently obvious oversight could have remained unnoticed throughout the lengthy design and construction process.

On April 3, 1912 the *Titanic* sailed into the southern English port of Southampton to prepare for her maiden voyage. Over the next week she was stocked with provisions, including 34 tons of meat, 5 tons of fish, 40,000 eggs, 40 tons of potatoes, 7000 lettuces, 36,000 apples, 2000 pounds of ice cream, and enormous quantities of tea, coffee, milk, cream, and liquor. There were also 57,600 pieces of crockery, 44,000 pieces of cutlery, 3364 mailbags, and more than 4400 tons of coal.

The *Titanic* goes down.

THE *TITANIC* SETS SAIL FOR NEW YORK

Just after noon on April 10 the *Titanic* embarked on her maiden voyage to New York. The accommodation was divided into three classes. Those in first class included the world's richest man, John Jacob Astor IV, who built the Astoria Hotel in New York. But most of the passengers, many heading to the New World in the hope of starting a new life, travelled in third class under the lowest deck. As the mighty liner left her moorings, the turbulence from her huge wake caused the nearby liner New York to pull loose from her berth. A collision was barely avoided as the New York was drawn to within about 3 feet of the *Titanic* before being hauled off by a tugboat. After this inauspicious beginning the *Titanic* steamed across the English Channel to pick up more passengers at the French port of Cherbourg, then made a brief stop at the Irish port of Queenstown (now Cobh). As she steamed into the North Atlantic Ocean, she carried eight hundred and ninety nine crew under the command of Captain Edward Smith, and one thousand three hundred and twenty-four passengers.

STARS DISAPPEAR

On April 14, four days into the voyage, the *Titanic*'s radio officers began receiving telegraph messages from nearby ships

Some of the lucky survivors—the Titanic was fitted with only enough lifeboat space for 1200 of the 2200 on board.

warning of icebergs in the vicinity. Smith made a slight southerly adjustment to the ship's course. Late that night, as stars shone brilliantly on a moonless night, ship's lookout, Frederick Fleet, was puzzled to observe that on the horizon stars were disappearing in groups of two and three. He soon realized, to his horror, that an enormous silhouette was slowly moving into the path of the great ship. Just before midnight Fleet sounded three warning gongs and telephoned the bridge with the words that all sailors dread: "Iceberg dead ahead!" First Officer Murdoch ordered that the *Titanic* stop its engines and turn hard to port (left)—but it was too late. At 11:40 p.m. the iceberg sliced into the ship's right side, sending a small avalanche of ice onto the well deck, buckling the hull, and tearing a thin gash about 300 feet long below the waterline. Water started pouring into the five forward compartments, and from this point the ship's fate was sealed. Just after midnight Captain Smith ordered that the lifeboats be prepared, and the first of many distress calls was sent.

Amazingly, the lookout officers were not provided with binoculars or a telescope, thus limiting visibility at night to about ½ mile. Researchers have calculated that the first officer's evasive manoeuvres would have been sufficient to avoid the iceberg had he received as little as half a minute's extra warning time. And binoculars would have provided several minutes more, at least.

A few minutes later crewman Samuel Henning heard an unusual whistling noise. As he walked among the anchor chains he noticed an open hatch cover, looked down into it and felt a stiff breeze against his face and hair. He realized that the rapid air escape must be caused by displacement from water entering below. He was the first to recognize that the *Titanic* was doomed.

The wireless operators began sending Morse Code distress calls in the traditional international signal "CQD". They received an immediate reply from the German steamer *Frankfurt*: "okay i must consult my captain. stand by." The British liner *Carpathia* then responded: "does the titanic know that there are some private messages waiting for her from cape race?" (the nearest land-based wireless station, in Newfoundland). The *Titanic* replied: "we need assistance. the titanic has struck a berg. this is a cqd old man. come at once." The Carpathia immediately changed course and sped through the perilous icebergs to the *Titanic*'s rescue. The Frankfurt's captain then sent the question: "what is the matter?" *Titanic*'s graceless response was "you fool, we're busy here. stand by." The *Frankfurt*'s captain, understandably outraged, repeated the question, drawing the reply: "you are jamming my equipment fool. stand by and keep out." The *Frankfurt*'s crew became even more enraged when they overheard the following exchange between the *Titanic* and its sister ship, *Olympic*, which was about 270 nautical miles further away than the Frankfurt: "what is the matter?" "we have struck an iceberg and need assistance." The British were responding politely to a distant British ship, but were insulting the Germans—who were actually in a much better position to render assistance.

TO THE LIFEBOATS

Soon the *Titanic* began listing to starboard as water poured into the hull. Gradually it began to dawn on the passengers that they were in great peril. They were ordered to don life jackets and make their way to the lifeboats, but many were reluctant to board them. Some of the first lifeboats, carrying women and children, were launched partially empty. As the list increased and the bow began disappearing under water, it became less difficult to fill the lifeboats. But the *Titanic*'s crew had never undergone a proper lifeboat drill, such was the

general confidence in the ship's indestructibility. Some of the sailors even had to be shown by passengers how to use oars, as court transcripts from the British government enquiry which immediately followed the disaster reveal:

A sailor was pushing his oar about every which way. "Why don't you put the oar in the oarlock?" asked Mrs White. 'Do you put it in that hole?'"he asked. "Certainly," she replied. "I never had an oar in my hand before," he explained. The men began arguing over how to manage the boat. One of them snapped at another: "If you don't stop talkin' through that hole in yer face, there'll be one less in this boat."

Although the boat carried insufficient lifeboats for all on board, it nonetheless carried more than were required at the time by the British Board of Regulations, whose rules were based on a ship's tonnage rather than the number of passengers on board. The last lifeboat was eventually launched just before the *Titanic* sank.

Meanwhile a light was visible on the horizon, less than an hour away. It belonged to the Californian, which had warned the *Titanic* (in vain) several hours earlier of the presence of icebergs in the area. But the Californian did not respond to the *Titanic*'s distress calls because her sole wireless operator was asleep. Nor did she respond to the distress flares that the *Titanic* was by now launching regularly, perhaps because it was deemed too hazardous to travel through the icy sea; perhaps because the crew mistook the flares for maiden-voyage celebration fireworks.

THE SEA POURS IN

At 1:20 a.m. water began to pour over the top of leaking boiler room 5 into boiler room 4. Until now, the rate of inflow had been slow, as the total surface area of the punctures in the hull was only about 1 square yard. But as the *Titanic*'s list increased, the sea began pouring through the anchor holes on the starboard side, which were now under water, doubling the rate of the inflow. Within a few minutes the starboard cargo bay doors and windows had also submerged, and the slow leaks were joined by raging torrents. Hindsight informs U.S. that if the watertight seals between the ship's compartments had been opened, she would have sunk slowly and evenly, rather than on a slanted angle, and the original gash would have remained the only leak. The *Titanic* would have remained afloat for at least another six hours, until the rescue vessel *Carpathia* arrived.

JUST BEFORE MIDNIGHT AN ICEBERG SLICED INTO THE SHIP'S RIGHT SIDE, SENDING A SMALL AVALANCHE OF ICE ONTO THE WELL DECK AND BUCKLING THE HULL.

By 2:10 a.m. the bow was submerged up to the base of the forward smokestack. Water began pouring down ventilators, stairwells, and lift shafts to the lower decks. Hundreds of passengers began instinctively clawing their way uphill toward the stern, which by now had lifted out of the water completely. No ship could possibly be designed to take such stresses—and at 2:18 a.m. the *Titanic* broke in half. The bow section plummeted over 2 miles to the bottom of the ocean, as the rear section momentarily regained equilibrium. Some lifeboat passengers thought the ship was miraculously righting herself, but after just two minutes the stern also sank. Imprisoned were many of the third-class immigrant families whose passage to the top deck had been barred, and the mostly French and Italian kitchen staff who had been locked into a room on E deck during the rush for the lifeboats. A massed, extended scream rent the air as hundreds of people were dumped simultaneously into the freezing water. A fortunate few managed to cling to wreckage until they were picked up by a lifeboat; anyone who remained in the water for even twenty minutes died of hypothermia. Captain Smith, having already ordered his passengers and crew to save themselves, jumped overboard just before the stern sank. He was last seen trying to assist a struggling child.

SURVIVORS ARE RESCUED

By 3:30 a.m. the *Carpathia* had reached the position sent by the *Titanic*'s radio officer, but nothing could be seen—no lights, no lifeboats, certainly no ship. Just after 4 a.m., as first light dawned, one of the crew saw a green flare sent up by one of the lifeboats. Elizabeth Allen, the first passenger to be rescued, confirmed to the amazed crew of the *Carpathia* that the *Titanic* had indeed sunk. Gradually the other lifeboats approached and more and more survivors came aboard, many screaming or sobbing. By 9 a.m. all the survivors were on board and the *Carpathia* resumed her voyage to New York. About one thousand five hundred perished in the disaster—about two-thirds of those who set out.

John Jacob Astor IV went down with the *Titanic*, but he ensured his pregnant wife, Medeleine, with her nurse and maid got into a lifeboat and were saved. The following year the first International Convention for Safety of Life at Sea was held in London. It made numerous recommendations, including that a lifeboat space be provided for each person on board ship, that lifeboat drills be held during every voyage, and that all ships maintain a 24-hour radio watch.

DISCOVERY OF THE WRECK

On September 1, 1985, after three search attempts over the previous five years by Texas oil billionaire Jack Grimm, the *Titanic* was discovered by a joint French–American scientific expedition. The wreck has since been explored by several manned and unmanned craft, and some small artefacts removed.

Although RMS *Titanic* sank nearly one hundred years ago and rests 12,000 feet below sea level, the ship's remains continue to fascinate people around the globe. On July 24, 2007, a U.S. Department of State media release entitled Proposed Legislation to Implement Agreement to Protect RMS *Titanic* Wreck Site Sent to Congress announced the government's intention to establish a protection zone around the famous wreck. By enacting this legislation and becoming a party to the agreement, the U.S. will become a leader in the international community in protecting perhaps the most important shipwreck in history, "in accordance with the most current standards of underwater scientific, historic and cultural resource protection, conservation and management."

FICTION FORESHADOWS THE TITANIC'S FATE

In 1898 Morgan Robertson published a novella titled *Futility, or the Wreck of the Titan*. It contains several eerie similarities to the fate of the *Titanic*, which had not even been designed at the time.

The *Titan* was described as the largest craft afloat, 800 feet long and displacing 75,000 tons; the *Titanic* was the world's largest liner, 880 feet long and displacing 53,000 tons. Both craft were equipped with three propellers and two masts. The *Titan* had a top speed of 25 knots, or nautical miles, per hour; the *Titanic* 24 knots. Both were travelling too fast for the prevailing treacherous conditions. The *Titan* was described as "indestructible"; the *Titanic* was announced as "virtually unsinkable" by its owners (only after its demise did the myth develop that the *Titanic* was considered "completely" unsinkable). Neither carried sufficient lifeboats for all those on board—the Titan carried twenty-four, 'as few as the law allowed', the Titanic twenty, less than half the number needed for three thousand people; each ship had a maximum capacity of three thousand people passengers and crew. Both set out on their maiden voyage from the English port of Southampton in April, both struck an iceberg on an April night in the North Atlantic around 350 nautical miles south of Newfoundland. More than half the two thousand two hundred on board the *Titan* drowned, their "voices raised in agonized screams"; more than half the *Titanic*'s 2200 passengers and crew died in the same gruesome fashion, according to survivors. ❧

1914

THE ASSASSINATION OF ARCHDUKE FRANZ FERDINAND

The assassination of the Austrian Archduke Franz Ferdinand and his wife on a visit to Sarajevo in June 1914 set in motion a series of events that led to the outbreak of World War I. Ferdinand was heir to the throne of the Austro-Hungarian Empire, and his assassin, nineteen-year-old Gavrilo Princip, was a Slavic nationalist. Princip believed that the death of the archduke was the key that would unlock the shackles binding his people to the Austro-Hungarian Empire, so he shot the duke and his wife as they drove in an open car through the city. What it did was lead Europe to war.

Gavrilo Princip was born to poor parents in 1894 in the Bosnian village of Obljaj west of Sarajevo, not far from the border with Croatia. His father, Petar, was a postal worker who married late in life and was fourteen years older that Gavrilo's mother, Marija, who gave birth to nine children, six of whom would not survive infancy. Marija wanted to name her fourth child Spiro but, because he was born on the feast day of St. Gabriel the Archangel, the local priest convinced his parents to name him Gavrilo.

At the age of thirteen he was sent by his parents to live with his older brother in Sarajevo, where it was hoped he would enlist in the army and one day become an officer. Princip, however, chose to enrol in a traditional high school in Tuzla northeast of Sarajevo and graduated in 1911. His life was a mundane and unremarkable one that most likely would have seen him continue to live in obscurity had not the Austro-Hungarian Empire annexed the Bosnian nation on October 5, 1908.

After his graduation, Princip's political convictions began to take shape at a time when anti-Austrian sentiments were rife and many students were beginning to form nationalistic associations, such as Young Bosnia and the increasingly militant Black Hand.

NATIONALISM IN THE BALKANS

The Black Hand movement was created on May 9, 1911, largely in response to the Bosnian Annexation Crisis, which saw Austria-Hungary annex Bosnia and Herzegovina as a strategic buffer in the aftermath of Bulgaria's declaration of independence on October 6, 1908. Serbs now living in Austrian-controlled and administered Bosnia were denied many basic political and civil rights, but although Serbia demanded the removal of foreign troops from the region it lacked the means to do anything else but protest. The Black Hand was led by Dragutin Dimitrijevic, a rogue Serb nationalist known to his inner circle as Apis, after the mythological bull-deity of ancient Egypt. Dimitrijevic was no stranger to assassination, having participated in the killing of Serbia's King Obrenovic and Queen Draga in 1903.

The idea of a united South Slavic state—with the unification of all South Slavic-speaking peoples throughout present-day Croatia, Bosnia, Macedonia, Serbia and Montenegro—was politically popular and the Black Hand waged a war of terror across Serbia. The organization had no qualms about using assassination to further their nationalistic aims; nor were they averse to using impressionable teenagers to act as their proxies.

Princip came to the attention of the Black Hand leadership through his association with Young Bosnia, whose members led austere lives free from tobacco, alcohol, and the distraction of sexual relationships. The founders of Young Bosnia were heavily influenced by the political strategies of the Italian unification movement headed by Giuseppe Mazzini. Mazzini had played a key role in the unification of Italian states almost forty years earlier and was a vocal advocate of political assassination as a legitimate tool in the struggle for independence. Princip was on his way to becoming a disciplined, hardcore revolutionary, and described his zeal in a note to a friend in 1912: "My flaming body will be a torch to light my people on their path to freedom."

THE ASSASSINS' TARGET
In June of 1914, Archduke Franz Ferdinand, heir to the Austro-Hungarian throne, received an invitation from General Oskar Potiorek, the governor of Bosnia-Herzegovina, to review a planned military exercise in his capacity as Inspector General of the Austrian Army. It seemed an odd request. Bosnia was the most dangerous, rebellious province in the empire. And only a month before the invitation was issued, the Serbian Prime Minister Nikola Pasic had relayed a warning to the Austrian government about the likelihood of assassination attempts on its visiting dignitaries. The selection of June 28 for the review seemed to doubly tempt fate. For this was St. Vitus Day, the day all Serbia stopped to reflect on the heroism of Milos Obilic, a medieval knight who, in the aftermath of the defeat of Serb forces by the Ottoman Empire in 1389, crept into the tent of the Turkish leader Sultan Murad I and stabbed him to death. A visit by any minister representing an occupying nation, much less an archduke, on the anniversary of such a key event in Serbian history, and with the nation going through a period of resurgence after having thrown off more than five centuries of Turkish rule, must to some have seemed almost like a dare.

Archduke Ferdinand and his wife Sophie Chotek, Duchess of Hohenberg, arrived in Sarajevo by train on the morning of June 28, 1914. In high spirits after having spent the previous day in the Tyrolean resort town of Ilidza, Archduke Franz Ferdinand and Duchess Sophie climbed into the car that would take them through Sarajevo's streets. Despite coming from an aristocratic family, under Hapsburg family law Sophie was considered a commoner, a ruling that had forced her and Ferdinand to elope and marry in secret in June of 1900. On returning to Vienna, Emperor Franz Joseph forbade Sophie to be seated alongside Ferdinand in a royal carriage or vehicle. Beyond Austria's borders, however, the reins of royal protocol were often loosened, and on this day Sophie sat proudly next to her husband in their brand-new, six-seater Gräf & Stift touring car. It was a decision that was shortly to cost the duchess her life. Six Bosnian assassins, including Gavrilo Princip, were waiting at various points along the royal route for the archduke to pass, armed with hand grenades and pistols—but the crowded streets were guarded by a complacent and woefully undermanned Sarajevo police force of just one hundred and twenty, who proved more interested in watching the procession than the crowds.

ONLY A MONTH BEFORE THE INVITATION WAS ISSUED, THE AUSTRIAN GOVERNMENT WAS WARNED ABOUT ASSASSINATION ATTEMPTS ON ITS VISITING DIGNITARIES.

A ROYAL PROCESSION
Franz Ferdinand looked every bit a royal as the procession set off along Appel Quay. Dressed in the blue tunic and black trousers of an Austrian cavalry officer, his chest was decorated with medals and a gold-braided waistband known as a bauchband. The plumage on his helmet and the three stars on his buttoned collar presented an unmistakable target to the six conspirators who were waiting along Appel Quay, Sarajevo's main thoroughfare, which already enjoyed the infamous nickname "the avenue of assassins". Unbeknown to Ferdinand or his Bosnian hosts, there was a veritable gauntlet of potential executioners lining Appel Quay awaiting the royal motorcade, which inexplicably was not given a police escort. But Ferdinand loved the city, and made a special request to his chauffeur, Leopold Lojka, to drive slowly so he could take his time and see something of its attractions.

The first in the line-up of conspirators was Mehmed Mehmedbasic, a twenty-seven-year-old carpenter waiting by the Cumuria Bridge, armed with a small bomb. He later claimed a gendarme was standing by him—and, furthermore, he couldn't get a clear shot at the archduke, and didn't want to act rashly in case one of his comrades might be better placed to strike. Mehmedbasic fled first to Montenegro and then to Serbia, and was the only one of the conspirators who managed to elude capture.

The archduke and the duchess, captured on film by a Sarajevo photographer just prior to their assassination.

Vaso Cubrilovic, a seventeen-year-old student who didn't want to harm Duchess Sophie, was standing a few feet down from the Cumeria Bridge. Cubrilovic was once expelled from his high school in Tuzla for storming out of an assembly during the playing of the Austrian national anthem. He, like Mehmedbasic, claimed to have been poorly positioned in the crowd.

The third man was Nedeljko Cabrinovic, a twenty-year-old anarchist and high school dropout. Cabrinovic, wearing a long black coat, asked a nearby policeman in which car the Archduke was travelling; and when the policeman told him he hurled his grenade at the slow-moving vehicle. The time was 10:10 a.m.

FERDINAND ESCAPES A GRENADE

Despite Franz Ferdinand's claim that he had knocked the bomb away with his hand, several witnesses recounted that it struck the car's folded-down roof-canopy before bouncing off and landing underneath the vehicle behind, which was carrying Count von Boos-Waldesk and the archduke's aide-de-camp, Colonel Morrizi. The grenade had an in-built ten-second delay and, when it detonated, killed two officers and wounded more than twenty bystanders. Cabrinovic then ingested a small vial of cyanide and leapt into the shallow waters of the river, but was quickly apprehended and placed under arrest. The cyanide, however, was old and only resulted in a severe bout of vomiting, not Cabrinovic's death. The archduke's driver responded to the attack by speeding up and racing through the stunned crowd towards the city hall, where Sarajevo's lord mayor, oblivious to the attack, was rehearsing the welcoming speech he had written earlier.

As the archduke's convoy sped by, the fourth man in the group, Cvjetko Popovic, later told investigators in an almost comical testimony that, because he was short-sighted, he couldn't make out which car was which and lost his nerve.

Gavrilo Princip was the fifth conspirator, positioned by the Latin Bridge. He heard Cabrinovic's bomb detonate, assumed the archduke had been killed and watched as the motorcade sped past. Waiting at the Imperial Bridge, the sixth man, Trifko Grabez, a friend of Princip's since high school, later confessed he lost the stomach to perform such a heinous act and had no intention of causing harm to innocent bystanders.

In the chaos that followed the failed assassination attempt, four of the assassins, seeing that their only opportunity to strike was gone, abandoned their posts and escaped, though all were eventually arrested. Princip, meanwhile, walked through the city's Turkish Quarter, and mulled over his missed opportunity to strike a blow for Serbian nationalism.

The royal couple arrived safely at the city hall, meanwhile, but Ferdinand was furious. "Mr. Mayor, I came here on a visit and I get bombs thrown at me. It is outrageous!" After much discussion Ferdinand then insisted, much to his wife's dismay, that rather than waiting for the arrival of troops to secure the remainder of the route through the congested streets and narrow lanes of the city's Turkish Quarter, they would instead be driven to the city's hospital so the archduke could pay his respects to those who had been injured by Cabrinovic's grenade.

A SERIES OF FATAL ERRORS

When the motorcade was leaving the hospital the chauffeur Lojka became disoriented, took a wrong turn and drove into the congested streets of the Turkish Quarter. When the cars turned right at the Bascarsija intersection and entered Franz Joseph Street, General Petiorek, who was riding in the archduke's car, ordered Leopold to stop and reverse out of the street. Then, in one of the more extraordinary quirks of history, Gavrilo Princip, who had been having lunch in Moritz Schiller's Delicatessen & Café, emerged onto the pavement just feet away. As Leopold was struggling to put the Gräf & Stift into reverse, he stalled the engine, thereby locking up its gearbox. Princip seized the moment, walked up to the car and fired two shots from his FN Model 1910 .38 Browning pistol. The first bullet hit Franz Ferdinand in the neck, severing his jugular vein. The second ricocheted off the door of the car and hit the duchess in her stomach.

The duchess immediately slumped forward in her seat. Ferdinand was heard to scream: "Sophie, don't die! Stay alive for our children!" but she died in his arms. The archduke survived his beloved wife only by minutes. Like Cabrinovic, Princip attempted to end his life by swallowing a capsule of poison but was arrested immediately after the fatal shots were fired.

THE ASSASSINS STAND TRIAL

Twenty-five men, including Princip, were tried for the murder of Franz Ferdinand and his wife. At the trial's conclusion, after all the testimonies had been heard and evidence gathered, the presiding judge asked the accused to stand if they felt any contrition for what they had done. Everyone stood except Gavrilo Princip. When asked why he chose to remain seated he replied that he felt remorseful that he had unintentionally killed Duchess Sophie and that because of his actions three children were now orphaned; but he refused to express regret at taking the life of the archduke. He rejected the suggestion that the group had to be encouraged by Cabrinovic and the Black Hand to strike, declaring that the idea to assassinate the archduke had come from within the group itself, and proclaimed that the

assassination was the work of men who loved their country and wanted an end to Austro-Hungarian colonialism.

Of the twenty-five accused, nine were released, eleven received terms of imprisonment ranging from three years to life, and five were hanged. Princip, too young at nineteen to be hanged under Austrian law, was sentenced to twenty years with hard labor, with the additional requirement that every year on the anniversary of the assassination his cell would be darkened and he would be refused a mattress and all meals. No evidence exists to suggest he ever regretted his decision to murder Archduke Franz Ferdinand; indeed at his trial Princip asserted: "I am not a criminal, for I destroyed a bad man. I thought I was right."

Cabrinovic received a twenty-year prison term and, like Princip, showed no remorse for his crimes. He died of tuberculosis in prison on January 3, 1916. Grabez, also imprisoned for twenty years, succumbed to tuberculosis in February of 1918. Vaso Cubrilovic was sentenced to sixteen years imprisonment but was released in November 1918, moved to Belgrade, and returned to teaching. Cvjetko Popovic was also released in November 1918 and went on to become a curator in the Sarajevo museum.

Gavrilo Princip was ordered to serve his sentence in Theresienstadt, an eighteenth-century Bohemian fortress north of Prague that had been converted into a military prison, but he would not be a prisoner for long. He was kept in solitary confinement in Cell 1 and became the prison's most famous inmate; but Princip had suffered from tuberculosis since he was a child, the disease was accelerated by the damp confines of his cell, and he died on 28 April 1918.

WAR IS DECLARED

The death of Archduke Franz Ferdinand was one of the defining moments of the twentieth century. Europe, leading up to World War I, was a tangle of "alliances". There was the Dual Alliance between Germany and Austria against Russia; the Franco-Russian Alliance to protect Russia against Germany and Austria-Hungary, and so on and so on. The assassination of the archduke was all that was needed as the trigger for their enactment. A month after Franz Ferdinand's death, Austria declared war on Serbia and began a bombardment of Belgrade, the Serbian capital, which led to Russia's Tsar Nicolas II coming to the assistance of his traditional Slavic brothers. France mobilized its military. Germany honored yet another alliance, the 1882 Triple Alliance with Austria and Italy, by coming to Austria's defence, and declared war on Russia. Germany then declared war on France and invaded Belgium, which meant that Great Britain, which had a treaty with Belgium to defend its independence, was obliged to declare war on Germany. The firing of Princip's .38 Browning pistol certainly seems deserving of the tag: "the shot heard around the world", for it precipitated much more than simply bringing the wrath of an empire down upon Princip's tiny Balkan nation. It ignited a world war. ❖

1915
THE BATTLE OF GALLIPOLI

In British history, the allied invasion of the Gallipoli Peninsula in Turkey during World War I, which began in February 1915, is regarded as an embarrassing military debacle and remembered chiefly for the fact that it almost cost the young Winston Churchill his career—Churchill was forced to resign from his job as First Lord of the Admiralty in May 1915 as a result of the failure of the campaign and then remained in the political wilderness for several years. However, for the peoples of Australia, New Zealand and Turkey, the intense, eight-month-long struggle at Gallipoli was, despite the carnage that occurred on the peninsula, something quite different, something much more positive and more important. It was the place where their national identities were forged.

In Australia and New Zealand, whose soldiers were so pivotal to the battle, Gallipoli acquired enormous importance as the place where the courage and spirit of the "Anzac" fighting man was demonstrated on a world stage for the first time. And for the triumphant Turks, defending their ancient Ottoman homeland, Gallipoli was a glorious victory that helped spur the nationalist fervor that would lead to the founding of the Turkish Republic, some eight years later.

METHOD IN THE MADNESS

Despite the campaign's later reputation, there was some sound reasoning behind the original plan for an attack at Gallipoli. By early 1915, the war that had begun only the previous August was stalemated, with long lines of trenches running from the North Sea all the way to the Swiss Alps. It was, furthermore, a horrendously violent stalemate: by November 1914, the Allies had suffered nearly a million casualties. Seeking to staunch this epic blood-letting, British strategists, and in particular Winston Churchill, the forty-year-old First Lord of the Admiralty, looked for ways to relieve the pressure on the western front. Soon, they turned their eyes to Asia Minor, and specifically to the Dardanelles Strait, part of the Ottoman Empire, an ally of the Central Powers—Germany and Austria-Hungary.

The Dardanelles is the narrow neck of water that connects the Aegean Sea to the Black Sea, via the Sea of Marmara and the Bosporus Strait, site of the city of Istanbul, formerly known as Constantinople. The British planners saw clearly that if they could gain control of the Dardanelles and thence Istanbul, they could not only neutralize the Ottoman Empire, but also funnel munitions to their ally Russia. This, in turn, could draw German troops away from the western front, allow the Allies to make a decisive breakthrough there and help achieve ultimate victory.

There were a couple of significant problems, however. The narrow strait of the Dardanelles, only ½ to 3¾ miles wide, has a very strong current that makes naval manoeuvres difficult. At the time it was also heavily guarded. The Turks had forts along both the Gallipoli Peninsula on the western, European side, and the Turkish mainland on the eastern, "Asiatic" side, and

Allied troops bathe during a rare moment of calm at Anzac Cove, while others move weaponry and assess the terrain above.

had mined the waters of the strait. There was nowhere in the entire 45-mile trip up the Dardanelles that a vessel could not be easily reached and sunk by shellfire.

ATTACK BY SEA

In the early winter of 1914–15, Winston Churchill managed to push through a plan to try to attack the Turkish forts along the Dardanelles using naval power alone. Like most British planners, Churchill considered the Turks to be inferior opponents with old munitions and guns that could not stand up to British firepower. In February 1915 and then again in March, a combined British and French force—the largest yet seen in the Mediterranean—sailed up the Dardanelles to bombard the Turkish defences, only to be pushed back, with heavy losses that included seven hundred dead, three battleships sunk and three others badly damaged.

Having lost to these "inferior" Turkish fighters, the British now pulled back to lick their wounds. The vice admiral in charge of the sea assault told Churchill that he could not silence the forts without the help of an infantry assault. And so the Gallipoli campaign began— as so many other disastrous campaigns have begun—as an escalation after a galling failure.

RESOURCES

Right at the start, there was a dispute over resources. The British commander of the campaign, General Ian Hamilton, asked Lord Kitchener, British Secretary of War, for one hundred and fifty thousand men. Kitchener, faced with competing demands for men and supplies from his commanders in France, would only allow half that number. And while he sent the veteran British Twenty-ninth Division to take part in the assault, a significant proportion of the Allied force was to be made up of the green and untried volunteer soldiers of Australia and New Zealand, who were currently 685 miles away, in Egypt, being trained to fight in France. Their units were subsequently combined into the Australian and New Zealand Army Corps (ANZAC), which consisted of the Australian First Australian Division and the Australian and New Zealand Division. Together with the British Royal Naval Division and the French Oriental Expeditionary Corps (which included four Senegalese regiments), these units made up the Mediterranean Expeditionary Force.

The British Twenty-ninth Division was to land at Cape Helles, at the tip of the Gallipoli Peninsula, where it was expected to advance inland and attack the Turkish strong points that guarded the Dardanelles. The job of the Anzac troops was to land further north on the west, or Aegean coast, of Gallipoli, at Gaba Tepe, move inland to block the expected Turkish retreat from Cape Helles or Turkish reinforcements moving down the peninsula, and assist with the attack on the Dardanelles narrows. The French corps would provide a diversionary landing on the south side of the Dardanelles to draw off Turkish forces and keep them pinned down; the British Royal Naval Division would also make a feint near the top of the Gallipoli Peninsula at Bulair.

A RECIPE FOR DISASTER

The Allied landings took place in the pre-dawn darkness of April 25. Amphibious landings were poorly understood at the time and the rugged, hilly landscape of much of Gallipoli, with its short, shallow gravel beaches overlooked by heights, was a recipe for disaster. The British took so long to plan their attacks that the German commander of the eighty-four thousand Turkish troops, Limon Von Sanders, was able to carefully dig in his men.

At Helles, the British landing was delayed and it was not until 8 a.m., in broad daylight, that the British soldiers arrived on shore. They approached on motor launches and on a transport ship, the River Clyde, which deliberately grounded itself and, through a special opening carved in its hull, debouched two thousand troops.

The Helles landing was a bloody mess, with the Turks bringing heavy firepower to bear on the invaders from only 55 yards away, blowing the men to bits in their boats. As the soldiers left the River Clyde along gangplanks, they provided easy targets for Turkish gunners who shot them down one by one. A British commander flying overhead in a small biplane was horrified to see the clear, bright blue water "absolutely red with blood" for 55 yards from the beach. Of the first two hundred soldiers who disembarked from the River Clyde, only twenty-one actually made it to the beach.

At other landing spots along Cape Helles, at beaches designated X, Y and S, the British had more luck, and found themselves landing almost entirely unopposed. By nightfall, thirty thousand soldiers were ashore. But at V and W beaches, heavily defended by Turks, the reception was hot. On W, 950 Lancashire Fusiliers landed; five hundred were killed or wounded that morning. Six Victoria Crosses were later awarded as a result of actions on W and V, and the Cape Helles landings in general were marked by extreme bravery. But a total of two thousand casualties were incurred by the British. In just one day, the slaughter had been horrific

> AT SUVLA AND AT ANZAC COVE, THE FIGHTING UP AND DOWN EACH HILLSIDE AND RIDGE TOP WAS HAND-TO-HAND AND BAYONET-TO-BAYONET.

and the Allied forces that did get ashore were left clinging desperately to the beachheads.

A group of Turkish senior officers observes the fighting at Gallipoli from a vantage point on a high ridge behind the front lines.

BIRTHPLACE OF THE ANZAC MYTH

The Australian and New Zealand troops were supposed to land at the somewhat wider beaches of the Gaba Tepe headland, but in the inky black of the predawn attack, their boats landed 1650 yards further up the coast at what would soon be immortalized as Anzac Cove. (Exactly why is still debated: it may have been human error, or possibly a last-minute change in plans that was not properly communicated.) Above the beach here towered the Sari Bair range of hills, which was creased with dead-end gullies and sharp ravines and covered with thick scrub brush, and almost impassable. Even so, the Anzac forces made inroads of 1650 yards. However, they were stopped by the quick work of the Turkish commander Mustafa Kemal Ataturk, who ordered a counterattack that drove the Anzacs back, forcing them to dig in on the hillsides, under unremitting fire and blazing sun. Here, too, the Allied forces suffered heavy casualties, with an additional two thousand killed and wounded that day.

To protect themselves against naval shellfire, the Turks built their trenches very close to the Anzac lines, in some cases only 30 feet away. To raise one's head above the parapets was suicide for either side, and thus much of the fighting was done by lobbing grenades over the tops of the trenches. The only defence against this was catching them and lobbing them back before they exploded, which some Anzacs became extremely good at.

STRETCHED TO BREAKING POINT

As the summer months wore on, they brought disease, thirst and privation. Every possible surface was covered by swarms of flies, which had been feeding on the corpses that abounded everywhere—in fact, corpses being the most readily available raw material, both sides built them into their defences, as parapets at the tops of the trenches. The Turks attacked numerous times, and each time were thrown back with great losses, yet still they kept coming. After a final Turkish attack failed on May 4, the Turks dug in again all around the Anzac defences. By then, the Turks had lost fourteen thousand men, the Anzacs almost ten thousand.

THE BATTLE OF GALLIPOLI

More than 3000 miles away from Britain, the Allied force was at the end of the food and supply chain, and was in danger of being forgotten by the public, whose attention was focused on the western front. Meanwhile, members of the British government fought with each other over the course of the campaign—two of its architects, including Winston Churchill, were soon forced to resign.

In Turkey, in contrast, the British threat reinforced the unity of the government of "Young Turks" (Mehmed Talat Pasha, Ismail Enver and Ahmed Djemal) who had taken control of the crumbling Ottoman Empire in a coup in 1913. For the Turks, a stalemate could be seen as a success. For the British, with their supply lines stretched thin, a breakthrough was essential; nothing less than victory would do.

THE AUGUST OFFENSIVE

On August 6, the British made one last-gasp attempt to break the increasingly stagnant and bloody stalemate at Gallipoli with a landing further north, at Suvla Bay. Two infantry divisions embarked and the Turks were caught completely by surprise. But unfortunately, Lieutenant General Frederick Stopford, in charge of the operation, moved far too slowly to exploit this advantage. Turkish reinforcements made it to the high ground, which the British troops were never able to take from them, despite repeated efforts.

At Suvla and at Anzac Cove, the fighting up and down each hillside and ridgetop was hand-to-hand and bayonet-to-bayonet. Often the scrub brush would catch fire from the munitions being expended, incinerating the attacking Anzac and British troops. But the Turks, inspired by the courageous leadership of Ataturk, continued to hold the high ground along the peninsula. With the stalemate enduring, the Allied campaign was effectively over—except for more bitter slaughter.

A SKILFUL RETREAT

A war of attrition continued over the next few months. At the beginning of September, it was suggested that the troops be pulled out. General Ian Hamilton resisted this, but was finally removed from command in October and replaced by Lieutenant General Sir Charles Monro, who began planning an evacuation. Meanwhile, in November, a terrible rain and snowstorm hit the battlefields, the worst in forty years. While the well-dug-in men at Helles and Anzac Cove had some

protection, those in more exposed positions, at Suvla Bay, for example, suffered mightily—many drowned in shallow trenches that caved in and flooded. So horrible was the disaster that the two sides almost forgot about fighting each other—the Turks and British hanging onto their parapets for dear life. By the time the storm finally blew itself out, two hundred troops had died of drowning and exposure, and thousands more were suffering from frostbite and illness.

This natural disaster, even more than the fighting, showed how precarious the Allied positions were. In December, the evacuation began. It turned out that nothing quite became the Allies at Gallipoli like their manner of leaving it. In a departure that salvaged some honor from the debacle, they were able to evacuate one hundred and five thousand men right out from under the noses of the Turks, and had everyone gone from the shambles of the battlefield by January 9, 1916.

A FOUNDING MYTH

The Gallipoli campaign became an inspiration for the peoples of Australia and New Zealand, and, in a different way, for the Turks. Known in Turkey as the battle of Canakkale after the port where the initial Allied sea invasion was blocked, Gallipoli was a triumph for the Ottoman Empire and personally for Mustafa Kemal Ataturk. His heroic performance saw him rise rapidly through the ranks during the battle and greatly expand his influence in military and government circles. After the Young Turks fled the country at war's end, he began an ascent to power that saw him become the founder of the modern state of Turkey in 1923, following the collapse of the Ottoman Empire and a war of independence.

But it is among Australians and New Zealanders, whose forces had performed so impressively and whose reputation as ferocious fighters was now undisputed, that the event had and continues to have its greatest influence. From the horrors of the peninsula, these former colonies, newly separated from their mother country of Great Britain, emerged as fully-fledged nations. The pride that Australians and New Zealanders took from Gallipoli and their reverence for their soldiers continue to be manifested as strongly as ever today. Not only is the landing commemorated solemnly in both countries every April 25, Anzac Day, but in recent years thousands have made pilgrimages, nearly 100 years after the event, to the Dardanelles. There they pay their respects on the hallowed ground where their heroes shed so much blood, even if it was for a lost cause. ❖

1916
THE BATTLE
OF THE SOMME

From June 24 to July 1, 1916, a total of 3000 British and French guns bombarded the German lines along the Somme River valley with such ferocity that many of the seven hundred and fifty thousand allied troops facing west from their trenches were quite certain that there could be no opposition when they went over the top to attack. At 7.20 on the boiling hot morning of July 1, ten huge mines went off in quick succession right under the German lines—mines that contained hundreds of tons of explosives. Then, as the poet John Masefield, who was present, later wrote, "the time drew near, [the British soldiers] … saw the flash of our shells, breaking a little further off as the gunners "lifted," and knew that the moment had come."

So certain was the Allied High Command that the Germans had been pulverized that they ordered the British troops to advance in waves, at a walk, behind one last rolling barrage—artillery fire that crept forwards ahead of the troops, clearing their way and concealing their approach. The soldiers' job would be merely to mop up, after which British cavalry would break through and finish off the retreating Germans.

Then, as Masefield wrote, "There came a whistling and a crying. The men of the first wave climbed up the parapets, in tumult, darkness, and the presence of death, and having done with all pleasant things, advanced across no-man's-land."

It took just a few moments for the slaughter to begin, but when it did, it changed British history and British consciousness forever.

GRISLY RECORDS

The battle of the Somme lasted from July 1 to November 13, 1916, and was the costliest battle in the history of the world, with a combined total of 1,265,000 British, French and German dead and wounded. The Somme also holds the record for the heaviest loss suffered in one day (July 1) by any British army: 57,450, with 20,000 of these dead.

It was at the Somme that the new British volunteer army of the Secretary of War, Lord Kitchener, was violently blooded. This army consisted for the most part of so-called "Pals Battalions"—ranks of volunteers recruited from the same rugby clubs, soccer teams and neighborhoods. The Pals had left their homes to bands playing and flags waving. It was as if they were marching off, not to war, but to a big game. At the time, Arthur Conan Doyle, author of the Sherlock Holmes stories, spoke for many patriotic Britons when he said: "If the cricketer [has] a straight eye, let him look along the barrel of a rifle." The enthusiasm of the Pals Battalions was overwhelming, and matched only by their naivety about war. The first day of the Somme would end all that.

The Somme was by no means the first bloody battle of World War I—the war had, after all, been going on for two years, and the terrible battle of Verdun was still being waged. But the way in which the British fell on the first day, steady wave after wave of eager Tommies tumbling like ninepins to the chattering German machine guns ("so many we didn't even need to aim," wrote one German soldier later), horrified all who saw it. The observers and participants included influential writers like Masefield, Siegfried Sassoon, Robert Graves and Liddell Hart. Historian Hart, who was gassed during the

battle, later made the Somme a cornerstone of his influential argument that direct attacks against an enemy holding a fixed position almost never work.

OVERWHELMING FORCE?

The Somme is a river in northern France whose name, in Celtic, means "tranquillity". It travels east through a gentle valley for about 150 miles, from the forested highlands of the Aisne to the Bay of the Somme in the English Channel.

In 1916, northern France was a prime battleground, where the Fourth and Fifth British Armies north of the Somme and the Sixth and Tenth French Armies south of the river faced off against the Second German Army. With superiority in numbers, French Field Marshal Joseph Joffre planned on attacking the Germans in a battle of attrition, to force them to commit and bleed their reserves. But the massive German attack at Verdun, beginning in February, had tied down most of the French Army, so the British, under their commander in chief Sir Douglas Haig, took over the planning and provided most of the manpower. Under pressure from the French, the start date of the attack was brought forward to take place on July 1 rather than August 1, and the goal now became to divert German resources from Verdun to relieve the pressure on the French.

The plan was for twenty British divisions to launch an attack on a 15-mile front north of the Somme, while seven French divisions charged along a 10-mile-wide line 10 miles south of the river. Massively powerful, this offensive should have made mincemeat out of the outnumbered sixteen German divisions. But Haig and Joffre made the crucial error of depending too much on their artillery. Not only did it destroy any semblance of surprise, but it barely damaged the Germans at all.

STOPPED IN THEIR TRACKS

The first day at the Somme stands as a microcosm of the dreadful cauldron that was World War I. As the artillery barrage entered its final moments, the British waited in their trenches carrying their heavy packs, smoking cigarettes. Some of them shook hands with each other. When the order was given to fix bayonets, the sound could be heard up and down the line, a metal clinking under the roaring of the shells and mines going off.

Officers blew their whistles, and the men then "stepped off". The British battalions attacked in four to seven successive lines, separated by perhaps three hundred or so feet, with the men instructed to walk almost shoulder to shoulder and upright, with their rifles held diagonally across their bodies. Officers wore different uniforms from those of the enlisted men and carried only pistols, which made them perfect targets for German snipers. Some of the men from the Pals Battalions went into battle that morning with puppies gambolling ahead of them as mascots. One company commander suggested his troops kick a soccer ball in front of them as they went, to mark their distance; they would "score a goal" by kicking it across enemy lines.

Sergeant Richard Tawney, a thirty-six-year-old writer and teacher in civilian life, jumped off with the first wave of British troops, following the rolling barrage. Initially, things seemed to be going swimmingly, as Tawney and his unit manoeuvred over four enemy trenches without a hitch. But then "when we'd topped a little fold in the ground, we walked straight into a zone of machine-gun fire. The whole line dropped like one man." The sights Tawney saw in that split second haunted him for the rest of his life. "My platoon officer lay on his back. His face and hands were as white as marble. His lungs were laboring like a bellows worked by machinery. But his soul was gone. He was really dead already; in a minute or two he was what the doctors called 'dead'."

Tawney was wounded twice but survived the day. Out of eight hundred and fifty in his company, there were only twenty-four left on the line by July 3. The Germans were supposed to have been pulverized. What had happened?

PERFECT POSITIONING
During the initial advance soldiers like Tawney were astonished to see Germans leaping from their trenches and setting up machine guns in still-smoking shell holes. While the bombardment had been stunning in its ferocity, the Germans' ability to fight had not been eroded. This was mainly because the Germans at the Somme had built not just trenches, but heavy dirt-and-concrete bunkers, some up to 40 feet deep, which no amount of shelling could destroy. Underground passages connected the bunkers (which had amenities such as electricity and wood-panelling). There were also field hospitals underground, and German reserves waited behind the lines in old caves that the French had used for years to mine chalk.

Adding to this, the German defensive positioning was nearly perfect. Their divisions were aligned along the mile-long crest of a low ridge, which reached out in numerous spurs towards the British lines. The spurs usually had forests or villages situated on them, and each of these had been turned into an armed strong point. The Germans had two forward lines and one line in reserve, each separated by heavy coils of barbed wire 65 to 100 feet thick. Because the German troops were at an elevation, they could easily see what the British were doing, while the British could only observe the Germans' front line.

Not that the offensive was a surprise, of course. The shelling had given it away, but, even before that, French newspapers, read avidly by German spies, had bragged of the coming offensive. And, at 2.45 on the morning of July 1, German forward listening posts picked up a message from the British commander of the Fourth Army, wishing his soldiers "Good luck". It was all the confirmation Berlin needed that the big attack was about to take place.

"THIS WAY TO ETERNITY!"
In a few places along the line, the soldiers were able to get as far as Tawney did before the machine guns opened up, but mainly the guns caught them only a few steps from their trenches, causing bodies to tumble backwards onto those who were climbing up behind. Since thousands and thousands of men were moving forwards, the dead and injured were trampled and the line kept moving, beyond the British wire, into no-man's-land. One battalion commander described "heaped-up masses of British corpses suspended on the German [barbed] wire while live men rushed forward in orderly procession … human corn-stalks falling before the reaper. 'This way to eternity!' shouts a wag behind."

The poet Siegfried Sassoon was in reserve that day (after earning the Military Cross the day before for a daring mission). He sat on a hill behind the lines and watched the British advance through field glasses. "I am staring at a sunlight picture of Hell," he wrote.

By three o'clock in the afternoon, up and down the line, there was no one moving in no-man's-land except the crawling, moaning wounded, still exposed to machine-gun fire—particularly from the elevated spurs—begging for water as the sun tormented them. Most of the others were dead or had stumbled back into their own trenches.

One fairly typical British division—Eighth Division of III Corps—suffered eighty percent casualties in the first ten minutes of the advance. It lost two hundred and eighteen out of three hundred officers, five thousand two hundred out of eight thousand five hundred soldiers. The German battalions on the opposite side of the wire from Eighth Division lost eight officers and two hundred and seventy-three men.

A few companies of the British managed to reach the German lines. But they became isolated survivors, who had, as one put it, been "playing leapfrog with death" and were generally unable to hold their positions. One exception was XV Corps, which was able to advance over two-thirds of a mile and seize its target, the village of Mametz. The cost,

> ONE BRITISH DIVISION SUFFERED EIGHTY PER CENT CASUALTIES IN THE FIRST TEN MINUTES OF THE ADVANCE.

though, was eight thousand dead and wounded. Nevertheless, on a horrible day for the British Army, this was viewed as a considerable success.

By nightfall of July 1, the British High Command had realized that the attacks of the first day had failed miserably. While some British officers, including Haig himself, refused to accept the blame for their failed planning—for attacking a well-entrenched enemy in broad daylight after giving ample warning that they were coming—the ordinary soldier knew what had happened. Sassoon's simple listing in his journal captures the state of affairs on the evening of July 1 succinctly: "C Company now reduced to six runners, two stretcher-bearers, Company Sergeant Major, signallers, and Barton's servant. Sky cloudy westward. Heavy gunfire on the left."

Most British soldiers now felt the attack would be called off, but Haig, despite the British army having suffered its worst-ever single-day casualty rate, decided to press on. In the next two weeks or so, he ordered dozens of "small-scale" attacks against the Germans, which nonetheless cost another twenty-five thousand casualties.

The British were finally able, on July 11, to capture the first line of German trenches. But then the Germans brought in reinforcements from Verdun and the contest degenerated into a bloody stalemate, as so many battles did in this slogging war of attrition, drawn out over the next four months. In November, the British began to make a slow, but steady advance forwards, but then bad weather brought the entire campaign to a halt. By then the casualty figure had reached 1.25 million for both sides. And the total amount of ground gained since July 1? Seven and a half miles.

DREAMS OF GLORY DASHED

In one respect, it could be said that the Somme had achieved its purpose: the fighting at Verdun shifted to the Somme and the Germans certainly lost irreplaceable manpower. Yet the battle will forever go down in history as a slaughter that shows what happens when inflexible and unimaginative planning meets rapid-fire automatic weapons.

More than that, the Somme was a turning point in British public opinion about the war. Never again would ordinary people look at the British government, specifically the British high command, in the same way. After all, it was the Pals Battalions from working-class towns who were decimated at the Somme. Half the British population saw a silent documentary film of the battle, which was made by the War Office as patriotic propaganda, but had an entirely different effect: viewers were left wondering why these working-class men had been sacrificed in what was evidently a pointless slaughter. Where was the glory of war now? Ever since, the Somme has represented the callousness of upper-class leaders prepared to turn soldiers into cannon fodder.

The transformation of mood, among British troops and among the public at home, was reflected in the diary of a nineteen-year-old British lieutenant named Edwin Campion Vaughan. He had entered the war with dreams of glory and had fought on the front lines for eight months. By the time of the Somme, his attitude had changed completely: "I sat on the floor and drank whisky after whisky as I gazed into a black and empty future." ❧

The bemedalled British commander in chief, General Douglas Haig, who planned the disastrous offensive at the Somme.

1917
THE BATTLE OF PASSCHENDAELE

Spring came late to northern France and Belgium in the first half of 1917. And so did summer. Instead of sunshine, unseasonable thunderstorms peppered the region throughout July. More than 5 inches of rain fell in August, more than twice the monthly average. A mercifully dry September brought some relief, but more rain fell through October and on into November. The area surrounding the town of Ypres in western Belgium was a low-lying region barely higher than sea level, with a high water table. Much of the area was either natural or reclaimed swampland, and was transformed by the constant rains into an unrelenting, sodden world of mud. It was a miserable place to fight a war.

Field Marshal Douglas Haig, the commander of the British Expeditionary Force (BEF) from 1915 until the end of World War I, was born in Edinburgh on June 19, 1861. As a teenager he studied at Brasenose College, Oxford, before enrolling in Sandhurst's Royal Military College, from which he graduated in 1884. His first military deployment was in India in 1887; from there he went on to command the 17th Lancers in South Africa before returning to India, where he was promoted to the rank of major-general in 1904 at the age of forty-three, becoming the youngest major-general in the history of the British army. After being appointed to an administrative post in London to assist in reforms to prepare the British army for a future war in Europe, he returned to India in 1909. In 1914 he assumed the role of aide-de-camp to King George V. War was declared in Europe in August 1914, and in December 1915 Haig became Commander-in-Chief of the BEF.

THE STRATEGIC IMPORTANCE OF YPRES
As early as January 1916, Haig believed a major assault in the Flanders region of western Belgium around Ypres was the key to victory on the Western Front. But any preparations for an assault were delayed due to the German offensive at Verdun in north-eastern France, which began in February 1916 and dragged on into December, resulting in the deaths of more than three hundred thousand men.

By the spring of 1917 Ypres was the only major Belgian town still in British and Allied hands. The Ypres Salient projected into German-held territory and its occupation denied Germany access to the Channel ports of northern France. If Ypres were to fall and the salient be taken, British shipping in the English Channel would come under increased threat from German U-boats, a third of which were already operating out of Belgian ports. Haig believed that an offensive from Ypres in the direction of Roulers and Passchendaele would not only eliminate the threat of German occupation in northern France and end the U-boat threat along the Belgian coast but might even act as a springboard into the Ruhr Valley to the east, Germany's industrial heartland, and bring about an early end to the war. Haig, promoted to the rank of Field Marshal in January, was convinced the will of the German army would collapse under the weight of an Allied offensive—although this turned out to be an overly optimistic assessment of German troop strength and morale, and closely resembled the opinion

British casualties litter the churned up battlefield during the Battle of Passchendaele.

Haig had entertained at the height of the Battle of the Somme a year earlier, a battle notable for unparalleled loss of life.

Prior to any advance on Passchendaele it was necessary to capture the strategic Messines-Wytschaete Ridge. The Messines Ridge offensive, meticulously planned and executed by the commander of the British Second Army, General Herbert Plumer, was one of the few World War I engagements that achieved its objectives quickly and with minimal loss of life. Eighteen months earlier, in preparation, Plumer had authorized the construction of twenty-two mine shafts that snaked their way at a depth of between 82 and 100 feet for a distance of over 5 miles beneath the German lines. The Germans were aware of the incursion, and there were even times when their own tunnels were intersected by those being dug by the Allies, resulting in several fierce hand-to-hand encounters. But the Germans failed to grasp the extent of the tunnels that Plumer had ordered to be packed with almost 500 tons of explosives.

DEVASTATION AT MESSINES RIDGE

At 3:10 a.m. on June 7, 1917, Plumer gave the order to detonate the explosives. The effect on the German lines was devastating. In excess of ten thousand soldiers were either killed or wounded, and the noise, probably until then the loudest man-made noise in history, created a shockwave that was felt as far away as Ireland. Nine divisions of British troops then advanced toward the German lines. In just under three hours every Allied objective had been secured and the battle was over. In excess of seven thousand German prisoners were taken, and Plumer was so delighted with the results that he approached Haig and pleaded with him to bring on his assault on the Passchendaele ridge, a strategic hill between Passchendaele and Ypres. Although the ridge was not scheduled to be attacked until the end of July, Plumer saw a rare opportunity to take advantage of the demoralized German troops and of the opening he had forced in their defensive lines. Unprepared, however, for the overwhelming nature of the Messines Ridge victory and the resultant opportunity it afforded him, Haig refused.

Haig had timed his offensive in the wake of the disastrous failure of the French-inspired Nivelle Offensive in May, which despite the deployment of more than 1.2 million troops and seven thousand guns had ended in complete failure and widespread acts of mutiny throughout the French army. The failure ended the career of the offensive's originator, French Commander-in-Chief Robert Nivelle. As disastrous as this was for Nivelle it cleared the way for Haig to launch his own

self-styled offensive, designed to bring an early end to the war. The strategy planned for the Third Battle of Ypres, or the Battle of Passchendaele, as it is more commonly known, involved the capture of Passchendale, a small village not far from Ypres; this would be followed by a push toward the region between the River Lys and the North Sea, ending the German occupation of the Belgian port cities and destroying their submarine pens.

DRENCHING RAINFALL IMMOBILIZES THE ADVANCE

On July 17, Haig ordered his artillery to begin a two-week long bombardment of the German defences around Passchendaele. Unfortunately, however, not only did the estimated 4.5 million shells fired from more than three thousand artillery pieces fail to dislodge the Germans, they also destroyed much of the irrigation works in the flat plains west of the town. The barrage pulverized the clay soil, creating tens of thousands of craters that immediately filled with water—and turned the landscape into a muddy hell.

Haig gave command over the advance on Passchendaele to General Hubert Gough, and the offensive began on July 31 with the Battle of Pilckem Ridge; after just two days, despite considerable gains in territory, persistently heavy rain brought the advance to a standstill. The heaviest rainfall for more than three decades turned the pockmarked clay into a sticky, knee-high quagmire that was so thick it drowned men and horses and immobilized anything that possessed wheels or an engine. Haig postponed the offensive after just a few days. A small break in the weather saw the advance resumed on August 16, but the terrain was deceptive. Areas that appeared to be stable were in reality little more than dry crusts over mud-filled interiors that collapsed the moment any weight was placed upon them.

On September 20, another easing of conditions resulted in a series of carefully orchestrated Allied assaults known as "bite and hold" advances that led to victories at the Battle of Menin Road Ridge, the Battle of Polygon Wood, and culminated on October 4 with the Battle of Broodseinde Ridge. The combined victories gave the Allied forces control of the ridgeline east of Ypres and a clear view to Passchendaele. These victories, however, had come at a staggering cost. Thousands had been killed and wounded, and the view from Broodseinde Ridge was of an endless sea of mud. Heavy rain began again late on October 4, making the bringing up of artillery to support the troops in their "bite and hold" offensive almost impossible.

RECORD RAINFALLS TURNED THE POCK-MARKED CLAY INTO A STICKY, KNEE-HIGH QUAGMIRE THAT WAS SO THICK IT DROWNED MEN AND HORSES.

HAIG ORDERS A RENEWED ASSAULT

On October 9, British and Australian divisions advanced on Passchendaele village in atrocious conditions. Although little ground was gained, Haig and Gough both felt enough progress had been made to justify a further assault on October 12. This assault, also known as the First Battle of Passchendaele (which has since gone down in history as little more than a slaughter), was led by the Australian Third Division and a division of New Zealanders, with the Australian Fourth Division in reserve. As expected, the shells from the preceding artillery bombardment that were meant to weaken the German defences exploded harmlessly in the mud as the Australian and New Zealand forces, armed only with rifles, machine-guns and grenades, were subjected to relentless heavy machine-gun fire coming from the German bunkers and "pillboxes."

Although several Australians managed to scramble their way to the very edges of Passchendaele, they failed to arrive in sufficient numbers to hold the position, and were soon pushed back to where the bulk of the Third Division had become mired along a small river valley. On October 12, the Third Division lost three thousand men, and the Fourth Division one thousand. New Zealand casualties were over eight hundred enlisted men and forty-five officers killed outright or lying mortally wounded in the mud—the single greatest loss of life

Soldiers struggle through muddy craters created by an onslaught of heavy artillery in perhaps the worst conditions of the war.

in a single day in New Zealand history. In total there were more than thirteen thousand Allied casualties, and at this point in the campaign total casualties were approaching one hundred thousand killed and wounded. In the midst of the carnage at Passchendaele, however, poignant acts of humanity and decency shone through. Stretcher-bearers were not only avoided as targets, but were permitted free rein by the German gunners, who even guided them to their fallen comrades as they scoured the battlefield for the wounded.

CANADIAN TROOPS RELIEVE THE ANZACS

The failure of the Australian and New Zealand assault to capture Passchendaele saw members of Field Marshal Haig's staff approach him with requests to call off the offensive, but Haig felt, or perhaps hoped, that the German will to continue the fight was close to ebbing away. On October 18, two fresh Canadian divisions arrived to replace the exhausted, decimated divisions of the ANZACS (Australia and New Zealand Army Corps).

The Canadian troops included many who took part in the great Canadian victory at Vimy Ridge in April 1917. In just thirty minutes at dawn on Easter Monday, after a three-week artillery bombardment on entrenched German positions, the Canadian First Division, under the command of General Arthur William Currie, ignored a snowstorm and swept away the ridge's first line of entrenched German defenders and then, a mere half hour later, overran the enemy's second defensive line. At the time Vimy Ridge represented the greatest single advance since fighting on the Western Front began, and the ridge remained securely in Canadian hands until the end of the war. Four Victoria Crosses were awarded for exceptional acts of bravery, and Currie received a knighthood. These were the soldiers who were about to be thrown into what history knows as the Second Battle of Passchendaele.

On October 19, the twenty thousand men of the Third and Fourth Canadian Divisions started moving into their positions, and on October 26, the first of two offensives began. The Third Division would attack through the northern approaches to Passchendaele along the high ground of Bellevue Spur, while the Fourth Division would approach from the south following the railway line from Roulers. The Third Division, despite seizing all of its initial objectives, was forced to give ground and link up with the British Fifth Army; meanwhile, the Fourth Division, which also had reached its objectives outside the town, was forced to withdraw in the face of a vicious German counter-attack.

THE SECOND PASSCHENDAELE OFFENSIVE

On October 26, the Second Battle of Passchendaele began. It had as its objectives the retaking of all ground lost in the first offensive and the capture of Crest Farm (a heavily defended farm to the south of town) as well as Meetcheele and the Goudberg area to the north. Crest Farm was taken and from there patrols were sent into the outskirts of Passchendaele itself, while the Third Canadian Division again fell short of its objectives. The Canadian Third and Fourth Divisions had suffered twelve thousand casualties for a gain of just a few hundred yards and were in desperate need of being relieved. Three days of sunshine from November 3 to 5 provided the Allies with the opportunity to organize their evacuation and, on November 6, the weary Canadians of the Third and Fourth Divisions were replaced by the troops of the First and Second Canadian Divisions. Despite the fact that German troops were still entrenched around Passchendaele, the Canadian First Division made a series of strong advances throughout the town and later that day, just a few hours after that final assault, Passchendaele at last fell into Allied hands.

When British and Canadian forces occupied Passchendaele on 6 November, Haig decided to call a halt to the offensive and claimed victory. But to the soldiers who had endured slogging their way through the interminable mud, stepping over the dead bodies of their comrades and horses protruding grotesquely from their muddy graves, all just to advance 5 miles—and in the process losing over three hundred and twenty-five thosand men killed or wounded—it must have seemed like anything but success.

A TERRIBLE VICTORY

By the time the fighting was over, the town of Passchendaele had ceased to exist. Aerial photographs taken after the battle showed that none of the town's farms, houses or commercial buildings remained. Even the majority of its roads were pulverized, becoming at one with the monotonous, featureless, moon-like landscape. All that remained were the vague outlines of one or two more prominent roads and the gutted remains of the town center. The patchwork of irrigated paddocks, the assemblage of the many geometric shapes that made up a typical European farming community, was gone.

PASSCHENDAELE HAD BEEN "DE-URBANIZED"

Some months later, in the spring of 1918, the German army launched Operation Michael, which culminated in the Battle of the Lys and the eventual retaking of Ypres by the Germans. Virtually all the ground that Field Marshal Douglas Haig had gained at the Battle of Passchendaele was given up.

When one thinks of the waste and futility of war, few battles in history typify this more than Passchendaele. Haig's stubborn determination to press on regardless of the atrocious weather and the intransigence of the town's defenders is difficult to excuse. The four million artillery shells fired by the Allies into the German lines did little to dampen the German resolve but utterly destroyed the irrigation system of the region, destroying rivers and streams, wrecking the water table and turning the very ground over which the Allies must cross into an impassable sea of mud. In the end, just over 2 square miles of territory was gained at the cost of half a million British and Allied soldiers killed and wounded.

Field Marshall Douglas Haig survived the Battle of Passchendale—not a difficult achievement considering he never visited the front lines—and died in 1928 at the age of sixty-six. He was given a state funeral. ❧

1917
THE OCTOBER REVOLUTION

On the morning of October 25, 1917, the American journalist John Reed and his wife, Louise Bryant, were staying at the Hotel Astoria in Petrograd—the former St Petersburg, grand city of the tsars. They awoke about 10 a.m. to the sounds of bells ringing and trucks racing up and down the street. Reed and Bryant dressed and went downstairs to find that the trucks belonged to the Bolsheviks, the small, leftist revolutionary party headed by Vladimir Ilich Lenin. They carried soldiers, who stopped at every street corner to plaster up a proclamation written by Lenin just that morning.

It stated, in ringing tones: "To the Citizens of Russia! The Provisional Government has been deposed. State power has passed into the hands of the organ of the Petrograd Soviet of Workers' and Soldier's Deputies … Long live the revolution of workers, soldiers and peasants!"

Actually, the provisional government of the moderate Alexander Kerensky not been deposed at all, but Lenin, ever impatient for action, had decided it wouldn't hurt to stretch the truth a little. And in one important respect, at least, he was right. That morning in Petrograd, the revolution that would change the face of a century—the revolution that "shook the world," as Reed would write in a famous book on the October Uprising—had truly begun.

The events of those ten days set in motion a seismic upheaval. Spreading out from the epicenter of this old imperial city, the earthquake of the Russian Revolution created a massive Communist empire. Ultimately, it would represent the strongest challenge ever to Western capitalism—a challenge that the West has only recently faced down.

CHANGE LONG OVERDUE

Could anyone have doubted that Russia was in need of a revolution as the twentieth century began? While serfdom had been officially abolished in 1861, peasants still worked twelve-hour days six days a week for the small number of wealthy landowners who owned most of the land in Russia. The country had been ruled for centuries by omnipotent tsars of varying abilities, and was mainly governed by a corrupt and crumbling bureaucracy. Common people were treated as little better than animals. Thousands of people existed on the edge of starvation.

Tsar Nicholas II—the "little father" of the country—was, even as tsars went, autocratic and conservative. Beginning his reign in 1894, he was unable to see that Russia was changing. The Industrial Revolution had transformed the landscape. Factories had drawn peasants to the cities, in turn bringing them into contact with radical theories. One of the most attractive was the idea that all men should be equal, that all should have a share of the Earth's bounty and no man have to work for an unjust wage or be a serf.

The country underwent a major upheaval in 1905, when thousands of unarmed Russian workers, carrying religious banners and pictures of the tsar, marched to the Winter Palace in St Petersburg to present a petition to Nicholas, telling him of their grievances. In response, the tsar's soldiers opened fire on this peaceful group, killing hundreds. The mass strikes that followed shut down the country's railways and businesses, and forced Nicholas to issue what was called his October Manifesto, which promised a democratic parliament. But the October Manifesto was merely an empty promise, as the

tsar subsequently undermined almost any serious effort at participatory government. Workers and radicals came to realize that yet more drastic action would be required.

BOLSHEVIKS AND MENSHEVIKS

The two men who would lead the revolution in 1917, Vladimir Lenin and Leon Trotsky, both spent years in exile as a result of earlier subversive activities. Born Vladimir Ulyanov in 1870, the son of a school inspector, Lenin worked as a lawyer in St. Petersburg and became radicalized after joining a Marxist group. In 1895, he was arrested for his activities, jailed for fourteen months and sent into exile in Siberia. After his release in 1900, he lectured on the socialist cause throughout Europe. During this time, he took on his revolutionary nom de plume.

At the Second Social Democratic Congress, a convention of Russian socialist groups that met in 1903 in London (for fear of being targeted by tsarist forces), Lenin led attempts to create a socialist political party. But the delegates split into two groups: the more radical and more numerous Bolsheviks (from the Russian for "one of the majority"), and the more moderate Mensheviks ("those of the minority"). Prominent on the Menshevik side was Leon Trotsky. Born Lev Davidovich Bronshtein in the Ukraine, Trotsky had become involved in Marxism while at school. In 1898, he was arrested for his activities, imprisoned and exiled to Siberia. He escaped to London in 1902 and then moved from country to country.

Both the Bolsheviks and Mensheviks played a part in the 1905 uprisings and their popularity increased steadily thereafter. Soon, all that was needed to fan the flame of revolution was social upheaval—and World War I provided that.

WORLD WAR I BECAME THE CATALYST FOR THE RUSSIAN REVOLUTION. DESERTERS RETURNED HOME AND BEGAN SEIZING LAND.

DEFEAT SPARKS REBELLION

The blood-letting of World War I became the catalyst for the Russian Revolution. Russia's entry into the war against Germany was an attempt by Tsar Nicholas to regain the prestige the country had lost in its disastrous defeat in the Russo-Japanese War of 1904–05, and to try to unite his increasingly fractious people in a common cause. But the attempt backfired as the Russian army took hundreds of thousands of casualties. By the winter of 1917, Russia had lost millions of soldiers—as casualties

In this early twentieth-century painting, the searchlights of the cruiser Aurora light up the Winter Palace as the Bolsheviks approach.

and prisoners of war, but also to desertion. These deserters, in no mood to knuckle down under the rule of the tsar, returned to their home villages and began seizing land from the wealthy.

In the meantime, food shortages were rampant in the country. In St. Petersburg, people were forced to wait in line a total of forty hours a week, just for bread. They began to riot, and this time the troops did not shoot them, as they had done in 1905, but instead joined them, tying red ribbons around their bayonets. With mounting losses from the war, and a complete lack of support from his own government and army, Nicholas II was forced to abdicate in March 1917, ending the three-hundred-year rule of the Romanov dynasty. He and his family were sent into exile in Siberia. A moderate provisional government took over, and a Constitutional Assembly was set up. The government was led by a thirty-six-year-old lawyer and politician, Alexander Kerensky.

Young, eloquent and charismatic, Kerensky was a threat to the more radical groups like the Bolsheviks, whose exiled leaders began making plans to return to Russia. In early April, Lenin was given safe passage homewards from Zurich through Europe in a "sealed" train (meaning it could not be stopped or searched) by the German government. Under pressure from Britain and France, Kerensky was then preparing for another Russian offensive against Germany (one that would result in failure and heavy losses for the Russians). The Germans hoped that a Bolshevik revolt would unseat Kerensky before he could mobilize his troops, and force Russia to sue for peace.

When he arrived at Petrograd's Finland Station, Lenin was met by a cheering crowd; he then began planning a revolution that would result in a government run by groups of workers, known as soviets. In May, Leon Trotsky also returned to Petrograd, to agitate on behalf of the Mensheviks.

FIGHTING IN THE STREETS

In June, Kerensky, pushed further to the right by criticisms from leftist groups like the Bolsheviks, launched his offensive against Germany—with disastrous results. As the summer progressed, conditions at the front deteriorated. Rebellious troops commandeered trains and forced the engineers to drive them to the rear of the lines. Returning to their farms, they murdered landlords and pillaged the bounty of the great estates. Factories in major cities such as Petrograd and Moscow ground to a halt as workers abandoned their machines and joined the Bolsheviks. There were food shortages everywhere.

Generally, Kerensky could do very little about the breakdown of law and order, but in July, when Bolsheviks and

THE OCTOBER REVOLUTION

Vladimir Ilich Lenin addresses a Moscow crowd. His famous ally, Leon Trotsky, is standing to the right of the podium.

anarchists launched violent street demonstrations in Petrograd (possibly instigated by Lenin), Kerensky was able not only to quell the uprisings but also to discredit Lenin by claiming he was a German agent. As a result, Lenin was forced to flee back to Finland.

With Lenin discredited, Kerensky might have moved forward, but in August he suffered a disastrous setback. His army commander in chief, General Lavr Kornilov, led an attempted coup in Petrograd. Kerensky was forced to ask the Bolsheviks for help; Kornilov was defeated, but not before the Bolsheviks gained large stores of arms and ammunition. Meanwhile, Trotsky was briefly jailed by the government and while there joined the Bolsheviks. His practical leadership complemented Lenin's theorising perfectly and the combination created a forceful partnership at the head of a movement that now had tremendous momentum.

THE REVOLUTION BEGINS

On October 24, Kerensky gave Lenin and Trotsky the opening they were looking for. In an attempt to nip the Bolshevik insurrection in the bud, Kerensky cut off the telephone service to the Bolshevik headquarters, raided the offices of the Bolshevik newspaper Pravda, and sent troops to patrol the

streets. He then appeared before a meeting of certain members of the Constituent Assembly, promising to pass reforms (such as turning over land to the peasants) immediately. At the same time, he claimed that he would defend his provisional government to the last.

But Kerensky received little support from the assembly. Sensing the true weakness of Kerensky's government, Lenin launched his revolution the next day.

By noon on October 25, Kerensky (who had awoken to find his own telephone lines cut) had decided that it would be dangerous to stay in Petrograd any longer. The Bolsheviks had seized key bridges, and his own troops, mainly inexperienced cadets, were deserting. He was almost certain to be captured and executed. Commandeering a car, he fled the city to attempt to find loyal troops to support him.

"NO MORE GOVERNMENT"

As John Reed and Louise Bryant walked the streets of Petrograd on October 25, trying to find out how events were unfolding, they found themselves surrounded by excited crowds and saw posters everywhere. "A whole crop of new appeals against insurrection had blossomed out on the walls during the night—to the peasants, to the soldiers at the front, to the workmen of Petrograd," Reed wrote. He and his wife came to the State Bank and queried the soldiers standing in front of it.

"What side do you belong to?" I asked. "The government?"

"No more government," one answered with a grin. "*Slava Bogu*! Glory to God!"

Kerensky's loyal ministers remained in the 1500-room Winter Palace, which was by then surrounded by Bolshevik troops. The subsequent siege became one of the strangest in history, with an almost farcical air. Reed and Bryant were able to stroll through the porous Bolshevik lines into the palace, which was guarded by Kerensky's cadets, whom Bryant called "poor, uncomfortable, unhappy boys'. There were also old tsarist retainers there, wearing their royal blue coats. Many of the defenders were drunk.

In the afternoon, two Bolsheviks came by on bicycles, demanding that the ministers give up by seven that evening. The ministers refused, thinking Kerensky might return with reinforcements. Then they sat down to a dinner of soup, fish and artichokes, although in the dark, since they had put all the lights out to hide their presence.

The Bolsheviks had seized a cruiser on the Neva River, the Aurora, and it was ordered to open fire on the Winter Palace. But because it was a training vessel it was equipped only with blanks, which it dutifully hurled at the defenders. The cadets responded with machine-gun fire until they realized the shells weren't hitting them. At about 11 p.m., the Bolsheviks fired on the palace using the guns of the Peter and Paul Fortress, an old tsarist fortress built on a small island in the Neva. Only two shots managed to hit the palace, however, the rest falling harmlessly into the river. They did little more, as Leon Trotsky put it in disgust, than "injure the plaster".

Finally, at about 1:30 a.m., the Bolsheviks rushed the palace. The first to notice they were coming was the palace switchboard operator, who called the ministers huddled in their chambers and said that "a delegation of three to four hundred is approaching". The Bolsheviks broke into the palace and, without bloodshed, arrested the weary cadets and ministers.

END GAME

The revolution was never so genteel again. Lenin, now in power, named as ministers the likes of Leon Trotsky and Joseph Stalin, a Georgian clerk who had worked for the Bolshevik newspaper *Pravda* and risen through the Communist ranks with Lenin's support. Lenin had the tsar and his family murdered, as well as other prominent Romanovs. He quickly made peace with the Germans, so that he could turn his attention to the civil war that was spreading across the nation, a vicious, take-no-prisoners battle between the newly formed Red Army and the "Whites", a coalition of tsarist supporters and other conservatives backed by the governments of Great Britain, France and the United States. These nations were extraordinarily worried about the threat that a Communist Russia might pose to their democracies and their imperial interests.

By 1920, the Bolsheviks, now officially renamed the Russian Communist Party, had triumphed. Kerensky fled to Paris and made his way to the United States, where he died in 1970. After Lenin's death from a stroke in 1924, there was a bitter power struggle. His obvious successor, Trotsky, was ousted and forced to flee by Joseph Stalin, who later had Trotsky assassinated in Mexico City.

Stalin became the premier of the Soviet state for the next twenty years, and was responsible for the deaths of millions of the very people the revolution was supposed to free from oppression. The idea of liberating Russia from the cruel and inept rule of the tsars had been a natural one. But the unfortunate result was the replacement of the tsars with an equally cruel and inefficient state. ❧

1929

THE WALL STREET CRASH

One man poisoned himself, his wife and his two young children. Another dropped dead in his stockbroker's office. Still another, who lived in a small town in North Carolina, went into his garage and shot himself, the echo careening around his quiet neighborhood.

Rich and poor alike were affected. Winston Churchill, staying at a fancy New York hotel, awoke to a commotion. "Under my very window," he later wrote, "a gentleman cast himself fifteen stories and was dashed to pieces." Irving Berlin, the famous songwriter, remembered it this way: "I had all the money I wanted for the rest of my life. Then all of a sudden I didn't."

It was "Black Tuesday", October 29, 1929. Earlier that morning, in the first thirty minutes of trading on the New York Stock Exchange, over three million shares of stock had changed hands, something that normally took five hours. All of the major companies—General Electric, Chrysler, Standard Oil—were plummeting.

Gradually, a crowd, later estimated at about ten thousand, filled the tiny winding streets around the exchange. Though the New York police commissioner placed extra security on the streets of the financial district, the people weren't violent. Instead, they seemed to be in shock. A reporter for the *New York Times* described the scene as "a sort of paralysed hypnosis". Inside the exchange, a broker, looking out a window, had the horrible feeling that he was surrounded by "haunted things".

And this was only the start. American companies, their stock prices collapsing, either went bankrupt or laid off employees, instituting sharp drops in the production of goods. As people lost their jobs, they went through their savings and often lost their homes, as well. Their purchases—of new cars, furniture, clothing—dropped, and more companies began to close. Without money from industries and personal savings (and without federal banking insurance, something that is mandatory in the United States today), banks began to fail.

The crash also had an international impact, too. With American businesses failing, the U.S. government instituted high tariffs on imported goods, hoping to stimulate the economy. The effect on foreign trade was disastrous. European countries, already experiencing their own financial difficulties due to over-speculation in their markets, found that the tariffs made it impossible for them to compete in the American marketplace. In response, they instituted their own tariffs, and international trade nearly ground to a standstill.

ROARING TOWARDS DISASTER

In America, along with the 1960s, the so-called Roaring Twenties is the twentieth-century decade most likely to be stereotyped. There, the name conjures up Prohibition, gangsters, flappers and bizarre fads. In fact, much of the stereotyping has a basis in fact. People were fad crazy in the United States. They held competitions to see how long they

A year after the Crash, in 1930, an unemployed man makes a heart-rending appeal for a job, on a street corner in Detroit.

could sit atop flagpoles.

They took part in dance marathons. They loved the new talking movies, the Marx Brothers, grand musical extravaganzas on Broadway and sneaking down to the corner "speakeasy" for a little snort of bonded Canadian whisky—or so the proprietor claimed—on the sly.

Driving all these fads was the greatest fad of all: playing the stock market. Prior to this era, the buying and selling of stock had been a rich man's game. But by the twenties, one million Americans (out of a population of about 120 million) owned three hundred million shares of stocks in U.S. companies. This was in large part due to the advent of radio, telephone and, especially, the ticker-tape machine—a small electronic machine from which a paper tape issued showing stock price quotations, allowing one to check each "tick" (upwards or downwards movement) of a stock, and communicate buy and sell orders almost instantly.

The practice of buying stock "on the margin"—paying only a portion of the stock's price yourself and borrowing the rest from a stockbroker—became so widespread that it seemed that you would have to be crazy not to play the market. As in the dot-com boom of the 1990s, stories abounded of ordinary people—the minister of the local church, a great-aunt, that quiet girl working behind the perfume counter at Sears—amassing fortunes. If you just stuck your money in a bank, you

An anxious crowd gathers on Wall Street on "Black Thursday", October 24, 1929. The final crash came on October 29, "Black Tuesday".

were, in the parlance of the day, a sucker.

THE BUSINESS OF AMERICA

In the mid-1920s, most Americans were quite happy with this situation—and with their government. Following the trauma of the Great War and what had been shown to be a corrupt administration under President Warren G. Harding, Calvin Coolidge became U.S. president in 1923. "Silent Cal" came across as a country bumpkin—a man of few but trenchant words who did not suffer city slickers gladly. Generally, voters approved of his "common man" approach, feeling that it mirrored their own feelings about themselves and their country. However, Coolidge was not quite what he appeared to be. In fact, he liked nothing better than to hobnob with the heads of major corporations in America at the time—John D. Rockefeller, Henry Ford, Andrew Mellon. "The business of America is business", Coolidge proclaimed. And: "The man who builds a factory builds a temple." Despite his working-man persona, Coolidge made basic changes that favored the wealthy over the working class—for instance, he made Mellon his Secretary of the Treasury and then allowed him to reduce income tax rates for big businesses and the rich.

Under Coolidge's presidency, business boomed. New technologies and procedures, which included Henry Ford's assembly line and improved techniques for refining oil, allowed companies to produce more iron, steel, gas and chemicals. But, unfortunately, this was a business and production boom, not an employment boom, since many of the new industrial methods had as their goal the elimination of manual labor. In a familiar story, the rich got richer as the poor got poorer—in the 1920s, according to historians, ninety percent of the nation's wealth was concentrated in the hands of thirteen percent of the population (today, roughly seventy percent of wealth is held by ten percent of the population).

Indeed, this so-called "New Era" of prosperity was to a large extent a chimera—as Mellon's tax cuts took effect, corporations which were making little in the way of profits had more money to spend, and they spent it on the stock market. And anyone in America who could afford to follow suit did so.

There were four million unemployed people in America by the end of 1928, yet the Twenties roared on unabated. When Coolidge refused to run for president again in 1928, his wife told a friend, "Papa says there's going to be a depression", but those who heard this just laughed, elected another pro-business leader, Herbert Hoover, and kept on speculating.

> IF YOU JUST STUCK YOUR MONEY IN THE BANK, YOU WERE, IN THE PARLANCE OF THE DAY, A SUCKER.

RIDING THE ROLLER COASTER

During the summer of 1929, the stock market reached an all-time high, with record numbers of shares being purchased. But the situation was beginning to give pause to sober observers. For not only were more and more shares being bought on the margin, but also, as of early autumn 1929, only a third of stocks—about four hundred of twelve hundred listed on the New York Stock Exchange—had grown in value since the previous January. It was also noted that the huge "stock trusts"—groups of wealthy investors who pooled their money to purchase stocks—could drive up almost any stock they wanted, simply by investing heavily in it.

In September, an influential economist named Roger Babson made a speech in which he said that a crash was coming, and that there would likely be "a stampede for selling which will exceed anything that the Stock Exchange has ever seen". Babson had been saying this for a year or so, but few had paid any attention to him previously. Now, however, his words echoed secret fears harbored by many, and a sell-off began. The market righted itself a few days later, but throughout September and into October it plunged up and down like a roller coaster.

A FEEDING FRENZY

When the stock market finally crashed on Tuesday October 29, it was one of the bleakest days in American financial history, becoming forever known as Black Tuesday. But five days prior to this, on October 24, a near-crash had already occurred. It became known as Black Thursday. Through early October, stocks had rebounded slightly as prominent bankers made calming statements to the effect that the market was simply adjusting itself. But late on the afternoon of Wednesday October 23 there was a sharp and terrifying plunge in the Dow Jones average (an index of select industrial stocks whose status is seen as an indicator of the health of the market in general) as brokers were flooded with sell orders by those who, like Babson, had finally decided the market was going to crash. In those days, unless they were wealthy enough to afford their own ticker-tape machine, people congregated in brokers' offices all over the country to watch the progress of their stocks. Stock panics, even in today's era of personal computers, are highly contagious. Think how much more virulent they would have been when your fellow investors were sitting right next to you, sweating and yelling "sell" orders.

By the end of trading on Wednesday, six million shares had changed hands, with losses of US$4 billion. That evening, stockbrokers began to make margin calls to those customers who had borrowed money to buy their stocks. In other words, the stockbrokers forced their clients to instantly repay the money they had borrowed to purchase the stock—the equivalent of a bank with whom you have a home mortgage suddenly contacting you to say that you need to pay off your entire mortgage at once or the bank will sell your house.

Shortly after the market opened on Thursday, it sped downwards like a space rocket plummeting back to earth. Panicked crowds in Wall Street and around the country pushed their brokers to sell and speculators dumped stock quickly. When those who had been called for cash to meet their margins were unable to come up with it, the brokers sold the stocks at once, to recover whatever part of their losses they could. It was a horrible feeding frenzy, made worse by the fact that the overwhelmed ticker-tape system broke down and most stock quotations were forty-five minutes late.

Since stocks were dropping twenty points in that interval, speculators and brokers were left in the dark about real values and began to sell blindly.

By mid-afternoon, stocks had crashed to the tune of US$11.25 billion. The only thing that saved the market for another "black" day was the fact that a consortium of bankers quickly pooled together about US$250 million and sent one of their members to walk the floor of the New York Stock Exchange making loud "buy" orders, often at above the asking price. By the end of the day, the market had stabilized, but was still down to the tune of US$3 billion dollars.

THE BLACKEST DAY

Between this penultimate day of tragedy for Wall Street and Black Tuesday, the Federal Reserve Board, prominent bankers and President Herbert Hoover worked feverishly to restore public confidence. "The fundamental business of this country … is on a sound and prosperous basis", Hoover said. (It was the kind of irrationally optimistic comment the nation would come to expect from this president. Later, when bankrupted doctors and businessmen were forced to sell apples on the street to make ends meet, he told a reporter: "Many people have left their jobs for the more profitable one of selling apples.") But many people had been wiped out on Black Thursday, and those who hadn't began to wonder if they hadn't better sell in order to hang on to whatever savings they had left. Consequently, on Monday, October 28, despite the reassurances, there was another plunge and near-crash.

And on Tuesday, October 29, the devastation really began. The day started with thousands of people congregating in Wall Street, as if they needed to be present at what they sensed was going to be a historic moment. All of the major stocks—those linchpins upon which the market depended—began to crash before the horrified eyes of those on the floor of the stock exchange. AT&T lost 105 points in a few hours that morning. RCA plummeted from 110 to 26. Brokers received sell orders from their clients, and went into a frenzy trying to place them. In two hours, eight million shares of stock were sold. One broker, apparently driven to a nervous breakdown by the pace of the activity, began screaming and rushed from the exchange, knocking over anyone who got in his way.

In the meantime, further margin calls ruined almost everyone who had borrowed to buy stocks. As the day wore on, people began to fall into shock. A reporter for the *New York Times* perceptively wrote that "to most of those who have been in the market it is all the more awe-inspiring because their financial history is limited to bull markets". In other words, these ordinary investors had never faced the full, clawing fury of a Wall Street bear market.

At three o'clock, after five hours of trading, the market closed. Sixteen million shares had been traded. The nation had suffered an estimated US$15 billion in losses. The Dow Jones had tumbled from 290 to 260 points, furthering its slide of 120 points since September.

The stories of suicides began—as the humorist Will Rogers was to write sardonically, "you had to stand in line to get a window to jump out of." While these tales are as exaggerated as some of the earlier boom tales of clerks gaining instant riches from stocks, there were some who took their own lives as a result of their financial ruin. Businesses began to die as well. The first to go were the investment firms, followed by companies that had over-speculated in stocks, and banks. Like a house of cards, the Roaring Twenties tumbled to an end.

RISKS REMAIN

Herbert Hoover had entered office in the greatest bull market of all time. By the time he left it, overwhelmingly beaten by Franklin Delano Roosevelt in 1932, he was surrounded by mobs chanting "We want bread!" These days, historians do not place the blame for the Great Depression only on the 1929 Crash, but also on the Hoover Administration. Its economic policies, including high tariffs that stifled international trade and not issuing enough money, created a shortage of cash and did little to help stimulate the economy.

There would be other stock market crashes, one in October 1987, another at the end of the dot-com boom after 2000 and again in 2008, but these did not have nearly so catastrophic an effect on the world. Among the lessons learned after the 1929 Crash was that margin lending had to be controlled, that the government needed to provide insurance to banks—the glorious "free market" needed in some sense to be regulated. Today, stocks, although they provide the highest return on the investment dollar, are still risky; and most ordinary investors cast concerned eyes upon their investment funds and pensions on a regular basis. The stories from 1929 of

1930
GANDHI'S SALT MARCH

here is an old Gujarat legend that says when a laborer on the salt flats of the Rann of Kutch dies, the only part of his body that survives the funeral pyre is the soles of his feet, which are baked so hard by a lifetime of walking its hot, dry saltpans that even the heat of the flames cannot make them burn.

In the aftermath of every monsoon season for the past five thousand years, salt has been harvested from the Rann of Kutch, an 7000-square-miles area of low-lying coastline in the Indian state of Gujarat. This vast desert of mudflats and salt marshes, with an average height above sea level of just 50 feet, has been mined by hundreds of generations of families. The salt it yields plays a vital role in replacing the natural salts that are taken each day from the bodies of India's laborers by the unrelenting heat and humidity of the Indian sun.

THE TAX ON SALT

Salt had been taxed in the subcontinent since the reign of the Mauryan emperor, Chandra Gupta, in the fourth century BC. In the sixteenth and seventeenth centuries the ruling Moguls placed a tax on salt in Bengal state as it passed through their territory on its journey up the River Ganges. Salt taxes under the Moguls, however, as they were throughout most of the country, were relatively light and imposed little financial hardship on the average Indian family. The taxation of salt was never a political or social issue so long as the amount at which it was taxed remained in the range of 2.5 to 5 percent.

In 1780 the manufacture of salt and the rate at which it would be taxed was brought under the control of the British government. (India had become a colonial possession of Great Britain in 1858, and would remain part of the British Empire until independence was achieved in 1947.) Government agents

were appointed and received a 10 percent commission on the revenues from the sale of salt. In the three years starting in 1781, tax revenues from salt increased from 2.6 million rupees annually to more than 6 million rupees. In 1788 the "fixed price policy" on salt that wholesalers had always been able to rely upon was abandoned in favor of government-run auctions. This forced up the price to the point where it became a genuine hardship for many Indian families, though arguments abounded as to just what constituted an average Indian family. It was even debated whether or not cattle should be included in calculating the needs of an average rural family. In 1880 the Madras Board of Revenue estimated that 18 pounds of salt (just over 8 kilograms) was the amount required to meet the needs of a family of six for a period of one year, and that purchasing it would take almost a month's wages from the pocket of a common laborer.

In 1885 the Indian politician and theosophist Swaminatha Iyer spoke in the National Congress against a proposed increase in the salt tax, calling it "unjust and unrighteous" and an unnecessary imposition on the poor of India. By this time the British monopoly on salt was total. The Salt Act of 1882 made the individual collection of salt illegal, and punishable by a prison term of up to six months as well as the confiscation of any vehicle or animal used to transport it. What had once been an abundant and vital natural resource available to all at a reasonable price had become a revenue tool to support and sustain the British presence, with little regard for the financial strain its artificially high price was imposing on the Indian people.

Calls for Indian independence, mostly in the form of militant nationalism, began in the early years of the 1900s, but it wasn't until the early 1920s that the Indian Congress Party adopted the non-violent policies espoused by Gandhi. In December 1929, under the leadership of Jawaharlal Nehru, the Congress Party adopted a resolution demanding complete and total independence from the British Empire and called for a campaign of civil disobedience across the nation. On January 26, 1930 the Indian National Congress issued a unilateral Declaration of Independence. History was being made, and everyone looked to Mohandas Karamchand Gandhi to see what he would do next.

GANDHI DEVELOPS A LIFELONG PHILOSOPHY

Mohandas Gandhi was born on October 2, 1869 in Porbandar on the coast of Gujarat, India. Porbandar was a princely state possessing nominal sovereignty and Gandhi's father was its prime minister. In 1883 at the age of thirteen, Gandhi wed Kasturbai Makhaji in an arranged marriage and together they had four children. In 1888 he travelled to London to study as a barrister and began to develop an interest in Christian and Hindu scriptures. In 1893 he and his wife went to live in South Africa where Gandhi became a victim of class and race discrimination for the first time in his life. He was taken off a train for refusing to travel third class despite having a first class ticket, was refused lodging at various hotels and was badly beaten by a stagecoach driver for refusing to surrender his seat to an English passenger. These events were a watershed in his personal development. He studied the effects of prejudice and pored over the principles of social justice, extending his time in South Africa to stay and fight for the rights of the country's Indian minority.

Gandhi returned to India in 1915 and in 1918 to 1919 achieved national prominence for organizing resistance in the state of Bihar to British demands that farmers grow cash crops such as indigo instead of the food crops required for day-to-day living.

Through the 1920s Gandhi became a uniting figure in the Indian National Congress, but at the same time he stayed aloof from internal politicking, preferring instead to fight the scourges of poverty and alcoholism, campaigning for the rights of the classless "untouchables", and promoting tolerance between Hindus and Muslims. At the close of the 1920s there was no leader more respected in all of India. He had been given the title of Mahatma, or "Great Soul", and was thought of as the Father of the Nation. If anyone could lead a protest movement to bring about the end of the British presence in India, it was he.

GANDHI PLANS THE MARCH

By February of 1930 Mahatma Gandhi had come to view the salt tax as an example of the "heartless exploitation" of India by the ruling British and, claiming to be inspired by "an inner voice", decided he would make the unpopular tax the focus of a symbolic non-violent protest. He would orchestrate a march to the sea, from his ashram in the Ahmedabad suburb of Sabarmati to the coastal village of Dandi in Gujarat on the shores of the Arabian Sea 242 miles away. The journey would take 23 days. When he arrived in Dandi he planned to kneel, scrape up a handful of saline mud from the ground, and tell those around him to do likewise and take it home and boil it to extract the precious salt. The illegal act would symbolize India's growing rejection of British rule and, he hoped, hasten the nation along the path to independence.

On March 2, Gandhi wrote to the viceroy, Lord Irwin, to inform him of his intentions. The letter read in part:

If my letter makes no appeal to your heart, on the eleventh day of this month I shall proceed with such co-workers of the Ashram as I can take, to disregard the provisions of the Salt Laws. I regard this tax to be the most iniquitous of all from the poor man's standpoint. As the Independence movement is essentially for the poorest in the land, the beginning will be made with this evil.

Irwin's response to Gandhi was merely to warn him that if he did anything that was in breach of the law, he would be held to account. Irwin was dismissive of Gandhi's planned march and said as much in a letter he wrote to London in February: "At present the prospect of a salt campaign does not keep me awake at night."

HISTORY WAS BEING MADE, AND EVERYONE LOOKED TO MOHANDAS KARAMCHAND GANDHI TO SEE WHAT HE WOULD DO NEXT.

THE COMMITMENT TO NON-VIOLENT PROTEST GROWS

Intent on achieving maximum publicity for his march, Gandhi announced his intentions to the media. The march would be a satyagraha, a synthesis of the two Sanskrit words satya (truth) and agraha (holding on to), which to Gandhi represented the sort of mix of love and firmness that comes from a commitment to non-violence as a means of personal expression and political action, and as a tool to wean one's opponents away from error—to convert your enemy rather than coerce him.

Gandhi was insistent that the march be conducted under the strict observance of the principles of satyagraha and according to his own rigid code of discipline, and for this reason preferred that those who would accompany him come from his own ashram and not from the Congress Party or other organizations.

On March 12, an estimated one hundred thousand people lined the streets of Ahmedabad as Gandhi and an initial seventy-eight satyagrahis (activists of truth and resolution)

Mahatma Gandhi addresses a rally in Calcutta during the early years of his opposition to British rule.

slowly made their way through the city streets. Press coverage reached saturation point. The Bombay Chronicle described the scene: "so enthusiastic, magnificent, and soul-stirring that indeed they beggar description. Never was the wave of patriotism so powerful in the hearts of mankind." The sixty-year-old Gandhi headed the procession, which soon grew to over 2 miles long. He carried a stick to help him walk at a brisk and determined pace. People climbed trees and rooftops so they would be able to one day tell their grandchildren they had seen him pass. In every village and at every halting station he stopped to speak to the assembled crowds, encouraging non-cooperation with the British and inviting them to join the growing ranks of his satyagrahis—and to return to the spinning wheels and to wear the khaddar.

The khaddar was a simple hand-spun cotton or silk covering, the manufacture of which Gandhi had long been promoting as a step towards reducing unemployment, particularly in the rural areas of India. It had become symbolic of India's struggle for independence, and was part of the early Swadeshi Movement, which began in Bengal in 1905 and grew from a desire to boycott British-made products and to promote indigenous industries. The more the khaddar was made and worn, the less demand there would be for British-made textiles.

THOUSANDS OF FOLLOWERS JOIN THE MARCH

The march took Gandhi through four districts and forty-eight villages. As he made his way from village to village, hundreds enrolled in the cause of civil disobedience. Many village elders resigned their posts and joined the march. Gandhi himself proclaimed he would refuse to return to his beloved ashram until the hated tax was repealed. To everyone who saw him he was an inspiration. Despite his advancing years he moved with the enthusiasm and purpose of a man half his age, an invincible juggernaut covering 12 miless a day without any obvious signs of fatigue.

The route was meticulously planned. Scouts were sent ahead to meet with the elders of every village on the route. Information on each community was relayed back to the approaching Gandhi—from the number of its "untouchables" to each person's salt consumption, from the number of spinning wheels it possessed to the number of cows the village had, from the quality of its drinking water to the state of its health care and educational facilities.

In every village through which he passed Ghandi spoke of the need to defy the British on the collection of salt and to boycott British cloth and return to the khaddar. He preached religious tolerance, and encouraged those in government positions to leave their jobs and join in the Salt Satyagraha. "Why are you afraid of such a government?" he asked in Buva village. "What could they do if there were eighty thousand volunteers?" At Ankleshwar village he spoke mockingly of British greed: "This government levies a duty on an item which is consumed by the poorest of the poor. We are lucky, at any rate, that there is no tax on the air we breathe!"

Twenty-three days later, on April 5, Gandhi and his initial group of seventy-eight devotees, now swelled to several thousand, arrived at Dandi. In an interview with an Associated Press reporter on the Dandi coast, Gandhi said: "it remains to be seen whether the [British] government will tolerate, as they have tolerated the march, the actual breach of the salt laws by countless people from tomorrow." On the following morning, April 6, Gandhi took a handful of mud and salt, raised his fist triumphantly into the air and declared: "With this I am shaking the foundations of the British Empire."

MASS DEFIANCE OF THE SALT TAX

The next day India erupted, as across the country tens of thousands of men, women and children ran to the coastline to gather salt in open violation of British law, salt which was then sold throughout cities, across the land, thus making accomplices of everyone who purchased it and swelling the ranks of the nation's passive revolutionaries almost overnight. The British responded in the only way they felt they could. Thousands were arrested and an unknown number were killed and beaten in the riots that followed.

On May 4, the District Magistrate of Surat, along with a small number of Indian officers and a squad of armed constables, came to arrest Gandhi at his small hut on Dandi beach. They had difficulty locating him amid the sea of white khaddar-wearing followers and had to be directed to the slight frame of the great man, who was in a deep sleep. "We have come to arrest Mr. Gandhi," the official said. "I am Mohandas Gandhi, and I am at your service", said the man, and when given some time to gather his things replied that he did not need any time to do so: "I am ready now. This is all I need." Gandhi gathered a few personal items into a small bundle at his feet and offered no resistance. After pausing briefly to brush his teeth, he was led away to Pune's Yerwada Jail where he remained until released in January 1931.

To the more than sixty thousand satyagrahis who were soon in prisons all over India, Gandhi was an inspiration. He was used to being imprisoned, and because he felt the entire world was a sacred place had little difficulty in adjusting to prison life. He also knew that each new day of his eight-month incarceration brought more converts to the cause of non-violent protest and the end of the British presence in India that much closer. Indian independence would finally be achieved in 1947, with Gandhi its champion. ❦

Gandhi's epic march was a world-wide media phenomenon, with Ghandi issuing regular statements along the way.

1933

FDR AND THE "NEW DEAL"

In October 1929, following a period of rapid expansion through the 1920s, a wave of panic selling swept through the financial markets of the United States. Within a week the value of all publicly listed American companies had collapsed, initiating a U.S.-led depression that would spread across the globe and drag all the world's economies down with it. Panic selling began on 24 October, but it was on "Black Tuesday", five days later, that investors crowding outside the New York Stock Exchange watched mutely as their life savings disappeared in front of their eyes. In New York, as evidence of plummeting stock values came out over the tickertape machines, many openly wept.

In just three years, from 1929 to 1932, the American economy went from relative prosperity to being on life support. Unemployment rose from three to twenty-five percent, which represented more than 13 million people, and the average family income fell by almost half. Farm foreclosures were being counted in the hundreds of thousands. In mining states such as Pennsylvania and West Virginia, two of the poorest states going into the Depression years, more than three out of four schoolchildren were reported as malnourished. Corporate profits across the nation fell by ninety percent, from $10 billion in 1929 to $1 billion in 1932. The number of new homes under construction fell by eighty percent and, by 1932, two in three Americans were classified as "poor" by federal government agencies. By 1932, 5000 American banks had gone out of business. It was an economic holocaust that seemed to have no end. One Manhattan-based Soviet trading company was receiving almost four hundred approaches every day from ordinary Americans enquiring after work in the U.S.S.R.

In the presidential elections of 1932, voters took out their anger and frustration on President Herbert Hoover, the Republican from Iowa who was the first occupant of the White House to be born west of the Mississippi. Unlucky enough to have won the 1928 presidential election, Hoover's name became synonymous with the crash and the Depression that followed. The thousands of slums that appeared almost overnight, it seemed, were nicknamed Hoovervilles, and he was lampooned in the press as a "do nothing" president. In fact Hoover did intervene, but the actions he took, particularly the raising of tariffs in a vain attempt to protect the economy, lengthened the Great Depression's impact.

THE NEED FOR A "NEW DEAL"

Franklin Roosevelt first mentioned the need for a "new deal" for the American people when he accepted the Democratic Party's nomination for the presidency in Chicago in July 1932:

> Washington has alternated between putting its head in the sand and saying there is no large number of destitute people who need food and clothing, and then saying the States should take care of them if there are. Throughout the nation men and women, forgotten in the political philosophy of the government, look to U.S. here for guidance and for a more equitable opportunity to share in the distribution of national wealth … I pledge myself to a "new deal" for the American people. This is more than a political campaign. It is a call to arms.

Roosevelt's subsequent election ended twelve years of Republican domination in Washington with a landslide victory, carrying forty-two states to Hoover's six (Hawaii and Alaska not yet having been admitted to the Union) and winning just over fifty-seven percent of the popular vote.

Few presidents had entered the White House bringing with them such a wealth of experience and tenure in public service. Elected to the New York State Senate in 1910, Roosevelt became

Roosevelt shakes hands with embattled farmers during his election campaign in 1932.

assistant secretary of the Navy in 1913 and played a key role in establishing the United States Navy Reserve. In 1920 he ran as the Democratic Party's vice-presidential candidate alongside the party's candidate for president, Governor James Cox of Ohio, who was defeated by Republican Warren Harding. In 1921 Roosevelt contracted polio while holidaying at the family home on Campobello Island, New Brunswick. The disease left him paralysed from the waist down.

Throughout the 1920s, Roosevelt never lost touch with his beloved Democratic Party, and in 1928 was persuaded to return to the political arena. He was narrowly elected governor of New York and, after a [eriod in office in which his integrity came to the fore, he was nominated as the Democratic Party's presidential candidate in 1932. Roosevelt's response to the raft of social and economic challenges he now faced would define a generation.

Roosevelt was elected the thirty-second president of the United States. In his inaugural speech on March 4, 1933 Roosevelt acknowledged the destruction that had brought the country's financial markets to its knees:

So first of all, let me assert my firm belief that the only thing we have to fear, is fear itself, nameless, unreasoning, unjustified terror, which paralyses needed efforts to convert retreat into advance …

On March 6, just forty-eight hours after assuming office, Roosevelt declared a mandatory five-day bank holiday to prevent panicked investors from withdrawing their savings, at the end of which the Emergency Banking Relief Act (passed in record time by a newly elected Democratic Congress) gave him the power to regulate and oversee all banking transactions. It was hoped this would bring to an end the horrific rate of bank closures (which had averaged almost fifteen hundred a year in the final two years of the Hoover presidency) and restore public faith in the financial sector. Then on March 12, Roosevelt spoke directly to an audience of fifty million for the first time in a series of live, reassuring "fireside chats" over the radio, laced with the optimism that would go on to become one of the defining hallmarks of his presidency.

THE NEW DEAL—FIRST STEPS TO RECOVERY

The New Deal that Roosevelt had first spoken of in his acceptance speech at the Democratic National Convention in July 1932 was to come in two stages. The First New Deal

The construction of the Hoover Dam—one of the massive public works ordered by Roosevelt as part of the New Deal.

(1933–34), which began with the passage of the Economy Act on March 20, 1933, slashed the salaries of public servants and reduced veterans pensions in an effort to limit the size of the budget deficit. But it only succeeded in reducing the deficit by $243 million—barely half the reduction the president was hoping for—and in the end had a negligible impact on either the size of the deficit or the economy. Roosevelt was a keen student of the economist John Maynard Keynes, who believed government spending should, in theory, "kick-start" a stagnant economy. He realized that, to stimulate growth in the absence of any meaningful investment from the private sector, massive injections of government money would be required. This put an end to any thoughts of returning the budget to surplus. The Economy Act was followed in May with the establishment of the Federal Emergency Relief Administration (FERA), whose job was to alleviate the debt incurred by the country's state and local authorities.

FERA was one of the many so-called "alphabet agencies" that Roosevelt created in the frenetic legislative agenda that characterized his first few months in office, and which collectively would be given the responsibility of implementing the policies of recovery. Such reforms and agencies included the Agricultural Adjustment Administration (AAA), the Civil Works Administration (CWA) and the Civilian Conservation

Corps (CCC). The CCC took unemployed young people, paid them a wage of $30 a month, and sent them to work on conservation and forestation projects around the country. During the CCC's nine-year existence it employed close to three million people. Other agencies, such as the Tennessee Valley Authority (TVA), were created by Congress to provide jobs for those regions that needed it most. In the Tennessee Valley, for instance, where one in three people suffered from malaria, generations of destructive farming practices had resulted in poor crop yields and unproductive soils. Farm incomes had been decimated, and its poorer communities were enduring living conditions typical of the developing countries of Latin America. The TVA was tasked with raising the living standards of the valley's residents, advising them on improved methods of crop rotation and new fertilizers.

Meanwhile reforms in the banking sector continued apace. On June 16, 1933 the second Glass–Steagall Act created for the first time a distinction between commercial and investment banks, made it illegal for banks to invest in the stock market and paved the way for the creation of the Federal Deposit

Insurance Corporation (FDIC) which insured the deposits of ordinary investors to the value of $5000.

UNPRECEDENTED GOVERNMENT INTERVENTION

In June 1933 Roosevelt also established the National Recovery Administration (NRA), an agency that was fundamental in implementing many of the early initiatives of the new government, including the building of soup kitchens and shelters across the country to feed and house America's new underclass. The NRA also had the power to exempt businesses from anti-trust laws if they complied with new government guidelines on working conditions and wage and price restraint. Throughout the year, federal government programs would usher in an era of government intervention on a hitherto unprecedented scale, designed to stimulate recovery in the industrial sector and to provide assistance to the millions of Americans whose livelihoods had been stripped from them.

June 1933 also saw the creation of the Public Works Administration (PWA), whose job it was to oversee the appropriation and allocation of funds for large-scale building programs, including highways and schools, and naval vessels from landing craft to aircraft carriers.

In 1934, in an attempt to control the sort of bad lending practices and rampant speculation that contributed to the 1929 stock market crash, the Securities Exchange Act saw the creation of the Securities and Exchange Commission (SEC)—in the hope the new agency would restore the public's faith in the banking system.

The Second New Deal (1935–38) was characterized by the passage of the National Labor Relations Act, essentially a workplace reform act designed to limit employer interference in the creation of labor unions and assist efforts by employees in the pursuit of collective bargaining and in the selection of representatives of their own choosing.

BURGEONING OPPOSITION TO NEW DEAL POLICIES

The Second New Deal saw a far heavier reliance on the deficit-spending theories of John Maynard Keynes. As the Democrats' deficit spending soared, opposition to the New Deal from both the socialist left and the conservative right began to grow. The radical Senator Huey Long (Democrat, Louisiana) attacked Roosevelt for not providing enough assistance—although his

ROOSEVELT WAS A KEEN STUDENT OF THE ECONOMIST JOHN MAYNARD KEYNES, WHO BELIEVED GOVERNMENT SPENDING SHOULD, IN THEORY, KICK-START A STAGNANT ECONOMY.

own Share The Wealth plan, which would see the confiscation of any personal fortune over the amount of $3 million dollars redistributed to the poor, would surely have ushered in a new American Revolution if actively pursued. Father Charles Coughlin, an anti-Semitic Roman Catholic priest with a national radio audience of over forty million, also became a thorn in Roosevelt's side. Coughlin, sometimes referred to as the "father of hate radio", referred to Judaism as "that synagogue of Satan' and to Roosevelt's New Deal as "the stinking cesspool of pagan autocracy".

Undaunted by the criticism, Roosevelt ploughed on. The first major legislative accomplishment of the Second New Deal was the Works Progress Administration (WPA), a body similar to the Public Works Administration (PWA) of the First New Deal in every respect except its scale—the WPA would eventually employ more then ten million Americans on new infrastructure projects across the country in a torrent of spending that saw Congress channel more than $10 billion into the scheme in ten years.

ROOSEVELT IS RE-ELECTED

On August 14, the Social Security Act of 1935 was passed, establishing a pension system for workers and introducing compensation for the victims of industrial accidents. The bill also included funds for vocational training to enable more people to enter the workforce, and assistance for the blind as well as for dependent and disabled children. Farmers benefited greatly from the Soil Conservation and Domestic Allotment Act, which paid subsides to farmers to limit overproduction and provided financial incentives to plant soil-enriching crops. There was barely a corner of American society that Roosevelt had not reached into with reforms and assistance, and in the presidential election of 1936 he was re-elected in the greatest landslide since the two-party system of government was established in 1850, winning over sixty percent of the vote and carrying every state in the union with the exception of Maine and Vermont. In fact, Roosevelt and the Democratic Party had become so synonymous with what was best for America that in the days after the election, on a highway as he crossed the border into Vermont, a prankster erected a sign that read: "You are now leaving the United States."

THE FINAL DEAL

In 1937 Roosevelt scaled back deficit spending. The economy, despite growing steadily since 1933, had not been strengthened sufficiently to continue prospering in the absence of any external stimulus and slipped back into a period of negative growth that opponents labelled the Roosevelt Recession. Midterm congressional elections in 1938 saw the Republicans claw back some representation and, although the Democrats still retained a two-thirds majority, the Republican resurgence spelled the end of the era of New Deal politics. In his State of the Union address in January 1939 Roosevelt offered no new domestic reform legislation, instead focusing on the prospect of war in Europe, a war that would see the United States return to a war economy footing, which would in turn erase the last vestiges of the Great Depression.

Not merely a response to difficult economic times, Roosevelt's New Deal also left a lasting legacy. It helped create a climate where those Americans striving for social justice could challenge more openly the notion of white supremacy.

African Americans began to believe the New Deal rhetoric that economic security was for all Americans. For Native Americans, gone were the days of cultural "assimilation" for the Indian New Deal of 1934 fostered the creation of tribal self-government. The foundation for America's post–World War II economic growth was laid in the New Deal's $6.5 billion public works projects that saw the creation of water projects, dams, sewerage plants, bridges, tunnels, schools, and highways. Many New Deal programs still exist today, including the Tennessee Valley Authority (TVA), the Federal Housing Administration (FHA), the Securities and Exchange Commission (SEC) and, of course, the nation's social security system, which gave Americans a system of welfare that brought the country closer to the true spirit of its own Constitution than it had ever been before, and changed forever the relationship between its people and their government. ✳

1934

THE NIGHT
OF THE LONG KNIVES

The phrase Night of the Long Knives was first used in the fifth century to describe a treacherous massacre—albeit quite likely an apocryphal one—in which a group of Celtic Britons were slaughtered by Anglo-Saxon soldiers while attending peace negotiations on Salisbury Plain in the south of England. Fourteen hundred years later, in November 1841, the phrase surfaced again, this time used to describe the assassination of Alexander Burnes, the great British explorer of the Indian subcontinent, in Kabul, Afghanistan. However, despite existing in literature for 1500 years, it wasn't until the bloody events that took place in Bavaria, Germany, in mid 1934, that the phrase at last found its terrifyingly appropriate place in history.

Adolf Hitler was sworn in as German Chancellor in the presidential offices of Field Marshal Paul von Hindenburg, the German head of state and guardian of the constitution, at midday on January 30, 1933. His inauguration marked the end of a brief, German fourteen-year flirtation with democracy known as the Weimar Republic. It was the culmination of a period of political and racial intimidation orchestrated by Hitler and achieved using his loyal Sturmabteilung (SA) or "assault detachment", a pseudo-military organization created in the early 1920s to intimidate and coerce his political opponents.

The SA had its genesis in the German Worker's Party (Deutsche Arbeiterpartei, or DAP), which was founded in January 1919 and which Hitler himself joined later that same year. Hitler's skills as a stirring, almost hypnotic orator saw him rise quickly through the party's ranks; and, in public meetings as early as 1921, whenever Hitler was subject to heckling from his audiences, armed party members would storm the crowd and throw the often bloodied and bruised hecklers into the street. These "stormtroopers" represented the beginnings of what would one day become the SA, Hitler's chief instrument of Nazi political persuasion.

THE RISE OF RÖHM AND THE SA

Banned by the German government in the wake of the Beer Hall Putsch in 1923 (a failed Nazi coup led by Hitler), the SA was reorganized in April 1924 by the fanatical Ernst Röhm and renamed the Frontbann. Composed essentially of those who formerly made up the SA, membership in the Frontbann grew to more than 30,000. In February 1925, when the ban on the Nazi Party was lifted, the Frontbann assumed its old title, Sturmabteilung, and new SA groups began to spring up right across the country and continued to grow in strength and numbers—until Hitler removed Röhm as its head and assumed personal control of the organization in September 1930.

Though Hitler was now in place at the head of the SA, it was Röhm who continued to enjoy the loyalty of his troops. Known collectively as the "brownshirts", the SA by 1930 had grown into a powerful political and military unit with well over a million members. In 1925, however, its original function of protecting the party's leaders had been taken from the SA and given to the newly formed Schutzstaffel (SS), an organization formed initially in 1925 to be Hitler's personal bodyguard. The SS demonstrated an unwavering and fanatical loyalty to Hitler and by 1941, under the command of Heinrich

Himmler, had grown to over a million men and exerted as much influence within the Third Reich as the German armed forces themselves. The SA, with Röhm as its chief of staff at Hitler's personal request, continued in its role as the party's enforcer in its running campaign against its real and imagined communist and Jewish opposition, pursuing increasingly violent street confrontations with the Communist Red Front, and terrorizing Jewish businesses and indeed anyone who demonstrated opposition to Nazi principles and ideals. Even among ordinary Germans there was a growing revulsion towards the tactics pursued by the SA.

Despite Röhm's demotion he retained the loyalty of the SA and had grown in stature to become one of the most powerful figures in the Nazi Party and, many thought, with enough of a following to become a threat to the leadership of Hitler himself. Nevertheless Hitler and Röhm had become close friends. Röhm was one of the elite group of Nazis (including Hermann Göring and Joseph Goebbels) who were able to address Hitler using the familiar and personal form of du, and one of the very few able to call him by his Christian name.

Upon Hitler's election as Chancellor, however, a rift began to emerge between the SA and the regular army. The SA was instrumental in consolidating the Nazi Party's grip on power in the wake of the 1933 elections and saw themselves as the vanguard in the coming National Socialist revolution. With its burgeoning number of recruits the SA also began to harbor thoughts of replacing the German Army (Reichswehr) itself. By early 1934 almost one in five of all German males over the age of fifteen were SA members, four million in all, and its potential to indoctrinate and coerce German society was second to none. With the Nazi Party now in power, all the restraints that kept the excesses of the SA in check were removed.

SA POPULARITY THREATENS NAZI DOMINANCE

Hermann Göring, with Heinrich Himmler (whom Hitler had made chief of the secret police, the Gestapo, in Prussia in April 1934), began to counsel Hitler that he must make a determined move against the SA before Röhm struck first. Himmler considered Röhm and the SA to be a threat to his own SS and wanted the power of the SA brought under control in order to prevent a leadership struggle that he felt had the

> WITH THE NAZI PARTY NOW IN POWER, ALL THE RESTRAINTS THAT KEPT THE EXCESSES OF THE SA IN CHECK WERE REMOVED.

potential to rip the party apart. The German High Command, which viewed the SA brownshirts as little more than vulgar, bloodthirsty thugs, also wanted Röhm and the SA leadership removed, especially in light of Röhm's publicly stated desire that a loyal, "nazified" SA should merge with the conservative and "ideologically suspect" Reichswehr and its class-ridden High Command. Even the country's conservative Vice-Chancellor Franz von Pappen urged Hitler to act. Although the SA was at the peak of its power, Röhm's stubborn independence had helped draw together some very powerful enemies.

Acting on the excuse that SA-led uprisings against the Nazi leadership in Berlin and the Bavarian capital of Munich were imminent, in the early hours of June 30, 1934 Hitler flew to Munich. With his entourage, he drove directly to the Bavarian Interior Ministry, where he ripped the epaulettes off the shoulders of Munich's chief of police, Obergruppenführer Schneidhuber, for failing to maintain order during an SA rampage through the city's streets the night before. After a group of SA stormtroopers were arrested and imprisoned on Hitler's orders, Hitler and a group of loyal SS members and a contingent of the Munich police drove to the Hotel Hanselbauer in the Bavarian spa town of Bad Wiessee where Röhm and the SA leadership were staying. The SA leadership consisted of far more than the stereotypical collection of street thugs and ideological misfits. Those who had risen to the top of the SA were often of high military standing and had trained and served in the old Imperial Army of Kaiser Wilhelm. One in three were professional soldiers whose years of service predated World War I, while two-thirds were decorated combat veterans of the war itself. They survived the brief communist revolution of 1918 that saw the overthrow of Kaiser Wilhelm, and in the early 1920s joined the fledgling SA movement because they possessed the leadership skills and military experience the SA was looking for. Hitler was of course well aware of the legacy of service to the nation the SA's leadership represented, but decided to move against it anyway, demonstrating to his rivals and to the world his ruthless treatment of anyone who opposed his autocratic rule, regardless of how good and loyal a German they might be.

Hitler's chauffeur, Erich Kempka, had flown with him to Munich and drove Hitler, at the head of a three-car motorcade, first to the Interior Ministry and then to Bad Wiessee to confront Röhm. The propaganda minister, Josef Goebbels, and the man Hitler has chosen to replace Röhm, Viktor Lutze, were sitting behind. Lutze had been involved in compiling the list of those SA leaders to be shot, but was not universally liked within the party. Goebbels himself once described him as possessing "unlimited stupidity". In an interview given in 1954, Kempka described what happened next.

SA Commander Ernst Röhm inspects his troops in Berlin in 1933.

HITLER CONFRONTS RÖHM

Hitler asked Kempka to ignore any SA guards that might be placed around the hotel's perimeter and to drive straight to the entrance. Kempka was then told the reason for coming to Munich was that Röhm was planning a coup and that he and the SA leadership had to be "removed". Kempka could hardly believe his ears but barely had time to comprehend what was happening before he found himself rushing into the foyer alongside detectives from the Munich police force who had been following in the cars behind. Röhm's staff guard, Standartenfuhrer Julius Uhl, was the first to be arrested and was locked away in the laundry room. Hitler himself, accompanied by two detectives with pistols drawn, went upstairs in search of Röhm, bursting into his room yelling: "Röhm, you are under arrest." Röhm, still in bed, pleaded his innocence but Hitler would have none of it. Röhm was spared incarceration in the laundry room. Instead he was taken down to the foyer, where he slumped into a large armchair and immediately ordered a black coffee. If, instead of a coffee, Röhm had decided to test the loyalty of his SA troops and ordered them to oppose their arrest, the history of Europe and of the world could have been very different.

SA leaders began emerging from their rooms and each was asked, individually, if they were participants in or had any

Adolf Hitler addresses the nation in a public broadcast a few months after the assassinations.

knowledge of Röhm's supposed "coup". One by one, they denied any knowledge of it, but their protestations had little effect. The laundry room filled up with the accused. One of Röhm's most senior officers, Edmund Heines, was found to be in bed with another SA officer and both were executed on Hitler's orders. Homosexuality had long been a part of SA practice, and Röhm himself was openly acknowledged to be a homosexual.

A bus was ordered to take those arrested back to Munich. Remarkably there was no resistance. Then a group of armed SA men arrived in a lorry and Kempka recalled at that point feeling certain that the operation would erupt in gunfire. As Kempka moved his hand slowly towards his sidearm, to his astonishment Hitler strode up to the armed group, negotiated with its leader, then ordered him to take his men and return to Munich—and, what's more, if they encountered the SS on the way were to permit themselves to be disarmed.

The arrested SA officers were then led from the laundry room to a bus, followed by Röhm himself, who offered no resistance and barely acknowledged Hitler's presence as he was marched past him, head bowed in an acceptance of whatever fate awaited him. Hitler then asked Kempka to return to their car, and again at the head of a column that had by now grown to include more than twenty vehicles, began to head back towards Munich.

Not all were similarly treated, however. When Ernst Röhm's personal doctor, SA Gruppenführer Ketterer, and his wife, walked from their room Hitler approached them and, after greeting them both cordially, advised them to leave the hotel immediately and not return.

THE MURDERS BEGIN

Over the following two days more than eighty-five of the SA hierarchy were murdered, although the actual number has been put as high as two hundred. Hitler also used the occasion to remove other selected opponents of the Nazi regime, including the man who preceded him as chancellor, Kurt von Schleicher, and Gregor Strasser, a former Nazi who had resigned from the party in 1932 after a dispute with Hitler over the political direction of the party. Strasser, a World War I veteran and Iron Cross recipient, was murdered in a prison cell in the basement of the Gestapo headquarters in Berlin, shot several times in the back of the head.

Ernst Röhm, the faithful Nazi who had stood by Hitler from the very beginning and against whom no charges or accusations of treason were ever proved, was taken to Munich's Stadelheim Prison, one of the country's largest gaols. Röhm was placed in cell 70, a celebrated address of sorts, whose previous occupants included the organizer of the overthrow of the Bavarian Wittelsbach monarchy in 1918, Kurt Eisner, and later Eisner's assassin, Anton Graf von Arco auf Valley, who was in turn moved to make room for Adolf Hitler, who called Stadelheim home for a month in 1922. Hitler was anything but eager to kill his old comrade, but was unable to imprison him indefinitely and felt him too dangerous and knowledgeable about the workings of the party to send him into exile. On July 2, at the personal request of Hitler, SS Brigadeführer Theodor Eicke, the commander of the Dachau concentration camp, and an SS officer, Michel Lippert, confronted Röhm in his cell and

left behind a loaded Browning pistol with the instructions that he had ten minutes in which to shoot himself; if he didn't they would return and shoot him themselves. When ten minutes were up, Eiske and Lippert returned to the cell to find Röhm still alive. Lippert picked up the pistol and shot the former head of the SA at point blank range. Röhm slumped to the floor, dead.

In a speech before the German parliament, the Reichstag, on July 13, 1934, Hitler announced the purge to the nation, claiming that Röhm and his other "conspirators" had come dangerously close to attempting to overthrow the government. His speech read in part:

> *In this hour I was responsible for the fate of the German people. I gave the order to shoot the ringleaders in this treason, and I further gave the order to cauterize down to the raw flesh the ulcers of this poisoning of the wells of our domestic life.*

ALL RIVALS VANQUISHED

Then, to ensure the legality of the massacre, retrospective legislation drafted by the former Bavarian and now German minister of justice Franz Gürtner was approved by cabinet on July 3. It made clear that the suppression of treasonous acts with deadly force was a legal and acceptable response in the safeguarding of the state. There was little open dissent. The German high command applauded the action that effectively ended the political and military aspirations of their SA rival, and even the ailing Hindenburg sent Hitler a telegram— whether coerced or not it is impossible to say—congratulating him for his expeditious handling of the matter.

Hitler ordered the new commander of the SA, Viktor Lutze, to clamp down on the drunken excesses, the homosexuality and the extravagant lifestyle that had become synonymous within the upper echelons of the SA leadership.

The night of the long knives was a turning point both for the Nazi Party and for Adolf Hitler personally. From the night of the long knives onwards, Germany was under the leadership of a despot who in every respect was above the law, able to do and say whatever he pleased in the absence of any organized opposition that might have dared to stand in his way. ❦

THE BATTLE OF BRITAIN

I n June of 1940, Great Britain was in mortal danger. Germany, under Adolf Hitler, had conquered all of Western Europe and was even now beginning preparations for an invasion of Britain. It was the most serious threat to its security that Great Britain had faced since the Spanish Armada in 1588. If Hitler's panzer divisions were able to cross the Channel and land on British territory, they would almost certainly overwhelm the exhausted British army.

Winston Churchill, the new Prime Minister of Great Britain, knew that his country faced a daunting challenge. On June 18, he stood before the House of Commons and said, "The Battle for France is over … the Battle for Britain is about to begin. Upon it depends our own British life, and the long continuity of our institutions and our Empire. The whole fury and might of the enemy must very soon be turned on us. Hitler knows that he will have to break us in this Island or lose the war … Let us therefore brace ourselves to our duties, and so bear ourselves that, if the British Empire and its Commonwealth last for a thousand years, men will still say, 'This was their finest hour'."

These were ringing and inspiring words—but the reality, for many in Great Britain, was that this was also their country's darkest hour.

OPERATION SEA LION

Operation *Seelowe*, or "Sea Lion", was the Nazi plan to invade Great Britain. As Churchill knew only too well, if the Nazis conquered Britain (and, therefore, its many colonial possessions), the war was over. The United States, which had not yet entered the war, would almost certainly be forced to accept Hitler's control over Europe as a fait accompli; the führer's "thousand-year Reich" might then become a reality.

German war planners fixed an invasion date for mid-September; the idea was to strike the south coast of England with a huge amphibious force while at the same time parachuting troops deep into the English countryside. German strategists knew that Britain had one major strength: a powerful navy consisting of fifty destroyers and numerous battleships and cruisers, a navy that outnumbered the German navy, the Kriegsmarine, and could blow any invasion fleet out of the water. Therefore, the Luftwaffe was charged with clearing the skies above the English Channel of British Royal Air Force (RAF) planes, so that it could then destroy the Royal Navy at will. Once that had occurred, the invasion could begin.

Reich Marshal Hermann Göring considered victory in the air to be a foregone conclusion. The German air force, the Luftwaffe, was stationed in three "air fleets" in bases in Norway, Belgium and France, and had about 2670 planes, including bombers and fighters—compared to a British fighter force of just 640, led by Air Chief Marshal Sir Hugh Dowding.

The battle of Britain—the first large-scale battle to be fought exclusively in the air—was about to begin.

SHIFTING STRATEGIES

The epic air battle, which for all intents and purposes lasted from July to September 1940, was fought in three successive phases, as Germany adjusted its tactics to try to beat the RAF into submission. In the first phase, the Luftwaffe launched heavy air attacks against Britain beginning on July 10, when bombers and fighters struck shipping, coastal convoys and ports

British pilots race to their fighters after receiving a warning of approaching German planes from coastal observation stations.

in the south of England. In addition, they went after Britain's new defensive weapon, RDF, "radio direction finding", now known as radar, which was able to give advance warning of German planes coming across the British coast.

These first attacks were intended to destroy the British capacity to resist an invasion, but they also had a further purpose: to draw the RAF into the air and destroy it. By all rights, the Germans should have achieved this. Not only was the Luftwaffe superior in numbers, but in pilot training as well. German pilots—many of whose combat experience had been honed in the Spanish Civil War, where Germany supported the Nationalists—had an average of at least six months' training, and usually a good deal more, and recent victories had instilled in them a strong sense of confidence.

Most of the British pilots, on the other hand, were inexperienced. Though the stereotype of the British pilot is of a dashing young man who had attended a top public school, only 200 or so of the 3500 British pilots who took part in the battle of Britain had received a public school education. Instead, these men who formed the front line of defence came from all walks of life: they included bankers, teachers, clerks, factory workers, shop assistants. What they shared, as one of them said, was a sense that, "You wanted action because you were twenty or so … You knew how to fly and you had to fly because there was a war on."

EAGLE DAY

It soon became apparent to the German high command that this first phase of their attack plan wasn't working. Despite the inexperience of the British pilots and the much larger Luftwaffe force, the RAF was more than holding its own. A great part of this was due to the superiority of the British fighter planes. The Germans depended on their Messerschmitt 109 single-engine and 110 double-engine fighters to protect their bombers and engage the RAF in dogfights. But the 110 in particular was relatively slow and had limited endurance compared to the British Hawker Hurricane, and, especially, the subsequently iconic Supermarine Spitfire, which gradually proved its superiority over the Messerschmitt 109, too.

On August 13—a day they codenamed *Aldertag*, or "Eagle Day"—the Germans shifted into the second phase of their offensive: targeting the RAF airfields with heavy bombing as well as dive-bombing attacks. This partially reflected Göring's mistaken impression that the Germans had knocked out the British radar system and had thus blinded its air defences.

The goal of the second phase was to force the RAF to abandon its air bases in southern England within four days, and to completely destroy the RAF within four weeks. But on Eagle Day the Germans lost forty-five planes, while the RAF had only thirteen downed. More importantly, half the downed

St Paul's Cathedral seen through the flames and smoke of blazing buildings after a German air raid on London.

RAF crews lived to fight again, since they had bailed out over friendly territory, whereas surviving German airmen were usually captured and thus lost to the Reich.

AERIAL COMBAT

This stage of the battle of Britain is the one most often portrayed in movies, with brave fighters putting down their cups of tea to race for their planes or dashing to their bases from a night of partying in London. In fact, this has some basis in fact. All across Britain, at dozens of air bases (but particularly at Fighter Command Group II, stationed in southeast England), pilots waited to "scramble" after enemy aircraft. One of them described having pyjamas on under his flight uniform, so that he could quickly take a nap on a bed if needed. Then the call would come—"Dover, 26,000 [feet], 50 bandits [German aircraft] coming from the south-east"—and he would race to his plane.

In the air, each side had varying tactics. The Germans flew in "fingers" of four fighters in line, or in widely spaced groups of four (to make them harder to spot at a distance). At first, the British fought in stiff, closely packed group but these were vulnerable to the more mobile Luftwaffe formations. So they changed their tactics to allow a few planes to function as "weavers", outlying planes that moved at will, searching for "bandits".

The experience of aerial combat was both beautiful and extraordinarily cruel. One pilot, Richard Townshend Bickers, wrote: "We struggled to gain every inch of height in the shortest possible time and we gradually emerged out of the filthy black haze which perpetually hung like a blanket over London. Suddenly at about 12,000 feet we broke through the smog and a different world emerged, startling in its sun-drenched clarity."

This crystal world was a murderous one, with no quarter given. One pilot described a head-on encounter between himself and an ME-109 pilot: "We appeared to open fire together and immediately a hail of lead thudded into my Spitfire". Then the German, though crippled, rammed directly into the British pilot's plane, sending him spiralling down to earth. He only just survived.

TARGETING CIVILIANS

Despite the initial British victories in this wave of the German attacks, the RAF was being slowly eroded by losses of both men and planes. By the end of August Dowding and his staff were making contingency plans to move the most important airfields north, there to await the inevitable invasion. Fortunately for the British, however, the Germans did not realize that the RAF was in such dire straits. And then something happened that changed the course of the campaign again.

In mid-August, German bombers, which had not heretofore been bombing British civilians, accidentally dropped a load of bombs over South London. The enraged British government retaliated on August 25 by bombing Berlin. The shocked German government, which had promised its civilian population that it was safe from the war, then decided to retaliate against British civilians, reasoning, too, that the direct attack on the RAF was not working.

What followed was the last phase of the battle of Britain. Beginning on September 7, two hundred German bombers a night assaulted London, using incendiary devices to create fires and high-explosive bombs to destroy structures. On September 15, two massive waves of German bombers attacked England—the largest air fleet ever to attack the country—but were repulsed by furious RAF counterattacks. German losses were sixty aircraft shot down, as compared to twenty-six RAF fighters. Another bomber force was repulsed two days later. As a direct result of this, Hitler postponed his invasion of Britain, and would finally abandon the idea altogether in December.

From June to September, the British had lost 915 fighters, with 481 men killed and missing (and another 422 wounded).

But the much-vaunted Luftwaffe had suffered 1733 planes lost (although the British claimed this number was closer to 2600).

The threat of invasion had been lifted, though the British were unaware of it at the time and the bombings continued. On the terrible evening of 15 October, nearly five hundred German planes dropped 350 tons of high explosives and an astonishing seventeen thousand incendiary devices on London. During this period, raids killed forty-three thousand British civilians and wounded perhaps five times that number. The "Blitz" of the winter of 1940–41 was particularly terrifying, and German planes continued to haunt the skies well into the following spring. One incendiary attack against London, on 10 May 1941, killed or wounded three thousand people. But it was the last major attack. Five weeks later, as Hitler invaded Russia, most Luftwaffe squadrons along the Atlantic Coast were redeployed for duty in the East.

The British people had not broken, and the battle of Britain had, indeed, been the country's "finest hour". Many things contributed to the eventual Allied triumph in World War II, including the entry of the United States into the conflict in December 1941. But without the RAF's desperate victory, the war would almost certainly have been lost in 1940. ❧

1941

THE ATTACK ON PEARL HARBOR

On November 26, 1941, the main Japanese aircraft carrier battle group, the *Kido Butai*, steamed out of the Kuril Islands (then part of Japan), in the gale-blown waters of the northern Pacific. The *Kido Butai* was made up of six aircraft carriers and numerous support vessels, and constituted the largest fleet seen to date in the Pacific, as well as the greatest number of carriers that had ever banded together. It was of the utmost importance that the fleet not be discovered, so much so that a force of submarines and escort aircraft spread out before the armada to destroy any ship that might stumble upon it.

The fleet was commanded by Vice Admiral Chuichi Nagumo, who had been tasked with the most momentous naval mission in Japanese history: to destroy the U.S. fleet at anchor in Pearl Harbor, on the Hawaiian island of Oahu, 1865 miles to the southeast of the Kurils. Eager to resume its empire-building in the East and stymied by the United States in its attempts to obtain badly needed resources, Japan had decided that war on the Western power was its only option. It expected that its attack would cripple America's naval capacity, allowing it to move in on other Asian nations. But although the raid would inflict a devastating military and psychological blow on the United States, it would—disastrously for the Japanese—fail to completely destroy the U.S. Navy, which would rapidly re-establish itself and help push Japan's armed forces back across the Pacific.

Japan's entrance as a major player upon the twentieth century stage had begun in 1905, when it had comprehensively defeated Russia in the Russo-Japanese War. Building up its navy, army and air force along Western lines, Japan soon had the finest military force in the Pacific Rim, and this build-up was accompanied by a parallel economic expansion. But to sustain its economic expansion Japan required additional natural resources, and it had long eyed off the bountiful neighboring lands of China and Southeast Asia. In 1931, Japan invaded Manchuria, populated the region with Japanese and used it as a base for incursions against other parts of China. Then, in 1937, it launched a full-scale invasion of China, beginning a prolonged war. Three years later, Japan signed the Tripartite Pact, effectively becoming an ally of the fascist states of Germany and Italy, which were already at war with Great Britain and France, and in 1941 it invaded Indochina.

CHOKING JAPAN

In response to these actions, the United States and Great Britain placed embargoes on shipments of oil and scrap metal to Japan. Enraged that the Western powers were objecting to the very type of expansion that they themselves had indulged in, and with supplies of oil dwindling, Japan felt it had no recourse but to take military action. But in order to buy time while its strategists formulated their plans, it began to discuss a possible truce with the United States.

The plan to attack Pearl Harbor was finalized by September 1941, but the Japanese continued extensive negotiations through their ambassador in Washington D.C., and President Franklin Roosevelt's Secretary of State, Cordell Hull. But the two sides were far apart—Japan wanting the United States to lift all trade embargoes and abandon the defences it was

preparing in the Philippines, and the United States demanding that Japan respect the boundaries of all Pacific Rim nations and pull back from expansion into Asia.

TOWARDS "CERTAIN VICTORY'

Late on December 6 (by Tokyo time; across the International Dateline in Hawaii it was December 5) the *Kido Butai* steamed along in the dark at 14 knots, bucking gale-force winds. The fog was so dense and the winds so high that five or six lookouts were washed overboard, never to be seen again. The ships had already undergone a successful but risky refuelling at sea—such manoeuvres are dangerous in rough weather as they can result in collisions. Yet the atmosphere aboard the Japanese ships was one of quietly intense excitement.

That same night, five Japanese midget submarines were launched from larger submarines. Just 80 feet long and carrying a two-man crew, they were to advance ahead of the fleet towards Pearl Harbor and rendezvous there with the air attack.

Before dawn on the morning of December 7, the main fleet reached its air-force launching point, 275 miles north of Oahu. The Japanese pilots and their crews were woke and ate a special ceremonial meal of *sekihan*, rice boiled with tiny beans. They put on their flight suits and headbands bearing the legend Hissho, or "Certain Victory', took emergency rations and went topside.

The big carriers had turned eastwards into the heavy wind for the launch of the planes, and they pitched heavily—dangerous conditions for taking off. Waving green lanterns as a signal, the ground crews on each carrier sent the planes aloft, timing the pilots' runs so that the carriers' bows were pointed up when the planes roared off the carrier decks. Within fifteen minutes, the first wave of 182 fighters and bombers—there would be two waves of 350 planes in all—had departed.

The sky in the east was turning pale. Under the command of Commander Mitsuo Fuchida, the Japanese planes turned south, towards Pearl Harbor. In Honolulu, the time was 6:15 a.m.

"TORA! TORA! TORA!'

It was a quiet, partly cloudy Sunday morning on Oahu, with very little movement on the massive naval and air base of Pearl Harbor. Skeleton crews manned many of the proud battleships along "Battleship Row" in the harbor, all, as tradition insisted, named after U.S. states: *Arizona, Oklahoma, California, Nevada, West Virginia, Tennessee, Maryland, Pennsylvania*. Some sailors were sleeping off a late night on leave; others were rising to prepare for church services.

Outside the entrance to Pearl Harbor, waiting for the massive anti-submarine net to swing open, was a navy minesweeper. Its captain saw a dark shape in the water and realized that it was a submarine. It appeared to be rolling slightly and was closer to the surface than a sub would normally be. He soon understood that this was not a friendly underwater apparition, however, but a Japanese midget submarine.

The minesweeper captain trained his guns on the sub and blew it out of the water before it could enter the harbor (two Japanese midget subs eventually did get inside the submarine net, and one may have torpedoed an American destroyer). The Americans had drawn first blood in the engagement, but the submarine probe was not seen as part of a larger assault, so no alarm was raised.

At 7:53 a.m., the first wave of Japanese planes flew in from the north, banked to circle around the west coast of the island and then, hopping over the volcanic peaks above Pearl Harbor, came roaring straight in from the south. Commander Fuchida radioed back to his carriers: "Tora! Tora! Tora!" *Tora* means "tiger" in Japanese and this was a prearranged code to signal to the Japanese commanders that the Americans had been caught completely by surprise.

HOPPING OVER OAHU'S PEAKS, THE JAPANESE PLANES SWOOPED, AND FOR TWO HOURS TORE PEARL HARBOR APART.

"I WISH IT HAD KILLED ME"

Admiral Husband Kimmel, naval commander of the Pearl Harbor base, watched from the window of a headquarters building as an armor-piercing Japanese bomb tore into the ammunition magazine of the *Arizona*, which blew up with a violent explosion, killing over one thousand American servicemen. A spent .50-calibre machine-gun bullet came through the open window and struck his left chest, but was deflected by his thick glasses case. Kimmel leaned over and picked it up: "I wish it had killed me", he said. Both Kimmel and his army–air force counterpart (at the time, those two wings were joined), General Walter Short, knew at once that their careers were over for having allowed Pearl Harbor to be caught so unawares by the Japanese attack. And, indeed, both were forced to resign in quick order.

For two hours, Japanese planes tore Pearl Harbor apart. Soon after the attack began, an American radioman sent out a message that was later to become famous: "AIR RAID PEARL HARBOR. THIS IS NO DRILL." The message was picked up by U.S. military installations from the Philippines to San Francisco.

On Battleship Row, a seaman on the *Oklahoma* heard an explosion and looked up to see his friend dead: "The boy just slumped over. Blood was all over everything. I still didn't know what happened'. Two bombs struck the *West Virginia*, greatly pleasing the Japanese pilot Matsumura Midorai, who had launched one of the torpedoes that hit the ship and who later recalled: "A huge waterspout splashed over the stack of the ship and then tumbled down like an exhausted geyser. What a magnificent sight." On board the *Utah*, seaman John Vaessen prayed as the ship capsized after being torpedoed: "I was hanging on to everything", he remembered, "the door and anything I could grab and the deck plates came flying at me, fire extinguishers and anything loose … I was just lucky that God was with me, that's for sure."

Guns pumping, fighters, bombers and torpedo bombers continued to pound the American base. On Hickham Field, the planes had been placed close together on the runway, to protect against saboteurs, which, however, made them an easy target. Only a few American fighters were able to take off, and all were shot down. In all, the army–air force lost 250 planes during the battle.

Along Battleship Row, great clouds of black smoke rose in the air. The Arizona had disintegrated, the *Oklahoma* had capsized, the *California* and *West Virginia* were sunk at their moorings. Eleven other vessels were sunk or damaged. The Japanese were uncanny in their aim, in part because they had developed a new type of dive-bomber-launched torpedo that skipped along the shallow waters of Pearl Harbor, and in part because a Japanese navy ensign, serving as a spy with the consulate in Hawaii, had carefully photographed the positions of the American vessels.

The American soldiers and sailors fought back bravely, managing to shoot down twenty-eight Japanese planes. But by the time the last Japanese planes had departed, the Americans had lost 2330 killed and 1145 wounded. Their grand Pacific Fleet was in tatters.

However, one vital component of the fleet had escaped the destruction. At the time of the attack, America's three aircraft carriers just happened to be out at sea, operating on manoeuvres to the west. Around this core, the fleet would quickly be rebuilt and play a leading role in the subsequent victory over Japan.

"A DATE WHICH WILL LIVE IN INFAMY"

At about 1.30 in the afternoon, Eastern Standard Time, Americans clustered around their radios to receive the news

that the Japanese had launched a surprise attack against their territory. At the same time, the Japanese had bombed the Philippines and Hong Kong, and landed troops in Malaya. On December 8, addressing a special joint session of the U.S. Congress, President Roosevelt called December 7 "a date which will live in infamy", and asked for a resolution of war against Japan, which was swiftly voted in. A few days later, the United States declared war against Germany as well. An enraged U.S. public was now completely behind Roosevelt, and the American nation quickly mobilized its massive industrial might and manpower for the conflict. 🐾

Smoke pours from wrecked U.S. warships.

1942–43

THE BATTLE OF STALINGRAD

On August 23, 1942, a warm Sunday afternoon, as families picnicked on the hills overlooking their modern, showcase Soviet city, World War II came to Stalingrad. In previous weeks, as the German Nazi war machine had closed in, air-raid sirens had frequently sounded false alarms, so few citizens were prepared for the Luftwaffe's onslaught. Two days of carpet bombing began, creating a firestorm 35 miles long that incinerated the small wooden houses of the suburbs and gutted city buildings, claiming the lives of tens of thousands. Massive fuel tanks along the River Volga were hit, sending volcano-like columns of flame into the air.

The Luftwaffe commander responsible for this carnage, General Wolfram von Richthofen (a distant cousin of World War I flying ace the Red Baron), surveyed his handiwork from the air when the bombardment was over. He wrote that Stalingrad had been "destroyed and [was] now without any further worthwhile military targets". As the elite German Sixth Army raced in to mop up what was left of the Soviet forces, it seemed to most that the fight for Stalingrad was all but over. But one of the bloodiest battles in history was only just beginning.

HITLER SETS HIS SIGHTS ON STALINGRAD

The city of Stalingrad lay over 2000 miles from the German border. What propelled the armies of the Axis powers (Germany and her European allies, Italy, Hungary and Romania) to that spot was "the limitless character of Nazi aims", as one of Adolf Hitler's henchmen later said during the Nuremberg war crime trials. Not only were oil, land and minerals abundant, but Hitler also considered Russia to be Germany's ultimate enemy—the headquarters of both communism and the "Jewish world-conspiracy".

During the first two years of the war, Hitler maintained a non-aggression pact with Soviet leader Joseph Stalin while he conquered most of Europe and reached a stalemate in his struggle against Britain. In June 1941 he was at last ready to invade the Union of Soviet Socialist Republics (U.S.S.R.). In what was possibly the most costly military mistake in history, he launched four and a half million soldiers across the border in an invasion that took the Soviets by surprise, largely because Stalin had dismissed all warnings (and obvious signs), thinking that the Allies were trying trick him into fighting the Nazis. The opening months saw millions of Soviet soldiers captured, along with the most fertile and developed western regions of the Soviet Union. The Axis forces came very close to taking Moscow, only to be repelled on the outskirts by massive counter-attacks. In the closing stages of that battle, winter descended with full force, almost literally freezing the invasion in its tracks for the next five months.

When campaigning resumed in the following spring of 1942, the focus was no longer Moscow but the oilfields near the Caspian Sea and the Volga that flowed into it. The river was Russia's main supply line, and Hitler planned to capture or destroy Stalingrad, the main city on the Volga, in order to cut this key artery and prevent the Soviets from defending their southern regions.

Hitler entrusted General Friedrich Paulus with the task of taking Stalingrad. Paulus was a former staff officer—a polite,

German prisoners of war marching out from the Red October factory amidst the ruins of war-torn Stalingrad.

impeccably well-groomed social climber with a passion for war games, whose hobby was making detailed maps of Napoleon's Russian campaigns. The general had proved to be an effective commander in recent battles on the vast Russian prairies and now, as the tattered Soviet armies pulled back towards Stalingrad, he advanced with over two hundred thousand highly skilled, well-equipped veterans at his command, along with the Fourth Panzer Army and the Fourth Air Fleet.

"COWARDS SHOULD BE EXTERMINATED"

Ranged against him were fifty thousand Red Army personnel, a mixture of raw recruits and soldiers cobbled together from various shattered armies. They had to defend a city 35 miles long and 5 miles wide, spread along the west bank of a broad river. Desperate measures were enacted to halt the endless retreats. Stalin's Order 227 declared: "Not one step back! … It is necessary to defend every position, every metre of our territory, up to the last drop of blood … cowards should be exterminated." Accordingly, machine-gun battalions were placed behind the front lines, ready to mow down anyone who broke and ran from the Germans, while the Soviet secret police, the NKVD, executed more than thirteen thousand soldiers for disciplinary offences during the course of the battle.

As the Luftwaffe struck, turning the city into an inferno, the citizens were mobilized. The Stalingrad Defence Committee organized students, and most of the workers, into militias, urging the populace to turn "each street, each house into an unassailable fortress". With brutal logic, Stalin forbade the civilian evacuation of the city early in the battle, calculating that the militias would fight even harder knowing that their loved ones were trapped there.

What the militias lacked in weapons, uniforms and training, they often made up for with suicidal determination, and their sacrifices bought the Red Army precious time to assemble in the city behind them. The first units to resist the Germans were made up of women, who operated dozens of anti-aircraft batteries at Gumrak, on the western outskirts of the city. As the panzer tanks charged across the plain towards them, the women levelled their anti-aircraft flak guns at them, destroying many and forcing the panzers to call in air support. The flak crews had never been trained to fire at ground targets, but they stayed at their posts for days until their ammunition ran out and they were overrun.

THE BATTLE OF STALINGRAD

The Germans were horrified and embarrassed to discover that they had been fighting women.

The layout of the city prevented the typical German tactics from being deployed. Denied the option of surrounding the Soviets, Paulus planned to drive several large wedges into Stalingrad, pushing through to the river bank and then systematically mopping up the isolated units. Panzers raced through farmland and orchards on the edges of Stalingrad to reach the Volga, where they shelled the river traffic and fought off heavy counter-attacks. On September 10, the Russian 62nd Army, ordered to hold the ruined city, found itself cut off from the other Soviet armies adjacent to Stalingrad, its only lifeline a river filling up with burning oil and bombed-out ships.

CHUIKOV EMPLOYS NEW TACTICS

Many on the Soviet side felt defeat was inevitable, including General Lopatin, commander of the 62nd Army. He was replaced by General Vasilii Chuikov, a rugged, crude and outspoken street-fighter from dirt-poor peasant stock. He had a broad, pockmarked face with a mouth full of glittering, gold-capped teeth and a deep booming laugh, and was so unkempt that he was frequently mistaken for a private. Chuikov crossed the river into the burning city, moving through the refugees and deserters crowding the river bank as he sought his headquarters on the Mamaev Kurgan—the ancient Tartar burial mound that formed a hill which overlooked the city.

On September 13, Chuikov had barely settled in to his HQ when Paulus launched a massive, coordinated assault on the heart of the city. Intense air and artillery bombardment came first, forcing Chuikov to abandon the Mamaev Kurgan, which was overrun by German infantry later in the day. Chuikov was now in great danger, because the hill would allow German artillery to control the river crossing and strangle his army. Just in time, the ten thousand men of the elite Soviet 13th Guards Rifle Division—veterans of the Spanish Civil War—arrived. They scrambled up the river bank, overcoming German units which had reached the river but had not yet dug in. The guards made frantic assaults to retake the Mamaev Kurgan, and they succeeded, saving the day. But almost a third of them were dead or badly wounded within twenty-four hours of arriving in Stalingrad.

IN WHAT WAS POSSIBLY THE MOST COSTLY MILITARY MISTAKE IN HISTORY, HITLER LUNCHED FOUR AND A HALF MILLION SOLDIERS ACROSS THE BORDER.

Chuikov had to think on his feet and direct an army reduced to twenty thousand men to defend positions he had never seen, against a very determined foe.

He also had to do something about the Luftwaffe's overwhelming air superiority, as the Red Army planes were fewer, slower and piloted by inexperienced crews. Chuikov directed all Soviet frontlines to be no further than grenade-throwing distance from the Germans, which meant that the Luftwaffe could not drop bombs without hitting their own. He also favored night attacks because, again, the Luftwaffe could not respond—and he wanted to heighten their terror.

Chuikov knew that the Germans were very efficient out in the open, where they could maintain their discipline and organization and draw upon the support of tanks and planes, so he encouraged his men to form small squads and fight vicious hand-to-hand battles, armed with grenades, light machine-guns, and even knives and sharpened shovels.

Soviet lines ran right through the city, through parks, yards and squares, and were anchored by strong points—usually four- or five-storey buildings. As the German attackers moved around these strong points, aiming to encircle them, they would enter minefields and take fire from camouflaged Russian tanks, or suffer sudden ambushes from small assault squads.

In late September the focus of the battle shifted to the factory complexes in the north of the city. During this assault, many Soviet units were surrounded for days and even weeks, the most famous being Sergeant Pavlov's twenty-five soldiers, who fortified an apartment block in the middle of the city and successfully held out against daily attacks for fifty-eight days.

In November of 1942, temperatures fell to −40°C (−40°F). The climax of the battle was drawing near; Paulus knew that his air support would be drastically reduced in the worsening weather, and his men would have to prepare winter quarters. For now, though, as the Volga froze, the weather gave the German forces an advantage. Large ice floes made the river crossing increasingly treacherous for Soviet reinforcements. Paulus' final offensive began on November 11. German soldiers fought their way through enemy lines down to the river bank behind the Red October factory, but many of the surrounded Soviets preferred to die rather than surrender.

ZHUKOV LAUNCHES OPERATION URANUS

Well over ninety percent of the city now lay in German hands, but the remaining defenders clung to the buildings along the

Newly promoted Field Marshal Paulus walks to the Russian command to surrender, February 1, 1943.

303

river bank as this final assault lost its momentum. Soon it was broken off altogether, for an excellent reason. Operation Uranus (also known as Operation Uran), the great Soviet counter-attack, had begun.

On November 18, the new German chief of staff, Kurt Zeitzler, convinced the Red Army was on its last legs, declared, "The Russians no longer have any reserves worth mentioning and are not capable of launching a large-scale offensive." But the next day, roughly a million Soviet soldiers plunged into the overextended and undermanned German lines far to the west and south of Stalingrad. Hitler had driven Paulus so hard to win the battle that the latter had been forced to commit most of the available German tanks and troops in the area to take the city, leaving their less-trained, under-equipped Italian and Romanian allies to hold the long front out on the frozen plains. Russia's greatest general, Georgy Zhukov, planned the counter-attack and kept the scale of it a secret from almost everyone until the moment it was unleashed. Paulus ordered his panzer tank crews to beat back the attacks, but the tanks held in reserve had been sitting idle in the snow, and most were now useless because rats and mice had eaten the insulation around the wiring in the engines. Three days after they began, the two great Soviet thrusts met up at the town of Kalach, and roughly three hundred thousand enemy soldiers were now caught in a vast pincer trap.

The besiegers had now become the besieged, caught in what the Germans called the Kessel, or cauldron. Paulus repeatedly requested permission from Hitler to break out of the Kessel, but this was never granted. Hitler had already made speeches declaring "No one will shift U.S. from the Volga," and Göring, commander of the Luftwaffe, ignored the doubts of his own staff and assured Hitler that the Sixth Army could be supplied by an airlift for as long as necessary. Luftwaffe crews desperately tried to carry out this task, but far too few planes made it through the blizzards, the anti-aircraft guns, and the rapidly improving Soviet air fleet. Trapped in the Kessel throughout the Russian winter, and running out of food, clothing, medical supplies and ammunition, the suffering of the German troops and their allies was extreme. Starvation, typhus, dysentery and frostbite claimed tens of thousands of lives, as did the constant attacks designed to force them to use up their ammunition and deny them any chance to rest. Additionally, the gun oil in German weapons froze, rendering most of them useless. The Russians—more experienced in low-temperature warfare—

mixed petrol in with their gun oil to lower its freezing point, thus preserving the effectiveness of their weapons.

Dead on their feet, the Germans were soon too weak to break out, even if they had been given the order. In any case, they would have had to fight through chest-high snow for 40 miles, in ragged clothing and carrying all their equipment.

Deserters started to cross over to Soviet lines in ever larger numbers, and around the airfields riots broke out as men tried to clamber onto outgoing aircraft, which were reserved for specialists and the wounded. Men sought to escape the Kessel by wounding themselves, or poking their hands up over the trenches to get the Soviets to do the job. But the military police guarding the airfields were aware of this ploy, and many soldiers grew even more desperate, shooting themselves (or each other) in the chest or abdomen instead.

SURRENDER ... AND A HORRIFIC TOLL

When Paulus requested permission to surrender in late January, Hitler told him, "Capitulation is impossible. The Sixth Army will do its duty to the last man." In an attempt to bribe Paulus to accept certain death, Hitler promoted him to field marshal, knowing that no German field marshal had ever surrendered. To his generals, Paulus remarked, "I have no intention of shooting myself for that Bohemian corporal." The next day, January 31, 1943, he surrendered, along with 23 generals, some 90,000 soldiers, 60,000 vehicles, 1500 tanks and 6000 artillery pieces. The toll had been horrific, almost too high to measure. Common estimates are that well over half a million casualties were suffered by the Germans and their allies, along with over a million Red Army casualties. No one knows how many civilians were killed, or how many escaped to safety, but the death toll certainly numbered in the hundreds of thousands, mostly as a result of indiscriminate Luftwaffe bombing. Stalingrad's population had been roughly 850,000 before the war; a 1945 census found only 1500 people in the city.

The battle was the turning point of World War II. The Germans never did return to the Volga or seize the oilfields they had coveted. Germany had never experienced a defeat like this, and it was now clear how the war would end. Germany's European allies—Italy, Hungary and Romania—had each lost almost an entire army in the battle, and they quietly began peace negotiations with the Soviets and the other Allies. And, on May 2, 1945, the Soviet Army would capture Berlin. ✢

1944
D-DAY

At about 2.30 on the grey, cloudy morning of 6 June 1944, three divisions of Allied paratroopers—about twenty thousand men of the American Eighty-second and One Hundred and First, and the British Sixth Airborne—took off from airfields in southern England, and flew east. Through breaks in the cloud cover, the pilots of the planes could look out to see the English Channel roiling darkly beneath them. The planes kept formation until they hit the French coast, when heavy anti-aircraft fire and machine guns reached up for them. Bullets passed through the thin skins of the lumbering C-47 transport aircraft, sounding, one man remembered, like "corn popping". The arcing tracers were brilliant—red, yellow, blue, orange—and mesmerizing in their beauty, until the soldiers remembered that for every colored bullet, six more followed, invisible.

Some planes were hit and exploded in mid-air. Others crashed into the ground below, burning. Still others took evasive action, scattering across the night skies. Levelling off where they could, the pilots gave the signal and the jumpmasters ordered the paratroopers out the door. The U.S. paratroopers' goal was to block off approaches to the Normandy beaches to keep the Germans from reinforcing their defences there. The British were to seize bridges over the Orne River. In the confusion, however, few men found their assigned drop zones—it has been estimated that only one in twenty-five landed where he was supposed to. Despite this, bands of men of different companies hooked up and began fighting the Germans wherever they found them.

One group of American paratroopers was captured just behind what would become known as Utah Beach, and placed as prisoners in a pillbox overlooking the waters. The Germans couldn't understand why the Americans kept begging to be taken further to the rear. But as dawn approached and the

mist began to lift slowly from the water, the German pillbox gunners finally understood. Blinking in disbelief, they looked out at the greatest amphibious landing force in the history of the world—6500 ships spread out in the English Channel along an 50-mile stretch of Normandy's coast, from Caen in the east to the base of the Cotentin Peninsula in the west. In those ships, and others still in port in England, a total of 150,000 soldiers waited to land. Overhead, just beginning a fierce bombardment, were B-17s, each carrying sixteen 495-pound bombs with which to pulverize the German coastal defences—just part of the force of 11,500 aircraft that would attack that day.

OPERATION OVERLORD

The Germans were witnessing the beginning of Operation Overlord, the long-awaited Allied invasion of France. Both sides had known for some time that the only way the Allies could destroy the German defences in Europe any time soon would be with a major land offensive. British and American forces were then moving north through Italy, but that was proving to be a hard, slogging conflict. On the eastern front, Soviet forces were pushing the Germans west, but making slow progress. American and British bombers were nightly pounding targets in Germany, but that alone wasn't going to crack the Germans either. Only a major ground offensive from the west was going to break the stalemate. And using Britain as a staging area for the hundreds of thousands of troops needed was the only possible approach.

The question for the Germans was: where along the Channel coast would the Allies attack? The Germans' Atlantic defences extended all the way from Scandinavia to Spain, but they could not possibly station enough troops to repel an invasion at every point along this line, so they kept a mobile reserve force back from the coast, ready to commit when the invasion began.

Most of this reserve—the Fifteenth Army, consisting of about one hundred thousand men—was stationed near Pas de Calais, the region around the port of Calais. The Germans had placed their bets that this was where the attack would come, as it was the area of France closest to England and could provide deep-water harbors for Allied ships, as well as a direct route to Paris.

Allied war planners, working since the summer of 1943, had decided to take advantage of these German preconceptions. They launched a massive disinformation campaign, code-named Operation Fortitude, involving fake radio traffic, dummy troop emplacements, and German "spies" in England who were really Allied agents, to make the Germans believe that an attack on the Pas de Calais was imminent. This highly successful subterfuge also convinced the Germans that any attack on any other part of the coast would be simply a diversion.

Meanwhile, the Allies developed a plan for a massive offensive on the Normandy coast, Operation Overlord. The commander of the operation was the U.S. General Dwight D. Eisenhower, who was in charge of SHAEF (Supreme Headquarters, Allied Expeditionary Force). General Bernard Montgomery of the British army led the Allied ground forces. Preparations at SHAEF were meticulous. Over a period of two years, men and materiel were built up all over Britain, so that the total number of combat-ready troops at the time of the invasion was eight hundred thousand, some forty-seven divisions.

Five beaches would be assaulted by Allied divisions: moving from east to west, they were code-named Sword (to be targeted by the British Third), Juno (Canadian Third), Gold (British Fiftieth), Omaha (U.S. First and Twenty-ninth) and Utah (U.S. Fourth).

THE TROOPS WHO WERE WAITING OFFSHORE FROM THE BEACHES IN THEIR LANDING CRAFT WATCHED THE SCENE IN AWE.

"THE MOMENT OF OUR LIFE"

After the Allied bombers had pounded the German shore defences, the navy began a massive bombardment in an attempt to destroy the gun emplacements along the shores, as well as mines and other obstacles at the water's edge. The troops who were waiting offshore from the beaches in their landing craft watched in awe as the shock waves from the battleships' blasts pushed the huge vessels sideways, in turn creating waves that rocked the landing craft up and down. One newspaper correspondent described the bombardment as "the loudest thing I have ever heard in my life". Listening

The view from inside one of the landing craft after the first wave of U.S. troops hit the water off Omaha Beach.

to it, "most of U.S. felt that this was the moment of our life, the crux of it."

At 6.20 in the morning, the bombardment let up and U.S. landing craft began to approach Omaha Beach, which was now shrouded in smoke. Shortly after, the invasions began at Juno, Sword, Gold and Utah. Unfortunately, the bombardment had done little to destroy the German defences. This was a testament to the work of Field Marshal Erwin Rommel, commander of the German Seventh and Fifteenth Armies, who had insisted that the German pillboxes be made of thick concrete reinforced with steel rods. Thus the defenders, while shocked and deafened, were able to rise as the bombardment lifted, and meet the Allies with stiff resistance all along the coast.

On Juno Beach, Canadian casualties in the first wave were fifty percent overall, but whether men lived or died depended to a great extent on which sector of Juno they landed on. The Regina Rifles, arriving on "Mike" sector, made it ashore backed up by the dependable amphibious tanks of the First Hussar Division, which were able to help neutralize the pillboxes that naval gunfire had been unable to destroy. By afternoon, they were off the beach and fighting house-to-house in the village of Courseulles-sur-Mer.

But less than half a mile away the Winnipeg Company on the western edge of the beach was severely battered by machine-gun fire from the pillboxes. There, the artillery bombardment had completely missed the mark and the tanks meant to support the men had landed elsewhere by mistake. The subsequent slaughter was terrifying. The Winnipegs finally made it past the beach defences, but lost three-quarters of their company. By the end of the day, however, the Canadian Third Infantry had pushed further into France than any other unit.

HELP FROM HOBART'S FUNNIES

On Sword Beach, the British Third were confronted with minefields and beach obstacles, but fortunately they came equipped with one of the oddest-looking weapons of the war: tanks known as Hobart's Funnies, after their inventor, Percy Hobart. Some of these vehicles had been modified to carry long arms like giant rolling pins, which whipped heavy chains into the sand, exploding mines harmlessly and allowing the infantry to follow in their wake. Others carried long extending platforms, rather like the extension ladders on fire trucks, with which to span ditches and walls. The British eventually managed to land twenty-eight thousand troops (suffering only six hundred casualties) and push to within 4 miles of their

target, the key town of Caen, before German counterattacks stalled them.

On Gold, the British Fiftieth suffered heavy casualties initially, in part because their tanks went astray. But by the end of the day, they, too, were advancing off the beach.

At Utah Beach, there was mass confusion. Stiffer currents than expected had carried the landing boats of the U.S. Fourth Division almost 1½ mile south of where they were supposed to be, so that the troops, trained via aerial photographs, had no idea where they were.

Landing in the wrong place turned out to be a stroke of luck, however, as the Fourth's original target was much more heavily defended than the sector where they now found themselves. The German defences were quickly silenced, the seawall breached, and men and materiel began to pour ashore. At eleven o'clock, forward elements of the Fourth linked up with paratroopers from the 101st, who had been dropped the night before. It was the Allies' first such link-up.

OMAHA'S DAUNTING DEFENCES

Historians have commented that if there was one place where the Germans might have stopped the Allied onslaught anywhere in Normandy, it was at Omaha Beach. Because it was the only

Allied commanders General Dwight D. Eisenhower (foreground) and General Bernard Montgomery (background) reviewing troops before the landing.

stretch of open beach for some way, it was considered to be an obvious target for landing, and thus was heavily defended. Yet the Allies had no choice but to attack at Omaha—if they picked a beach further west, there would be too great a gap between them and the British sectors.

Omaha Beach is about 6 miles long and perhaps 400 yards across at low tide, which is when the invasion was occurring. Much of the ground was shingle, or small, round stones, which would not support the weight of tanks. There were high bluffs facing the beach and on either side of it, making it into a kind of amphitheater. The Americans could not therefore outflank the German defences; they had to go right at them.

And what defences they were. Interlocking firing trenches made sure that every inch of ground along the beach was pre-sighted by machine guns, mortars and artillery. A trench system on the tops of the bluffs gave soldiers cover as they moved between pillboxes. Underground ammunition chambers protected the supply of shells. Five "draws", or small ravines, led up the cliffs; overlooking each was a strongpoint containing the dreaded German 88, the ubiquitous light artillery gun.

When the German defenders saw the Americans swarming ashore that morning, they almost felt sorry for them. "They must be crazy," one of them said. "Are they going to swim ashore? Right under our muzzles?"

WITHERING FIRE

But right under their muzzles the Americans came—forty thousand of them over the course of the day. Once again, few units landed where they were supposed to, due to the heavier than expected tidal currents caused by the strong winds. By the time that A Company (First Division) landed, the soldiers had been in their boats for four hours and were wet, seasick and exhausted. When the first landing craft hit the beach, it was literally pulverized, either by a mine or German artillery fire, killing all on board. Other GIs hit the beach at the same time, but withered under the volume of fire (one German machine-gunner alone fired twelve thousand rounds that day). As the navy coxswains brought the landing craft in, many were stopped by the barrage and let their ramps down too early, causing the heavily loaded troops to disembark into deep water. A good many soldiers drowned.

Men ran onto the beach and then froze in fear. Long snaking lines of soldiers formed behind the X-shaped beach obstacles. One survivor remembered: "The beach was covered with bodies, men with no legs, arms—God it was awful." Bad as the fire was, if the attackers simply stayed where they were, they would die. They had to move, and, one by one,

groups of men (often without officers to lead them) raced for the seawall near the base of the cliff, where the machine-gun fire from above could not reach them, although they were still subject to murderous mortar fire. As subsequent waves of men came in, the GIs were able to force their way up the draws and, once on top of the cliffs, attack the German fortifications from the rear.

There were more than three thousand casualties on Omaha Beach that day, and most occurred in the first few hours. By nightfall, however, the Americans had a precarious toehold.

A FATAL DELAY

Allied forces suffered eleven thousand casualties on D-Day, but managed the most important thing in any amphibious assault: not to be driven back into the sea. Over the next week or so, the troops cleared German opposition between the beachheads and linked their forces, forming a secure area 80 miles long and 10 miles deep. The German commanders, many of whom thought the real invasion was still to come at Pas de Calais, were slow to react, and by the time it finally dawned on them that Normandy was the Big One, the Allies were too securely ensconced to drive out.

In late July, the British and Canadians finally secured the city of Caen and then mounted major offensives. These drew more and more German reserves, allowing the Americans, further to the west, to break out from the coast. Allied forces then pushed through France en masse and by August had captured Paris. The success of the D-Day landing meant that Hitler's Third Reich was all but doomed.

1944

THE BATTLE OF THE BULGE

A momentous military engagement that took place on the European western front between December 16, 1944 and January 17, 1945, the battle of the Bulge was one of the biggest and bloodiest battles of World War II. It involved over one million soldiers—half a million Germans, six hundred thousand Americans and fifty-five thousand British—and cost the combatants almost two hundred thousand killed and wounded. The American casualties of eighty-one thousand, which included nineteen thousand killed and almost twenty-four thousand captured, made the Bulge the most costly U.S. engagement of the entire war. Yet ultimately the battle was a triumph for the Allies, for it broke the back of the German defence of western Europe, paving the way for an attack on Germany itself, and for ultimate victory.

The battle's curious name is another reason why people remember it. The "bulge" was the dent, or, in military terms, salient, punched into the thin Allied line by the surprise German counteroffensive that began the battle—a bulge that protruded as much as 50 miles in some areas. Not that this was, technically speaking, a single battle at all, but rather a series of small and large encounters that took place over the following five weeks between a determined German Army making a last-ditch attempt to win the war and an equally determined Allied force trying to stop it. Most historians call it the Ardennes Offensive, after the rugged, wooded Ardennes area of southeastern Belgium where the dramatic events unfolded.

THE SUMMER OF '44

Beginning in early June with the Allied invasion of Normandy, the summer of 1944 had been a long, hot and weary one for the German army. At the end of July, the Allies broke out of Normandy, where they had been contained by ferocious German fighting. With the Americans, British and Canadians proceeding on three separate fronts, two German Armies were sent reeling back towards their homeland, suffering ten thousand dead and leaving behind fifty thousand prisoners. On the eastern front, an entire German Army group in Poland had been shattered by a massive Soviet offensive, while two more German Armies were retreating back up the Italian boot and more American forces were landing in the south of France.

But in early September, the Allied offensive in the west came grinding, almost literally, to a halt. The reason? Supplies. The Allied army, moving at a faster rate than anticipated, could not be provided with as much fuel, ammunition and spare parts as it needed. This was in part because of the extensive damage done by the Germans to France's infrastructure of railways and bridges, but also because the only deep-water port the Allies held was Cherbourg, at the tip of the Cotentin Peninsula in Normandy. They had also captured the port city of Antwerp, but it could not be used until the Germans were pushed away from the surrounding area, which would not happen until late November.

German troops, some in winter camouflage, surrendering to members of the U.S. First Army during the fighting in the Ardennes.

With the Allies having paused, the Germans stopped their flight. The two Armies then faced each other across the Ardennes, and the ever-resourceful Germans sought for a way to take advantage of the situation.

SENT REELING

About 5.30 on the morning of December 16, sleepy American troops on the 75-mile-long Ardennes front, extending from Monschau in the north to Echternach in the south, were awakened by a massive artillery bombardment that shattered trees in the rugged terrain, blew soldiers out of their foxholes and scrambled communications systems. Much to the Americans' surprise, the Germans—whom many in the U.S. ranks considered to be licking their wounds after being pushed back through France—were attacking, and attacking in force.

Even the scattered and confused reports reaching the headquarters of Supreme Allied Commander Dwight Eisenhower indicated multiple German divisions (there were in fact twenty—hundreds of thousands of men) attacking along the entire front. Soon reports came through of whole American regiments surrendering and others reeling back.

The bombardment haunted many a survivor's dreams thereafter, for it involved over 600 light, medium and heavy guns, as well as 347 Nebelwefer (multiple rocket launchers), whose screaming missiles were terrifying to hear. The German Sixth Panzer Army, commanded by General Sepp Dietrich, attacked in the northernmost part of the sector, supported to the south by the Fifth and Seventh Panzer Divisions. At the same time, two special units were brought into play. Colonel Friedrich von der Heydte led a thousand paratroopers in a drop behind Allied lines, planning to fight off any reinforcements coming from the north. Colonel Otto Skorzeny disguised a small group of Germans in U.S. uniforms and led them through to the American rear, where they disrupted communications and sowed confusion.

The quiet hills and forests, covered with snow, became a terrifying killing ground. One American non-commissioned officer, raising his head after the bombardment, realized the telephone lines had been cut at the same time as he saw, coming through the early morning snow and darkness, "opaque figures", who turned out to be German soldiers in snowsuits. (The Americans had no such camouflage gear.) Ferocious running battles began all along the American lines, but many of the GIs were green replacement troops and gave up without firing a shot.

ALL AT ONCE THE QUIET HILLS AND FORESTS, COVERED WITH SNOW, BECAME A TERRIFYING KILLING GROUND.

HITLER'S DARING GAMBLE

The massive German counteroffensive against the Americans in the Ardennes was the brainchild of one man: Adolf Hitler. During a September briefing at his headquarters at Wolf's Lair, in East Prussia, Hitler was told that, following the halt of the Allied advance due to dwindling supplies, German forces had made a few small and successful counterattacks. A briefing officer pointed to a map of the Ardennes and the Netherlands as he described these small successes—some of the few the German army had experienced lately. Suddenly, Hitler stood up. "I have come to a momentous decision," he said. "I shall go over to the counterattack!"

Striding to the front of the room before his surprised officers, he took the pointer and tapped the map. The counteroffensive would originate "out of the Ardennes", just where the successful German thrust into Belgium had begun in 1940, and its goal would be Antwerp. If German troops could break through to Antwerp, they would starve the Allied army of supplies while splitting it in two, with the Americans to the south and the British and Canadians to the north. Such a bold stroke might make the western Allies sue for peace and allow the Germans the chance to turn all their attention to fighting Russia in the east.

The plan was on paper not strategically unsound, but in practice extremely perilous. It depended on total secrecy, on bad weather to halt the Allied bombers and spotter planes, and on one assumption that Hitler took as gospel: that the Americans were inferior fighting troops and would be easily overwhelmed.

SKYLINE DRIVE

In fact, while many Americans did surrender, many more carried on the fight of their lives. During the early days of the attack, the veteran Twenty-eighth Infantry Division held half of the ground attacked by the Germans, from St Vith in the north to Medernach in the south. Part of their line was the so-called "Skyline Drive", a road running along a ridge for about 10 miles. When the Germans attacked in force, the Twenty-eighth held their ground. Some American soldiers, manning machine guns, noted that the German infantry attacked in columns rather than in line abreast, making it easy to mow them down. This was a sign of a major German weakness: although the Germans held the numerical advantage, many of their troops were green conscripts, either very young or very old, and often poorly led and trained.

The Germans' immediate goal was to reach the Meuse River and protect the river crossings in order to allow the panzers to break through and drive towards Antwerp, which was held

by British forces. To protect the Meuse crossings, the British assembled a makeshift group of air-force personnel, rear-echelon clerks, and cooks. Meanwhile, members of the British Twenty-ninth Division, which had been refuelling in the rear, fought their way back to the front. Units of the British Corps also fought bitter actions at the Meuse crossings of Dinant, Givet and Namur, sustaining heavy casualties but successfully holding off the Germans.

The Americans, in the meantime, fought desperately at the village of St. Vith, on the north side of the "bulge". There, the Seventh Armored Division put up a roadblock that held the German panzers in place from December 17–23, inflicting enormous casualties and destroying their timetable. With precious time running out, Field Marshal Walter Model, the German commander in chief who had been instructed by Hitler to oversee the offensive, decided to redouble his efforts to push through the Allied lines further south.

THE ELEMENT OF SURPRISE

How had the Americans not noticed that twenty divisions of the German army with 2600 artillery pieces, 1400 tanks and self-propelled guns had gathered only a short distance across the front from them? There were several reasons for this. One

An American Sherman M4 tank creeps through the Ardennes Forest. Conditions were hazardous for armored vehicles.

was that the Americans had long come to depend on their top-secret code-breaking program, known as Ultra. Ultra only read radio traffic. With the Germans back in their native land, they could and did impose radio silence while at the same time using their excellent and extensive telephone and telegraph systems to communicate.

The Germans were also extremely clever at disguising their troop movements, making them appear to be defensive preparations (the code name for the entire attack Wacht am Rhein, meaning "the Watch on the Rhine", was deliberately devised by Hitler himself to connote homeland security rather than aggressive action). In addition, the Allies had also become a little complacent. The prevailing point of view of many high-ranking officers was that the Germans were too beaten to attack. A few days before the German offensive, an American staff officer told top brass, "The enemy divisions … have been cut by at least fifty percent … the [German] breaking point may develop suddenly and without warning."

Finally, there was the weather. Here the Germans got a lucky a break. Although the skies in that part of Europe

THE BATTLE OF THE BULGE

are usually cloudy in December and January, in 1944–45 they were unusually so, and parts of the front were covered in dense fog and snow—it was one of the worst winters in decades. Allied planes were grounded, and therefore unable to follow German movements.

A DEFIANT RESPONSE

With the German attack slowed in the north around St. Vith, Model directed the Fifth Panzer Division to attack and seize a vital road junction at a village called Bastogne. But the U.S. 101st Division, along with elements of other divisions, dug in around the village and fought back valiantly against German attacks that began on December 20.

The defenders of Bastogne were under the command of a tough, no-nonsense officer named General Anthony McAuliffe. Some of his troops wore only summer uniforms (resupply of winter ones had been slow) and had little ammunition— McAuliffe had had to order his artillery to fire only ten rounds per day. A few did not even have guns. Nevertheless, under heavy snow and leaden grey skies, they repulsed attack after attack. Gradually, however, German armored troops advanced around the village and soon it was surrounded.

On December 22, a four-man German delegation, carrying a white flag, came into the town and demanded to see McAuliffe. They carried a note, in German and English, asking for his "honorable surrender", since "the fortunes of war" had changed. If this surrender were not forthcoming, the Germans would destroy Bastogne.

When McAuliffe was informed of this, he wrote down the following reply:

To the German Commander:
Nuts!
The American Commander

Word of McAuliffe's response spread around the troops at Bastogne, stiffening their morale, even though they expected a heavy attack at any moment. Fortunately for the Americans, on December 23 the skies finally cleared. Tons of ammo and supplies were airlifted into the town, while U.S. fighter planes provided close support. When the Germans finally did attack, they were repulsed.

THE TIDE TURNS

With the skies clearing and American reinforcements pouring in, the tide began to turn against the Germans. On Christmas Day, the U.S. Second Armored Division struck the Germans at the center of the bulge and after a two-day battle began pushing them back where they had come from. In the meantime, U.S. General George Patton's tanks forged a narrow corridor to Bastogne, through which relief was able to flow. In early January, Model began to pull back his troops on every front, breaking contact with the Allied lines so skillfully that the Allies didn't know the Germans had gone from some areas. By January 17, the Allies had eliminated the salient in their lines and reformed an unbroken front.

The lengthy campaign had delayed the Allies from moving forwards for six weeks, but had cost the Germans casualties and materiel that they could not replace. As a result, Hitler was left with almost no reserves at all, and, with the Russians pressing in from the east, it was only a matter of time before the Allies would secure the total defeat of Germany. ❧

1945

THE BOMBING OF HIROSHIMA

The atomic bomb that the United States dropped on the Japanese city of Hiroshima on August 6, 1945—as well as the one unleashed three days later on Nagasaki—changed the world utterly. In the short run, these massive weapons of destruction ended World War II almost immediately, a not inconsiderable consequence for a single weapon. In the long run, the unleashing of atomic weapons shaped global history, giving rise to the Cold War, during which the great superpowers of the United States and the Soviet Union engaged in a nuclear arms race. In turn, and even after the end of the Cold War, it affected the consciousness of almost everyone on Earth.

It wasn't as if, in the summer of 1945, Hiroshima was untouched by the war. At least fifty thousand people, many of them children, had been evacuated from this, Japan's seventh largest city. Military fire marshals had demolished hundreds of houses to create firebreaks, hoping to protect Hiroshima from the fate suffered by other places during the ongoing and intense U.S. bombing campaign that had already targeted sixty Japanese cities—Tokyo had been devastated in March by a firestorm. Yet, except for an incident when an American bomber had accidentally jettisoned its bombs on the city, Hiroshima had fared far better than many comparable urban centers.

Despite having a population of some 250,000 people, Hiroshima still had the feel of a small, peaceful town. Located in the western part of Japan's main island of Honshu, it was a pleasant place. Mountains flanked the city on three sides and seven rivers flowed through it (Hiroshima means "wide

island"). More than forty bridges crossed these rivers, the largest and most famous one being the Aioi Bridge.

Why hadn't the Americans bombed them, the people of Hiroshima often asked themselves? There were certainly military-supply industries in the city, although not necessarily the most crucial ones. A rumor sprang up that President Truman had an aunt who lived in Hiroshima and thus wanted to spare the city. It is a measure of how much people wanted to grasp at straws in the summer of 1945 that many of Hiroshima's residents believed this.

As July turned into early August, Hiroshima's luck continued, so much so that the town's children, when they saw the silver shapes of the U.S. B-29 bombers high in the sky, winging their way elsewhere in the country, would laugh and cry out, "B-san!" Which means, "Mr B".

A RUTHLESS CAMPAIGN

After initial successes in China and Southeast Asia, the Japanese had been slowly pushed back towards their homeland as American forces retook island after island in the Pacific in vicious, no-holds-barred combat. With the capture of the Mariana Islands in June of 1944, the Americans arrived within striking distance of Japan and were able to unleash the might of their air force. The mainstay of that force was the four-engine B-29 Superfortress, which featured cutting-edge innovations—a pressurized cabin, a fire-control system and remote-control machine-gun turrets. It could fly as high as 63,000 feet, higher than most fighters and anti-aircraft guns could reach.

At first, however, the bombing results that came from Japan were disappointing to the American high command. High above Japan, strong prevailing tailwinds made the planes hard to stabilize and the B-29's chief weakness—an engine that could overheat under stress—proved to be a significant problem. But then General Curtis E. LeMay was appointed to take over the bombing campaign.

Later to become infamous to another generation of Americans for threatening to "bomb Vietnam into the Stone Age" during the 1960s, LeMay was an inspirational figure in the U.S. military during World War II. He conceived the tactic of low-level, night-time bombing raids using incendiaries. Since Japan's air defences were mainly visual ones, operational only in daytime, night-time bombing helped neutralize whatever Japanese anti-aircraft resistance was left.

LeMay's perfect storm of tactics came together on the night of March 9–10, 1945 during the bombing of Tokyo, when 335 B-29s, stripped of most of their defensive armaments to allow them to carry extra bombs, went in low and slow, dropping incendiaries or napalm every 50 feet. Within two hours, Tokyo was engulfed in a firestorm. Estimates of the dead civilians that night range from seventy thousand to a hundred thousand. One million Japanese were left homeless.

During the raid, American pilots were forced to wear oxygen masks to filter out the stench of burning flesh. Even the American planners were aghast at the devastating results of the campaign. (LeMay acknowledged later: "I suppose that if I had lost the war, I would have been tried as a war criminal.")

The purpose of this bombing campaign aimed directly at Japan's civilian population was to force the country to surrender. However, the ferocious fighting on the Japanese islands of Iwo Jima and Okinawa that spring had made the American high command realize that Japan would not capitulate easily. Even more extraordinary force was needed.

"THE PERFECT AIMING POINT"

The morning of August 6 dawned partly cloudy and warm in Hiroshima. Nurses in Shima Hospital, a small, private medical institution next to the Aioi Bridge, gently awakened their patients for breakfast. Children and their teachers gathered at the adjacent Honkawa Elementary School. Around 7.30, an American B-29 flew overhead and seemed to circle, but the children playing in the Honkawa school playground paid "Mr B" little heed.

Just after eight o'clock, another U.S. bomber appeared. This one, too, was ignored by the nurses, teachers and children, and by the citizens of Hiroshima who hurried across the Aioi Bridge to work. To them the bridge was a familiar object of pride, the longest of Hiroshima's spans, joining the east and west sections of the city.

At the same moment, high above Hiroshima, a twenty-six-year-old American bombardier named Major Thomas Ferebee, aboard the second B-29 (the first had been a weather-monitoring plane), squinted through his bombsight, searching for that very same bridge. Ferebee had personally selected the Aioi Bridge from reconnaissance photographs as his Aiming Point, or AP. His commander, Colonel Paul Tibbets, the pilot of the B-29, had agreed with his choice, saying, "It's the most perfect AP I've seen in the whole damned war."

It was just after 8:15 a.m. The "perfect AP" filled Ferebee's precision bombsight and he said: "I've got it."

A DEADLY DILEMMA

The 4.5-tone bomb whose release Ferebee was about to trigger was called, with typically sardonic American humor, "Little Boy", and it was the first of only two atomic bombs in history to be used in conflict. Little Boy was the end result of the most extraordinary secret program of the war.

After nuclear fission had shown a select group of scientists around the world that enormous energy could be released by splitting an atom, Germany had begun developing an atomic bomb. In response, the Americans, Canadians and British had initiated the Manhattan Project in 1942 to develop one, too. The Nazis, as it turned out, never got very far with their bomb, but the Americans, driven by the spectre of atomic weaponry in Hitler's hands, proceeded at a furious pace, spending over two billion U.S. dollars and eventually producing a nuclear weapon. The "gadget", as the scientists called it, was successfully detonated in New Mexico on July 16, 1945.

The new weapon gave U.S. President Harry S. Truman a chance to end the war quickly. But was dropping such a bomb on Japanese civilians morally permissible, even in wartime? This was an immensely problematic issue, the morality of which is debated to this day. Truman was aware of the power of the bomb and its potentially devastating effect. But he was also under intense pressure to limit further loss of life as a result of a prolonged conflict. Though the war in Europe

THE AMERICAN B-29 FLEW OVERHEAD AND SEEMED TO CIRCLE, BUT THE CHILDREN PLAYING IN THE HONKAWA SCHOOL PLAYGROUND PAID LITTLE HEED.

The mushroom cloud from 'Little Boy', the first atomic bomb, dropped on Hiroshima on August 6, 1945, rises above the city.

A man stands by a gutted tram amid the Hiroshima ruins, a few months after the dropping of the atomic bomb.

had been over since April of 1945, the human toll in the continuing war against Japan was still soaring. On top of the almost 300,000 Americans already killed in both theatres of war, recent fighting against the Japanese on Okinawa had cost 72,000 American casualties, as well as 125,000 Japanese deaths, of which over 40,000 were civilians. If the Americans went ahead with Operation Olympic, their planned invasion of the Japanese mainland, projected for the fall of 1945, they expected casualties in the hundreds of thousands, as well as millions of Japanese deaths.

On July 26, America joined with its allies in issuing the Potsdam Declaration, demanding Japan's unconditional surrender. Japan refused and seemed to dismiss the Allied demands out of hand. (In fact, Japan was in turmoil and its leaders were terrified that the Soviet Union might enter the war against it—which it did, on August 8.) Even at this point, Truman still had alternatives to dropping the atomic bomb immediately, including demonstrating its power on a non-civilian target. But, tiring of the Japanese delays, he decided to proceed with the most forceful demonstration possible.

After some discussion, the peaceful city of Hiroshima was picked as the target. It had not yet been bombed, so the destruction caused by Little Boy could be well studied, and it

was thought that the mountains on three sides of the city would have a "focus effect" on the blast, causing more casualties.

SHOCKING DESTRUCTION

As soon as Little Boy fell out of its bomb bay doors, the B-29—the Enola Gay, it was called, after Paul Tibbets' mother—dived sharply and to the right before gaining altitude and heading back west, towards the sea. Ferebee watched the bomb as it fell, at first sideways, then turning nose down. It was set to detonate in forty-three seconds and the crew waited breathlessly. They were wearing dark goggles to protect their eyes from the glare of the explosion, which they had been told could scorch their retinas. Since this first dropping of the bomb was a historic occasion, the intercom exchanges between the crew members were being recorded (and Tibbets had warned them to watch their language).

Nothing happened after the forty-three-second count, and many of the crew thought the bomb was a dud. But then there came an extraordinary flash of light and a shock wave so fierce that Tibbets thought the plane had been hit by anti-aircraft fire. A huge column of smoke began to rise from a fiery red core, forming a mushroom-shaped cloud. Tibbets told the whirring recording device that he was "shocked" by "a destruction bigger than I imagined." But perhaps a more honest response came from the co-pilot, Captain Robert Lewis, who wrote in his notes as the plane sped from the target: "My God, what have we done?"

GROUND ZERO

Ferebee missed the Aioi Bridge by about 250 yards, and Little Boy exploded at 18,000 feet above Shima Hospital. The hospital courtyard was directly under the explosion and was thus the Ground Zero, or "hypocenter", of the blast. All hospital staff and patients were instantly vaporized. Eighty-eight percent of people within 500 yards died instantly. Heat waves at temperatures of 3000 degrees Celsius caused first-degree burns within about 2 miles of Shima Hospital.

The Aioi Bridge buckled but was not destroyed. At the Honkawa Elementary School about 325 feet away, teacher Katsuko Horibe was tossed through the air but survived, as did the only other survivors near the blast, because the school had concrete walls. The children in the playground were burned beyond recognition.

Everyone close to Katsuko Horibe suffered horrible burns. As she wandered with her surviving children onto the streets, she noticed that the burned men and women were holding their arms straight up in the air, a natural response to prevent the raw skin rubbing on the body, but one that made it look as if the whole city were a hell full of supplicating people.

The Ota River, spanned by the Aioi Bridge, was the first place these people raced to, to dive into the water, but the river itself seemed like it was on fire, being filled with burning debris and burning bodies. Scenes of horror abounded. One survivor, sixteen years old at the time, remembered that "what impressed me very strongly was a five- or six-year-old boy with his right leg cut at the thigh. He was hopping on his left foot to cross over the bridge." Another noted that a black rain began to fall an hour after the attack, yet it did not put out any of the fires.

Hiroshima was so short of manpower that thousands of high school students had been mobilized to operate telephones and trams. Seven thousand of them were to die that day. One who survived, a fifteen-year-old girl who was disfigured by the blast, remembered: "I saw something shining in the clear blue sky. I wondered what it was, so I stared at it. As the light grew bigger, the shining thing got bigger as well. And at the moment when I spoke to my friend, there was a flash, far brighter than one used for a camera. It exploded right in front of my eyes ... I thought the bomb had been dropped on the central telephone office. The dust was rising and something sandy and slimy entered my mouth." It was her blood mixed with the dust.

Looking down from his weather station on a hill above the city, Isao Kita, a meteorologist, wrote: "I could see that the city was completely lost. The city turned into a yellow sand. It turned yellow, the color of the yellow desert."

"THE GREATEST DAY IN HISTORY"

Estimates of the death toll vary, but perhaps one hundred thousand people died in Hiroshima almost immediately, and another thirty thousand, due to burns and radiation poisoning, by the end of the year. This was a far greater toll than the Manhattan Project planners had expected. Nevertheless, President Truman immediately declared August 6 "the greatest day in history", and again called on Japan to surrender, promising "a rain of ruin from the air" if it again refused.

But the shocked Japanese government did not respond immediately and on August 9 another atomic bomb was dropped, this time on Nagasaki, where the death toll reached sixty to seventy thousand. After this, on August 15, Japan finally surrendered.

The war was over. But the use of the nuclear bomb echoed through subsequent generations. After August 6, 1945, human beings would always be possessed of the knowledge that there exists a weapon that can do awful damage, and can be carried in a missile-tip or even a suitcase. Not only that, but the use of one of these weapons might cause yet more of them to be unleashed, so that the world might ultimately be destroyed. This consciousness—nuclear anxiety—is a fixture of our modern age, and is here to stay. ❧

1951–present

THE COLD WAR AND BEYOND

The Almost Complete Records

MISSILE TRANSPORTERS

12 PROB GUIDELINE MISSILES.

5 MISSILE DOLLIES

20' LONG CYLINDRICAL TANKS

MISSILE TRANSPORTER

OPEN STORAGE

1962
THE CUBAN
MISSILE CRISIS

Very early in the morning of October 15, 1962, a U-2 spy plane took off from McCoy Air Force Base in Florida, in the United States. The U-2 was the best aerial reconnaissance plane in the world—sleek and lightweight, supersonic and capable of snapping clear pictures from heights of 65,000 feet. Yet it was not without flaws, one of them being its vulnerability to well-aimed surface-to-air missiles, or SAMs. In one incident in May of 1960, a U-2 had been shot down over Russia, becoming a major public embarrassment for the Eisenhower Administration in its waning days. And on September 9, 1962, another had been shot down over western China, tarnishing the image of the new administration of President John F. Kennedy. U-2 flights were therefore considered risky from a public relations point of view, but the one taking place over Cuba on October 15 was deemed too important to forgo.

The U-2 crossed Cuba at almost exactly 7 a.m., just the right time for spy photos as the sun is high enough to create shadows which give dimension to objects on the ground. The camera in the plane's belly clicked and hummed. In fifteen minutes, the U-2 had finished its job and turned back towards its base. By the middle of the day, the pictures were in the hands of analysts at the CIA headquarters in Langley, Virginia.

This reconnaissance photograph, taken over Cuba on October 15, 1962, highlights the features of a Russian missile base.

At 7:30 on the following morning, McGeorge Bundy, President Kennedy's National Security Adviser, met with the CIA analysts in his office in the White House basement to review the images. They directed Bundy's attention to a rectangular-shaped clearing in the Cuban jungle. Military trucks could be seen, as well as some long sheds. Based on their knowledge of similar sites in the Soviet Union, the analysts were sure that some of the shapes were missile ramps. Indeed, it was the CIA's conclusion, they told Bundy, that the Soviet Union was installing medium-range nuclear missiles in Cuba.

The briefing chilled Bundy to the bone. For this meant that Russia had, or would soon have, nuclear weapons in place less than 90 miles from America. Bundy called the president.

TO THE BRINK

For fourteen days in the middle of October 1962, the world came the closest it has ever come to nuclear war. During those fourteen days, a nuclear holocaust was a very, very real possibility, so much so that one Russian participant in these events said that at one point he was "counting the minutes"—not days or hours—until missiles were fired. Americans bought food supplies with which to stock "bomb shelters" (usually cellar rooms) in their homes, while schoolchildren practised taking cover under their desks. Around the world, people nervously read newspapers and watched the crisis on television. Demonstrations demanding a peaceful resolution to the standoff took place in Paris and London.

When the crisis eventually subsided, John F. Kennedy, the charismatic and youthful President of the United States, would be hailed in America as a hero for having faced down the Russians. Yet what many people do not know to this day is that Kennedy made a secret deal with Premier Nikita Khrushchev, the leader of the Soviet Union, to get the Russians to dismantle their missile sites—a deal even some intimates in his administration were not aware of.

What became known as the Cuban Missile Crisis was caused by a number of factors. They included Russia's unsettling knowledge that the United States had it completely outgunned when it came to nuclear missiles, and the Kennedy Administration's near-clinical paranoia about having a socialist state in Cuba. But, as with many dramas, both on the world stage and in our own backyards, the chief cause was hubris.

"THERE IS NO EVIDENCE"

It is part of the many myths surrounding the Cuban missile crisis that President Kennedy woke up on the morning of October 16 to be told for the very first time that Khrushchev had installed nuclear missiles in Cuba. In fact, the warnings had been arriving for some time. In early August, CIA director John McCone had received a highly reliable report that at least one such missile had been installed in a cave with a hole drilled through its ceiling near the little Cuban harbor town of Mariel; McCone personally told the president this on August 20. U-2 reconnaissance flights in early September had also revealed the presence of SAM missile sites, submarine pens and Soviet MiG fighters in Cuba. Further reports indicated that five thousand to ten thousand Soviet troops were also present.

SINCE LATE 1961, THE CIA HAD BEEN MAKING SMALL RAIDS ON CUBA, HOPING THAT CASTRO WOULD LASH BACK.

Despite this, Kennedy had said at a press conference in early September: "There is no evidence of any organized combat force in Cuba from any Soviet bloc country." The main reason for his secrecy was that the Americans were then planning an attack on Cuba to rid themselves of this taunting presence. An earlier attempt to do this, the so-called Bay of Pigs invasion, in 1961, carried out by Cuban exiles and funded by the CIA, had been a poorly planned disaster. The new invasion, however, was to be an all-American one, with the full power of U.S. military might behind it. But the Kennedy Administration could not simply invade Cuba; it needed to provoke President Fidel Castro into some belligerent act that justified such a response. Since late 1961, the CIA had been running Operation Mongoose, in which operatives made small hit-and-run raids on Cuba, hoping that Castro would lash back.

TIT FOR TAT

Khrushchev's decision to place nuclear warheads in Cuba had been prompted by numerous considerations. One was the United States' far greater nuclear firepower—at the time, America had 27,297 nuclear warheads to Russia's 3332. Another was Castro's request, made in January of 1962, that Russia station men and weapons in Cuba in case of another American attack. The Russians believed the Americans would attack again, as well—one Russian diplomat later told a historian that "in the spring of 1962, we in Moscow were absolutely convinced … that a new military invasion of Cuba was at hand—but this time with all the American military might, not only with proxy troops."

But what had finally convinced Khrushchev to position his missiles close to America's shores was the decision by the Kennedy Administration to place fifteen intermediate-range ballistic missiles in Turkey in 1961. From then on, any Soviet official vacationing along the shores of the Black Sea could easily imagine an American nuclear warhead arcing across the shore and 1550 miles into Russia. From the Russian point of view, these missiles were a direct challenge to Soviet security.

THREE OPTIONS

The president's reaction to the call from Bundy on October 16 was swift. He ordered an immediate top-secret meeting of a dozen leading foreign policy officials, including Bundy, Secretary of State Dean Rusk, Secretary of Defense Robert S. McNamara, and the president's brother, Attorney-General Robert Kennedy, whose influence on the president went beyond the domestic purview of normal attorneys-general. Also part of the group were Chairman of the Joint Chiefs of Staff General Maxwell Taylor, Vice President Lyndon Johnson, and the Ambassador to Russia, Chip Bohlen. Known as the Executive Committee, which would soon be shortened to "Excomm," this group would meet daily for the next two weeks. The meetings were taped—U.S. presidents had been taping important moments in office since World War II—and the tapes are now a matter of public record.

At the first meeting, President Kennedy was told the extent of the build-up in Cuba. The Russians were constructing nine missile sites, which could launch SS-4 and SS-5 missiles a distance of almost 2500 miles into America. There were indications that up to forty launching sites were planned, which would mean nearly seventy per cent of the Soviet nuclear capability was resting right on America's doorstep. The scale of the build-up came as a surprise, even to Kennedy.

Three types of response were discussed. One, advanced by Maxwell Taylor, was an air strike: "We're impressed, Mr. President, with the great importance of getting a … strike with all the benefits of surprise … Hit 'em without any warning whatsoever." Another option was a blockade, to keep any more

Anxious Americans listen to President Kennedy's analysis of the tense standoff. Scenes like this took place the world over.

Soviet men and materiel from entering Cuba. And then, as Robert Kennedy put it, "we have [a third choice] … which is the invasion." At the same time as he said this, Robert Kennedy passed a note to his brother, which read: "Now I know how Tojo felt when he was planning Pearl Harbor" (a reference to the popular, but inaccurate, perception that Japanese Prime Minister Hideki Tojo had personally planned the surprise attack on 7 December 1941).

THE BIGGER PICTURE

On October 18, out of a secret location deep in the Russian steppes, the Soviets launched Cosmos X, their very first spy satellite. Primitive by today's standards, and less advanced than U.S. satellites, Cosmos X rose to a height of about 125 miles and headed off on a course which put it directly above U.S. military bases, on land and at sea, in the southern and southwestern United States. As a result of this, the Soviet Union was able to see for the first time at close quarters the massive American military build-up that had been going on since October 16. A day later, the official Soviet newspaper, *Isvestia*, published a warning: if America attacked Cuba, the Soviets would go to war against the United States. This warning was without a doubt approved by Khrushchev.

On October 22, President Kennedy went "live" with the crisis. Addressing the American nation and an anxious worldwide audience on television, he announced the discovery of the missile installations and proclaimed that he was placing a naval blockade—or "quarantine," as he called it, since blockades were illegal under international law—around Cuba. Kennedy had fought off the military demands for a massive bombardment or invasion of Cuba, mainly because he felt Khrushchev would retaliate with military action in Berlin (then still divided into Eastern and Western sectors), which would call for a U.S. response, thus escalating the situation even further.

Khrushchev responded by declaring the quarantine illegal (which it was) and vowing that Russian ships would ignore the blockade. The Russians, through Soviet Ambassador Anatoly Dobrynin, also claimed that there were nothing but "defensive" weapons in Cuba, which the Americans knew to be a lie.

On October 24, the blockade went into effect. U.S. intelligence knew that nineteen Soviet ships were at that moment en route to Cuba. As the Western world held its collective breath, the Strategic Air Command (SAC) went to

THE CUBAN MISSILE CRISIS

a DEFCON 3 alert. (In American military lexicon, DEFCON alerts gauge the readiness of the country's defences against attack. DEFCON stands for Defense Readiness Condition, with DEFCON 5 meaning normal peacetime conditions and DEFCON 1, which has never been used, standing for imminent attack.) Sixteen of the ships turned away. Two moved towards the 180 U.S. ships strung out around Cuba, escorted by a Russian submarine. As a U.S. destroyer prepared depth charges to blow the Russian sub out of the sea, the two surface vessels stopped dead in the water and waited.

EYEBALL TO EYEBALL

At this point, famously, Dean Rusk is said to have turned to McGeorge Bundy and said: "We're eyeball to eyeball, and I think the other fellow just blinked." But this wasn't quite the case. On the evening of October 24, Khrushchev sent a private message to Kennedy, continuing to claim that the quarantine was "an act of aggression." This caused Kennedy to order the Strategic Air Command to DEFCON 2, for the first (and only) time in its history. By the morning of October 26, Kennedy was convinced that he needed to invade Cuba and increased the frequency of reconnaissance flights over the island to one every two hours. But then Kennedy received a letter from Khrushchev—one that Bobby Kennedy described as "very long and emotional"—which stated that Soviet missiles and personnel would be removed if Kennedy announced that he would not invade Cuba.

As Kennedy considered this, a U-2 was shot down over Cuba on October 27, killing its American pilot, and other reconnaissance planes were fired on. These attacks were nevertheless against Khrushchev's orders, but tensions rose extraordinarily, leading the American military to once again push for war. On the evening of October 27, Khrushchev sent yet another missive, this time demanding that Kennedy remove the American nuclear warheads from Turkey.

The official version at the time had it that Kennedy simply chose not to respond to the second letter, only replying to the first and agreeing not to attack Cuba. But, in fact, through a secret avenue of communications Kennedy also agreed to remove the missiles from Turkey. This agreement was known only to a few intimates, because Excomm at large was against the deal, which was felt to undermine NATO and Turkey.

WINNERS AND LOSERS

However the agreement had been achieved, people around the world breathed a huge sigh of relief. The crisis had shown how close the planet could come, at any time, to nuclear war,

and it caused many people around the world to join peace movements, particularly those that sought the banning of nuclear arms.

While Kennedy—who would be president for only little more than a year, before being shot down in Dallas—was not the all-out victor he was initially credited with being, he can be applauded for resisting military urgings to go to war, urgings that could very well have led to a nuclear holocaust. But it was American hubris, in thinking it could invade Russia's ally Cuba with impunity while positioning missiles in Turkey, so near Russia, that had initiated the crisis.

Khrushchev had also made mistakes, however, in thinking he could get away with placing missiles in Cuba and in underestimating American resolve. Afterwards, he lost face around the world and in October 1964 was forced to resign, at least in part because the Soviet Union had been cast as the loser in this ultimate global confrontation.

All in all, for the statesmen the result could be seen as a draw. The true winners, however, were the citizens of the world, who had only narrowly escaped being vaporized by atomic weaponry.

THE BAY OF PIGS

On April 15, 1961, a CIA-backed invasion force of Cuban exiles hit the beaches of the Bay of Pigs (Bahía de Cochinos) in southwestern Cuba in an attempt to overthrow the new government of Fidel Castro. After initial successes, the invasion force, lacking promised support from the U.S. Navy and Air Force, was soundly defeated and most of its members imprisoned. (The U.S. was later forced to ransom them for U.S.$53 million.)

The Bay of Pigs was the worst disaster of the Kennedy Administration and haunted U.S.–Cuban relations for decades to come. The plan had originated and been approved during the Eisenhower Administration, prior to Kennedy's term in office. Even then, U.S. government officials were seeking a way to overthrow the unfriendly socialist government that had come to power in a neighboring country that had previously been an ally—indeed, almost a colony.

On coming to office, Kennedy gave his approval for the invasion. But once he realized that the United States would have to take a public, rather than a covert role in the fighting, he baulked and withdrew military backing at a late stage. This was one of the main reasons why the invasion failed. Another, revealed in 2000, was that the Soviet Union and Cuba knew about the invasion, including its date, all along, thanks to a KGB mole in the CIA. ❧

1963
THE ASSASSINATION OF PRESIDENT KENNEDY

Almost everyone in the Western world who was an adult on November 22, 1963 can remember where they were and what they were doing when they heard the news that President John Fitzgerald Kennedy had been assassinated in Dallas, Texas. The young American president had won international renown as the gracious, charming symbol of the Second World War generation's coming of age; of a hoped-for end to the Cold War; and of the beginning of what Kennedy himself called a "New Frontier" that would include the eradication of poverty and the spread of democracy worldwide. The shock of his death reverberated far and wide.

Without doubt, the assassination is the single most controversial event in U.S. history. Well over two thousand books have been written on the subject. Two government commissions have studied it in depth. Numerous movies and documentaries have been devoted to dissecting that day, those scant six seconds, those three (or four, or five) shots.

It all boils down to this. If we have to believe that a lonely, maladjusted, arrogant sociopath like Lee Harvey Oswald was alone responsible for killing the charismatic, altogether extraordinary JFK—just Oswald himself, without the aid of some massive and covert machinery of conspiracy—then we have to believe that we live in a world where random luck can fall on the side of creeps as well as handsome heroes.

If, on the other hand, we believe, as some conspiracy theories suggest, that the Mafia, Fidel Castro, the Soviet Union or the CIA—or Kennedy's own vice president, Lyndon Johnson, for

that matter—used Oswald as a pawn (a "patsy" is what Oswald said he was) to get to the president, then we can believe that JFK was killed for a purpose, that he died because his perceived goodness threatened the wrong people or global interests. And that is truly a hero's death.

GOING ON A CHARM OFFENSIVE

The day of the assassination began for the glamorous presidential couple in Forth Worth, Texas, about 30 miles from Dallas. It was cool and overcast, raining slightly. A crowd of twelve thousand people gathered in front of the Hotel Texas, where the Kennedys were staying. Coming out without Jackie—a fact that he knew disappointed the crowd—Kennedy made a few short remarks before commenting wryly that his wife's tardiness was due to the fact that "she always looks so much better than the rest of us."

This was not the first time that Kennedy had used his cultivated young wife—she was thirty-three to his forty-six—to charm slightly hostile crowds. And this trip to Texas was in fact one huge charm offensive. The following year, 1964, would be a re-election year for Kennedy, and Texas was one of the states in the country not swayed by his aura, since along with it came many stances—including civil rights and his reluctance to re-invade Castro's Cuba—that did not endear him to the heart of conservative Texans. This was not merely a matter of polite political disagreement. Numerous violent fringe groups were known to exist in Dallas, and security along the president's motorcade route would be stringent.

A VIOLENT LONER

As Kennedy was preparing to leave Fort Worth, a twenty-four-year-old man named Lee Harvey Oswald—who sometimes used the pseudonym Lee Hidell—was preparing to leave for his job at the Texas School Book Depository, a textbook distribution center located in Dealey Plaza, a small park on the outskirts of Dallas' downtown. Oswald had a bland, almost meek appearance that disguised numerous secrets. Born into a poor New Orleans family, he had never known his father, who had died two months before his birth. He grew up to be a lonely child—"lone" or "loner" were words that would follow him all his short life—who was fascinated with guns. As a teenager, he developed leftist views. He could also be violent, striking his mother, Marguerite, on several occasions; once he pulled a knife on her.

Despite his early socialist leanings, Oswald joined the U.S. Marines when he was seventeen, in 1956. By the end of 1956, after only a few weeks of training, he had attained a "sharpshooter" qualification on the firing range. That meant he could hit a 10-inch bull's-eye from 220 yards away, eight times out of ten, without the aid of a telescopic sight.

THE FATEFUL JOURNEY

President Kennedy and his entourage—which included Vice President Lyndon Johnson, a native Texan, and his wife, Lady Bird, as well as Texas Governor John Connally and his wife, Nellie—flew into Dallas' Love Field to be greeted by cheering crowds. Special plaudits were reserved for a smiling Jackie Kennedy, lovely in a pink suit and pillbox hat. The Kennedys and Connallys then entered their limousine (the Johnsons would follow two cars behind) for the motorcade to the Dallas Trade Mart, where Kennedy would make a speech. The Kennedy car was an open-topped Lincoln Continental.

The skies had cleared, the weather was warming and crowds had already begun to gather along the motorcade's route, which had been published in the local newspapers. The penultimate leg of the trip took it through Dealey Plaza, in front of the Texas School Book Depository building. Some of the depository workers gathered at the windows for a bird's-eye view of the proceedings. Lee Harvey Oswald was alone on the sixth floor, in the southeast corner of the building. None of his fellow workers saw him, because he was hidden behind cartons of books he had placed there.

In his hands was an Italian-made Mannlicher-Carcano rifle, complete with telescopic scope, which he had purchased for $24.45 from a Chicago mail-order rifle and ammunition company.

> LEE HARVEY OSWALD WAS TRAINED TO HIT A FAR-DISTANT BULL'S-EYE, EIGHT TIMES OUT OF TEN, WITHOUT THE AID OF A TELESCOPIC SIGHT.

Conspiracy theorists would later disparage the Mannlicher-Carcano as a poor rifle, impossible to use to hit a moving target, but FBI tests found it to be extremely accurate. It fired a 6.5-mm bullet at about 2000 feet a second. The Mannlicher-Carcano could also be broken down and reassembled quickly; Oswald had walked into work that day with a long brown package that contained, he said, "curtain rods."

By 12 noon, Oswald was ready.

THE MAN BEHIND THE BOXES

A study of Lee Harvey Oswald reveals a personality typical of lone assassins. After a short, unhappy time in the Marine Corps, where he was bullied for his socialist sympathies, his Marxist leanings became more pronounced. He attempted unsuccessfully to renounce his citizenship, and moved to the Soviet Union, where he worked in a factory in Minsk and met and eventually married Marina Nikolayevna Prusakova.

But after an attempt to obtain Soviet citizenship failed, he tried to kill himself and was placed in a mental asylum.

Upon his release, upset over his rejection by the Russian government, Oswald returned to America and settled in the Dallas-Fort Worth area with Marina and their new daughter, June. When he wasn't working in a series of menial jobs, Oswald made fitful attempts to live out his socialist beliefs. He volunteered briefly for an organization called Fair Play for Cuba, and went to Mexico, where he visited both the Cuban and Soviet embassies, trying to get visas to live in their countries.

All of this later provided fodder for conspiracy theorists, who believed that Oswald was working for the Russians or the Cubans, or even the CIA. A problem with all these theories, however, is Oswald's extraordinary instability, which impressed almost everyone with whom he came into contact. He was just too weird for professional intelligence operatives to use as a spy, let alone as an assassin.

In any case, Oswald had already carried out a similar act, alone. In April of 1963, he had sneaked into the backyard of a former U.S. Army general and arch-conservative segregationist named Edwin Walker, who had recently made an "anti-Communist" speaking tour—and shot at him. The shot hit a wooden windowsill and was deflected, although bullet fragments grazed Walker. Oswald's involvement was not suspected until after the Kennedy assassination,

---

President Kennedy addressing the press in 1963.

when police found surveillance photos Oswald had taken of Walker's house. Having missed Walker, Oswald's restless anger—at the world, at authority figures to both the right and the left of the political spectrum—had gone unassuaged.

THE ZAPRUDER TAPE

Even today, explanations of the assassination that posit Oswald as the "lone" shooter can prompt a vitriolic response from passionate conspiracy theorists. "Ridiculous!" they say, or "What about Umbrella Man?" Umbrella Man is a figure who appears in a famous film of the assassination and who, for no apparent reason, on a sunny day opens and closes his umbrella just as JFK's motorcade passes and shots ring out. Many conspiracy theorists suggest that this man must have been signalling to someone.

The film in question was made by Abraham Zapruder, a fifty-eight-year-old clothing manufacturer, who had offices in the Dal-Tex building in Dealey Plaza. He was an avid Democrat and supporter of President Kennedy, and he made a point of going home in the middle of the day to get his 8-millimetre film camera to record the president's visit.

He then went with his secretary to Dealey Plaza, walked down Elm Street past the book depository and climbed up

The President and Jackie Kennedy at the start of the motorcade.

on a concrete pergola near the grassy knoll and the triple underpass through which Kennedy's motorcade would drive. The innocent and enthusiastic film Zapruder subsequently made has become essential evidence in all investigations of the assassination.

KENNEDY'S LAST MOMENTS

At just before 12:30 p.m., Kennedy's motorcade entered Dealey Plaza on Main Street, turned right on Houston Street, travelled one block and turned left onto Elm Street beneath the book depository. This was a 120-degree turn, which slowed the motorcade down to a speed of just about 10 miles per hour.

First came two motorcycles, then Kennedy's limousine, with the President and First Lady in the back seat and John and Nellie Connally in the front seat. The crowds along Elm Street began to scream and wave. "Mr. President," Nellie Connally said at that moment, "you can't say that Dallas doesn't love you." "No, you certainly can't," the president said.

At this point, as Kennedy and his wife smiled and waved, Oswald fired his first shot. It missed. While no remnants of the bullet have been found, it appears that it nicked the branch of an oak tree and ricocheted against a kerb—a chip of concrete flew off and grazed the cheek of a bystander.

Within three seconds, Oswald had fired again. This second shot entered Kennedy's upper back. Although it didn't touch his spine it created a shock wave that damaged his sixth cervical vertebra, which in turn caused a neurological reflex sometimes called Thorburn's Position. This can be seen quite clearly in Zapruder's film: Kennedy's arms go up almost parallel to his chin, elbows jutting out and fists clenched, and remain locked there. The same bullet then struck John Connally, seriously injuring him.

Watching the Zapruder film at this point, one sees the situation in the lead limousine quickly unravel into chaos. The driver, disastrously, slows the vehicle to a near crawl. Governor Connally has collapsed with his head on his wife's lap. Kennedy is leaning towards Jackie, his arms locked. She reaches to him, trying to pull down his left elbow from this strange position.

Then, suddenly, a large portion of the right side of Kennedy's skull flies off. In the film, it looks like the bullet has hit him on that side, but what can be seen is really an exit wound. The bullet had entered the back of Kennedy's head and exploded outwards. Nellie Connally remembers Jackie Kennedy saying, "His brains are in my hand."

The film captures Jackie, her pink suit blood-spattered, trying to climb over the back of the car, where a Secret Service man was reaching to her. Some speculated that she was trying to escape the carnage, but she later provided a simple explanation: a piece of her husband's skull had blown back over the car. She wanted to get it, in case it was needed.

"JUST A PATSY"

Oswald hid the rifle behind some boxes and sprinted down a rear stairwell of the book depository. A police officer who had already entered the building, gun drawn, stopped him, but Oswald's supervisor identified Oswald as an employee, and he was allowed to leave. He returned to a rooming house where he had been staying, picked up a pistol and headed out once more. He was seen acting suspiciously enough—ducking into storefronts as police cars went by—that an officer named J.D. Tippet stopped him for questioning. Oswald shot him four times and killed him.

By this time, the rifle had been found in the book depository and an all-points bulletin had been issued for Oswald's arrest. Soon, he was caught in a movie theatre where he was hiding and booked on suspicion of murdering both President Kennedy and Officer Tippet. Reporters saw him briefly; he claimed he was innocent, "just a patsy," he said, arrested because he had lived in the Soviet Union.

Meanwhile, the enormity of the assassination was sinking in. Film taken of the crowd in Dealey Plaza after the motorcade rushed the mortally wounded president to the hospital shows men and women standing around in stunned silence, hands over their mouths, or with tears unashamedly running down their cheeks. The same reaction of shock, disbelief and grief quickly spread worldwide.

OSWALD IS SILENCED

In his short time in custody, Oswald continuously wore a smug grin or sneer. Although he continued to deny killing the president, he seemed to be enjoying himself immensely—right up to the moment when, while being transferred to another jail, he was shot and killed by a strip club owner named Jack Ruby.

Ruby's motive appeared to be simple revenge: he had idiolized JFK. His friendship with members of the Dallas police force had allowed him to be on hand as Oswald was being moved. This was more fodder for conspiracy theorists, who postulated that the supposedly Mob-connected Ruby had been hired to shut Oswald up. But Ruby's Mafia connections were never proven, and most of those close to him scoffed at the notion that he was part of a conspiracy. They considered him unstable—after he shot Oswald, Ruby cried, "This should show the world that Jews have guts!"—and to be acting out of violent emotion.

Ruby was convicted of murdering Oswald in 1964, then granted a new trial on appeal (over a technicality). But he died in jail of lung cancer in 1966, before the new trial, insisting on his deathbed that "there was no one else" involved in Oswald's murder.

Despite this, and the findings of the 1966 Warren Commission, which stated that Oswald had been the lone gunman, theorists continued to pore over pictures of Dealey Plaza on that day, looking for accomplices. They found smoke coming from the grassy knoll, which turned out to be leaf shadows. They found CIA men disguised as tramps, who turned out to be tramps. Shots that seemed to have come from all over the plaza turned out to be acoustical echoes.

Oh, and Umbrella Man? The simple truth about Umbrella Man is that he was a guy named Louie Witt, who came forward in 1978 when he heard of his notoriety among conspiracy theorists. Witt was an eccentric who waved his umbrella to heckle Kennedy; he still had the umbrella.

And the simple truth about the assassination appears to be that Lee Harvey Oswald, acting on a deranged impulse, was the sole killer of John F. Kennedy. Not a terribly satisfying answer—as mundane, in fact, as an old umbrella—but, nonetheless, unless new evidence is found, almost certainly the correct one. ❧

THE ASSASSINATION OF PRESIDENT KENNEDY

1967
THE SIX-DAY WAR

It was Moshe Dayan, the charismatic Israeli Defence Minister, who first began referring to Israel's "War of Independence" against its Arab neighbors in June 1967 as the Six-day War. The name quickly stuck, and it was a brilliant stroke, bringing with it echoes of the Book of Genesis: God had made the Earth in six days, and Israel had asserted itself as a nation in the same amount of time in a lightning war that saw it defeat Egypt, Syria and Jordan. The difference was that in the biblical story God rested on the seventh day, whereas Israel's epic triumph brought it no rest at all. Today, Israel remains the occupier of the land it won in the Six-day War, but, as a result, it is faced with repeated terrorist attacks, and its borders seem no more secure than they were prior to that conflict. Some might wonder, has Israel's victory turned to ashes?

Beginning in roughly the mid-nineteenth century, the Zionist movement called for Jews in Europe, Russia, America and the Middle East to return to their ancestral homeland of Palestine—especially to their sacred city of Jerusalem—and settle there. At the time mainly populated by Arab peoples, the region had been under Ottoman rule since the early sixteenth century. When Great Britain took control of Palestine after the First World War, it promised through the Balfour Declaration, a formal statement of policy intentions in the postwar Middle East issued by its Foreign Secretary Arthur James Balfour, to create a Jewish state. However, each successive wave of Jewish immigration was met with violent resistance from Palestinian Arabs, some of whom were then

From the opposite side of the Suez Canal, an Israeli soldier studies an oil refinery at Port Suez set alight by Israeli shelling.

seeking independence for Palestine, and Britain soon reneged on its promise.

After the Second World War, when the Holocaust created sympathy worldwide for the Zionist cause, the British handed over the Palestine problem to the United Nations. It sought to resolve the situation in November of 1947 with General Assembly Resolution 181, which partitioned Palestine into two states, one Arab, one Jewish. Zionists welcomed this proposal, but Arabs rejected it because large numbers of Palestinian Arabs would be left living in the Jewish state. The day after the resolution was passed, Palestinian fighters attacked Israel, and what Israel called its War of Independence began.

Fighting through 1948 against Palestinian nationalists and their Arab supporters from Iraq, Syria, Egypt and Transjordan—all of its neighbors—Israel eventually conquered 30 per cent more territory than the partition had given it. Although the Old City of Jerusalem ended up in Jordanian hands—a blow to the Jews, who had been expelled from this ancient city by the Romans in the first century AD—and the Israelis suffered heavy losses, by the end of 1948 the Israeli state had been born.

COUNTDOWN TO WAR

It would take almost another decade of war—through to the Israeli victory in the second Arab-Israeli war of 1956—for the Israelis to solidify their position. After 1956, Palestine settled into an uneasy calm. However, in a manner typical of the Middle East, the two successive and overwhelming Israeli victories simply sowed the seeds of another war. Pan-Arabism—the philosophy that the Arabs, no matter what their country, were all one people—took hold in the region at this time and found its chief proponent in Gamal Abdel Nasser, President of Egypt, who had driven the British out of the all-important Suez Canal and nationalized it for his people.

For the next ten years, Nasser made preparations for a new and final war against Israel. He joined forces with Syria, to Israel's east, and spoke of liberating the Palestinians living in land held by the Israelis. The radical Baathist Party controlling Syria was even blunter: it wanted, a spokesperson said, "to push Israel into the sea."

Meanwhile, the Israeli Defence Force (IDF) continued to build up its army and air force with munitions and planes from the United States and France. Egypt and Syria did the same, with weaponry supplied by the Soviet Union.

"A CHILD'S GAME"

By 1967, Israel was ringed by thousands of miles of hostile borders and more than thirty Arab divisions. With a few simple strokes, Egypt could close off Israel's vital shipping links through the Strait of Tiran to the Red Sea. Jordan talked openly of diverting the Jordan River, Israel's main water supply. One Egyptian government official said that his peers in the military considered "the destruction of Israel a child's game." A Syrian general thought that the Arab allies could conquer Israel in four days.

In May of 1967, Egyptian forces began to concentrate in the Sinai Peninsula to the southwest of Israel. Under intense pressure from Nasser, the United Nations agreed to remove its Emergency Force, which had acted as a buffer in the area since 1957. On the night of May 22–23, the Egyptian navy blockaded the Strait of Tiran, something Israel had always said would be tantamount to a declaration of war. Israeli Prime Minister Levi Eshkol pleaded unsuccessfully to Britain, America and the United Nations for help.

At the end of May, Nasser signed a defence pact with King Hussein of Jordan, and Jordanian troops began massing along the border with Israel, while Syrian forces massed on the Golan Heights. "Our basic objective will be the destruction of Israel', Nasser said on May 27.

Conferring with Yitzhak Rabin, commander of the IDF, Eshkol finally realized that Israel had no choice: it had to go to war to survive. And it was quickly established that the best way to do this was to take pre-emptive action against the Arab states that threatened it.

The decision was so nerve-wracking that Rabin suffered a nervous breakdown and was treated for acute anxiety and depression. But with chief of staff Ezer Weizman running operations—and the aggressive Moshe Dayan pushing for a massive surprise attack—the Israelis made their move.

FLYING LOW ACROSS THE DESERT, MAINTAINING RADIO SILENCE, THE ISRAELI PLANES FLASHED INTO EGYPTIAN AIR SPACE AND LAUNCHED DEVASTATING ATTACKS.

OPERATION FOCUS

At about 7.30 on the morning of June 5, 250 Israeli French-made fighter-bombers rose from their airfields, flew out over the Mediterranean, and then banked and headed straight for Egypt. This was the start of Operation Focus, one of the most carefully planned and complete surprise attacks of this or any other war.

Flying low across the desert—sometimes just 30 feet above the ground—and maintaining strict radio silence, the planes flashed into Egyptian air space and launched devastating attacks against Nasser's airfields. The raid was perfectly disciplined and methodical: the first planes dropped huge concrete-busting bombs to destroy the runways, then other fighters roared in to bomb and strafe.

The attack caught the Egyptians completely off guard. Within two hours, after twenty-five Israeli sorties against eleven airfields, the Egyptians had lost more than half of their air force—approximately three hundred fighters, bombers, and helicopters.

Operation Focus was a brilliant move. Striking first against their most powerful enemy brought the Israelis time to turn and face Jordan and Syria. And Israel's resulting domination of the skies allowed its forces to advance against the dug-in Egyptian troops in the Sinai. There, the Egyptian army was quickly pushed back all along the line.

In the east, despite Israeli diplomatic efforts to keep their eastern neighbors from attacking, the Jordanian's launched an offensive against IDF forces, shelling and bombing targets within Israel, which included Tel Aviv and the Jewish portion of Jerusalem. But another quick Israeli air strike destroyed much of the Jordanian air power.

By nightfall, Israeli forces held strong positions along all their borders. Ironically, citizens in Cairo were told that the Egyptians were destroying the Israelis and celebrations there went on into the night.

EGYPTIAN ERRORS

Despite these Israeli victories on the first day, the Egyptians were far from defeated. Nasser sent out a desperate plea to other Arab countries for more planes and soon fifty Soviet-built MiGs were on their way from Algeria. Since most Egyptian planes had been destroyed pilotless and on the ground, scores of pilots stood ready to fly the replacement fighters.

But Egyptian generals now made several tactical mistakes. Instead of digging in to repel the advancing IDF (which was tired and suffering from ammunition shortages), they decided to retreat through the Sinai towards defensive positions along

the Suez Canal, thus ceding great amounts of territory as they went. On June 6, however, Nasser began a propaganda war that was more effective than his war on the ground, claiming that the attacks were being made by waves of American bombers, piloted by Americans. Protests sprang up against the United States all over the Arab world.

In the meantime, fighting was occurring between the IDF and Jordanian forces in Old Jerusalem. The Israeli attack had begun early in the morning of June 6, as huge searchlights behind Israeli lines illuminated the dug-in Jordanian forces and blinded them. The fighting was vicious, bunker to bunker, machine-gun nest after machine-gun nest, hand to hand.

By the end of the day, the Israelis had taken all of Jerusalem except the Old City, where the Jordanians were still entrenched. Early the following morning, Israeli artillery bombarded these positions, driving the Jordanians back across the West Bank, and then IDF paratroopers entered the Old City en masse. It was a time of extraordinary emotion for the Israelis. The assault commander, Colonel Motta Gur, sent a message to his officers: "The ancient city of Jerusalem, which for generations we have dreamt of and striven for—we will be the first to enter it."

The Israelis took the Old City with little resistance, moving to the site of the First and Second Temples, a place of pilgrimage for both Muslims and Jews. Despite sniper fire, they made

Israeli paratroopers stand reverently beside the Western Wall of the Old City of Jerusalem, after its capture on June 7, 1967.

their way to the Western Wall, one of the most sacred places in the Jewish religion, the only portion of the Second Temple still standing, the rest having been destroyed by the Romans in 70 AD. There, General Shlomo Goren, chief rabbi of the IDF, blew his shofar, a traditional Hebrew trumpet used in religious ceremonies, and proclaimed: "I have come to this place never to leave it again."

On the evening of June 7, the United Nations was successful in arranging a ceasefire between Israel and Jordan. King Hussein of Jordan, who had lost half of his kingdom in a few days—the half that brought him a good deal of tourist revenue—retired to lick his wounds.

SLAUGHTER IN THE SINAI

In the Sinai, the Israelis raced after the retreating Egyptians. They stopped taking prisoners, advising any Egyptians they encountered to run in the direction of the Suez Canal and attempt to cross back into Egypt. But when they caught and trapped Egyptian troops in the mountain passes leading back towards the canal, they indulged in great slaughter. Israeli artillery poured fire down on traffic jams of Egyptian trucks and tanks, and soon wrecked machinery and dead bodies littered the narrow passes—in Mitla Pass, on June 8, thousands of Egyptians lost their lives.

On that same day, the IDF in the Sinai, having heard of the recapture of Jerusalem, sought some glory for itself. Despite having standing orders to stay 12 miles away from the Suez Canal, and despite the fact that the retreating Egyptians had blown the bridges over the waterway, some Israeli soldiers jumped into the canal and bathed gleefully in its all-important waters.

Egypt now accepted a ceasefire, too, leaving Syria as Israel's only undefeated enemy. Syria remained in control of the strategically important Golan Heights, east of the Jordan River, from whose summits it could pour down artillery fire on Jerusalem. On June 9, the IDF attacked the Syrian positions. The fighting was as vicious as that for Jerusalem, but on June 10, driven by their grand successes and racing now for as much territory as they could gain before the expected ceasefire, the Israelis drove the Syrians out and captured the Golan Heights.

PEACE REMAINS ELUSIVE

It had been an incredible war, an astonishing six days unlike any other six days in history. Eleven thousand Egyptian troops had been lost, as well as six thousand Jordanians and one thousand Syrians, while the IDF had suffered only seven hundred dead. The territory Israel had gained was beyond its wildest expectations a week before—26,000 square miles, which included the Sinai and the Gaza Strip from Egypt, East Jerusalem (including the Old City) and the West Bank from Jordan, and the Golan Heights from Syria. The Arab nations and President Nasser (who was to die in 1970) had been totally humiliated.

In November of the same year, the United Nations passed an American-backed resolution that called for Israel to withdraw from the occupied lands; in return, the Arab combatants would recognize Israel's statehood. But the Arabs would not agree to this "land for peace" deal, so Israel not only remained in the so-called Occupied Territories, but also began to fortify them and populate them with Jewish settlers.

Such settlement, some of it illegal, has ever since fuelled the rise of Palestinian nationalism and sparked terrorist attacks on Israel, which has responded on many occasions with military strikes on the homes of Palestinians and their supporters. "Land for peace" continues to be the operative philosophy when other countries try to broker peace in the Middle East, but it has not worked terribly well. After forty years, Israel remains an occupying power. And no matter how just its cause may have been in 1967, as such it has caused a good deal of harm to Palestinians living within and close to its borders.

War goes on now, as it did in 1967, but it is a far different war, and one whose eventual victor—if there can be one—is anybody's guess.

1968
THE TET OFFENSIVE

arly in the morning of January 31, 1968, Michael Herr, an American war correspondent, was visiting Special Forces troops at their base camp near Can Tho in South Vietnam. As he sat smoking marijuana with the Green Berets, he heard the sound of fireworks coming from the nearby town. It was Tet, the annual Vietnamese celebration heralding the beginning of the lunar New Year. That year, 1968, would be the Year of the Monkey. All over Vietnam, similar celebrations were going on.

But as Herr and the Green Berets sat there, the fireworks got closer and closer and louder and louder, until they realized that these were not fireworks at all, but grenade explosions and automatic weapons fire. The Americans were under attack.

That night, as he describes it in his classic work of war reportage, Dispatches, Herr changed from observer of war to participant, fighting alongside the Special Forces troops, who were surrounded on all sides and under heavy fire: "I slid over to the wrong end of the story, propped up behind some sandbags at an airstrip in Can Tho with a .30 caliber automatic in my hands."

A PYRRHIC VICTORY
The attackers were the Viet Cong and North Vietnamese Army (NVA), the Communist forces fighting for control of Vietnam against the South Vietnamese Army of the Republic of Vietnam (ARVN) and their U.S. allies. As their massive and historic Tet Offensive began, numerous noncombatants like Herr, from journalists to staffers at the U.S. Embassy to civilians in the ancient and elegant city of Hue, found themselves on the front lines of the war. The journalists quickly relayed their experiences home. Vivid reports made front pages around the world; scenes of carnage were shown nightly on television.

The impact of the offensive and the effect of these images would ultimately force the U.S. president, Lyndon Johnson, not to seek re-election—a shocking result for the leader and his advisers, given that the offensive would end with an American victory, the devastation of the Viet Cong as a fighting force and the severe mauling of the NVA. But this would be the public's way of making the president and the military pay for their propaganda—for lying about the war. They had told the public that the battle was almost won. Tet, with its attacks right at the heart of U.S. interests in Vietnam, showed graphically that it wasn't.

THE IDEOLOGICAL BATTLEGROUND
The war in Vietnam that became such a flashpoint of the 1960s was a continuation of a war that had been going on since the Second World War ended. After the Japanese surrender, the French attempted to take back their former colony, but the Viet Minh, Vietnamese nationalists led by the Communist Ho Chi Minh, defeated the French at the battle of Dien Bien Phu in 1954—a battle that signalled the end of Western colonialism in Asia. In the peace settlement that followed, Vietnam was divided into two separate states at the seventeenth parallel, in recognition of gains made by the Viet Minh. In the North, Ho Chi Minh, with aid from the Chinese, set up a Communist state. In the South, a democratic Western-backed state was born. A demilitarized zone (DMZ) was created in order to keep the two sides apart, but from the start the Viet Minh infiltrated the South and launched hit-and-run guerilla raids meant to undermine the South Vietnamese government. The United States, fearful that a North Vietnamese annexation of South Vietnam would lead to Communist takeovers of other nations in Southeast Asia —the so-called "domino theory"—ramped up the supply of military aid, advisers and support troops.

The first American ground combat troops, 3500 in all, landed in Vietnam in 1965. By December, faced by a wily and determined guerilla foe, the United States had increased its presence to two hundred thousand troops. By November 1967, despite protests in the United States against the war, there were nearly half a million Americans fighting the Viet Cong and the NVA.

To counter the protests at home, a carefully orchestrated "success offensive" was set in motion. General William C. Westmoreland, commander of the U.S. Military Assistance Command, Vietnam (MACV), claimed to anyone who would listen that America was winning the war. President Lyndon Johnson appeared on the deck of the aircraft carrier U.S.S. *Enterprise* in late 1967 and declared that the war would not last "many more nights."

Within weeks, the Tet Offensive would highlight the absurdly misplaced optimism of these words.

THE EMBASSY ATTACK

At about 2:45 a.m. on the night of January 31, at the same time as Herr and his Green Berets were roused from their stoned state by the attack, a group of nineteen highly trained Viet Cong guerillas struck at the prime symbol of the American presence in Vietnam: the U.S. Embassy in Saigon. Blowing a hole in the outside wall of the embassy compound, they stormed the buildings and killed five U.S. Marine guards and numerous military police (MPs).

Many of the attackers had worked by day as gardeners and drivers at the embassy and thus knew the layout intimately. While the highest-ranking American diplomat present—the Deputy Chief of Station—was pinned down in his house, the attackers fought a six-hour gun battle with reinforcing marines. By the end of it, the attack had been halted and the attackers wiped out. But television footage of the battle and pictures of the Viet Cong dead littering the embassy grounds were flashed around the world. Many Americans were left wondering how such a thing could have happened in a war they were supposed to be winning.

PLANNING TET

The operating genius behind the Tet surprise attack was North Vietnamese General Vo Nguyen Giap. It was his belief that the previous two years of guerilla warfare against the Americans had done nothing to appreciably change the fortunes of North Vietnam and had in fact left the country, through attrition, in a steadily weakening position. Despite the fact that the conventional wisdom behind guerilla warfare is not to engage the enemy in set-piece battles (and, in fact, at places like the Ia Drang Valley in Vietnam's Central Highlands in 1965, the NVA had done just this and been battered by U.S. firepower), Giap wanted to shake up the enemy with a dramatic attack. Giap also believed that the population of South Vietnam was sick of the Americans and the corrupt South Vietnamese puppet government, and that the planned Tet Offensive could be the spark that would fan the flames of a broad popular uprising. In this last calculation, however, the normally pragmatic Giap was well wide of the mark.

Under Giap's plan, preparations for the Tet Offensive had already begun in the autumn of 1967, when North Vietnam struck at U.S. bases such as Khe Sanh and Con Thien along the DMZ, attempting to draw U.S. reinforcements away from South Vietnam's cities. But the main offensive was to be launched at the time of the Tet celebration. While secretly planning this attack, North Vietnam announced that it would participate in a truce for the duration of the festival. In response, the South Vietnamese Army gave half of its troops permission to go on leave.

> GIAP BELIEVED THAT THE TET OFFENSIVE COULD BE THE SPARK THAT WOULD FAN THE FLAMES OF A BROAD POPULAR UPRISING.

AN INTELLIGENCE FAILURE

There has long been a myth that the United States was completely surprised by Tet, but in fact this was not the case. Such a huge build-up—for an attack that would involve almost two hundred Viet Cong and NVA battalions hitting over one hundred targets in South Vietnam— could not be kept secret for long. In fact, a Viet Cong soldier's notebook, containing a fairly precise description of the attack, was even captured on January 5.

However, in what one U.S. Army general later called "an allied intelligence failure ranking with Pearl Harbor," the MACV failed to put two and two together. And although a heightened state of alert was called for, it was in the main ignored by American commanders. After all, it was estimated that they were on high alert nearly fifty per cent of the time, anyway.

On the night the Viet Cong guerillas blasted their way into the U.S. Embassy, two hundred U.S. colonels went to a raucous party at a fellow officer's quarters in Saigon. Only one extra guard had been assigned to the embassy.

RUNNING BATTLES LIVE ON SCREEN

In the days before the attack, thousands of NVA and Viet Cong stripped off their uniforms and infiltrated Saigon.

Bewildered residents returning to the city of Hue soon after North Vietnamese forces were forced out by U.S. bombing.

Thousands more did the same in other cities. Still more waited in the countryside, ready to attack military bases. Overall, about seventy thousand North Vietnamese and Viet Cong were involved. These fighters hit hard, and with a vengeance, attacking thirty-six of forty-four provincial capitals, five large cities and about one hundred other towns. Twenty-five military bases were assaulted. In and around Saigon, the enemy blew up a good portion of the massive Long Binh ammunition dump, briefly took over the national radio station, and attacked the Presidential Palace. General Westmoreland found himself under siege at the MACV headquarters and ordered his personal staff to find weapons to aid in the defence of the perimeter. The Saigon suburb of Cholon—inhabited mainly by Chinese—was turned by the NVA into a virtual staging ground for their attacks. In one running gun battle, U.S. military police—whose role normally was restricted to rousting drunken marines out of bars—fought better-armed, better-trained guerillas in a side alley near the U.S. embassy. Sixteen MPs were killed and twenty-one wounded.

Thousands of people on both sides were to die in the ensuing days. The United States was faced with an enemy that had dug in, literally in its midst, and would fight to the death.

In the meantime, the world saw a constant barrage of television images of battles going all over the southern half of

US troops wounded during the Tet Offensive. Images like this one shocked the American public and heightened opposition to the war.

the country—battles in which the U.S. forces appeared to be being overwhelmed. The war had been beamed to American television and around the world since the first U.S. troops had arrived in 1965, but most of the early reports contained very little combat footage, since obtaining it involved extreme risks for reporters. Now, however, all reporters had to do was point their cameras through their hotel windows in Saigon and viewers would see street battles in progress and hear the sound of gunfire.

This was where Lyndon Johnson's "success offensive" worked against him; expectations had been set so high that the American people simply could not comprehend how the North Vietnamese could pull off such a coup. After the few first days, the U.S. television presenter Walter Cronkite said, "What the hell is going on? I thought we were winning the war." It mattered little that within weeks the North Vietnamese were being pushed back, with heavy losses. The dramatic images stuck in people's minds.

THE BATTLE FOR HUE

After the embassy raid, the battle that became most emblematic of the Tet Offensive was the pitched combat that took place for a month, beginning in early February, as American and South Vietnamese forces attempted to recapture Hue City, in central Vietnam. Situated on the banks of the Perfume River, Hue is the ancient "Imperial City" of the Nguyen Dynasty and is filled with historic artifacts and the tombs of the ancient Vietnamese dynastic rulers. In 1968, it had a population of about 140,000 people, and was also noted for its graceful parks and a French-designed university campus, whose student body included a large number of Catholics.

When the Tet Offensive began, a division of NVA and Viet Cong attacked and seized much of the city. The North Vietnamese hoisted their flag over the Citadel, the fortified inner city of the ancient kings, and quickly reinforced it with ten thousand troops. Then they commenced another mission: to cleanse the city of those who had spoken out against the Communists in the north. NVA commanders carried lists of these people, who included government officials, teachers, priests and others, many of them foreign-born. Many were rounded up and executed, some by shooting, others by being buried alive. Thousands of graves were dug.

In early February, however, three under-strength battalions of U.S. Marines, aided by the South Vietnamese, counter-attacked. The weather was cold and rainy. The Americans engaged in running battles with their NVA counterparts, fighting for the city block by block—the only house-to-house fighting seen in Vietnam.

At first, out of respect for the historic value of the ancient city, the Americans did not bomb Hue, but the NVA was so well dug in that they finally decided they had no choice. Plane after plane then hit enemy positions with napalm and high explosives, turning seventy per cent of the city to rubble and making 116,000 civilians homeless. For many watching at home, it was another example of an ill-advised and counterproductive U.S. policy of using massive amounts of firepower to achieve a pyrrhic victory. This strategy was famously summed up in a television interview by a U.S. major involved in heavy fighting for another town, Ben Tre on the Mekong Delta. "It became necessary to destroy the town to save it," he said.

VICTORY FROM DEFEAT

The popular uprising that Giap expected did not eventuate. By the beginning of March, the NVA and Viet Cong forces had been pushed back from every position they had seized on January 31, and suffered a staggering forty-five thousand men killed. The offensive became a calamitous defeat for Giap and for North Vietnam. After Tet, the Viet Cong ceased to function as a fighting force and the NVA struggled to rebuild itself.

But although they had lost on the ground, the North Vietnamese had won where it counted: in the hearts and minds of the public in the West. Americans in particular now saw that their government's strategy was resulting in massive casualties, both American and Vietnamese, and that the war seemed to have no clearly defined goal and no end in sight.

Shortly after the offensive, the news was leaked that General Westmoreland wanted an additional 206,000 troops in Vietnam. Westmoreland saw the situation from a military point of view—after defeating the enemy he wanted to press home the attack. But Americans saw it as sacrificing more precious lives for a lost cause.

In the presidential election year of 1968, Lyndon Johnson became so unpopular that after narrowly winning the important Democratic primary contest in New Hampshire—normally a shoe-in for a sitting president—he announced in March that he would not run for another term of office. He also declared a halt to U.S. air strikes above the twentieth parallel in an attempt to bring the North Vietnamese to the negotiating table.

After tumultuous months that saw yet more angry antiwar protests in the United States and elsewhere, formal peace negotiations began in Paris, in November of 1968. It was the first step in the de-escalation of the war, which would eventually lead to a full U.S. withdrawal in 1973.

From the point of view of Giap and his commanders, the forty-five thousand men lost in the Tet Offensive had not died in vain. ❧

1969
THE FIRST MOON LANDING

It's always been up there, nice and yellow and juicy, an allure to lovers, waxing and waning, in charge of tidal pulls, rhyming with "June" and "spoon." Human beings have worshipped it, steered by it, and been driven mad by it. There are rock drawings five thousand years old that depict it. In the second century AD, the Roman writer Lucian wrote a romance in which travellers went to the Moon—the first of many efforts in the genre that would eventually be known as science fiction. People right into the twentieth century imagined there might be extraterrestrial life of some kind there, teeming away beneath the surface or on the so-called "dark side." Yet, for all of human history, no one had ever landed on it. Two hundred and thirty eight thousand miles away, it sat there, tantalizing us.

It took two things to make a lunar expedition possible in the late 1960s. First, technology had to advance to a point where rocketry could hurl capsules out of the Earth's gravitational field and into the much weaker gravitational pull of the Moon. Secondly, the Russians had to act like they were going to get there first. For, first and foremost, landing a man on the Moon was, in those days at the height of the Cold War, a political act. With the United States and Russia competing in every aspect of life, from education and technology to the arms race, such an achievement would demonstrate the superiority of one

system, democracy or Communism, over the other. And not only to the citizens of the U.S and the U.S.S.R., but also to other nations, most notably developing nations taking their first steps towards political independence.

In this contest of one-upmanship, science, ironically, was sidelined. And in this lay the seeds of the demise of lunar discovery exploration.

BEATING THE SOVIETS

On July 16, 1969, three astronauts lay strapped on their backs in their space module atop a massive *Saturn V* rocket. Neil A. Armstrong, Edwin "Buzz" Aldrin Jr. and Michael Collins were the finest products of the National Aeronautics and Space Administration (NASA), and they—like the pioneers of the Age of Exploration, to whom admiring editorial writers often compared them—were going on a journey into the unknown. In a few moments, they would lift off into the bright Florida sky and head for a landing on the Moon.

The mighty U.S. Apollo space program had begun just eight years before, in April of 1961. On the twelfth day of that month, the Russian cosmonaut Yuri Gagarin had become the first person to travel into space and orbit Earth. This had stirred U.S. President John Fitzgerald Kennedy's strong competitive streak. Shortly after Gagarin's single, ninety-minute orbit, Kennedy wrote to Vice President Johnson, then chairman of the National Space Council, asking: "Do we have a chance of beating the Soviets by putting a laboratory in space, or a trip around the Moon … or by a rocket to go to the Moon and back with a man?"

Apollo 11 takes off from Cape Canaveral, Florida. The tip of the rocket carried the command module, *Columbia*, and the lunar module, *Eagle*.

At the time, the American space program was not far behind the Russians in its ability to launch a man into space—on May 5, 1961 Alan Shepard became the first American to orbit the Earth—but lagged in developing the technology to reach the Moon. The Russians had succeeded in launching at least three so-called hard-landing rockets—unmanned spacecraft that had been shot up with the goal of simply hitting the Moon—and America was at least two years away from achieving this. But buoyed by Shepard's triumph, Kennedy issued a famous challenge when addressing a Joint Session of Congress that summer: "I believe this nation should commit itself to achieving the goal, before this decade is out, of landing a man on the Moon and returning him safely to Earth."

HEADING INTO ORBIT

With a mighty roar which thrilled the million people who had gathered on the beaches around Kennedy Space Center near Cape Canaveral, Florida, and the millions more watching on television, *Apollo 11* lifted off into space. Only eleven minutes after blast-off, it was in orbit with the three astronauts aboard beginning to feel the sensations of weightlessness.

They were used to it. Neil Armstrong, the commander of the mission, was thirty-eight years old, a veteran of seventy-eight combat missions during the Korean War, a test pilot of some of America's most advanced rocket airplanes, and a veteran of an earlier Gemini space flight. Armstrong had been selected to become the first man to walk on the Moon.

Thirty-nine-year-old Buzz Aldrin would be Armstrong's partner on the Moon landing. He, too, had been a Korean War fighter pilot and was a Gemini veteran. Aldrin would pilot the lunar module, *Eagle*, which would separate from the command module, *Columbia*, once in the Moon's orbit and bring the two astronauts down to the surface of the Moon.

The third man was Michael Collins, thirty-eight, pilot of *Apollo 11* and the *Columbia* command module. Another Gemini veteran, Collins would not get a chance to touch the Moon's surface but had the essential job of making sure the *Eagle* was launched correctly and ensuring that it redocked safely for its journey back to Earth.

A TURBULENT DECADE

While only eight years had passed since Kennedy's challenge, they had been tumultuous ones. Kennedy was dead of an

WHILE MILLIONS WATCHED THE JOURNEY OF APOLLO 11 WITH ADMIRING EYES, OTHERS FELT SPACE TRAVEL WAS A KIND OF VANITY PROJECT.

assassin's bullet, as was his brother, Robert, and another iconic figure of the sixties, Martin Luther King, Jr. The war in Vietnam had torn the United States apart, pitting patriotic conservatives against those who thought the conflict misguided or immoral. The counterculture of drugs, sex and rock 'n' roll was in full swing. And America was riven by racial divisions and, in some places, crushed by poverty.

Therefore, while there were millions who watched the journey of *Apollo 11* with admiring eyes, there were others who felt that space exploration, at the cost of billions of dollars, was a kind of vanity project meant to enhance the image of the United States abroad at the expense of the ten million people who lived below the poverty line at home.

But nothing deterred NASA from attempting to reach its goal. With Project Apollo, named after the Greek and Roman god of the Sun (among other things), it devoted all its energies to finding a way to land a man on the Moon and began a series of unmanned and manned missions. Efforts intensified in 1966, when the Russians managed to reach the Moon with a so-called soft-landing module—a rocket-launched landing vehicle that did not crash on impact and was able to send back lunar pictures.

In 1967, tragedy struck the U.S. program when three astronauts on *Apollo 1* the first manned launch, which was intended merely to test systems by sending the men into Earth orbit—died in a fire on the launching pad. By July 1969, however, Apollo had made four successful manned flights, which had put spacecraft in orbit around the Moon and tested the lunar module.

Unfortunately for the Russians, at this crucial stage one of their chief scientists died and their N1 rocket exploded at least four times during top-secret launch attempts. The Soviet program quickly unravelled, and even Soviet politicians privately ceded the race to the Americans.

Now, on July 16, 1969, with Armstrong, Aldrin and Collins speeding to the Moon, and with the eyes of the world upon them, the United States was about to publicly claim its prize.

"YOU CATS TAKE IT EASY"

It took the astronauts three days to reach the Moon. On July 19, in the command module *Columbia*, they passed behind the Moon and while on its "dark" side initiated rocket burns that slowed the spacecraft down and corrected its course so that it could enter lunar orbit, about 60 miles above the surface of the Moon. Armstrong and Aldrin then entered the *Eagle*, and, on July 20, separated from *Columbia*. "You cats take it easy on the lunar surface," Collins told them, his jocularity masking a real concern, for his fellow astronauts were literally going where no human being had gone before.

After it coasted down to an altitude of 20,000 feet, the *Eagle* began a powered descent at the rate of about 12,000 feet per second. The surface of the Moon began to appear around the astronauts, pocked with deep craters and with boulder fields scattered on all sides. Suddenly, a computer overload alarm went off, meaning that one of the navigational computers was in danger of malfunctioning. Mission Control in Houston, confident it was a false alarm, never even thought of stopping, however. "Roger, we're GO on that alarm" was their response, meaning that the mission would continue.

The computer was bringing the *Eagle* down into a deep, wide crater, about 650 feet in diameter, called West Crater. The area around the crater was covered with boulders as much as 10 feet high. Noting this, the astronauts decided

---

This famous image of Buzz Aldrin walking on the Moon was taken by Neil Armstrong, who is visible in the reflection on Aldrin's visor.

to override the computer. "We elected to overfly this area in preference for smoother spots a few hundred yards farther west," Armstrong said after the mission. Their final approach took them between two boulder fields, where they touched down.

Since lunar gravity is only one-sixth that of Earth, and since the *Eagle*'s rockets had blown dust everywhere, Aldrin and Armstrong were not entirely sure they had landed until a contact light lit up on one of the *Eagle*'s landing pads. "Houston, Tranquility Base here," Armstrong reported. "The *Eagle* has landed." There was pandemonium in Mission Control in Houston—joyous celebrations, hugging and kissing, the lighting up of cigars. It was 4:18 p.m., U.S. Eastern Daylight Time, on June 20, 1969.

"ONE SMALL STEP"

While the world waited in awed wonder, the two astronauts rested and checked their gear. The *Eagle*'s cameras sent back ghostly, almost surreal images of a moonscape that was stark and lifeless. At 10:40 p.m., after resting, Armstrong put on his backpack with its portable oxygen system and began climbing down a nine-rung ladder to the surface. Before stepping down, he prudently looked at the ground below him. "The surface appears to be very, very fine-grained," he said. Then his left foot touched the ground. "That's one small step for man, one giant leap for mankind."

This utterance, heard through hissing static, immediately became famous around the world. But Armstrong always insisted, with irritation, that he had said "one small step for a man," and so his words were officially changed to this, although the recording does not reflect it. Whatever he said, Armstrong—a man of few words, not comfortable with rhetoric—had made history.

Around the world people watched in astonishment. Some held "moon parties" and toasted the yellow orb with champagne, or stood on rooftops, staring up at the Moon, trying to imagine that human beings were, right at that moment, walking on its surface. It was hard not to feel that something had changed irrevocably in the universe.

MEN FROM PLANET EARTH

Soon after, it was Aldrin's turn to climb down to the Moon's surface. The two men then began their scientific tasks, which consisted of taking soil and rock samples and setting up a sort of aluminium-foil windsock, designed to capture solar wind particles (charged particles ejected from the upper atmosphere of the Sun).

The two men also set up seismic equipment, to measure moonquakes, and a laser mirror. The latter would reflect back a laser beam sent by an observatory telescope in California, allowing scientists to determine the precise distance between the Earth and the Moon; even more importantly, scientists could use the laser mirror to monitor movements of the Earth's crust.

The astronauts also planted an American flag and placed a stainless-steel plaque that read: "Here men from Planet Earth first set foot on the Moon. July, 1969." It was inscribed with the names of the three astronauts and that of President Richard Nixon.

Finally, after over two hours on the surface of the Moon, Aldrin and Armstrong climbed back up the ladder and into the *Eagle*. It was just after 1 a.m. At 12:54 p.m. that day, after resting and preparing for another twelve hours, Aldrin fired the *Eagle*'s ascent engine and the craft climbed into the sky, where it rendezvoused with the *Columbia*, piloted by Michael Collins. Then all three astronauts flew home.

After splashing down in the Pacific Ocean on July 24, 1969, Collins, Aldrin and Armstrong were placed in quarantine for three weeks, just in case they had brought unknown microorganisms back from the Moon with them. They re-emerged to fame and adulation.

THE END OF APOLLO

Most people assumed the success of *Apollo* 11 would pave the way for not only more trips to the Moon but also manned voyages to other planets. As it turned out, there were four more manned missions to the Moon, including one, in 1971, in which America's premier astronaut Alan Shephard famously stroked a few golf balls. But following the return to Earth of *Apollo* 17, on 19 December 1972, the program was scrapped.

A telling fact about that last mission was that it was the only one whose crew included a real scientist, geologist Harrison Schmitt. All other *Apollo* astronauts were military men, talented and savvy in many areas, but not scientists. The program had been driven by political ambition—the desire of an American president to beat a rival. It had never really become the scientific fact-gathering program it ought to have been.

The public's attention span, never long, soon shifted in another directions. Moon walks became old hat. Moreover, as the 1970s and recession set in, there was no longer the money to fund this incredibly expensive program. And with the Russians having fallen out of the race, there was a growing sense that the Americans had sealed their victory and had nothing more to prove.

Human beings have not been to the Moon since 1972, and the beautiful orb in the sky has returned to the world of our imaginings, only a little marred by a stainless-steel plaque and one or two golf balls. It seems only fitting. ✸

1972
THE MUNICH OLYMPICS
TERRORIST ATTACK

At 9 p.m. on the evening of September 4, 1972 nine men assembled at a restaurant in Munich's central railway station. Eight of them had arrived in the German city of Munich in pairs, shortly after the commencement of the Games of the twentieth Olympiad. A ninth, Abu Daoud, a Palestinian Liberation Organization (PLO) militia leader and member of the militant group Black September, had helped plan the assault that would soon take place and was now in Munich to give his assassins one last, final briefing.

The men selected for their "unspecified mission" were mostly young Palestinians known as shababs, recruited from various refugee camps throughout Lebanon and flown to Libya in North Africa where they trained in hand-to-hand combat. Daoud had spent the earlier part of the evening stuffing eight bags, each with the Olympic logo clearly visible, with weaponry including Russian-made AK-47 Kalashnikov assault rifles and hand grenades, food, nylon stockings to disguise their identities, lengths of pre-cut rope for binding their victims and first-aid kits.

Two days prior to the opening ceremonies, Daoud and Luttif Afif (also known as "Issa"), the Palestinian commander, had lied their way into the village, pretending to be Brazilians with a lifelong dream to one day visit the Jewish nation—and were shown around the Israeli apartments by an unsuspecting member of the Israeli delegation. They took note of the configuration of the apartments, the location of stairwells, telephones, windows, and the various exit and entry points of the complex, and when they were finished were given a handful of miniature Israeli flags to take back to Brazil. That night in the railway restaurant, Daoud and Issa told the young Palestinian shababs that from that moment onwards they should consider themselves to be dead—killed pursuing the PLO's objective of establishing a Palestinian state in Israel. They were each given a duffel bag and a track suit, on the back of which was printed the name of an Arab nation; they gave Abu Daoud their passports and, some time after 3 a.m., left the restaurant in taxis bound for the Olympic Village.

THE ISRAELI TEAM ARRIVES

When the Israeli Olympic team boarded their flight in Israel bound for the Munich Olympics, twenty-seven years had passed since the end of World War II. Israeli participation in the German games was significant. Several of the twenty-three Israeli athletes and officials had lost family members in the Holocaust. The horrors perpetrated by the Nazi regime were still fresh and vivid, and the West German government was keen for the world to see their divided nation as having come to terms with its past and facing the future with optimism and hope.

When the Israeli team arrived there was a joyful and almost cavalier atmosphere throughout the Olympic Village. Security was deliberately lax and passes were often ignored. Some athletes were even seen scaling the village's 6-foot-high perimeter fencing to bypass the official checkpoints. In addition, as if to emphasize the fact that the nation had moved away from its militaristic past, there was not a single armed guard to be seen anywhere. Adding to the concerns of Shmuel Lalkin, the head of the Israeli delegation, the Israeli team would be housed in

31 Connollystrasse, a small building near an access gate in an isolated part of the village that would be difficult to defend in the unlikely event of an assault. Not entirely oblivious to the likelihood of a breach of security, the German authorities had drawn up a list of twenty-six possible threat scenarios, of which Scenario 21 eerily paralleled the shocking events that were to come—but it was dismissed by security analysts as simply too unlikely to be taken seriously.

On the evening of September 4, the Israeli team returned to their rooms late, after attending a performance of the musical Fiddler On The Roof and, later, posing for a group photograph.

THE TERRORISTS GAIN ENTRY TO THE VILLAGE

Just after 4 a.m. in the morning on September 5, five Palestinians belonging to the Black September terrorist organisation scaled the chain wire fence that surrounded the Olympic Village and rendezvoused with three accomplices who had already gained access. The five men had concealed their weapons in athletic bags and, although several witnesses watched as they climbed over, there seemed nothing overtly suspicious or out of place, as athletes had been routinely scaling the makeshift fence since day one of the games without incident. The eight men then used stolen keys to gain access to the apartments that housed the Israeli team.

At just after 4:30 a.m. in apartment 1 the team's wrestling official, Yossef Gutfreund, heard a series of scratches at the door and went to investigate. To his horror he was confronted by three masked gunmen. He immediately used his 300-pound bulk to keep the door closed long enough to shout out to his teammates to get out any way that they could. Weightlifting coach Tuvia Sokolovsky leaped from the balcony to safety, thanks to Gutfreund's heroic efforts to keep the terrorists at bay. After ten seconds or so of stubborn resistance they were able with their Kalashnikov assault weapons to pry open the door and force Gutfreund to the floor—but Gutfreund had been able to hold the door closed long enough to allow Sokolovsky to run across an open patch of lawn and take refuge behind a garden bed. Sokolovsky later recalled how he could hear the "whizzing" of bullets flying past his ears as he fled.

CHAOS AND HORROR IN APARTMENT 1

Chaos erupted throughout the apartment. Amitzur Shapira, Israel's premier track and field coach and father of four children,

was hauled from his bed, as was Kehat Shorr, a Romanian who had fought against the Nazis and lost his wife and daughter in the Holocaust. In 1963 Shorr emigrated to Israel and became the coach of its national shooting team. When the terrorist group's commander Luttif Afif (soon to be known the world over as "the man in the white hat") burst into the bedroom of burly wrestling coach Moshe Weinberg, Weinberg responded swiftly. He grabbed a knife from his bedside table and lunged at Afif, slicing open the breast pocket of his jacket and wrestling him to the floor. As the two were struggling another terrorist entered the room and shot Weinberg through the mouth.

The athletes and officials, including Weinberg, then had their wrists and ankles bound and were forced up the stairs into the bedroom shared by Jacov Springer, a weightlifting judge, and Andre Spitzer, the Romanian-born fencing master who had arrived in Munich only the previous evening. Spitzer had earlier amazed his fellow athletes by walking up to a group of Lebanese athletes in the Olympic Village to ask them about their results. Israel was at war with its northern neighbour, Lebanon, but Spitzer believed that the Olympic ideals of brotherhood and of the unifying power of sport embedded in the Olympic Charter would be more than capable of overcoming the politics of division and hate. The Lebanese group greeted Spitzer warmly, asking him about his results and wishing him well. It was exactly how Andre Spitzer had always dreamed the Olympic Games would be, and he returned to his teammates full of optimism and hope for a better world.

WHEN THE ISRAELI OLYMPIC TEAM BOARDED THEIR FLIGHT, TWENTY-SEVEN YEARS HAD PASSED SINCE THE END OF WORLD WAR II.

After securing the hostages in the first apartment the terrorists began their search for more hostages. Inexplicably walking past apartment 2, which housed five athletes including Shaul Ladany, a race walker who had survived the horrors of the Bergen-Belsen concentration camp, they moved on to apartment 3, cocked their weapons and burst in.

FURTHER HOSTAGES—AND AN ESCAPE

Inside apartment 3 were the weightlifters David Berger, Zeev Friedman, Eliezer Halfin, Yossef Romano, Gad Tsabari and the most gifted and youngest member of the team, eighteen-year-old Mark Slavin, who in 1972 prior to emigrating to Israel had become the top middleweight Greco-Roman wrestler in the Soviet Union. Some had been woken by the gunshot that had

Dramatic images of the siege were broadcast around the world as the hostage crisis was played out.

injured Weinberg but had failed to recognize the sound for what it was. As the group was being led back to apartment 1, Tsabari, with no way of knowing whether he would be murdered or simply be used as a bargaining chip in a political negotiation, made a bold bid for freedom. As the group passed a stairway that led down to an underground parking lot, Tsabari shoved aside one of the masked gunmen and threw himself down the stairs. With a terrorist in hot pursuit, the pillars and support columns of the car park provided Tsabari with the cover he needed to make good his escape. Attempting to take advantage of the melee, Weinberg also tried to break free, but was not as fortunate. Despite disarming one of his captors Weinberg was killed in the ensuing scuffle. As the hostages were being taken into apartment 1, Yossef Romano, a Libyan-born weightlifter and hero of the 1967 Six Day War, was killed as he too attempted to disarm one of the terrorists.

At 5:08 a.m. two sheets of paper were thrown from the apartment's second-storey balcony. They listed the names of 234 prisoners who were incarcerated in Israeli gaols. The terrorists demanded that they be released by 9 a.m.—a hopelessly unrealistic demand—and warned that if this were not done they would begin to execute their hostages at the rate of one every hour and throw the bodies into the street for the world to see.

The Israeli delegation parades during the opening ceremony on August 26, eleven days before the attack.

WEST GERMANY'S RESPONSE TO THE CRISIS

The immediate West German response was to gather together a crisis team comprising the interior minister Hans-Dietrich Genscher, his Bavarian counterpart Bruno Merk and Munich chief of Police Manfred Schreiber. Together they struggled to formulate a response. Schreiber offered the terrorists an exorbitant amount of money. Genscher pleaded with them not to cause the spilling of yet more Jewish blood on German soil and even offered himself in return for the hostages' release. Hopes of sending in police disguised as chefs were abandoned when the terrorists ordered all deliveries of food and supplies to be dropped at the entrance to the building's foyer.

NEGOTIATIONS FAIL

At 8:45 a.m. the mayor of the Olympic Village, Walther Troga, Schreiber and an Egyptian International Olympic Committee (IOC) official were allowed into apartment 1 to discuss the details of the terrorists' demands and to meet the hostages. As they approached the apartment block the archetypal image of the kidnappings, the image of a terrorist on the second floor balcony with a balaclava over his head to hide his identity, was flashed around the world. Schreiber remembered being incensed that the man had pointed a machine gun directly at him. "Towards me! The Munich Police Chief!" he later recounted indignantly. Once the German officials were inside, it quickly became apparent there would be no negotiating the hostages' safe release. Issa kept repeating his demands "in a staccato-like fashion," Schreiber later recalled. "He sounded like one of those people who aren't completely anchored in reality or totally aware."

Plans to infiltrate via the heating ducts were also abandoned when it was realized television cameras were broadcasting police attempts to enter the building's air-conditioning system live to the entire world—including the television sets being watched closely by the athletes' captors. As negotiations progressed the initial 9 a.m. deadline was extended, first to 3 p.m. and then to 5 p.m., when the terrorists issued a fresh demand to be flown with their hostages to Cairo, where they believed the chances of negotiating a release of the 234 prisoners in Israel would have a greater chance of success. Issa issued his demands to the German negotiators: they were all to be taken to an airport and transferred onto a waiting plane; he expected the freed prisoners in Israel to be on the runway at Cairo airport by 8 a.m. the following morning; and, if the prisoners were not delivered, all the hostages would be executed.

Adding to the tension, no one in the German government, including Chancellor Willy Brandt, was able to get Egyptian president Anwar Sadat to answer the phone and discuss the possibility of Egypt providing a more optimistic haven for the negotiations. Eventually Brandt got through to Egyptian prime minister Aziz Sidky, but he failed to provide Brandt with a promise that if the hostages were flown to Cairo they would not be harmed. In the absence of a guarantee of the hostages' safety, Brandt felt unable to permit them to be taken off German soil. The mood of the negotiators in Munich had become one of total despair. For better or worse, it seemed, the drama was destined to unfold before their eyes in the Bavarian capital. The negotiators were reluctantly forced to take the view that the only possible alternative to a bloodbath was to allow the kidnappers to believe a plane had been prepared for them, and hope that an opportunity to act would somehow surface.

At 10:10 p.m. a bus pulled up at the doors of the apartment complex and took the terrorists and their hostages to two waiting Iroquois helicopters, thus depriving the German sharpshooters the chance of any clear shots. German authorities in a third helicopter preceded the two Iroquois to the NATO airbase at Fürstenfeldbruck. Meanwhile, in the back of the aircraft waiting for the terrorists at the airfield, a so-called strike force was concealed. Incredibly, they had just taken a vote to abandon the mission—and had failed to consult or inform their superior officers about this extraordinary action. As a legacy of World War II, Germany had no special forces units trained to handle such a situation and the lack of professionalism would eventually doom the hostages. All that now threatened the terrorists at Fürstenfeldbruck were two Bavarian riot police and three Munich police officers (none of them sharpshooters) positioned on the roofs of the airport buildings, and chosen simply because they belonged to clubs that shot competitively on weekends.

SIEGE ENDS AT FÜRSTENFELDBRUCK AIRFIELD

At 10:35 p.m. the two helicopters arrived at Fürstenfeldbruck and their pilots emerged, accompanied by six kidnappers. Issa immediately inspected the waiting jet. On discovering that the plane was crewless and realizing he had been deceived, Issa ran back to the helicopters and ordered their pilots be held at gunpoint. At 11 p.m. the German snipers opened fire, killing two terrorists. The German pilots escaped to safety in the confusion, but policeman Anton Fliegerbauer, stationed in the airport's control tower, was hit and killed. When a number of armored personnel carriers arrived just after midnight, Issa seemed to have realized his time was up and murdered Friedman, Springer and Halfin. He then threw a grenade into one of the helicopters, which exploded and incinerated all those inside. Although events at this point are somewhat blurry, the consensus is that another kidnapper, Adnan Al-Gashey, killed the remaining five hostages in the second helicopter. None survived.

Three hostages were arrested on the tarmac, all of them feigning death, while a fourth was cornered in a nearby parking lot and shot dead by police.

Abu Daoud, the mastermind behind the massacre, avoided all Israeli attempts to kill him and lives today in Syria. He published his autobiography, Palestine: From Jerusalem to Munich, in 1999. 🕊

1974
THE WATERGATE SCANDAL

Richard Milhous Nixon entered public life in America as a congressman from California in 1946, before being elected to the Senate in 1950. Chosen as Dwight D. Eisenhower's running mate in 1952, he served as the nation's vice president under Eisenhower for two terms before becoming his party's choice to face the Democratic senator from Massachusetts, John F. Kennedy, in the 1960 presidential election. Defeated by Kennedy in the closest result in U.S. history, Nixon continued to fight for Republican causes and candidates in the years that followed, including the disastrous and always doomed Goldwater campaign of 1964, travelling across America and speaking at countless Republican rallies and fundraisers. In 1968 he was given his party's endorsement as their presidential candidate in the upcoming November elections and defeated his Democratic opponent Hubert Humphrey by just 500,000 votes. On January 20, 1969 he was sworn in as the nation's thirty-seventh president.

Richard Nixon spent his entire adult life making speeches, and in the process gave Americans some of the most memorable moments in postwar politics. No speech, however, could compare to the one he gave on August 9, 1974, his last day in office, his presidency having been consumed and eventually destroyed by the Watergate scandal—many of his former aides were in jail, and his own reputation was in tatters.

ONE FINAL, MEMORABLE SPEECH

On his final morning in office, Richard Nixon spoke for the last time as president to his cabinet and the assembled White House staff. He said how he wished he'd been by their offices a little more, to ask them about their work, to shake their hands and ask their advice on "how to run the world." He just didn't have the time, he said. Sniffling continually, Nixon fought his emotions as his wife Pat and daughters Trisha and Julie looked on, realizing their husband and father was at last speaking from the heart after a lifetime of rhetoric and debates, letting America see him as he really was. He spoke of how no one in his administration, not one man or one woman, profited as a result of being there. "Not one single man or woman," he said. His mannerisms were different. The political colossus of America's postwar years seemed close to tears.

He spoke of his father's lemon ranch with affection and a rare dose of comic timing. "It was the poorest lemon ranch in California I can assure you. [Pause.] He sold it before they found oil on it." The room was engulfed in laughter. His voice broke as he spoke of his mother, whom he called "a saint," losing two sons to tuberculosis, and with a halting voice said what a tragedy it was that she would likely have no books written about her. After a lifetime of not allowing the world to see the man beneath the politician, and in the wake of his resignation speech to the nation the previous evening, Nixon was finally baring his soul. Grown men in the audience were crying. Nixon had saved the greatest speech by an American political figure in the twentieth century for his final hours as president, speaking for over twenty minutes without notes. "Always give your best.

A humble President Nixon gives his farewell speech to White House staff on August 9, 1974.

Never get discouraged. Never be petty. Always remember: others may hate you, but those who hate you don't win unless you hate them, and then … you destroy yourself."

Richard Nixon was the most complex, contradictory and paradoxical man ever to occupy the White House. Was this speech, as eloquent and moving as it was, an insight into the real man, or was it—as the former White House aide, author and speechwriter William Safire once said—just one last, final expression of a man with more layers than a layer cake, an enigma that defied explanation?

NIXON'S 1972 LANDSLIDE WIN

In the 1972 presidential election the incumbent Richard Milhous Nixon defeated the Democratic challenger George McGovern in a landslide. Nixon received 18 million more votes than the senator from South Dakota, won forty-nine out of fifty states, and his victory margin of more than 23 per cent was the fourth highest in U.S. history. Almost from the moment McGovern announced his candidacy there was never any real doubt who would win. Nixon had wrestled with how best to extricate the United States from the mess that was Vietnam, had established a relationship with the People's Republic of China, and his administration was presiding over a healthy economy.

President Nixon in happier times—campaigning for a second term in the 1972 election that he won in a landslide.

The irony of what would become known as Watergate is that if ever a president didn't need to covertly acquire information on his opponents and engage in political dirty tricks in order to win an election, he was the one. Nixon was always going to win in a landslide.

On June 17, 1972 five men were arrested breaking into the offices of the Democratic National Committee in the Watergate hotel and office complex in Washington, DC. The story was broken by two Washington Post reporters, Carl Bernstein and Bob Woodward, and the trail of laundered money, wiretapping, corruption and various abuses of power led first to the Committee to Re-Elect the President (CREEP), and eventually all the way to the White House itself.

The suspicions of the Post reporters were further raised in August when a cashier's cheque for $25,000 ended up in the bank account of one of the Watergate burglars, Bernard Barker. Then, in September, they broke the story that the former U.S. attorney-general, John Mitchell, now Nixon's campaign manager, had been in control of a Republican slush fund that saw money appropriated for intelligence gathering operations.

Mitchell vehemently refuted the claim. "That's the most sickening thing I've ever heard," he was quoted as saying.

CONSPIRACY, BURGLARY AND WIRETAPPING

An FBI investigation in October concluded that the break-in was the result of a larger, coordinated campaign of sabotage and excess by the Nixon re-election committee, and in January 1973 two members of the committee, G. Gordon Liddy and James McCord, were found guilty on eight charges of conspiracy, burglary and wiretapping by Judge John Sirica, Chief Justice for the U.S. District Court for the District of Columbia. In April, the fallout reached deep into the White House itself when three of Nixon's most senior advisers, H. R. Haldeman, John Ehrlichman and John Dean III, as well as Attorney-General Richard Kleindienst, offered their resignations. Nixon accepted them because, as he said the following day in a live telecast to the nation, "There can be no whitewash at the White House," and promised he would act to purge American politics of the sort of abuses that had occurred on his watch. Nixon appointed his defense secretary Elliott Richardson as attorney-general in place of Kleindienst and gave him specific instructions to uncover "the whole truth" of the scandal that was engulfing his administration. Nixon himself, however, was far more involved in the cover-up than he was prepared to admit.

On May 18, the Senate Watergate Committee, a special committee set up to investigate the burglary and other aspects of the scandal, began a series of nationally televised hearings, but the sort of explosive testimony some were hoping for was slow in coming to the surface. Jules Witcover, a Washington Post staff writer, likened the opening day's proceedings to watching grass grow, a boring ordeal of "snail's pace testimony" and "yawn-inspiring recounting."

THE OVAL OFFICE IS IMPLICATED

On June 3, however, the trail at last led directly into the Oval Office when John Dean, Nixon's former special adviser, acknowledged to prosecutors and Senate investigators that the President had discussed aspects of the Watergate cover-up with him on at least thirty-five occasions between January and April, and agreed to testify at upcoming Senate hearings, regardless of whether or not he would be granted immunity from prosecution. In another damning Washington Post exposé, Woodward and Bernstein quoted reliable sources as saying Dean had confessed to investigators that Haldeman and Ehrlichman had both been present in the Oval Office with

PEOPLE HAVE GOT TO KNOW WHETHER OR NOT THEIR PRESIDENT IS A CROOK. WELL, I'M NOT A CROOK. I'VE EARNED EVERYTHING I'VE GOT.

Nixon when details of the cover-up were discussed. Then on July 17 it was revealed Nixon had been secretly tape-recording his conversations in the Oval Office, Cabinet room and the Executive Office Building since the spring of 1971, and that a telephone in the Lincoln sitting room in the White House and another on the presidential desk at his retreat at Camp David, Maryland, had also been modified.

Although much was made of Nixon's clandestine wiretapping, the practice was hardly new to Washington. Wiretapping began with Roosevelt in 1940 and every president since has made use of it. Truman endorsed wiretaps in matters of domestic security and presidents Kennedy and Johnson authorized wiretaps on Martin Luther King Junior. Nixon's conversations, however, would later prove to be damning indictments of his involvement in the cover-up. On July 18 he reportedly ordered the system to be disconnected, and on July 23 he refused requests to turn the tapes over to the Senate Watergate Committee.

The so-called Saturday Night Massacre of October 20 represented the most traumatic and far-reaching development in the crisis to date. Nixon discharged special prosecutor Archibald Cox (the former Harvard lawyer who had been appointed special prosecutor by Attorney-General Elliot Richardson to investigate the alleged Watergate cover-up), and on the same day accepted the resignations of Attorney-General Richardson and his deputy, William Ruckelshaus, after they refused his order to fire Cox. With the demise of the office of special prosecutor, all investigations and prosecution of suspects became the responsibility of the Justice Department. The crisis had been precipitated by a directive from Nixon to Cox not to request any further tapes beyond those Nixon had already agreed to provide. Cox replied he was unable to comply with the president's request, and Nixon, after failing in his attempts to get Richardson and Ruckelshaus to sack Cox, exercised his own executive authority and promptly discharged him. Late that night Cox issued a statement which read in part: "Whether ours shall continue to be a government of laws and not of men is now for Congress and ultimately the American people."

NIXON MEETS THE PRESS

The noose was tightening around the president. On November 17, in the face of persistent questioning over his personal finances, Nixon was compelled to go on television in an hour-long question-and-answer forum with hundreds of journalists and editors from the Associated Press, during which he said: "People have got to know whether or not their President is a crook. Well, I'm not a crook. I've earned everything I've got." When asked what occupation he might pursue when he left office, after joking that that would depend upon when he left, Nixon replied that he would like to write or perhaps return to practising law. He ended the discussion claiming the White House tapes would exonerate him of any prior knowledge regarding the July 1972 break-in at the Watergate complex. In defending his personal finances he said while it was true that he paid only a nominal amount of tax in 1970–71, it was also true that he was the first occupant of the Oval Office since Harry Truman who didn't own any stock, having divested himself of his holdings in 1968. "I made my mistakes, but in all of my years of public life I have never profited from public service."

On April 30, 1974 the Nixon White House handed over more than 1200 pages of edited transcripts of the tapes, in two halves, to the House Judiciary Committee, a standing committee within the U.S. House of Representatives whose duty it is to oversee the administration of justice in federal courts, transcripts which the White House claimed would offer proof that the president had not engaged in any criminal plots to obstruct justice. The White House PR machine went into overdrive, telephoning editors and others in the press to "convince them" that the transcripts absolved Nixon of any wrongdoing. The second half of the transcripts were damning, with Nixon clearly discussing topics such as blackmail payments, abusing the "national security" option in the defence of White House staff called to testify before the House Judiciary Committee, and the recording of continual references to the laundering of money. An extract from a March 21, 1973 meeting between Nixon and John Dean left little room for interpretation when Nixon said, in response to the likelihood of raising $1 million in "hush money": "We could get that. On the money, if you need the money you could get that. You could get a million dollars. You could get it in cash. I know where it could be gotten."

In July, Cox's replacement as special prosecutor, Leon Jaworski, no longer content with the White House–sanctioned transcripts and having unsuccessfully tried to subpoena the tapes, approached the Supreme Court to bypass the Court of Appeals (to which Nixon had gone in his attempts to deny Jaworski access to the tapes). Supreme Court Chief Justice Warren E. Burger, reading from a thirty-one-page document that reflected a unanimous 8–0 ruling, deemed that Jaworski as Special Prosecutor had the right to sue the President and ordered Nixon to hand over sixty-four tapes "forthwith." He rejected the president's claims of executive privilege. Nixon handed over the tapes, which included the infamous "smoking gun" tape that led to the erosion of the last vestiges of support for Nixon in Congress. Over the next several days the House Judiciary Committee passed three articles of impeachment (sets of charges drafted against public official) on the charges of obstruction of justice, misuse of powers, failure to adequately respond to House Judiciary Committee subpoenas and violating the presidential oath of office. Nixon, realizing he could no longer stave off impeachment, resigned the office of president on August 8, 1974.

A HISTORIC LETTER OF RESIGNATION

Nixon's letter of resignation was typed on a single sheet of White House stationery and was addressed to Secretary of State Henry Kissinger, the man who, together with Nixon, had engineered some of the greatest foreign policy triumphs in American history, triumphs few American politicians possessed either the instincts or the daring to even attempt.

Dear Mr. Secretary:

I hereby resign the Office of President of the United States.

Sincerely,

The Honorable Henry A. Kissinger
The Secretary of State
Washington, D.C. 20520

AFTERMATH

Watergate had many victims, but none more so perhaps than Nixon himself. After his record-breaking election victory in 1972 he seemed to have garnered the will of the people, his Silent Majority, and was looking at a second term full of challenges and opportunities to grow in stature, to mend old political fences, perhaps achieve a rapprochement with the nation's press, which he always felt had unfairly maligned him, and to become the statesman that seemed so befitting the man. Instead he allowed his own foibles, insecurities, decades of accumulated political baggage, and his need to vanquish enemies, both real and imagined, to rouse his inner demons and blur his judgement. For those who supported him to the end, how they must have wished that the humanity, grace and eloquence that he displayed as he haltingly bade farewell to his White House Staff on August 9 had been perceived as strength rather than weakness and not been kept hidden from the American people.

On September 8, new president Gerald Ford granted Richard Nixon a 'full, free, and absolute pardon', thus bringing to an end any possibility of indicting the former president over his involvement in the Watergate affair. . ❧

1986
THE CHERNOBYL NUCLEAR DISASTER

In the 1980s it would have been difficult to imagine the citizens of any nation in the world, nuclear or not, being quite as enthusiastic and at ease at the prospect of living alongside nuclear reactors as the citizens of the Soviet Union. Ever since the U.S.S.R.'s first reactor came on line in 1954 at Obninsk, 66 miles southwest of Moscow, the Soviet government and its scientists had been assuring the people of the safety and unlimited benefits of the "peaceful atom" that was nuclear energy. Concerns raised about the dangers and environmental impact of nuclear power plants were deemed to be attacks on science itself, and government and academic assurances that the industry was all but accident proof went largely unchallenged for more than thirty years.

The magazine Ogonyok, which first went to press in Russia in 1899, was for generations at the very center of Moscow's intellectual and literary life. In 1980 Ogonyok carried a story by the academic M. A. Styrikovich that was typical of the over-simplified and condescending approach the nuclear industry had towards the public it was meant to be serving. "Nuclear power stations," he wrote, "are like stars that shine all day long … they are perfectly safe." Styrikovich likened nuclear reactors to steam engines, and characterized the technicians who ran them as little more than stokers. It was an outrageous comparison, but by simplifying the technology in the eyes of the public it not only helped lessen concerns over the technology, but also meant the government could pay nuclear technicians much the same as they paid employees at a steam-fired thermal power station.

EARLY NUCLEAR ACCIDENTS

The disaster that would soon unfold at Chernobyl was without a doubt the world's worst nuclear accident, but it was by no means the first. The accidental removal of control rods at the Chalk River reactor near Ottawa in Canada in 1952 resulted in a partial meltdown of its uranium fuel core. In 1957 a fire in the reactor of Windscale Pile 1 (north of Liverpool, England) led to the contamination of more than 200 square miles of the surrounding countryside, and the sale of milk products from cows in the fallout zone was banned for a month. At the Three Mile Island plant in Harrisburg, Pennsylvania, in April 1979, a sudden loss of coolant in two of the reactors caused radioactive fuel to overheat, resulting in a partial core meltdown and the release of radioactive material into the atmosphere. In the face of these highly publicized incidents in the West it must have seemed, in comparison, as though the Soviet nuclear program was after all the clean, cheap, incident-free operation its government had always said it was. In reality, of course, the Soviet nuclear program was an accident waiting to happen.

In September 1957, at a nuclear power plant at Chelyabinsk, a city to the east of the Ural Mountains on the Miass River, a chain reaction in some spent fuel rods resulted in a large amount of radioactive material being released into the atmosphere. The residents of Chelyabinsk were evacuated and a barbed wire fence was erected around the exclusion zone. In 1966 there was a power surge at a reactor in Melekess (now Dimitrovgrad). In October 1975 a partial core meltdown at a nuclear power station outside Leningrad resulted in the temporary closure of the reactor and, in 1977, a meltdown of fuel assemblies at the Byeloyarsk power

plant in Sverdlovsk Oblast irradiated the plant's staff. Though the irradiation levels were low and nobody died, the meltdown resulted in repairs having to be made to the reactor that took more than a year to complete.

Unlike Canada, Great Britain and the United States, the Soviet Union had little trouble in keeping its nuclear misadventures well hidden from the prying eyes of the world's media. The time was coming, however, when the accident to end all nuclear accidents would, by its sheer scale, force its disclosure to the world. Even so, at 1:23 a.m. on April 26, 1986, when Chernobyl's No. 4 reactor exploded and started a chain reaction that released more than thirty times the amount of radiation into the atmosphere than was released by the Hiroshima and Nagasaki atomic bombs combined, the outside world was not informed that a radioactive cloud was spreading across the landscape until two days after the event.

CHERNOBYL'S GENESIS IN THE 1970S

Construction of the Chernobyl plant had begun in the early 1970s and would include a total of four nuclear reactors, each capable of generating 1 gigawatt of electricity. The first reactor was commissioned in 1977, and No. 4 reactor came on line in 1983. At the time of the accident two more reactors were under construction, but in the wake of the explosion were never completed.

Chernobyl is located in northern Ukraine in an area known as the Belorussian–Ukrainian Woodlands. In early 1986, 110,000 people lived within a 18-mile radius of the plant in seventy-six towns and villages. As many as 50,000 of these lived in the town of Pripyat, just over a mile away, with the stacks of the power station easily visible in the distance. Chernobyl was a high power channel-type reactor, or RBMK 1000. RBMK reactors were 1950s technology built around a massive graphite block assemblage known as the "moderator" which slowed the neutrons produced by fission. These "boiling water reactors" used the radioactive steam produced from nuclear fission to power massive turbines. There were, however, many flaws inherent in the RBMK design, chief of which was the absence of the concrete containment structure common to other reactors. Such a structure wrapped around the reactor and would act as a final barrier to the release of any radioactive material in the wake of a core meltdown or other accident.

A helicopter surveys the devastation at the Chernobyl plant on April 26.

THE REACTOR EXPLODED WITH THIRTY TIMES THE AMOUNT OF RADIATION RELEASED BY THE HIROSHIMA AND NAGASAKI ATOMIC BOMBS COMBINED.

On April 25, 1986, Chernobyl's number 4 reactor was shut down in preparation for the testing of an emergency core cooling procedure. In the event of an external power failure that would cut power to the reactor's cooling pumps, it was thought the plant's slowing steam turbines could be harnessed to produce enough electricity for 45 seconds, that is, until the plant's diesel-powered generators could come on line to compensate for the loss of power. Approval for the test came only from the Chernobyl plant director, without consultation with either the reactor's designer or its scientific heads.

At 1:06 a.m. on April 25, technicians began to gradually reduce the power level of the number 4 reactor by inserting control rods into the core of the reactor to control the rate of fission. For the purposes of the test the reactor output should have fallen to between 700 and 1000 megawatts but, due to an oversight by a plant operator who forgot to properly set a controller, the output by 12:30 a.m. on April 26, nearly twenty-four hours later, had fallen to just 30 megawatts. Attempts to increase the reactor's power were hampered by a combination of graphite cooling and xenon poisoning, but by 1:03 a.m. the reactor had been stabilized at about 200 megawatts which, despite being far lower than was considered ideal, was nonetheless thought high enough for the experiment to be continued. The reactor's automatic shutdown system was taken off line to permit the reactor to continue operating under abnormally low conditions.

A MASSIVE STEAM EXPLOSION

In an RBMK reactor, about thirty control rods are required to maintain control of the reactor's temperature, but, on this occasion, most were removed to compensate for the xenon buildup and only six rods were actually used—which led to the reactor becoming extremely unstable. To maintain steam pressure the operators also decided to reduce the feedwater rate. This resultant loss of cooling increased the reactor's instability and led to a massive power surge that ruptured the fuel and hot fuel particles and, at 1:23 a.m., culminated in a steam explosion. The explosion tore apart fuel channels, causing the reactor to suffer a catastrophic water loss. This water loss contributed to a second and far more powerful explosion, the precise cause of which is still a matter for debate, but which many scientists believe could have been a small nuclear explosion caused by the rapid release of neutrons. The explosions were so violent that the foundations of the reactor fell by 13 feet.

Approximately 25 per cent of the graphite blocks from inside the reactor, as well as various pieces of substructure and

core components, were ejected through the reactor's roof—along with radioactive material and smoke that reached more than half a mile into the atmosphere and began to be carried by the prevailing winds in a northwesterly direction. Radiation levels soared dramatically, immediately reaching levels as high as 20,000 roentgen per hour. With a lethal dose calculated at around 500 roentgen over a five-hour period of exposure, it took only a few minutes for any unprotected workers in the reactor to receive a fatal dose. Radiation dosimeters, devices used to measure exposure to ionizing radiation, were either unavailable or lacked the capacity to read anything over 0.01 roentgen. They would simply have been interpreted as being off the scale—though no one could have possibly imagined the levels of contamination that were now invisibly swirling about them as more than 180 tons of irradiated fuel was being released into the atmosphere.

More than a hundred firefighters from Chernobyl and Pripyat attended the fire, with the first arriving within five minutes, and it was this group that suffered the greatest degree of exposure and the highest casualties. The first firefighters to arrive were not even warned that the smoke and debris were radioactive. None of them had any idea what graphite was, and several later commented how they picked up chunks of graphite that had been ejected form the reactor off the ground.

Liquidators, wearing suits that offer no protection against radiation, set up "No Entry" signs in the no-go zone.

There were not only fires in and around number 4 reactor itself but also on the roof of the adjacent turbine hall, and various spot fires were burning in fuel storage areas and other areas throughout the plant. These external and conventional fires were mostly under control by 5 a.m., but the graphite fire in the reactor itself was another matter. It continued burning until May 10.

In excess of 5000 tons of sand, clay, lead and boron to absorb neutrons were dropped into the reactor by more than eighteen hundred helicopter sorties in an effort to extinguish the fire and prevent any further contamination. An unintended side effect, however, was that much of the material failed to be deposited on its intended target. In fact, it may have provided an insulative effect that a week after the event led to an increase in the fire's temperature and another sudden, though isolated, discharge of radionuclides (atoms with an unstable nucleus) into the atmosphere.

The following announcement was aired on Pripyat local radio in the hours preceding the town's evacuation. The wording was deliberately vague and intended to convey the impression that the "accident" and any after-effects were confined to the plant and posed no immediate threat.

An accident has occurred at the Chernobyl Nuclear Power Plant. One of the atomic reactors has been damaged. Aid will be given to those affected and a committee of government enquiry has been set up.

THE WORLD'S FIRST RADIOACTIVE HIGHWAY

The town of Pripyat had been built to house the families of those who worked at Chernobyl. Within two days the entire population of 50,000 was evacuated in 1100 buses, a massive column that stretched for more than 12 miles along the Pripyat–Chernobyl road. What nobody paused to consider as the convoy took the residents of Pripyat away forever, effectively turning their home into a ghost town, was that the vehicles' tyres were picking up radioactive material from the road and were about to transform the Pripyat–Chernobyl road into the world's first radioactive highway.

Seven days after the evacuation of Pripyat, Chernobyl was abandoned. A 19-mile exclusion zone known as the Zone of Alienation was established, and remains in force to this day. In the absence of human activity, populations of wild boar, deer, wolves and the rare lynx have exploded in recent years in what has become a people-free enclave, save for the few hundred mostly elderly residents who either refused to be relocated or moved back to their homes in the months that followed. In 2009 the population inside the Zone of Alienation was estimated to be between 350 and 400.

WIDESPREAD CONTAMINATION

As the radioactive cloud made its way across Europe, governments urged their citizens to remain indoors. In the German state of North Rhine–Westphalia, parents were told to stop their children from playing in sandpits. The London Festival Ballet voted to cancel an upcoming tour of the Soviet Union. It took just four days for the cloud to reach Monaco and the French Riviera.

In the 2006 Torch Report, an independent report commissioned by the European Greens, it was found that those parts of Europe most contaminated were Belarus (twenty-two per cent of its total land area) and Austria (thirteen per cent). High levels of radiation were also found in Finland, Sweden and Ukraine. Lower levels of contamination fell across eighty per cent of Moldovia, Slovenia, the Slovak Republic and Switzerland.

THE AFTERMATH

The hasty construction of a ferroconcrete shelter around number 4 reactor was begun almost immediately in an attempt to prevent further contamination. Also known as the "sarcophagus" it was completed on November 19, 1986 and, out of necessity, was constructed in part using remote control methods, which immediately led to questions over its structural integrity. There was a massive amount of hardware and fuel to contain: 10,000 tons of irradiated metal, 10 tons of radioactive dust, core fragments, more than 180 tons of fuel, and 4400–5500 gallons of contaminated water in the basement of the reactor. Not all of its seams were properly sealed, however, and its exterior walls are already showing signs of cracking. A new Safe Confinement Structure, made possible with funds from the European Bank for Reconstruction and Development and the Chernobyl Shelter Fund, is scheduled for completion in 2012, and ongoing work inside the original sarcophagus has stabilized its rate of decay.

The region's rivers and lakes were made bitter with radioactive fallout. Across the western Soviet Union rain became contaminated as it fell through the radioactive cloud, and sediments became so thick at the bottom of the Pripyat River by 1988 that the sludge was officially classified as radioactive waste. It took a decade for the swift-flowing currents in those rivers within the exclusion zone to disperse their waste and be declared clean.

More than four hundred and forty employees were present at Chernobyl at the time of the explosion and, of those, three hundred were admitted to hospital. One hundred and thirty-four were diagnosed with Acute Radiation Syndrome (ARS) consistent with exposure to iodine-131, cesium-134 and various plutonium isotopes, and twenty-eight died of their injuries. In the absence of a universally accepted methodology to calculate the final, continuing number of deaths, estimates range from a United Nations figure of between four thousand and nine thousand to a Greenpeace study that suggest the final toll could be as high as ninety-three thousand.

1989
THE TIANANMEN SQUARE INCIDENT

Tiananmen Square lies in the geographical center of Beijing and is the largest city square in the world. Its 526,000 square yards can accommodate in excess of one million people. It was on the rostrum of the Tiananmen Gate (Gate of Heavenly Peace) on the square's northern perimeter that Mao Zedong declared the establishment of the People's Republic of China on October 1, 1949. There are few places in modern China that possess greater cultural and social significance.

DEATH OF A REFORMER

Beginning in 1978, a new era of economic and political reforms was initiated throughout China by Premier Deng Xiaoping, the ageing comrade of Chairman Mao and a hero of the Long March. The economic reforms proved popular among China's peasants who saw increases in real wages and demonstrable improvements in their day-to-day lives. Political reform, however, was proving more elusive, and the intelligentsia and student organizations in the country's large cities were becoming increasingly impatient for change. When the progressive political reformer Hu Yaobang, the Communist Party's sixth general secretary, died of a heart attack on April 15, 1989 many viewed his death as extinguishing the last hopes for real democratic reform. Hu's funeral was to take place in Tiananmen Square on April 22, and fifty thousand students planned to participate, using the occasion to deliver a petition to Premier Li Peng critical of the Party's veiled disapproval of Hu's support of both freedom of speech and freedom of the press. The Party saw Hu as uncomfortably close to the nation's "bourgeois liberals" and left-leaning middle-class intelligentsia. Hu had been forced by Party hardliners to resign his position as general secretary in January 1987, and compelled to write a humiliating letter of "self-criticism" of his reformist principles.

Hu's funeral arrangements, along with official government pronouncements of his importance in helping shape modern China, seemed to many to be a little subdued. He had after all fought to rehabilitate those who had suffered under the communists during the Cultural Revolution, and was a supporter of greater autonomy for Tibet, from which he once ordered the withdrawal of thousands of Chinese soldiers and ordered those who remained to learn the Tibetan language. Although Hu's official death announcement contained all the usual communist rhetoric, such as saying he had been a "staunch communist warrior" and a "proletarian revolutionist," he was also said to have made unspecified "mistakes."

On the eve of the funeral, in excess of a million people had gathered in Tiananmen Square and its approaches. The events that were to follow, known within China as the June Fourth Movement, would be the culmination of a protest movement that first began in earnest in December 1986. Students began to take advantage of the first loosening of political control to ask for the right to study abroad as well as greater accessibility to Western culture and influences. Speeches against the slow pace of reform were suddenly being made across the country by leading figures such as Professor Fang Lizhi of the Univer-

A sea of student protesters gather in Tiananmen Square on May 4.

sity of Science and Technology in Anhui Province, one of the founders of the pro-democracy movement who had been expelled from the Communist Party in 1987. Fang and his wife took refuge in the U.S. embassy in Beijing on June 5, 1989 and remained there for more than a year before fleeing to England and then on to the United States.

MASSACRE—OR PROTEST?

"The Tiananmen Square Massacre" has become one of those phrases that has entered the world's lexicon and refuses to go away, despite the historical fact that although there were undeniably protesters killed in the square on June 4 and 5, video footage of the melee shows little actual fighting. CBS news correspondent Richard Roth, who was standing on the south portico of the Great Hall of the People that constitutes one of the square's boundaries, was driven in a jeep through the square together with another journalist, Derek Willis, just 40 minutes after they had both heard the sound of gunfire. But they saw no bodies, no injured students or soldiers, and no ambulances. Live on air later that day with the celebrated news anchor Dan Rather of CBS, Roth stuck to his story and referred to the violence that he had witnessed in the square as an "assault" rather than a massacre. Roth, of course, spoke only of what he himself

Tank Man blocks the path of a military convoy along the Avenue of Eternal Peace near Tiananmen Square.

had seen, and had no first-hand knowledge of the violence that had occurred throughout the city. Historians have long shied away from the term Tiananmen Square Massacre and now speak instead of a broader Beijing Massacre.

So what exactly did happen in the Chinese capital on June 4 and 5, 1989?

Although portrayed in the Western media as largely a student movement, the demonstrations that began on April 27 touched a nerve with the Chinese populace. In cities across China millions began to appear in their streets in open revolt. They were elderly people, children, labourers, people representing every level of society, who took their lead from the students and dared to show dissent. It was almost a "carnival" of protest. Large-scale protests that erupted in Guangzhou, Hong Kong and Shanghai included doctors, nurses, scientists—even elements of the Chinese navy were protesting. The Chinese press was reporting events freely and relatively unhindered, and hundreds of thousands of protesters were converging on the capital. What had begun as a student protest was evolving into a country-wide phenomenon.

On May 4, one hundred thousand protesters converged on Beijing to march in support of freedom of the press and to open a dialogue between their own elected representatives and the government. The government rejected their overtures, claiming it would speak only to the leaders of recognized, pre-existing student organizations. On May 13, just two days before a state visit by the architect of the Soviet Union's own period of openness and reform, Mikhail Gorbachev, the students decided that in order to maintain the momentum they had generated so far, they would initiate a hunger strike. Initially involving just hundreds, the hunger strike soon took on a life of its own. Protesters from regional cities flocked to Tiananmen Square to join it. The protesters were for the most part peaceful, even cooperative with the soldiers and authorities who were monitoring them. When three students threw ink over the portrait of Chairman Mao that overlooks the square, students assisted police in arresting them.

THE STUDENTS MEET WITH PREMIER LI PENG

It was a time of unprecedented freedoms in which confrontations between the communist leadership and ordinary citizens that would have been considered unthinkable just days earlier were played out on television screens across the nation. On May 18, the Chinese media televised a meeting between Premier Li Peng and two of the student movement's most prominent advocates, Wu'er Kaixi and Wang Dan. Wang was a history student at Peking University, one of the birthplaces of the student movement. Wu'er, an ethnic Uyghur and student of Beijing Normal University, interrupted the premier in the midst of his opening remarks and promptly made history: "I understand it is quite rude of me to interrupt you, Premier, but there are people sitting out there in the square, being hungry, as we sit here and exchange pleasantries."

Li broke in to accuse Wu'er of being impolite, but Wu'er realized he must seize the moment and speak not only his own mind, but also on behalf of all those in China who were seeking freedom: "Sir, you said you are here late, but we've actually been calling you to talk to us since April 22. It's not that you are late, it's that you're here too late. But that's fine. It's good that you are able to come here at all ..."

At 5 a.m. on May 19, without warning, the general secretary of the Communist Party, Zhao Ziyang appeared among the students in Tiananmen Square and delivered a speech that had not been sanctioned by the Party leadership. Zhao asked the students to end their hunger strike and their protest

ESTIMATES OF THE NUMBER OF DEAD AND INJURED WILL FOREVER BE DEBATED AS THE CHINESE GOVERNMENT NEVER MADE PUBLIC ITS RECORD OF THE INCIDENT.

before the Party's patience ran out. He promised them that the leadership would continue to discuss their grievances and said that it was wrong for them to put their young lives in jeopardy over issues that he believed could be settled in time through negotiation. It was an extraordinarily conciliatory speech, but the students did not abandon their protest. The following day Zhao was stripped of his position and placed under house arrest. His motivations for pursuing such a unilateral act in defiance of his party have remained a subject of debate ever since.

MARTIAL LAW

On May 20, the day after Zhao's speech, Premier Li Peng imposed martial law across Beijing. Three hundred thousand troops were ordered to occupy Tiananmen Square, but as the armored personnel carriers and trucks laden with troops moved into the city they found their way forward blocked by hundreds of thousands of protesters. Columns of army transports filled with troops were mobbed by citizens demanding to know why they were entering their city. "Brother soldiers, you should be defenders of the people!" one elderly woman cried out to a group of seated soldiers. After four days of this impasse, enduring an unprecedented loss of face in the process, the army withdrew to bases outside the city. The protesters had won a memorable triumph. The authorities, however, had not only lost face but were beginning to wonder how long it would be until they lost control—and were determined that such a humiliating event, in full view of the world's media, would not happen again.

Meanwhile the demonstrations continued to spread. Three hundred thousand people thronged Hong Kong's famous Happy Valley Racecourse on May 27 to sing democratic songs of encouragement for the Beijing protesters, and the following day a rally involving 1.5 million people, representing twenty-five per cent of the territory's population marched through its streets.

On June 1, troops from the 27th and 28th Armies were despatched from their barracks outside Beijing and ordered into the city, this time with orders to clear the square by dawn on June 4. In the western suburbs of the capital, every time the troops broke through a blockade, the protesters would fall back and form another blockade further down the street. But inexorably the armed forces—the People's Liberation Army (PLA)—forced their way through blockade after blockade, making their way toward Tiananmen Square.

THE MILITARY FIRE ON DEMONSTRATORS

On the night of June 3, the troops entered the city proper from the surrounding provinces. In response, protesters barricaded the streets leading to the square with buses, trucks and earth-moving equipment. In comparison, the atmosphere in Tiananmen Square itself seemed almost surreal. It was a scene of relative peace on the evening of June 3 compared with the carnage unfolding in the surrounding streets, a place of order and calm in the midst of a gathering cyclone. At around 9:30 p.m. armored personnel carriers began to ram and break through the barricades, and the populace could not believe that the PLA was firing live ammunition upon the very people it was meant to defend. Beijing's citizens were shocked, looking down from their balconies onto troops using battlefield weapons against ordinary men, women and children. Away from the square, in the streets of the capital, people were being shot. Large numbers of casualties were ferried to local hospitals on bicycles, on carts, on anything that moved. Western journalists were being begged to take photos and to film what was happening, and to show the images to the world.

At 5:40 a.m. on June 4, armored personnel carriers and soldiers with bayonets fixed entered Tiananmen Square en masse; several incidents of indiscriminate fire were reported by Western journalists and other eyewitnesses. Some students took refuge in buses but were pulled from them and set upon. The troops effectively blockaded access to the square, and the protesters made several attempts to enter, only to be shot at. Many were shot in the back as they first rushed and then retreated from the soldiers, who were now under orders to have the square cleared of protesters by 6 a.m. on June 5 (the following morning).

On the morning of June 5, a line of eighteen tanks was making its way from Tiananmen Square along the Avenue of Eternal Peace. An unidentified man suddenly appeared from nowhere, in the full view of the international media. Carrying what looked like shopping bags, he stood defiantly in front of the advancing tanks, forcing them to stop. After several attempts were made by the lead tank to go around the man, the engine was turned off. Those behind it did the same. Tank Man (as he is now known) climbed on top of the lead tank and seemed to yell at its crew to turn around. A soldier emerged and after a brief conversation the man climbed down from the tank but again stood before it. He was eventually taken from the scene by what looked like ordinary civilians concerned for his safety. He has never been located or identified. Four photographers—Jeff Widener of the Associated Press, Stuart Franklin of Magnum Photos, Charlie Cole of *Newsweek* and Arthur Tsang Hin Wah of Reuters—all captured the Tank Man's defiance on film, and the next day the image made headlines across the world. In 1998 *Time* magazine named the man one of the one hundred most important people of the century.

THE PROTESTERS LEAVE THE SQUARE

Inside the square, meanwhile, a debate had broken out between two student factions, one wanting to stay, the other wanting to leave. The soldiers held their fire and offered amnesty if the protesters agreed to vacate the square. Thousands left Tiananmen Square by its southeast corner, singing the "Internationale," the great revolutionary song of workers and communists, and vowing to carry on the fight. A wholesale massacre had been avoided.

Estimates of the number of dead and injured will forever be debated as the Chinese government never made public its record of the incident. The Chinese Red Cross put the figure at 26,000 people killed and more than 30,000 injured, a total that was of course disputed by the government, which put the number killed at 300 with 7000 injured. Perhaps the most accurate assessment comes from the assembled foreign media who witnessed the attacks from a range of differing perspectives and whose estimates were three thousand killed, close enough to the Red Cross estimate as to represent the most plausible outcome.

The student leaders of the rebellion, many of whom were from affluent and well-connected families, largely escaped execution or long-term prison sentences. Wu'er Kaixi escaped to live in Taiwan and Wang Dan was imprisoned but permitted to emigrate to the United States. Others were imprisoned but released after serving relatively short sentences. Chai Ling, one of the leaders in the latter stages of the protest and one of the chief organizers of the hunger strike, escaped to France in 1990 and eventually settled in the United States.

As to what extent the Tiananmen Square protests affected government policy and acted as a catalyst for real change, the answer is: very little. The government continued its repressive policies and, even today, the subject of the student protests of 1989 is a taboo subject in the media. The notion of freedom of speech in China remains elusive. ✜

1989
THE FALL OF THE BERLIN WALL

Most famous walls in history—the Great Wall of China, Hadrian's Wall, the walls of Troy, to name a few—were constructed to keep people out: Mongols, barbarians, Greeks, whoever. However, the purpose of the Berlin Wall, built in 1961, was the exact opposite: to keep people in. Specifically, it was designed to prevent the people living in the eastern half of the German city of Berlin, which, since the Second World War had been part of the Communist German Democratic Republic (GDR), from leaving for the western, democratic, "free" half of the city, then part of West Germany, or the Federal Republic of Germany.

Of course, the powers that be in the GDR at the time would not admit to this and told the world that their only goal had been to build a protective shield against Western espionage agents and other pernicious influences. But the people who lived in East Berlin knew differently—which is why thousands sought a way over or under the wall and why about two hundred died doing so.

In the end, the wall amounted to a propaganda victory for the West and a failure of imagination on the part of the Communist regime for, during the twenty-eight years that it stood, it became symbolic of the fact that a person living in the Eastern Bloc lacked the freedom to move about as he or she chose, a basic tenet of democracy. The wall also severely restricted the East Berlin economy by limiting the free flow of goods and currency, so that while West Berlin boomed, East Berlin stagnated.

The end of the nightmare of the Berlin Wall was a long time in coming, but when it came it was accompanied by one of the most joyous celebrations of freedom the world has ever witnessed.

LIVING IN A DIVIDED CITY

After the end of the Second World War, Berliners got used to living in a divided city. The victorious Allies divided Germany into four zones, one each for the Americans, British, French and Soviets. Although Berlin lay inside the zone belonging to the Soviets, it was also divided into four sectors, so that the victorious powers could govern the country jointly from the capital.

But the beginnings of the Cold War interfered with this setup. In 1948, responding to the reality that they were united against Joseph Stalin and Soviet Russia, the three Western powers merged their German zones into one, creating, in 1949, West Germany. In response, the Soviet zone became East Germany. West Berlin in turn became a part of West Germany, and consequently an island of Western control at the heart of a Communist state.

Berliners made the best of the situation, making shopping trips back and forth, visiting relatives and landmarks, going to theatres. Everyone needed to carry identity cards and the checkpoints were a nuisance, but those who had lived through the Second World War had lived through far, far worse.

THE TRAP IS SPRUNG

At about midnight on Saturday August 12, 1961, the S-Bahn trains travelling from East Berlin to West simply stopped running. West Berliners who happened to be spending the evening in East Berlin were forced, grumbling, to get out and walk. When they reached the checkpoints, they were stopped by East German border guards, and only allowed back into the Western part of the city after their papers had been checked and double-checked. Any East Berliners trying to get over to the West were firmly turned away. East Berliners who happened to be in the West at that point realized that they had to make a daunting decision: they could return—to family and friends—but never cross into the West again; or they could start a new life, alone, and never turn back.

Meanwhile, the generally quiet streets along the West Berlin-East Berlin border filled with troop carriers, armored cars and Soviet tanks. Then trucks arrived, carrying pneumatic drills, barbed wire and concrete posts. In an obviously carefully planned operation, GDR troops began tearing up the pavement just inside the East German border, sinking the posts, stabilizing them with poured concrete and stringing barbed wire between them. The tanks fanned out to block any movement along East–West boulevards, and other streets were ripped up to hinder any possible attacks from the West.

When the people of East Berlin awoke on Sunday August 13, they quickly realized they were completely cut off from the West. No longer could they visit relatives or go shopping in the Western part of the city. No longer could the sixty thousand East Berliners who worked in the West reach their jobs. The "iron curtain," a metaphor that Winston Churchill had famously used in a 1946 speech to describe the division between Communist nations and the West, had become reality.

HOW THE OTHER HALF LIVES

During the 1950s, the citizens of East Berlin, able to view the city's Western half at first hand, had gradually realized that it had a far better standard of living. In fact, in that decade, infused with American aid, West Germany experienced a phoenix-like rise from the ashes of the Second World War. By 1960, West Berlin had built (and publicly celebrated) its one hundred thousandth new apartment; raised luxury hotels; constructed museums, galleries and concert halls; and seen numerous industrial plants—many destroyed during the war—resume production.

In East Berlin and the GDR, in contrast, the economy was stagnant. Basic human needs—food and clothing—were sometimes hard to come by, and the ruins of buildings bombed

by the Allies during the war remained as a stark reminder of the city's failure to advance. Little wonder then that during the 1950s a total of two and a half million East Germans fled to the West, almost half of whom were under the age of twenty-five. One million of these refugees escaped through East Berlin, where there were no walls or barbed wire because the agreement between the four occupying powers specifically prohibited this.

It became clear that if this situation were allowed to continue, not only would East Berlin be almost entirely drained of workers, but also the claim that the GDR was a happy socialist state would be disproved. So Walter Ulbricht, Chairman of the Council of State of the GDR, and his boss in all but name, Soviet Premier Nikita Khrushchev, decided to build themselves a wall.

WORK IN PROGRESS

The Berlin Wall was a work in progress that the GDR sought constantly to perfect. At first, it was just barbed wire. Where houses or apartment buildings lined the boundary, GDR troops (no Russian troops were involved, lest it seem like a Soviet initiative) initially bricked up just the ground floor and windows. But East Berliners jumped across the barrier from upper windows or climbed from them along ropes to the windows of neighboring apartments, so the authorities responded by bricking up entire buildings.

Through the autumn of 1961 and into the early winter, the barbed wire gave way to a concrete-slab wall 13 feet high. Soon this barrier extended for nearly 100 miles, completely encircling West Berlin. (Twenty-eight miles of the wall were directly between East and West Berlin, the rest between West Berlin and East Germany.) Only eight crossing points were left—one specifically for the transfer of deceased persons to relatives in the other half of the city (which were allowed to pass in either direction every Wednesday, after their coffins had been carefully checked), one for the mail, and the rest for foreigners or East Berliners with special passes. One crossing—in the middle of the broad and busy Friederichstrasse—became famous as "Checkpoint Charlie," where spies were exchanged, where East met West with an air of steely tension.

Beneath the Brandenburg Gate, Berliners celebrate the fall of the wall. The Brandenburg Gate was reopened in s 1989.

> EAST BERLINERS WHO HAPPENED TO BE IN THE WEST HAD TO MAKE A DAUNTING DECISION: RETURN—TO FAMILY AND FRIENDS; OR START A NEW LIFE, ALONE, AND NEVER TURN BACK.

RUSH FOR FREEDOM

At first, when the barrier was mere barbed wire and gaps still existed, frantic East Berliners escaped in droves—almost fifty thousand in that first month of August 1961 alone. They slipped through the wire at night, swam across canals, sneaked across the boundary clinging to the undercarriages of cars. But then the local East Berlin GDR guards, some of whom turned a blind eye to such escapes, were replaced by guards from Saxony and other parts of the country, who had no ties to the city. These men, the Volkspolizei or "Vopos," were ordered to shoot escapees on sight. Sixteen had died by the end of the year. Several deaths were witnessed by helpless Western authorities, even the media, and became notorious symbols of the suffering caused by the wall.

Despite the fact that the wall was a violation of the agreement between the Allies, the Western powers weren't willing to confront the Communists over it. There were simply larger issues at stake: the division of Berlin paled in comparison to the space race and the attempts by both sides to control the outcomes of civil wars in various emerging countries. However, the wall did give U.S. presidents, from John F. Kennedy to Ronald Reagan, a perfect symbol of a dictatorial Communist regime.

Over time, the two sides of the wall developed distinctive characters. The Western side was covered with bright graffiti

An East German border guard patrols a checkpoint in Berlin, soon after the construction of the Berlin Wall in 1961.

and became a kind of tourist attraction. In contrast, the Eastern side became a desolate death zone, the wall separated from the adjoining streets by a 100-yard-wide "no-man's-land," every inch of which was covered by Vopos guns. As a result, escape attempts dwindled dramatically.

The only citizens who travelled from East to West on a regular basis were East German pensioners, who were allowed to visit their families in the West and stay as long as they liked. While the GDR presented this as a humanitarian gesture, many people pointed out that every pensioner who stayed in West Berlin was one less the East German government had to pay for.

COMMUNISM RESTRUCTURED

In June of 1985, twenty-four years after the construction of the wall, facing the reality that the Soviet Union had fallen far behind the rest of the world in economic output, Premier Mikhail Gorbachev introduced reforms under the heading of perestroika, or "restructuring." The reforms included the introduction of private ownership of businesses, the expansion of foreign trade, and permitting foreigners to invest in Soviet business ventures.

In turn, the states that made up the Soviet Union loosened their own trade laws, while nationalists in Eastern Bloc nations began clamoring for more freedom and a say in their own government. In 1989, for instance, the first free labour union was founded in Poland. In August of that year, Hungary removed its border restrictions with Austria. Thereafter, for any East German to escape to the West, he or she needed simply to get to Hungary, which was fairly easy.

Yet, even as most observers began to think that a change was soon to come in the long-static situation in Berlin, Erich Honecker, who headed the East German Socialist Party, decried perestroika and promised that nothing of the sort would take place in East Germany. The wall, Honecker said, would last "a hundred years." But Honecker and his other ageing politicians were soon being left behind by a new reality. Gorbachev had heralded a new era of détente, where there would be no need for an armed line between the two Germanys. And no need for a wall.

THE WALL COMES DOWN

In the autumn of 1989, thousands of demonstrators marched the streets of East Berlin—an unheard of sign of independence among the citizenry—demanding "Wir wollen raus," or "We want to leave." Finally, on 18 October, Honecker, lacking support both within and without East Germany, resigned, citing health reasons.

After Honecker's resignation, more and more East Germans streamed to recently liberalized countries such as Hungary and Czechoslovakia, so many that the governments of these countries pleaded with East Germany to do something about the flow of refugees. On November 8, the East German government decided to issue passports to any East German who wanted one; all the citizens had to do was ask.

This decision was announced the next day at a press conference given by the East Berlin Minister of Propaganda, Günter Schabowski. In an almost offhand way, he said that people would now be able to cross between the two Germanys whenever they wanted and not have to go through any other countries. When asked when this would take place, Schabowski said: "As far as I know, effective immediately, right now."

Schabowski's announcement was carried live by radio and television at about 7 p.m. Within twenty minutes, thousands of East Berliners had flocked to checkpoints, carrying their identification papers and demanding to be let through to West Berlin. At first, the Vopos attempted to turn them back, then to sort through the papers, but finally, they gave up, opened the gates, and a mass of humanity swarmed through.

There followed one incredible party, carried live on television around the world, as mobs of people, waving bottles of wine and beer, cheering and hugging and kissing, thronged the wall. One of the most remarkable scenes was the moment when a young man wearing a backpack walked through the no-man's-land on the eastern side of the wall, near the Brandenburg Gate, climbed on top of it, and began walking back and forth in a nonchalant fashion. For the crowds on both sides, this was a moment of extraordinary tension: no citizen had got this close to the wall for years without being shot. But, aside from drenching the young man with a hose, the Vopos did nothing. Soon he was joined by hundreds of others, dancing atop the most hated symbol of oppression in postwar Berlin history.

The party lasted for weeks. On Christmas Day, the American composer and conductor Leonard Bernstein led a concert which included Beethoven's Ninth Symphony (Ode to Joy), performed by an orchestra of musicians drawn from East and West Germany, as well as from around the world. People chipped away at the wall with hammers and pickaxes, taking away chunks of it for souvenirs. In 1990, heavy equipment was brought in to tear down the rest. The only portions of the wall left now are parts of memorials and a section in a Cold War museum.

GERMANY REUNITED

German reunification was officially declared on October 3, 1990, but the citizens of Berlin knew that the real uniting had begun on November 9, 1989, when the hated wall was at last breached for good.

Since reunification, the road has been a rocky one for East Germany and for many former Eastern bloc countries. In part, this is because, economically, the Communist states had fallen a long way behind the West during the time the wall was in place. Some economists estimate that even with a five to six per cent annual growth rate, they will need another twenty years to catch up. Though Germany is still one of Europe's leading powers, its recent economic growth has been greatly hindered by reunification, and unemployment remains at high levels in the former East Germany. For some, the shadow of the Wall remains. ✦

1990
THE RELEASE OF NELSON MANDELA

Rolihlahla Mandela was born in the small village of Mvezo in the Transkei region of South Africa on July 18, 1918. He became the first in his family to attend school when he was sent to the Clarkebury Boarding Institute, then on to a Wesleyan secondary school in Healdtown. A teacher at Clarkebury gave him the name Nelson, which in time came to be used in place of his birth name Rolihlahla, which colloquially means "troublemaker."

EARLY YEARS WITH THE ANC

In 1940 Mandela ran away to Johannesburg to escape an arranged marriage. There he met Walter Sisulu, a future African National Congress (ANC) collaborator, who helped him find work as a clerk in a local law firm. The ANC had been formed in 1912 as a broad-based coalition of concerned black South Africans, including tribal chiefs, church leaders and various community organizations. They were determined to fight for equality and freedom for black South Africans in the face of decades of increasing racial segregation.

It wasn't until 1948, however, in the wake of the South African general elections, that the process of segregation became enshrined as an official policy of the newly elected Nationalist Party. This official policy became known as apartheid.

In 1941 Mandela completed a bachelor of arts degree by correspondence from the University of South Africa. When he began legal studies at the University of Witwatersrand he met future anti-apartheid activists, such as the former German-Jewish refugee turned lawyer Harry Schwarz, the future ANC theoretician Joe Slovo and activist Ruth First. It was people like these, along with others such as Oliver Tambo and William Nkomo, who realized it was necessary to transform the ANC from a conservative organisation content to work within the law into a radicalized movement prepared to pursue civil disobedience and violence to achieve their aims.

In 1952 the ANC initiated its Campaign for the Defiance of Unjust Laws, and Mandela crisscrossed the country organising opposition to South Africa's discriminatory legislation. That same year Mandela and Oliver Tambo opened their own law firm in Johannesburg and, throughout the 1950s, were involved in a series of highly publicised trials. These included representation of blacks forcibly resettled under the government's Western Areas Removal Scheme and opposition to the Bantu Education Act (1953), which forced separation of all races in the country's schools and universities.

Nelson Mandela first saw Nomzamo Winnie Madikisela in 1957, albeit briefly, as she waited for a bus while he sped past driving a friend to hospital. Even so, he couldn't help but notice her. She was a beautiful and confident-looking twenty-two-year-old, a social worker, and he was thirty-eight. Mandela had divorced his first wife, Evelyn Mase, with whom he had four children, earlier that year, and shortly after the divorce was finalized he and Winnie were married. Winnie involved herself intimately in the ANC's struggle and soon became accustomed to police raids on her home, enforced separations from her new husband, and the endless routine of political gatherings.

Nelson Mandela addresses an ecstatic crowd in Cape Town the day after he is released.

While pregnant with their first child she was arrested during a demonstration on behalf of the ANC Women's League and almost miscarried in prison.

Women demonstrate in front of the Law Courts in Pretoria after the verdict in the Rivonia trial.

MANDELA'S FIRST PRISON SENTENCE

The ANC was outlawed in 1960. The following year Mandela was elected leader of the ANC's armed wing, Spear of the Nation (Umkhonto we Sizwe—the term was Mandela's). This was a significant development in the history of the ANC which had been for the most part a non-violent organization. But within the ANC there was growing scepticism that peaceful protests would bring effective change; in fact, each confrontation with the police seemed only to result in further erosion of black rights.

In 1962 Mandela travelled abroad for several months, speaking and generating political support for the ANC cause in Ethiopia, Sierra Leone, Senegal and Ghana. He then flew to London where he sought out former comrades and met with ANC recruits about to travel to Ethiopia to begin training in guerilla tactics. On his return to South Africa on August 5, 1962 Nelson Mandela was arrested and found guilty of illegally leaving the country and of incitement to strike. He was sentenced to five years' imprisonment and sent to Robben Island.

Robben Island's isolation, 12 miles out from Table Bay, had always made it an ideal human dumping ground. Just 3 miles by a mile and a half in size, the windswept, low-lying island was first seen by Europeans when Vasco da Gama's fleet sailed by in 1498; twenty-seven years later, it became a prison when the first Portuguese convicts were sent there. South Africa was subsequently colonized by both Britain and the Netherlands. From 1652 to 1795 the Dutch East India Company used Robben Island as a prison and added a quarantine station, while during the British colonial period from 1806 to 1910 it served first as a prison, then as a hospital for lepers, the mentally ill and the chronically sick. From 1939 to 1959, the island was used by the South African army and navy as a training center. In 1960 it was transformed into a maximum security prison for political and criminal prisoners.

MANDELA'S SECOND PRISON SENTENCE

Nelson Mandela had been on Robben Island only a few months when he was taken back to Pretoria as a defendant in the Rivonia Trial, which saw Mandela and nine other ANC leaders tried on a total of 221 counts of sabotage and "fomenting violent revolution." The trial began on November 26, 1963 and the defendants, realizing from the outset that it was a show trial, endured it with stoicism and strength. Three of the accused, Mandela, Govan Mbeki and Walter Sisulu, made a pact that if at the trial's conclusion they were given the death penalty, none of them would lodge an appeal. The verdict was delivered on June 11, 1964. Mandela and seven other ANC leaders, including Walter Sisulu, were all found guilty and given life sentences. Nelson Mandela was found guilty on four charges of sabotage, and most of the prisoners were flown to Robben Island the next day.

LIFE ON ROBBEN ISLAND

Although Mandela was to spend the next twenty-six years behind bars, his time there was crucial in forming the man who, in the wake of his release on February 11, 1990, would become the first president of a free and democratic South Africa. He was the 466th prisoner to be incarcerated on Robben Island and was given the prisoner number 466/64. Mandela's cell, in a purpose-built part of the prison called Section B, measured just 6 feet x 6 feet with a straw mat for a bed, a bucket for a toilet, and a small barred window. Breakfast was usually corn porridge, with just a few vegetables for dinner. Suffering almost daily harassment from the prison guards, who were anything but sympathetic to his cause, he nevertheless continued his struggle and was constantly at odds with the prison authorities over demands for better food, clothing and conditions.

Nelson Mandela was a Category D prisoner, which was the most restrictive category, reserved for political prisoners. Category D prisoners were permitted just one letter and one visit every six months. All mail was subject to extensive censorship and could be a maximum of only five hundred words in length. Nevertheless, Winnie's letters and visits sustained him, and Mandela later praised her for the love and encouragement she provided him. In a letter written from his cell in May 1979 he said to her: "Had it not been for your visits, wonderful letters and your love, I would have fallen apart many years ago."

The daily routine of life on Robben Island was harsh and repetitive. At 5.30 am the guards would wake the prisoners and the next hour was spent cleaning their cells, washing and shaving, and emptying their sanitary buckets into a communal toilet. A few minutes were allowed for exercise in the prison courtyard prior to breakfast, which was washed down with a roasted maize and hot water mixture that the prison guards called "coffee." Mandela and the other prisoners then spent the bulk of their day seated in rows, smashing the island's ubiquitous limestone rocks with small hammers weighing around 2.2 kilograms (5 pounds). The work was relentless. A one-hour lunch break may have been a welcome respite from the tedious labour but not from the boredom and sour aftertaste of prison food, with lunch consisting of a mixture of maize and yeast added to water to make a broth only slightly thicker than water. After lunch work continued until 4 p.m. when the prisoners were marched to their communal shower, then dinner at 5 p.m. There was no such thing as "lights out" on Robben Island, with each cell lit by its own 40-watt light bulb. Prisoners such as Mandela, who was studying to complete his law degree by correspondence, were permitted to work as late as 11 p.m. Reading newspapers was forbidden, although Mandela and others found ways of bribing the guards so they could keep abreast of political developments on the mainland.

Beginning in 1965, Mandela and several other prisoners were made to extract lime from a nearby quarry using nothing but a pick and shovel and with no protection from the island's hot summer winds or the ice-cold northwest gales that blew in throughout the winter. The sun reflected harshly off the white limestone, but repeated requests for sunglasses to shield their eyes from the glare went unheeded for years until the prisoners were eventually given permission to purchase their own glasses. The glare was so intense that it damaged Mandela's tear ducts. Despite the conditions and the exposure to the elements, Mandela preferred working the limestone seams to the four monotonous walls of the prison courtyard, and he looked forward to the daily 20-minute walk to and from the quarry.

IN FEBRUARY 1990 NELSON WALKED FREE FROM VICTOR VERSTER PRISON—TWENTY-SEVEN YEARS, SIX MONTHS AND FIVE DAYS AFTER HIS ARREST.

OPPOSITION TO APARTHEID GROWS

In 1968–69 Mandela's mother and his son from his first marriage passed away, but on neither occasion was he permitted to attend the funeral. In 1980 the ANC and the exiled Oliver Tambo began a Release Mandela campaign, and in 1982 Mandela was transferred from Robben Island to Pollsmoor Prison on the mainland. During the 1970s he rejected various offers of early release because of the conditions attached.

Anti-apartheid demonstrations gathered strength throughout the 1980s, and by 1985 massive protests opposing the South African regime were occurring across the United States and Europe, raising awareness of its injustices and of the continuing imprisonment of Mandela and other ANC leaders. Mandela continued to remain resolute, refusing to renounce violence in exchange for another offer of early release. By June of 1986 increased violence in black townships forced President P. W. Botha to declare a state of emergency; in 1987 Mandela began a series of personal negotiations with an increasingly politically and economically isolated South African government, a development that angered many of the ANC hierarchy who were living in exile in Zambia.

MANDELA IS RELEASED FROM PRISON

After being treated for tuberculosis in December 1988, Mandela was transferred from Pollsmoor Prison near Cape Town to Victor Verster Prison near Paarl, where he swapped a prison cell for a small cottage with a swimming pool and vegetable garden. Persistent high blood pressure saw him provided with his own personal chef who prepared a special low-sodium diet, and he began receiving visits from old friends such as Harry Schwarz. Botha suffered a stroke and was forced to resign as president in August 1989. He was succeeded by the conciliatory Frederik Willem de Klerk, who released many of those who had been imprisoned in the wake of the infamous Rivonia Trial. De Klerk was very different from the white South African politicians who had come before him. In discussions with Mandela he came to accept the principle of power sharing, and opposed the settlement of blacks into certain designated homelands. De Klerk engineered the transformation of South Africa from a racially segregated state into a respected multi-racial democracy, reversing the ban on the ANC on February 2, 1990 and at the same time announcing Nelson Mandela's imminent release. On February 11, 1990, at 4:15 p.m., Nelson walked free from Victor Verster Prison—twenty-seven years, six months and five days after his arrest outside Durban for illegally having left the country. The historic event was televised live across the world, and Mandela made a speech that left the millions listening in no doubt that the struggle was far from over:

> Our resort to the armed struggle in 1960 with the formation of the military wing of the ANC was a purely defensive action against the violence of apartheid. The factors which necessitated the armed struggle still exist today. We have no option but to continue. We express the hope that a climate conducive to a negotiated settlement would be created soon, so that there may no longer be the need for the armed struggle.

Nelson Mandela was already a great leader when he began his period of imprisonment on Robben Island in 1964. At forty-six he was also arrogant, easily embittered and impatient for change. The man who emerged from prison in February 1990 was very different. He had undergone a metamorphosis. His years in prison had given him humility, patience, an inner peace and an abiding certainty that things were about to change. He was at once more restrained yet every bit as determined, had "begun to feel the power of prayer," and slowly, almost imperceptibly, had evolved into a statesman. Mandela admitted as much, saying upon his release: "I came out mature."

In the days that followed, the world's media all but besieged Mandela's home in the Johannesburg suburb of West Orlando. Supporters of the ANC thronged the streets, singing songs of protest and celebration day after day, from dusk until dawn. But despite the buoyant mood, there was much that needed to be done. Over the term of his imprisonment, conditions not dissimilar to anarchy had come to reign in many of South Africa's black townships. Children were refusing to go to school and vigilantism was rife, particularly by blacks on blacks. In his speeches over the coming days Mandela was openly critical of those fellow blacks "who use violence against our people."

MANDELA IS ELECTED PRESIDENT OF THE ANC—AND OF SOUTH AFRICA

On February 27, Mandela flew to the exiled ANC leadership in the Zambian capital of Lusaka and assured them he would not seek to become a lone voice in the cause of freedom. In the months to come he flew to more than twenty countries, building up incalculably valuable reservoirs of goodwill and admiration wherever he went and, despite receiving pressure from foreign dignitaries to renounce the use of violence, he never once stepped back from the ANC's stated aim of using armed struggle to attain political objectives. In 1991 Mandela was elected president of the ANC at its first national conference held inside South Africa since the organization was banned in 1960. The following year he divorced Winnie Mandela in the wake of her conviction on charges of accessory to assault and kidnapping. In 1993 Nelson Mandela and Frederik Willem de Klerk were awarded the Nobel Peace Prize.

He voted for the very first time in his life on April 27, 1994 at the age of seventy-five. The ANC won a landslide victory with 62.6 per cent of the vote, and Nelson Mandela was elected president of South Africa on May 10, 1994.

1997 THE DEATH OF PRINCESS DIANA

On August 30, 1997, Diana, Princess of Wales and her companion Dodi Fayed, son of Mohamad al-Fayed millionaire Egyptian businessman, were dining at the exclusive Hôtel Ritz in Paris. Mohamad al-Fayed was the owner of the landmark Parisian hotel, and Diana and Dodi, who had spent the previous nine days holidaying together on Mohamad al-Fayed's yacht *Jonikal*, in the waters off the French Riviera, had arrived in Paris earlier that day. They planned to spend the night at Dodi's apartment not far from the Arc de Triomphe on the Rue Arsène Houssaye, with Diana due to return to her Kensington Palace home, and to her sons, William and Harry, the following day.

ESCAPING THE PAPARAZZI

Diana was the most photographed woman in the world, and the ever-present paparazzi were circling outside the hotel. Dodi sent two decoy cars to the hotel's front entrance in an attempt to distract them while he, Diana, their chauffeur Henri Paul and Dodi's bodyguard Trevor Rees-Jones left by a rear exit on the Rue Cambon in a black Mercedes S280. Initially followed by at least one photographer on a motorcycle, the car drove past the Jardin de Tuileries and Place de la Concorde before turning right onto the Cours la Reine, which runs parallel to the River Seine.

At 12.23 am, approaching the underpass beneath the Pont de l'Alma, and now with three motorcycles in hot pursuit, Henri Paul picked up speed and sped into the tunnel, coming up quickly behind a Citroen BX sedan and a white Fiat Uno. The driver of the Citroen, Mr. Medjahdi, saw the car "slewing out

of control' as it was "hurtling towards me." He accelerated in an attempt to put some distance between the two cars, and the next thing he heard was the deafening sound of impact as the car carrying the Princess of Wales slammed into the substructure of the underpass. It was reported that part of the Fiat's taillight had been found in the tunnel, which raises the possibility that it may have been struck by the Mercedes as Henri Paul attempted to swerve around it, and that this may have contributed to his losing control of the vehicle. The Mercedes hit the right wall of the tunnel as it attempted to pass the Fiat, ricocheting across the two west-bound lanes of the tunnel and into a bridge pylon.

The Fiat Uno was the accident's "mystery car." Scratches of paint from it were found on the Mercedes S280 so there is no doubt the two vehicles came into contact but, despite an extensive search by French authorities, the car has never been found. Dodi Fayed's father maintained that its driver was a French photo-journalist, Jean-Paul Andanson who, he believed, was in fact a British secret agent involved in the so-called "plot" to kill Diana. Andanson, however, had an alibi for the night of the crash, and he committed suicide in 2000. The driver of the Fiat Uno, whoever he or she may have been, has never come forward.

THE MERCEDES PLOUGHS INTO THE THIRTEENTH PYLON

The Pont de l'Alma's concrete support pylons were not protected by guardrails and the Mercedes ploughed headlong into the thirteenth pylon. The impact was so severe the car

DODI DEAD, DIANA CRITICAL

BADLY INJURED: Diana

By Millicent Brown

PRINCESS Diana's lover Dodi Fayed was killed early today in an horrific car crash in Paris.

Diana was "terribly hurt" and was rushed to hospital after the accident, believed to be near the Ritz Hotel.

Witnesses said Dodi had been trapped inside by the side of the road and described the inside of the couple's limo as being "full of blood".

Their chauffeur is believed to have lost control as their car hit...

JOURNEY TO DISASTER: Pages 4 & 5

THE SUNDA

No 9,027   31 AUGUST 1997

Dodi is killed, D injured in Paris

Paparazzi pursu

by Andrew Alderson and Charles Masters
Paris

DIANA, Princess of Wales, was seriously injured and Dodi Fayed, her new millionaire boyfriend, was killed in a car crash in Paris early today as they holidayed in France.

Police said the crash was caused by a group of six paparazzi following the couple's Mercedes on motorcycles shortly after midnight. The couple have been pursued round the clock by the media since they began their relationship two months ago.

The driver of the princess's car, a security officer from the Ritz hotel, Paris, was also killed, officials at police headquarters said. The princess's bodyguard was cut from the wreckage of the car and seriously injured.

Diana, was in intensive care with a broken arm, a thigh injury and concussion early today in La Pitié hospital, close to the scene of the accident. Michael Jay, the ambassador, was at her side.

Fayed, 42, an Egyptian with a playboy reputation and son of his father Mohamed al-Fayed, the multi-million-pound, was believed to have been sitting next to Diana in the car. The accident took place in a short tunnel beside the

Tragedy ends the affair: Diana is in a Paris hospital — Dodi died in the road tunnel

Romance that

Blair backs power
bid... Mandelson

The Mail
ON SUNDAY

AUGUST 31, 1997   85p

Dawn tragedy shakes the world

DIANA DIES IN PARIS CAR CRASH

THE CARING PRINCESS — NO LO

Mail on Sunday Rep

PRINCESS Diana and her boyfriend Dodi Fayed were killed after a car crash caused by a high-speed chase.

She died at 4am Paris time after doctors fought to save her.

Diana was found slumped in...

The Sunda

NO. 1,890   AUGUST

Princess D
Dodi are
Paris ca

Paparazzi
blamed as
Mercedes
smashes
into wall

by GREG NEALE
HELEN JOHNSTONE
TOM BALDWIN
CATHERINE ELSWORTH
and ROBERT SHRIMSLEY

DIANA, Princess of Wales, was killed with her boyfriend Dodi Fayed early today after their car crashed in Paris while being chased by press photographers.

was turned around 180 degrees before careering across the tunnel into the concrete wall on the other side and coming to rest over the center dividing line. The front half of the car had been crushed beyond recognition and the engine pushed almost into the front seat. The rear of the car, by comparison, remained relatively secure—it was later determined that if Diana and Dodi had been wearing their seatbelts at the time of the accident both of them would probably have survived.

Henri Paul, 41, was the Ritz's assistant director of security and the man upon whom much of the blame for the accident was to fall. Although he had been employed at the Ritz since 1986 he was not working as Dodi Fayed's personal chauffeur, despite recently receiving training in defensive driving. He was not meant to be driving Diana and Dodi anywhere that night. At 7 p.m. he had left the hotel, thinking he had finished for the night, but was called back because Dodi wanted to use his usual driver to drive a decoy car so he and Diana could elude the paparazzi. Thinking he was free for the evening, Paul had been indulging his fondness for a drink with other employees, something he almost certainly would not have done if he had been able to foresee the whims of Dodi Fayed.

In the wake of the accident his blood alcohol level was tested and shown to be 1.75 grams per litre, three times over the legal limit of 0.5. In the hour or so before the accident Paul had drunk two Ricards, an anise-based liquor equivalent to four shots of whisky. Forensic tests also showed high levels of prescription drugs in Paul's system, including the anti-depressant Prozac, and Tiapridal, an anti-psychotic drug often used to suppress mood disorders, which led the English toxicologist Dr Robert Forrest to remark: "If I knew that I was going to be driven by someone in that condition, I would not get into the car with them. No way."

Witnesses to the chase agreed that the Mercedes was travelling at 90 miles per hour or more as it entered the tunnel, at least three times the speed limit of just under 30 miles per hour. Though it seemed to dash the hopes of conspiracy theorists the world over, it appeared the accident was the result of the very same two ingredients that lead to road deaths every other day—speed and alcohol.

James Huth, a former dental surgeon turned feature filmmaker, had been watching scenes from his first film in his parents' apartment on the Cour's Albert Premier when he heard the sound of screeching tires followed by three loud impacts. He ran outside where a friend told him there had just been a car accident in the Pont de l'Alma tunnel. Huth ran to investigate. With no idea who the victims were, he approached the mangled wreckage of the Mercedes and saw Henri Paul slumped forward in an airbag in the driver's seat, dead. Aware of the danger of moving injured people suffering

spinal injuries, Huth advised others who had arrived seconds before him not to touch the bodies. Reports by other witnesses claimed, at about this point, they had heard the woman in the rear of the car murmur: "Oh my God" and "Leave me alone." Huth told Trevor Rees-Jones, who was in a state of near panic in the front passenger seat, to stay quiet, that someone would be there shortly to help him. Rees-Jones' wrist was broken and his jaw was, according to Huth, "hanging off."

DIANA CONSCIOUS

Huth moved around to the rear of the car and saw Dodi Fayed's lifeless body slumped between the car's two front seats, his leg broken in two places below the knee the only obvious sign of trauma. The only occupant of the car he didn't clearly see was Princess Diana herself. Diana, still conscious, was thrown to the floor by the impact and lay crumpled in the rear footwell, largely obscured from Huth's view by Dodi's body. Neither Diana, Dodi Fayed nor Henri Paul were wearing seatbelts at the time of the accident.

Physician Frederick Mailliez was among the first on the scene and used his mobile phone to call for an ambulance. He too failed to recognize the woman in the rear footwell, later testifying that she seemed unconscious but at the same time

In an overwhelming outpouring of grief, mourners left over one million bouquets of flowers at Kensington Palace.

was able to move her limbs. Photographers had by this time surrounded the car and were taking pictures. None of them offered to assist. Mailliez lifted up the head of the princess and placed an oxygen mask over her mouth to help her breathe. Although her internal injuries were life threatening she showed few external injuries save for some lacerations about the face. Jack and Robin Firestone, two American tourists on holiday in the French capital, also arrived in the seconds after the crash and were horrified to see photographers standing less than a metre away from the car taking pictures of a blonde woman lying on the back seat.

Within seven minutes of the accident a military emergency vehicle arrived and treatment of the injured began. At 12.40 am a SAMU ambulance (a hospital-based emergency service) arrived and its physician immediately inserted an intravenous drip into Diana, who was able to move her right leg and left arm. Dodi Fayed was pronounced dead at 1.32 am. Henri Paul was declared dead not long after being dragged from the wreckage. Both he and Dodi had suffered a ruptured aorta. Trevor Rees-Jones was taken to Pitié-Salpêtrière Hospital, a teaching hospital and one of the largest hospitals in Europe, with injuries to his brain and chest, and although initial reports suggested he might have been wearing his seatbelt, two subsequent inquiries both determined that he had not.

At 1 am Diana was removed, still conscious, from the wreckage but immediately went into cardiac arrest. External chest massage saw her cardiac rhythm return and she was transferred to the waiting ambulance at 1.18 am. Diana's injuries were horrific—the impact would almost certainly have caused major deceleration injuries such as internal lesions. Yet the ambulance crew treated her only for the outward measurable symptoms, namely falling blood pressure, while ignoring its cause. They attended her for almost an hour.

The force of the impact had shifted her heart from the left side of her chest to the right, tearing her pericardium (the double-walled sac inside which the heart rests) and partially, though not wholly, rupturing the pulmonary vein. The ambulance left the tunnel at 1.41 am and arrived at Pitié-Salpêtrière at 2.06 am, a twenty-five-minute trip to a hospital just over 4 miles away on a largely deserted expressway that should have taken just five to ten minutes. Diana was fast running out of time, but the ambulance driver, unaware of the extent of her internal injuries, deliberately drove slowly so as not to subject the patient to unnecessary bumps and movement. At one point the ambulance had to stop when her blood pressure fell to a dangerously low level.

DIANA FINALLY REACHES THE EMERGENCY ROOM

Diana didn't arrive in the emergency room of Pitié-Salpêtrière until 104 minutes after the crash. Ten minutes after arriving she suffered a second cardiac arrest. Epinephrine was injected directly into her heart and an incision was made in the chest so the attending surgeons could gain manual access to the heart. Diana's left pulmonary vein was hemorrhaging where it came into contact with the left atrium, and had been losing blood for more than an hour and a half. Unlike the aorta, however, which takes blood out of the heart and where the pressure is high, the pulmonary is a "low pressure" vein and can often partially clot if ripped. This is almost certainly what happened with Diana and is the reason she was able to survive as long as she did. The tragedy was that in Diana's case she had an injury that was impossible to repair in the field, and the French emphasis on treating people at the scene, as distinct from the U.S. approach of "scope and run" and of getting patients to an emergency room as soon as possible, probably cost Diana her life. Despite being sutured, and with the hemorrhaging brought under control, two hours of open heart massage and electric shock therapy could not reestablish a heartbeat. The Princess of Wales was pronounced dead at 4 am, and her death was announced at a news conference ninety minutes later. If

she had arrived at Pitié-Salpêtrière an hour earlier, would she have survived? It is a moot point.

Prince Charles and the rest of the royal family were on their traditional summer holiday at Balmoral Castle in Scotland when the accident occurred. Charles and his mother, Queen Elizabeth, decided not to tell his sons, William and Harry, the news of their mother's death until they woke the next morning. Charles and Diana's two sisters, Lady Sarah McCorquodale and Lady Jane Fellowes, travelled to Paris and accompanied Diana's body back to England.

Princess Diana's death caused an outpouring of grief around the world but particularly in Britain. More than a million people lined the route of her funeral procession from her home at Kensington Palace at the western end of Hyde Park to Westminster Abbey, throwing flowers in front of the gun carriage, drawn by six horses, that bore her coffin. On top of the coffin were three wreaths placed there by her brother, Earl Spencer, and her two sons, Prince William (fifteen) and Prince Harry (twelve). It was mostly a silent procession, or as quiet as a million people can be, a silence broken only by the tolling of Westminster Abbey's Tenor Bell, once every minute, and the sounds of the horses' hooves as they struck the pavement. A particularly memorable and heart-rending image is of Diana's two sons walking solemnly behind their mother's coffin, displaying a quiet dignity that belied their tender years and flanked by their father, Prince Charles, their grandfather Prince Philip, and their uncle, Earl Spencer.

MILLIONS ATTEND DIANA'S FUNERAL

Two thousand people had been invited to attend the funeral, with some having to be ushered into St Margaret's Church adjacent to Westminster Abbey in order to accommodate everyone. Luciano Pavarotti, a personal friend of Diana, had been asked to sing at the service but had refused, saying he would have been unable to make it through any song without breaking down in tears. Elton John, who was to perform his song "Candle in the Wind" with reworked lyrics in honor of Diana, entered the abbey alone.

The funeral service began at 11 am. An hour later, after a minute's silence, Diana's coffin was placed in a hearse and for the next two hours was taken on a prearranged route through the streets of London before it began its final, 80-mile journey to Althorp Estate in Northamptonshire, the Spencer family home for more than five hundred years. Twenty generations of Diana's family are buried in the cemetery of the Church of St Mary the Virgin in the nearby town of Great Brington, but it was decided the Princess of Wales' final resting place would be in the gardens of the estate itself, to spare the residents of Great Brington the inconvenience of the presence of the millions of well-wishers that would have transformed her shrine into a place of pilgrimage.

2001 9/11

They were four energetic and intense young men, the oldest of them born in 1968, the youngest a decade later. Three of them had studied city planning and engineering. All were well travelled, not only in their native Middle East but also throughout Europe and the United States, where all four, on temporary work visas, took pilot-training lessons. During the last days of their lives, they acted like anyone else might do in America—drawing cash from ATMs, eating at fast food places, even having a few drinks at a bar. They might easily have been taken for recent immigrants, young professionals enjoying a new lifestyle and looking forward to a bright future in their adopted country.

But they were anything but. For on September 11, 2001, Mohammed Atta, Marwan al-Shehhi, Ziad Jarrah and Hani Hanjour would lead fifteen other men onto four passenger planes. Turning these jets into deadly weapons, they would inflict the most devastating terrorist attack in history on the United States, in the name of an Islamic jihad, or holy war.

In doing so, they would transform the world. The 9/11 attacks not only led to a war in Afghanistan and a contentious and divisive conflict in Iraq, but also changed the way many people viewed their lives. After 9/11, travel became fraught. Danger could lurk on airlines, in nightclubs, on railway trains and buses. A lost suitcase could be a bomb, an approaching guard might arrest you at any moment. Public anxiety was—and to some extent remains—at its highest since the worst days of the Cold War.

PRIME TARGET

By the end of the twentieth century, the United States had become a prime target for Islamic terrorists, due to its long-term support of Israel and of Saudi Arabia, which it had supplied with funds, military equipment, and training. Chief among these was Al-Qaeda, an Islamic militant group, led by Osama bin Laden, which seeks to install fundamentalist regimes in all Muslim countries and eradicate all foreign, non-Muslim influence from those nations. As noted by the 9/11 Commission, a bi-partisan U.S. government group that looked into the September 11 attacks, "Islamist extremists had given plenty of warning that they meant to kill Americans indiscriminately and in large numbers." Indeed, 9/11 was not the first time American interests, and even the country itself, had been attacked by such extremists, including Al-Qaeda.

The first attack on U.S. soil was the 1993 bombing of the World Trade Center, which caused some damage but failed due to bungles by the terrorists, most of whom were caught and jailed. In 1994, a plot to blow up thirteen American passenger jets over a two-day period was foiled. The following year, terrorists attacked a U.S. military base in Riyadh, Saudi Arabia, killing nineteen American servicemen and wounding hundreds of others. The U.S. embassies in Kenya and Tanzania were bombed in 1998, with a total loss of 260 lives; and in October of 2000 seventeen American sailors were killed when a motorboat filled with explosives was ignited next to the U.S. destroyer Cole, in the port of Aden in Yemen.

Al-Qaeda learned from these successes and failures. Having in the late 1990s re-established its headquarters in Afghanistan—then ruled by the Islamic fundamentalist Taliban regime—the group began planning a grand attack on the United States. According to the 9/11 Commission, preparations began as much as eighteen months before September 11 occurred, and the operational mastermind was bin Laden's right-hand

---

The south tower of the World Trade Center starts to collapse at 9.59 a.m. The north tower would crumble half an hour later.

man, Khalid Sheikh Mohammed. Khalid was captured in Pakistan in 2003, and remains in custody in the U.S. prison at Guantanamo Bay, Cuba.

The devastated remains of the World Trade Center in Manhattan, subsequently known as the "Ground Zero" of the terrorist attack.

TRIAL RUNS

The four pilots had been in America for some time, perhaps from as early as January 2000, funded by Al-Qaeda money laundered through numerous sources and deposited regularly in their bank accounts. In early 2001, Osama bin Laden met with subordinates in Afghanistan in order to pick what the 9/11 Commission later referred to as "the muscle": the hijackers who would subdue and threaten the passengers while the trained pilots flew the planes. Twelve of the fifteen men selected came from Saudi Arabia, where bin Laden originated. Most of them were unemployed, with at most a high school education, and single. For the most part, they had been recruited after attending mosques that practised a more austere and radical form of Islam.

After undergoing basic training in Afghanistan, these men were sent to the United States. They began arriving there in pairs, on tourist visas, in April of 2001, and met up with the pilots, who helped them find places to live, open bank accounts, and become accustomed to American life.

During the summer of 2001, the pilots took cross-country reconnaissance flights, carrying knives through airport security and, once on a plane, watching to see when the cockpit doors would be opened.

In June of 2001, the hijackers received final word from bin Laden regarding their targets. They were to be the World Trade Center in New York, the Pentagon in Virginia, and either the White House or the Capitol Building in Washington DC—the nation's headquarters of finance, defence and government.

A BEAUTIFUL DAY FOR FLYING

Up and down the eastern seaboard of the United States on September 11, people awakening and getting ready to go to work remarked on what an extraordinarily beautiful day it was. The sky was clear, the air nearly translucent and the temperature mild, almost balmy. It was a beautiful day for flying.

At around 7:30 a.m., Mohammed Atta and his four muscle men boarded American Airlines Flight 11, bound for Los

Angeles, at Boston's Logan International Airport. The plane took off at 7:59. At another terminal at Logan Airport, Marwan al-Shehhi and his four companions checked in for United Airlines Flight 175, also heading for Los Angeles. This plane took off at 8:14. Meanwhile, at Dulles International Airport in Washington DC, Hani Hanjour and his four-man team boarded American Airlines Flight 77, bound for Los Angeles. This plane lifted off at 8:20. At that same moment in the same airport, Ziad Jarrah and three companions boarded United Airlines Flight 93 to San Francisco, which rose up into the air at 8:42.

The flights had been chosen with great care. Each was bound for the West Coast, which meant that the planes would have plenty of fuel. The airplanes were Boeing 757s or 767s, simulators of which the pilots had trained in.

The terrorists took their first-class seats, in most cases two at the back of the first-class section and two at the front. Then they waited.

FLIGHT 11

At 8:14 a.m., American Airlines Flight 11 out of Boston reached 25,000 feet, at which point the pilots had a routine conversation with the Logan control tower. By 8:25, two attendants on the flight, Betty Ong and Amy Sweeney, were making cell phone calls to American Airlines offices. Ong reported: "The cockpit is not answering … somebody is stabbed in business class. I think there's mace … we're getting hijacked."

Most likely, the muscle men had risen up as soon as the cockpit door was opened and stabbed two of the unarmed flight attendants in order to create terror. Another man, who had formerly been an Israeli army soldier, was also killed, probably because he tried to stop the terrorists. Then the pilots were killed or incapacitated and Atta took over the controls. The plane executed a sweeping turn over Massachusetts and New York State's capital city of Albany, and headed south, down the Hudson River. Betty Ong reported that the plane was flying "erratically."

At around this time, air traffic controllers began to hear voice transmissions from Flight 11. At one point, a voice said: "Don't try to make any stupid moves. Just stay quiet and you'll be okay." A terrorist—possibly Atta—had tuned into the wrong transmission channel and instead of talking through the cabin intercom was broadcasting his message over the air traffic control channel.

At 8:29 a.m., air traffic control notified the FAA that a hijacking had occurred. But it was too late for military aircraft to intercept. Flight 11, swooping down to 985 feet, was speeding

over Manhattan Island at 450 miles per hour. Flight attendant Sweeney, looking out the window, cried out on her cell phone: "We are flying low. We are flying very, very low. We are flying way too low … Oh my God we are way too low."

Then the phone went dead as American Airlines Flight 11 crashed into the north tower of the World Trade Center, tipping its wings at the last second to create maximum damage to the structure. The exact time was 8:46:40.

FLIGHT 175

The flight crew on United Airlines Flight 175, which had also taken off from Boston's Logan airport, heard what they considered to be a "suspicious transmission" from another plane (which turned out to be Flight 11) and reported this to air traffic control. Then Flight 175 itself stopped responding to enquiries from air traffic. At 8:51 a.m., the flight left its normal altitude and also began flying erratically.

As with Flight 11, passengers made panicked calls on their mobile phones. One man, Peter Hanson, called his father to say, "I think they've taken over the cockpit … the plane is making strange moves." A flight attendant reported that both pilots were dead. At nine o'clock, Peter Hanson called his father again. "It's getting very bad on the plane," he said. "Passengers are throwing up and getting sick. The plane is making jerky movements … I don't think the pilot is flying the plane … I think we are going down … Don't worry, Dad: if it happens, it'll be very fast—my God, my God."

Flight 175 crashed into the south tower of the World Trade Center at 9:03:11.

FLIGHT 77

Before boarding American Airlines Flight 77 for Los Angeles at Washington's Dulles International Airport, two of the hijackers had set off metal-detector alarms. But they had then passed through manual checks with a hand-held metal detector and were allowed to proceed, although their luggage was held as a precautionary matter until it was ascertained that they were indeed on board. Videotape of one of the hijackers viewed later appears to show a Stanley knife buttoned into his back pocket.

The flight reached its cruising altitude of 35,000 feet at 8:46. At around 9:16, one of the passengers, Barbara Olson, wife of Theodore Olson, the U.S. Solicitor-General, called her husband to say that the plane had been hijacked by men with a Stanley knife. Ted Olson told his wife about the two earlier crashes into the World Trade Center, but then the call

THE TARGETS CHOSEN BY THE TERRORISTS WERE AMERICA'S HEADQUARTERS OF FINANCE, DEFENCE AND GOVERNMENT.

was cut off. At about 9:30, the autopilot of the plane was disengaged when it reached 69,000 feet and then Flight 77 made a sweeping turn, descending to 2100 feet. Hani Hanjour, the hijacker pilot, pushed the throttles to full power as the plane dived down into Arlington, Virginia, across the Potomac from Washington DC. When it hit the Pentagon, at 9:37:46, Flight 77 was travelling at more than 530 miles per hour.

FLIGHT 93

The last of the airlines hijacked that day, Flight 93, carrying thirty-seven passengers, was twenty-five minutes late in taking off, finally departing at 8:42. It became the only plane out of the four in which all the passengers had full knowledge of what had occurred previously and time in which to attempt to do something about it.

At 9:26 a warning was sent out to all planes in the sky to beware of any "cockpit intrusions," along with the news that two planes had hit the World Trade Center. The puzzled pilot of Flight 93 asked for a confirmation of this strange message, but before that could occur, the plane suddenly dropped altitude and began putting out a Mayday distress call. Air traffic control in Cleveland heard the pilot crying, "Hey, get out of here!" The plane then turned back east.

As they did on the other planes, the hijackers told the passengers that there was a bomb on board and that if they didn't cause trouble they would be all right. But from mobile phone conversations the passengers soon knew that it was only a matter of time before the plane would be crashed into a building.

One caller told his wife that they had voted to rush the hijackers. They were planning to use anything they could as weapons. At 9:57, the passengers began their assault, the sounds of which were recorded on the cockpit voice recorder, which was recovered after the crash. The terrorist pilot Ziad Jarrah yelled at another hijacker to block the door and then rolled the plane side to side and pitched it up and down.

On the cockpit voice recording, at exactly ten o'clock, Jarrah says in Arabic: "Is that it? Shall we finish it off?" Another terrorist tells him to wait. Then a passenger is heard to yell, "In the cockpit. If we don't, we die." There are further sounds of commotion and then Jarrah yells: "Allah is the greatest!"

At 10:03, the airliner rolled over on its back and crashed at a speed in excess of 500 miles per hour into a wooded area outside Shanksville, Pennsylvania, about twenty minutes" flying time from Washington. Because of the efforts of the passengers, either the Capitol Building or the White House was saved.

THE WAR ON TERROR

The 9/11 attacks took the lives of 2749 people in the World Trade Center, 125 at the Pentagon, and 256 on the four planes. It was the worst-ever attack on the United States in its history, with a death toll greater than that of Pearl Harbor, when 2330 died. The 9/11 Commission called it "a day of unprecedented shock and suffering in the history of the United States."

The attacks were witnessed on television by millions around the world. The reaction of the United States was swift. Based on evidence that Al-Qaeda and Osama bin Laden were operating in Afghanistan, President George W. Bush ordered an attack on that country by the United States and a coalition of allied nations, which began on October 7, 2001. It was successful in displacing the Taliban, although not in discovering the whereabouts of Osama bin Laden. In 2003, the United States and Britain also launched an invasion of Iraq, claiming that Saddam Hussein had links to Al-Qaeda (a claim since hotly disputed), sparking a long, bloody and divisive conflict in that country.

Around the world, nations tightened up security in airports, along borders and on public transport. This in turn gave rise to a debate about how to balance security and civil liberties, a debate that still rages as new terrorist attacks take place and new plots are uncovered.

The shock waves from 9/11 are still reverberating around the world. They will do so for decades to come. ❧

2003
THE BATTLE OF IRAQ

What possible connection could an urbane Swedish diplomat and politician, from a family of scholars, have with the U.S. invasion of Iraq? Hans Martin Blix was born in Sweden on June 28, 1928. He studied at the University of Uppsala in Sweden and New York's Columbia University, and earned a PhD from the University of Cambridge in England. Through the 1960s and 1970s he rose through Sweden's diplomatic ranks, and became foreign minister in 1978. In 1981 he was appointed head of the International Atomic Energy Agency, an independent international organisation with links to the United Nations, and held this position until 1997. In March 2000 he was chosen to be the head of the new United Nations Monitoring, Verification and Inspection Commission (UNMOVIC), and in 2002 was ordered to focus his agency's efforts on disarming Iraq. According to American and British intelligence, Saddam Hussein had been stockpiling weapons of mass destruction (WMDs) that threatened the strategic interests of the West. Hans Blix was ordered to find them.

SADDAM "PLAYING GAMES OF CAT AND MOUSE"

On November 8, 2002, United Nations Security Council Resolution 1441 required that Iraq compensate Kuwait for widespread looting by Iraq's troops after its invasion of 1990 and that it halt its continuing importation and acquisition of prohibited weapons. The resolution also provided Saddam Hussein with one last opportunity to comply with a string of previous resolutions calling for full disclosure of the presence of WMDs. UN inspection teams under Hans Blix were running out of patience with Saddam's stonewalling, and Blix was quoted as saying that had Saddam complied with UN resolutions after the 1991 Gulf War he would have saved his country ten years of harsh economic sanctions. Hussein had been "playing games of cat and mouse" with UNMOVIC, Blix said, and he had warned the Iraqi government there would be serious consequences if his disarmament teams continued to be harassed and fed bogus information on the whereabouts of the country's WMDs.

Nevertheless, Blix came to believe that the case arguing for the presence of WMDs was, at best, flimsy. Despite Iraq's intransigence Blix's teams had managed to search more than seven hundred suspected WMD sites across the country in the months leading up to the invasion—and had uncovered nothing of substance. UNMOVIC's lack of evidence of WMDs was, however, in stark contrast to what was coming out of the intelligence agencies of Britain and the United States, and at odds with the talk of war coming from the White House and No. 10 Downing Street. Unable to see the case for war, Blix later confided that he thought British prime minister Tony Blair and U.S. president George W. Bush were behaving "like seventeenth-century witchfinders" in their determination to remove the Iraqi dictator.

In the two years following the tragedy of 9/11, it is estimated that George W. Bush and seven of his most influential aides—including his defense secretary Donald Rumsfeld, his national security adviser Condoleezza Rice and his secretary of state Colin Powell—made more than nine hundred false or misleading statements regarding the threat posed by Iraq and its supposed links to the terrorist group Al-Qaeda. Examples of the deliberate pattern of so-called irrefutable facts that Bush administration officials were using to bolster its case for war are legion. On August 26, 2002 Vice President Cheney declared: "Simply stated, there is no doubt that Saddam Hussein now has weapons of mass destruction. There is no doubt he is amassing them to use against our friends, against our allies, and against

us." In September 2002 President Bush declared on radio: "The Iraqi regime possesses biological and chemical weapons, is rebuilding the facilities to make more and, according to the British government, could launch a biological or chemical attack in as little as forty-five minutes after the order is given. This regime is seeking a nuclear bomb, and with fissile material could build one within a year." In February 2003 secretary of state Colin Powell said: "What we're giving you are facts and conclusions based on solid intelligence." No matter that, years later, the Duelfer Report concluded that Saddam Hussein had virtually terminated Iraq's nuclear program in 1991 and had made no attempt whatsoever to resurrect it. The American people and the world were being psychologically prepared for war, and there wasn't anything they, or Hans Blix and his dedicated teams of weapons inspectors, could do about it.

COALITION PREPARES FOR INVASION

The coalition of armed forces led by the United States and Great Britain, assisted by troops from Australia, Poland, Spain and Denmark, had spent months assembling at staging posts in neighbouring countries in and around the Persian Gulf, and were poised to invade Iraq with the aim of achieving three stated objectives: to end the regime of Saddam Hussein and

US Marines from the 3rd Battalion engage Iraqi troops on the outskirts of Baghdad.

its support of terror, to locate and neutralize once and for all its "weapons of mass destruction," and to free the Iraqi people from tyranny and oppression.

The beginning of the invasion, code-named Operation Iraqi Freedom, was under the command of U.S. army general Tommy Franks. It involved more than three hundred thousand troops and an estimated seventy thousand Kurdish troops, and its intent was signalled on March 19, 2003 with a U.S. air strike on the Presidential Palace in Baghdad. Forty-five minutes later, at 10:15 p.m. Eastern time in the United States, President George W. Bush addressed the nation, declaring that the U.S. and coalition forces were in the early stages of a campaign to disarm Iraq and free its people, that the United States was going into Iraq "with respect for its citizens, for their great civilization, and for the religious faiths they practice." It would be a swift campaign based on mobility, superior technology and the precise application of overwhelming force. And it would begin in the south around Basra.

On March 20 coalition troops entered Basra Province in the south from their assembly points within Kuwait while commandos launched a seaborne strike to capture the port city of Basra itself. More than eight hundred cruise missiles rained down on Iraqi targets in and around Baghdad and the cities of Mosul and Kirkuk in the invasion's first forty-eight hours in a tactic known as "shock and awe." This tactic was designed not merely to hit designated targets but also to deal a psychological deathblow to the Iraqi armed forces and extinguish their will to fight. In the first two days of the conflict more missiles were launched against Iraqi targets than were fired during the entire forty days of the 1991 Gulf War. Unlike the "dumb bombs" of 1991, however, these were satellite-guided high-precision bombs, and their targets were not the Iraqi army so much as its leadership—in accordance with a U.S. battle plan that was expressly designed to bypass Iraqi divisions rather than confront them, to instead eliminate the ability of Saddam Hussein and his generals to communicate with and coordinate their armies.

As U.S. troops headed towards Basra on March 21, Iraq's 51st Mechanized Infantry Division, a force of eight thousand to ten thousand soldiers sent to the south of the country to guard the area bordering Iran, surrendered virtually without a fight. It was typical of the many poorly equipped regular army units encountered by coalition forces. The U.S. 5th Corps and the 1st Marine Expeditionary Force converged upon Baghdad from the east and south. In the north, a late decision by Turkey not to allow coalition forces to use its territory to mount an assault meant that the fifteen thousand troops of the 4th Mechanized Infantry Division had to be redeployed to the south, and in their place the U.S. 173rd Airborne Brigade was to be airdropped on the outskirts of Kirkuk, linking up with Kurdish forces to help secure the north of the country and keep the thirteen divisions Saddam had deployed there at bay.

THE BEGINNING OF THE INVASION, CODE-NAMED OPERATION IRAQI FREEDOM, INVOLVED MORE THAN THREE HUNDRED THOUSAND AMERICAN TROOPS.

BOMBING MISSIONS DISMANTLE IRAQ'S AIR DEFENCE

Coalition ground forces were able to advance with relative impunity due in no small part to the cover provided by coalition aircraft. The success of the air war had reduced by hundreds the number of targets that ground forces would otherwise have had to deal with and kept the Iraqi air force out of the sky. The U.S. air force alone flew more than fifteen hundred sorties on March 21–22, and another fifteen hundred on March 22–23, of which more than eight hundred were bombing missions that dismantled Iraq's air defence network, command bunkers and control centers.

The coalition's advance slowed on March 23–24, and twenty-six soldiers were killed in what would be the worst single day's fighting in terms of casualties. Another two thousand sorties flown by coalition aircraft saw approximately eight hundred precision-guided bombs dropped onto five hundred targets. The Iraqi air force, as it had been from day one, was nowhere to be seen. Meanwhile, in the south, the Basra airfield had been secured and mine-clearing operations in the waterways surrounding Umm Qasr were progressing well.

On March 24–25 the 5th Corps and 1st Marine Expeditionary Force were continuing their push towards Baghdad and the Iraqi army was already showing clear signs that it was no longer functioning as a cohesive fighting force. The Iraqi leadership started stripping Republican Guard units from wherever it could gather them and redeploying them to the south of Baghdad in a desperate attempt to slow coalition progress. Their deployment, however, brought them out into the open and made them vulnerable to coalition air strikes throughout March 25–26.

US forces had been advancing on average 80 miles a day over the first four days of the campaign, one of the most rapid armored advances in military history. They achieved this by avoiding, where possible, large concentrations of the enemy's armed forces as well as large towns and cities.

THE NOOSE AROUND BAGHDAD STARTS TO TIGHTEN

On March 30 sandstorms that had been hampering air sorties for two days finally cleared and more than twelve hundred precision-guided bombs were dropped on specified targets, more than half of which were the rapidly disintegrating units of the Republican Guard positioned in and around the Iraqi capital. The 3rd Infantry Division secured a bridge across the Euphrates River at Al Handiyah while the 101st Airborne Division captured the airfield at An Najaf 100 miles south of Baghdad. The way to Baghdad opened on April 2 with the near-destruction of the Medina Division of the Republican Guard by the 5th Corps. The coalition advance was relentless. Fifteen hundred sorties were being flown every day, focusing on eliminating Republican Guard units and clearing the way for land forces to continue their advance on the capital. The much anticipated Battle for Baghdad was, thanks to the coalition's massive air superiority, little more than a series of smallish skirmishes fought against Iraqi troops who had been deprived of their will to fight. Helicopters were able to fly in close support to slow-moving A-10 attack aircraft in the face of almost non-existent anti-aircraft fire.

The 5th Corps took Baghdad Airport in the face of demoralized defenders and, together with the 1st Marine Expeditionary Force, was now able to initiate raids by armoured vehicles deep into Baghdad itself, further sapping the morale of those scattered Republican Guard units that had managed to escape the carnage from the air and ground and had fallen back into the hoped-for safety of the suburbs. The air campaign by now was routinely flying fifteen hundred sorties every day and mercilessly targeting the Republican Guard around the clock.

By April 5, U.S. forces had consolidated their hold on Baghdad and its airport, and controlled both the southeastern and southwestern approaches to the city. The following day, April 6, a coalition announcement claimed it now enjoyed air supremacy over all Iraqi airspace and the 5th Corps and 1st Marine Expeditionary Force had all but surrounded the Iraqi capital, preventing any reinforcement of Iraqi positions from its forces to the north of the city.

FEDAYEEN SADDAM AMONG THE LAST TO SURRENDER

The International Institute for Strategic Studies estimated that the Iraqi forces opposing the invasion totalled approximately 536,000, of which 375,000 were regular army, eighty thousand were Republican Guards, with a further forty thousand belonging to the Fedayeen Saddam, literally "Saddam's Men of Sacrifice," an ultra-loyal paramilitary force that reported directly to Saddam and operated outside of the normal parameters of the military hierarchy. Although hopelessly outgunned and outnumbered, the Fedayeen Saddam were among the last to surrender and continually hampered the advance of coalition forces towards Baghdad using subterfuge and guerilla tactics.

In the end it seemed as though the U.S. and coalition forces had achieved a magnificent victory. The Iraqi government and its military, the world's twelfth-largest standing army, had completely and utterly collapsed in just three weeks. Baghdad fell on April 9, and Saddam Hussein fled the city as U.S. forces took control of Ba'ath Party government and administrative buildings. A successful amphibious assault by the British Royal Marines on the Al-Faw Peninsula and around the outskirts of Basra had seen the country's vast network of southern oil fields seized relatively intact, and Polish commandoes had successfully taken all of Basra's offshore oil platforms.

Fighting continued in the country's north after the fall of Baghdad, with Kurdish forces capturing the town of Kirkuk on April 10, and Mosul the following day. The invasion came to an "official" end with the fall of Saddam Hussein's home town of Tikrit on April 15. Saddam's Ba'ath Party and its military apparatus had been toppled with significantly less loss of life than had been anticipated, and the overwhelming technology possessed by the U.S. punished any Iraqi mistakes in the field with overwhelming severity. Coalition casualties included one hundred and thirty-nine U.S. personnel and thirty-three from Great Britain, as opposed to an estimated nine thousand two hundred Iraqi soldiers and almost seven thousand three hundred civilians killed.

"MISSION ACCOMPLISHED"

An undeniable and spontaneous outpouring of gratitude towards coalition personnel was evident on the streets of Baghdad and few seemed immune from the euphoria of victory. On May 1, President George Bush flew in to address sailors aboard the aircraft carrier U.S.S. *Abraham Lincoln*. In a speech that would later be pilloried in the world media when it became apparent that any thought of victory was premature to say the least, the president made his famous declaration: "In the Battle of Iraq, the United States and our allies have prevailed." As if to emphasize the point, a giant banner hung on the carrier's superstructure behind him read MISSION ACCOMPLISHED. While Bush had nothing to do with the banner's deployment (it was requested by the navy and the banner itself was made by members of the White House staff), its very existence made it seem that the president clearly associated himself with the sentiments it expressed. For the war's critics, the speech summed up the arrogance of an administration that had raced into a war the critics felt America had no right to wage, then prematurely declared its closure without regard to any need to "win the peace."

Saddam Hussein went into hiding and was finally dragged out of a hole in the ground by soldiers of the U.S. 4th Infantry Division at a farmhouse in Tikrit. He was found guilty of crimes against humanity and the former dictator was hanged on 30 December 2006. ❧

President George W. Bush addresses the nation on Iraq beneath a banner reading Mission Accomplished on May 1.

CREDITS

CHAPTER CREDITS

Joseph Cummins: chapters 5, 6, 9, 13, 14, 16, 17, 19, 20, 21, 24, 25, 30, 32, 34, 35, 37, 38, 40, 41, 42, 43, 48, 49, 51, 52, 56, 57, 59, 60, 61, 62, 63, 64, 65, 66, 71, and 74

James Inglis: chapters 1, 2, 3, 4, 7, 8, 10, 11, 12, 15, 18, 22, 23, 26, 27, 28, 33, 36, 46, and 58

Barry Stone: chapters 29, 31, 39, 44, 45, 47, 50, 53, 54, 55, 67, 68, 69, 70, 72, 73, and 75

IMAGE CREDITS

Australian War Memorial: page 253 [AWM A05297]

Australpress/Topfoto: pages 33, 70, 126, and 129

AKG: pages 10, 16, 26, 124, 166, 320, and 358
Corbis: pages 23, 29, 40, 44, 59, 118, 136, 144, 151, 155, 204, 230, 236, 263, 277, 278, 281, 282, 288, 329, 352, 354, 360, 362, 364, 372, and 380

Getty Images: cover, pages 8, 12-13, 18, 22, 30, 32, 37, 38, 47, 50-51, 52, 54, 56, 63, 67, 68, 72-73, 76, 78, 80, 82, 85, 88, 91, 94-95, 96, 98, 100, 104-105, 108, 112, 115, 123, 132, 135, 138, 141, 146, 156, 158, 160-161, 164, 170, 172, 174, 178, 184-185, 195, 196, 199, 201, 206, 210-211, 215, 220, 228-229, 234, 238, 242, 247, 248, 250, 256-257, 260, 266, 268, 270, 272, 286, 291, 292-293, 296, 298-299, 301, 302, 306, 308, 310, 213, 317, 318, 322, 325, 339, 340, 342, 345, 349, 350, 369, 370, 374, 378-379, 382, 384, 388, and 390

National Library of Australia: pages 188 and 190

Picture Desk/The Art Archive: pages 60, 148, and 240

The Library of Congress: pages 181, 218, 225, and 330

INDEX